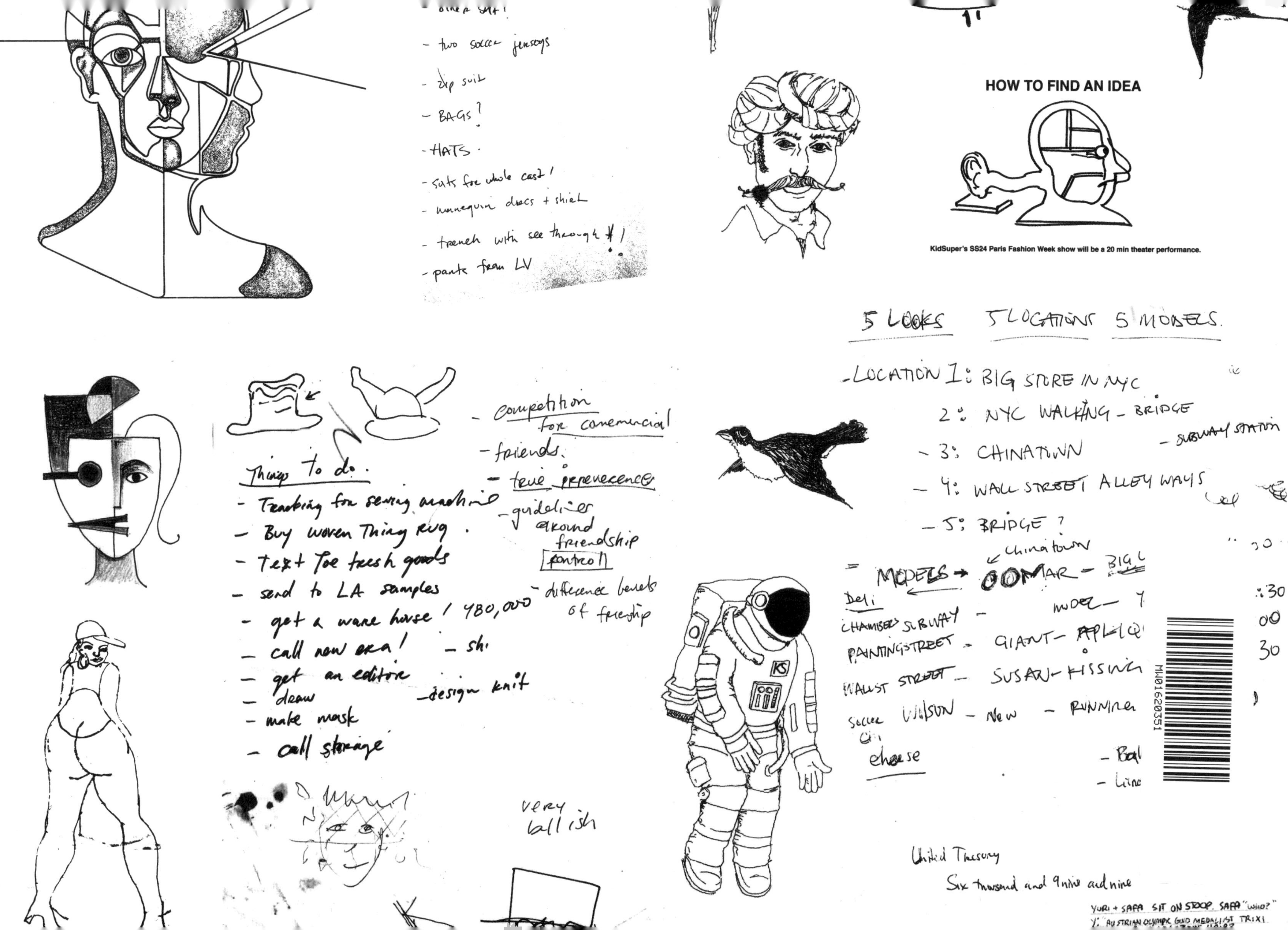

- two soccer jerseys
- zip suit
- BAGS?
- HATS
- suits for whole cast!
- mannequin dress + shirt
- trench with see through #!
- pants from LV
HOW TO FIND AN IDEA
KidSuper's SS24 Paris Fashion Week show will be a 20 min theater performance.
5 LOOKS 5 LOCATIONS 5 MODELS.
- LOCATION 1: BIG STORE IN NYC
2: NYC WALKING - BRIDGE
- 3: CHINATOWN - SUBWAY STATION
- 4: WALL STREET ALLEY WAYS
- 5: BRIDGE ?
- competition for commercial
- friends
- true preference
- guideliner around friendship
control
- difference levels of friendship
Things to do.
- Tracking for sewing machine
- Buy woven Thing rug.
- Text for fresh goods
- send to LA samples
- get a ware house / 480,000
- call new era!
- get an editor
- draw
- design knit
- make mask
- call storage
MODELS → OOMAR
Deli
CHAMBERS SUBWAY
PAINTING STREET - GIANT
WALL ST STREET - SUSAN - KISSING
Soccer WILSON - New - RUNNER
cheese
very tallish
United Treasury
Six thousand and 9nine and nine
YURI + SAFA SIT ON STOOP. SAFA "WHO?"
:30
00
30
MW01620351

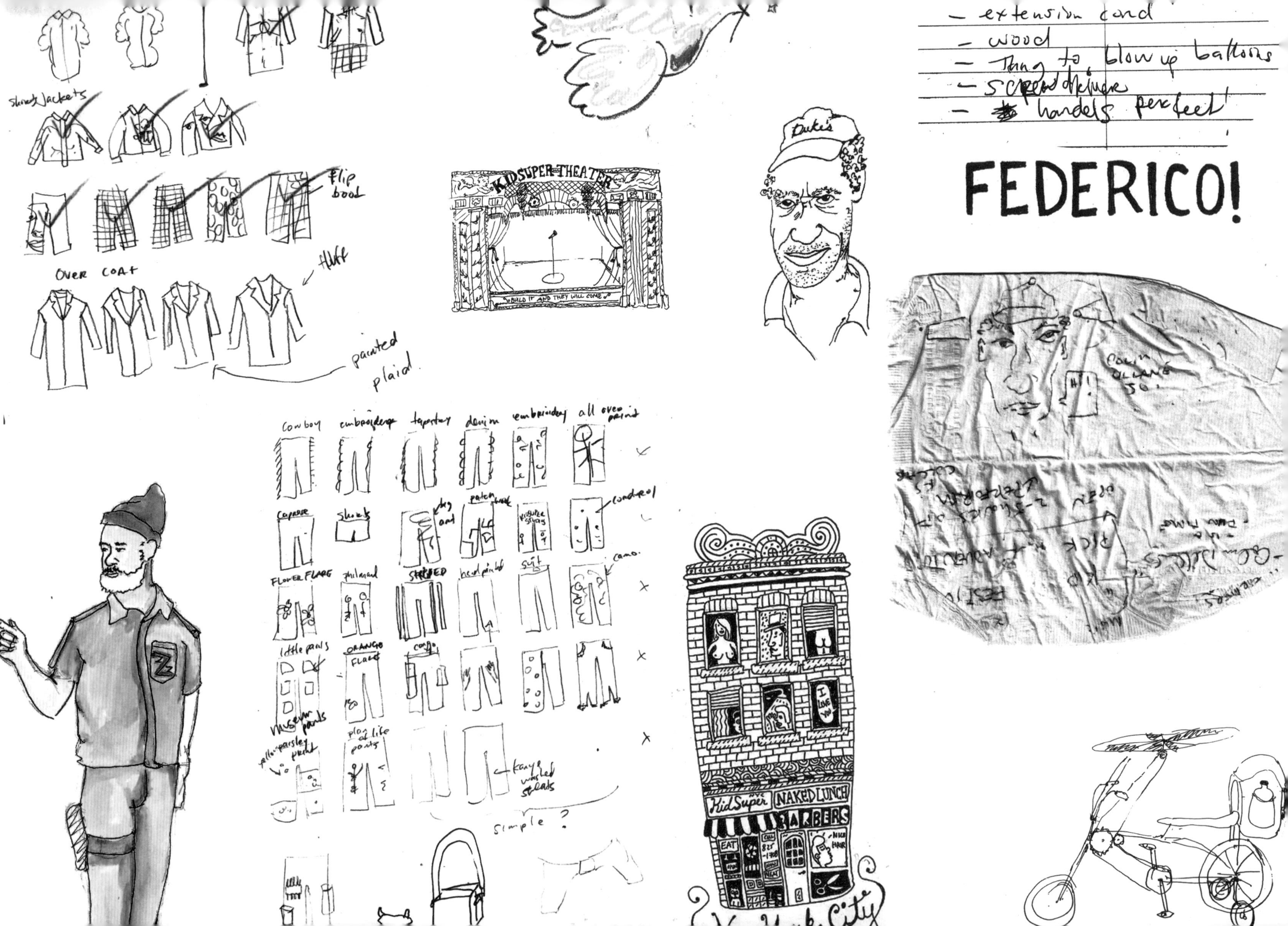

- extension cord
- wood
- Thing to blow up balloons
- screwdriver
- handels perfect!
FEDERICO!
Duke's
KIDSUPER THEATER
BUILD IT AND THEY WILL COME
OVER COAT
flip book
painted plaid
cowboy
tapestry
denim
embroidery
all over print
shorts
patch work
hand painted
suit
camo.
corduroy
FLOWER FLARE
STRIPED
ORANGE FLARE
little pants
plan of life pants
simple ?
KidSuper NYC
NAKED LUNCH
BARBERS
EAT
NICE HAIR
I LOVE YOU

KidSuper Studios

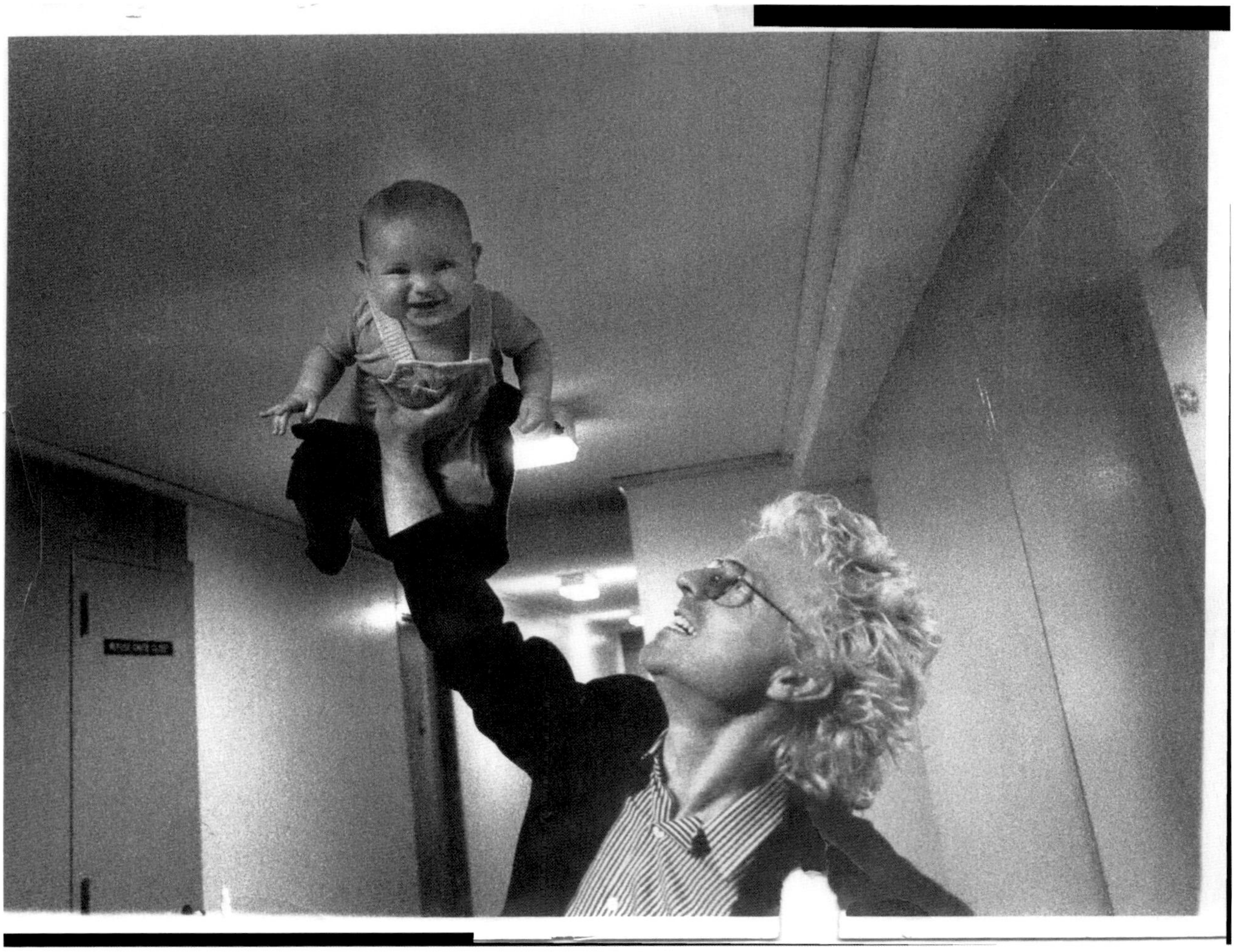

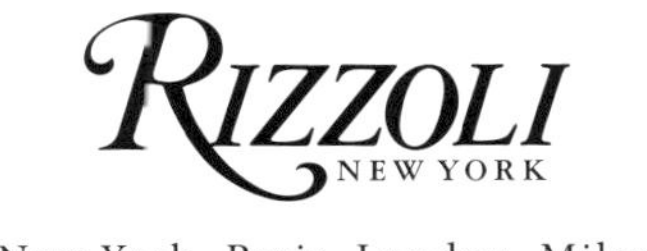

New York · Paris · London · Milan

THE MISADV
KIDS

ENTURES OF

UPER

First published in the United States of America in 2025 by Rizzoli International Publications, Inc.

49 West 27th Street
New York, NY 10001
www.rizzoliusa.com

Editor: Jenna Blaha
Book Design: Keir Novesky, Victor Williams, Michael Houtz, Colm Dillane, and Adham Foda
Front cover image: © Estelle Sweeney
Back cover image: © Colm Dillane

Rizzoli International Publications, Inc.

Publisher: Charles Miers
Editor: Ian Luna
Project Editor: Joe Davidson
Production: Barbara Sadick & Eugene Lee
Proofreader: Mary Ellen Wilson

Printed in Singapore
2025 2026 2027 2028 2029 /
10 9 8 7 6 5 4 3 2 1
ISBN: 978-0-8478-7564-1

The authorized representative in the EU for product safety and compliance is Mondadori Libri S.p.A., via Gian Battista Vico 42, Milan, Italy, 20123
www.mondadori.it

Visit us online
Instagram: @RizzoliBooks
Facebook.com/RizzoliNewYork
Youtube.com/user/RizzoliNY

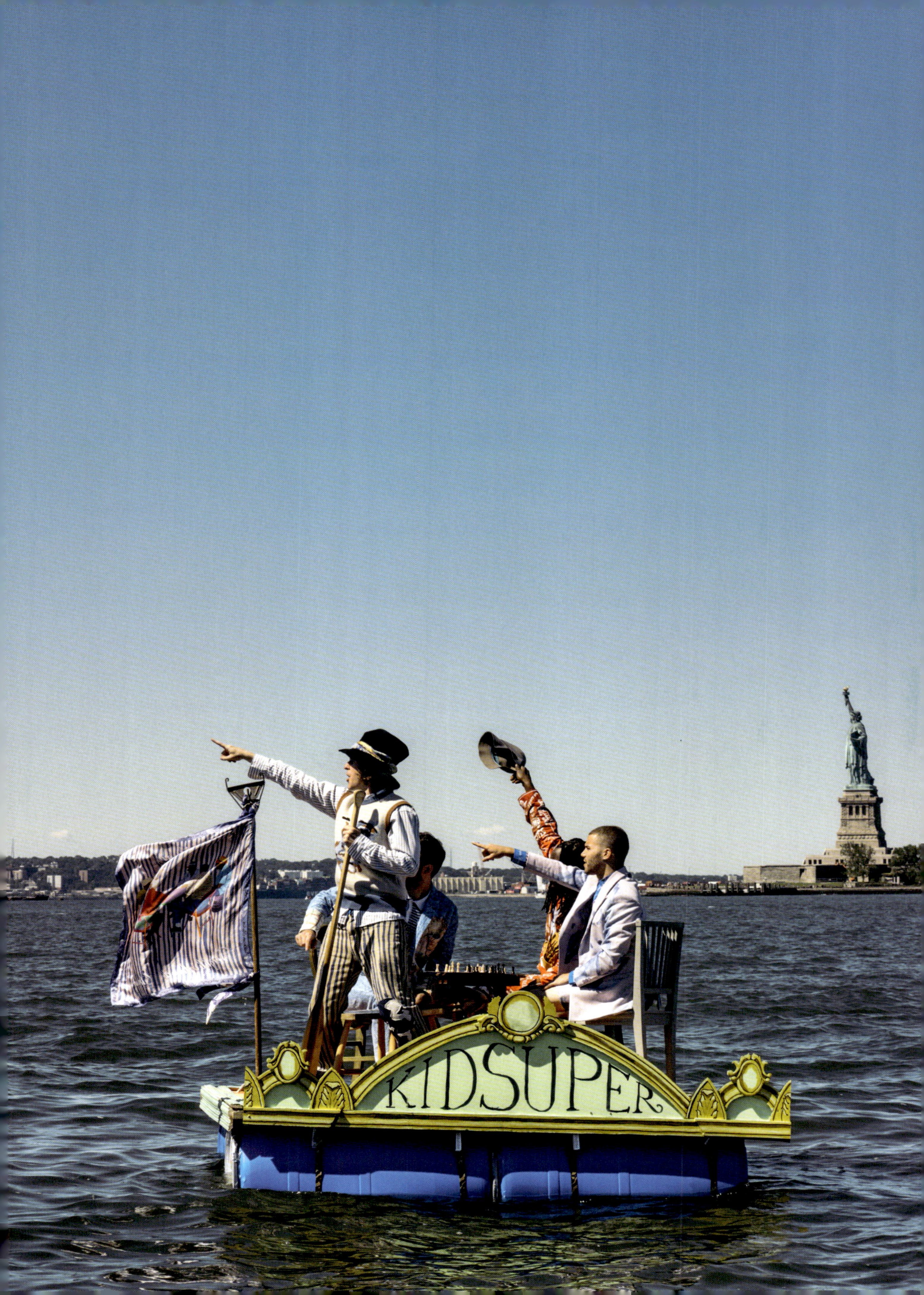
KIDSUPER

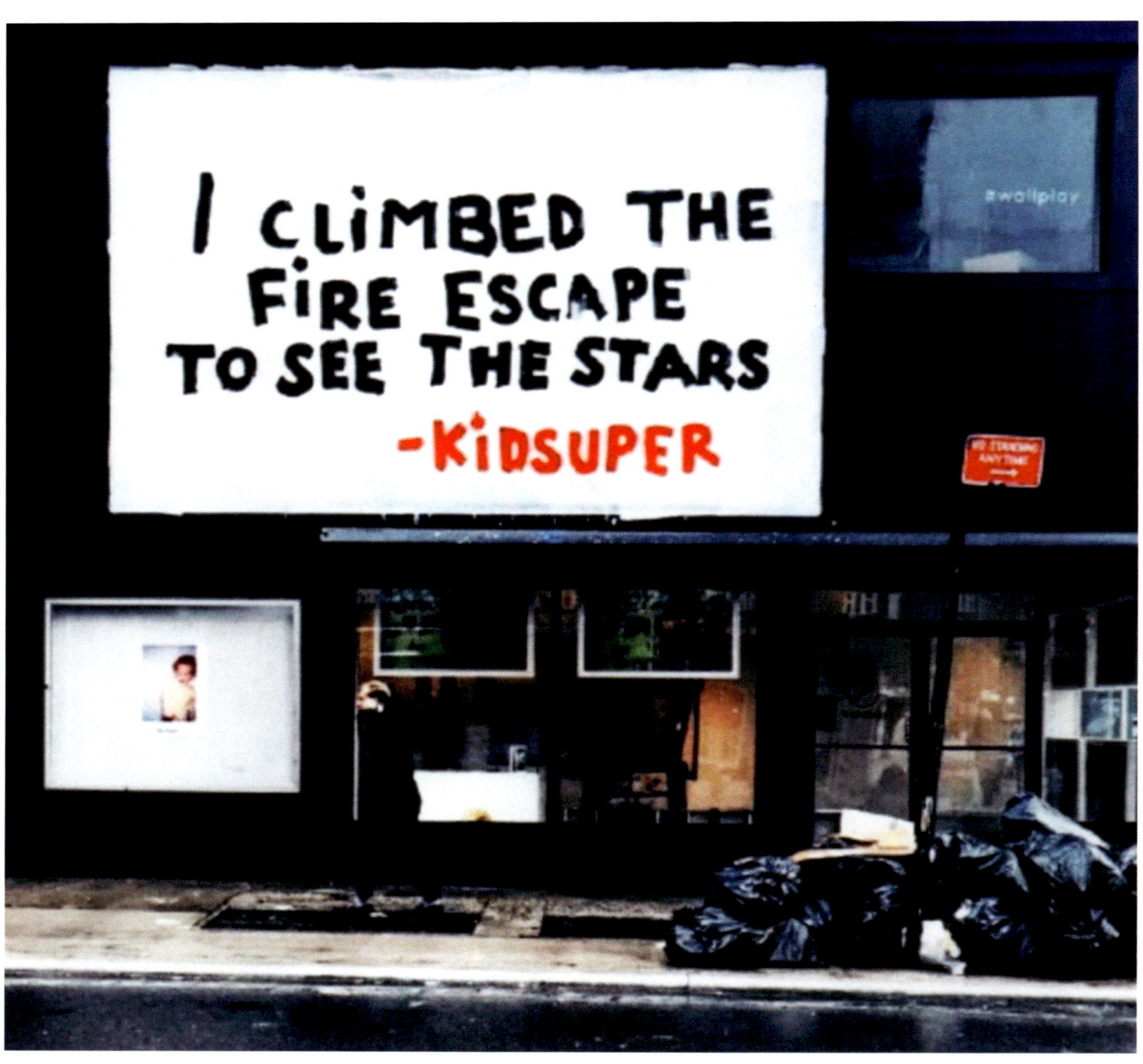

When I was a teenager I used to climb up scaffolding and explore buildings and spaces in New York City. This was my wilderness. When I was 19, I was caught and arrested for trespassing. When the cops asked me and my friends where the drugs, graffiti, tools were, I responded "I climbed the fire escape to see the stars." It became a mantra of KidSuper, using what I have to try to reach my goals.

PROLOGUE:

THIS ISN'T A BOOK ABOUT MY WORK, OR A RETROSPECTIVE OF ALL THAT I HAVE DONE...

I'M NOT OLD ENOUGH for that and I have not done enough. We can get to that later. This is the exact opposite of that: this is a book about how to live. A book about life. What do I know about life? Who knows. But what I do know is ideas. And what's more important than ideas?

When I get an idea, it never leaves and I work tirelessly to try to accomplish it. And that is what I think life is about. It is the pursuit that brings meaning to life. It is making a to-do list and checking it off, whether it is just a small or big idea.

This is a book about a way of thinking that might inspire you to make your own book.

I know ideas are hard to come by, but I give power to small ideas and big ideas equally. I am satisfied by them in the same way. Figuring out my next fashion show, or planning the next business move, or creative directing for the biggest brand in the world gives me the same satisfaction as fixing the scanner that broke while making this book. I just enjoy problem solving.

There is and always might be a naivety to everything I do. Someone asked me the other day why I am a rule breaker in the fashion industry. I didn't even realize I was breaking the rules because I did not know the rules.

When Orson Welles was asked about why his first film, *Citizen Kane,* was such a monumental hit, he responded, because "I did not know any better." "You don't know what cannot be done."

Everything I have learned in life is from trial and error, from my stubbornness and fearlessness, from the act of just plain action!

This book will go through the twelve fashion shows that I have done to date. Each of them is completely unique in its own way and has taken my creativity to places I didn't even know existed. I see them as magnificent, colossal mountains I tried to climb.

Each one of these fashion shows will act as a pillar for how to live: the twelve steps of my hero's journey.

If my life so far can give any sort of guidance or inspiration, it is from all the things I have attempted.

KIDSUPER

TABLE OF

CONTENTS

INTRODUCTION:

The Misadventures of KidSuper
A Manifesto of Ideas

THE 12 RUNWAY shows were never just fashion shows. Each one felt like a mountain I didn't know how to climb—no map, no real plan. Just a belief that the idea was worth chasing.

Looking back, every show was its own episode. A stand-alone story. A near disaster. A tiny miracle. But taken together: It started to feel like a journey—a completely backwards, upside-down, misfit version of the hero's journey.

So, here it is:
The KidSuperHero's Journey.

12 fashion shows.
12 misadventures.
12 steps to doing the impossible, or at least trying.

NOTES: You might wonder why I am using Fashion Shows as my guiding pillars.

I think fashion is an interesting art form because of the constant demand to produce. Every season, no matter what happens, even through COVID, you have to produce and release items or else your business fails. Within this constant demand—though sometimes incredibly draining—there is this opportunity to try new ideas; to constantly test and receive feedback from new attempts. Because of this, you are constantly improving and learning. Fashion is interestingly enough capturing the current zeitgeist, equally as much a business as an artistic pursuit, especially when you are the designer and the CEO. There is an artistic freedom in being a business and an artist. I can make the executive decisions to fund my ideas.

Colm Dillane's ~~Desig~~ DESIGN RULES

1) What if ____ was possible?

2) STORY INFORMS PRODUCT INFORMS STORY
PRODUCT TO UNLOCK CULTURE
STORY
PRODUCT

3) ORIGINAL ART USE YOUR HANDS AND/OR IMAGINATION

4) COMPETITION BREEDS CREATIVITY
(AND TEAMWORK, TEAMS HAVE CAPTAINS)

5) INSPIRATION FROM ACTION ~~TAKE RI~~ TAKE RISKS

6) TINKER (WITH FORM, HISTORY, CONVENTION)

7.) ART IS MATH!! PROBLEM SOLVE
(OBSTACLES INSPIRE ANSWERS)

8) UTILITY CAN BE DESIGN NOT FUNCTION
(AERODYNAMIC CHAIR)

9) HUMOR IS PROGRESS
MISTAKES ARE FUNNY
BOREDOM IS LAZINESS

10) NEW YORK CITY IS PERFECT IN ITS MESS
PEOPLE ARE EVERYTHING

11) DEADLINES ARE OUR NORTH STAR! ★

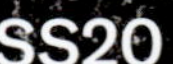

SS20

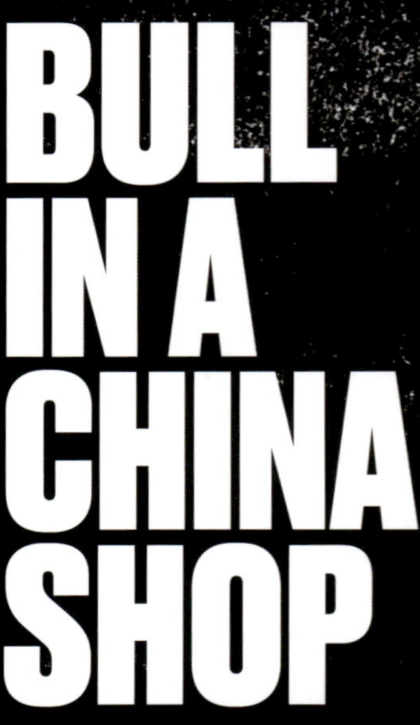

BULL IN A CHINA SHOP

Make as much noise as possible. Fuck it—what's the worst that can happen, some broken china?

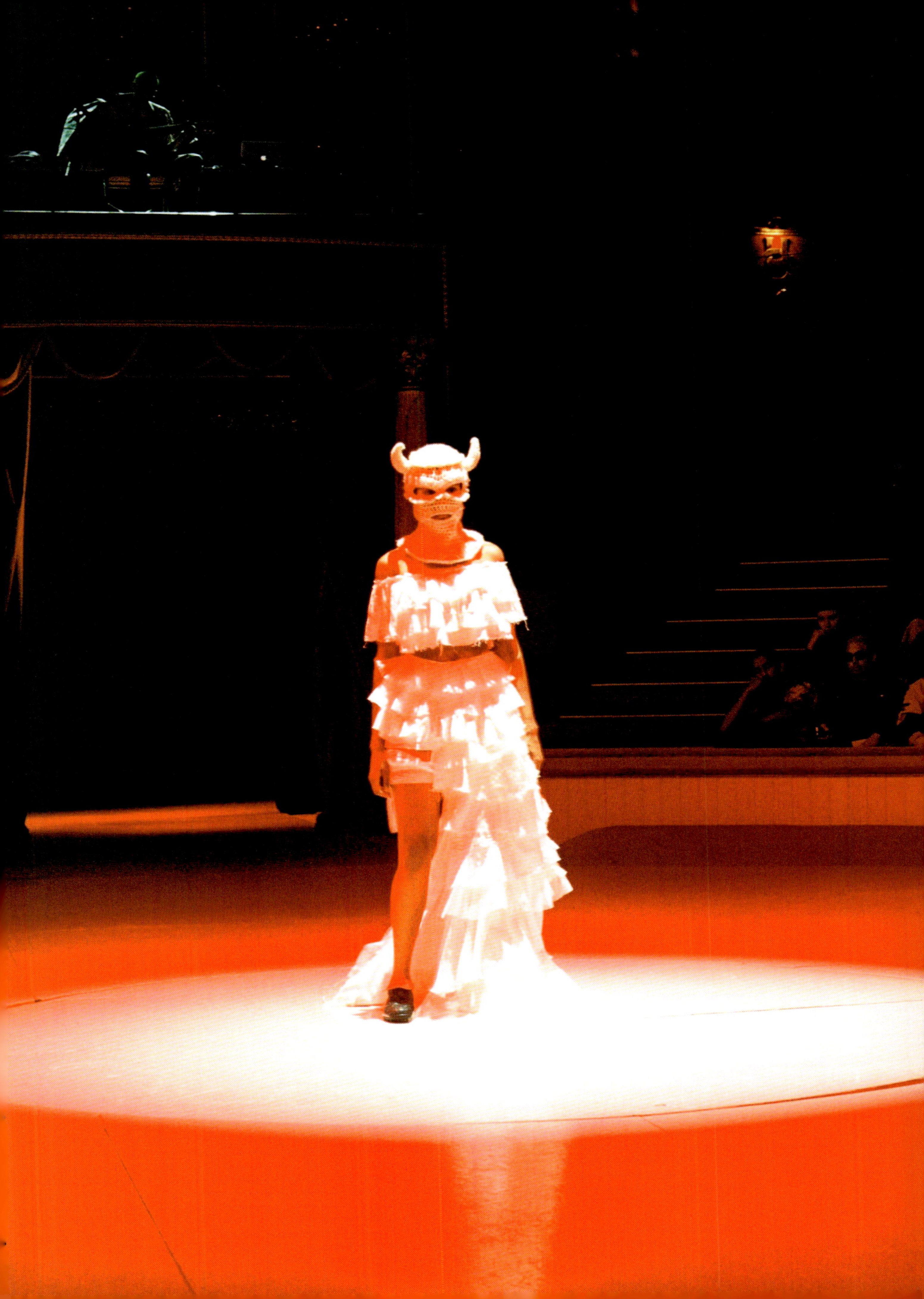

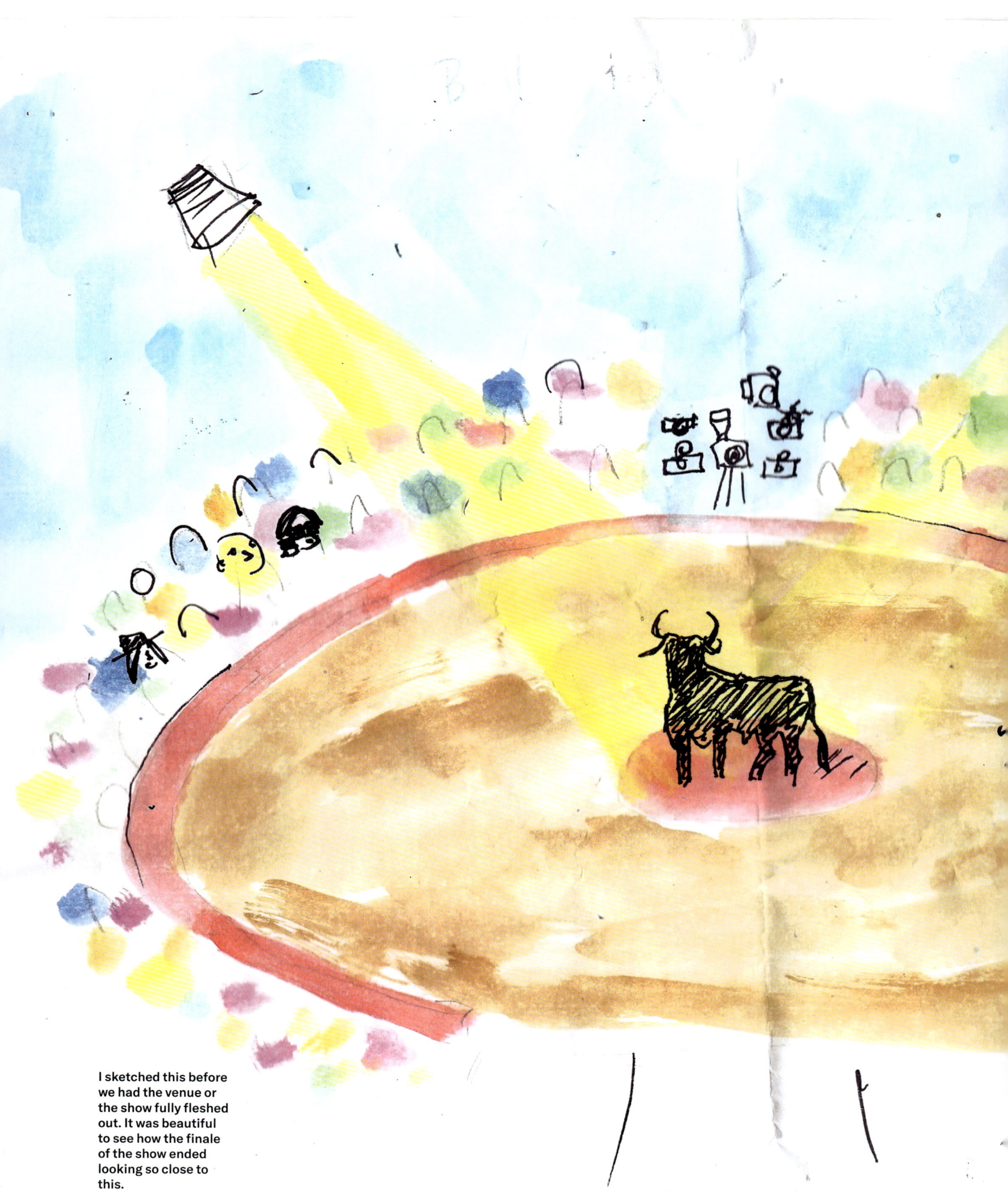

I sketched this before we had the venue or the show fully fleshed out. It was beautiful to see how the finale of the show ended looking so close to this.

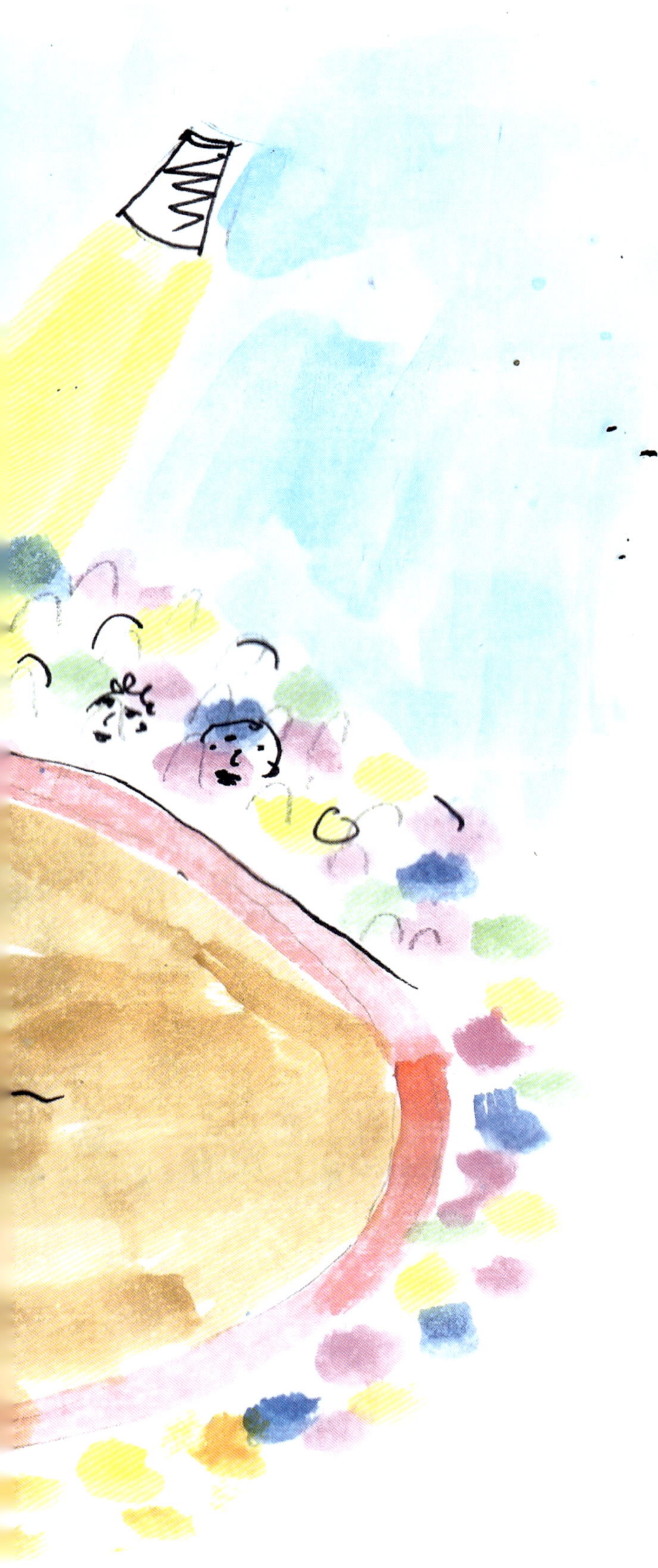

MY FIRST FASHION SHOW EVER

IT WAS 2019 and I had been doing all kinds of different creative projects under the moniker KidSuper—clothing, art shows, album covers, photoshoots, music videos, graphic design, merch, even billboards. I was starting to gain recognition as someone who could pull off ambitious projects.

One day, two girls walked into my store, where I was also living at the time. One was a stylist named Taisha, and the other, Brit, worked in PR. They asked me, "What's next for KidSuper?" Jokingly, I said, "Paris Fashion Week."

Brit then mentioned that she worked for a French PR company and asked if I wanted to meet her boss. At that time (and even now), my philosophy was to say yes to everything—enthusiasm is contagious. So, of course, I said yes.

When I met her boss, there was some miscommunication—he thought I was actively planning a show and asked, "What venues are you considering in Paris?" Not wanting to look unprepared, I started making things up on the spot. I blurted out, "Most runways are straight. What if we did a circular one? It could be themed like a bullfighting ring—my mom is from Spain, so I could tie in that iconography of the bull. I am in a way a Bull in a China Shop. I don't belong here but I am going to make some noise."

I left the meeting thinking, What was that? But every few weeks, the PR guy, now known as Florent, would check in, saying, "Hey, Paris Fashion Week is two months away . . . a month and a half away . . . a month away." I kept brushing it off, thinking, I can't believe he actually thinks we can do this.

But my friends, who had seen me pull off crazy things before, were all in. They believed in the KidSupermentality—that anything was possible. And I thought to myself, If I named the brand KidSuper, I have to live up to it. I have to take risks.

So, I called him back and said, "Let's do Paris Fashion Week, whatever that means."

AT THE TIME, I had no idea what a fashion show entailed—where to get models, how many looks I needed, nothing. This wouldn't just be the first fashion show I organized—it would also be the first one I ever attended. We applied to be on the official Paris Fashion Week calendar and were (as I expected)

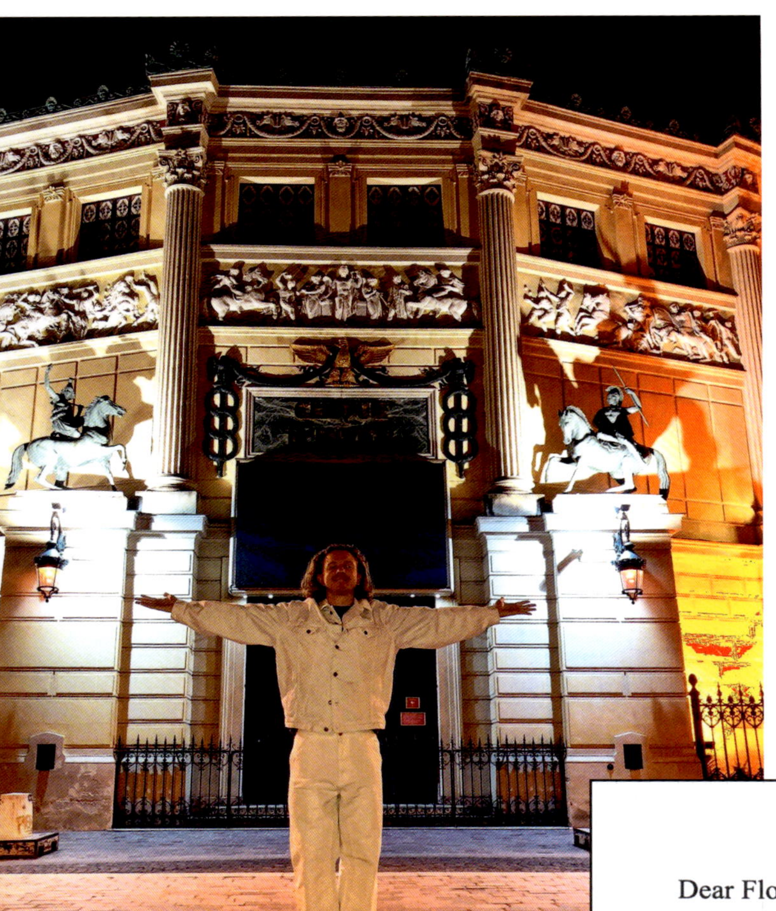

In front of Cirque d'Hiver Bouglione, the venue for the first show. This felt so big, so monumental.

rejected. So we did an off-calendar show, which is when you put on a show at the same time in Paris and hope (for me, beg) people would show up.

I called my friends: "We have a month to create thirty looks." I figured that was a solid number from my research on *Vogue*'s website—some shows had twenty, some had seventy. I started pulling together pieces from past collections, screen-printing patterns, hand-knitting sweaters, and working with Big L, a sixty-year-old Senegalese tailor who had worked with Dapper Dan. I asked him, "Do you want to come to Paris with us?" He immediately said yes. I brought him, my friends, and anything that looked like it would work on a runway to Paris.

IN PARIS, we searched for a venue. One caught my eye—a beautiful, old French circus that perfectly fit the bullfighting theme. But it was 30,000 euros for the day. I told the PR guy it was too expensive, so he showed me cheaper options—5,000, 10,000, 15,000 euros—but I couldn't get the circus out of my head.

I thought, If we rent this space, I don't even need to decorate it—it already looks perfect. So I made the call: Go big or go home. We booked the circus.

Dear Florent,

Following the meeting of the Advisory Men's Committee organized yesterday, unfortunately we are sorry to inform you that your application was not selected for the official schedule (show and presentation) of the Men's PFW SS20.

Thank you for your interest.

We remain at your disposal should you need any further information,

Best regards,

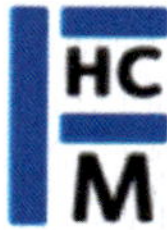

FÉDÉRATION
DE LA HAUTE COUTURE
ET DE LA MODE

The Rejection Email that we didn't make the official calendar

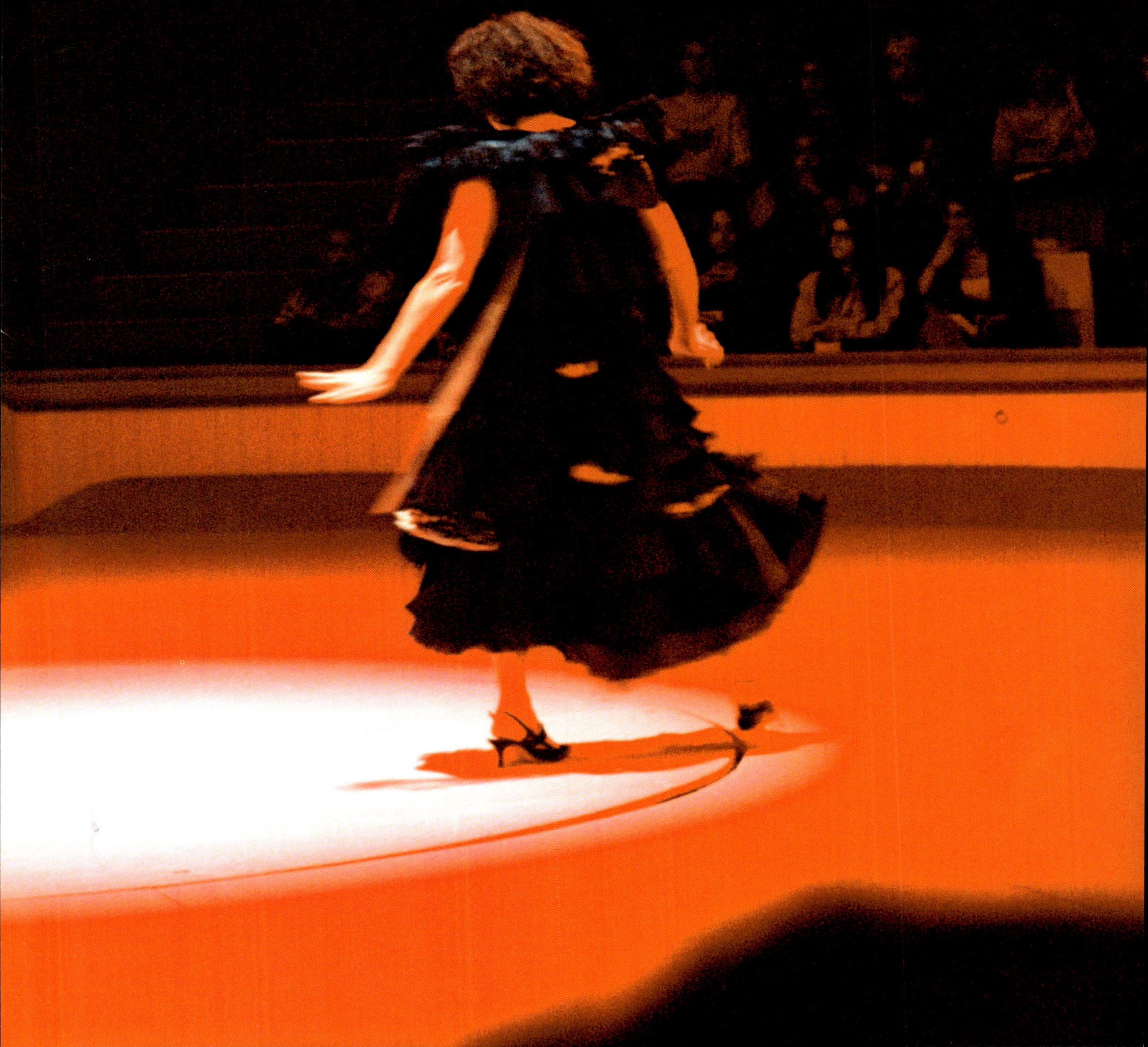

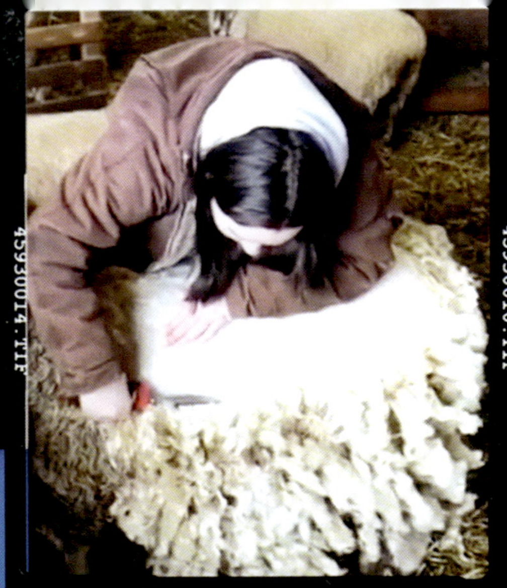

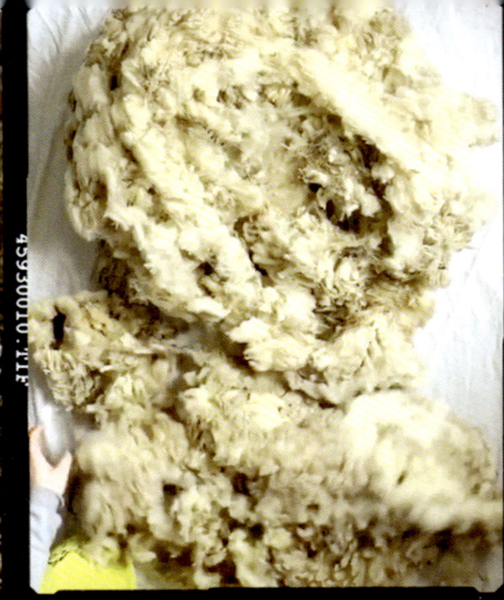

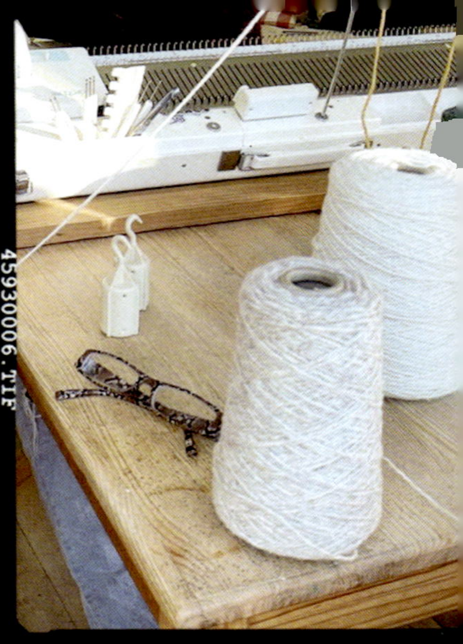

THIS SWEATER WAS MADE FULLY FRO
DIFFERENT CREAM SHADES ARE THE

HOW TO MAKE
KNITS

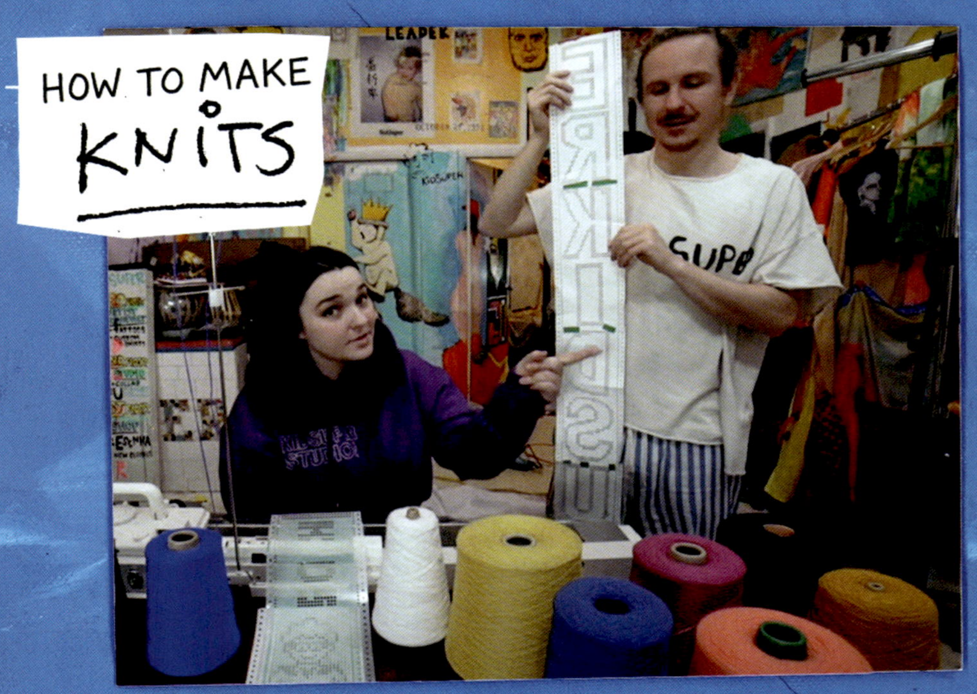

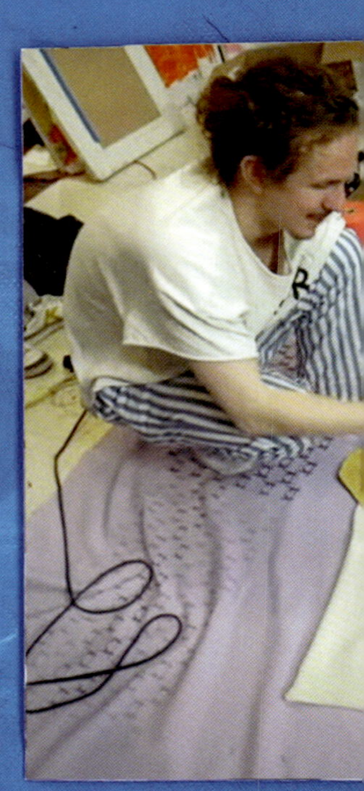

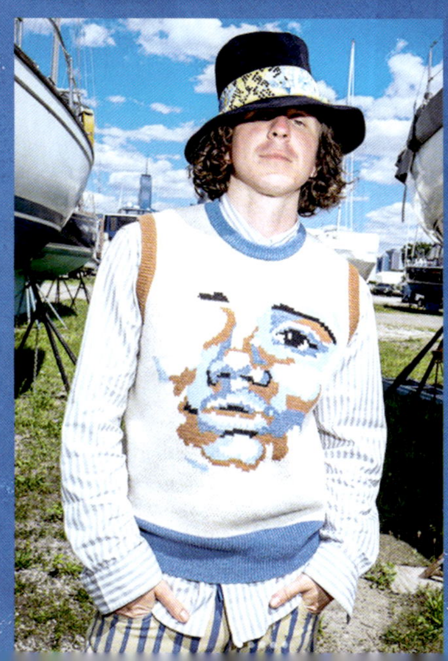

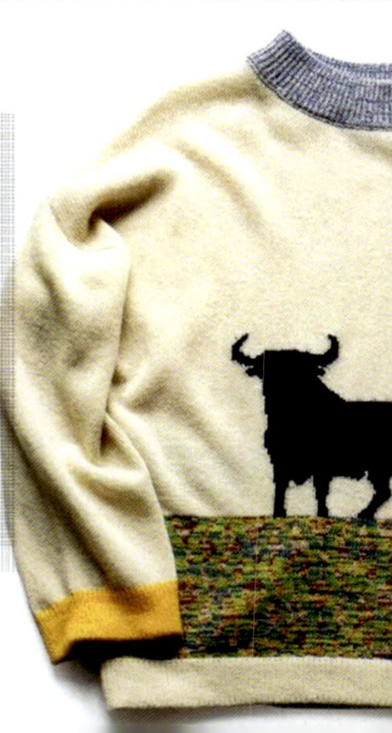

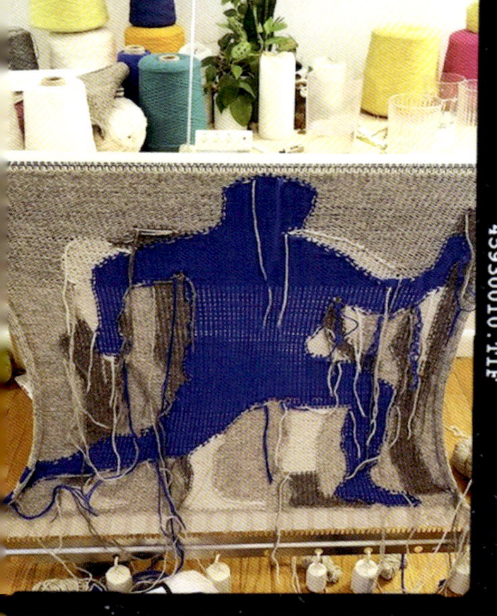

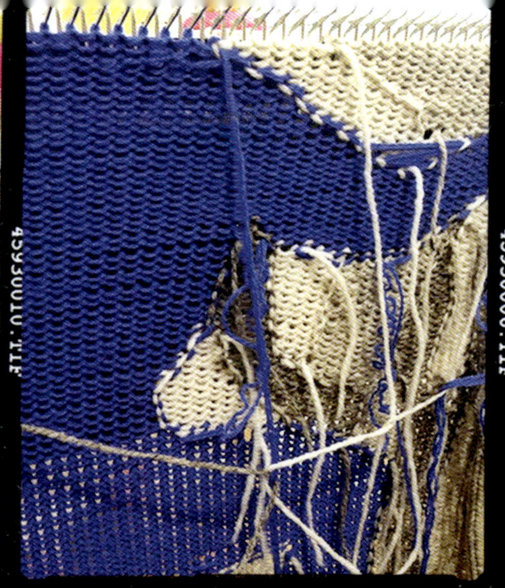

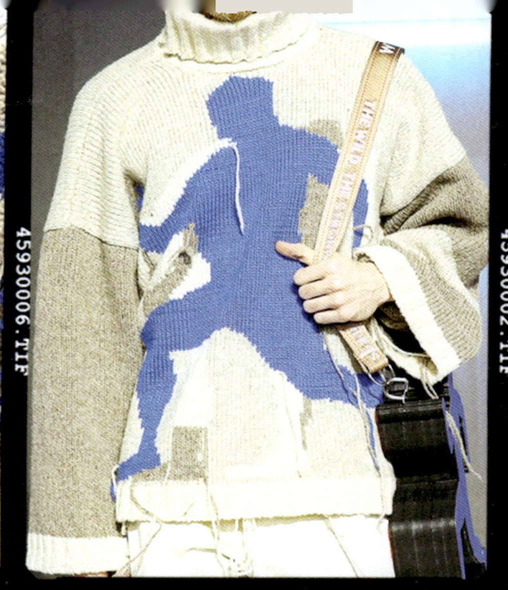

LOCAL SHEEPS IN THE USA THE
ATURAL UNDYED COLOR OF THE WOOL

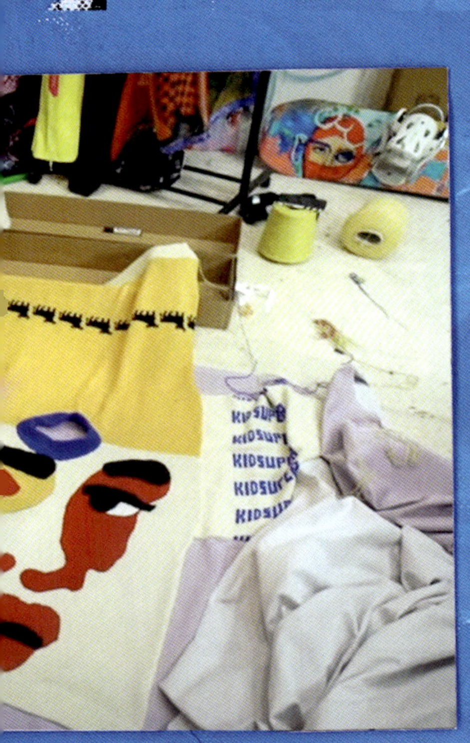

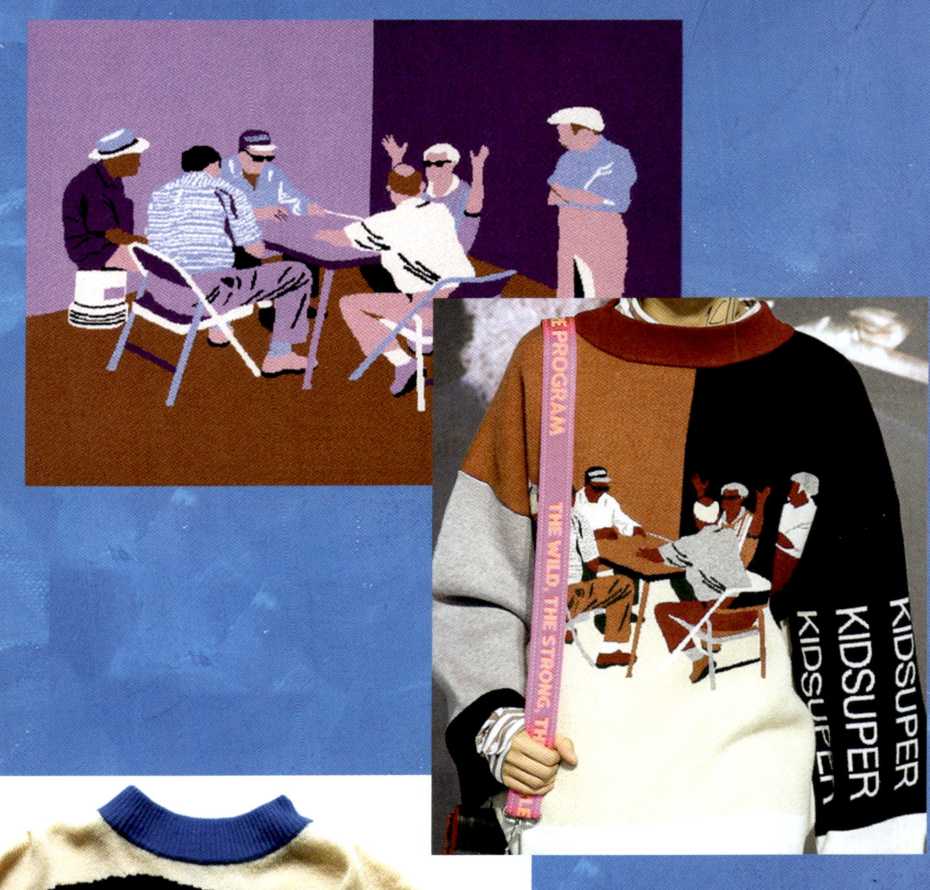

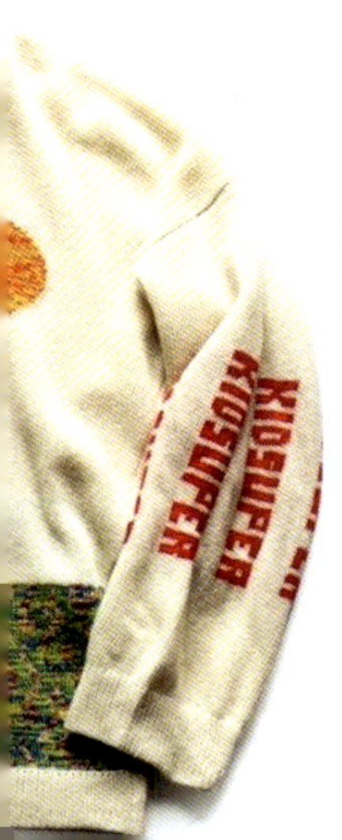

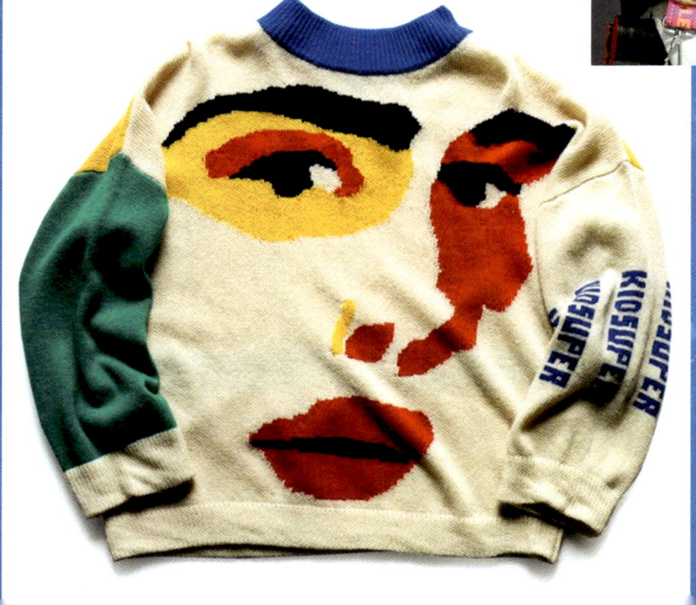

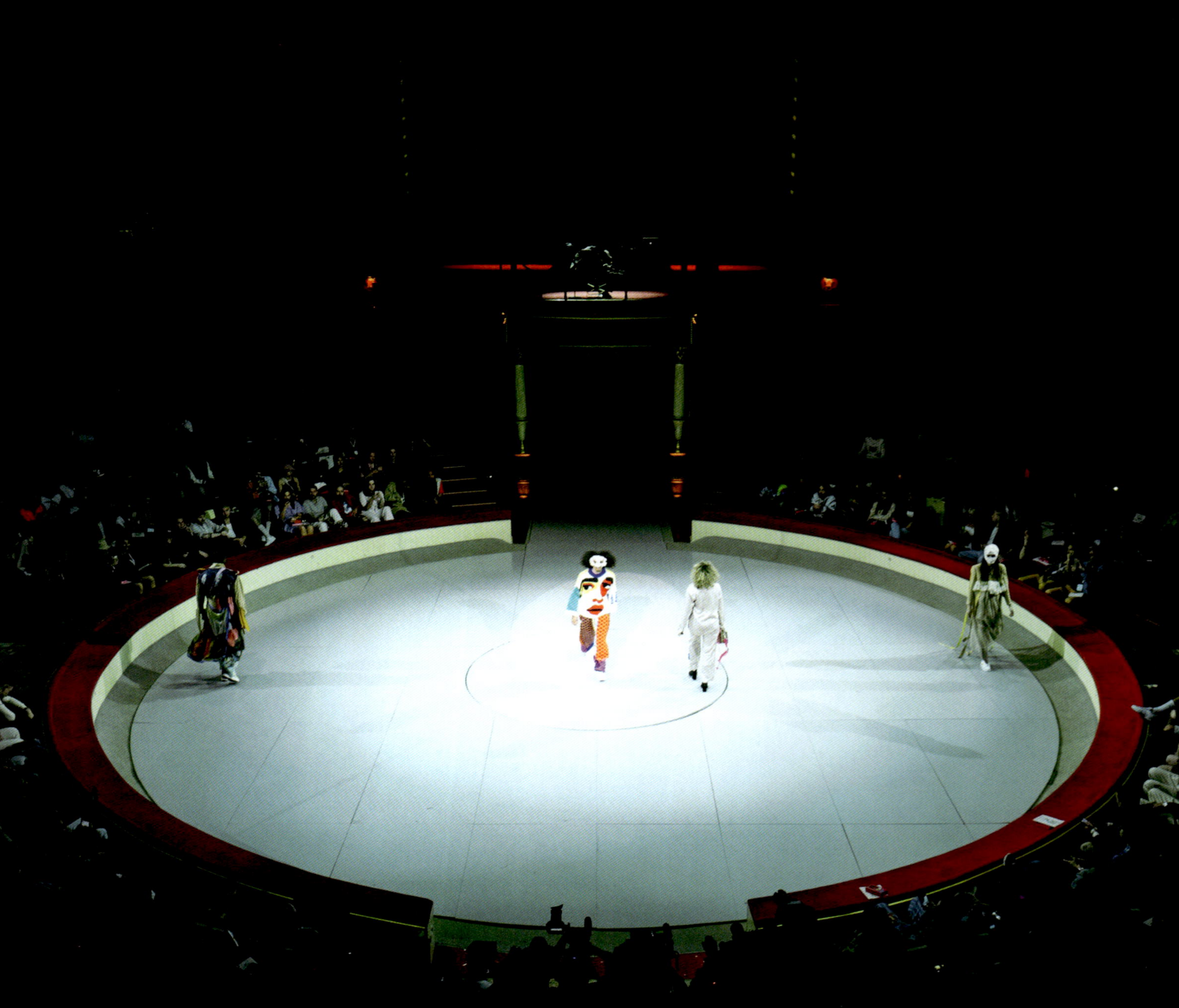

I STILL DIDN'T know where to get models, so I looked around and decided: friends, rappers who wore my clothes, anyone who fit the vibe—I cast them all. We needed more models.

A few hours before the show, my parents arrived. Looking at them, I thought, It would be amazing if they opened the show. I told them, "Mom, Dad, you're walking."

They weren't sure if I was joking. My mom started practicing her walk, but in her head she was Naomi Campbell—way too much strutting. I told her, "Mom, just walk normally." But she couldn't. So I finally said, "Forget it—just dance."

I had hired a flamenco guitarist for the show's music, and I figured if my mom danced flamenco down the runway, you would assume she was a professional dancer. And if she messed up, she's smooth enough to make it work. It would be beautiful.

THIRTY MINUTES BEFORE the show, the guitarist bailed. Total panic. Then I remembered Dominic Fike, an artist who had come to Paris with us to walk the show. I asked him, "Don't you play guitar?"

Dominic Fike closing the show playing the flamenco that he learned an hour before

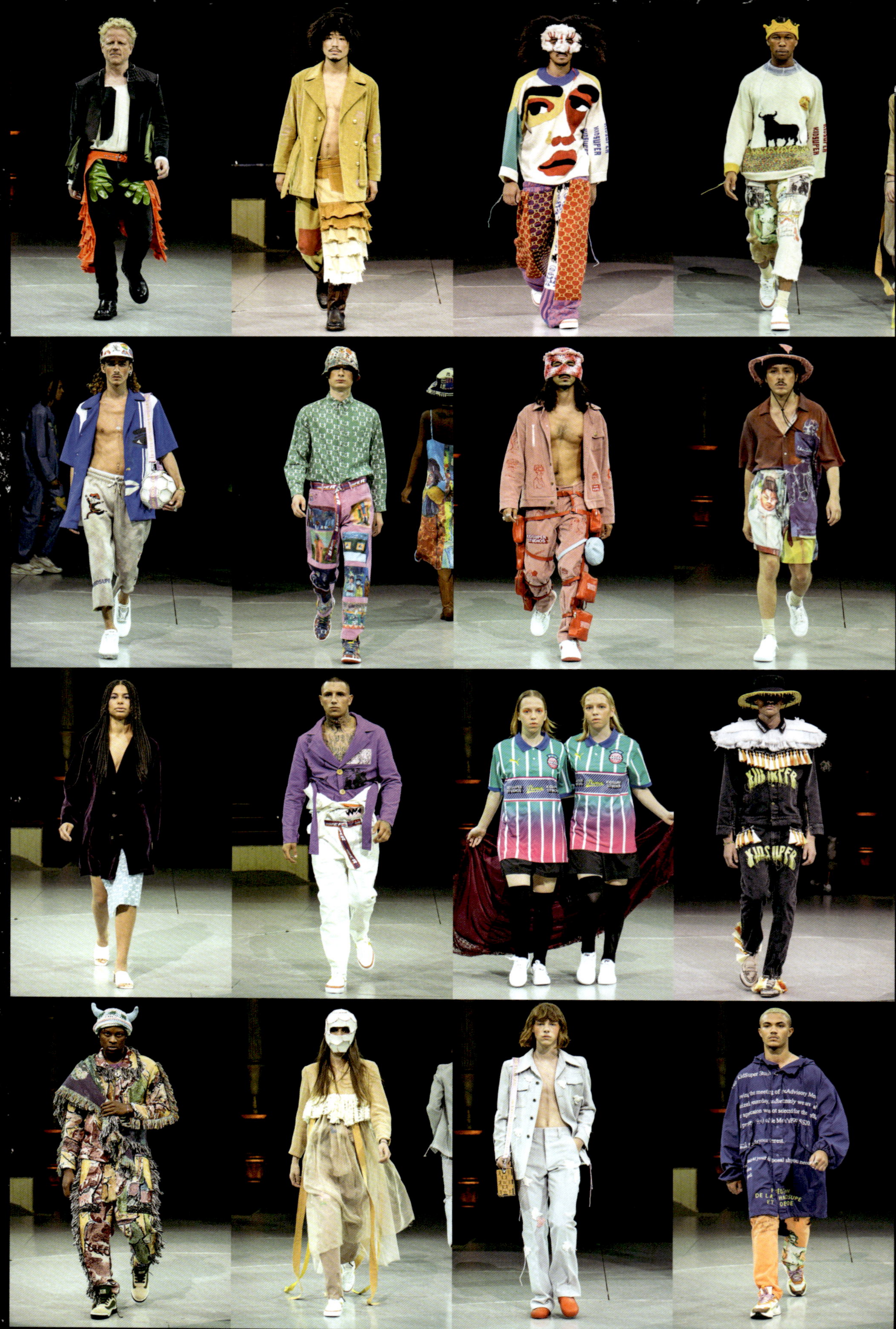
KIDSUPER

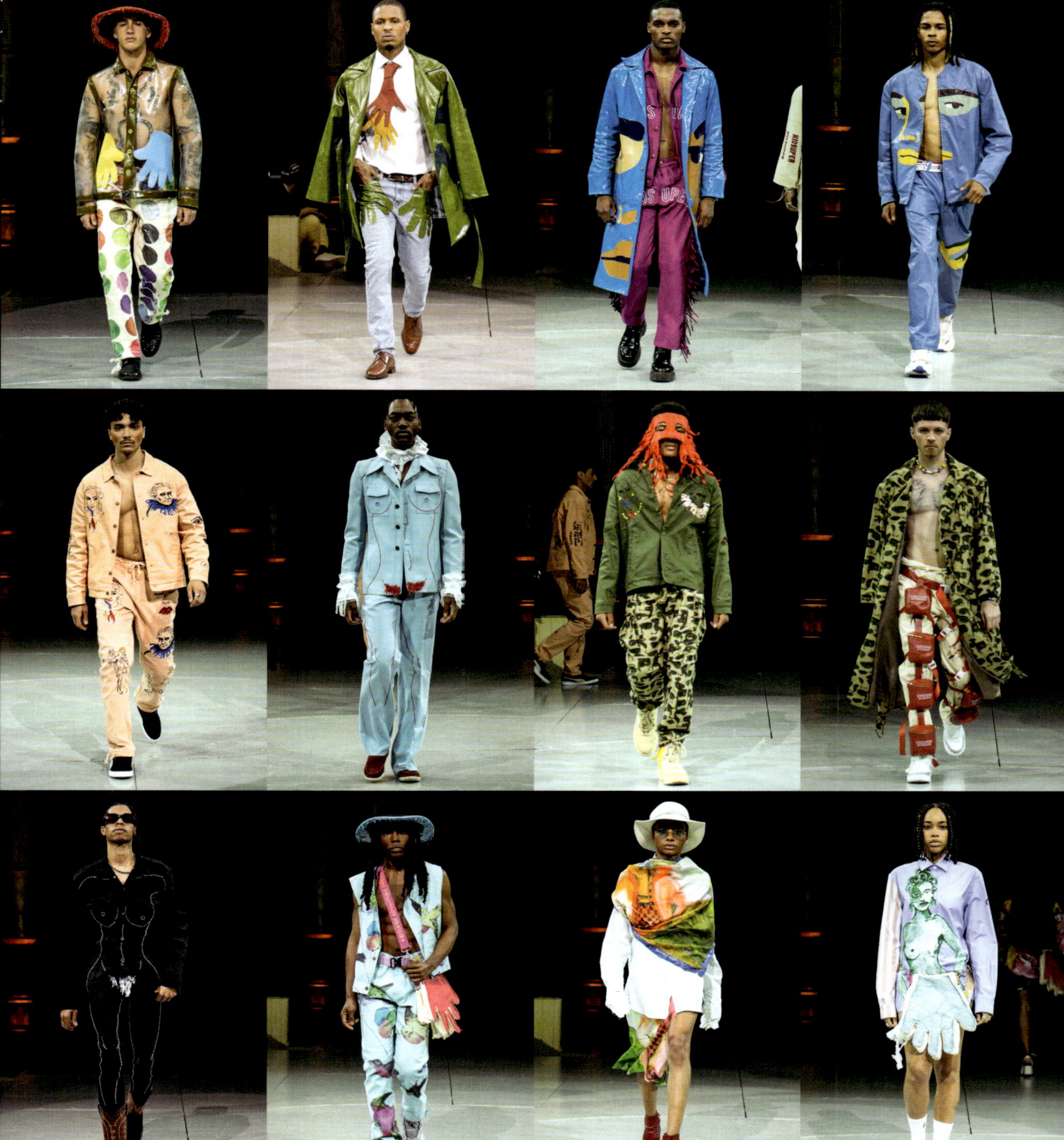

He picked up the guitar and started trying to play flamenco. And just like that, we had live music again.

The show started: Dominic playing guitar, my mom dancing down the runway, my dad walking after her, followed by thirty models and a finale of a breakdancer dancing around a girl in a bull mask and gown. The energy was unreal.

Before the show, I had told the PR guy, "I don't care if a million people come—I just need someone from *Vogue* to see it and review it." After the show, I rushed backstage in celebration and Florent came up to me and said, "A woman from *Vogue* is here to speak with you."

I was ecstatic. She came backstage in a red jacket, and I excitedly walked her through everything: "This is where my mom walked, I made this all by hand, Big L helped me, these are my best friends."

The next day, she published an article titled "KidSuper Show Is the Breakout Surprise of the Paris Menswear Shows So Far."

GO big or go home.

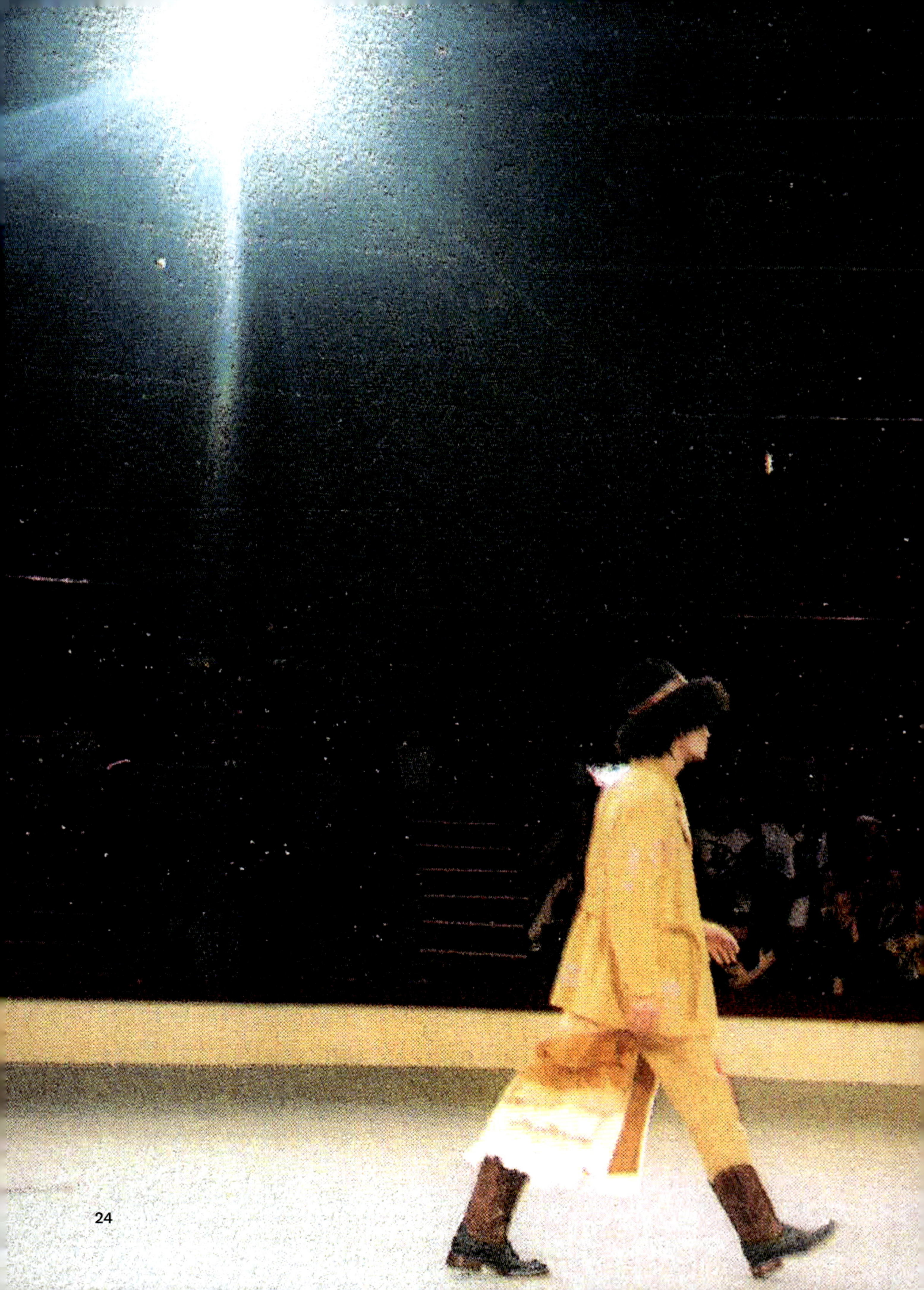

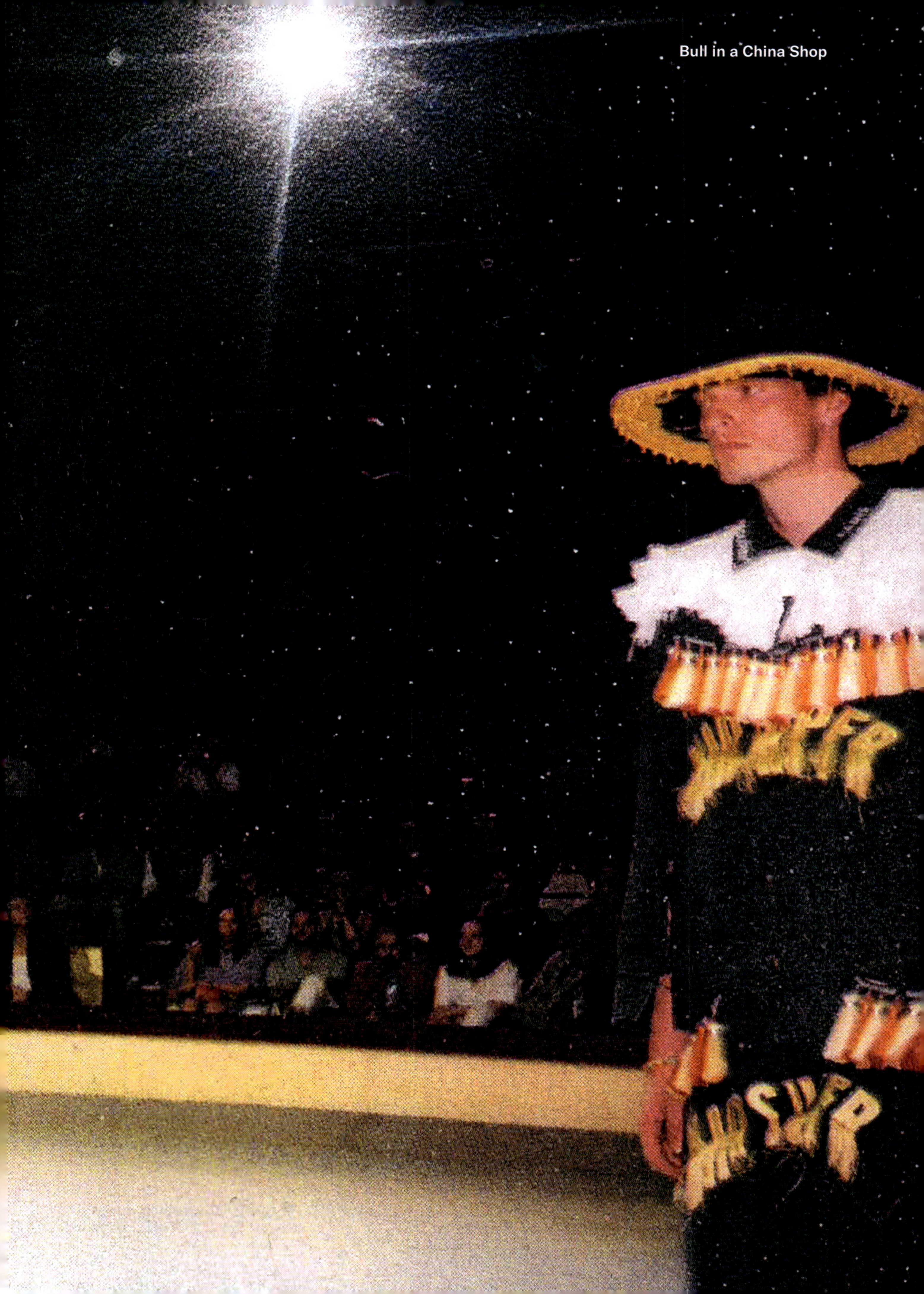

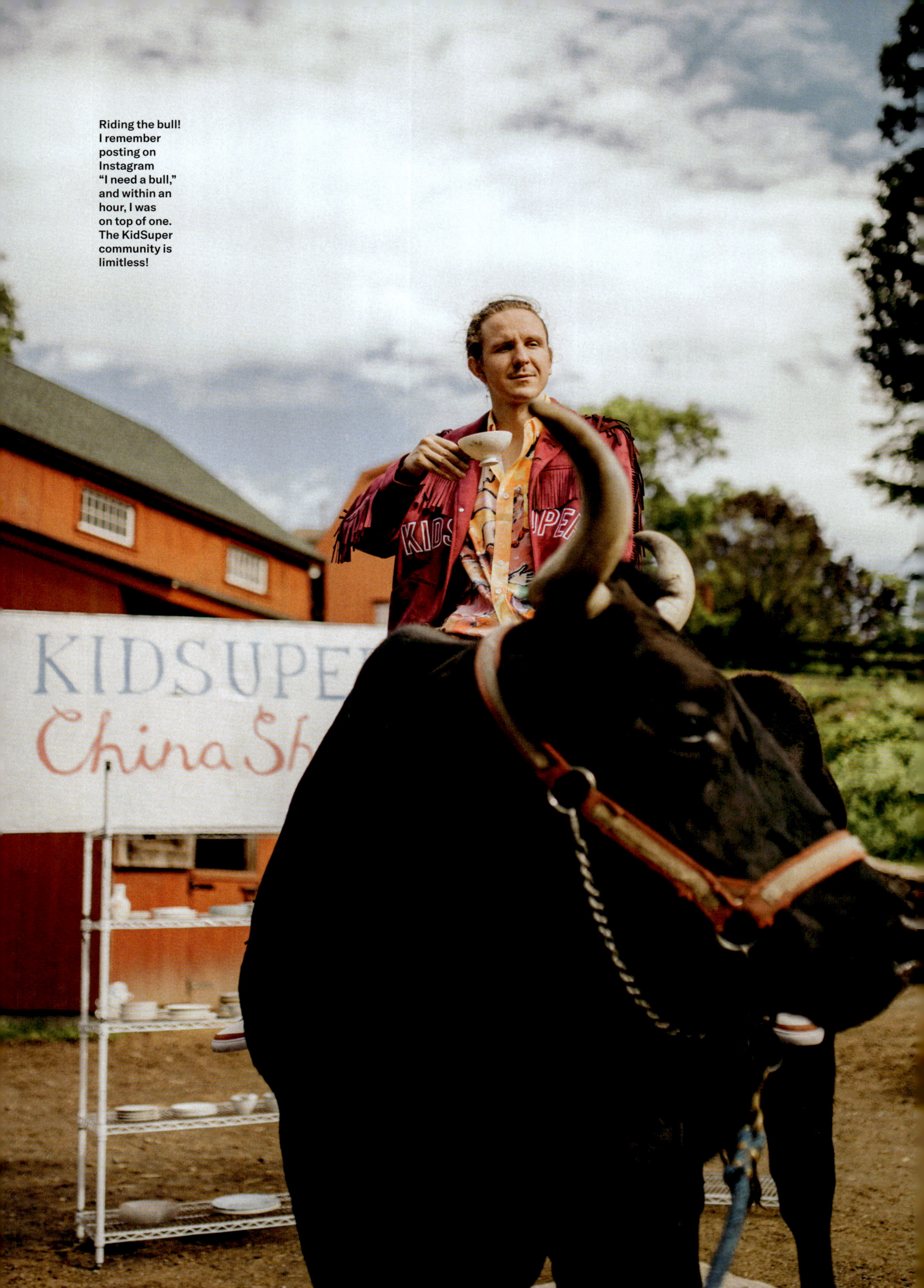

Riding the bull! I remember posting on Instagram "I need a bull," and within an hour, I was on top of one. The KidSuper community is limitless!

VOGUE

FASHION BEAUTY CULTURE LIVING WEDDINGS RUNWAY MORE

RUNWAY

Colm Dillane's KidSuper Show Is the Breakout Surprise of the Paris Menswear Shows So Far

BY AMY VERNER
June 21, 2019

Whatever unofficial accolades get doled out during these men's collections, KidSuper's "Bull in a China Shop" show on Thursday should be recognized for its go-big-or-go-home pluck. Founded by native New Yorker Colm Dillane, the streetwear-centric label is part of this season's mini migration of American brands testing Paris as a launchpad. The show took place at the Cirque d'Hiver Bouglione, a theatrical venue built during the Second Empire for circuses and other performances in the round. And between his parents doubling as models and the breakdancing matador, it attested to his unhinged imagination.

"When you think of fashion, you think of Paris. It's like going to Hollywood if you're an actor. So bringing the collection here is wild," said the 27-year-old who sold T-shirts in his high school cafeteria but went on to study mathematics at university. "For me, math is the essence of creativity; you can't change the rules, but how can you think creatively to solve the problem?"

Breaking out in Paris would certainly qualify as such. Even the boldface names who have worn his clothes—J Balvin, Shawn Mendes, Young Thug, Mahershala Ali, and Khalid—have done so with little song and dance. But this didn't matter because, well, he had the circus. Plus, he had his crew: Beyond his mom and dad, several longtime friends took a spin around the stage. Rapper Russ Vitale sang a catchy, custom song with lyrics that repeated KidSuper's name over and over again.

The combined men's and women's collection played up Spanish influences while loading the looks with arts-and-crafts details. Patchworks and direct placements of Dillane's hand-drawn illustrations felt like wearable outsider art; an accumulation of materials that benefited from the workmanship of a veteran Dapper Dan tailor who goes by the name Big L. If some leaned too clownish for everyday comfort, they also were delightfully daring. After the finale, in which a girl in an asymmetric, tiered bridal-style dress was seduced by the breakdancing matador, Dillane came out to express his gratitude, acknowledging that this wasn't the fashionable thing to do: "Guys, you have no idea how much work and effort went into this. I love all of you." We look forward to his return.

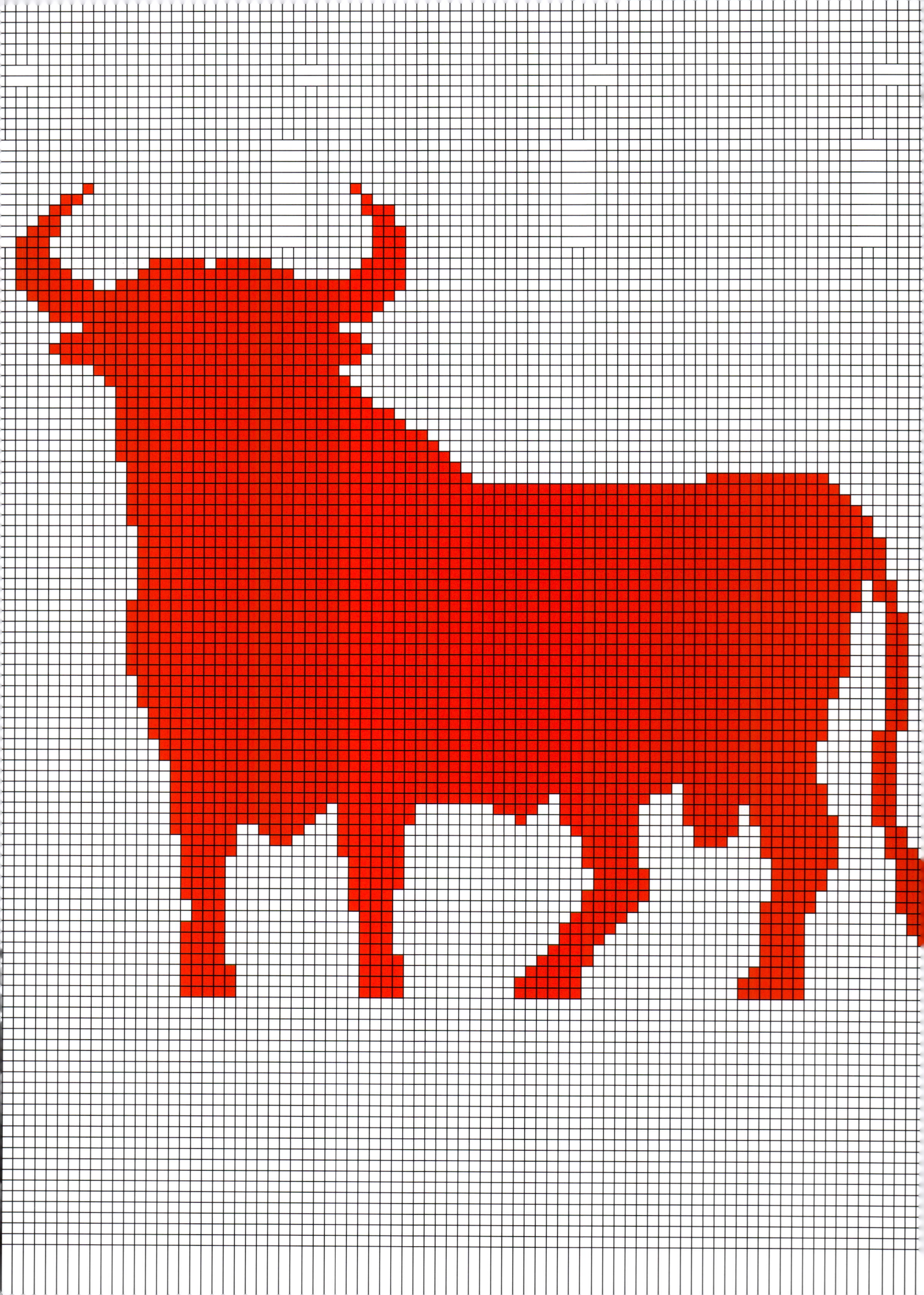

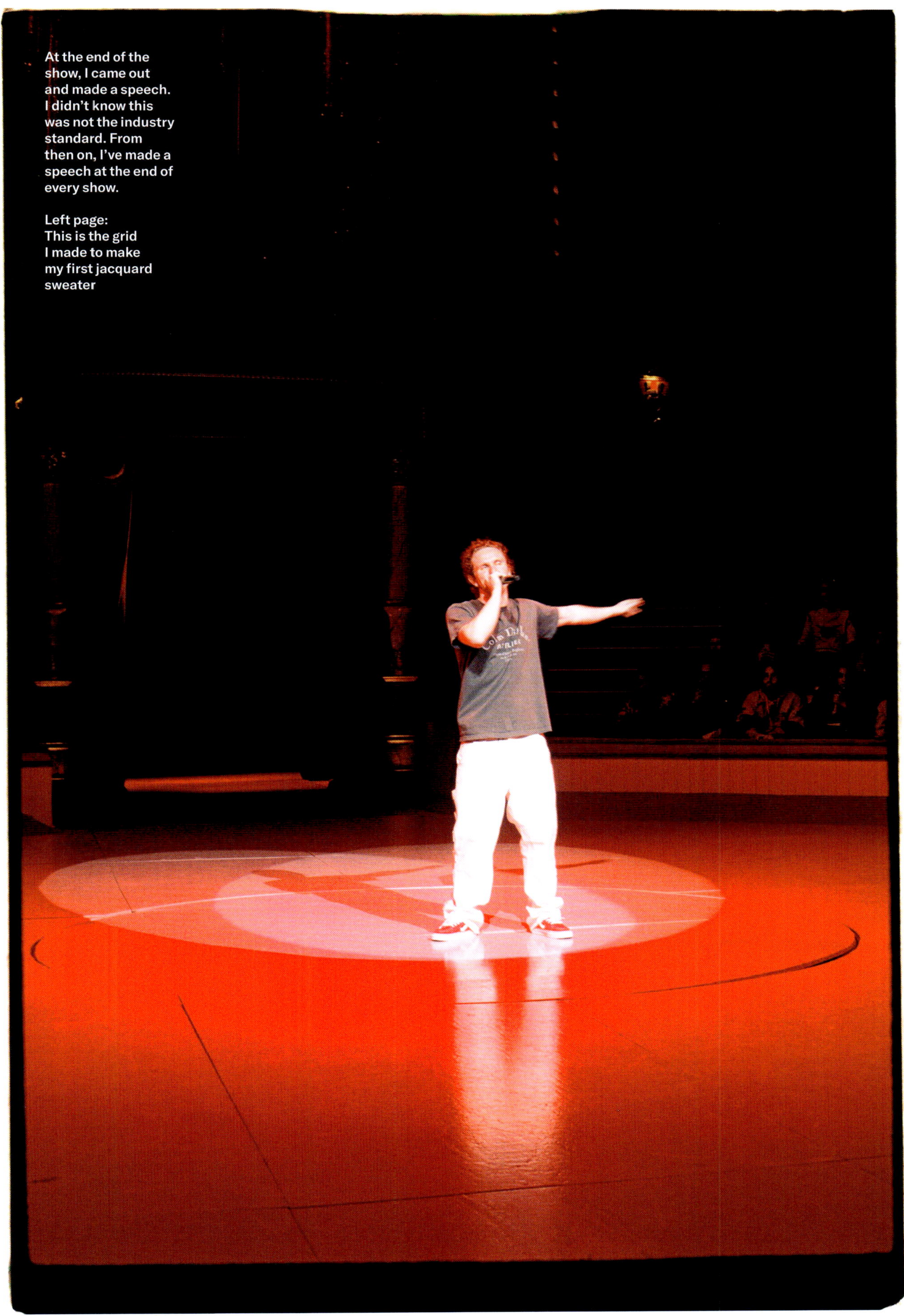

At the end of the show, I came out and made a speech. I didn't know this was not the industry standard. From then on, I've made a speech at the end of every show.

Left page:
This is the grid I made to make my first jacquard sweater

SS20

RECYCLING: A FASHION SHOW

Make the most out of what you have.

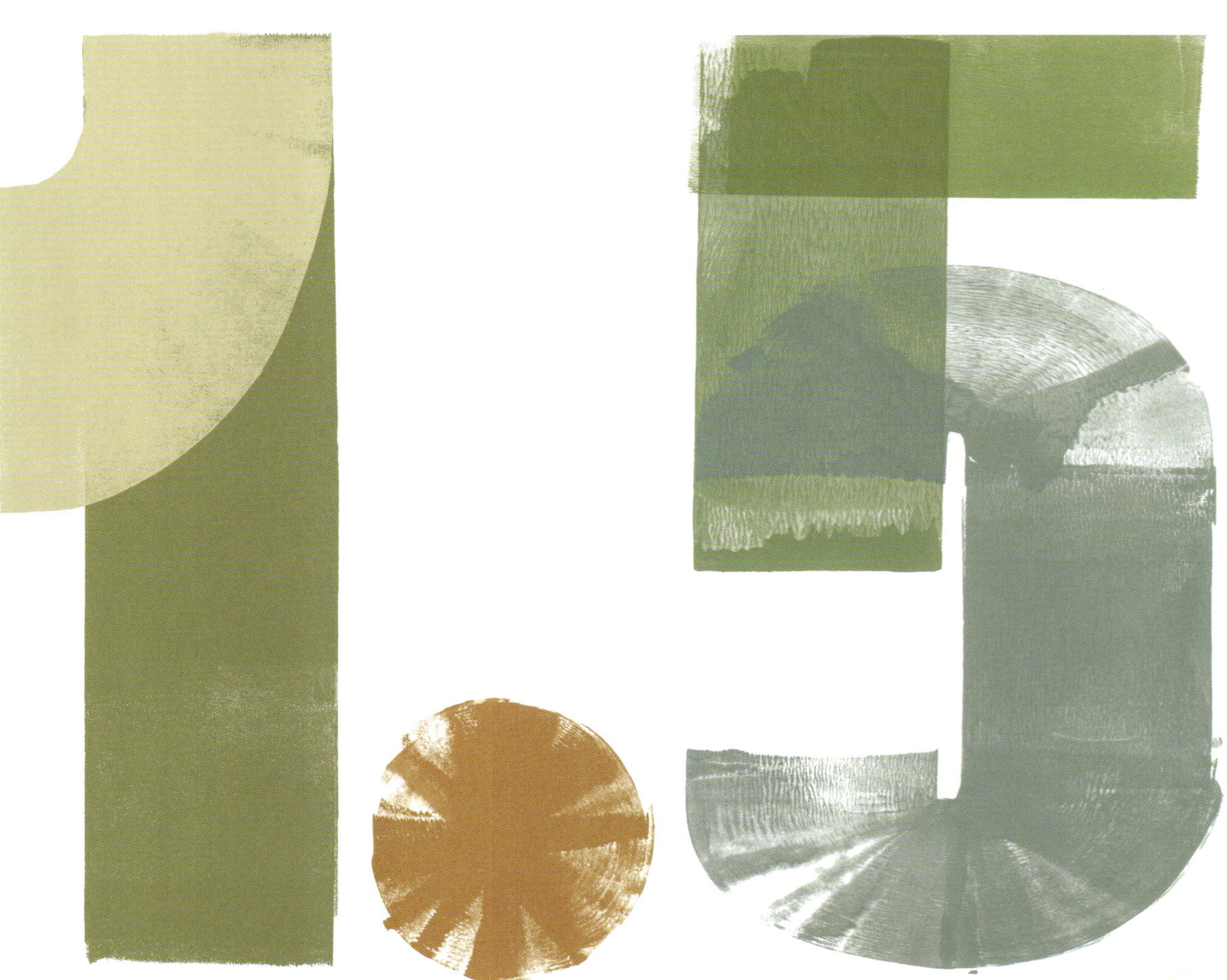

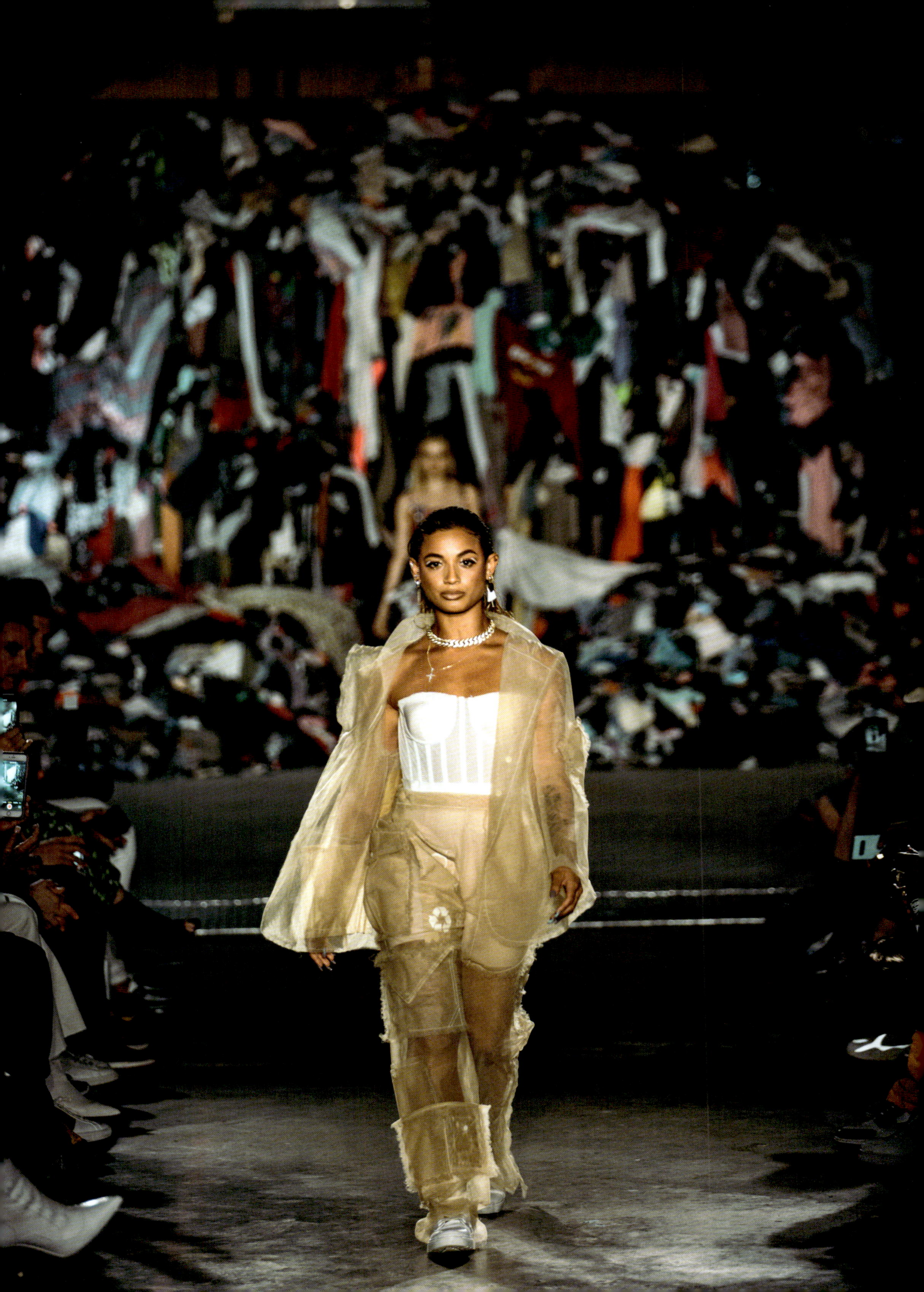

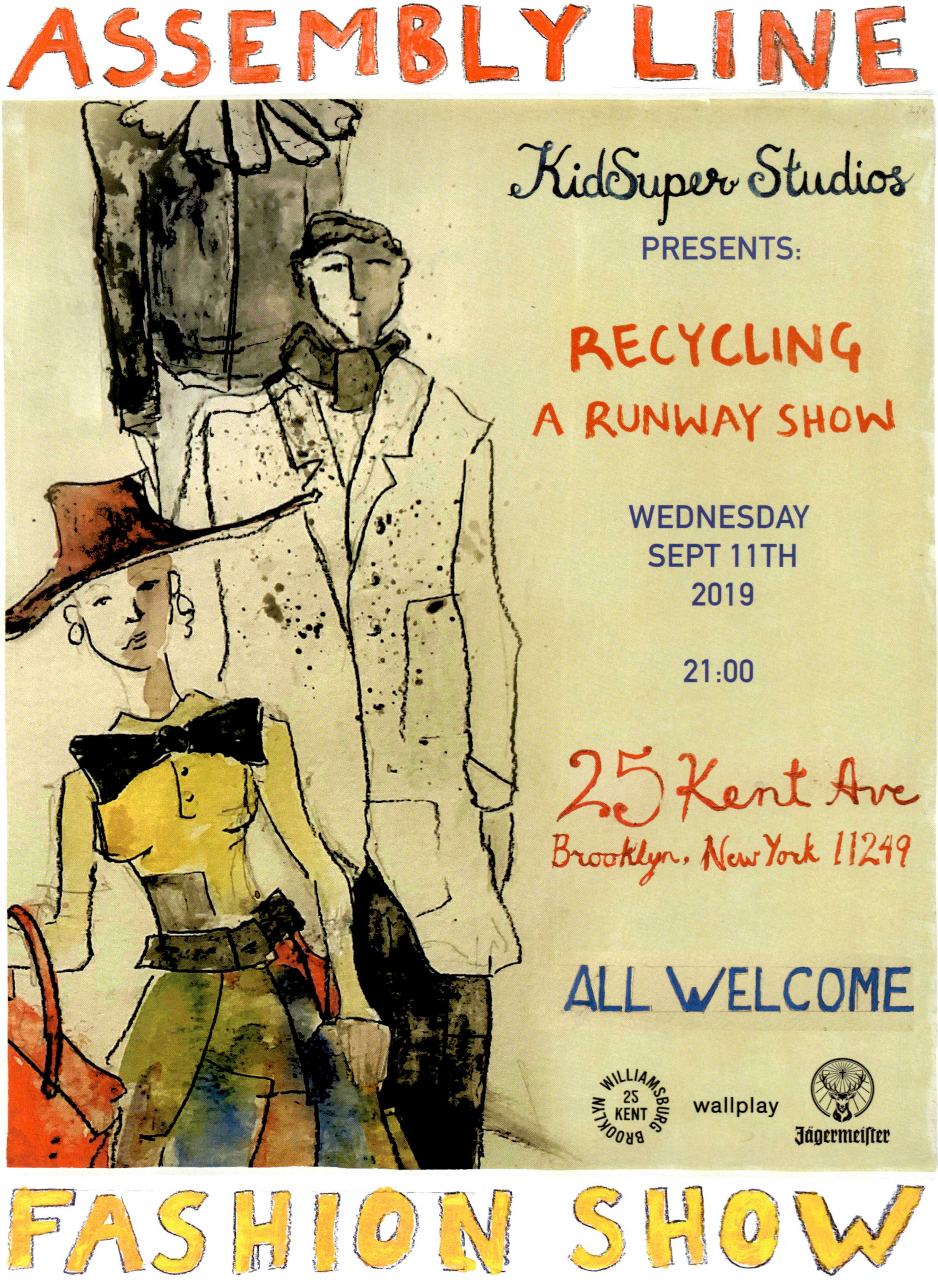

ASSEMBLY LINE

KidSuper Studios

PRESENTS:

RECYCLING

A RUNWAY SHOW

WEDNESDAY
SEPT 11TH
2019

21:00

25 Kent Ave
Brooklyn, New York 11249

ALL WELCOME

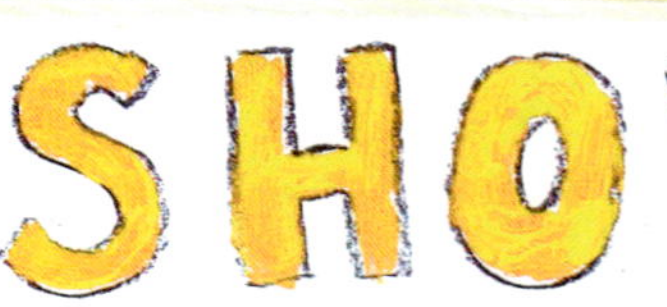

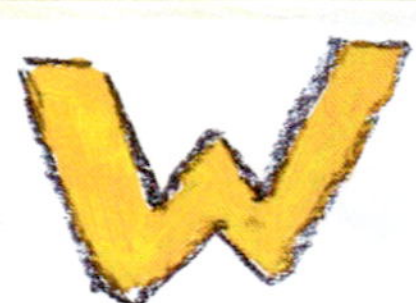

FASHION SHOW

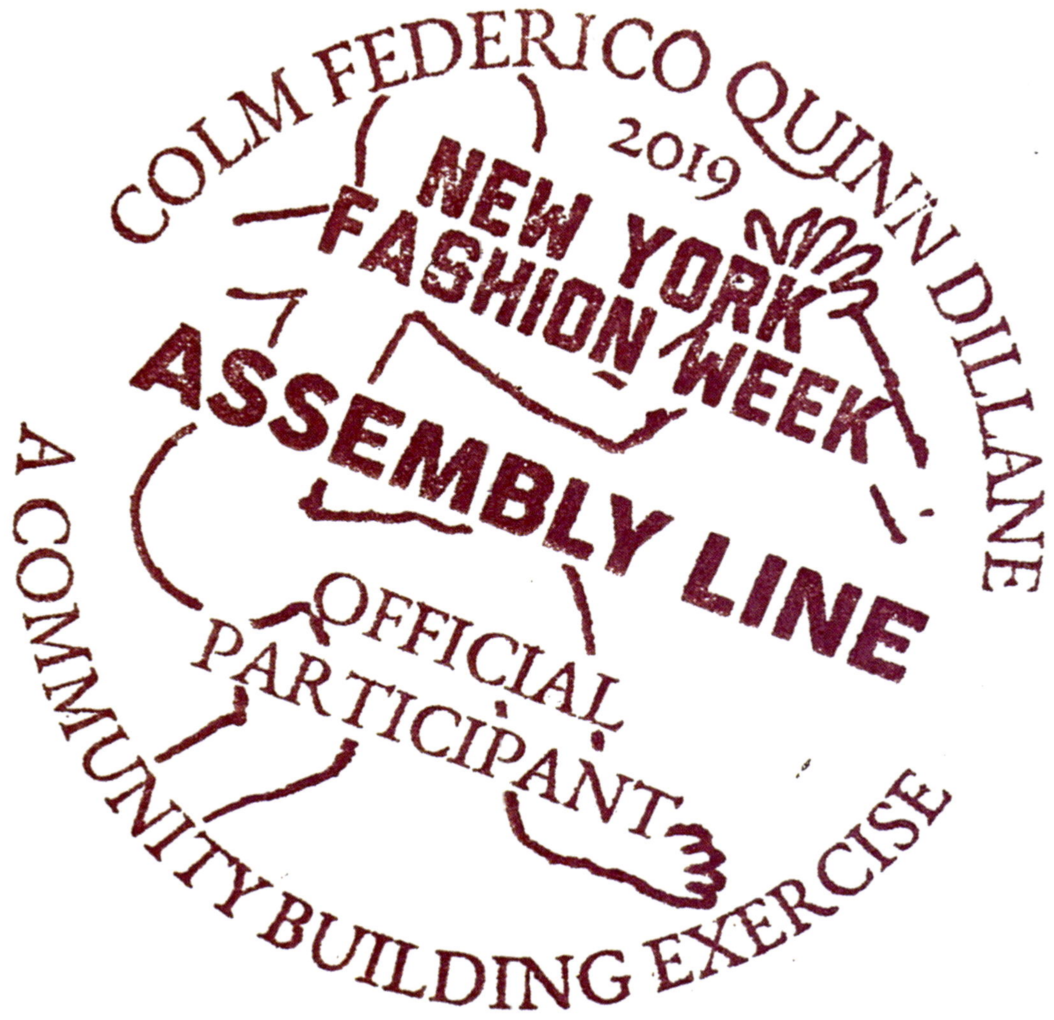

Left page:
The flyer for the fashion show open to the public

I HAD JUST RETURNED from Paris, my first-ever fashion show, and the *Vogue* article had come out. In my mind, it was life changing. In reality? Nothing changed. I was still an outsider, and no one really knew who I was. The only thing that shifted was, I guess, a little glimpse that this whole thing was more possible: I had not only been in *Vogue* but raved about.

Back in New York, people started asking, "Are you doing New York Fashion Week?" Fresh off the Paris high, I thought, Of course. I just did Paris—I can't leave New York behind.

New York Fashion Week was in September, which meant I had about two months to figure it out.

Years before, I had worked with an organization called WallPlay, which worked with local New York City landlords to offer their vacant storefronts to artists for free. The idea was to transform these empty spaces into artists' hubs and ultimately generate attention to the area. A win-win for everyone. I had turned some of these spaces into incredible experiences—one was even a full-blown theater (a story for another chapter). Because of this, WallPlay trusted me.

So when they landed a 20,000-square-foot space in Brooklyn, they called me, knowing I was maybe the only artist crazy enough to do it justice.

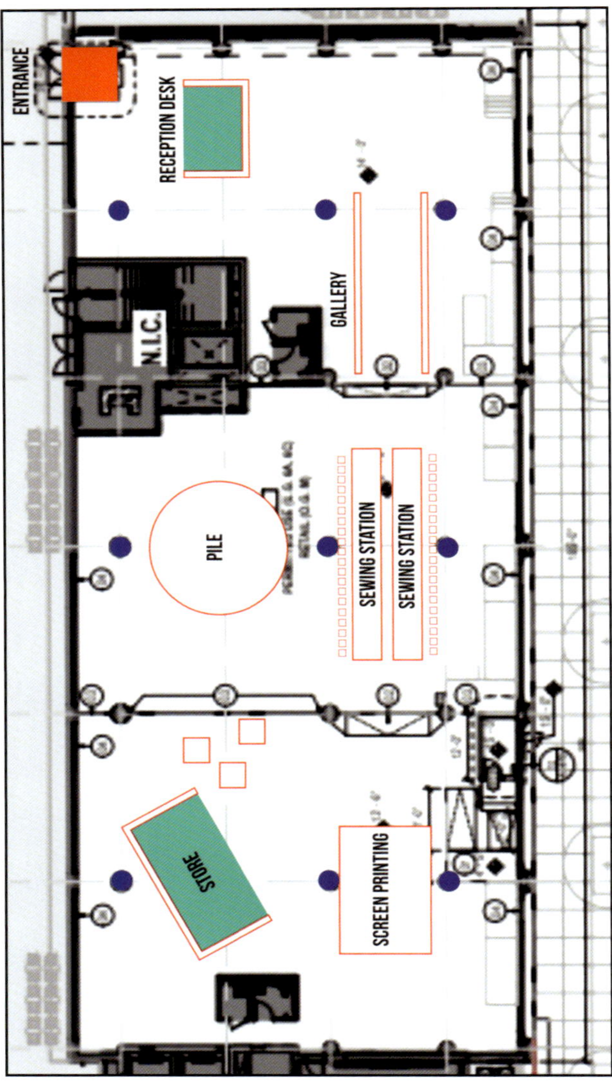

The layout for the space

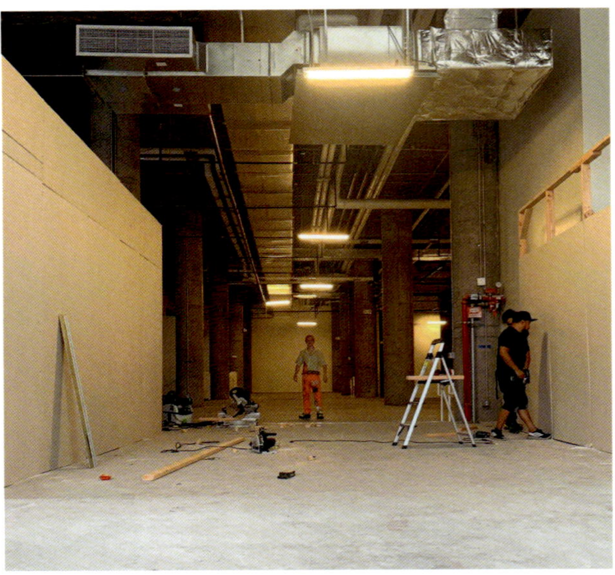
20,000 square-foot space

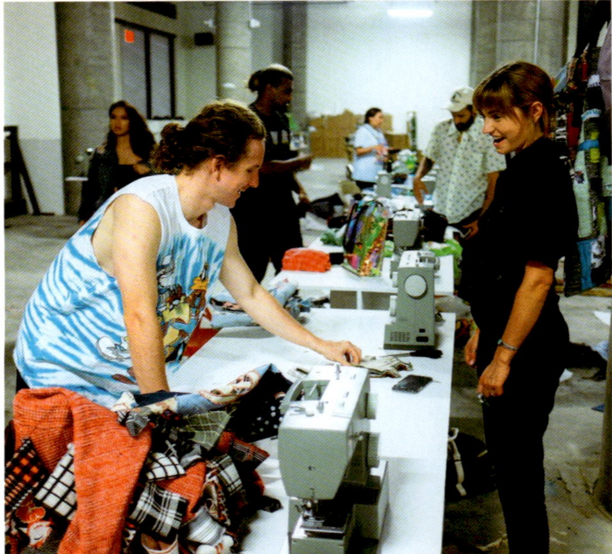
Singer's sewing machines

The problem? I was completely broke. I couldn't even afford an Uber home from the airport when I landed from Paris (thank you to Dekel for loaning me some money). And now I had 20,000 square feet to figure out what to do with.

I DECIDED TO make the space an open creative hub—somewhere anyone could come and be part of something. If I was given this opportunity, why not share it?

I got Singer to donate fifty sewing machines. I had everyone in New York donate old clothing. I built a massive pile of clothes—actually, I built a pyramid underneath to make it look even bigger. Then I set up a screen-printing section.

The idea was simple: people could come in, grab old clothing, cut it up, sew it back together, screen-print it, and walk away with a one-of-a-kind piece. My artwork covered the space, and to make things even funnier, I built a fake secretary booth at the entrance where people had to "check in." (During the final show I dressed up as Stacy the Secretary, complete with a skirt, suit, nails and prosthetics. The reason? I have no idea.)

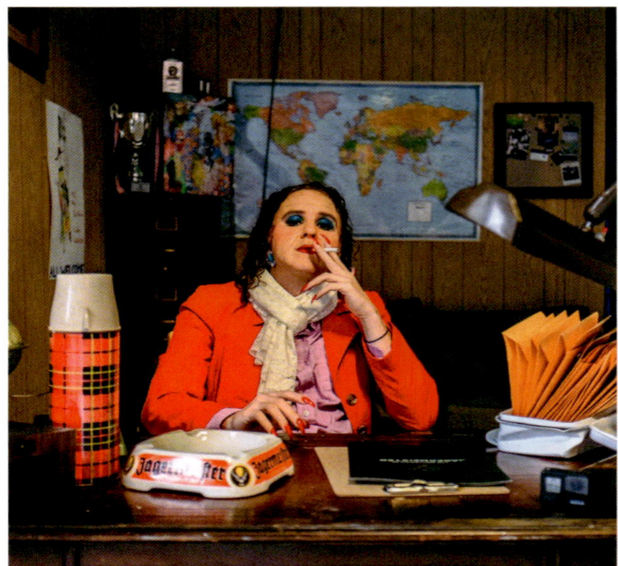
I dressed up as "Stacy" to be the front desk lady of the gallery during the opening

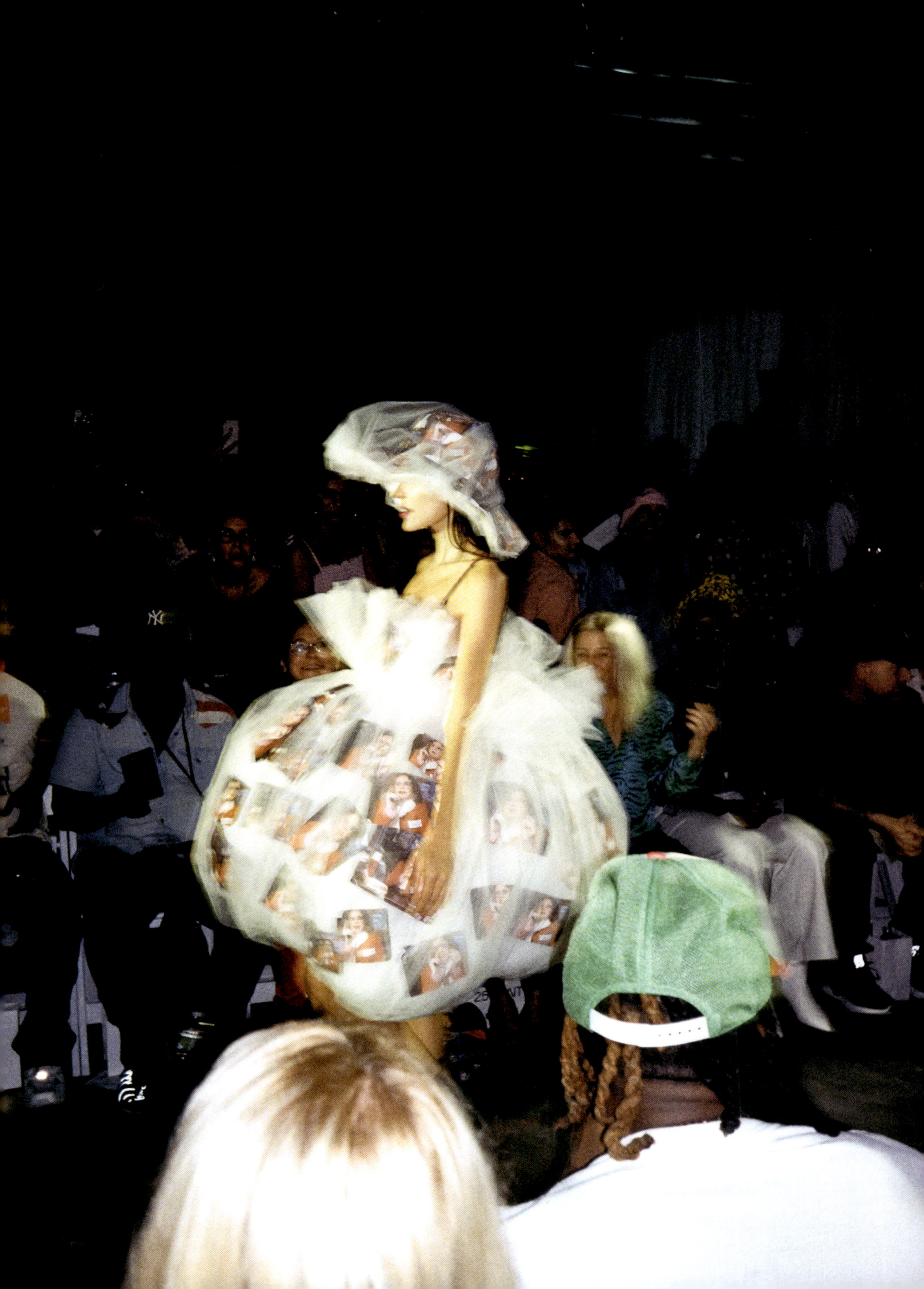

PATCHWORK

FASHION SHOW MADE FROM DONATED CLOTHES

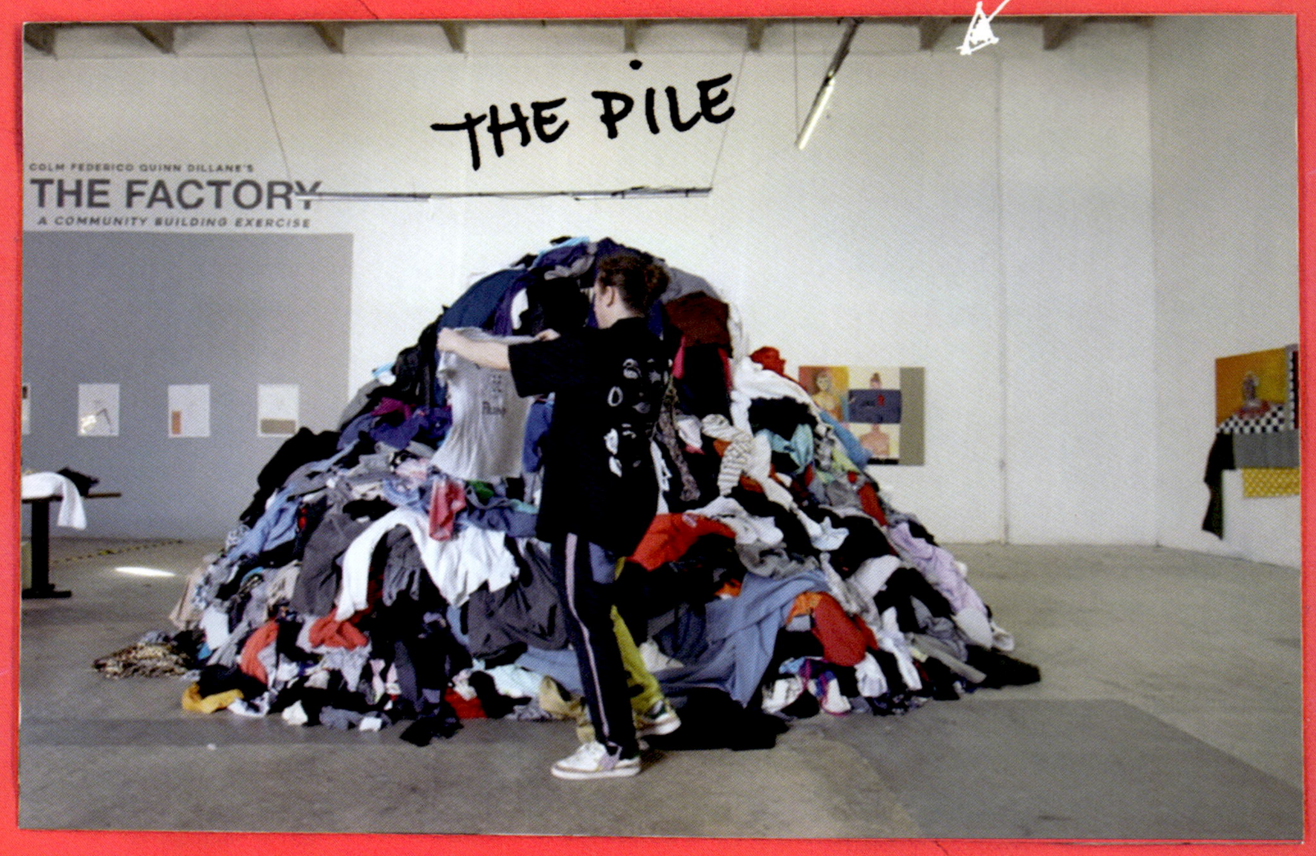

THIS RECYCLED SHOW INSPIRED PATCHWORK IN FUTURE COLLECTIONS

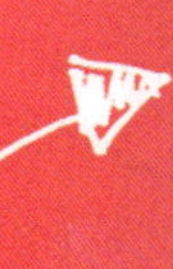

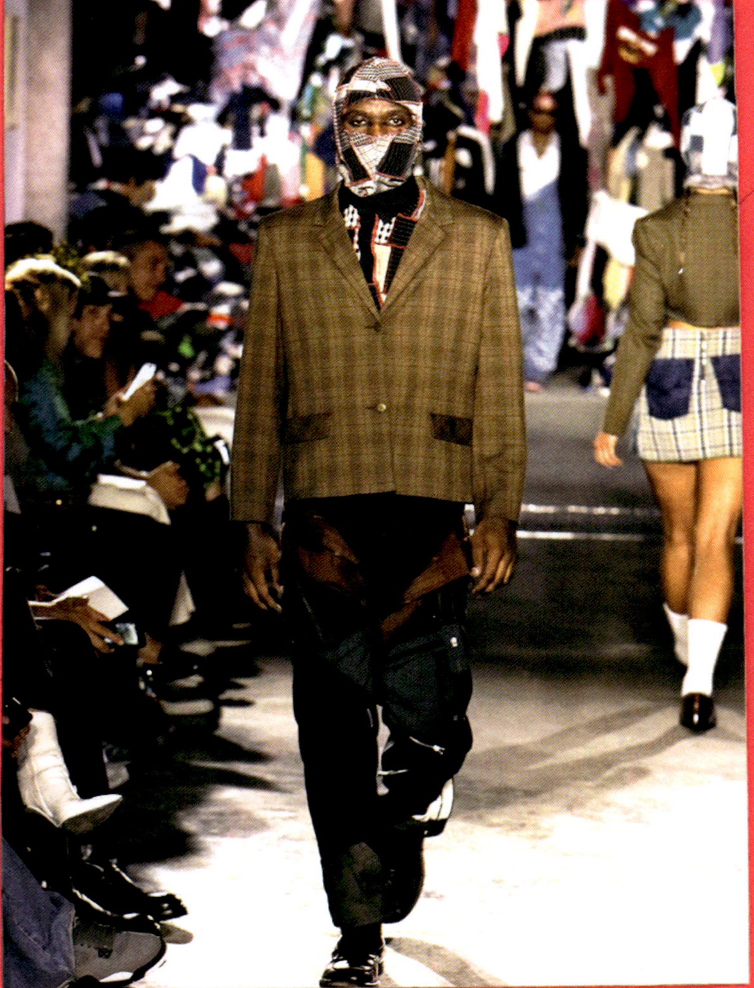

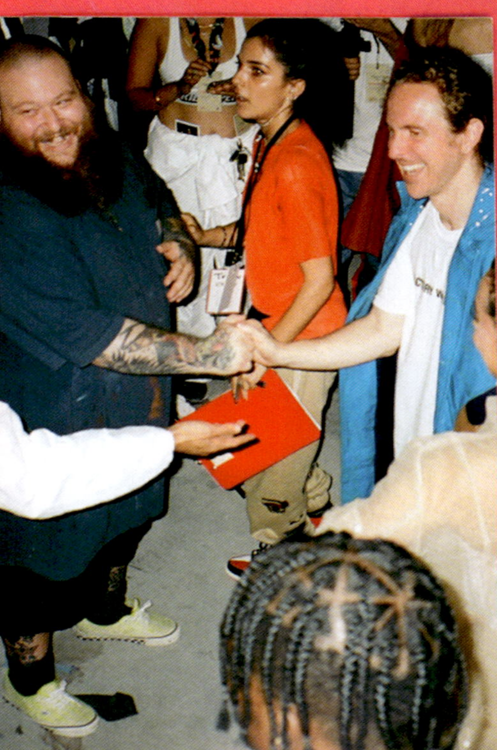

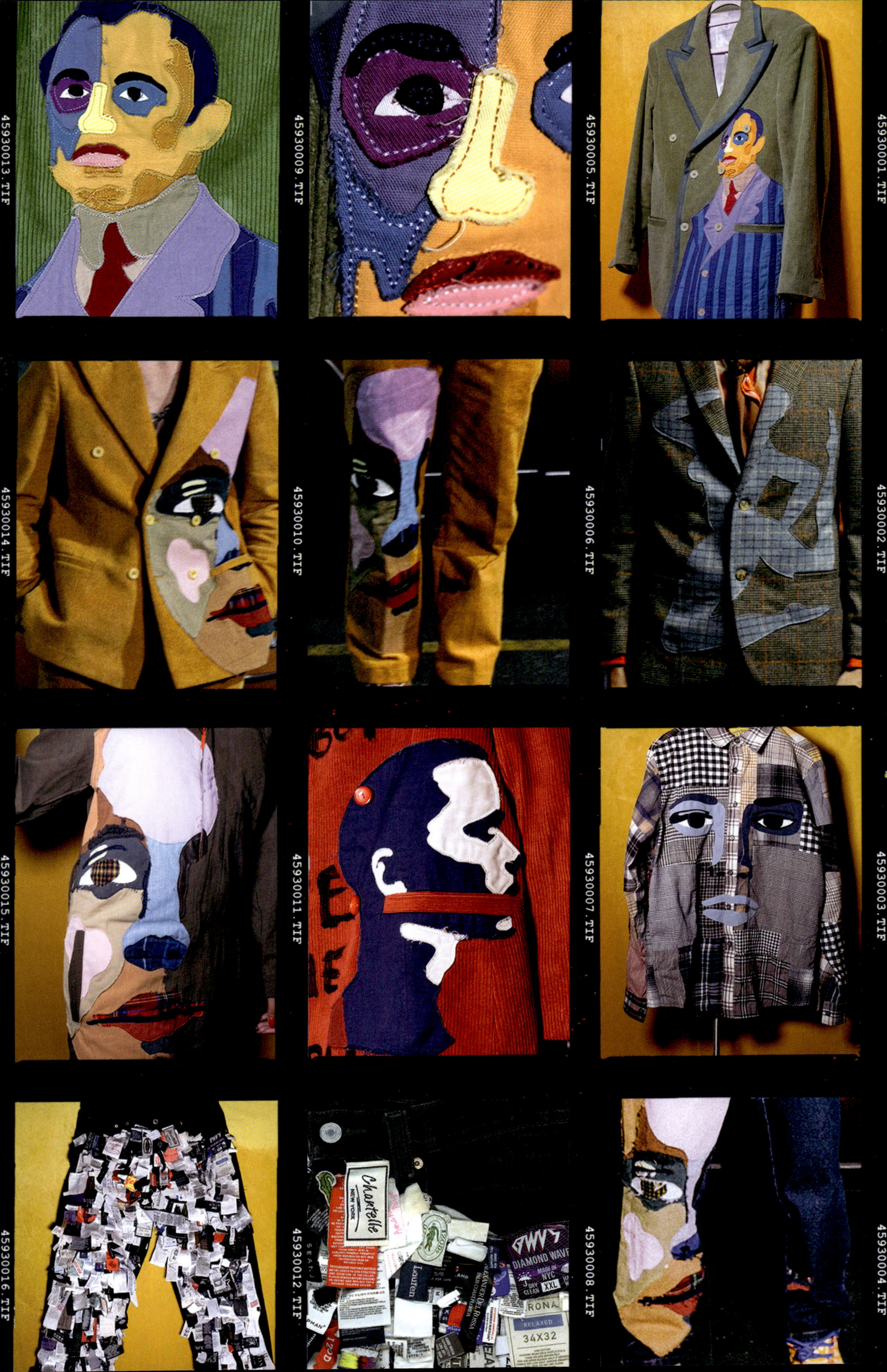

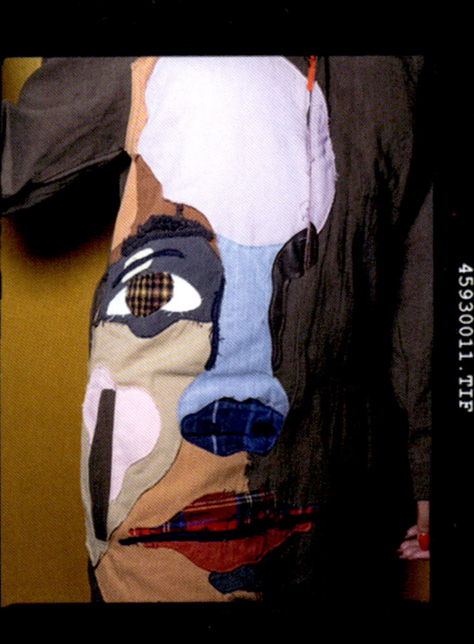

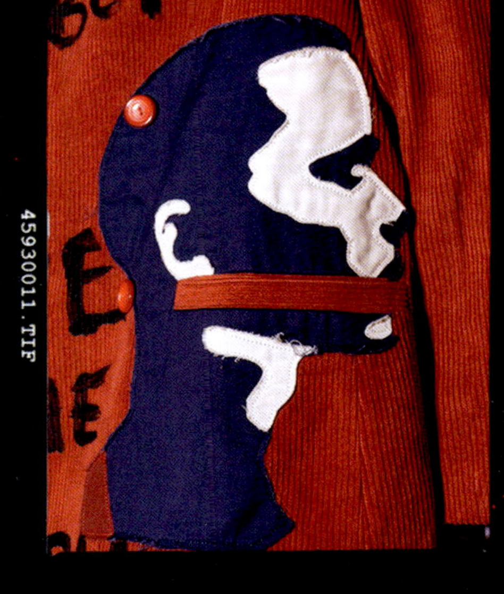

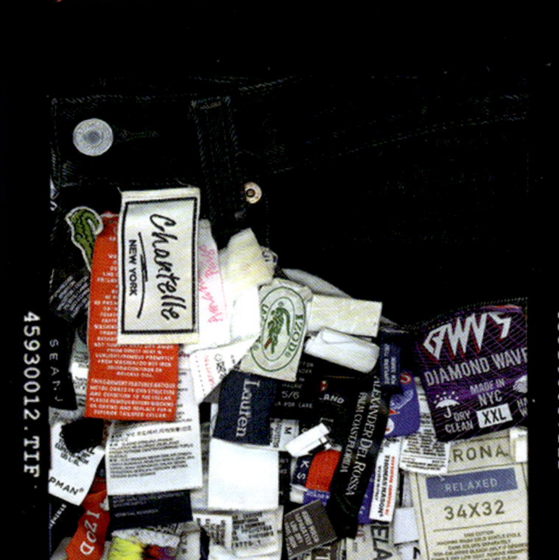
Chantelle
NEW YORK
Lauren
DIAMOND WAVE
RELAXED
34X32

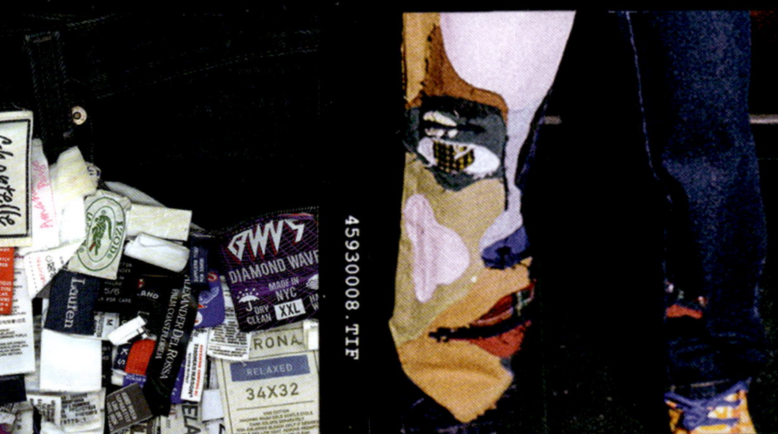

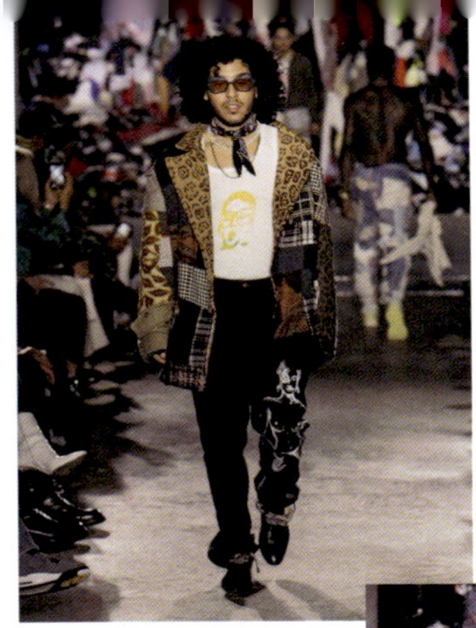

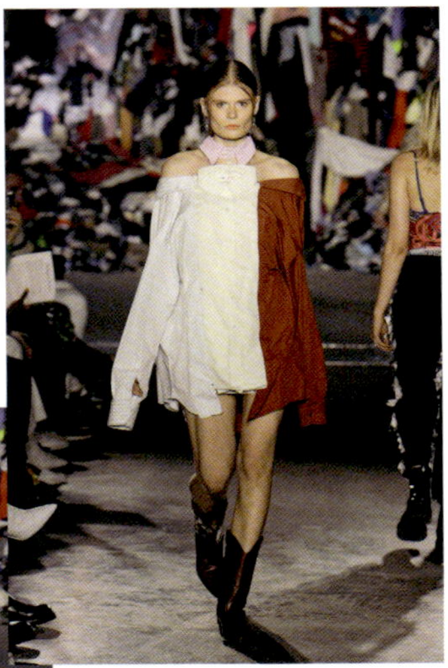

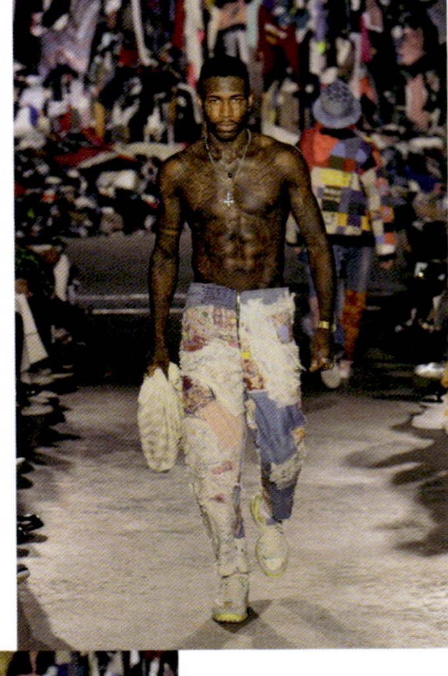

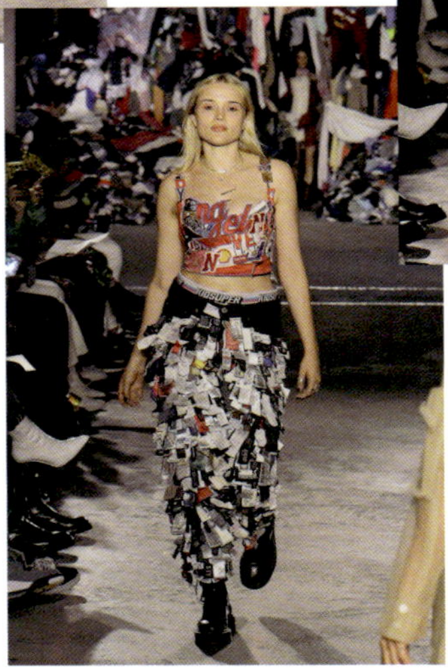

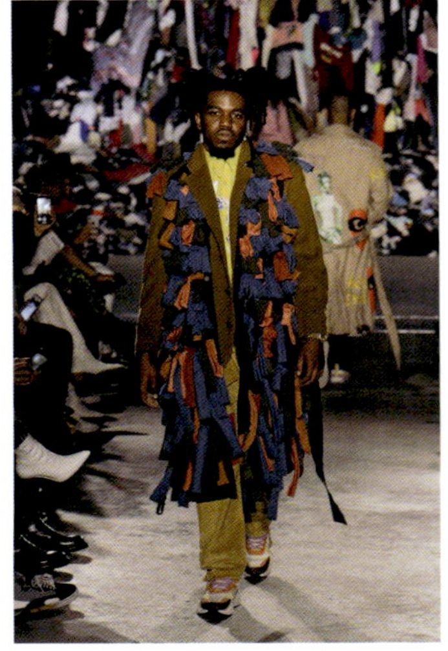

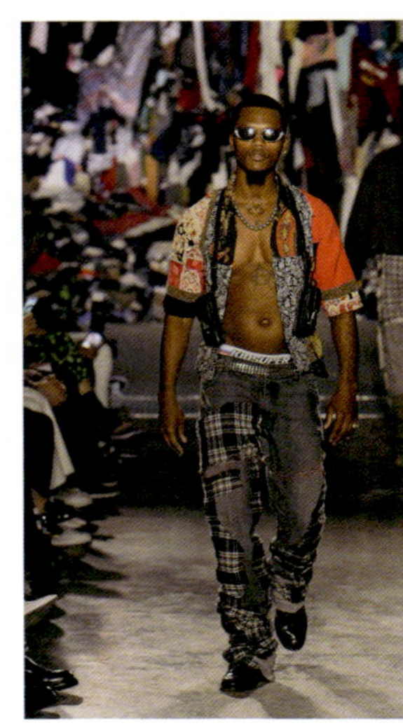

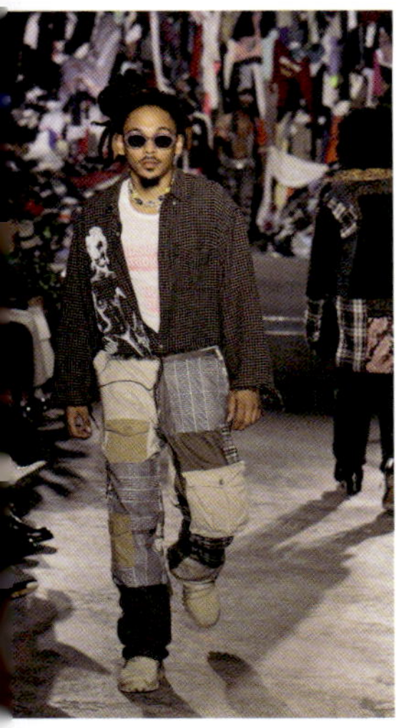

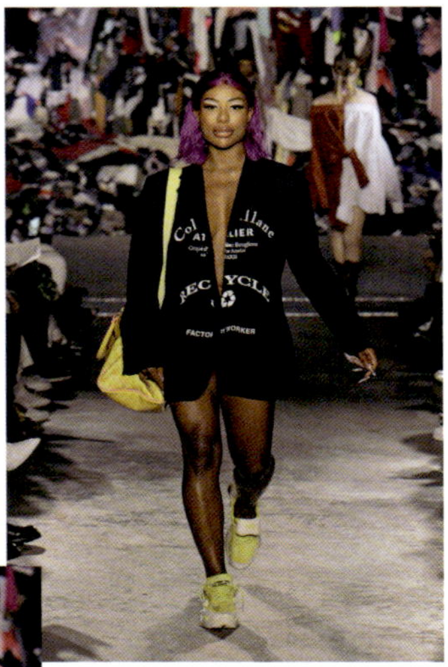

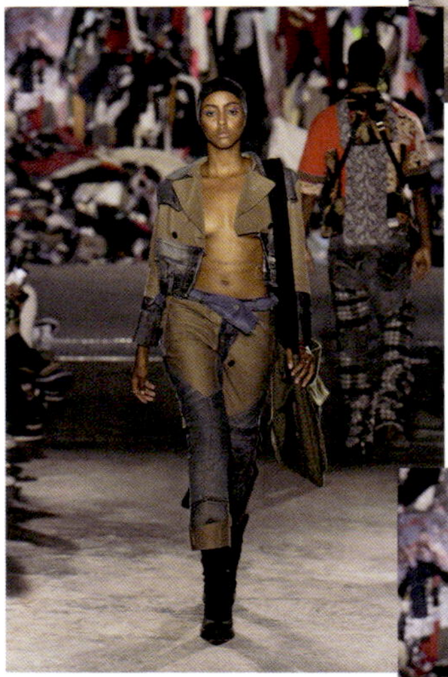

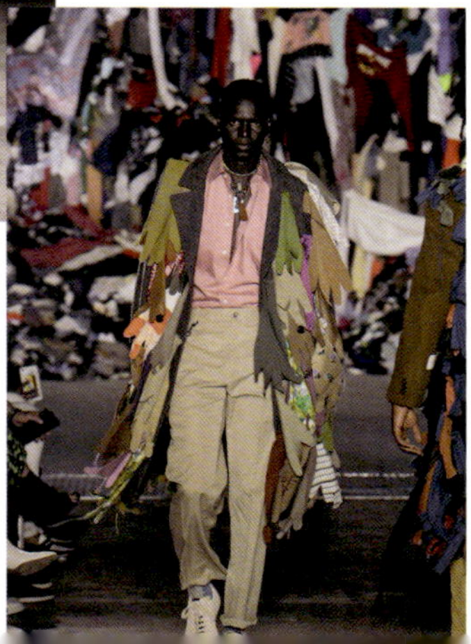

I posted on Instagram: Anyone who wants to be part of this month-long exhibition, pull up.

I DIDN'T EXPECT MUCH, but on the first day, a crowd of people showed up, excited to sew. The next day, thirty more came. And then another thirty. And another.

A week in, I realized I had accidentally built a creative summer camp. A rotating group of people—aged 17 to 30—were showing up every day, spending hours sewing, designing, and creating.

I looked at them like, Don't you have jobs? Responsibilities? Maybe they thought this was their big break into fashion. What they didn't know was, I had no money. But from the outside, it looked like I had everything—this giant space, an operation running full-time. I felt like I had a responsibility to make this . . . whatever this was . . . worth it.

Then I thought: New York Fashion Week is a month away. Why not turn this into a New York Fashion Week show?

I pitched it to the group: What if we use all the donated clothing and work together to make a full runway collection?

They were all in.

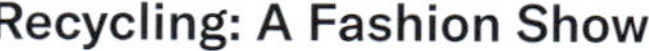

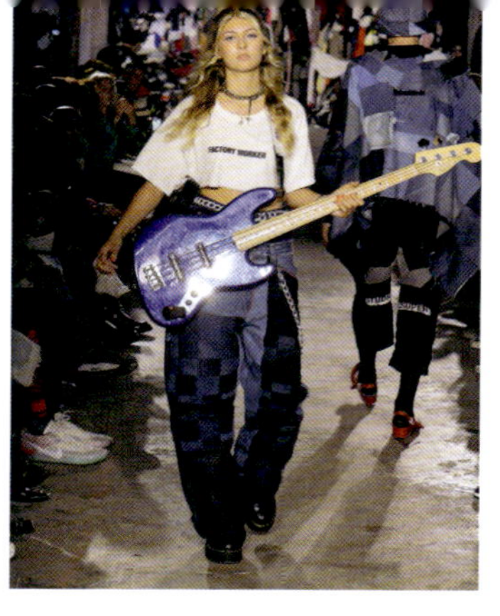

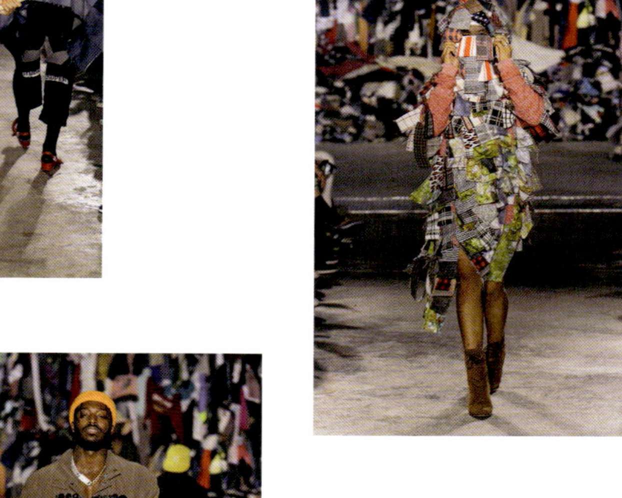

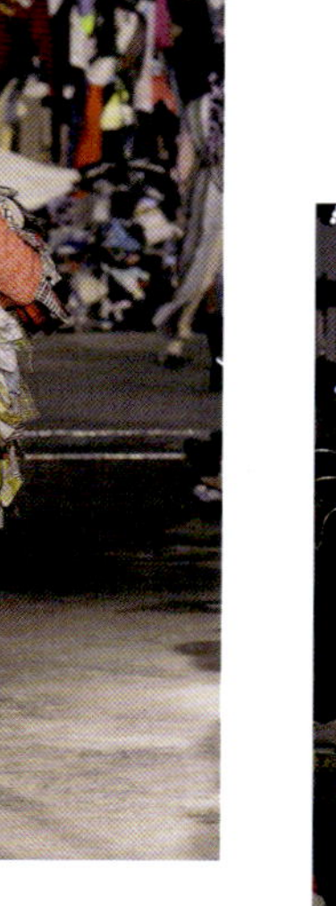

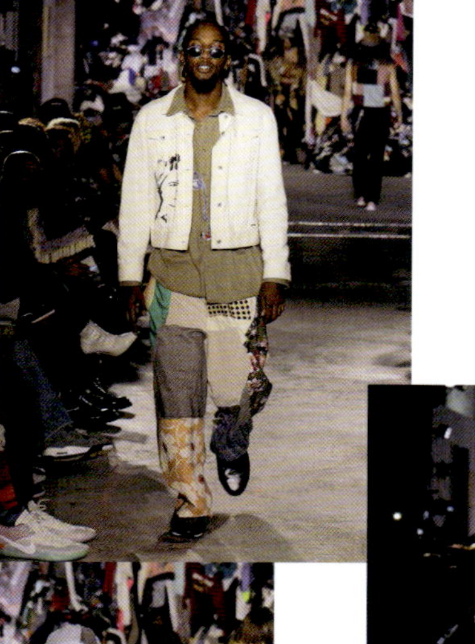

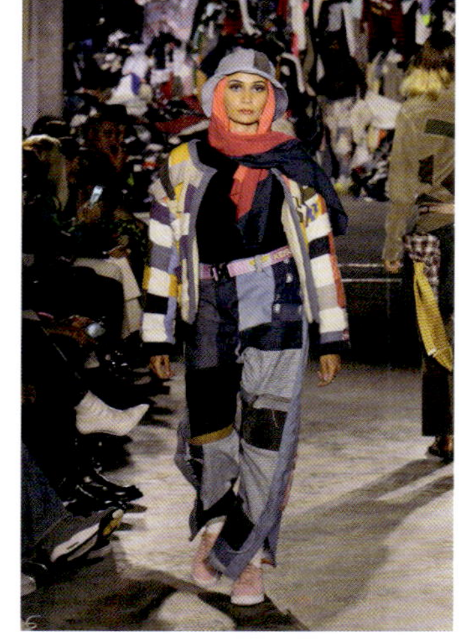

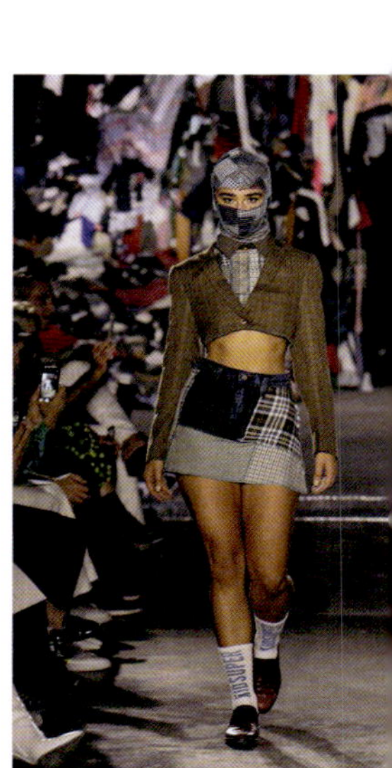

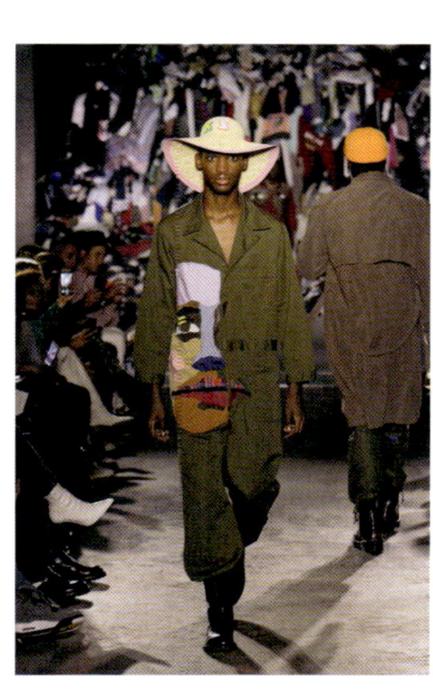

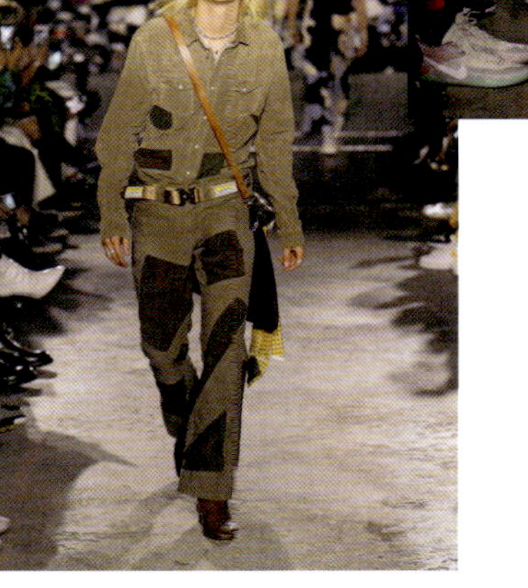

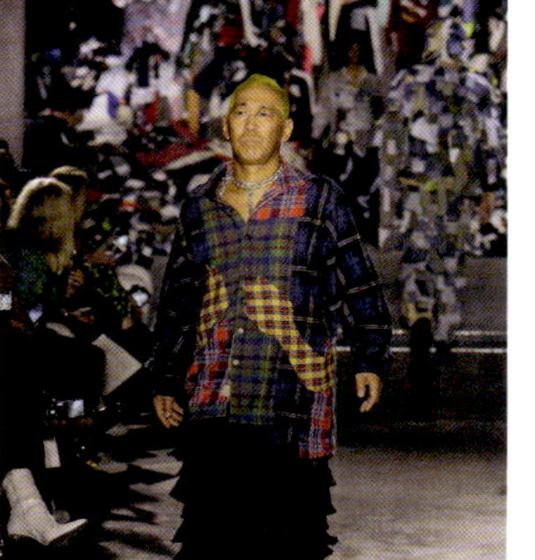

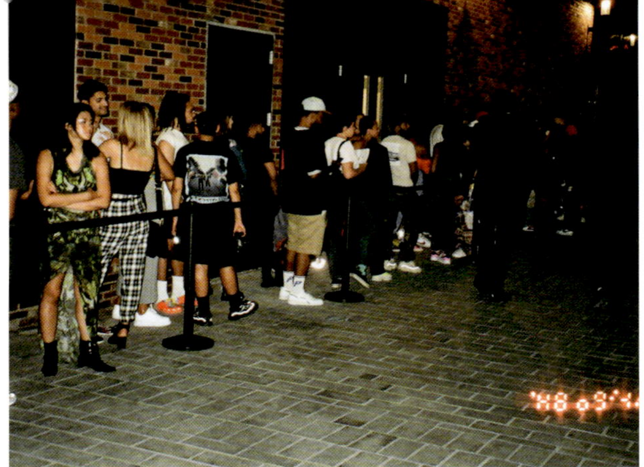

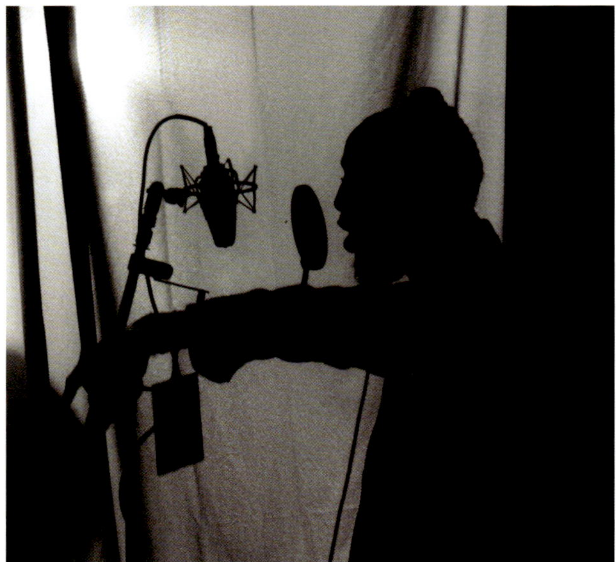

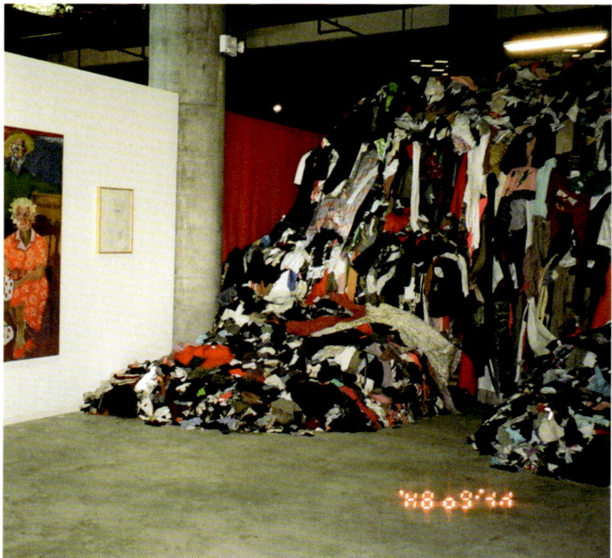

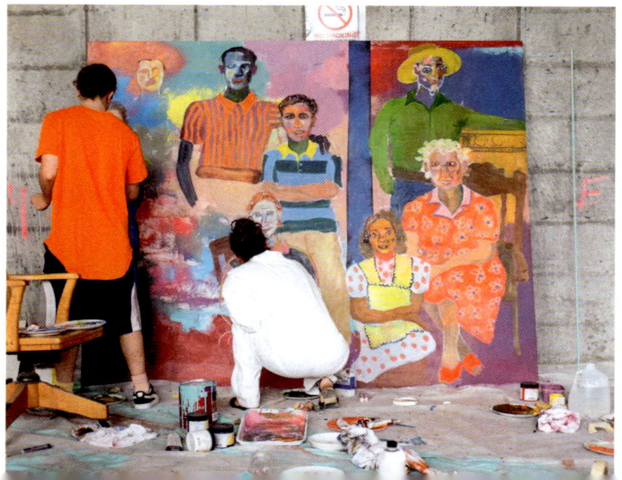

EVERY DAY, we worked. I helped each person design their own piece. But I still had no money. I started pitching sponsors, trying to get anything—at the very least, food for everyone working nonstop.

It got out of control. More people kept showing up. Expectations kept growing. And suddenly we weren't just making clothes—we had to figure out lighting, sound, and logistics for a full-blown fashion show.

As Fashion Week approached, the space felt like a family. Some people even slept in the space. I even crashed there a few nights myself, working until morning.

We decided to make the models walk out of the massive clothing pile—like they were emerging from it. We street-cast everyone. No professional models. The construction worker who built the pyramid? I thought he looked amazing, so I cast him. Action Bronson wanted to walk. Of course, he did.

Then we decided: Let's break a world record.

We looked up the Guinness World Record for longest coat, made ours a few inches longer, and officially broke the record.

THE DAY OF the show, we still didn't have music. So I set up a recording booth in the space. Artists started laying down tracks while we styled and prepped models. The music was literally being made in real time.

The show was for the people, so we made it completely open to the public. Three thousand people showed up. It was chaos at the door. It was pure New York energy. Strangers, friends, rappers, creatives—all packed into this wild, makeshift space.

At the end, the "summer camp" we had built for a month was over. But the impact lasted.

- Some of the kids who worked on the show went on to start their own brands.

- The construction worker I cast? He got signed as a Prada model. Another girl who walked got signed to *Wilhelmina Models*.

- Some of the workers still work with me to this day.

- Some became superstar musicians.

This was fashion for the people, by the people. It felt like everything New York should be. And one day, I want to do it all over again.

I wonder what that first Instagram post looked like inviting everyone to participate.

The funniest thing was, after my rave review from *Vogue* I was expecting an even better review for this show. I asked the publicist where the reviews were. Not one. He said, "Colm, this is the same season as the Paris show. You did two Spring/Summer 2020 collections."

I thought to myself, no wonder that seemed so difficult. Two shows in three months. And another one to come.

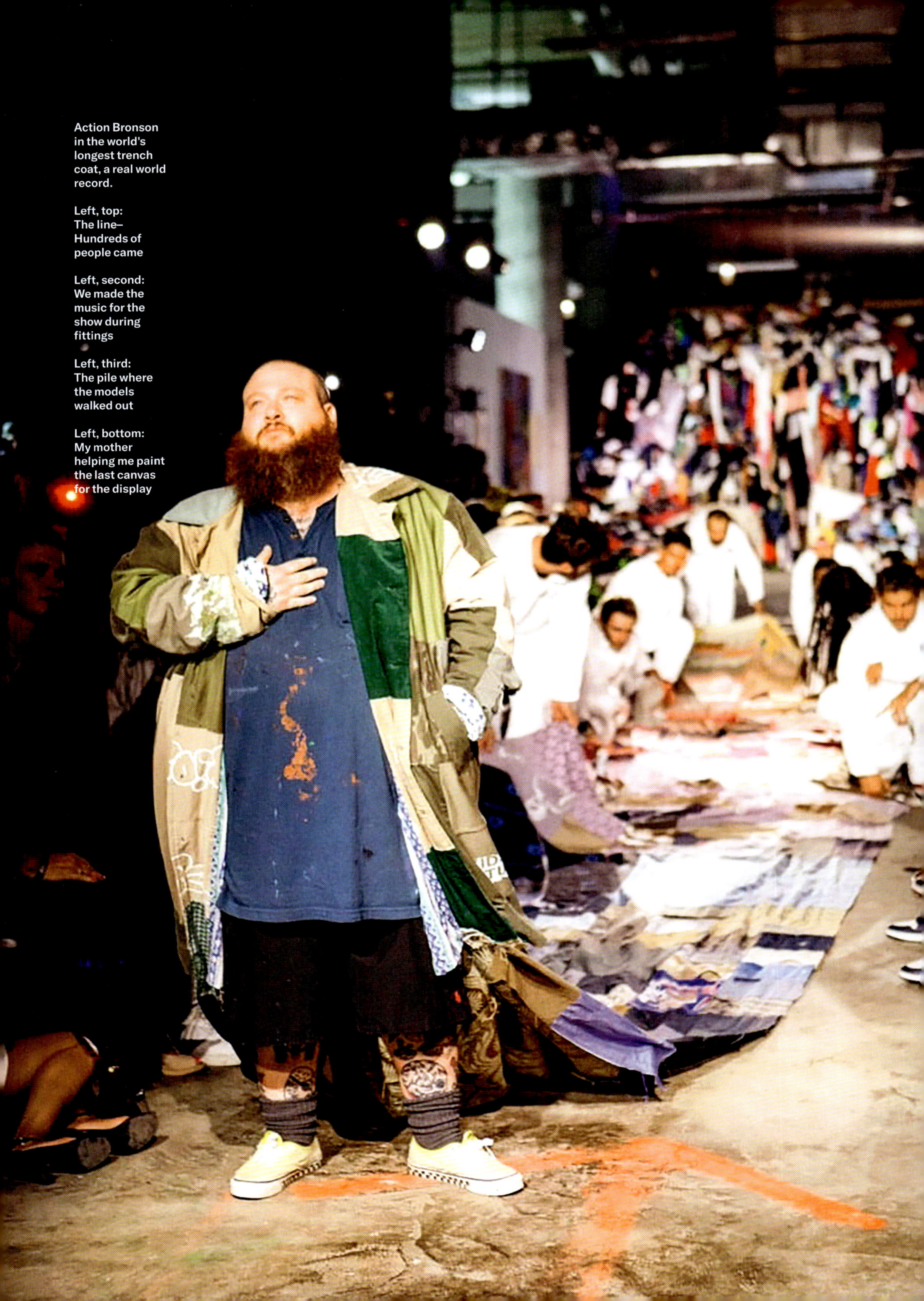

Action Bronson in the world's longest trench coat, a real world record.

Left, top: The line–Hundreds of people came

Left, second: We made the music for the show during fittings

Left, third: The pile where the models walked out

Left, bottom: My mother helping me paint the last canvas for the display

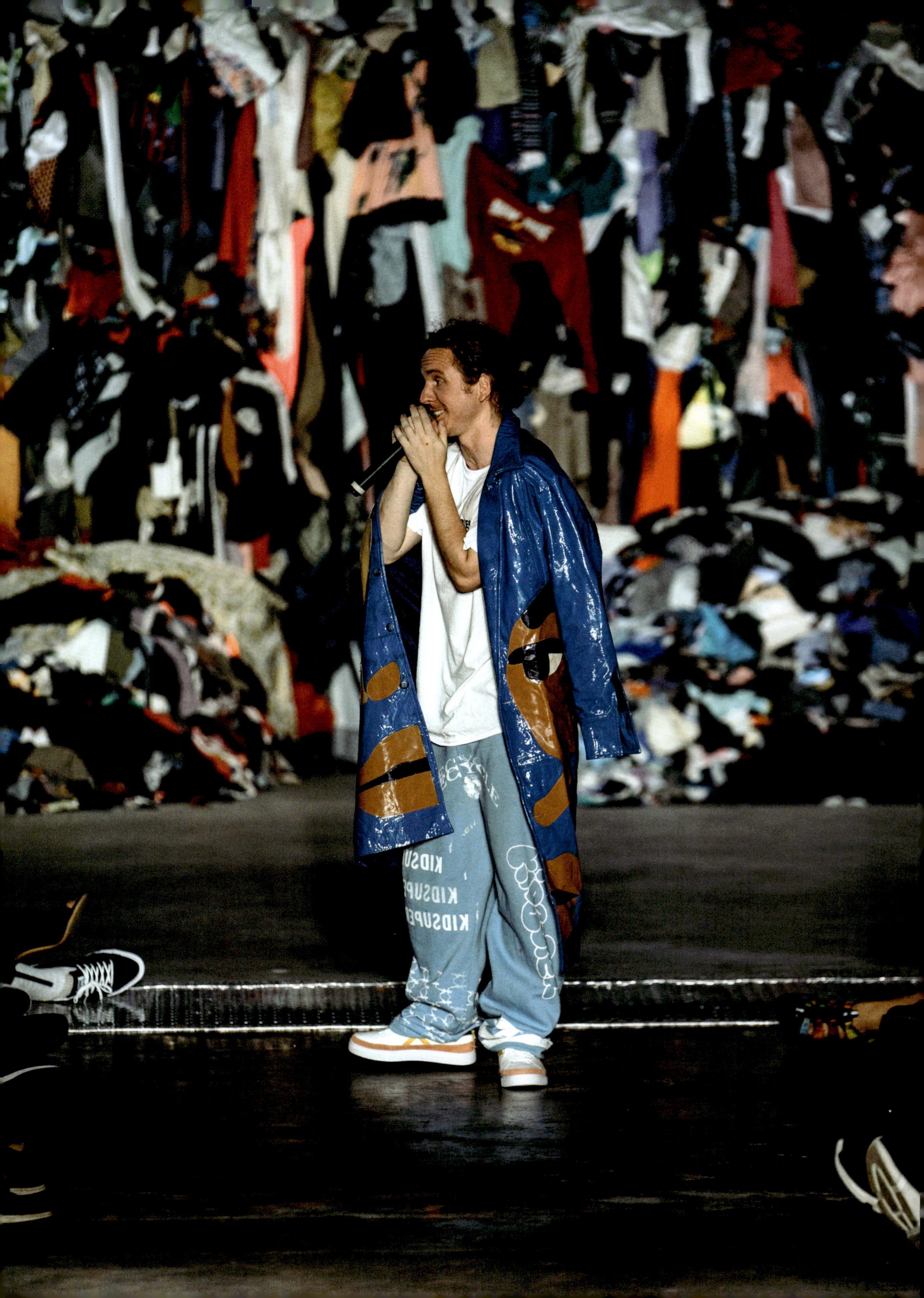
KIDSU
KIDSUP
KIDSUPE

Another speech. I brought out all of the sewers and workers that participated in the show to walk at the end.

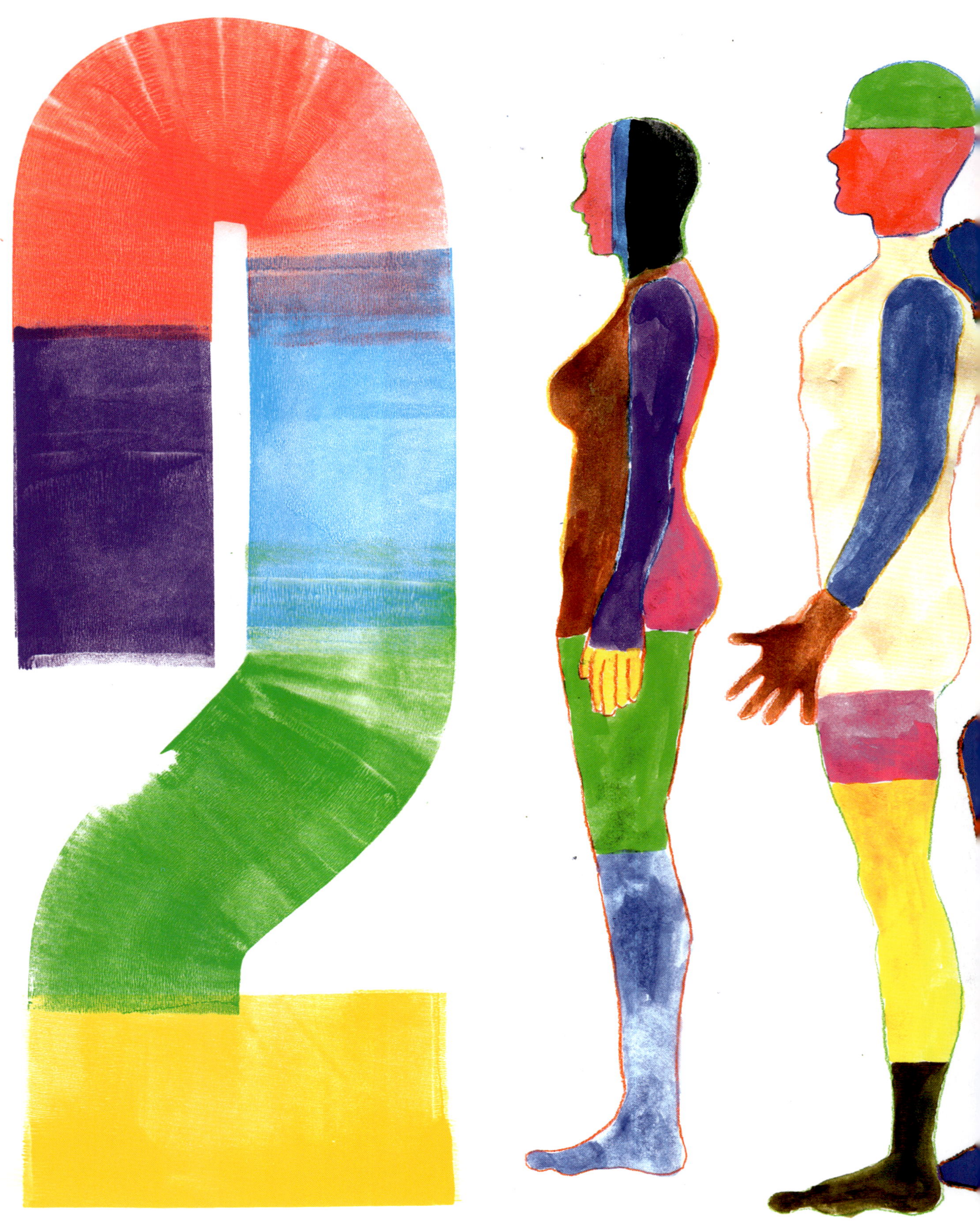

RUNNING AS FAST AS YOU CAN

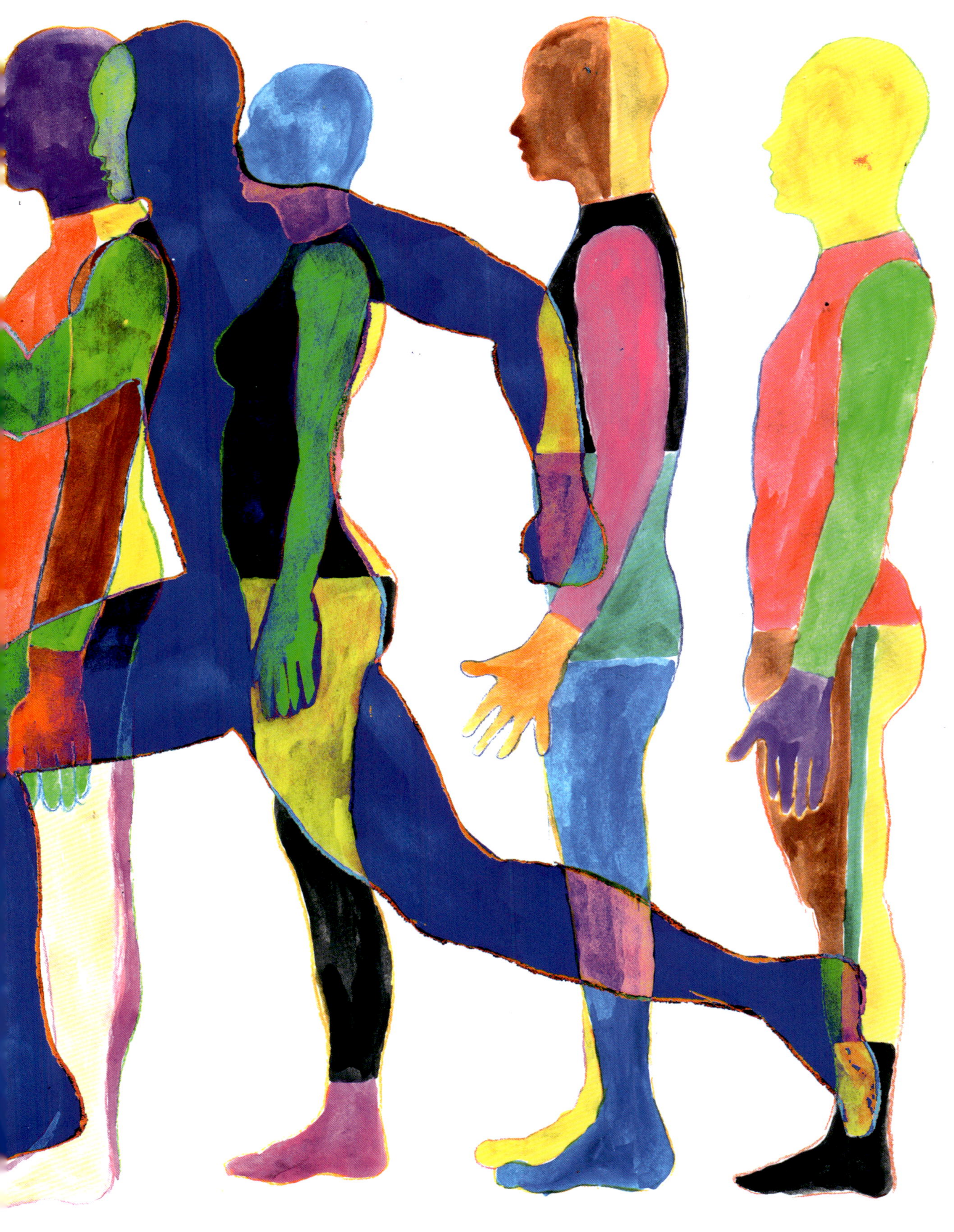

AW20 If you're gonna try something, you better try as hard as you can.

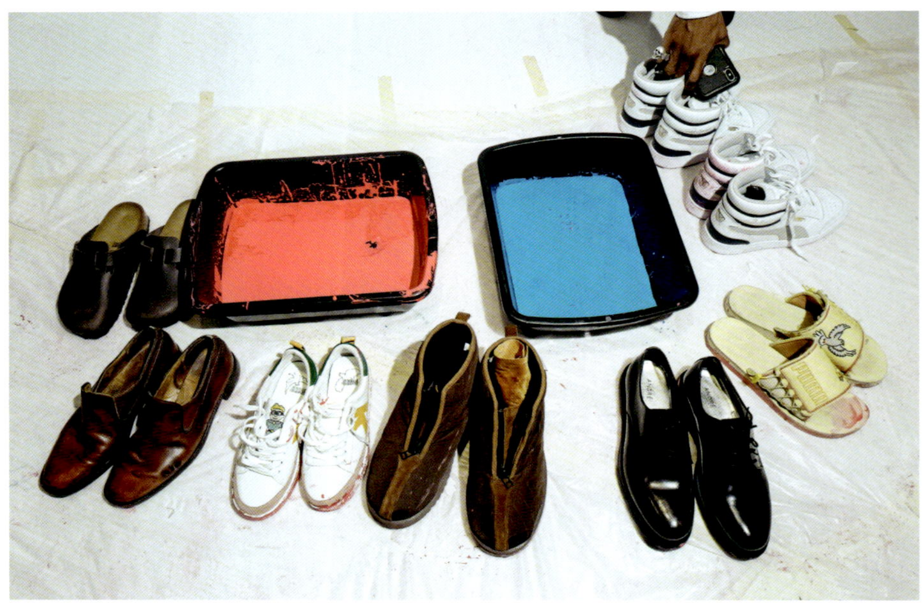

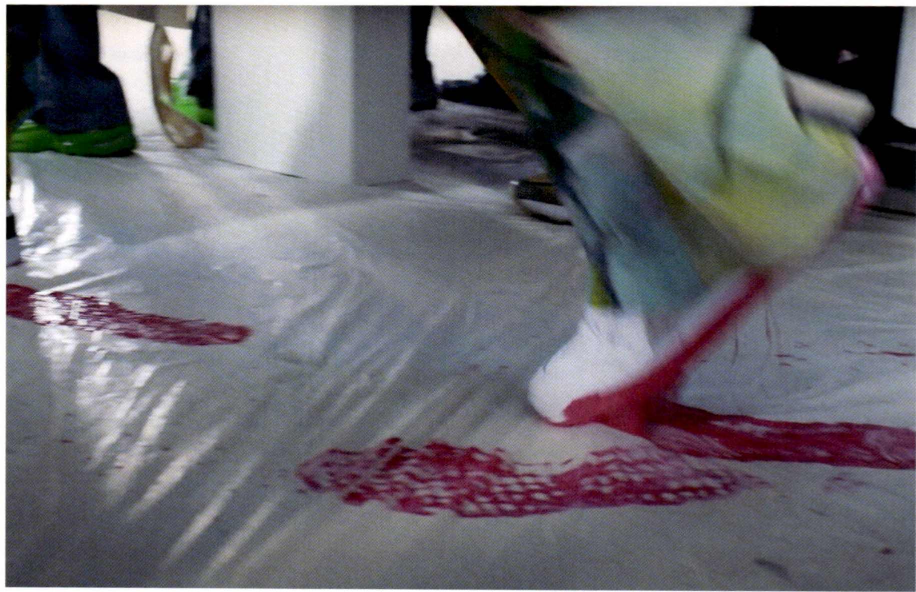

The paint that the models stepped in before the show

THIS SHOW FELT like more of a make-or-break moment than the first one. I had already done two fashion shows in three months, and now, just three months later, I had to do another one. That meant three fashion shows in six months—and I was still completely broke.

I was also feeling a bit disheartened. I had received an incredible review for my first show, yet my life hadn't changed. Then I did this huge NYC show where thousands of people showed up, and I got no review at all. I wasn't even dropping new clothing because I was so overwhelmed with the shows that I didn't have the money—or even the time—to order more. The thing about fashion is you always need a reservoir of money to order your next collection. I was struggling. The only thing keeping me afloat was sponsorships from Jägermeister and one-off gigs like album artwork and music videos.

I started questioning the purpose of these fashion shows. What were they actually accomplishing? I talked to my PR agent and others in the industry, and although there was momentum building, I wasn't sure if another show was worth it.

Then I had to remind myself—I didn't do the first show for a review. To be honest with myself I didn't even expect *Vogue*

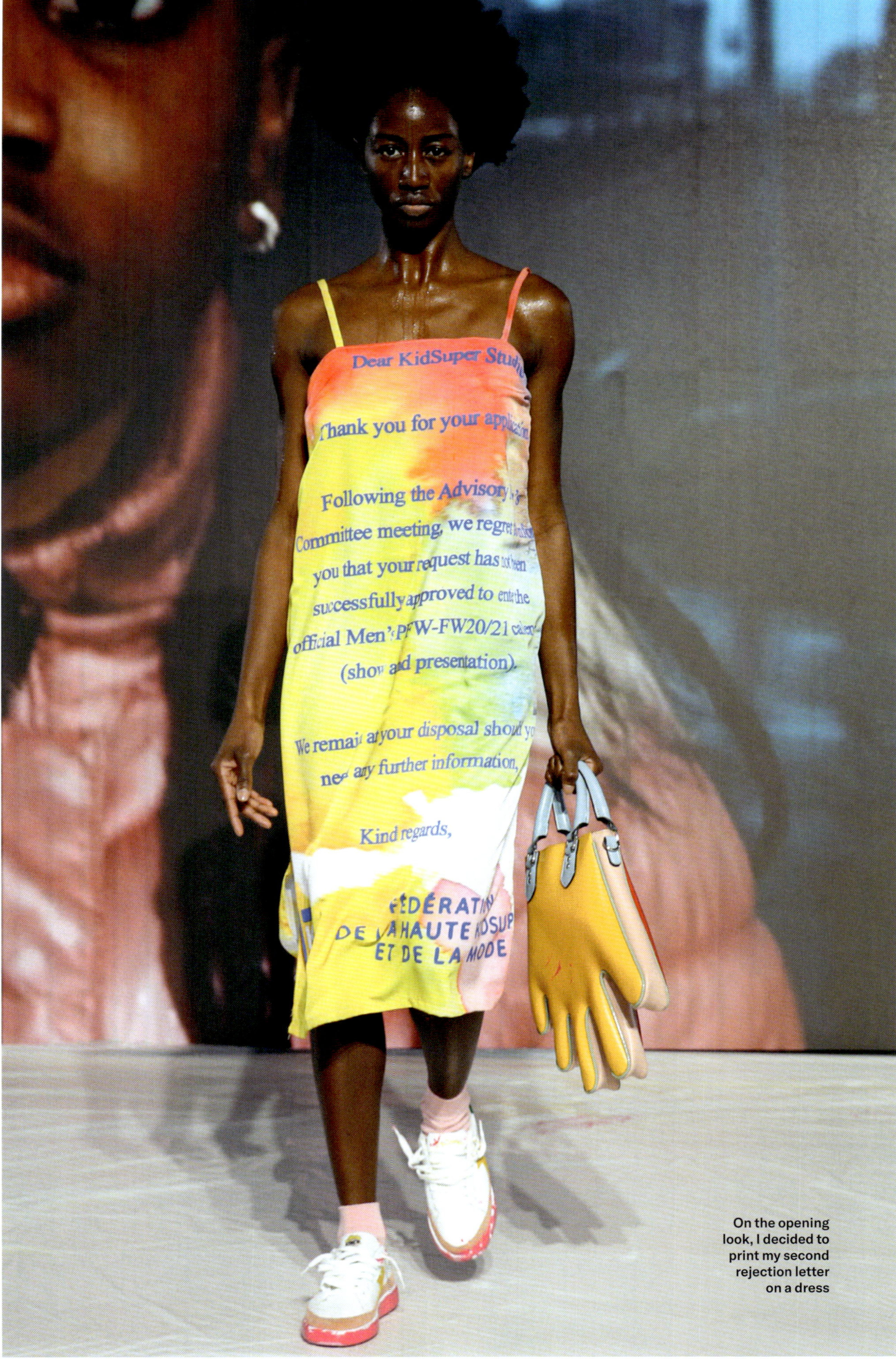

On the opening look, I decided to print my second rejection letter on a dress

PAINTING → IDEATING →

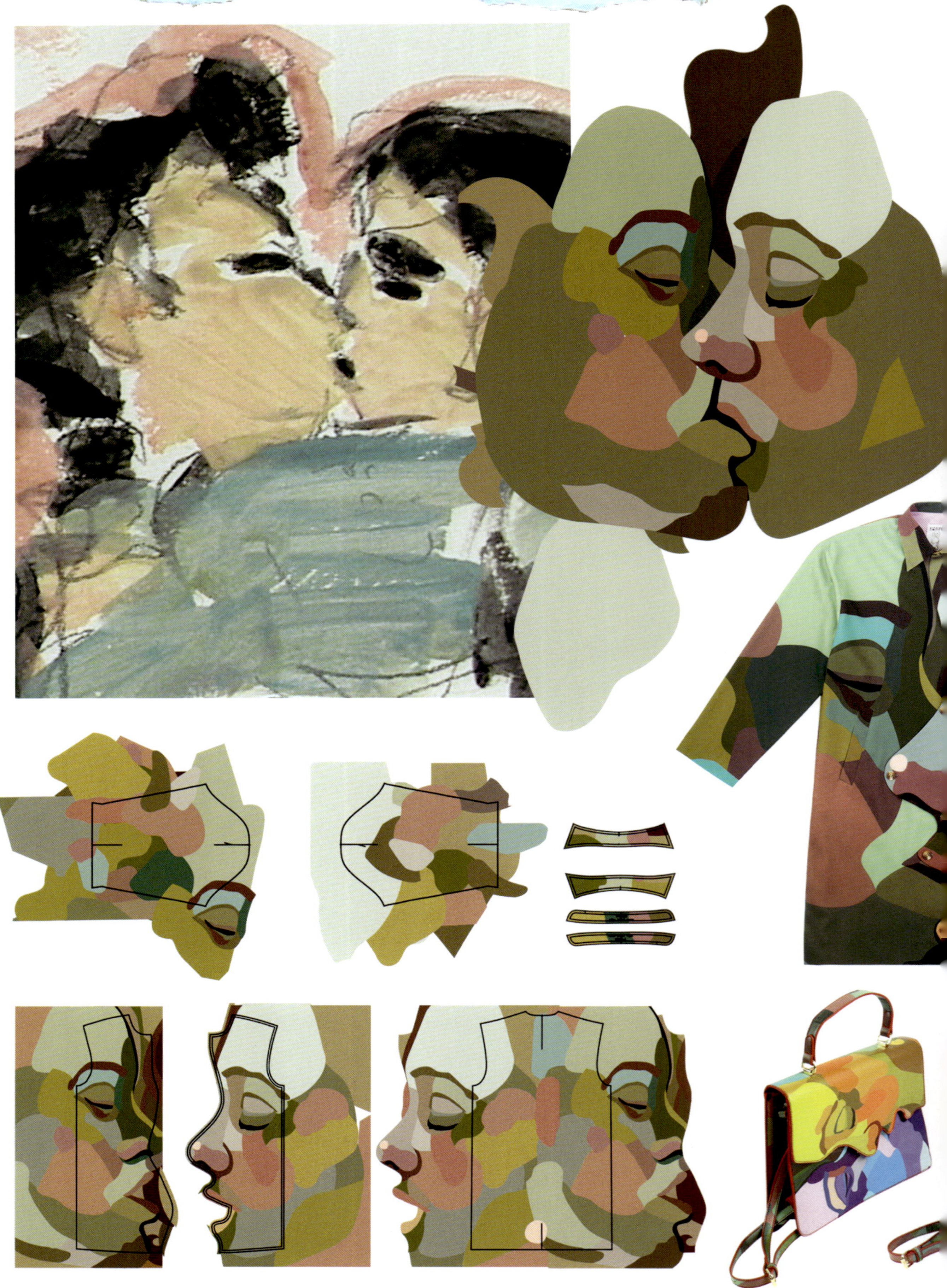

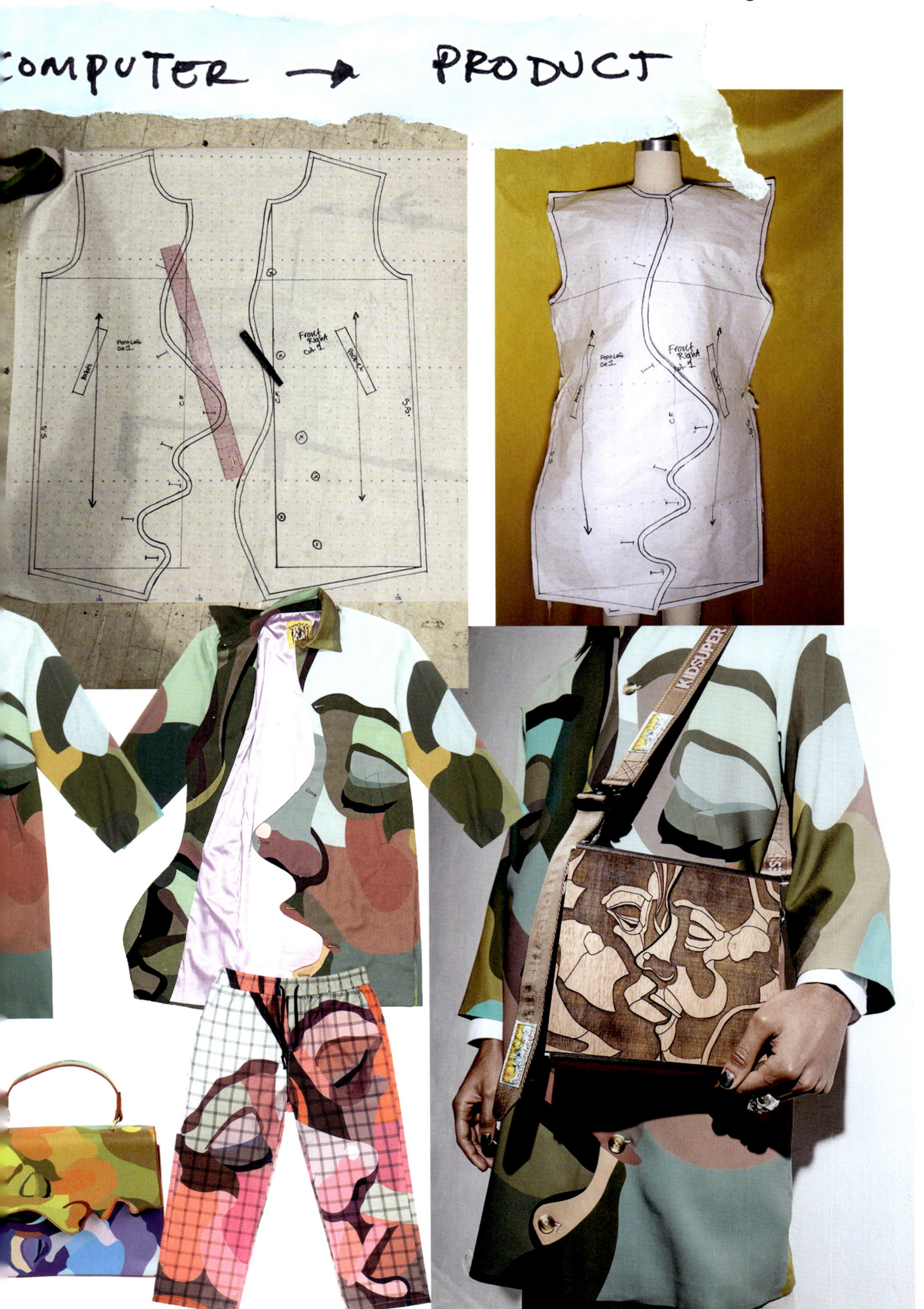
COMPUTER → PRODUCT
KIDSUPER

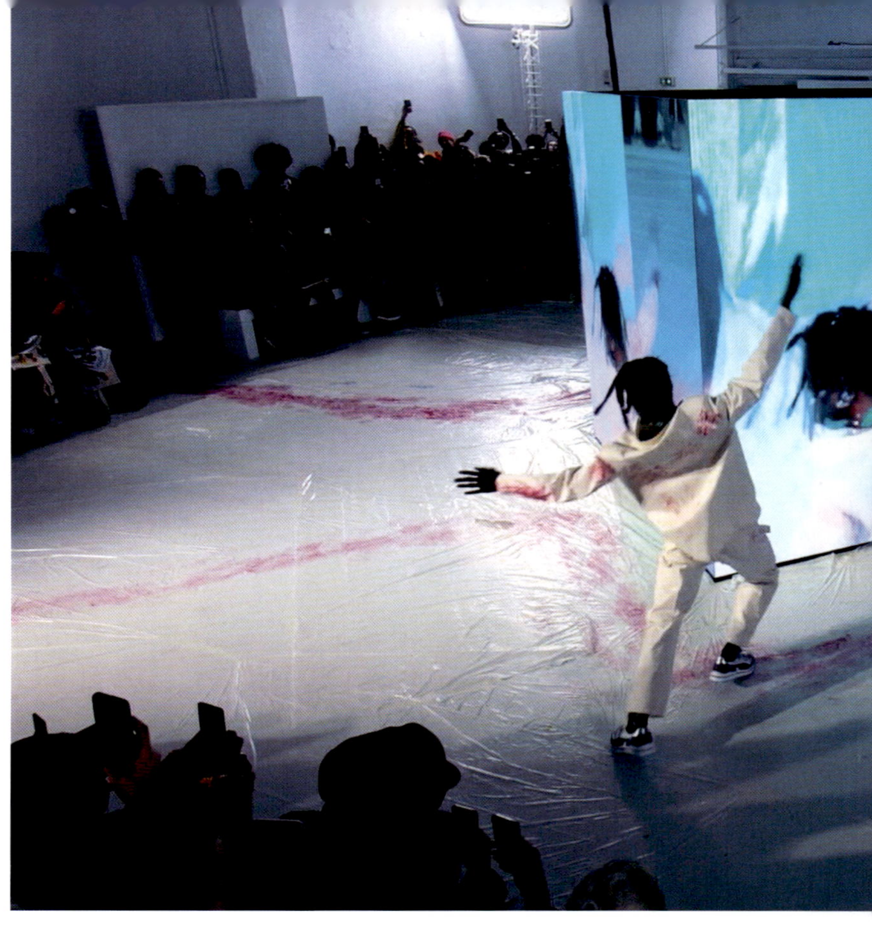

to show up to that first show at all. I did it because it was a creative challenge, because the ceiling for creativity in fashion shows was so high, and because I wanted to prove something to myself. I never expected that first review, so why was I now obsessing over getting another one?

At the same time, I had just been rejected again from Paris Fashion Week. That rejection lit a fire in me—it set a clear and defined goal, and I wasn't going to stop until I was accepted. I've always had this mentality of never quitting. Even back when I was at NYU, studying math while running my brand, people questioned why I didn't change my major or drop out. But for me, if I start something, I see it through. One of my father's unspoken commandments.

That mindset shaped the theme of the show: "Running as Fast as You Can." If you're going to do something, give it everything. If you're going to run, run as fast as you can.

The concept was simple but powerful: models would step in paint and walk in a circle around a video cube playing footage of people running. The music would mimic the sound of someone out of breath over an instrumental. With each step, the models would leave a trail of footprints, and as more models came through, the path would become clearer. The final model,

The final look of the show. It worked to everyone's surprise – including mine – it actually came together!

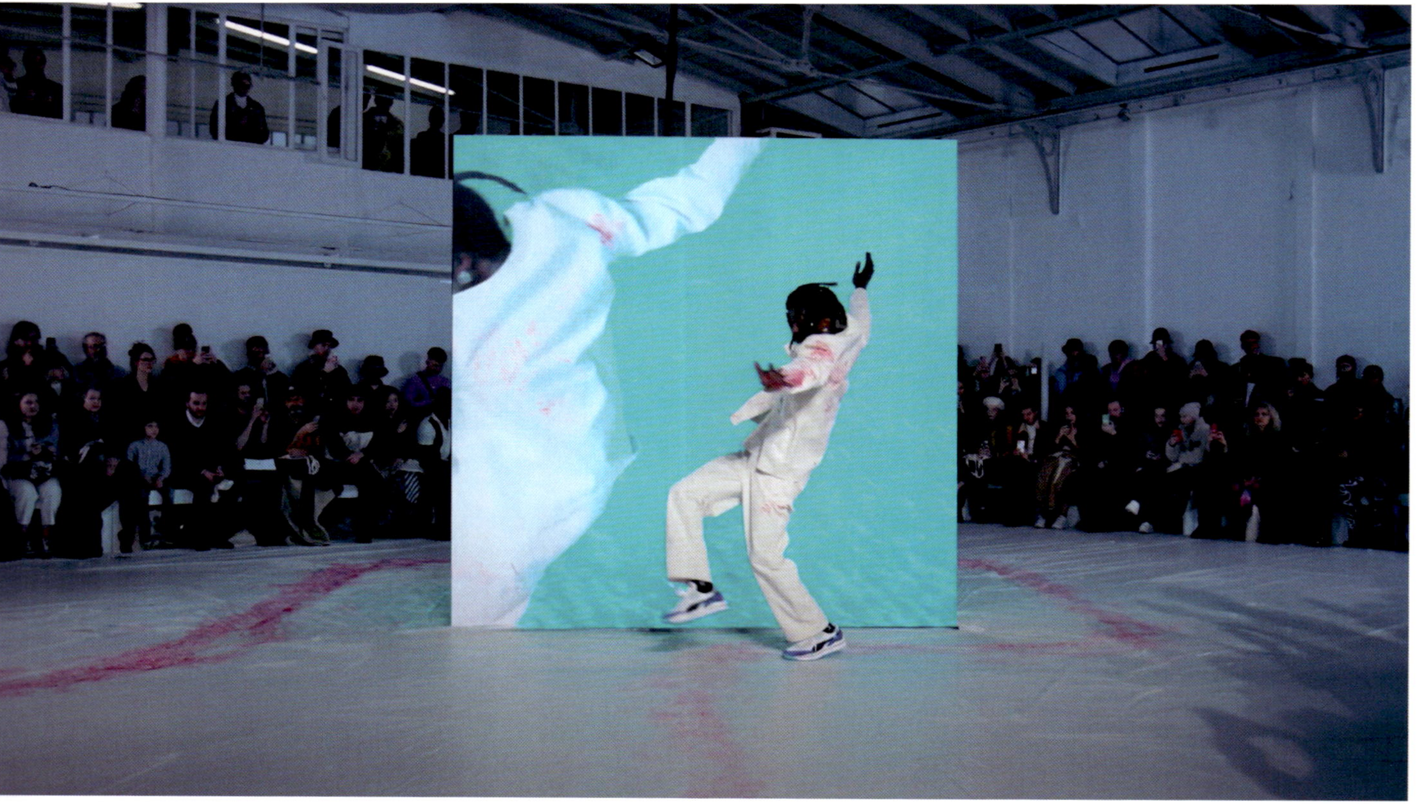

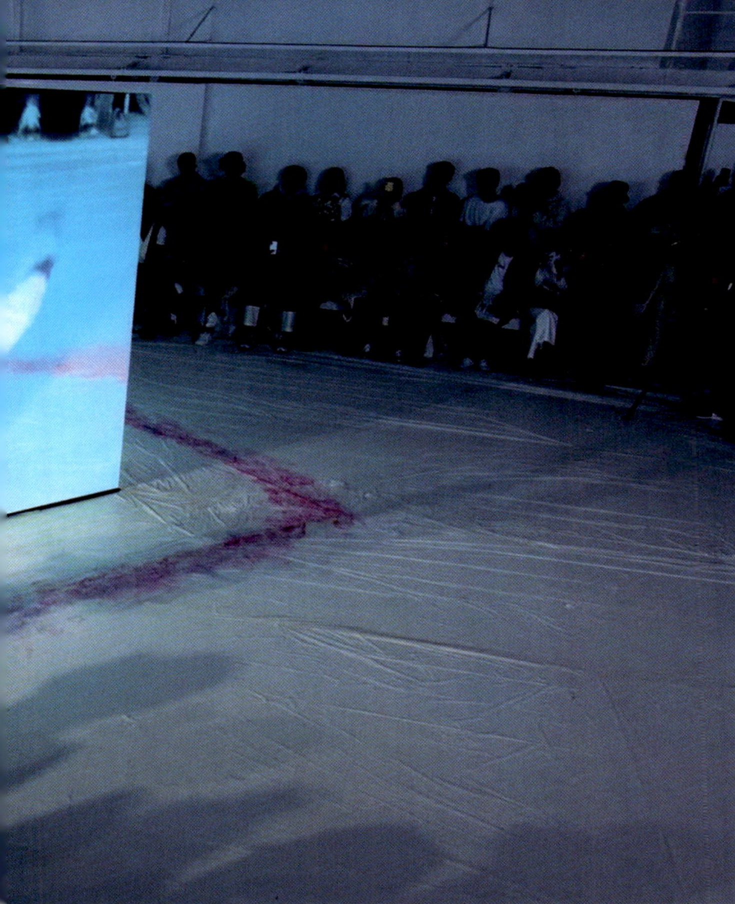

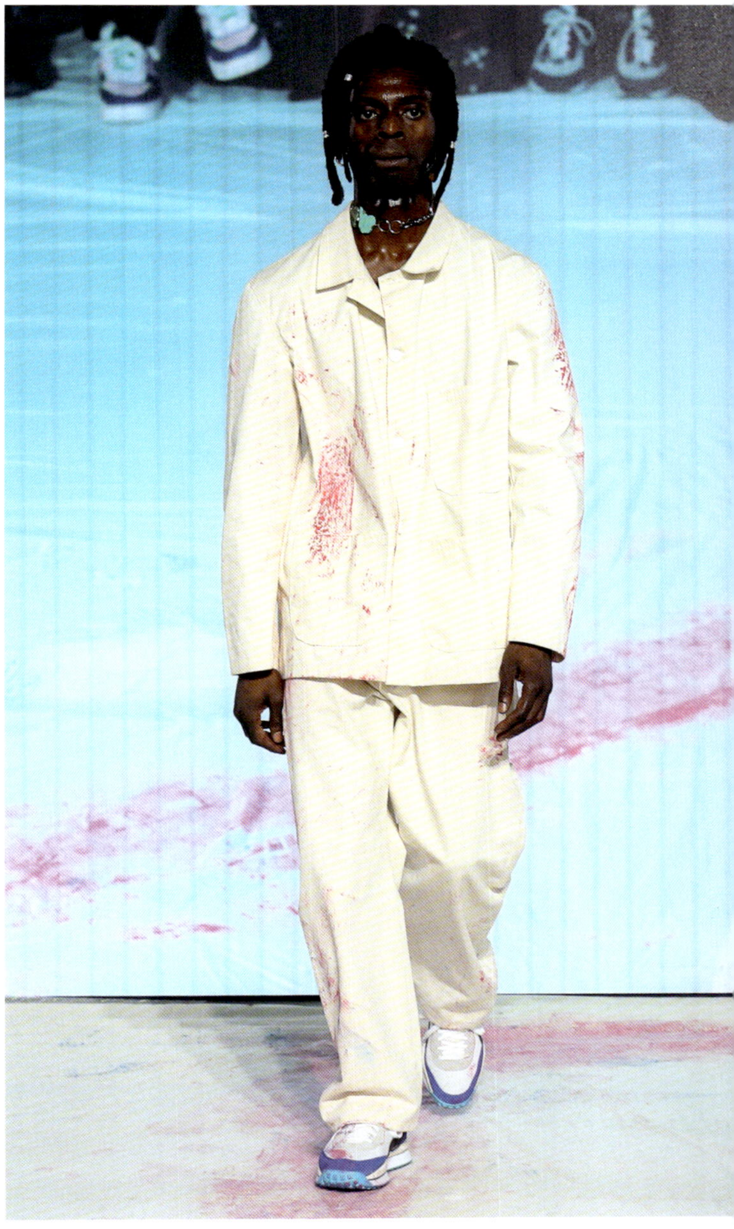

dressed in a pristine white suit, would be a breakdancer. As he danced, rolling and spinning on the floor, the painted footprints would create a unique pattern on his suit—turning the performance into the design itself.

An hour before the show, the venue owners pulled me aside: "Colm, this is bullshit. You can't have paint on the floor."

The entire concept revolved around the paint. Without it, the show, in my mind, would be the worst show ever. We went back and forth, back and forth, and finally I made a last-ditch offer: "What if I cover the entire floor in plastic?"

They agreed, but with a warning: "If there's even one drop of paint on the floor, you'll owe us thousands of dollars." With less than an hour to go, I told the production company and

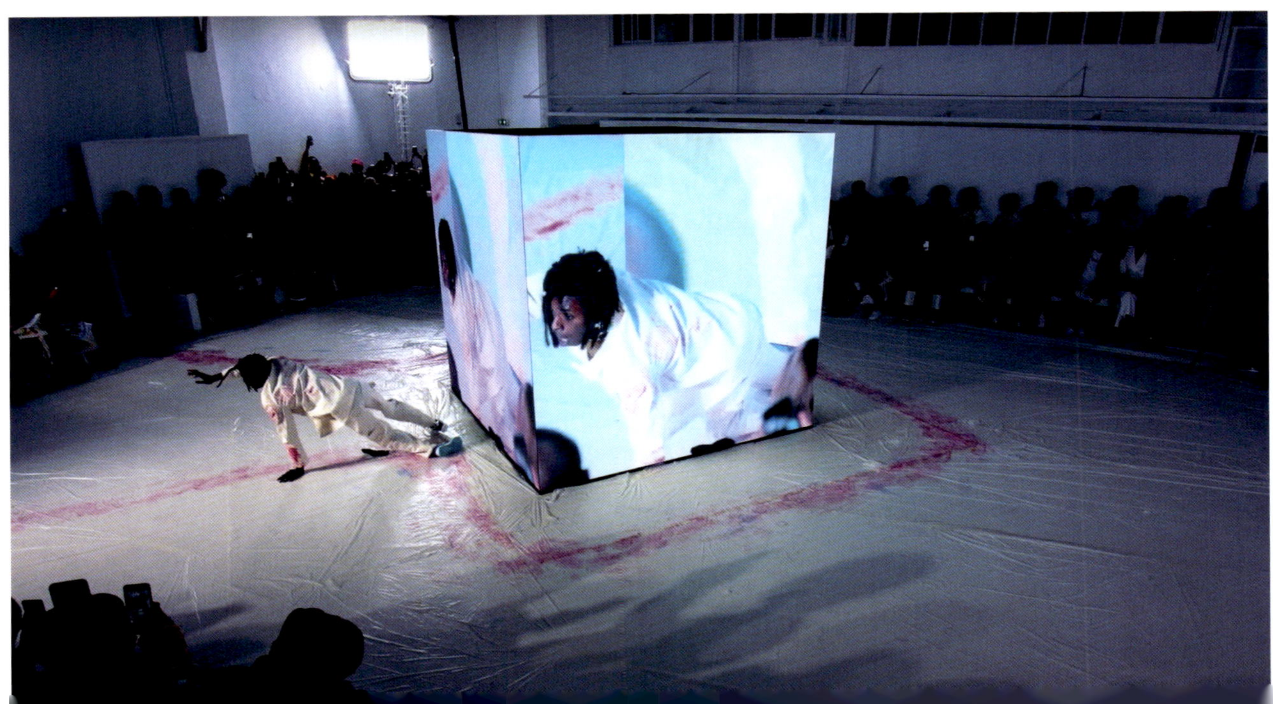

FELTING

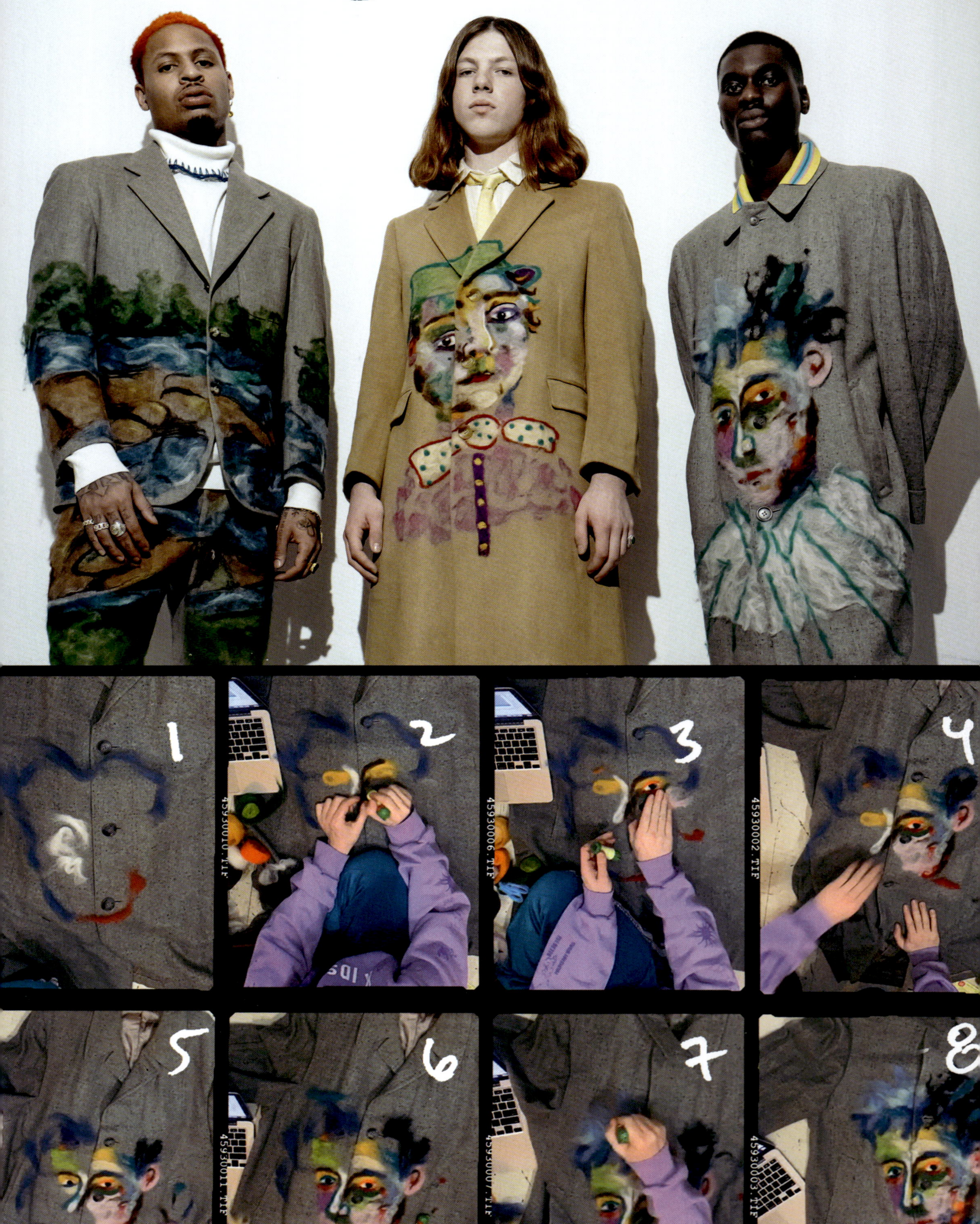

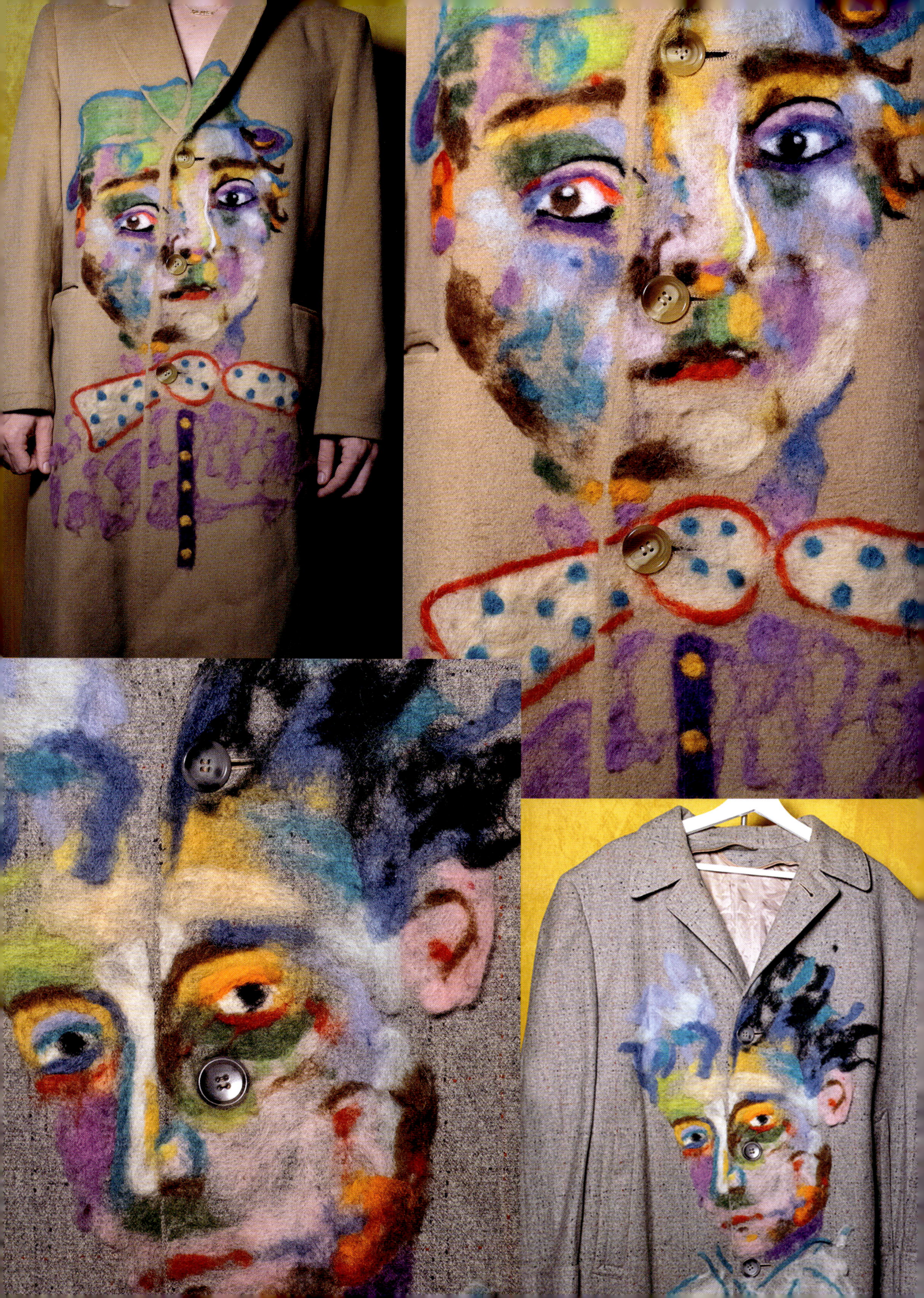

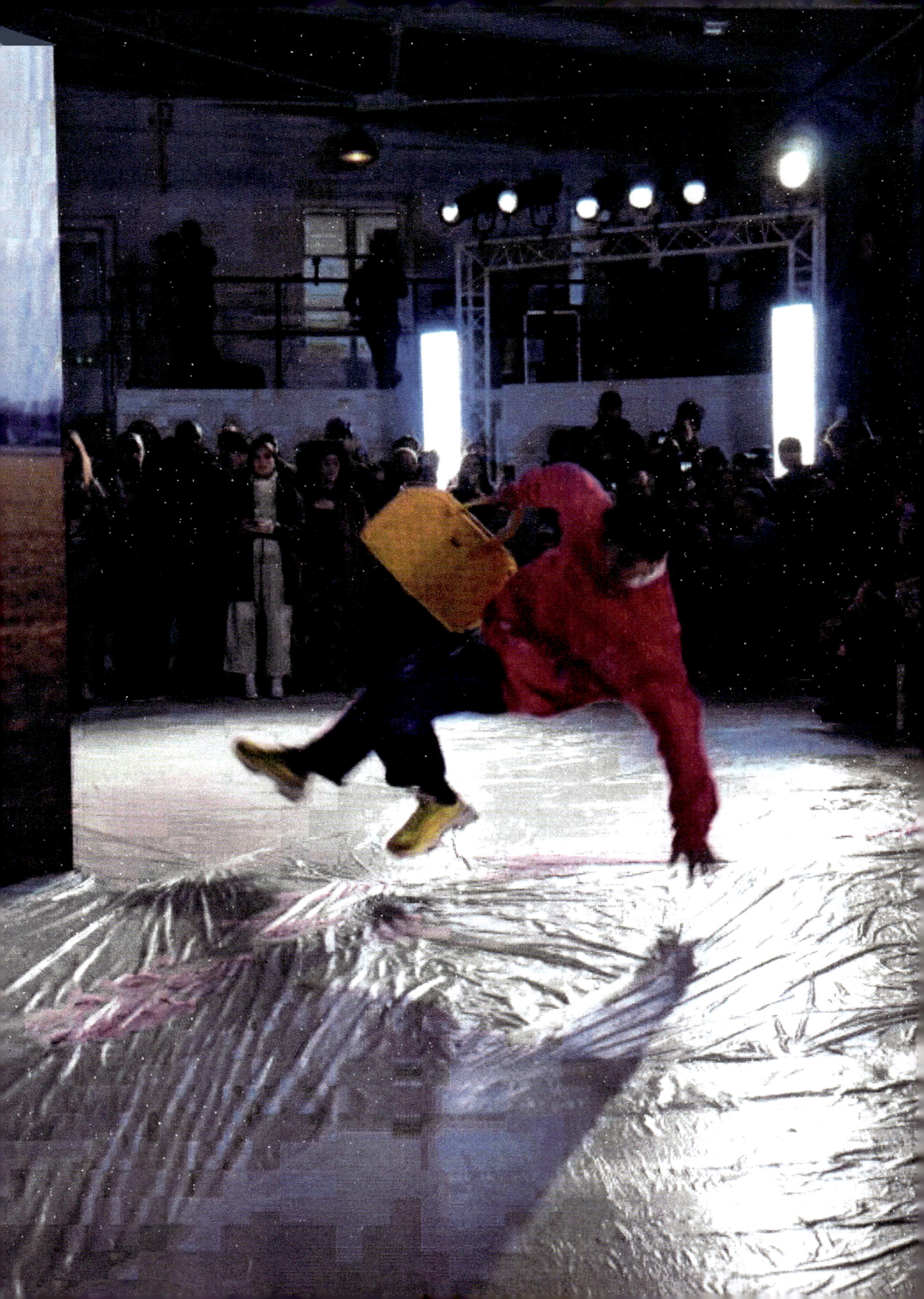

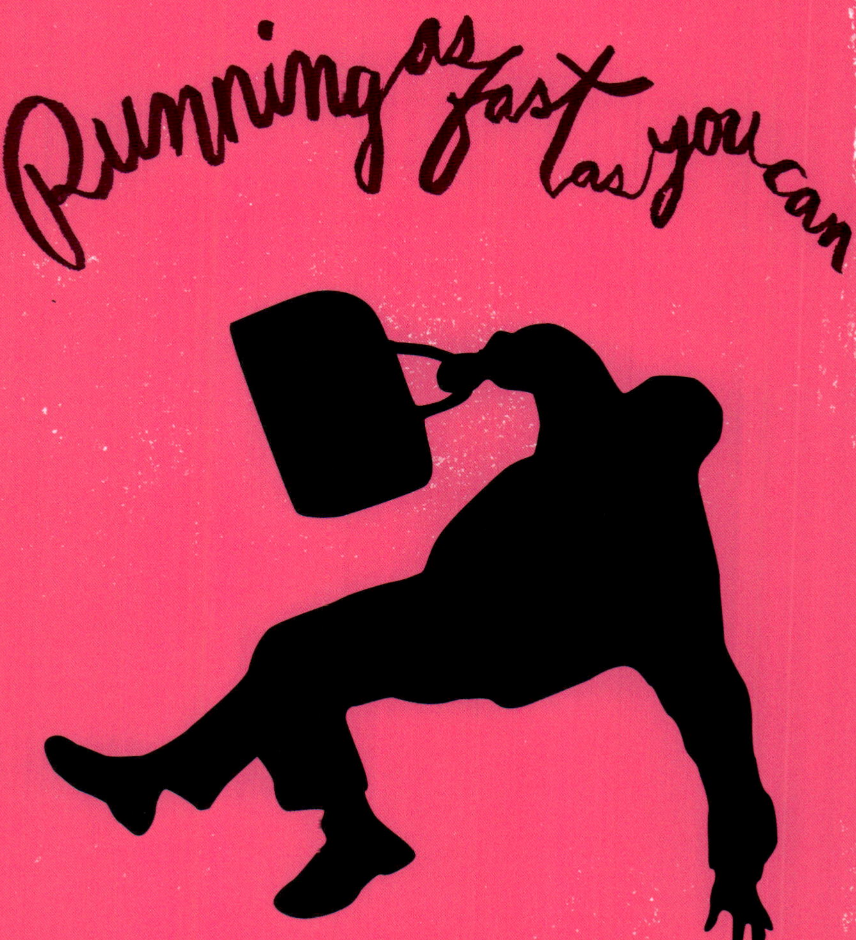

GET UP, GET GOIN’

A model falling caught while in midair. I turned it into a logo later on. It represented everything about KidSuper: falling forward.

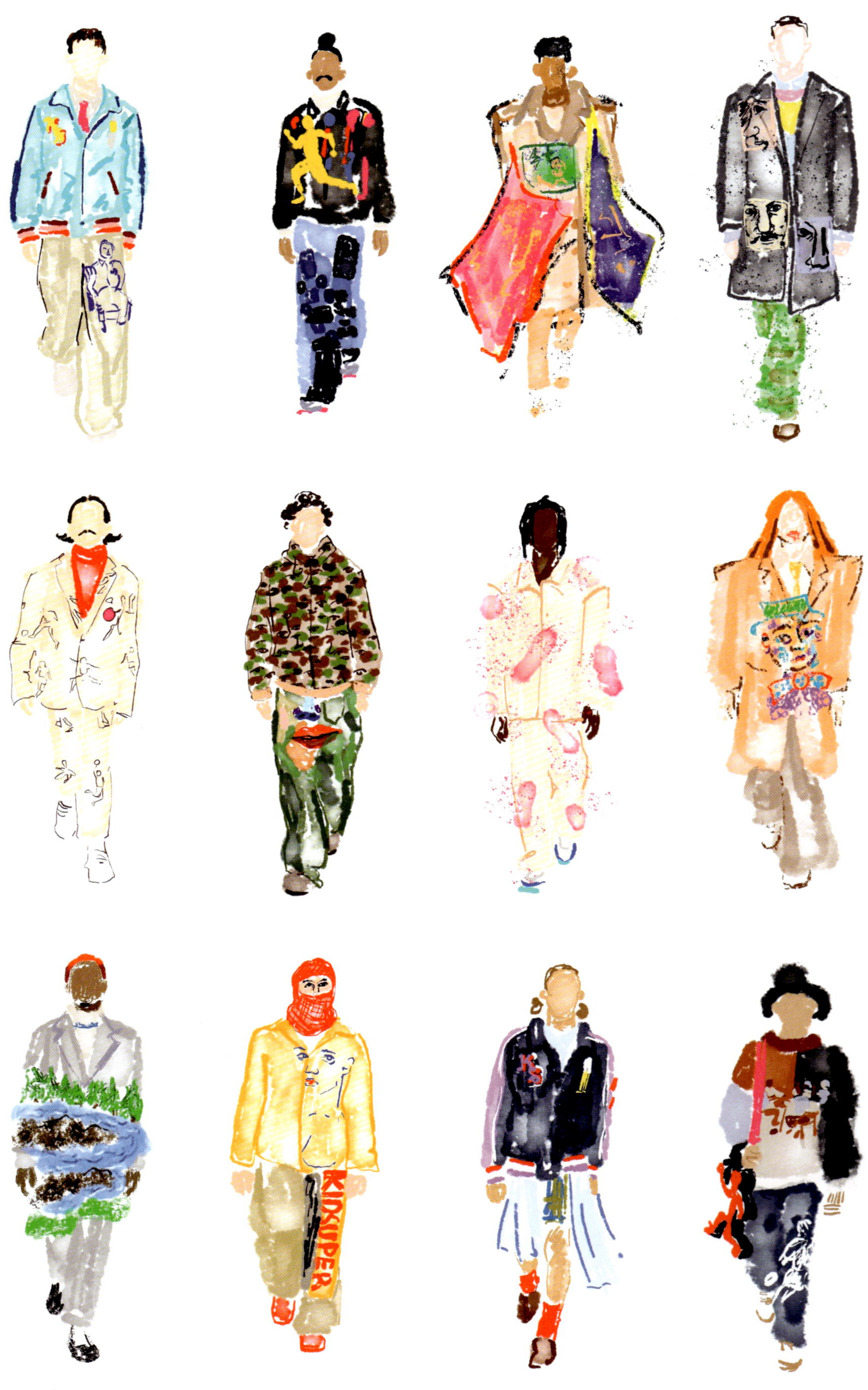
KIDSUPER

called every friend I could and got them to help cover the floor in plastic. We scrambled to get it done, and obviously we couldn't test if it worked.

The show started and the first model stepped onto the paint, then onto the plastic . . . and immediately started slipping. What I hadn't realized was that I had just created a human slip-and-slide. Now, if one model falls at a fashion show, it's considered a disaster. But here? One hundred percent of the models were slipping. Backstage, models were furious. "Who thought of this? This is bullshit!" I had my hands over my head, thinking, everything is going wrong that could go wrong.

After 30 or so slipping models . . . the finale started.

The breakdancer came out, and because of the slippery surface and his breakdancing style, it seemed like the slipping was intentional. He exaggerated the slipping and made it part of the show. He received huge applause to end the show and when it was time for me to come out, I didn't just walk—I slid out onto the runway. Up until then I had still never been to a fashion show, and I didn't know that designers didn't make speeches at the end. So I grabbed the mic and said: "Sometimes you slip and fall, but you have to remember to get back up and run as fast as you can. I'm Colm Dillane—thank you for coming to my show!"

The crowd went wild. The speech was the glue that tied it all together.

After the show, someone from *Vogue* came up to me and said: "That decision to have the models slip—it created such a visceral experience for the audience and perfectly reinforced your concept. Brilliant." I looked her dead in the eyes and said, "I'm so glad you understood my vision."

A few months later, I finally got accepted onto the official calendar for Paris Fashion Week.

Sometimes, nothing goes as planned. Sometimes, everything seems to be falling apart. But remember to always try to *Run as Fast as You Can.*

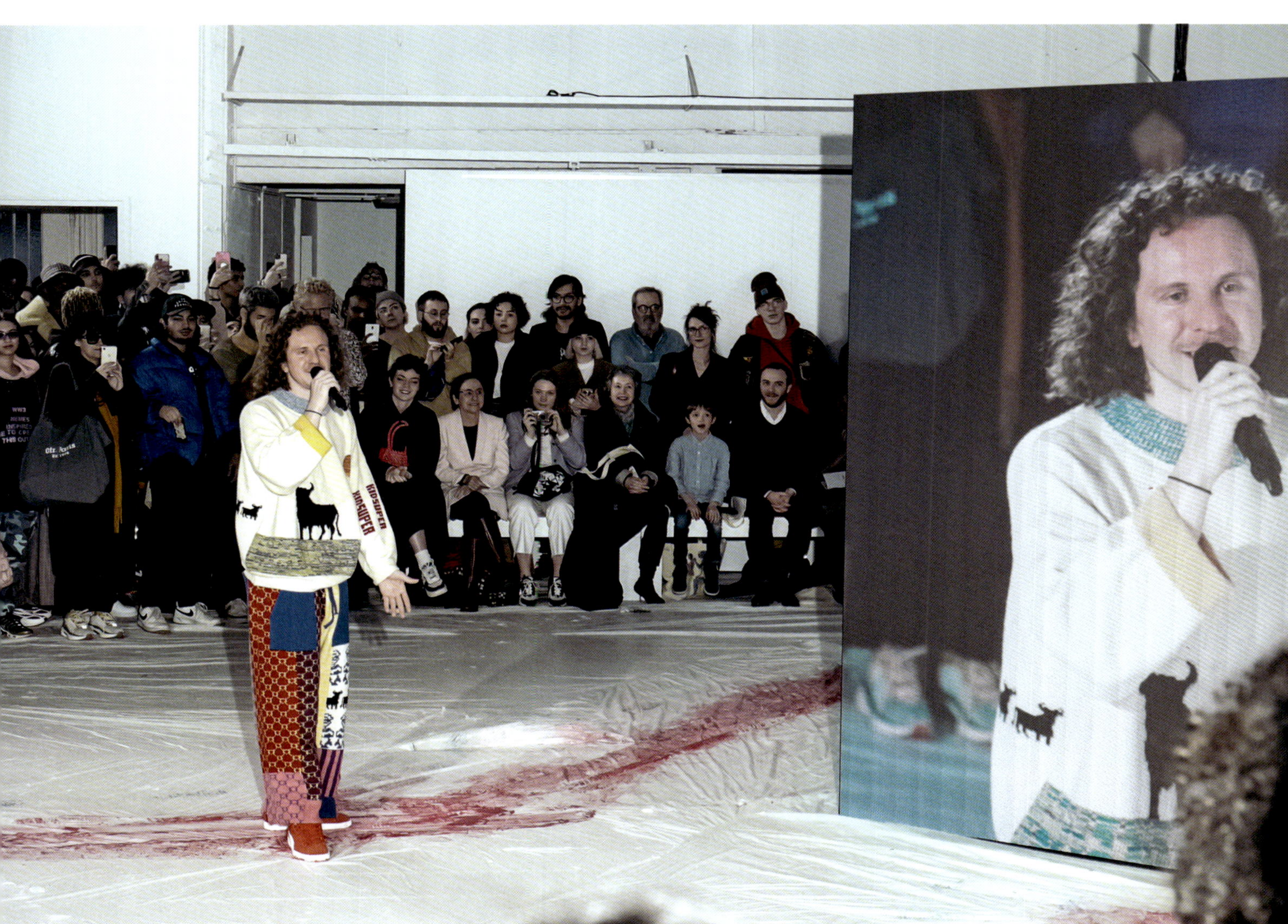

My most important speech of all the speeches, really tied the show all together.

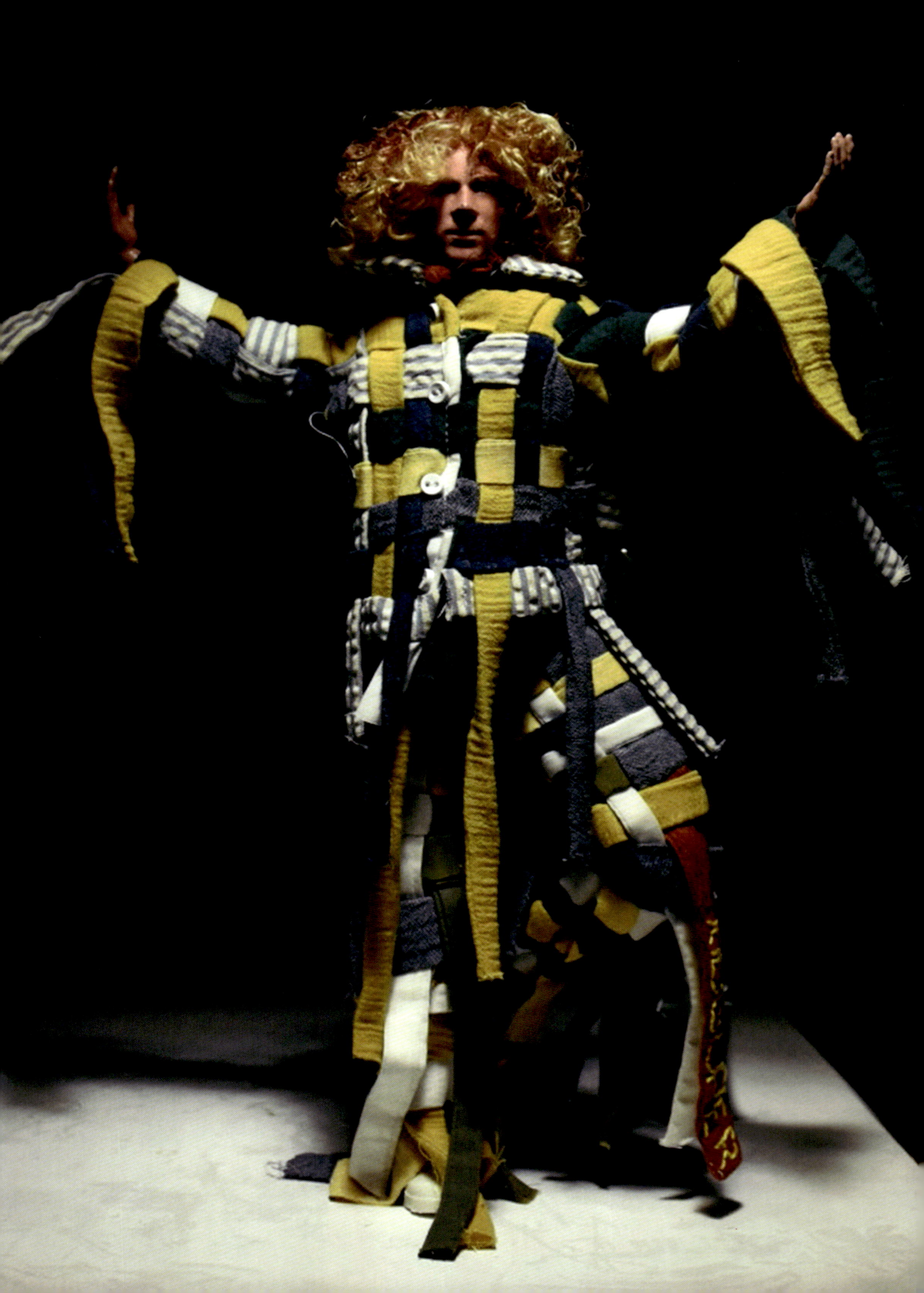

SS21

EVERYTHING'S FAKE

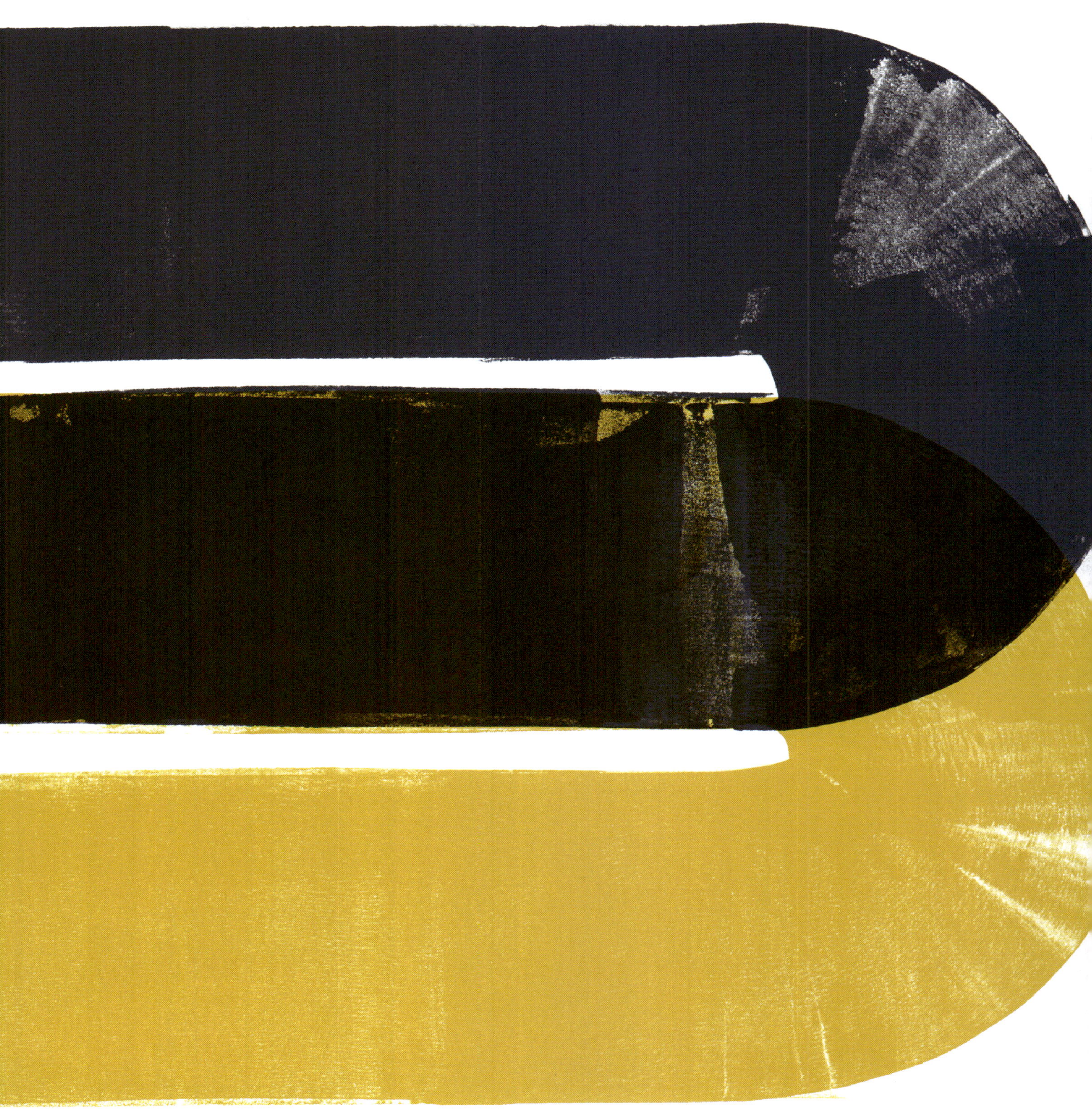

UNTIL IT'S REAL

Turning
nothing into
something.

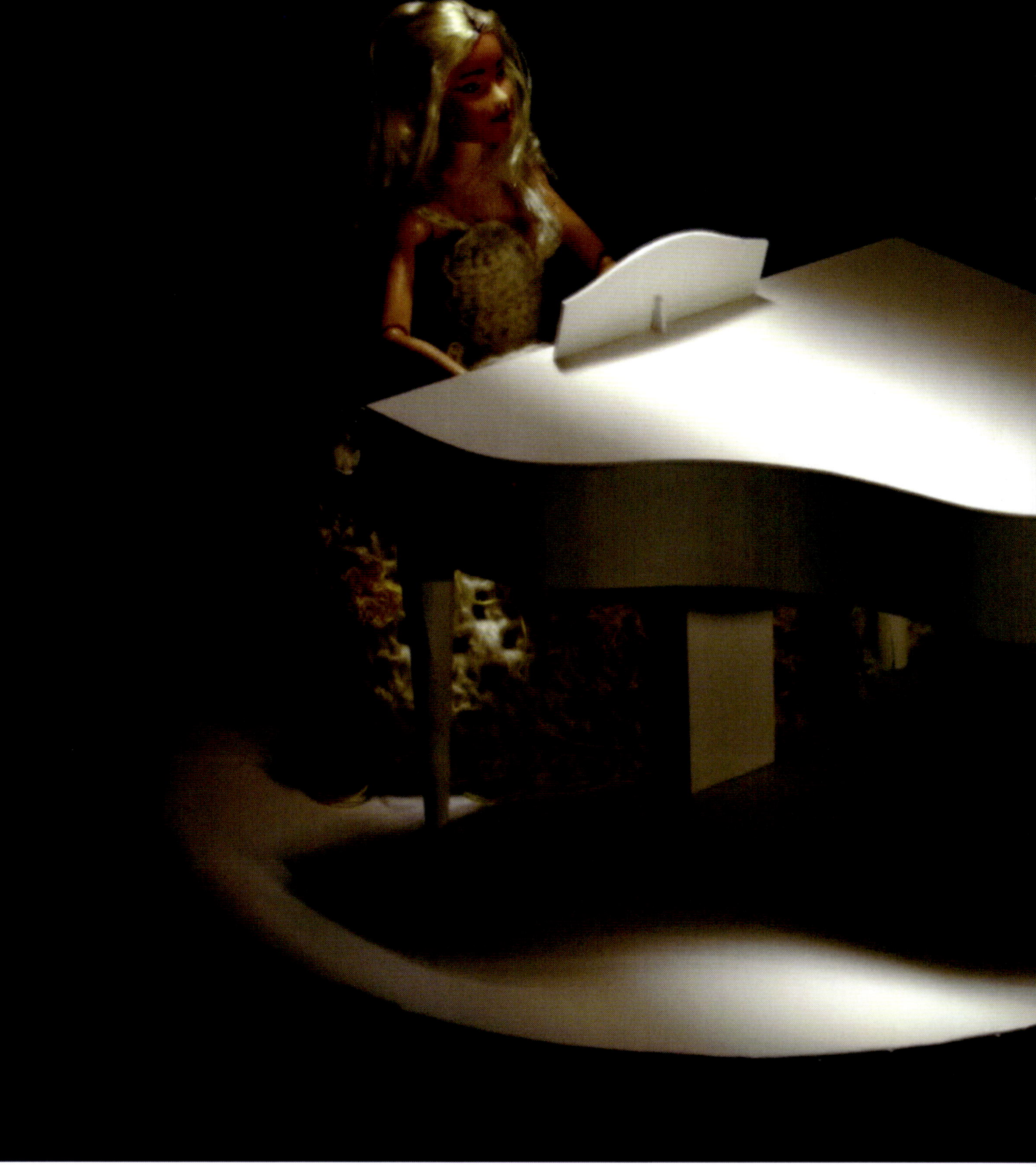

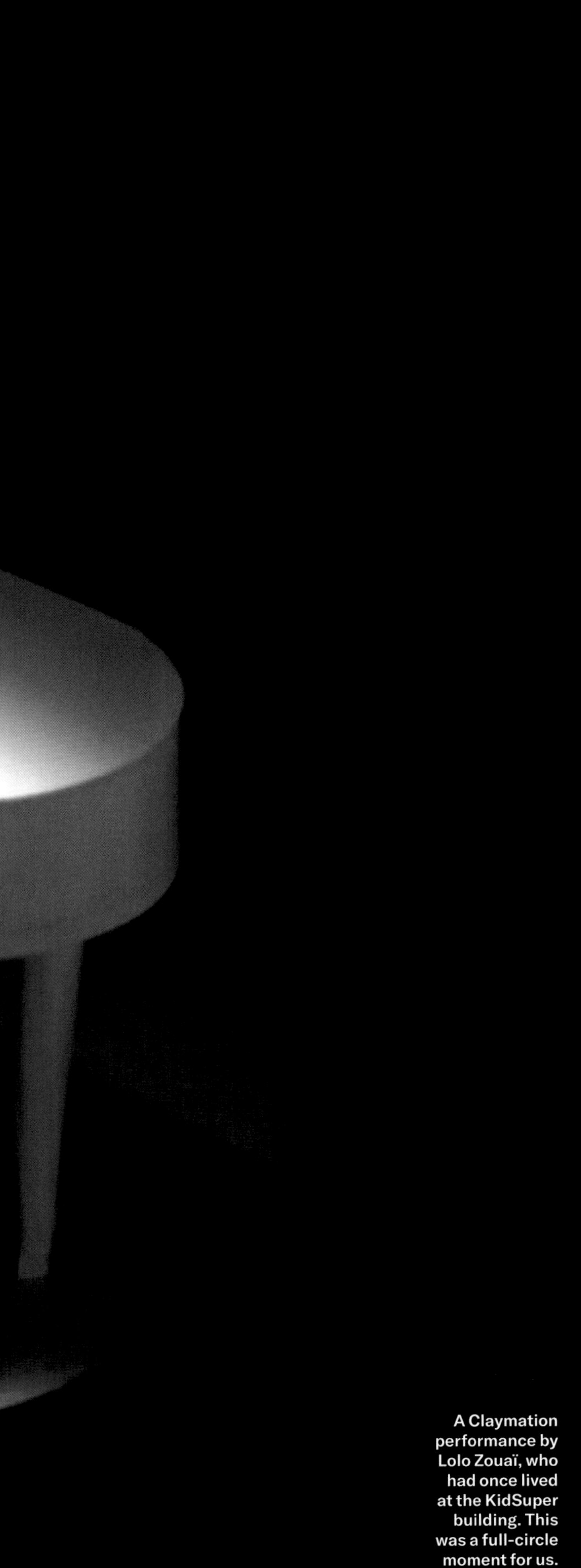

A Claymation performance by Lolo Zouaï, who had once lived at the KidSuper building. This was a full-circle moment for us.

I RECEIVED AN EMAIL and I had done it—I was officially on the Paris Fashion Week calendar.

And then . . . COVID hit. And in a weird way this saved my business.

Looking back, I don't think I would have even had enough money to do an in-person show. I probably would've had to say, "Thank you for the acceptance, but I can't participate." Or maybe I would have sold a kidney and figured it out. (I just can't imagine myself quitting.) Who knows, but with the pandemic, everything changed. Suddenly, fashion shows were virtual—and no one really knew what that meant.

All the fashion shows now had to be in a video presentation. There was no precedent and, in my mind, no rules. And for the first time, big budgets didn't matter as much—you couldn't rent a palace, fly out a celebrity, or hire the world's top models. Everyone was stuck at home. For the first time, it felt like a level playing field. It wasn't about money; it was ideas versus ideas. And if you're competing with me on ideas, I like my chances.

I had already been making music videos and short films, and I'd always loved stop-motion animation. I had done two stop-motion music videos prior: Russ, "Cherry Hill," and The Mind, "Mercury Rising." (The Russ music video has 15 million views, and The Mind video won at a film festival.)

If I had to pick one art form that truly embodies the KidSuper spirit, it would be stop-motion—it's about taking inanimate objects and bringing them to life. That's exactly what KidSuper is about.

So I decided to make a stop-motion fashion show.

Instead of real models, I used Barbie dolls—12-inch-tall figures dressed in our own KidSuper handmade miniature outfits. I ripped off all the heads of the dolls and 3D-printed and sculpted the faces of my idols so they could walk the show. Salvador Dalí, Ronaldinho, 50 Cent, Picasso, Jackie Chan, Jennifer Lopez, and more all showed up to walk my show.

Each doll walked in a perfectly choreographed stop-motion

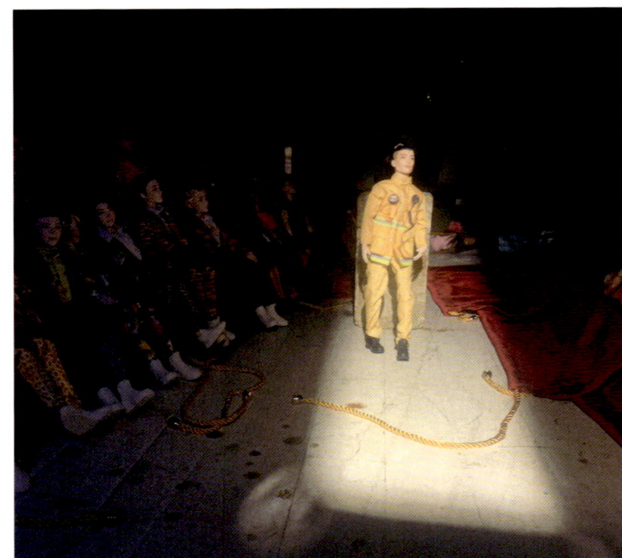

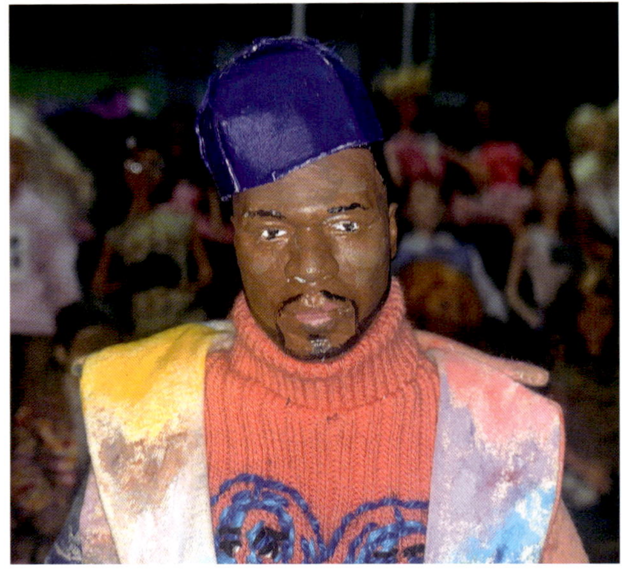

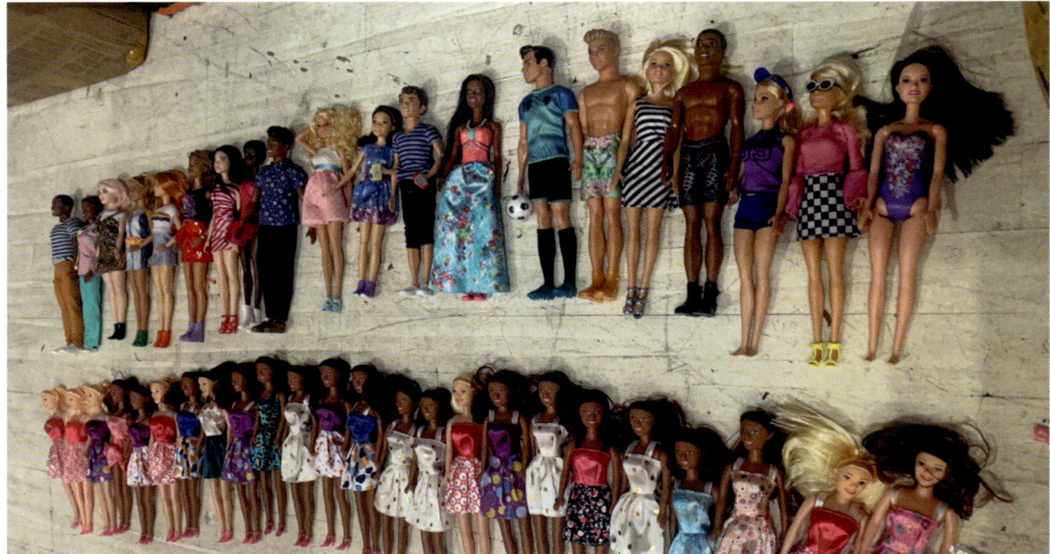

The process of making the dolls, from finding Barbie dolls, ripping off their heads and 3D printing, painting and sculpting our "heroes" heads.

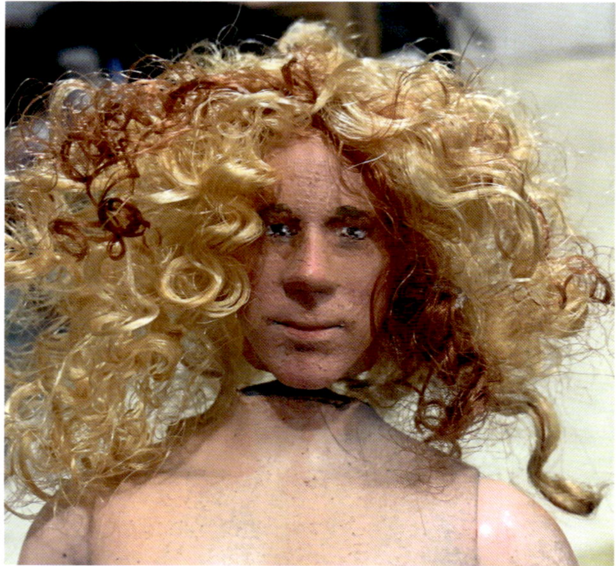

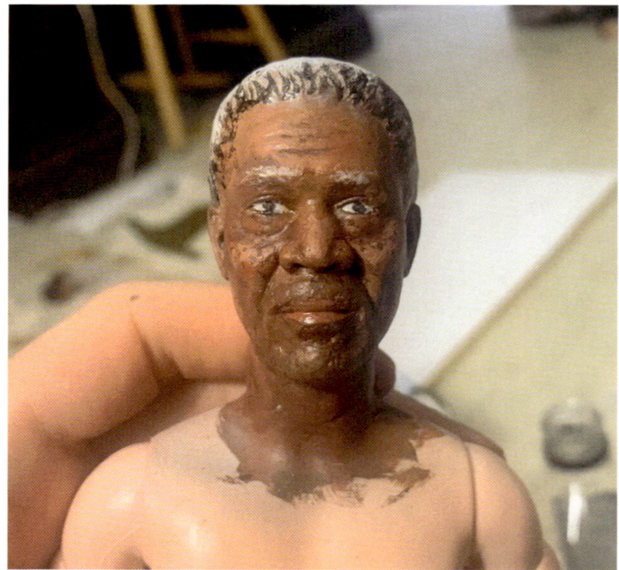

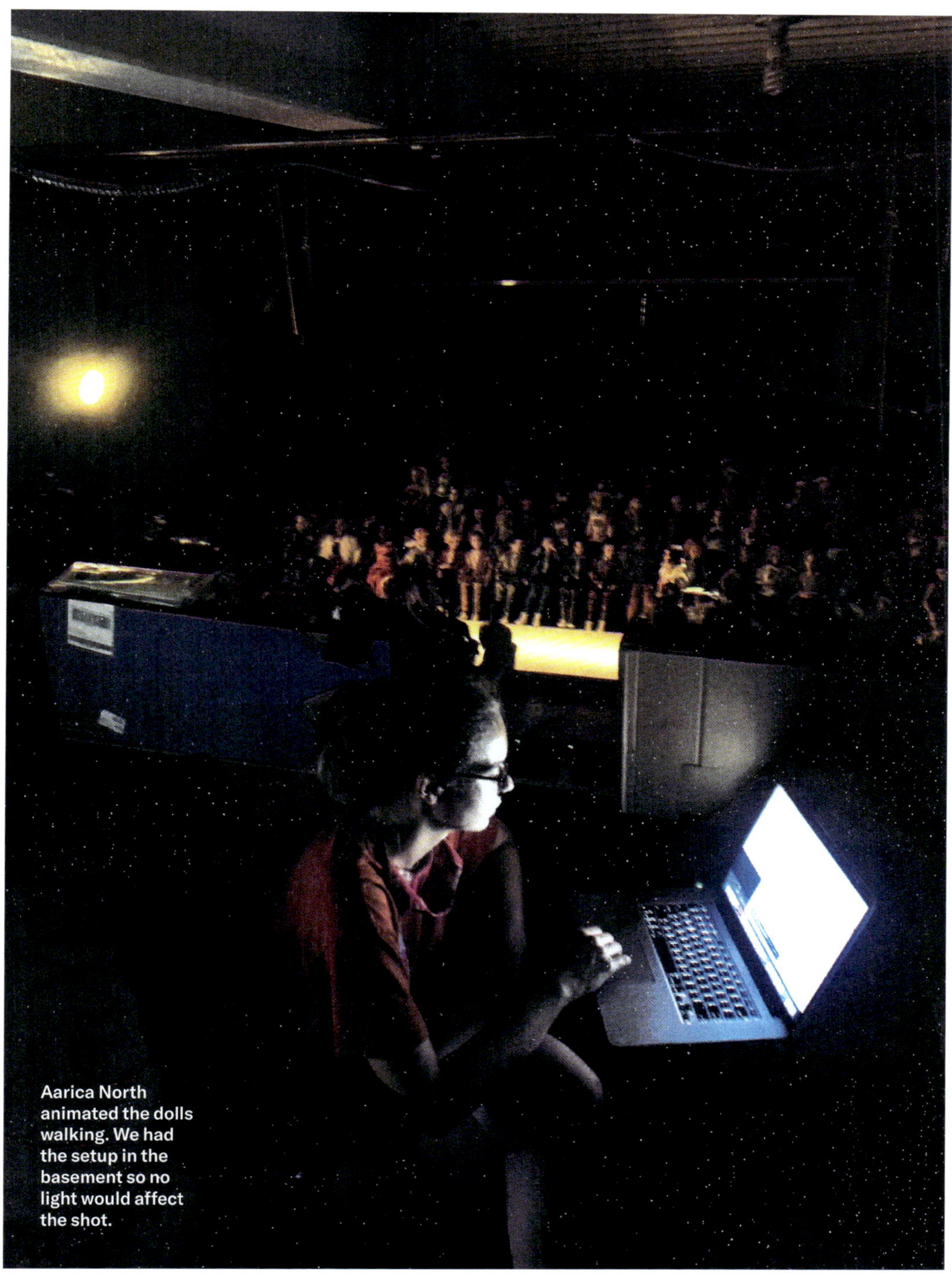

Aarica North animated the dolls walking. We had the setup in the basement so no light would affect the shot.

runway show, just like a real Paris Fashion Week presentation. The audience? Also Barbie dolls.

Instead of spending the minimum $70,000 that even a cheap fashion show costs, I made this entire show for $5,000—shot in my basement. Me, Aarica, Jon, Nate, Stav and Lucy made it happen.

It was the most KidSuper thing I could have done—breaking the mold, thinking differently, proving that creativity wins over budget.

And this time, since I was on the official Paris Week calendar, people were actually watching. Before, I was breaking the mold in places where no one cared. But now? I was on the same stage as the greats. And I had their attention.

I named the show "Everything's Fake Until It's Real"—because that's what KidSuper is. It's a real business built on unreal ideas. It was all fake until, suddenly, it wasn't. It was an idea I had in high school and now we have a Rizzoli book.

The show was not easy to make, eleven days nonstop. It was COVID, so most of us never left the KidSuper store. It was a machine: as one doll was being finished, one was being

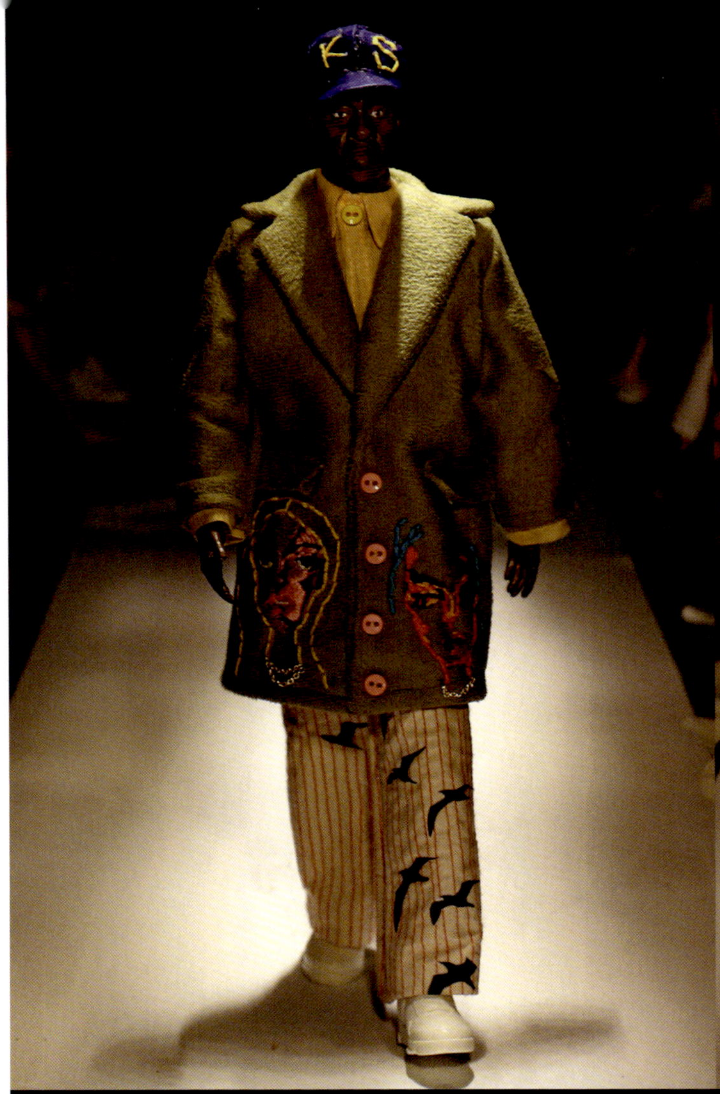

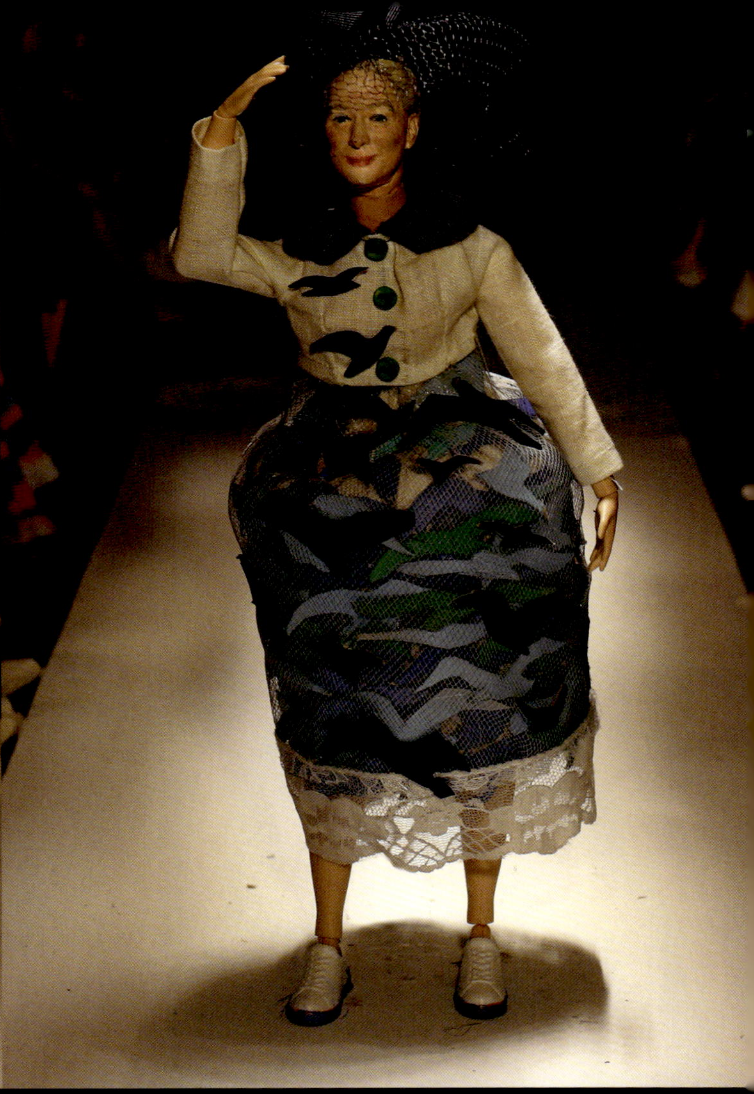

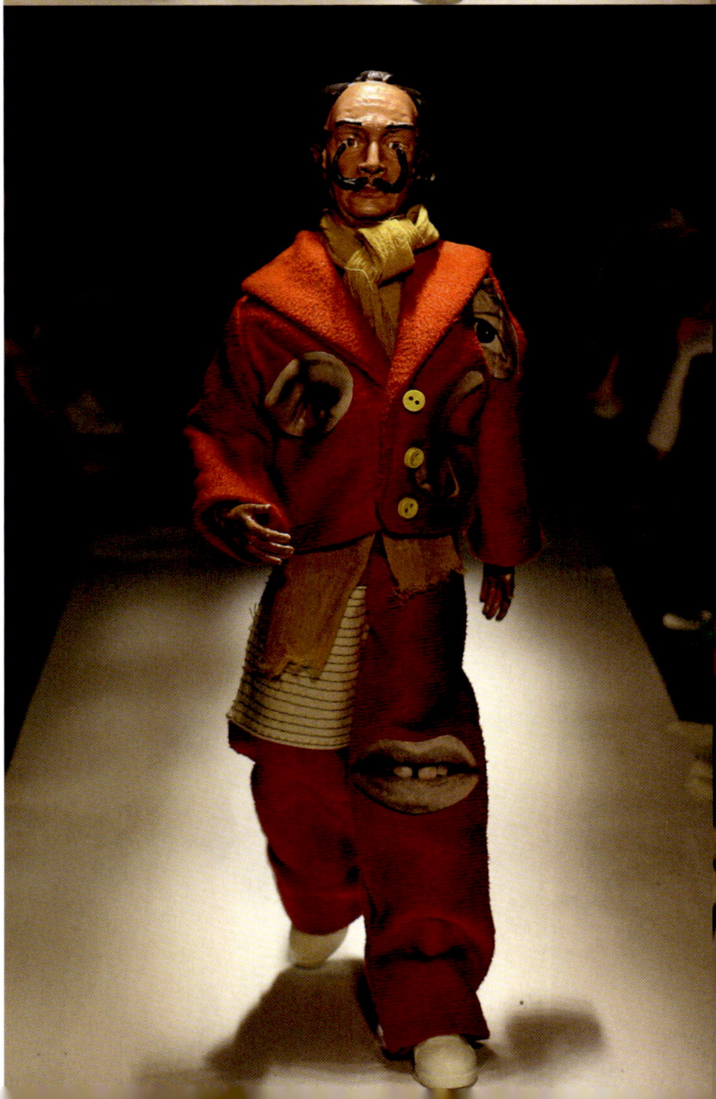

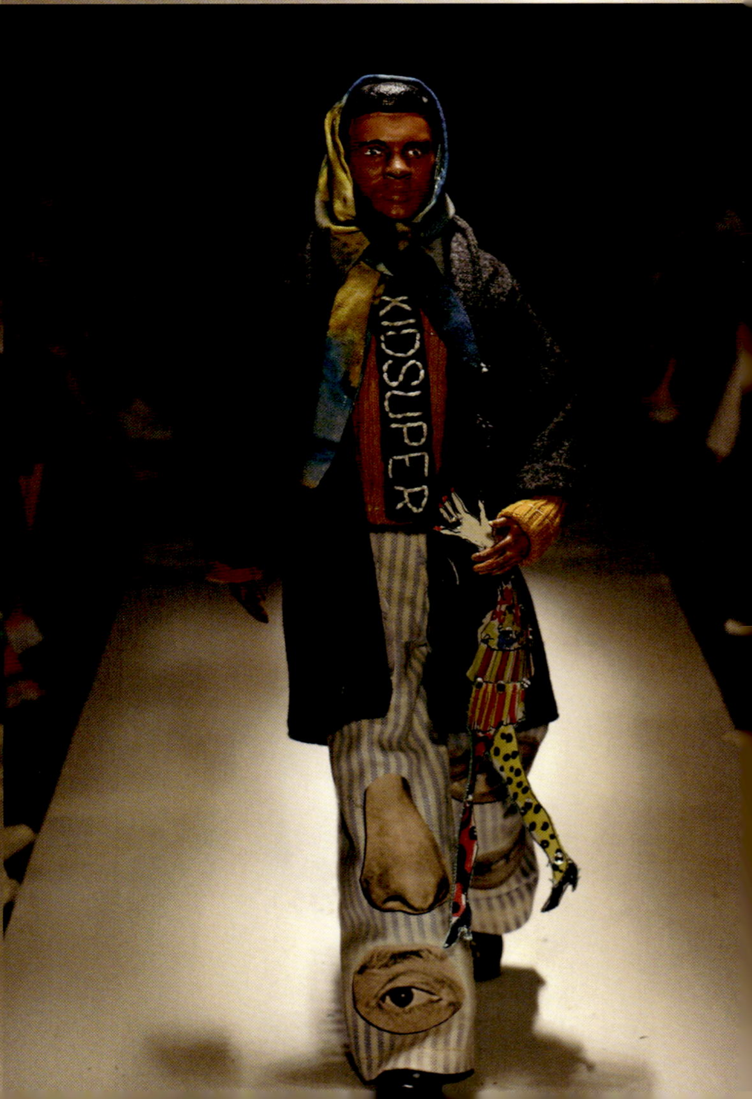

KIDSUPER

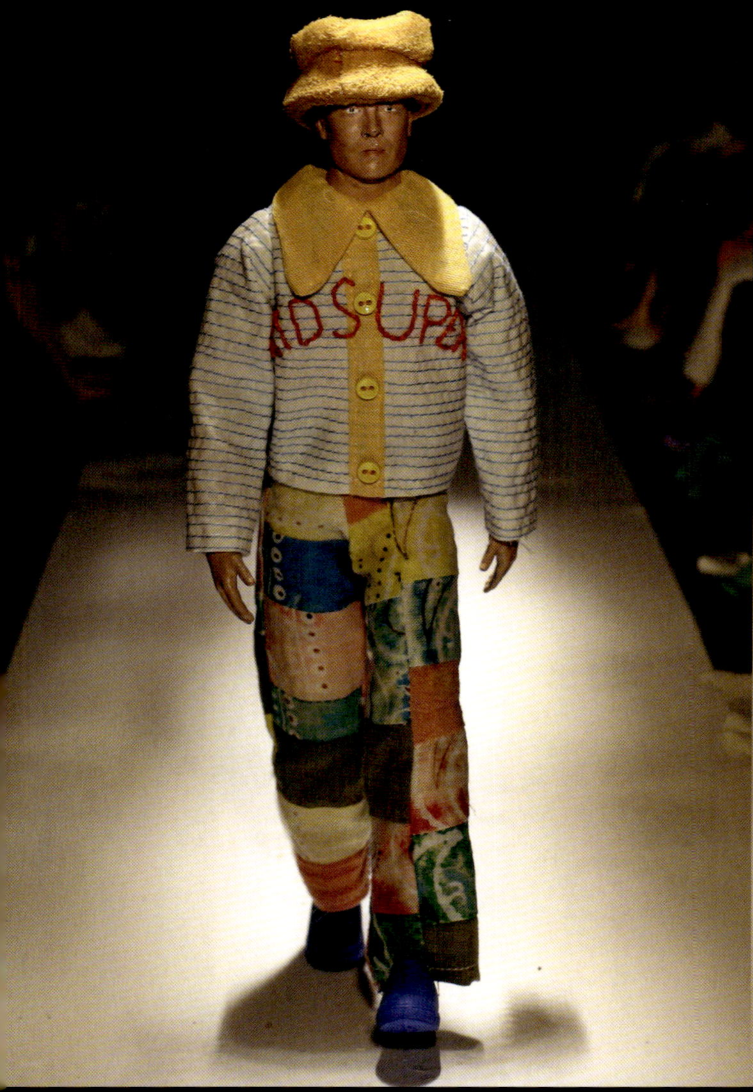

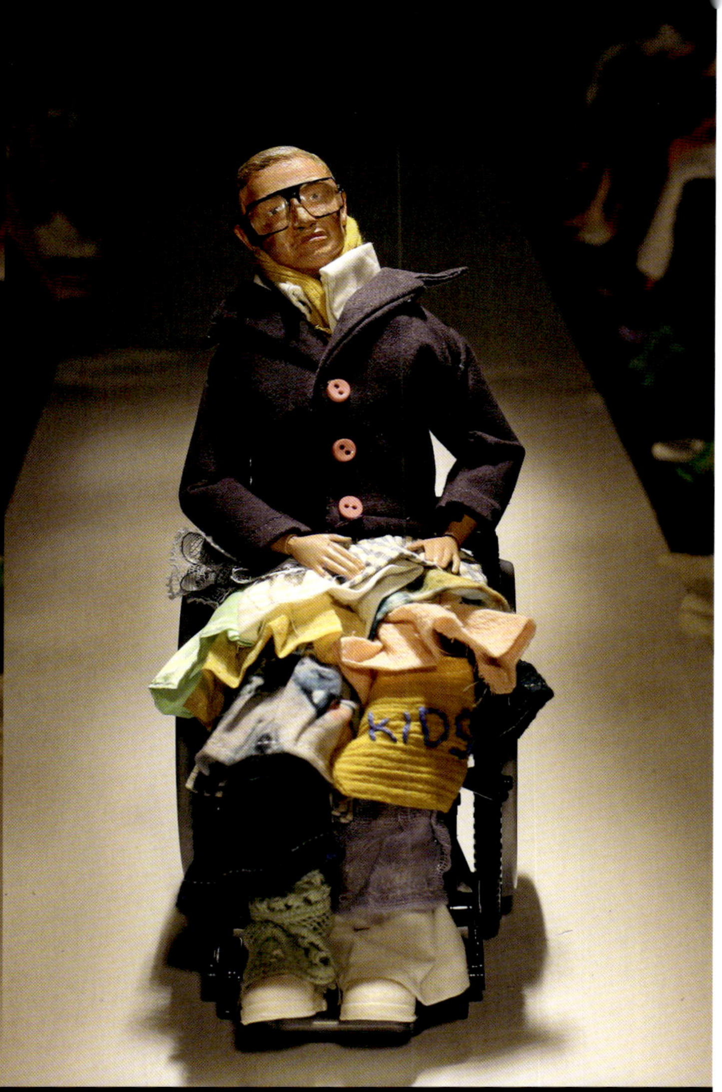

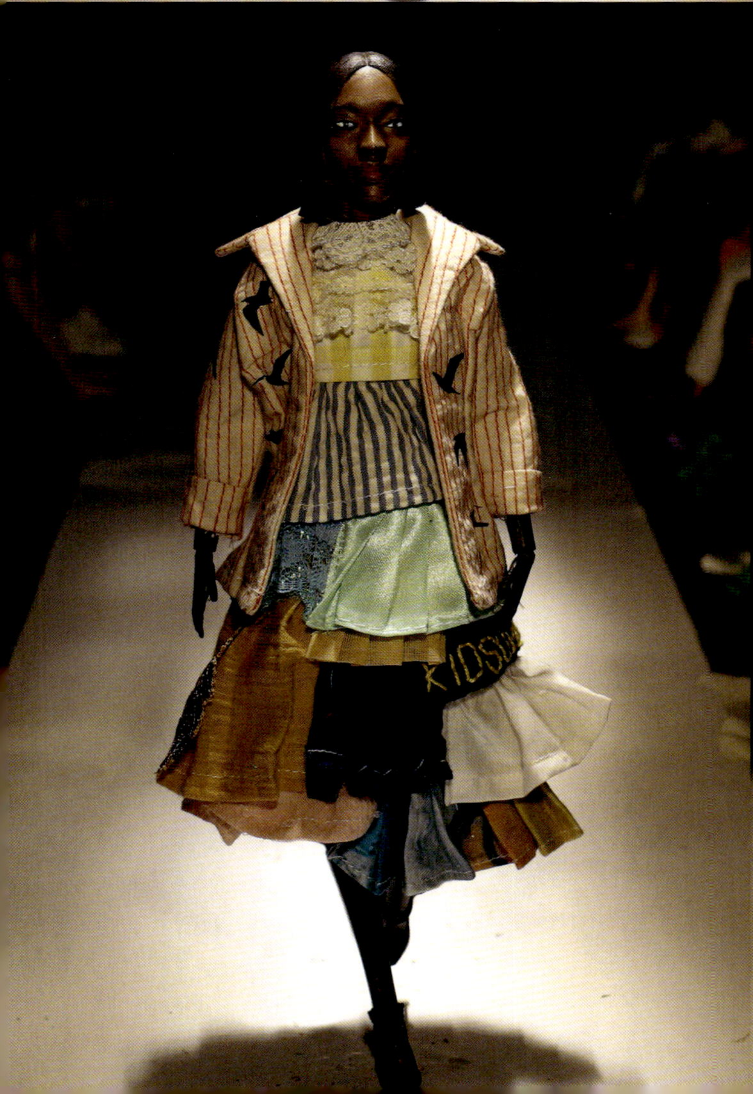

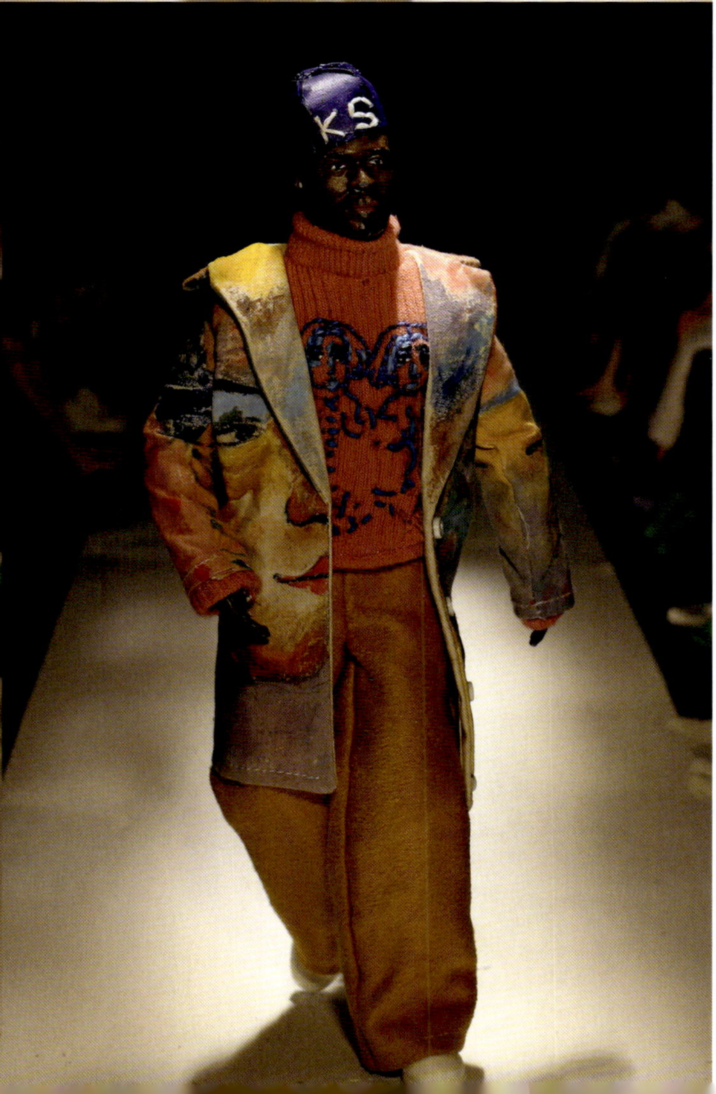

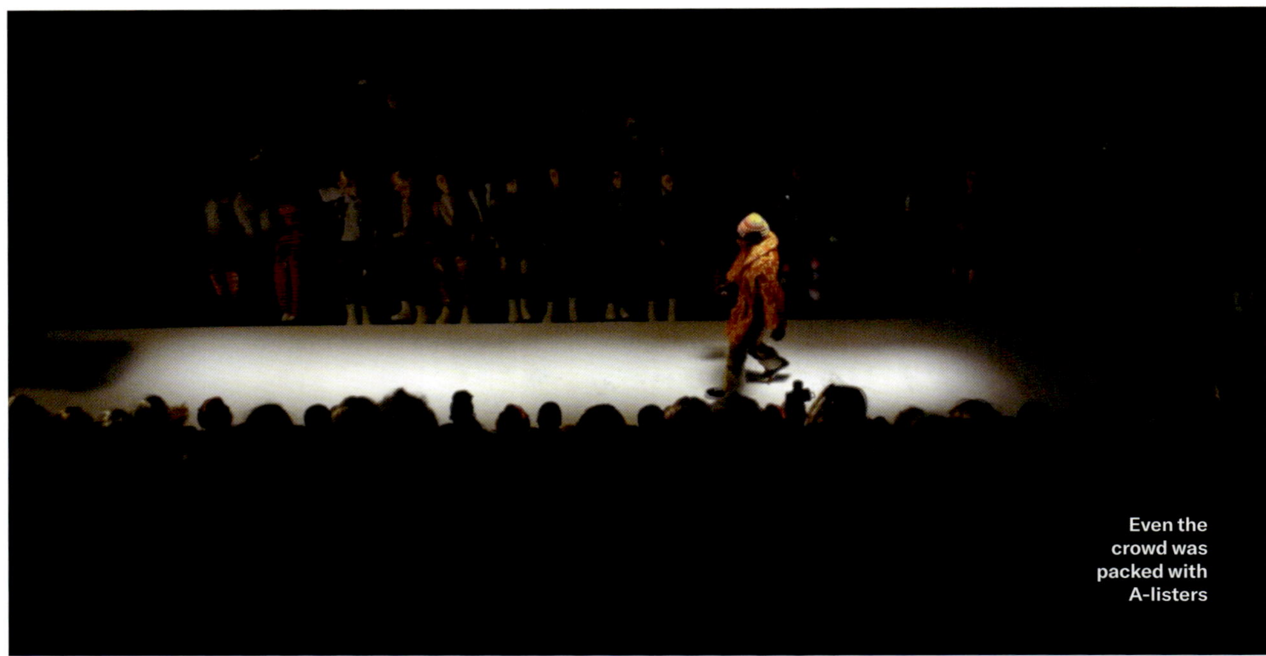

Even the crowd was packed with A-listers

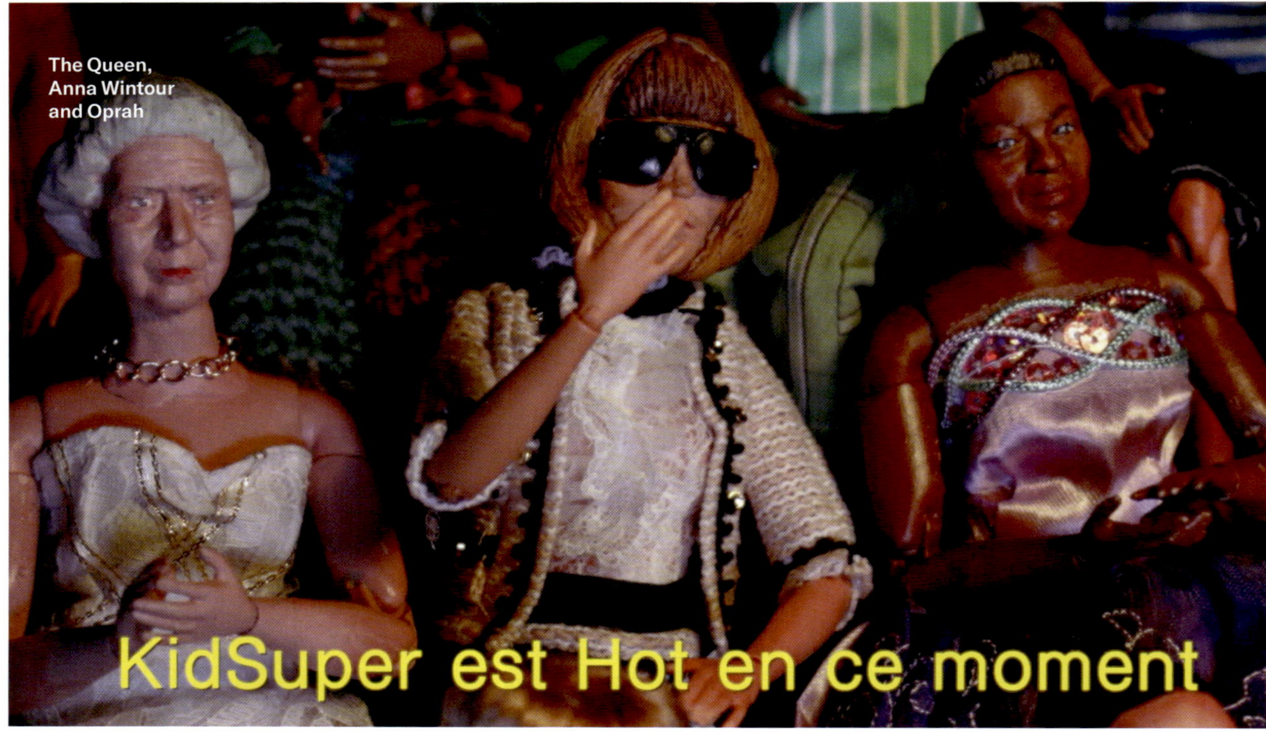

The Queen, Anna Wintour and Oprah

animated. Leading up to the last second, when it was due for Paris Fashion Week's online calendar. Even though the show was animated, I ended it in a speech—well, a doll version of me ended it in a speech: "People say the fashion world is filled with fake and plastic people... but today, we proved them wrong."

Which was funny because—well, I did use fake people. And they were plastic. But in some way, this was the most real thing I had ever done—because it was the most authentically KidSuper.

When Paris Fashion Week launched its online showcase, all the designers released their videos at the same time. And my show stood out. It became my first real hit in the fashion world.

For the first time, fashion insiders started reaching out: Mike Amiri from Amiri hit me up, Rei Kawakubo from Comme des Garçons wanted me in Dover Street Market—something I had dreamed of. The LVMH prize told me I should apply.

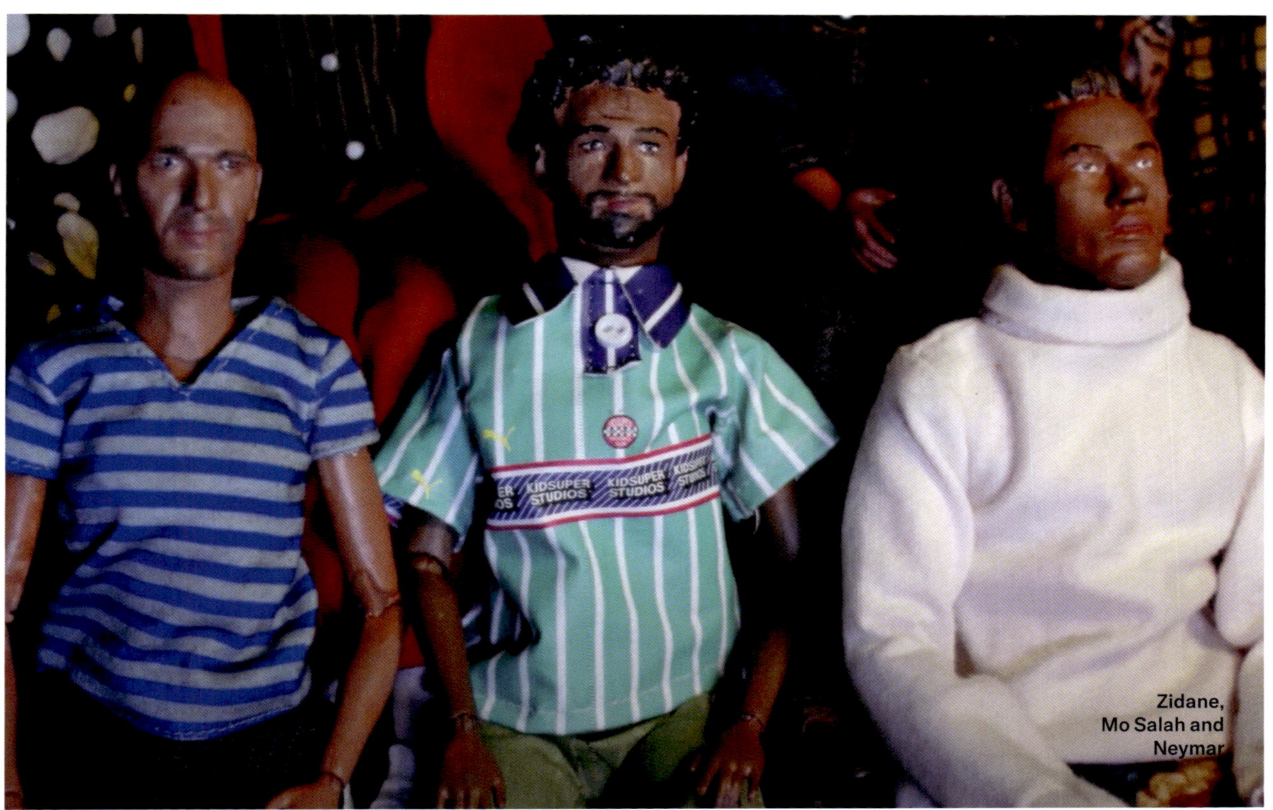

Zidane,
Mo Salah and
Neymar

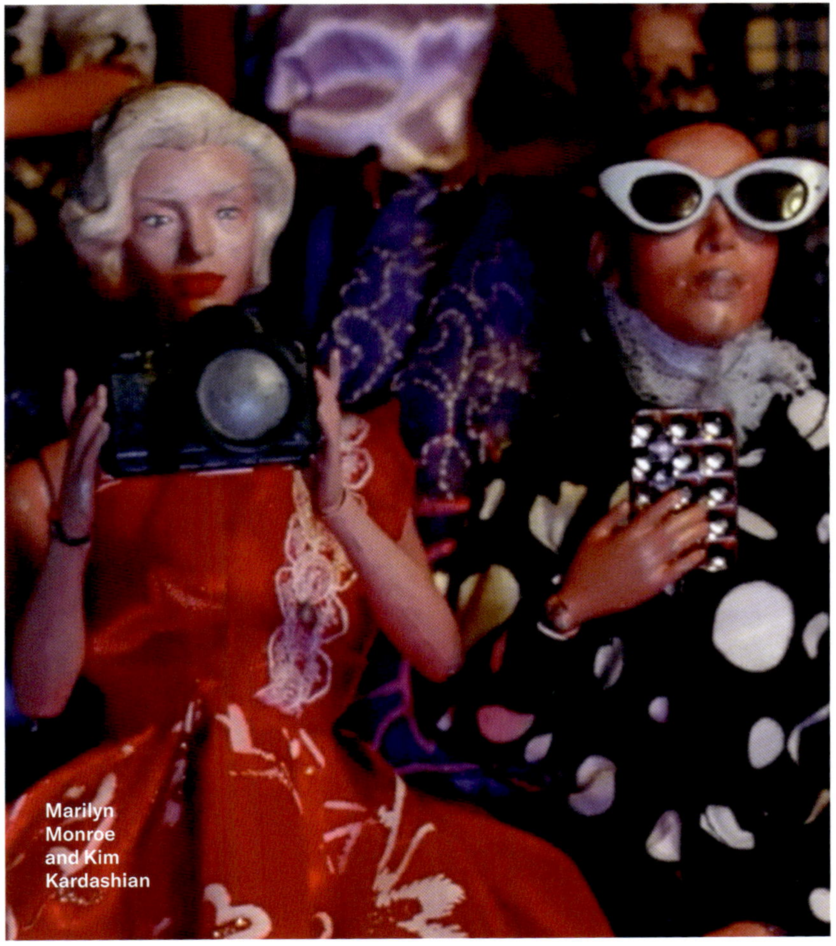

Marilyn
Monroe
and Kim
Kardashian

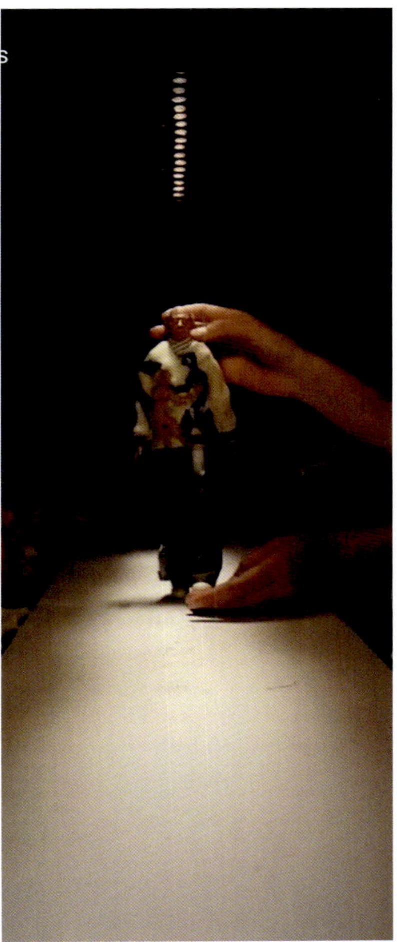

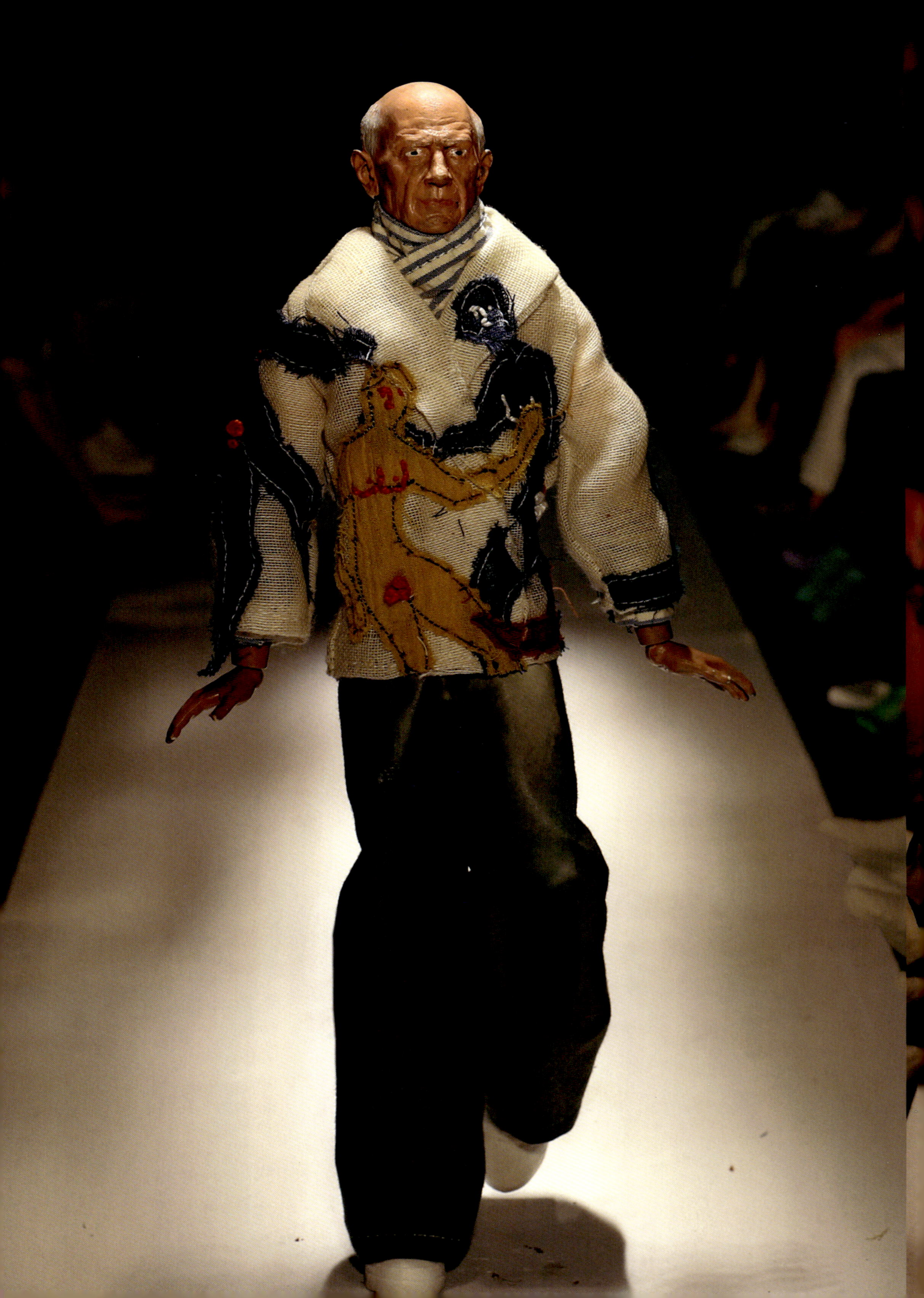

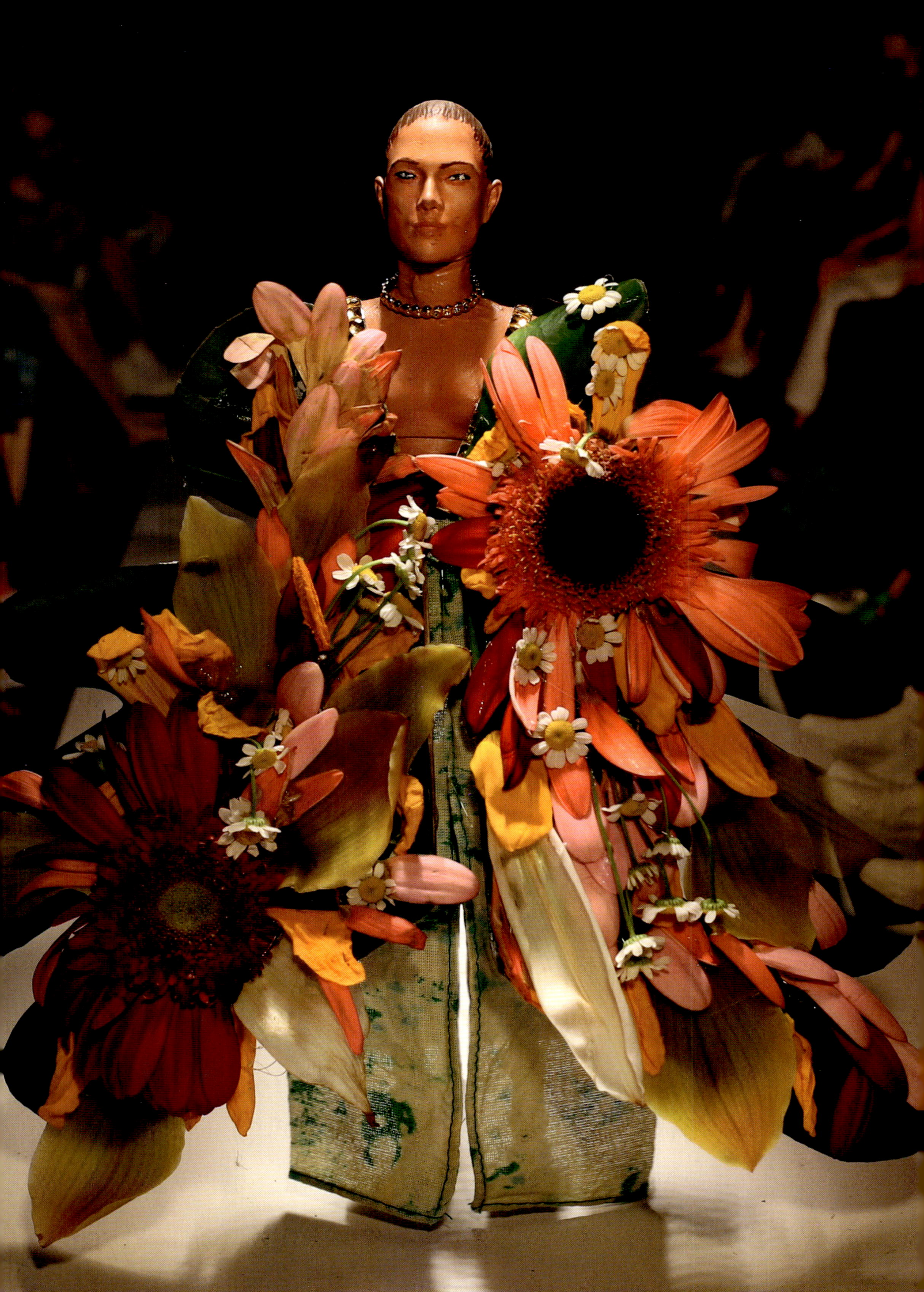

It was a turning point.

And the craziest part? I remember telling my friends, "Well, we're definitely getting kicked out of Paris Fashion Week for this. It's not even life-sized clothing. But at least we're going out our way."

But instead of getting kicked out . . . it became my biggest success up to that moment.

And that's what made it even better—the moment I was the truest to myself was the moment that worked the best.

Months later the Metropolitan Museum of Art requested a look from the show. They did not realize the look was twelve inches tall, so I had to remake it in life-size form; from a basement to the museum. It is still currently in archival storage in the museum's permanent collection.

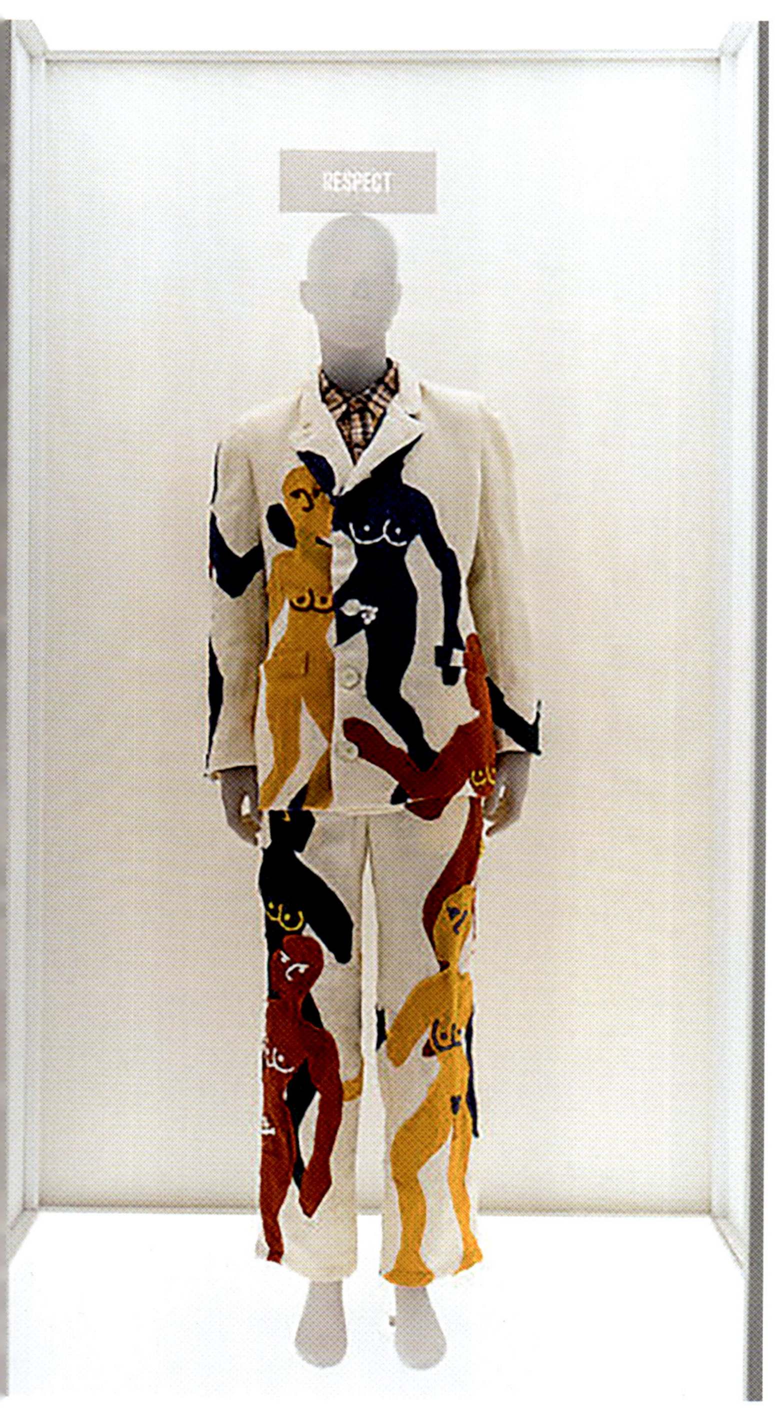

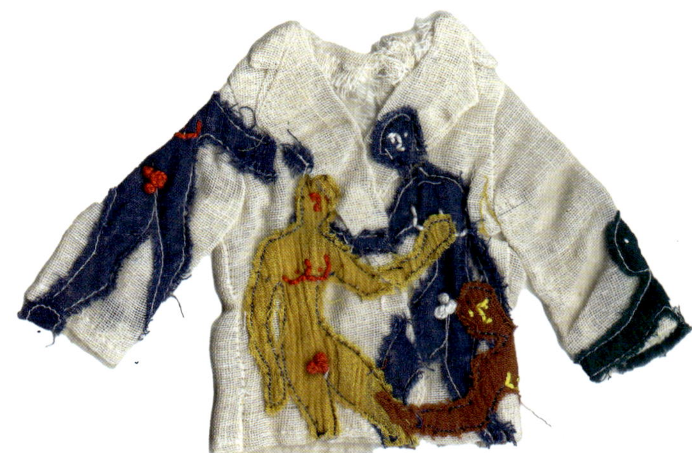

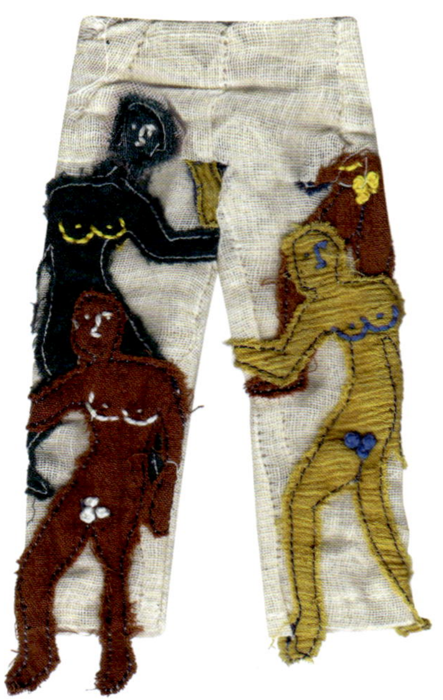

We got asked by the Metropolitan Museum of Art if they could display our look from the show. They had no idea it was only 12 inches tall. I had to remake the outfit into life size before they found out.

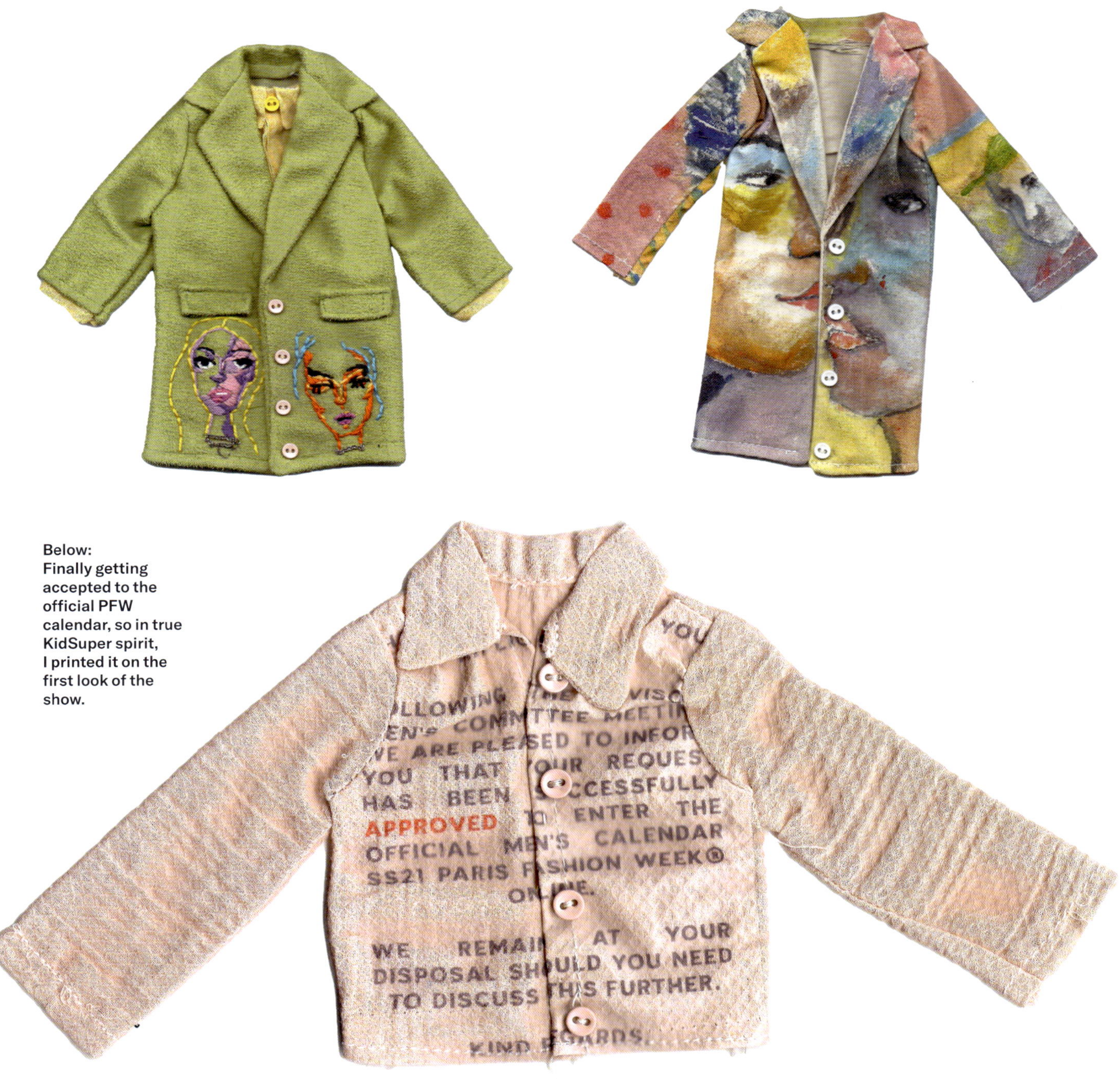

Below:
Finally getting accepted to the official PFW calendar, so in true KidSuper spirit, I printed it on the first look of the show.

Thank you for your application.

Following the Advisory Men's Committee meeting, we are pleased to inform you that your request has been successfully approved to enter the official Men's calendar SS21 Paris Fashion Week® online.

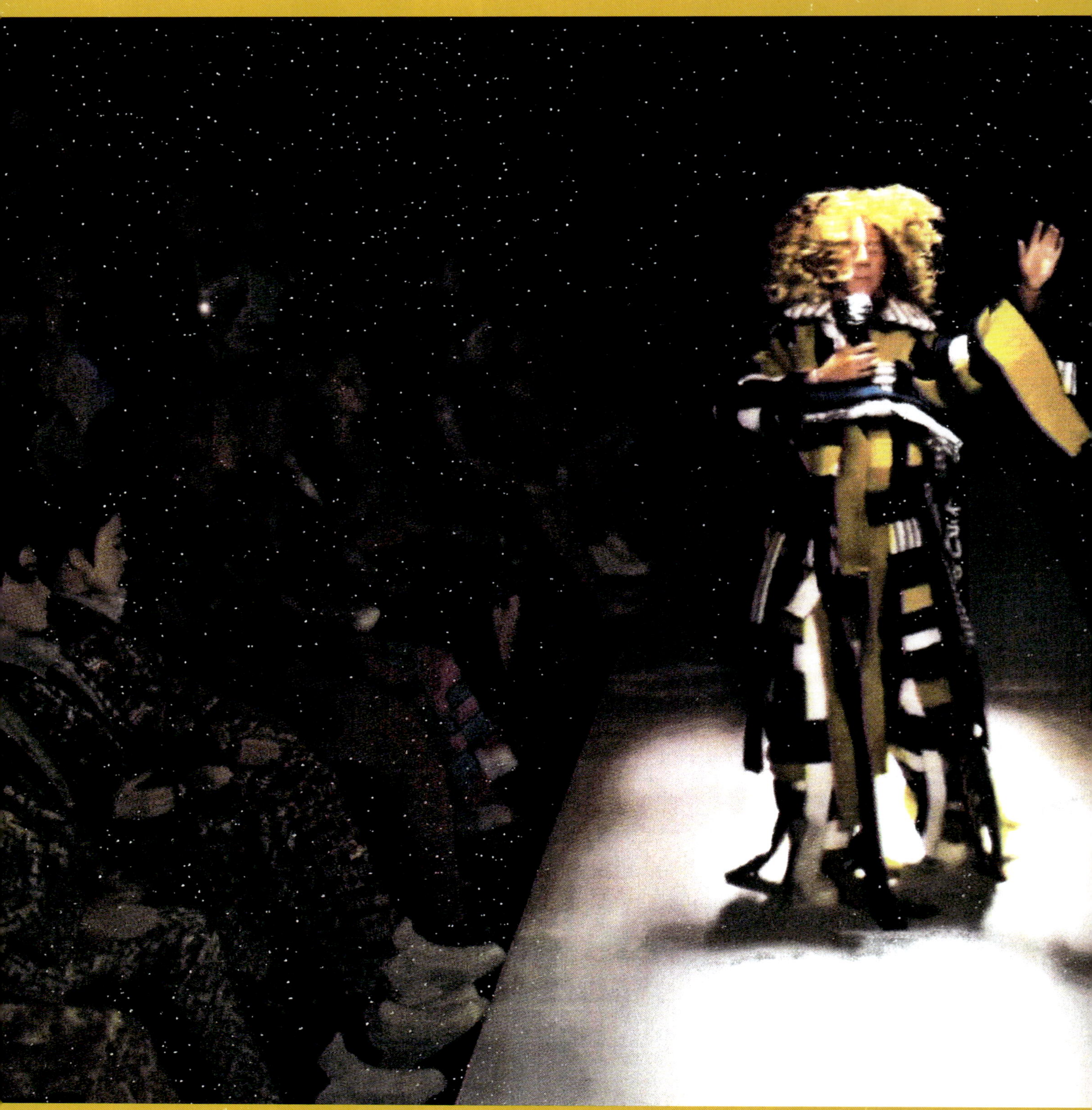

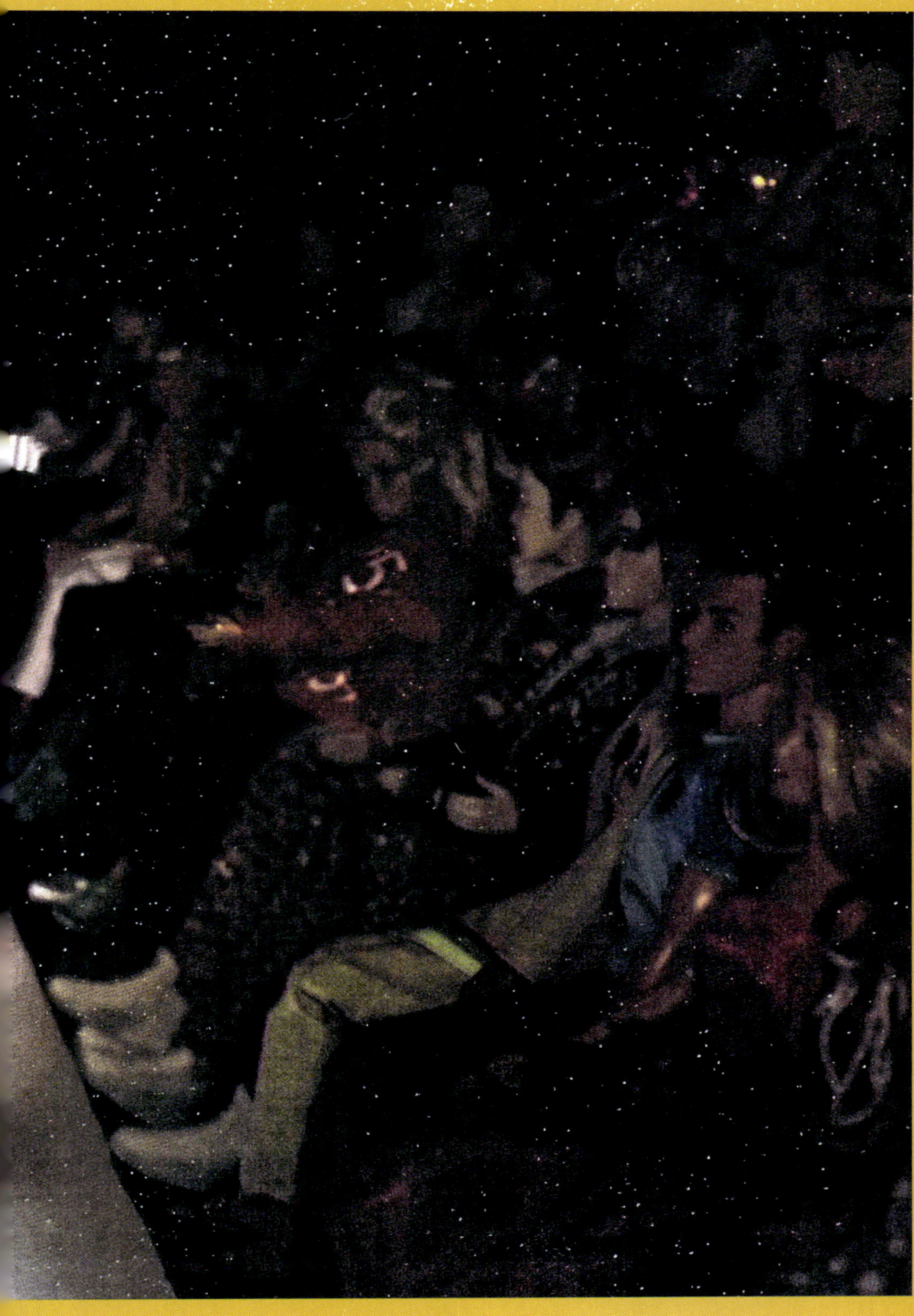

Even in doll form...
I made a speech

IF THE PLAN DOESN'T WORK YOU'RE INSANE,

AW21

I will either be insane or a genius.

IF THE PLAN WORKS YOU'RE A GENIUS

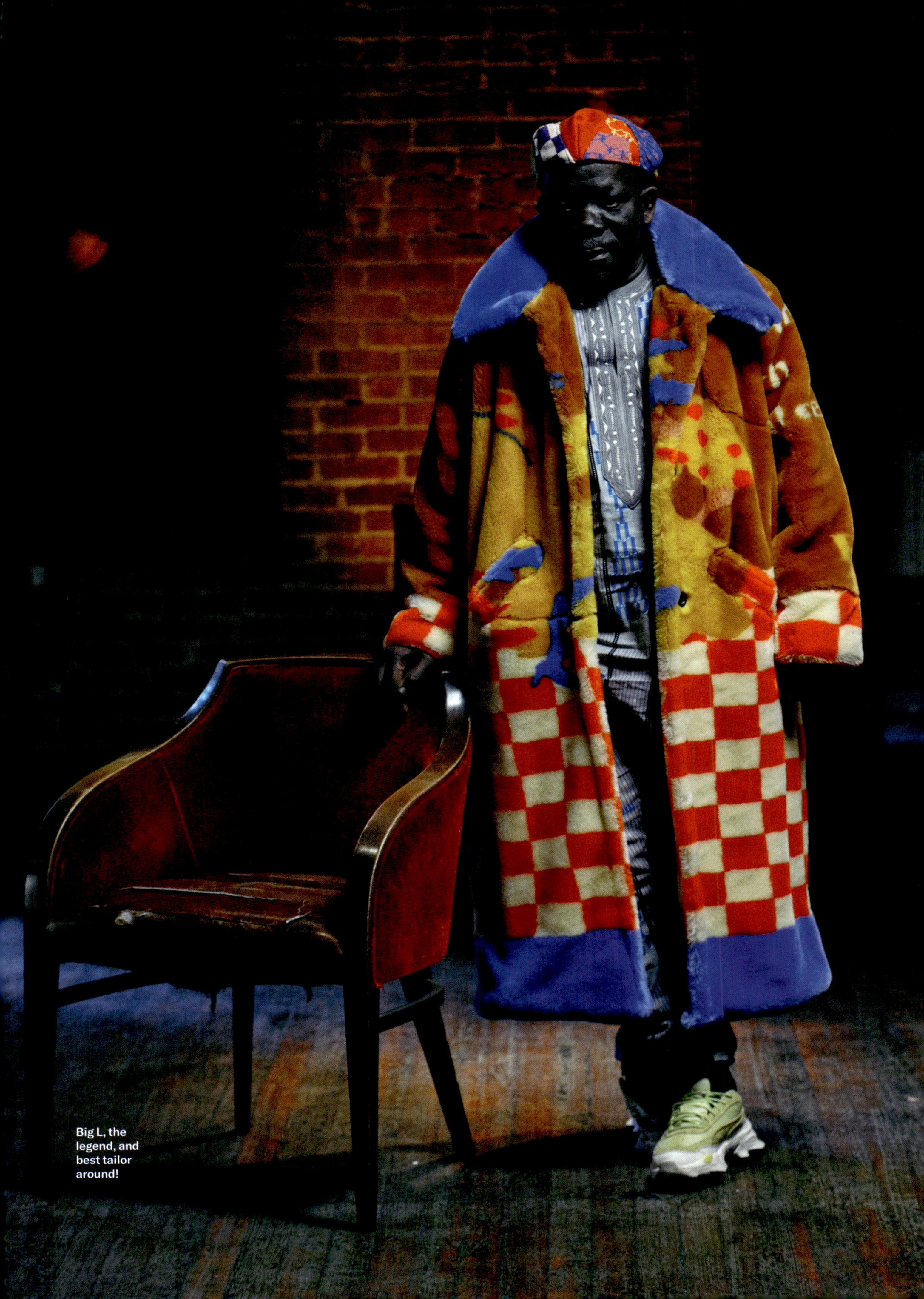

Big L, the legend, and best tailor around!

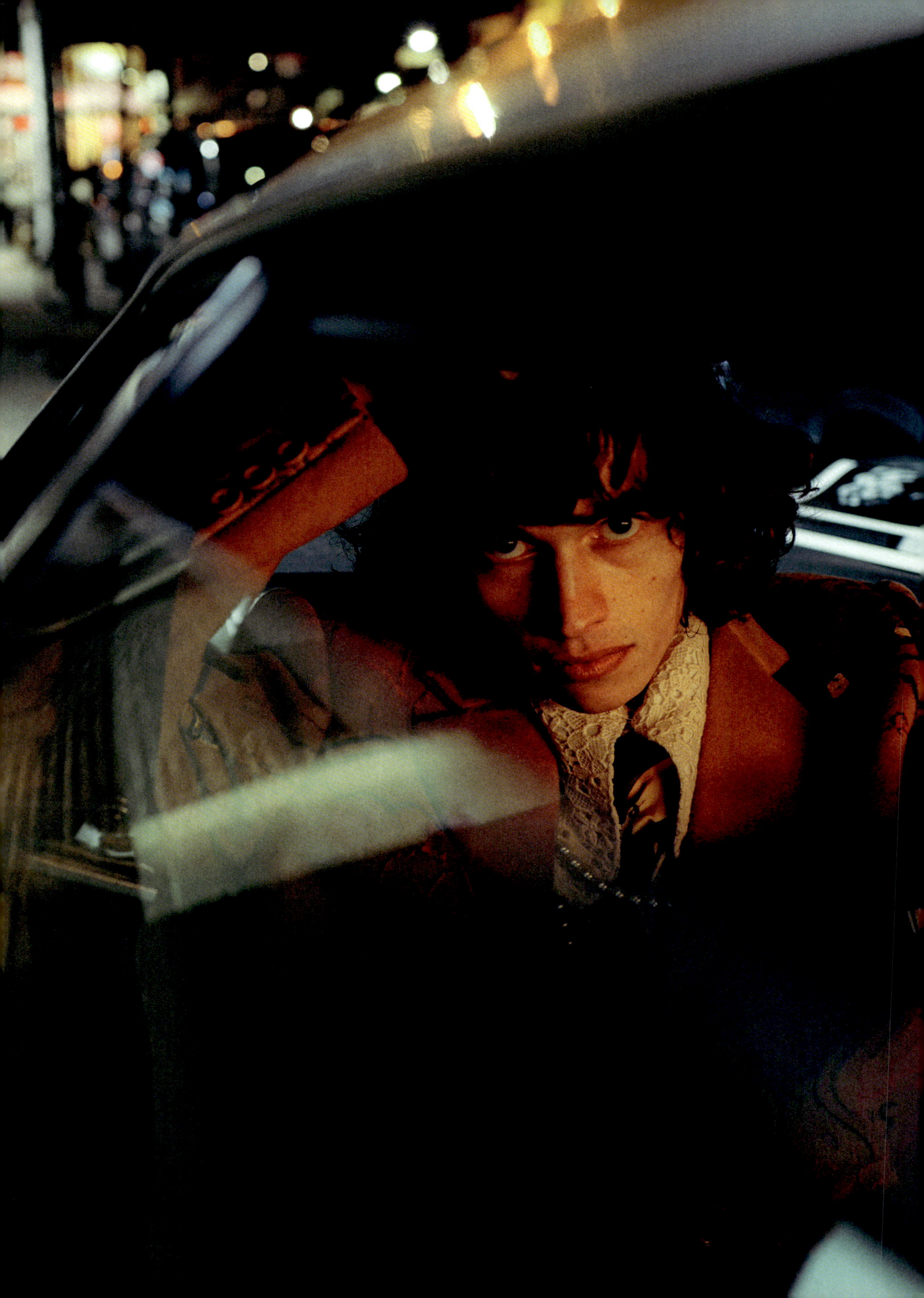

I'D ALWAYS WANTED TO write, act in, and direct short films. I'd done small skits with friends, but nothing high level. Then Paris Fashion Week went virtual, and suddenly I had a platform and a budget (KidSuper budget)—about $50K. I thought, "What if I put that into a short film? Maybe it'll feel like a real production."

So I started writing a script inspired by New York City—the characters, the places, the energy. From Chinatown to Big L, from high school friends to the corner butcher shop, I wanted to capture moments that felt uniquely New York.

And as the script came together, it naturally started inspiring the clothing too.

Up until then, most of my video work had been music videos—cool visuals but no dialogue. Any dialogue I had done was just for random skits. This was my first time tackling something more structured, with an actual narrative.

Originally, it was supposed to be one long story, but as we shot and edited, it got a little out of hand. It wasn't really working as one piece. So I decided to break it into seven short stories—each unrelated but tied together by the spirit of New York. Each story with its own theme:

Chapter 1: The Pickpocket — Socrates was misunderstood

Chapter 2: The Butcher and The Three Daughters — There's only two things that drive someone to change: self preservation and self promotion

Chapter 3: Bodega Politics — I have never said a nice thing to my best friends

Chapter 4: Chinatown Showdown — If the plan doesn't work you're insane, if the plan works you're a genius.

Chapter 5: Tunnel Twins — I never got good advice from anyone who didn't take risks

Chapter 6: Big L's Speech — I didn't learn English, I learn how to get money

Chapter 7: Gran Theft Autonomy — Happiness lies in the pursuit of happiness

This was my first real cinematic project, and I wanted it to look the part. I told the DP, "I want it to feel like a Wes Anderson film. Let's use the same lenses he uses."

And honestly? It was an amazing experience—but everything that could go wrong . . . did.

- We had a hijack scene planned with my friend's car. The car broke down, so we had to move the entire shoot to where the car was stranded.

- During Big L's scene, he fainted from the heat of the lights. For a second, we thought he'd died. (He was fine, just panicked. Terrifying in the moment, though.)

- An intern driving the rental truck left the door open. A car drove straight into it.

It was absolute chaos and we went way over schedule. I gathered the crew, saying, "Put your hands in if you're down to finish this. Off the clock. No extra pay." Everyone did. That moment of collective passion was unforgettable.

And when I saw the final cut? I knew.

In the end, it turned out beautiful. The characters, the colors, the dialogue—I was proud. It was my first real taste of filmmaking, and it felt like proof that I could do more. The title said it all: "If the plan doesn't work, you're insane. If the plan works, you're a genius."

That's what this whole project was about.

No one was making short films for fashion shows. I was risking my own money on an idea that didn't even make business sense. But I wanted to do it anyway.

And in the end, it worked.

Next step? A full movie. Hopefully soon.

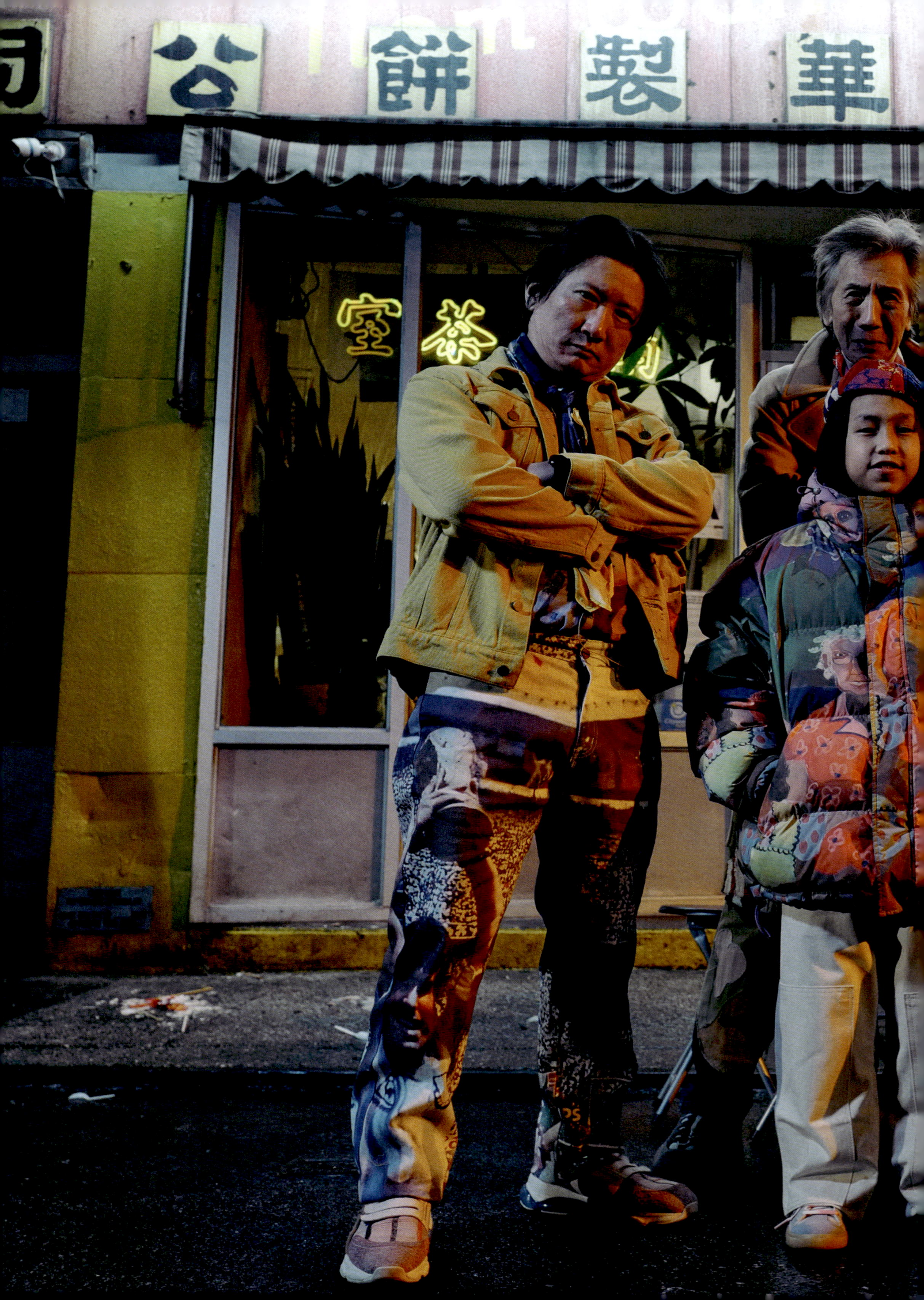
華製餅公
茶室

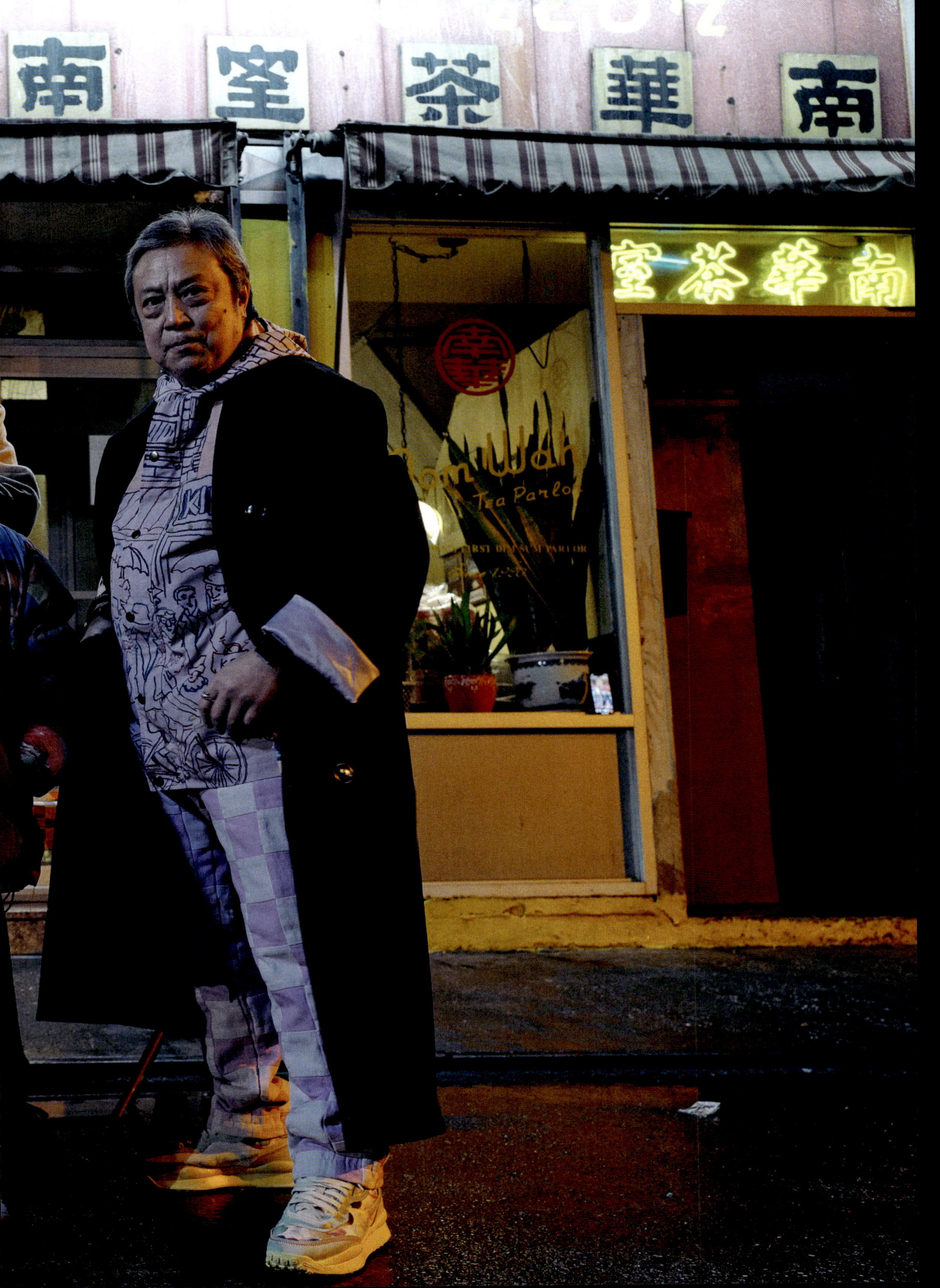
南華茶室
Tea Parlo

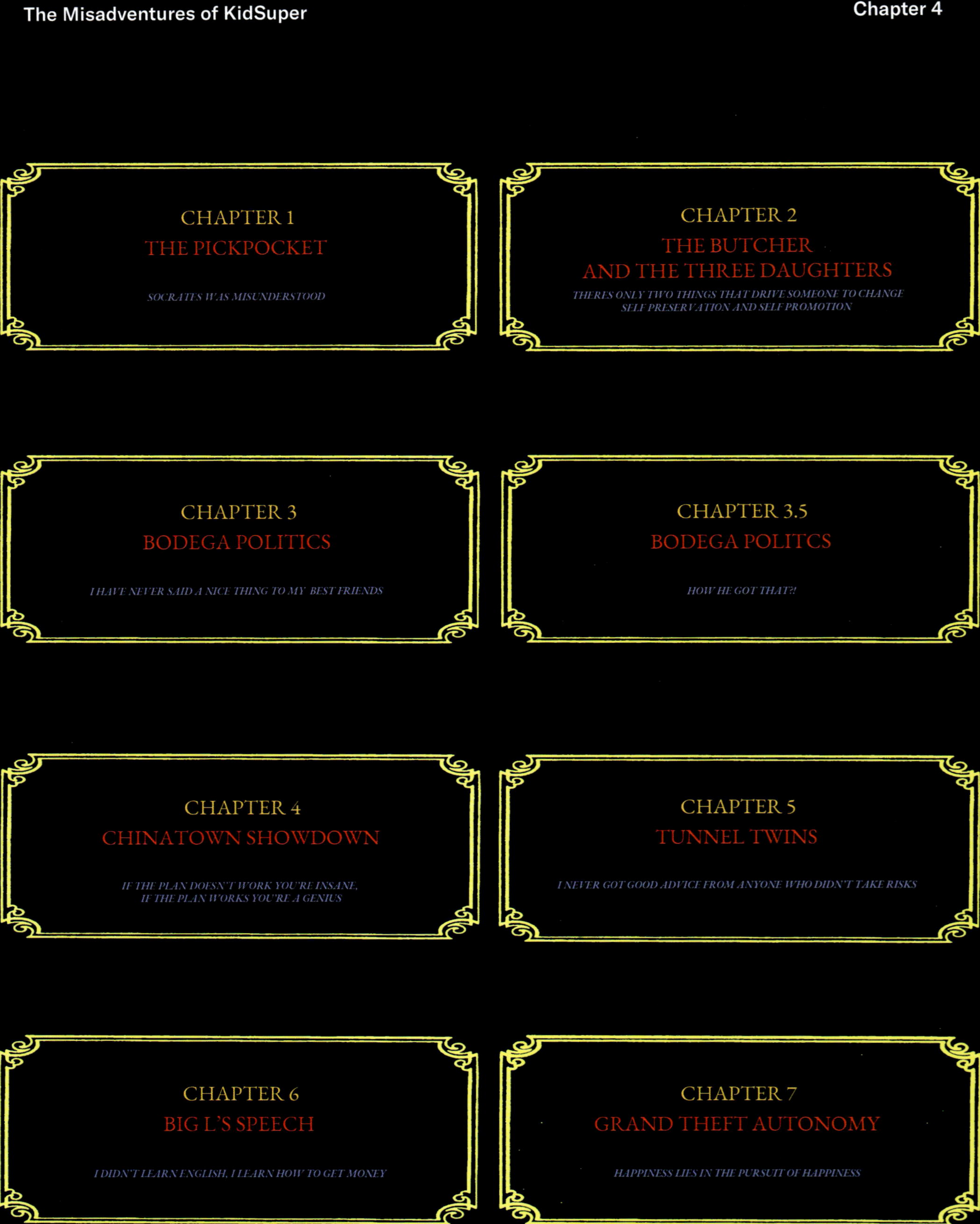
CHAPTER 1
THE PICKPOCKET
SOCRATES WAS MISUNDERSTOOD
CHAPTER 2
THE BUTCHER
AND THE THREE DAUGHTERS
THERES ONLY TWO THINGS THAT DRIVE SOMEONE TO CHANGE
SELF PRESERVATION AND SELF PROMOTION
CHAPTER 3
BODEGA POLITICS
I HAVE NEVER SAID A NICE THING TO MY BEST FRIENDS
CHAPTER 3.5
BODEGA POLITCS
HOW HE GOT THAT?!
CHAPTER 4
CHINATOWN SHOWDOWN
IF THE PLAN DOESN'T WORK YOU'RE INSANE,
IF THE PLAN WORKS YOU'RE A GENIUS
CHAPTER 5
TUNNEL TWINS
I NEVER GOT GOOD ADVICE FROM ANYONE WHO DIDN'T TAKE RISKS
CHAPTER 6
BIG L'S SPEECH
I DIDN'T LEARN ENGLISH, I LEARN HOW TO GET MONEY
CHAPTER 7
GRAND THEFT AUTONOMY
HAPPINESS LIES IN THE PURSUIT OF HAPPINESS

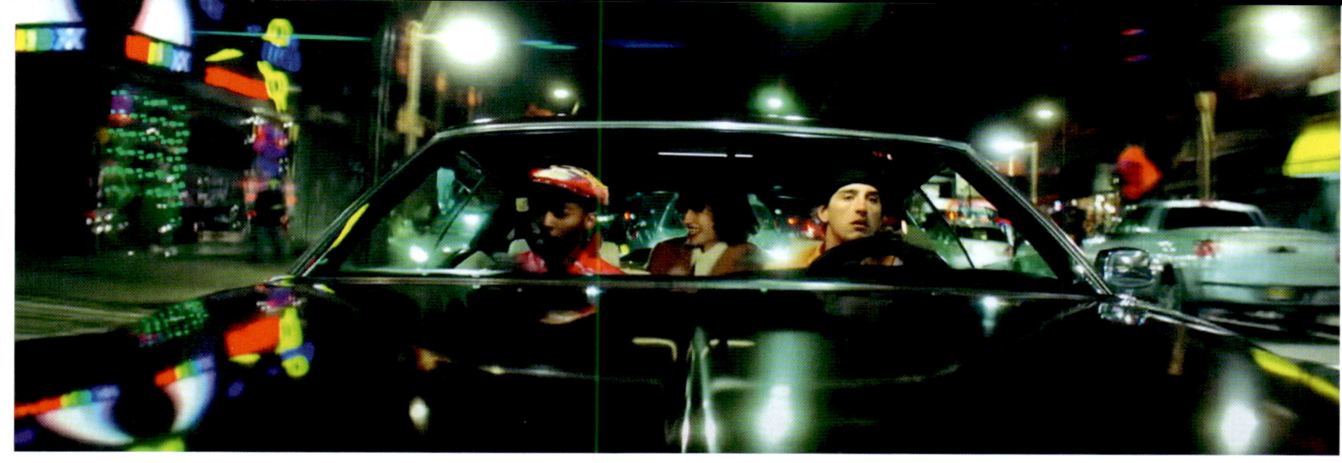

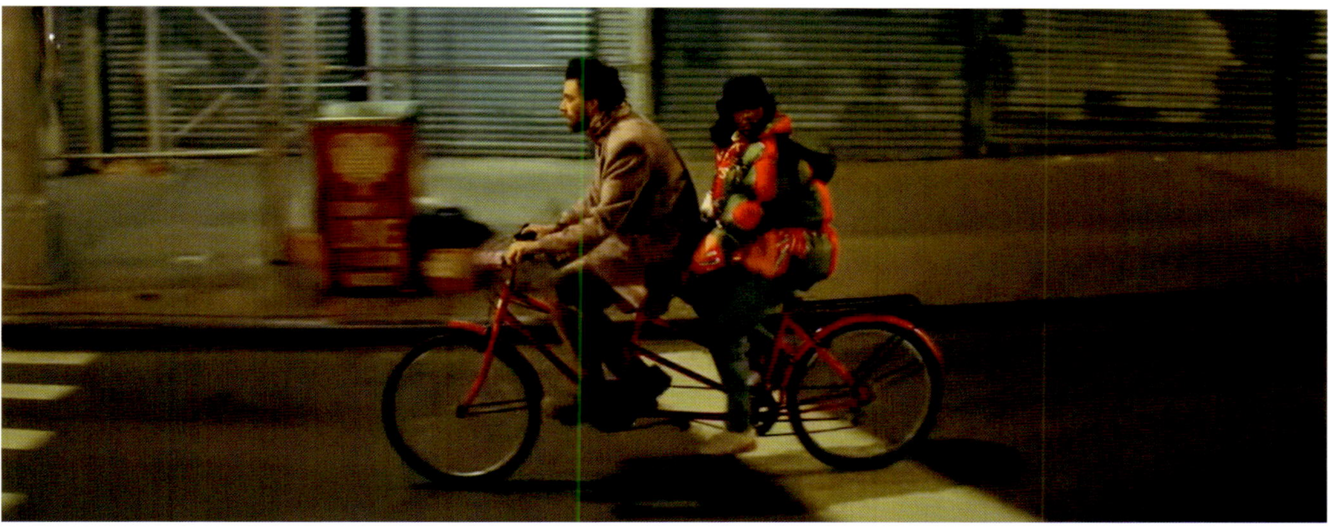

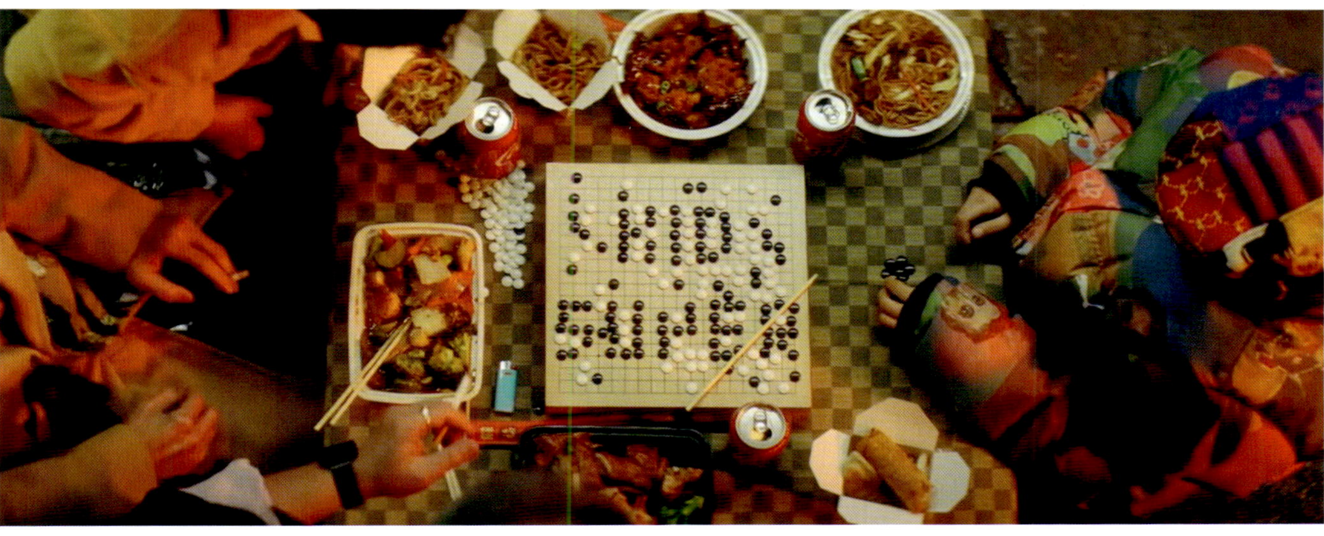

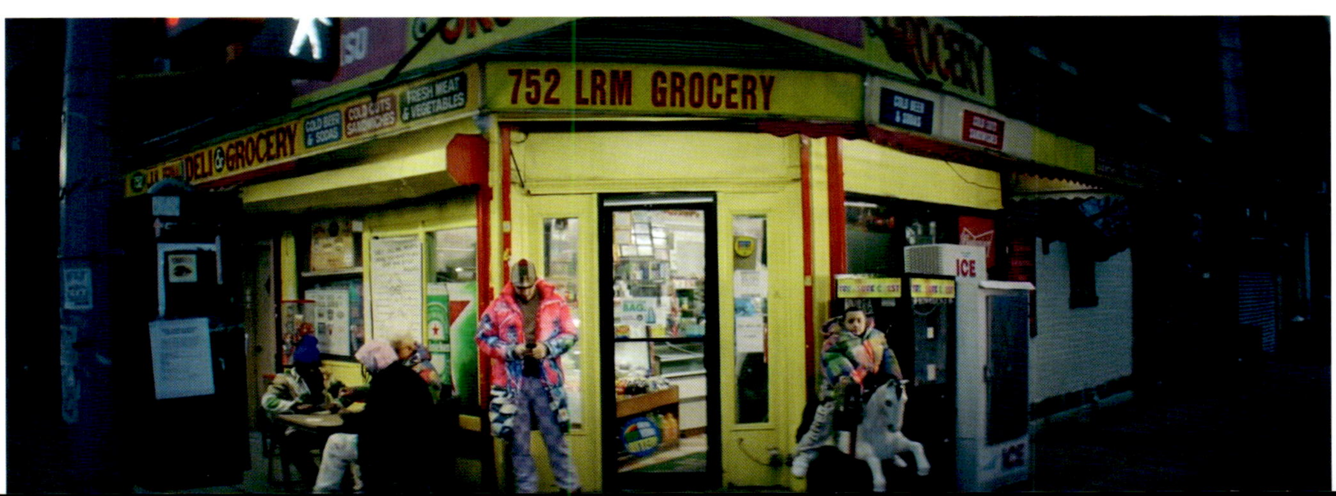
752 LRM GROCERY
DELI GROCERY
COLD BEER & SODAS
COLD CUTS SANDWICHES
FRESH MEAT & VEGETABLES
ICE

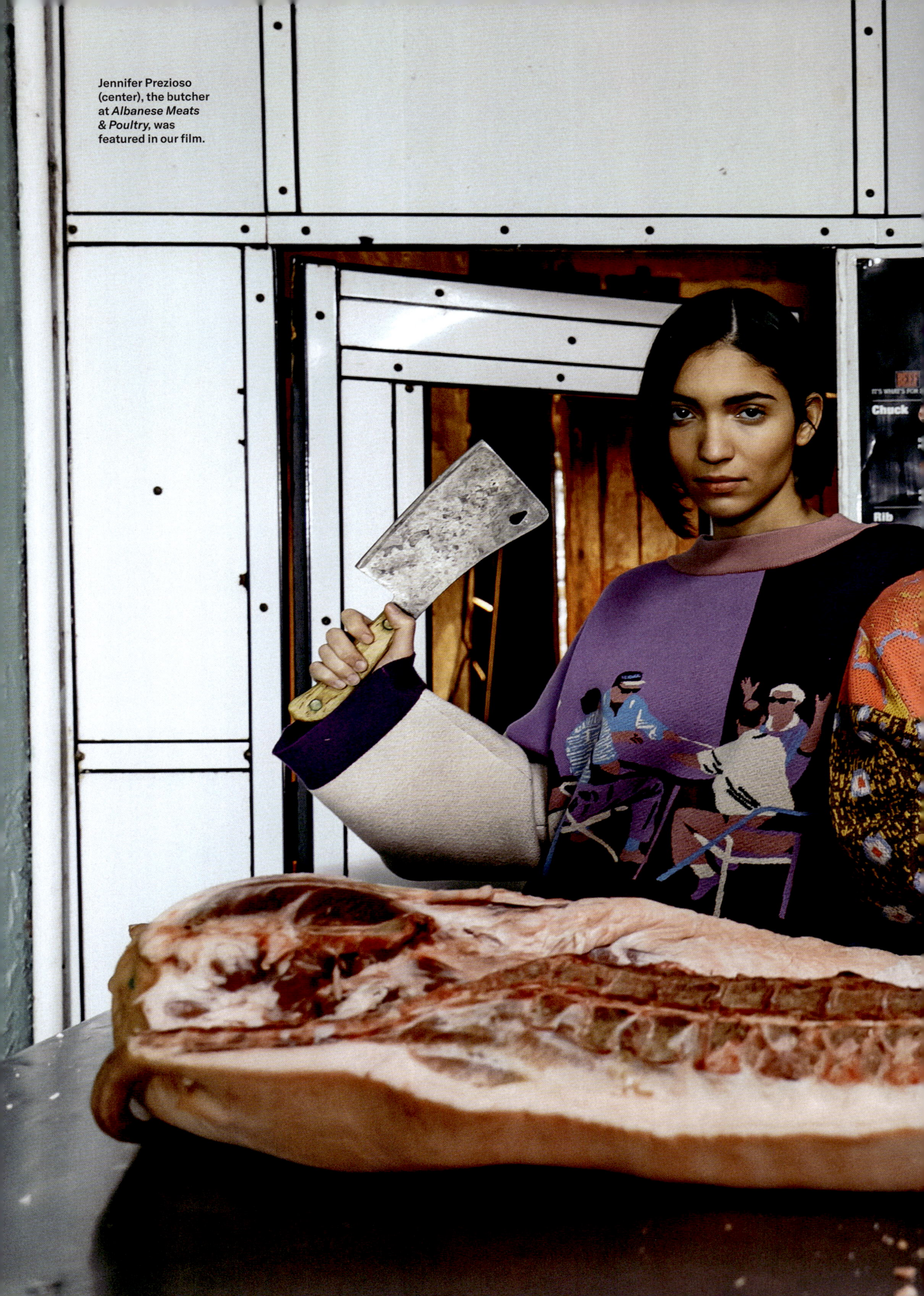

Jennifer Prezioso (center), the butcher at *Albanese Meats & Poultry*, was featured in our film.

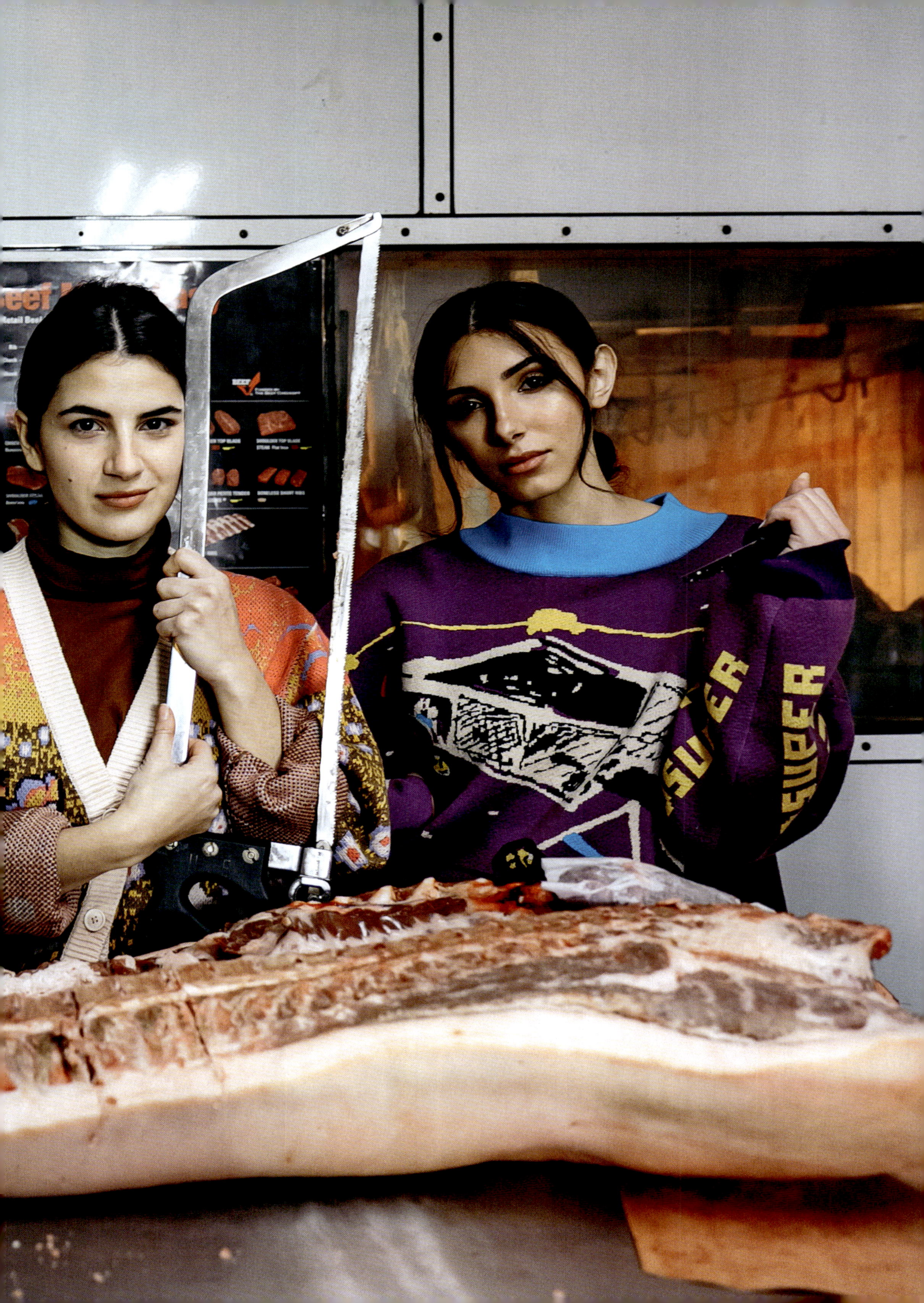
SUPER
SUPER

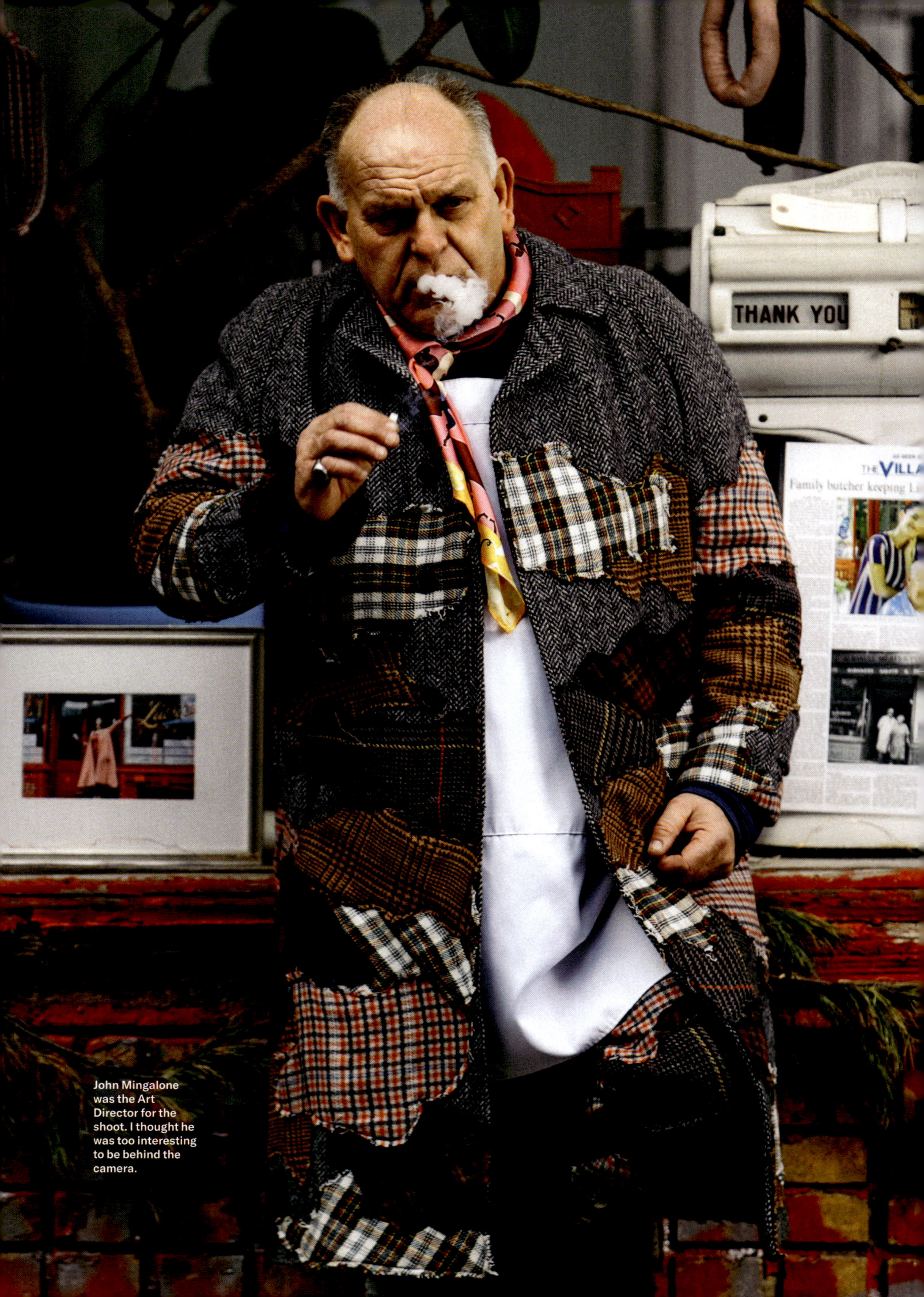

John Mingalone was the Art Director for the shoot. I thought he was too interesting to be behind the camera.

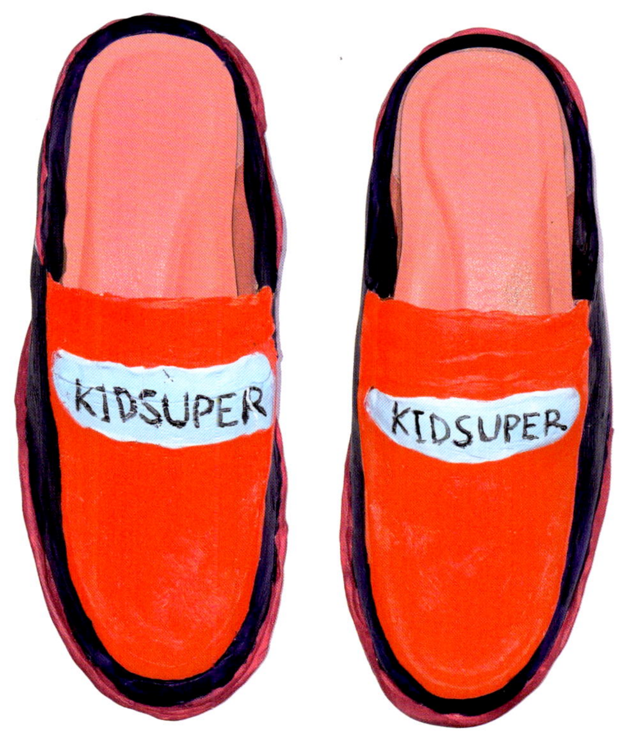
KIDSUPER
KIDSUPER

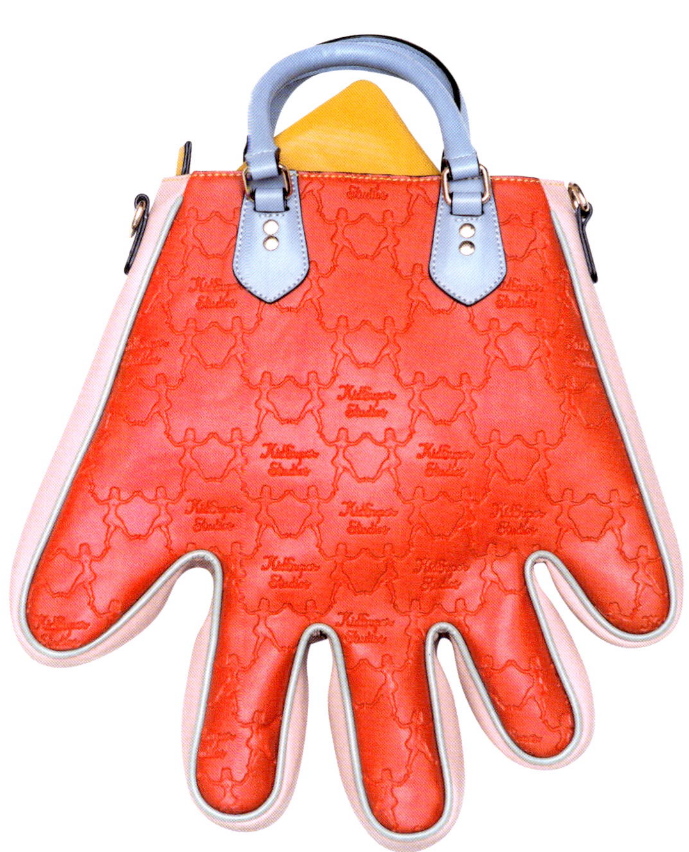

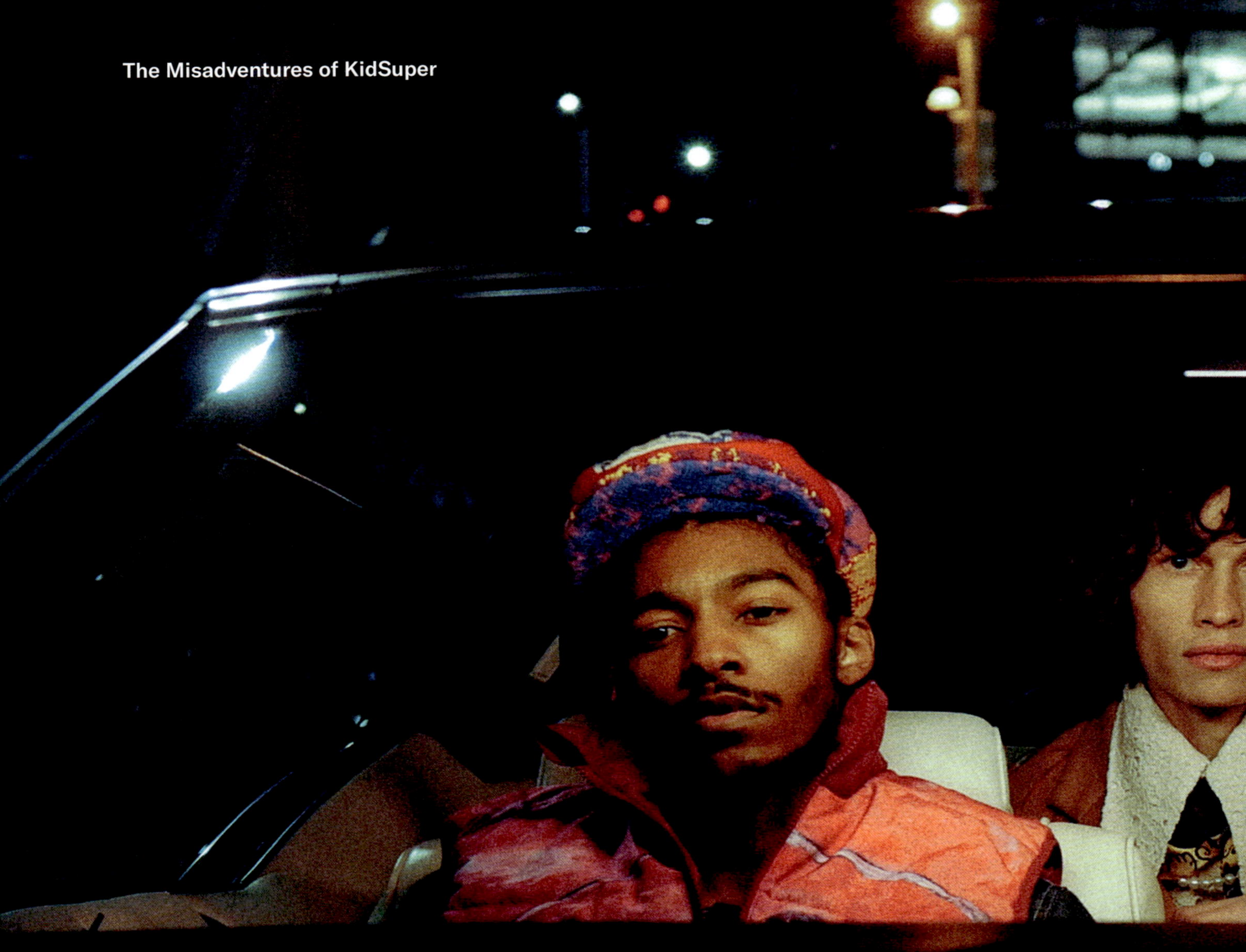

CAR SCENE

cut to the outside of car, at and angle, three misfits trying to jack in the window of the car with a coat hanger, they are going back and forth.

VOICEOVER
John Locke said "No man's knowledge here can go beyond his experience" which i couldn't agree more, but he never stole a car in broad daylight on broadway and myrtle, so what does he know. My favorite philosophers were people of conviction

close up on thief leaning over the car, we see the shoulders of the other two actors.

THEIF 1
Aristotle says that happiness is the ultimate good, but is this a personal happiness or a collective happiness? And Is this moral pursuit for a collective happiness detrimental to ones personal growth?

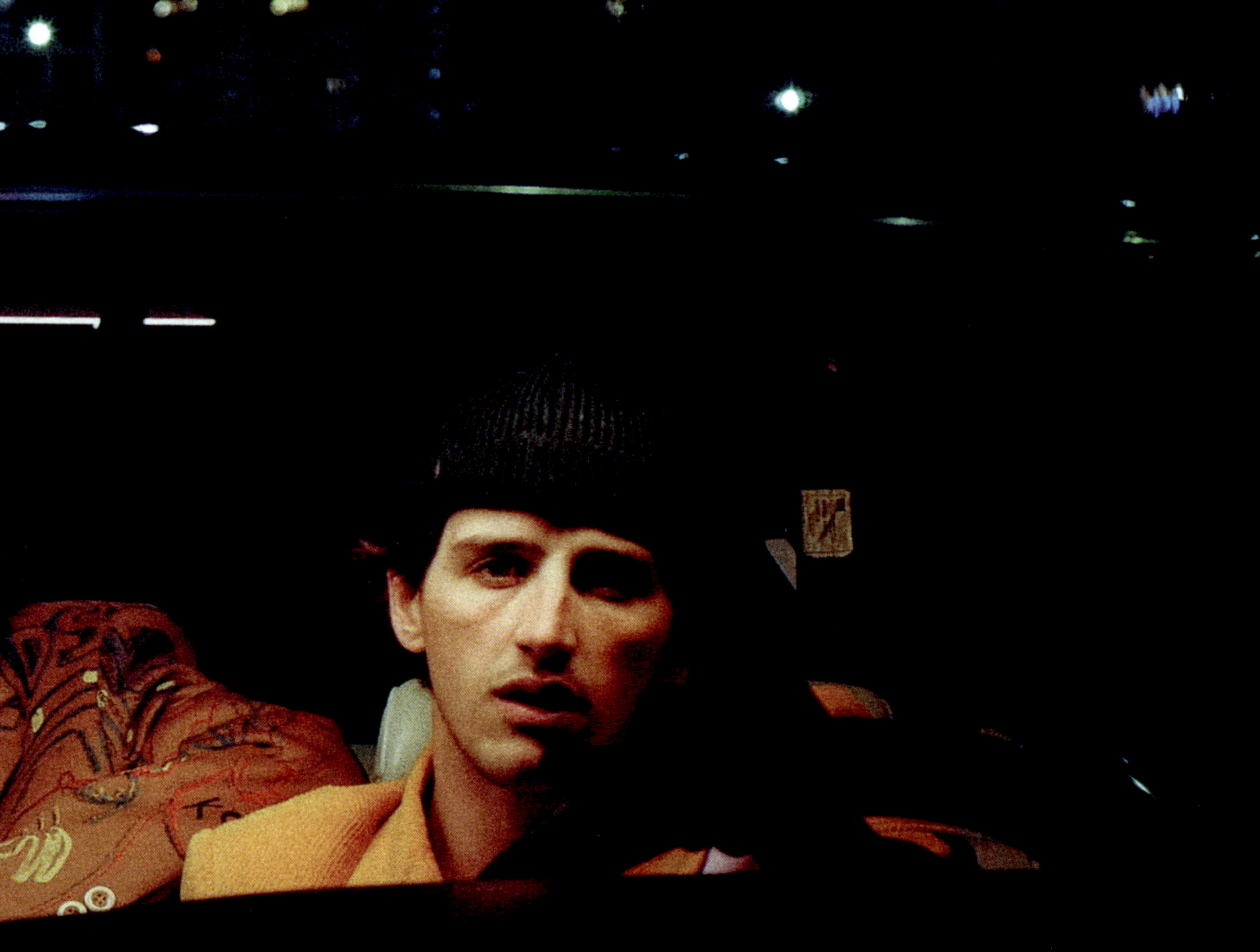

cut to thief 3 who is hanging out next thief 2. Thief 2 is in front of the passengers seat trying to jimmy the window.

THEIF 3
it depends what you deem important, is there a moral strength in choosing the collective over the self?

cut to thief 2 crow bar in hand trying to jimmy the window.

THEIF 2
(the one with the metal stealing)

Our pursuit of morality is based on a belief in god, you take away that belief and you are left with a little more options

door clicks open, both get in the car,

THEIF 3
or toooo many options leaving everything a little pointless

close ups on getting in the car, lock opening, doors opening

I acted in the
short film, so
I didn't deliver
a speech at
the end.

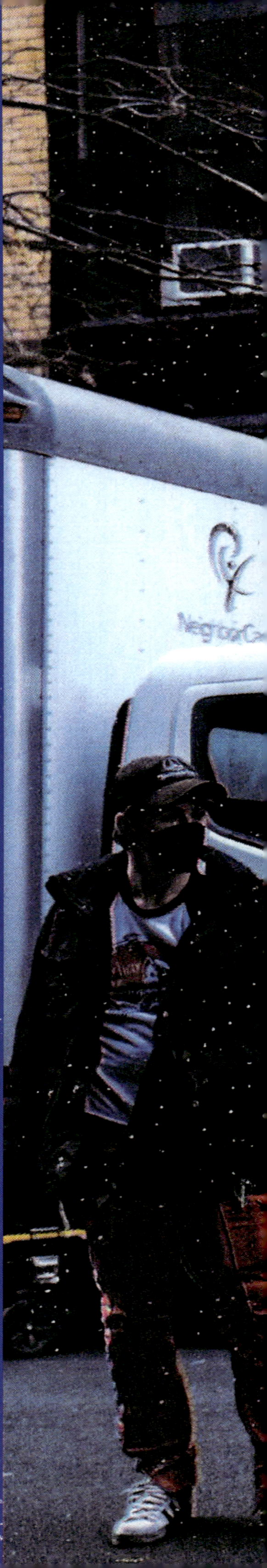

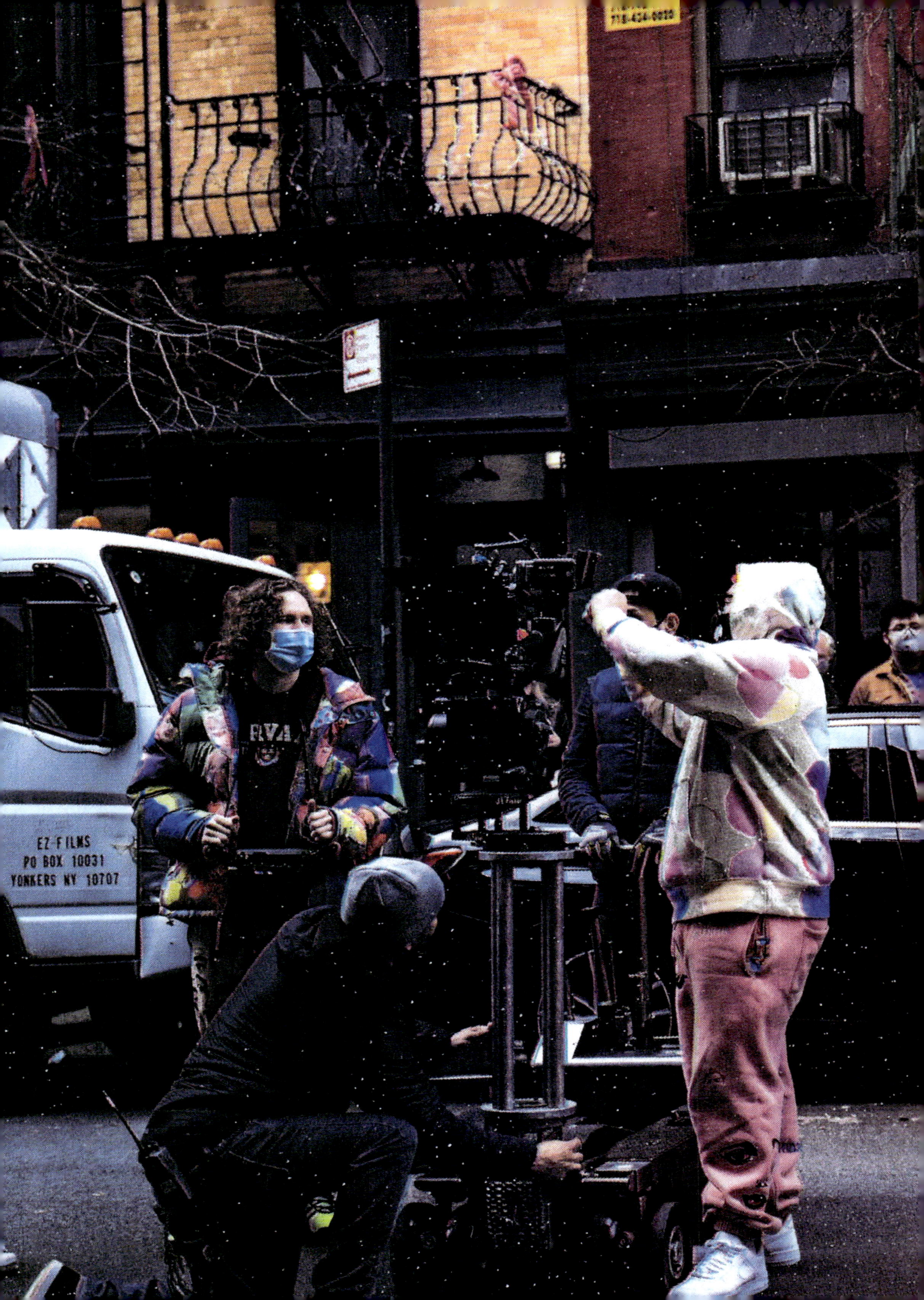
EZ FILMS
PO BOX 10031
YONKERS NY 10707

SS22

WHAT DO YOU WANT TO DO

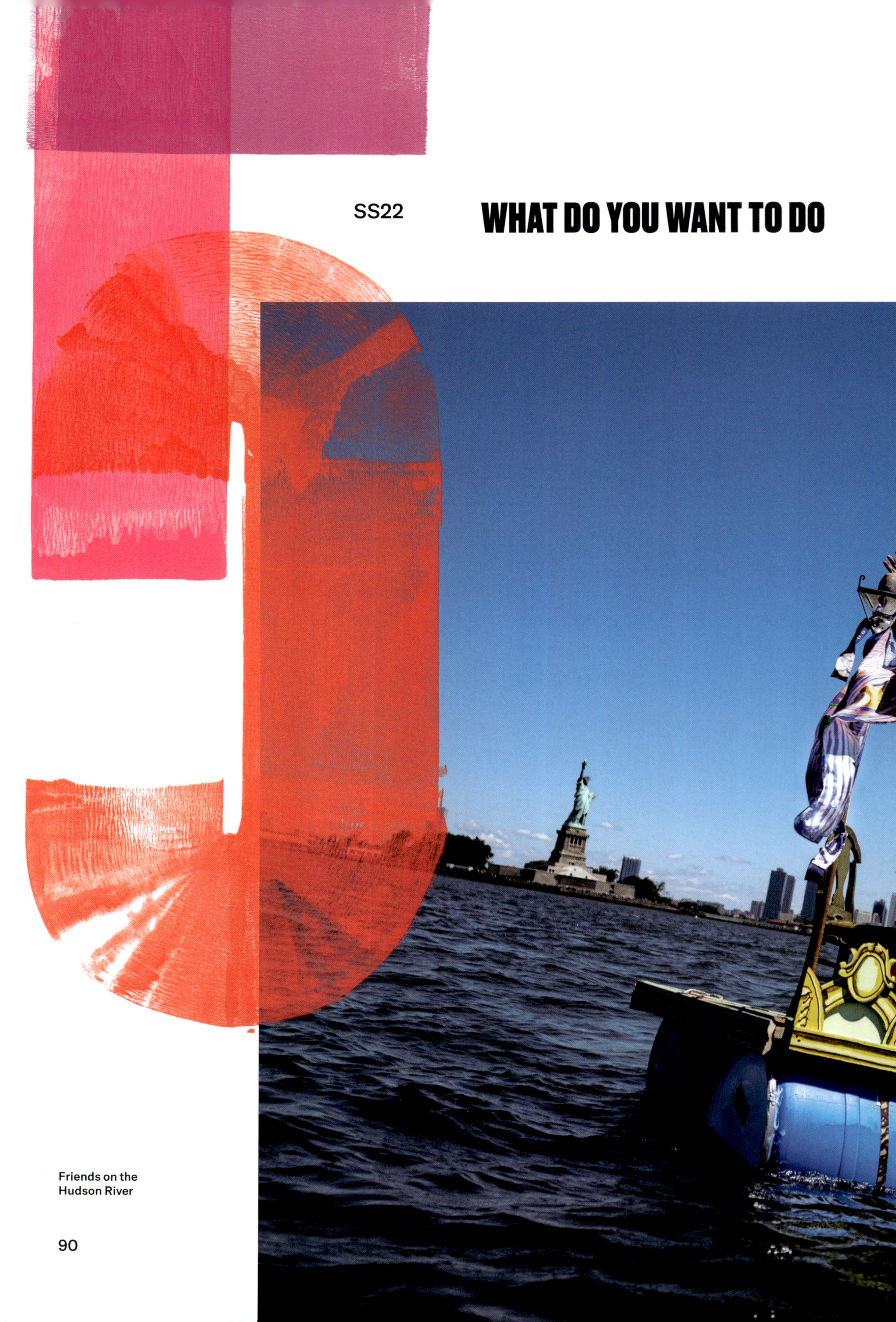

Friends on the Hudson River

BEFORE YOU DIE?

Keep asking yourself that question.

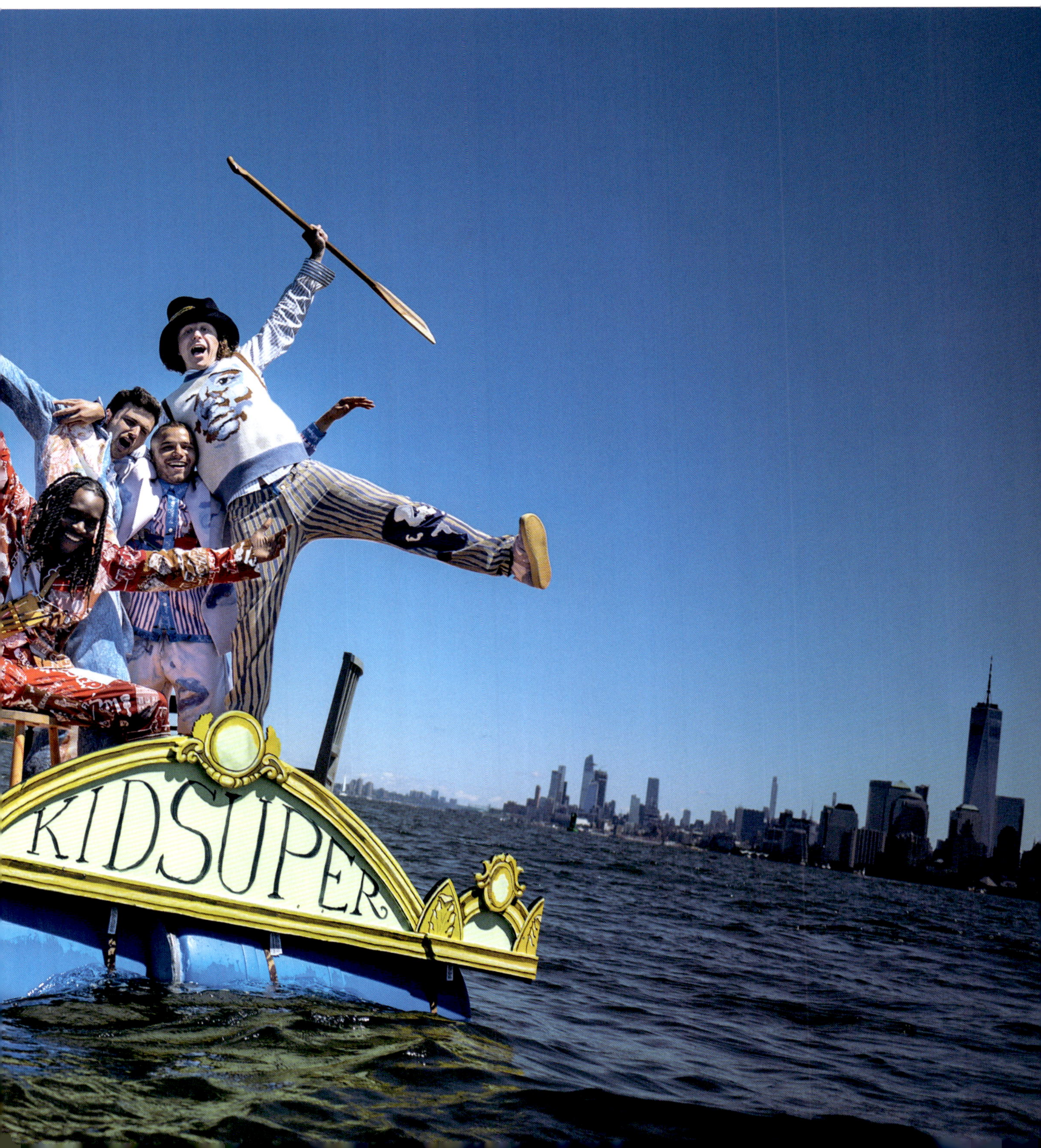

VIRTUAL FASHION WEEK was rolling, and I'd already pulled off two out-of-the-box concepts—a stop-motion runway show and a short film. Both were getting attention in the fashion world. For the first time, people were championing my wild ideas.

So why not keep thinking outside the box: COVID won't last forever. This virtual format won't last forever. We can literally do anything and call it a fashion show.

So I asked my friends: "If you could do anything before you die, what would it be? Let's make that the fashion show."

I said we could "climb Mount Everest wearing KidSuper puffer jackets and call it a fashion show." I actually looked it up. Six months of training, $200K each. Unfortunately out of budget. So I kept asking people, "What do you want to do before you die?" I found myself more interested in the answers people gave than in the dreams themselves—like little windows into who they were.

That's when the idea hit.

1. Set up a booth in Washington Square Park.
2. Ask passersby what they want to do before they die.
3. If the dream was possible, try to make it happen—while wearing some of the collection and call it a Fashion Show.

SIMPLE ENOUGH IN THEORY. In practice? Total chaos. We were completely at the whim of New York.

The thing about New York is that everyone who lives here—or moves here—is already chasing something. A dream, an escape, an experience. If you're not open to spontaneity,

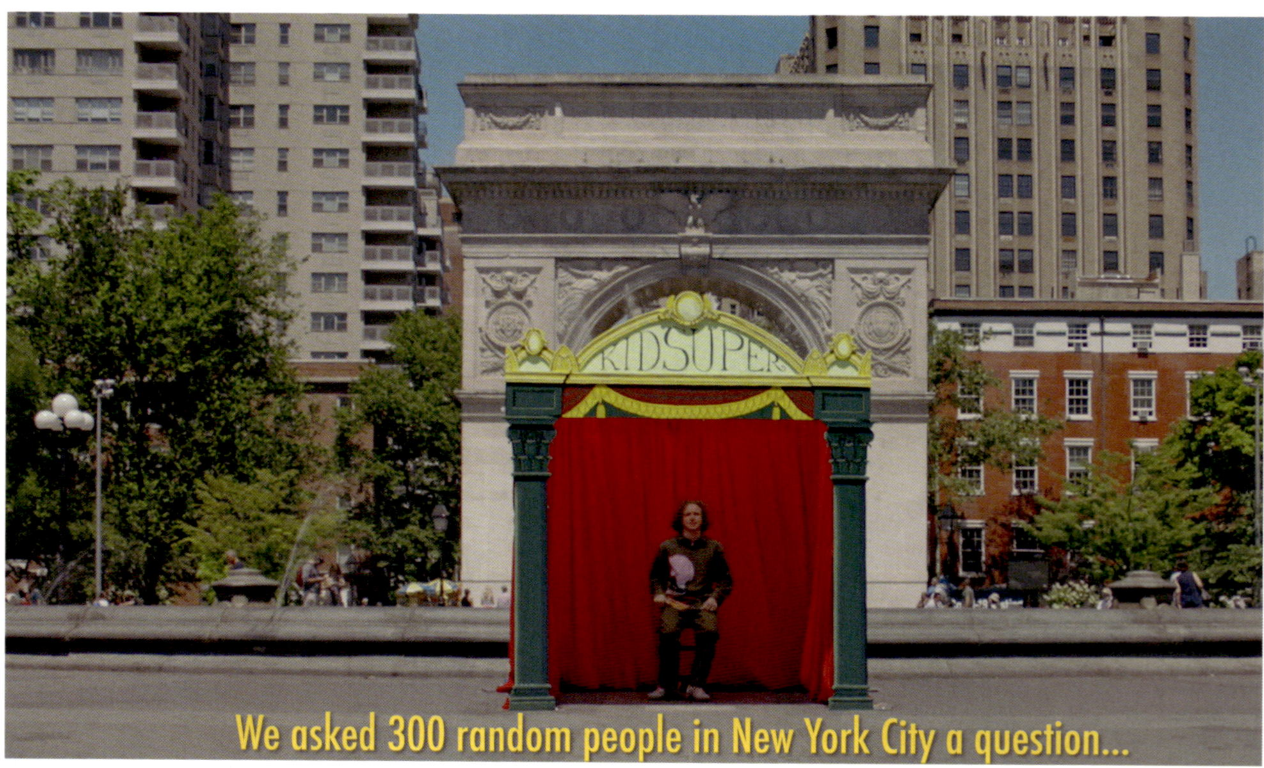

This was the setup in the middle of Washington Square Park.

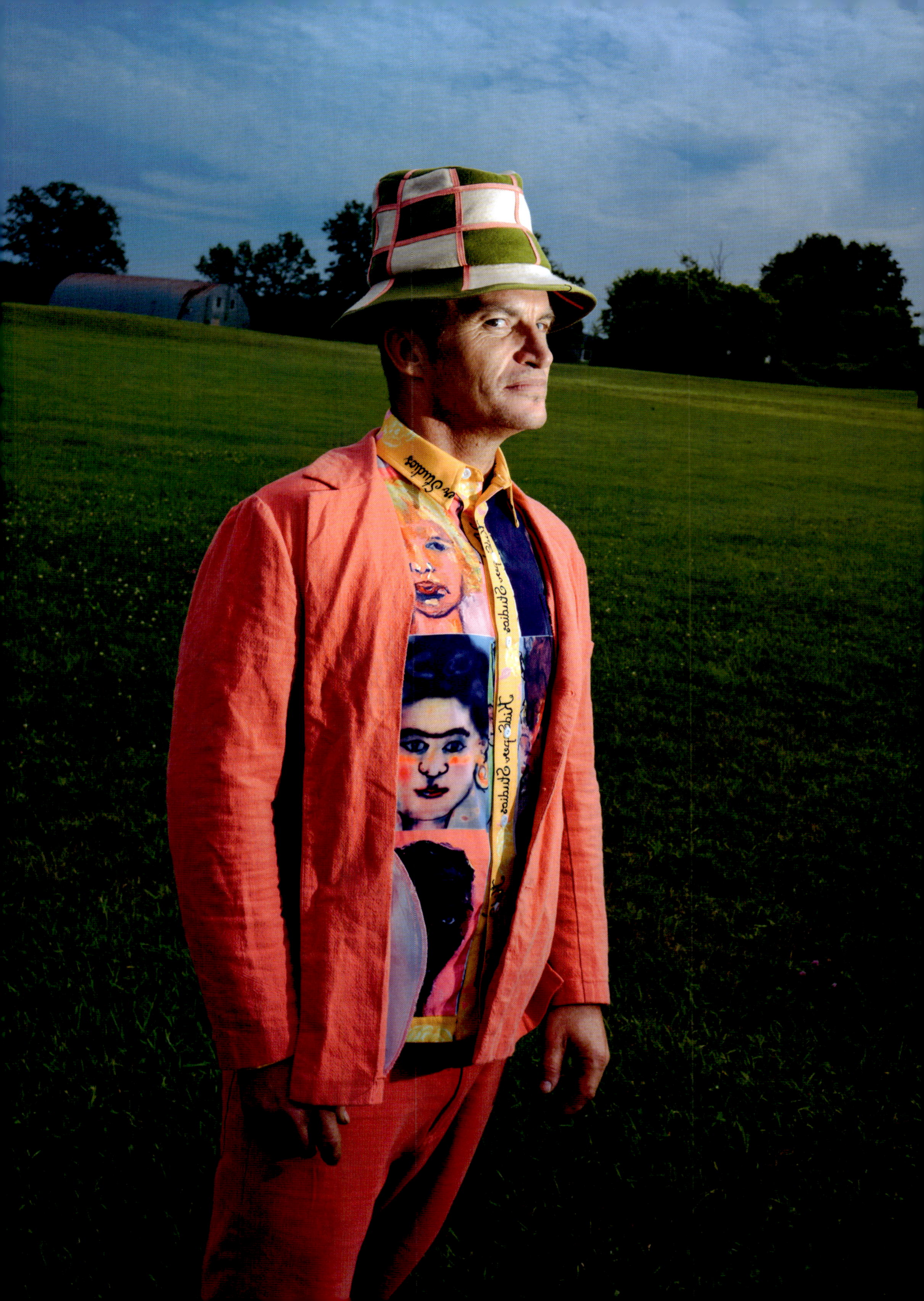

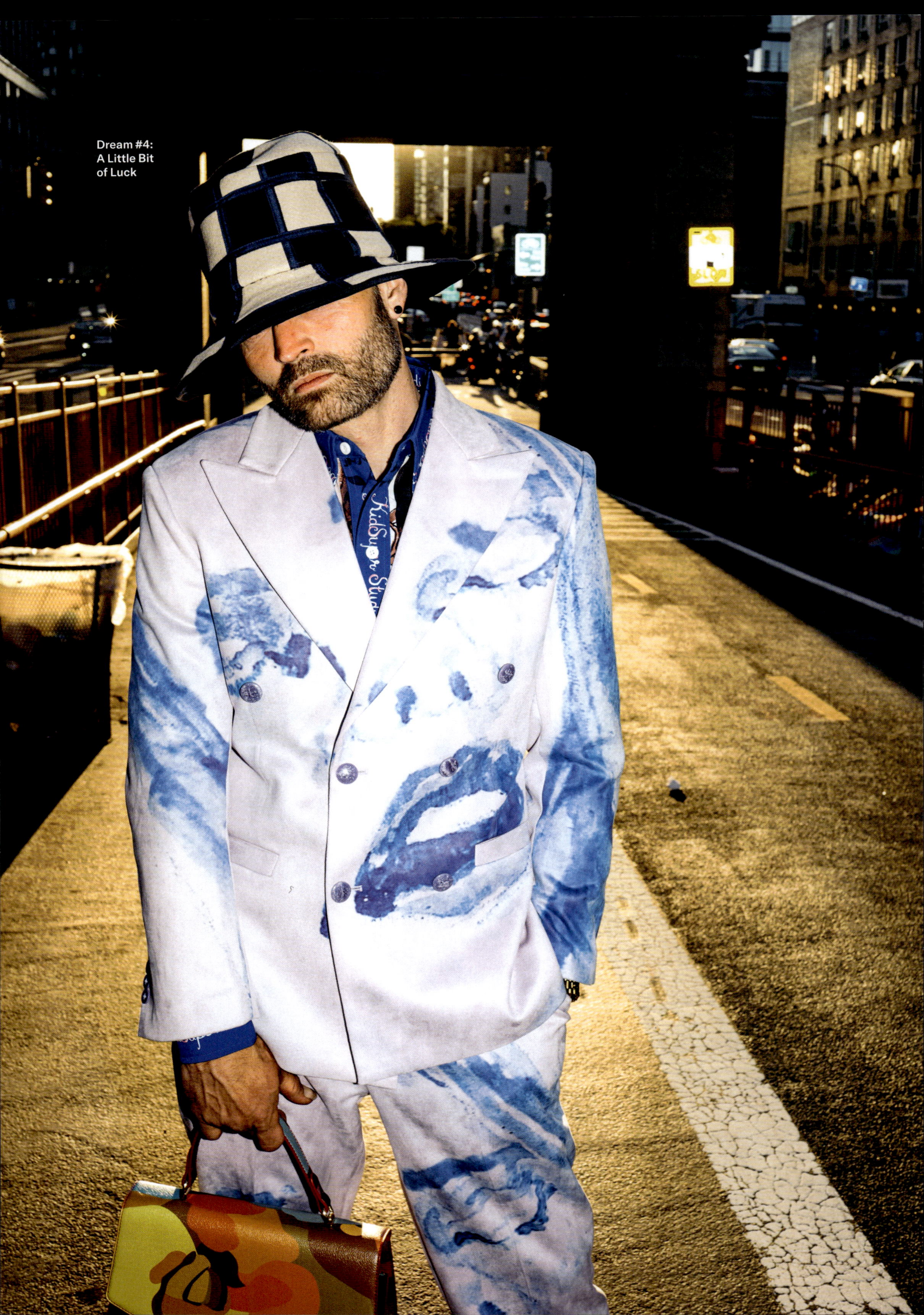

Dream #4:
A Little Bit
of Luck

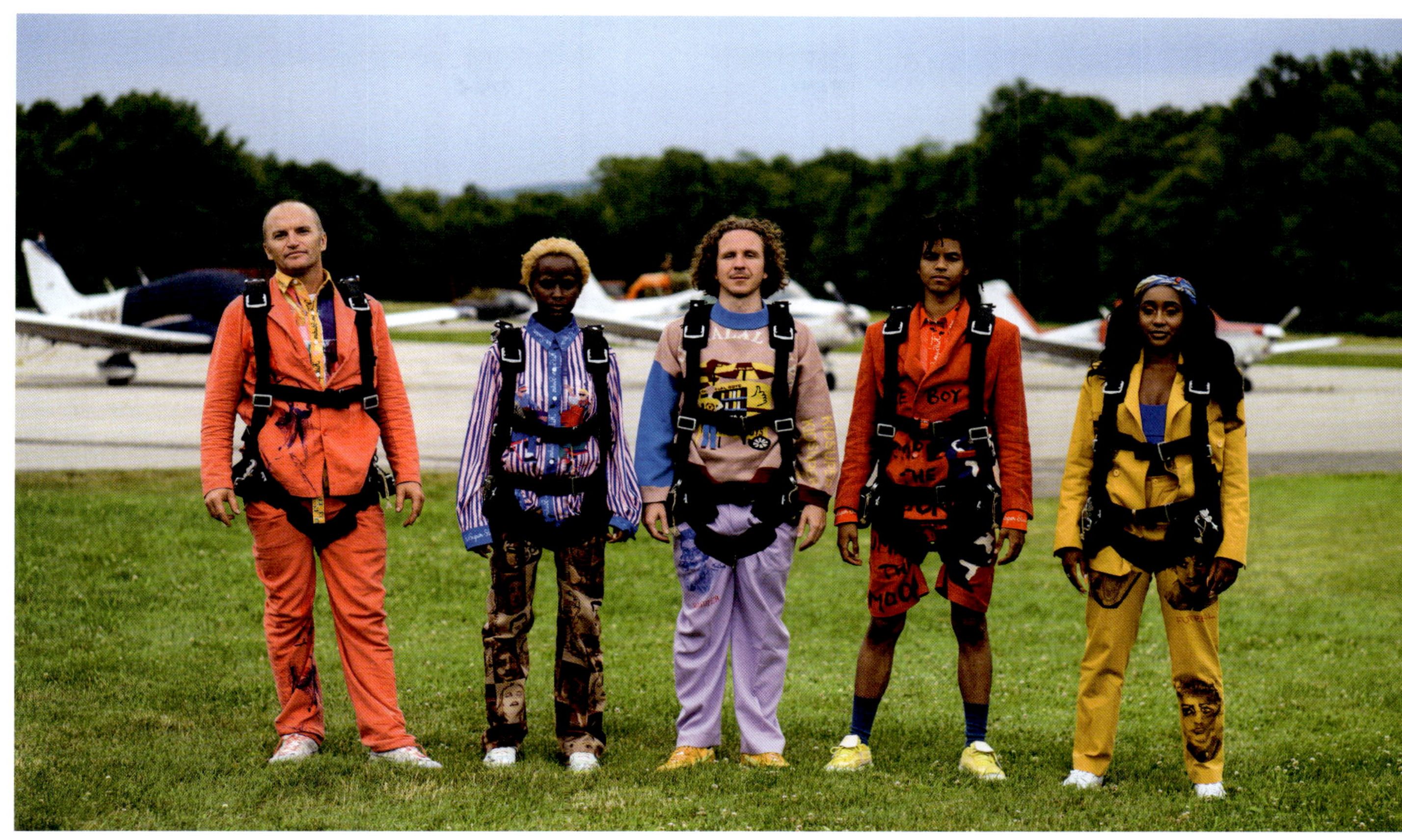

Dream #1: Skydiving

why live in the most spontaneous city in the world?

So when we asked, people actually answered. And if someone mentioned a dream that seemed remotely possible, I'd follow up: "Do you actually want to do this?"

A lot of people said skydiving. That one seemed easy—book a jump and fall out of the sky. When it came to it, I was just there to facilitate. I really did not want to go skydiving, but the group we assembled—total strangers—became like a little family. All in or all out. Backing down wasn't an option. So against my will, and in true KidSuper spirit, I jumped.

The more personal the dreams, the more moving.

One guy, down on his luck, just wanted a fresh start. So we gave him one: a shower, a KidSuper outfit, and a place to sleep. We bought him a bus ticket home and a phone to stay connected. We followed up with him for months after, and then one day he stopped answering the phone we'd gotten him. I like to think he just didn't need us anymore.

We put on a blind date for two people searching for love. I am not exactly sure how it ended, but she did drive him home.

Another person wanted to reconnect with their mom, so we flew them both to Paris. Watching them explore the city together was like seeing a weight lift off someone's shoulders in real time.

And then people started asking me: "What about you? What's one thing you want to do before you die?"

I've got a long list of dreams, some less do-able in a day, but I had always wanted to raft down the Mississippi River.

There's nothing more visually free to me than floating

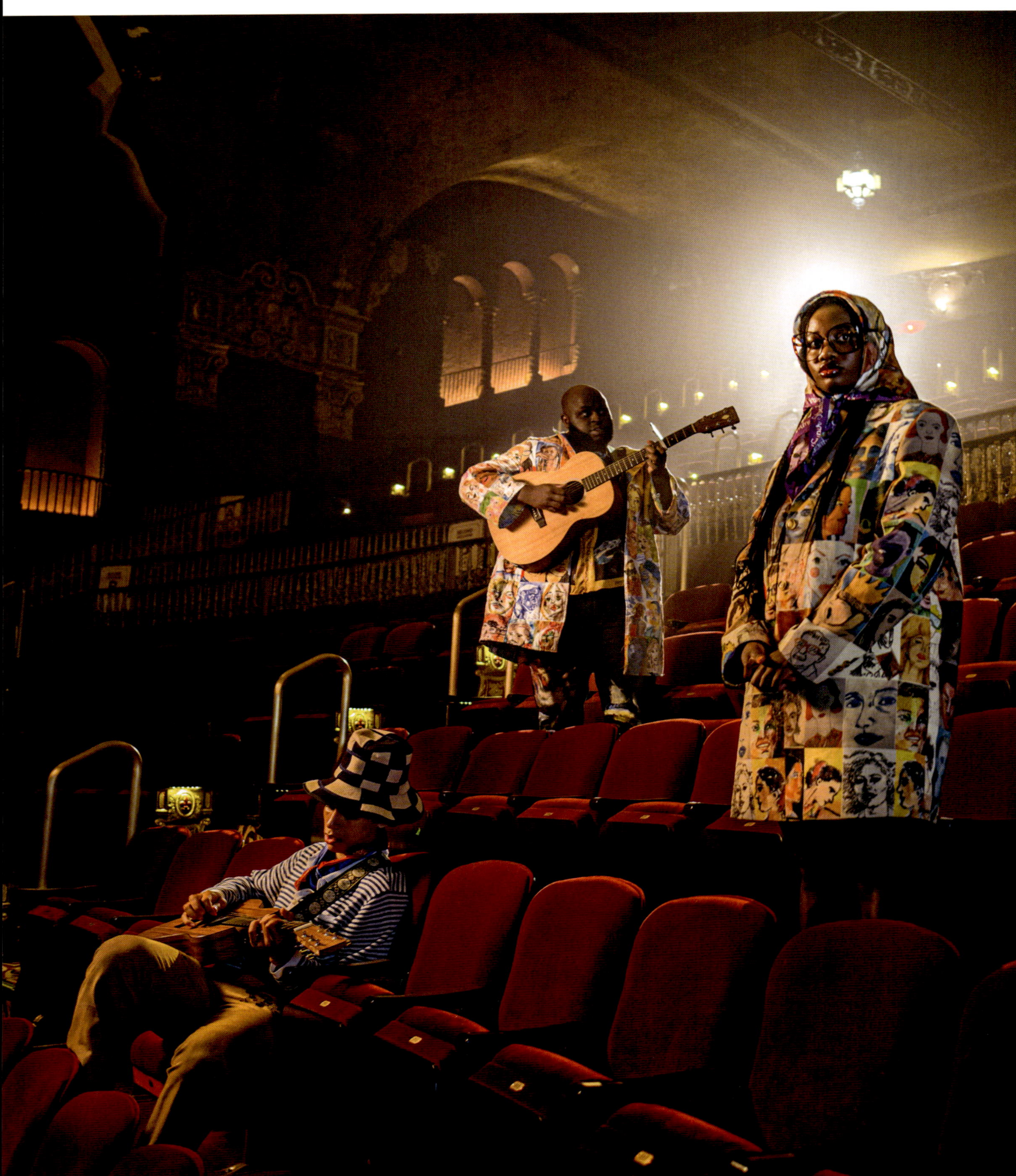

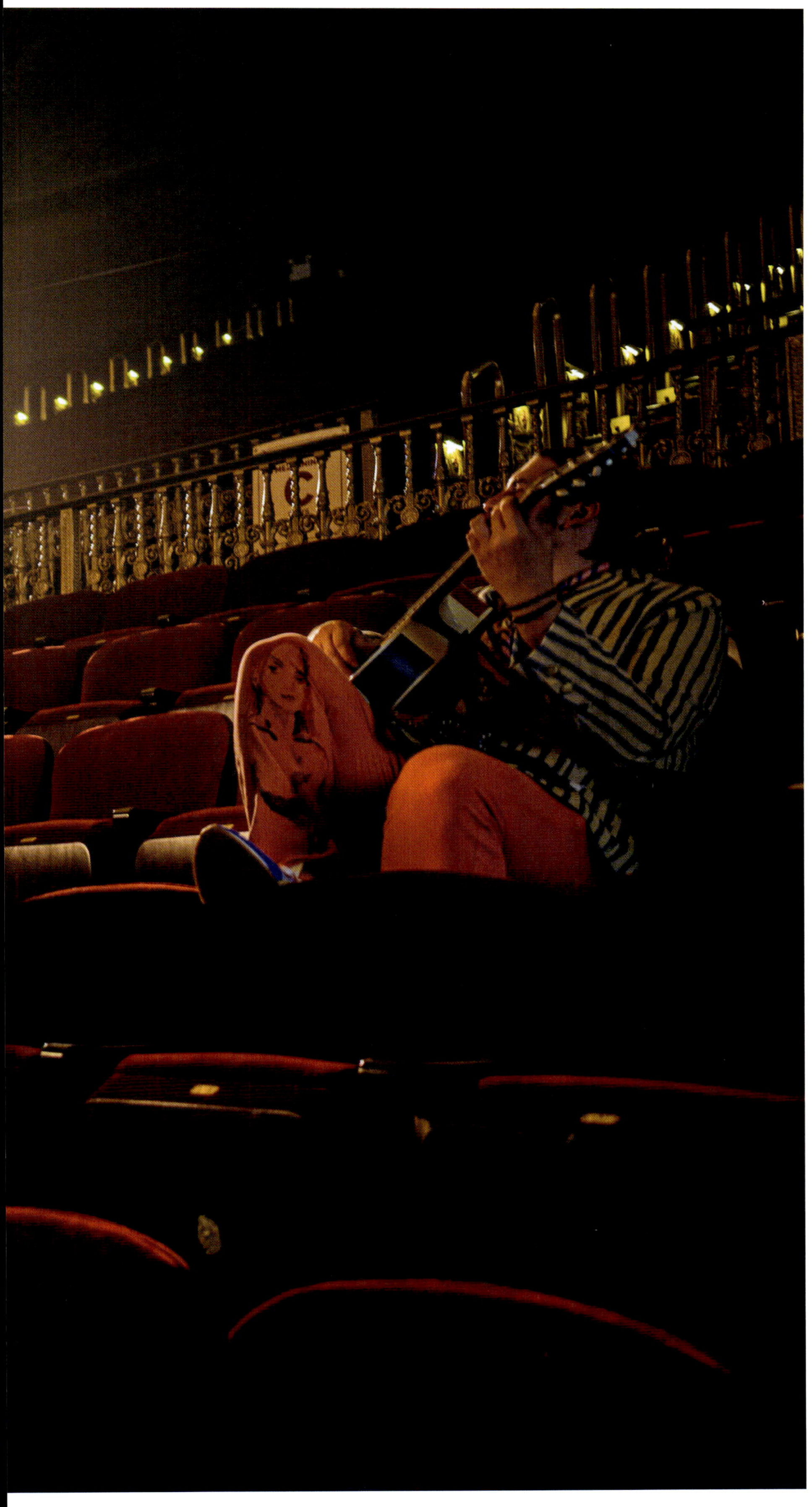

Dream #7: Showtime.
Performing at St. George
Theatre in Staten Island

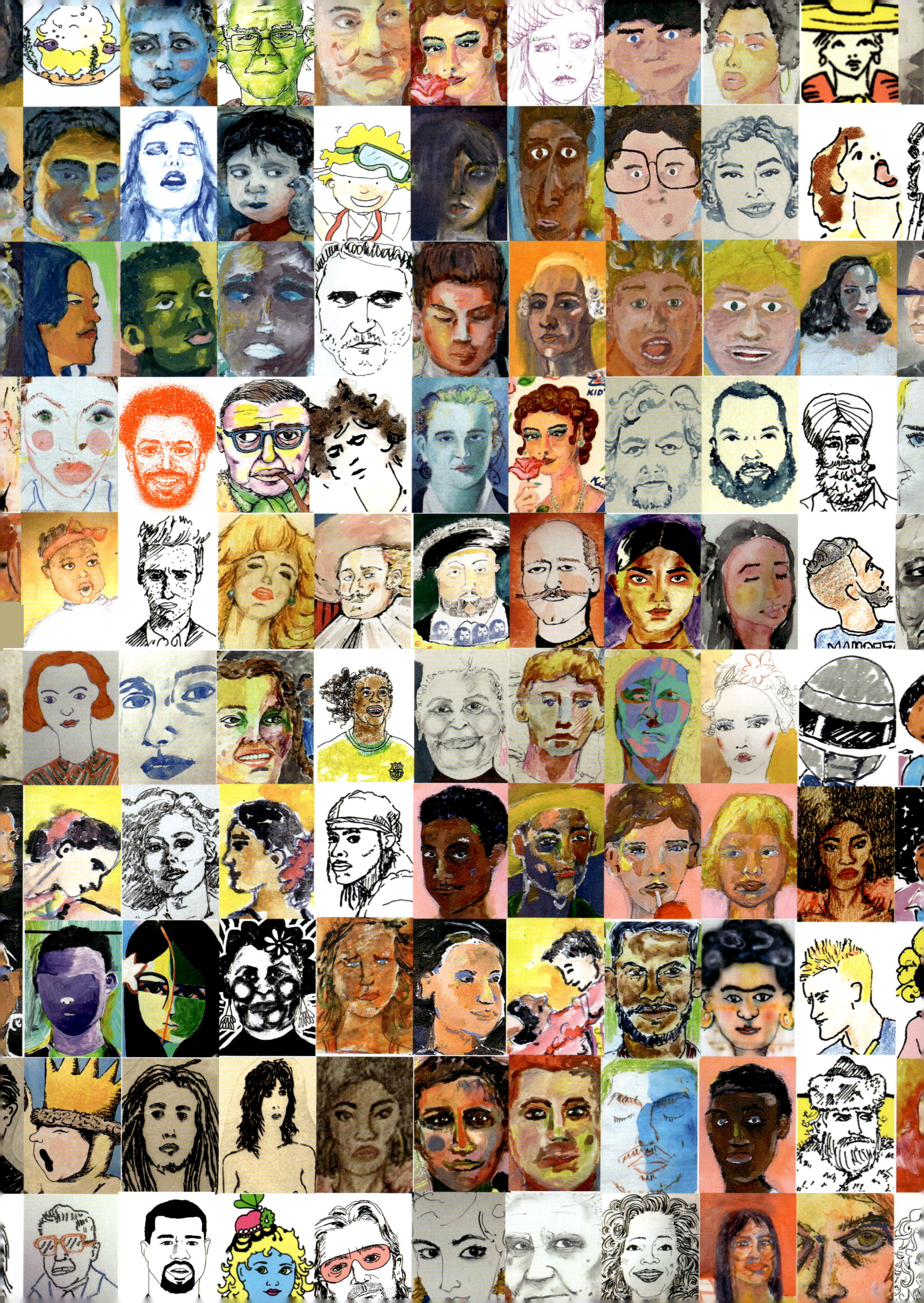

Dream #6: Everest. This dress was made out of hundreds of fans' faces that I doodled

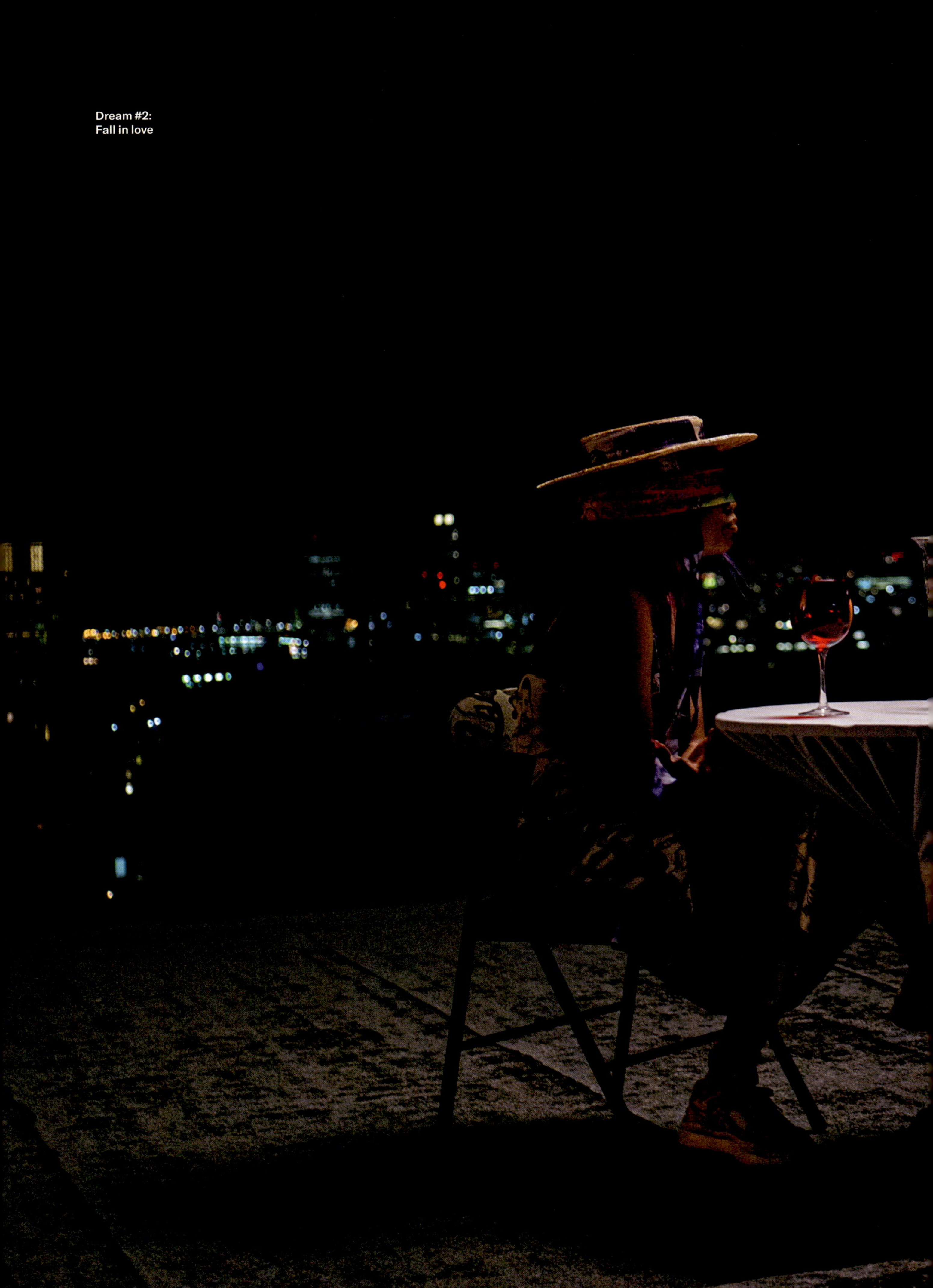

Dream #2:
Fall in love

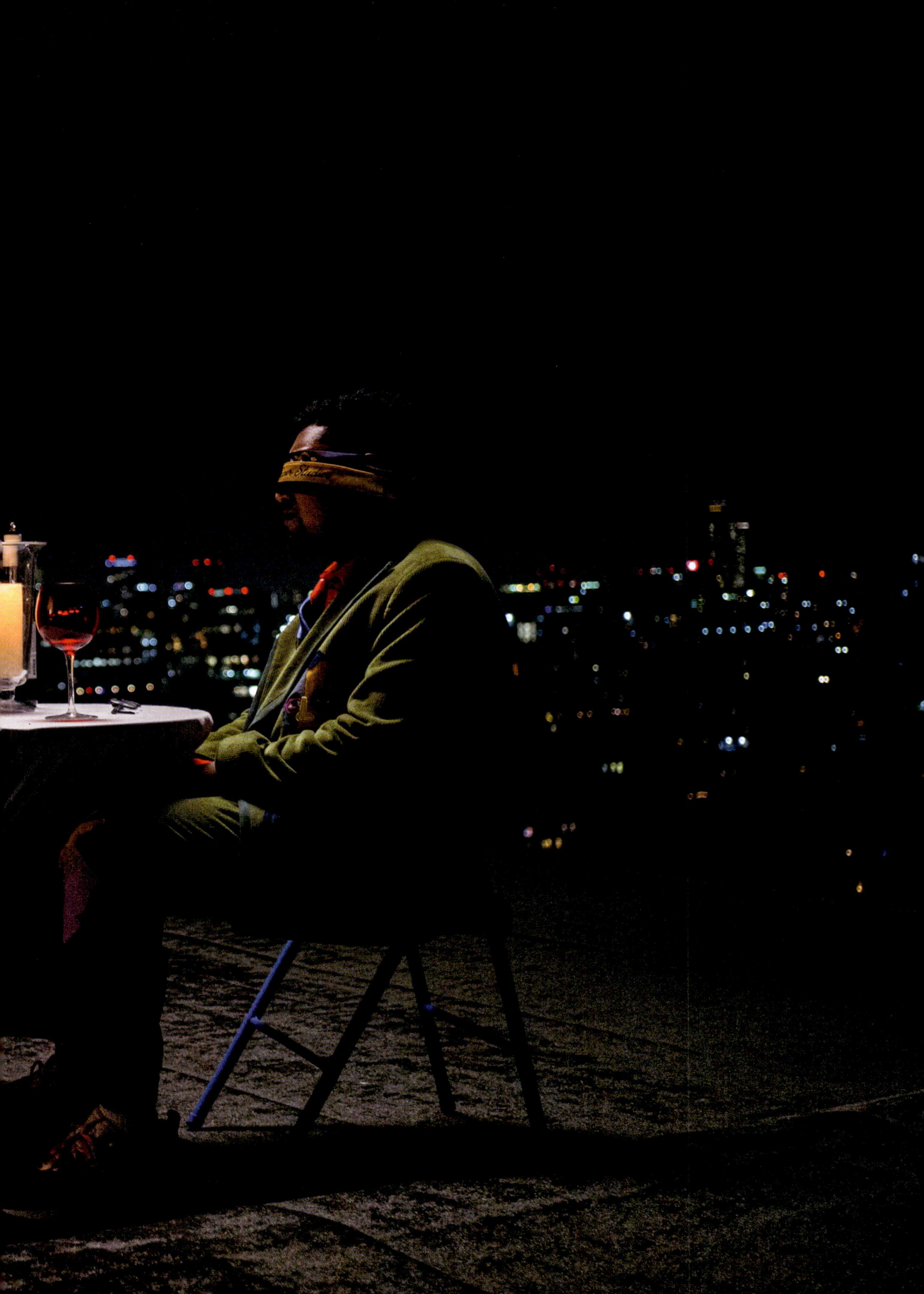

down a river, no destination, just drifting. I had read *Huckleberry Finn* as a kid and the image of going on an adventure down the river always stuck with me. I did some research: The Mississippi River is far from me, and I had no idea where I would get on. On top of that, the Mississippi's current is incredibly fast, and you'd end up stranded in the middle of nowhere.

Then I looked out my window. Why not the Hudson?

I googled "how to build a raft," drove to Home Depot, and built the whole thing in the parking lot. Any tool I needed, I would just walk to Home Depot and "rent" (buy and return) it.

The raft, of course, was completely untested. How could I test it? I was in a parking lot.

THE MORNING OF the launch, I told my friends to meet me under the Brooklyn Bridge at five a.m. I didn't explain much—just "Show up."

They showed up, half-asleep, and before they could question it, we were pushing the raft into the water.

Luckily, our producer found a boat-tour guy last minute. He offered to follow us and get footage. My goal was simple: to get as close as possible to the Statue of Liberty.

But I hadn't accounted for how fast the Hudson moves.

Within ten minutes, we were stranded in the middle of the river, paddling furiously and going nowhere. The current was dragging us straight toward the ocean.

My friends—who hadn't even known really what they were signing up for—were now stuck on a homemade raft at sunrise in the middle of the Hudson River. But like many of the past KidSuper misadventures, they had a feeling that it would all work out.

Eventually, the tour boat had to tow us back. But we got the shot.

Looking back, it's funny how a fashion show turned into something so much more. It wasn't just about clothes. It was about people chasing dreams—however big, small, or ridiculous.

After the whole thing, we followed up with participants and asked them how their experience was. One story stuck with me.

One of the guys who went skydiving said, "You wouldn't have recognized me a month before this project. I've been sober for one month. Every time I get my shit together, something good happens. This feels like a sign."

When we took him skydiving, the instructor he was strapped to was a former addict himself. He'd found skydiving after getting clean—said it scratched the same itch without self-destruction.

After the jump, the guy was buzzing. "That feeling," he said, "that's what I've been chasing. I'm gonna keep skydiving."

It's been almost five years since we filmed that project.

But the energy of it—the spontaneity, the vulnerability, the way strangers came together to make each other's dreams happen—that still sticks with me.

Maybe it's time to do it again.

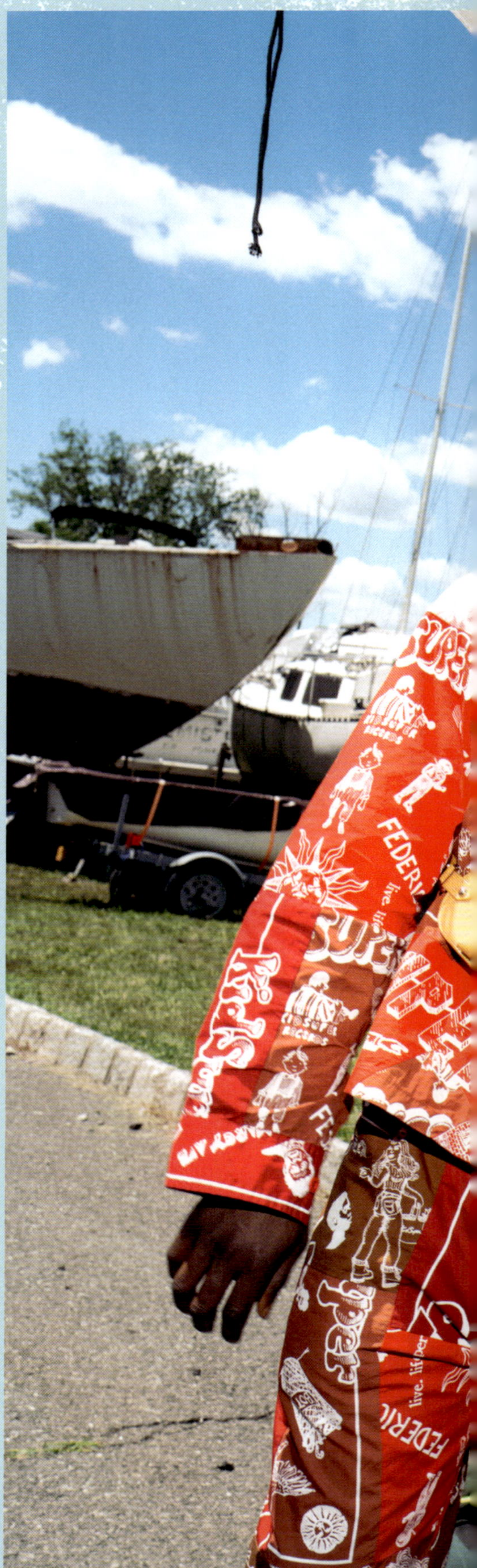

The boys. I ended this video with my trying to accomplish my own dream they came with

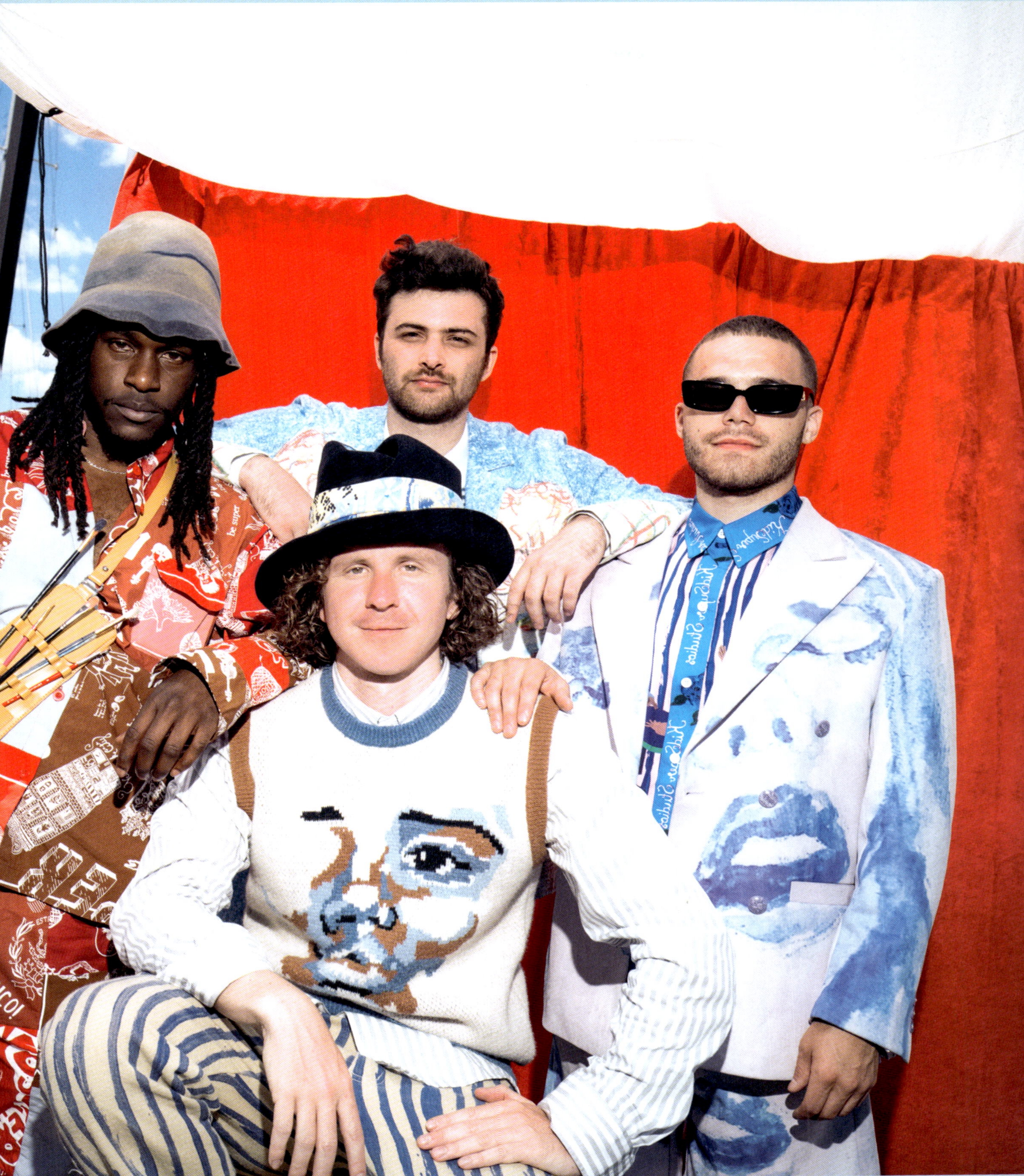

6

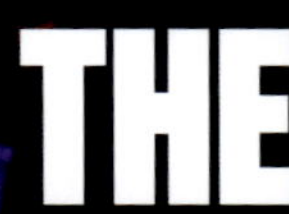

THE MISADVENTURES OF

I am constantly tripping forward.

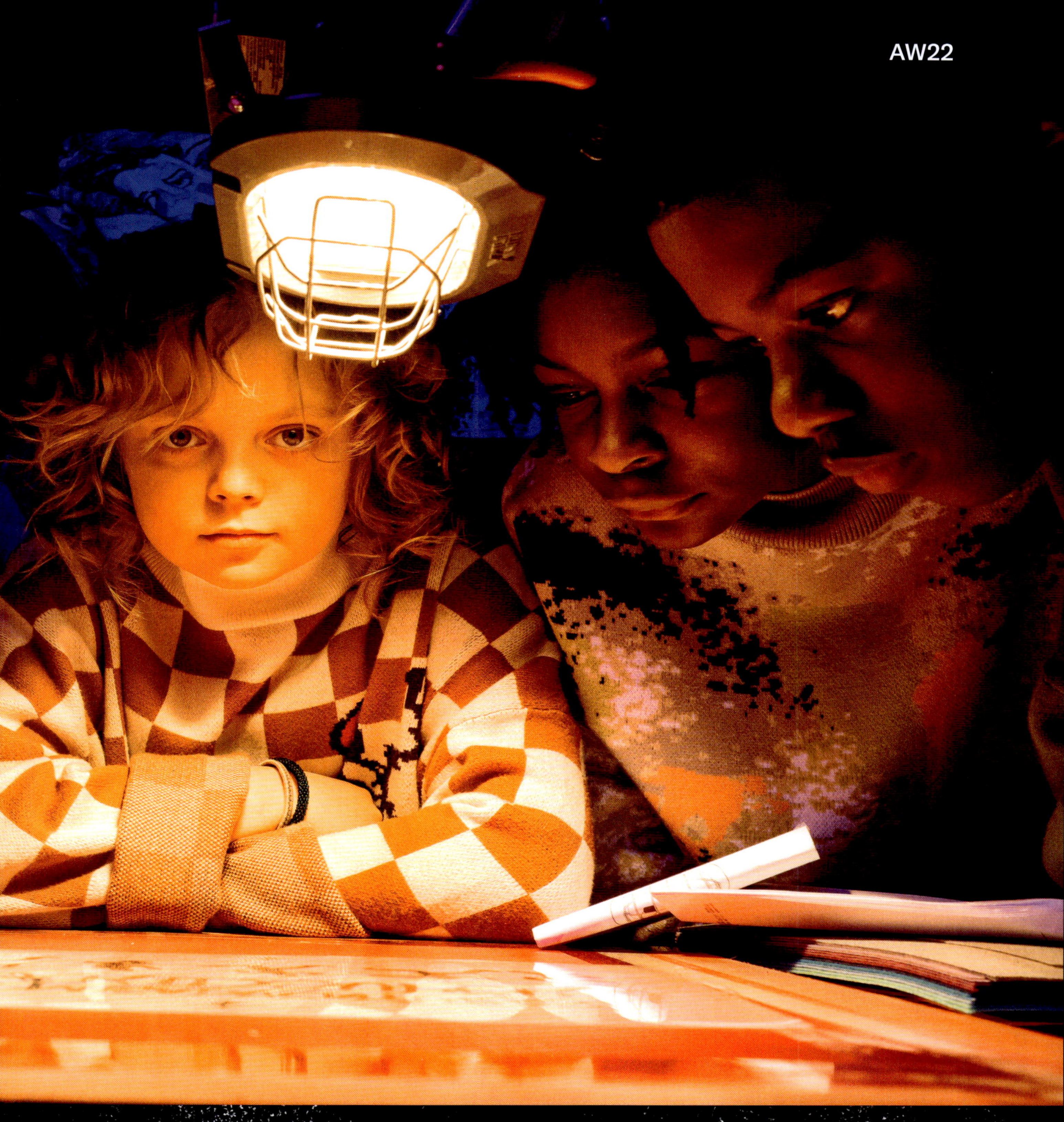

KIDSUPER

TWO YEARS INTO COVID the world was reopening, and the fashion world wanted everything back to normal. Some local brands had already started to do in-person fashion shows again, but I was in no rush.

The virtual fashion show medium treated me well. They were limitless—stop-motion, short films, wild concepts that'd never work on a traditional runway. And let's be real, they were cheaper. No flights to Paris, no venue rentals, none of the usual insanity. So when Paris Fashion Week reached out, I said, "I'll do one last virtual show."

But if it was my last virtual show, it had to be something unforgettable.

For years I'd had this idea: the KidSuper story would make a great TV show—something like *Entourage* or *How to Make It in America*. A group of friends trying to build the biggest brand in the world, based in New York and fueled by ambition, chaos, and pure creativity.

So I did some digging. I looked up the IMDb pages for those two shows. One name popped up on both: Rob Weiss.

Through Instagram, friends of friends, and perseverance, I got Rob on the phone and pitched the idea: "A TV show about KidSuper—the fashion world, the hustling, the misadventures. It's similar to the stories you have done before." He was cool about it. "Sounds interesting. Send me the pilot script."

It was a Friday. I panicked and said, "Ah, man, I'm not home right now. Can I send it Monday?"

"No problem," he replied. So I locked myself inside all weekend and wrote the entire pilot episode from scratch. Monday morning, I sent it off, fingers crossed.

That night, Rob called me. "I never finish scripts people send me—but I actually liked yours. It's good."

I'm thinking to myself, "That's it, we've got a TV show."

Princess Nokia—
some of those
hands are mine

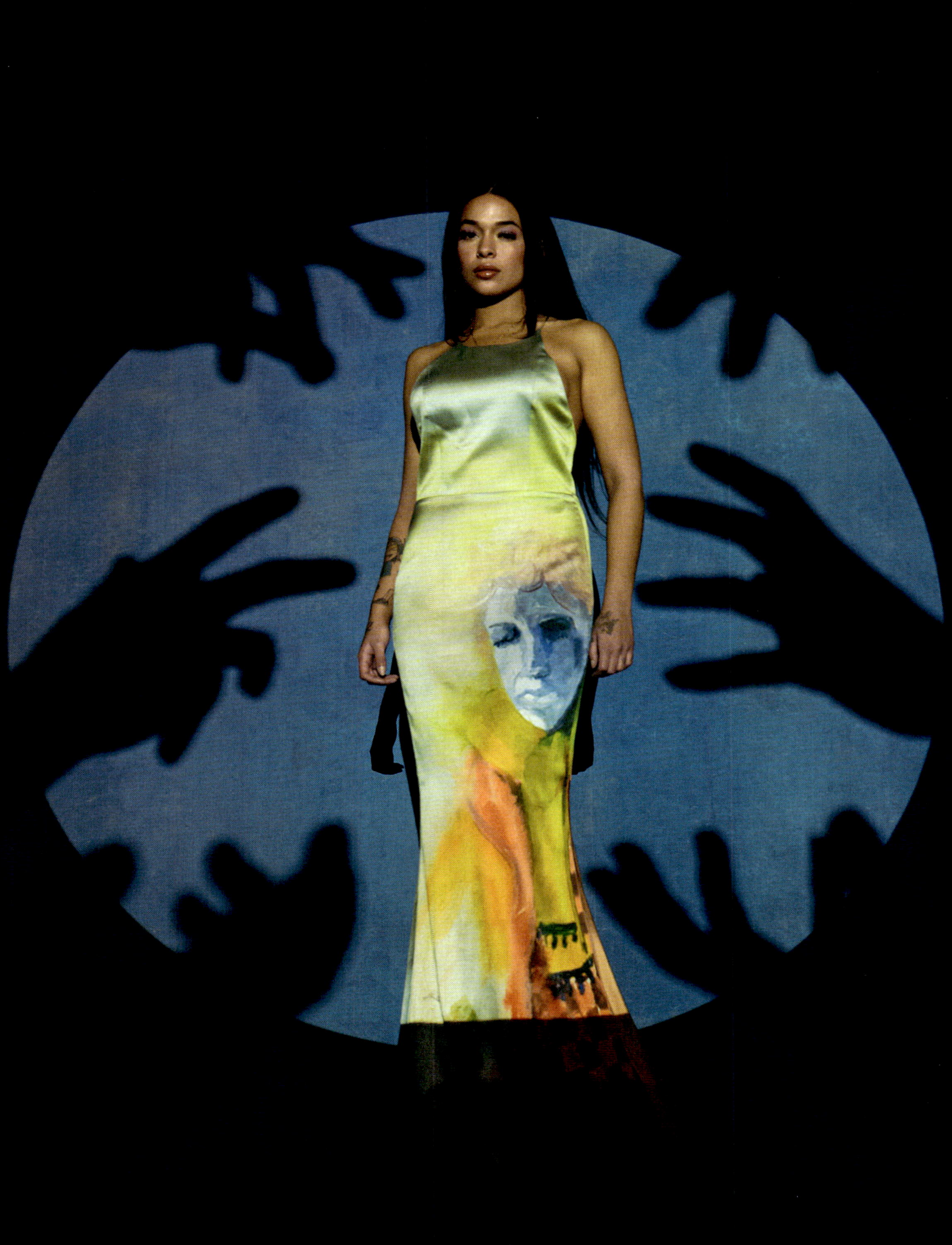

THE BEGINNIN

#1
OPENING SCENE

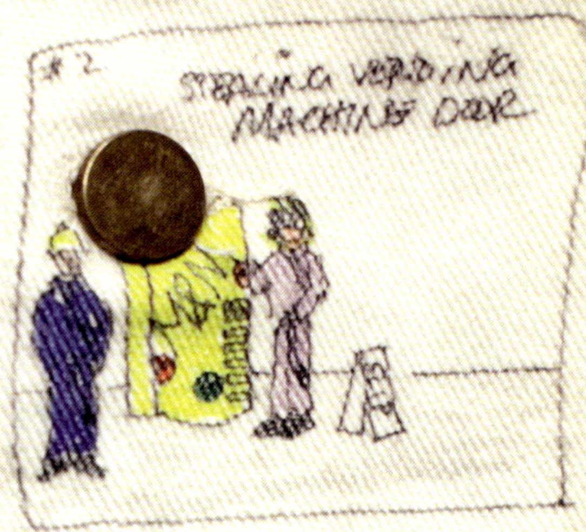

ESTABLISH THE CHARACTE
FRIENDSHIP AND BRO

#3 THE FAMILY VAN

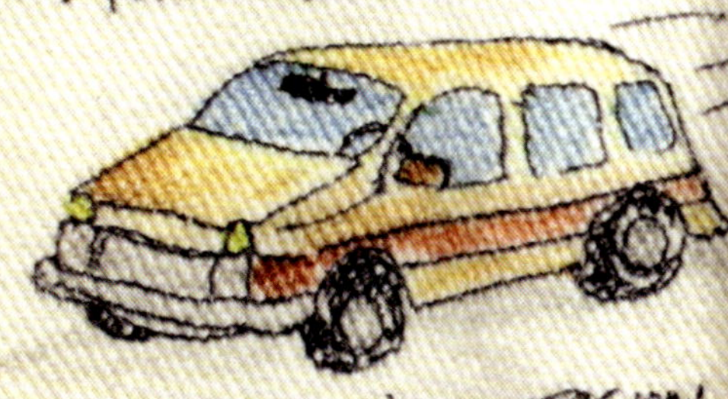

STOP MOTION VERSION
THROUGH THE CITY

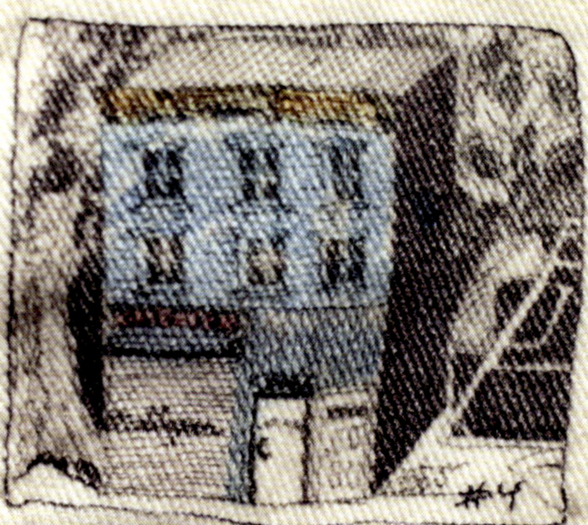

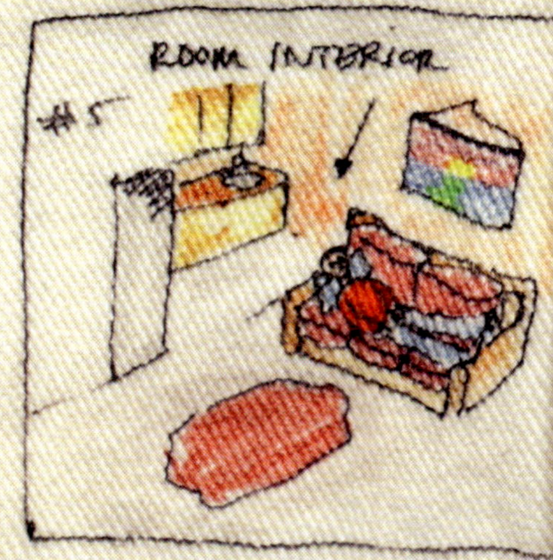

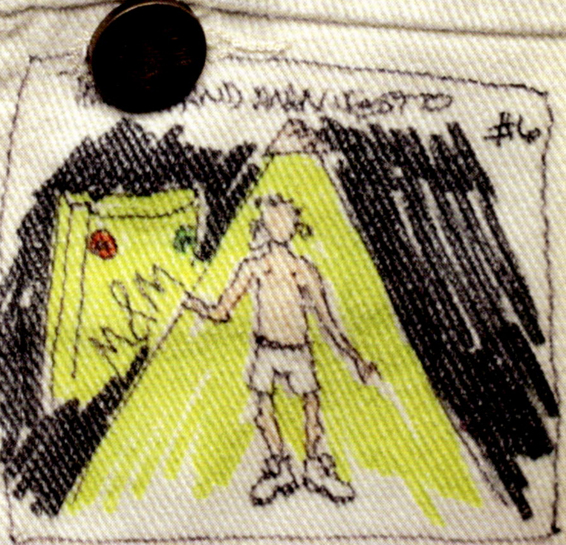

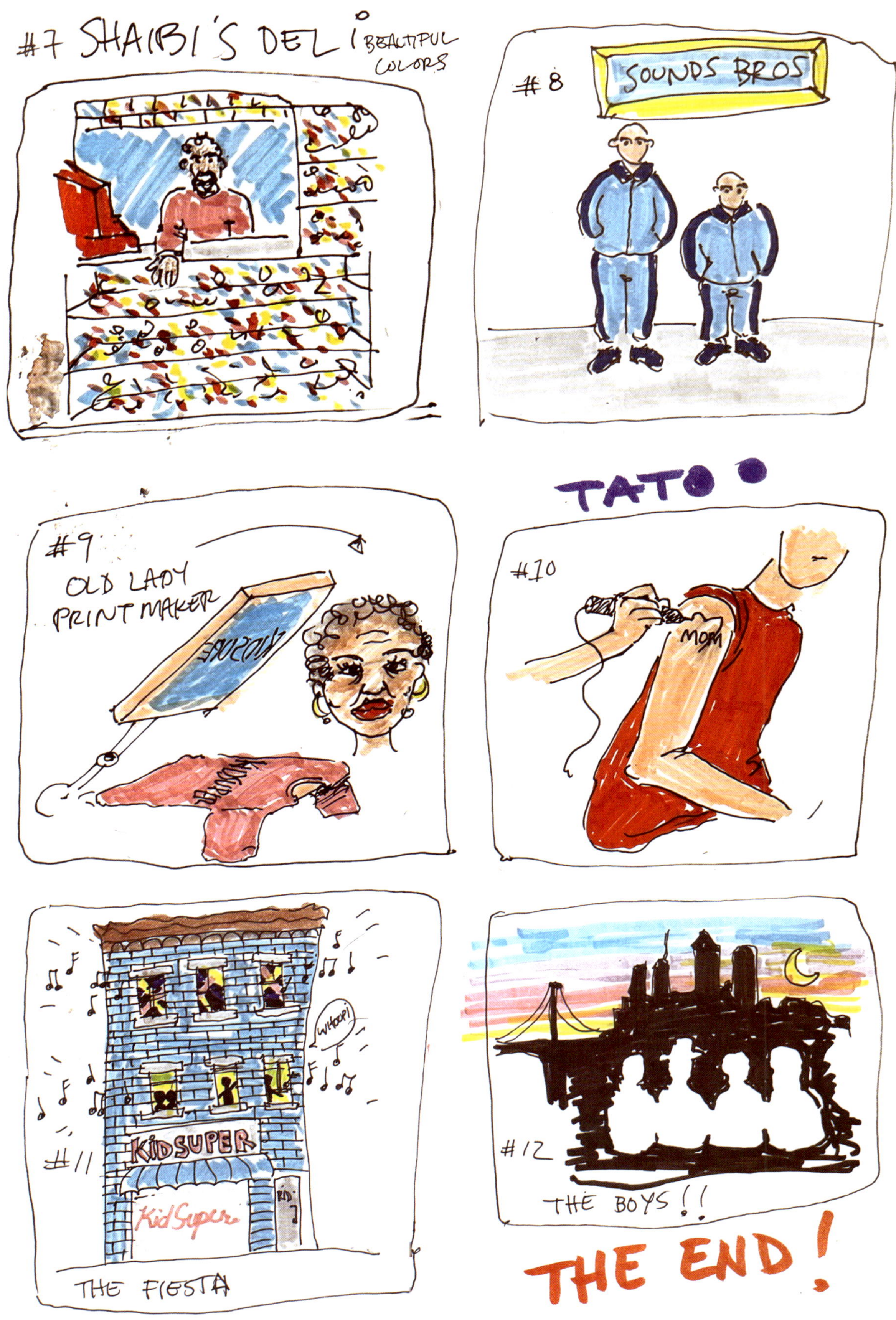

The storyboard from the short film screen-printed onto a checkered jacket from the collection

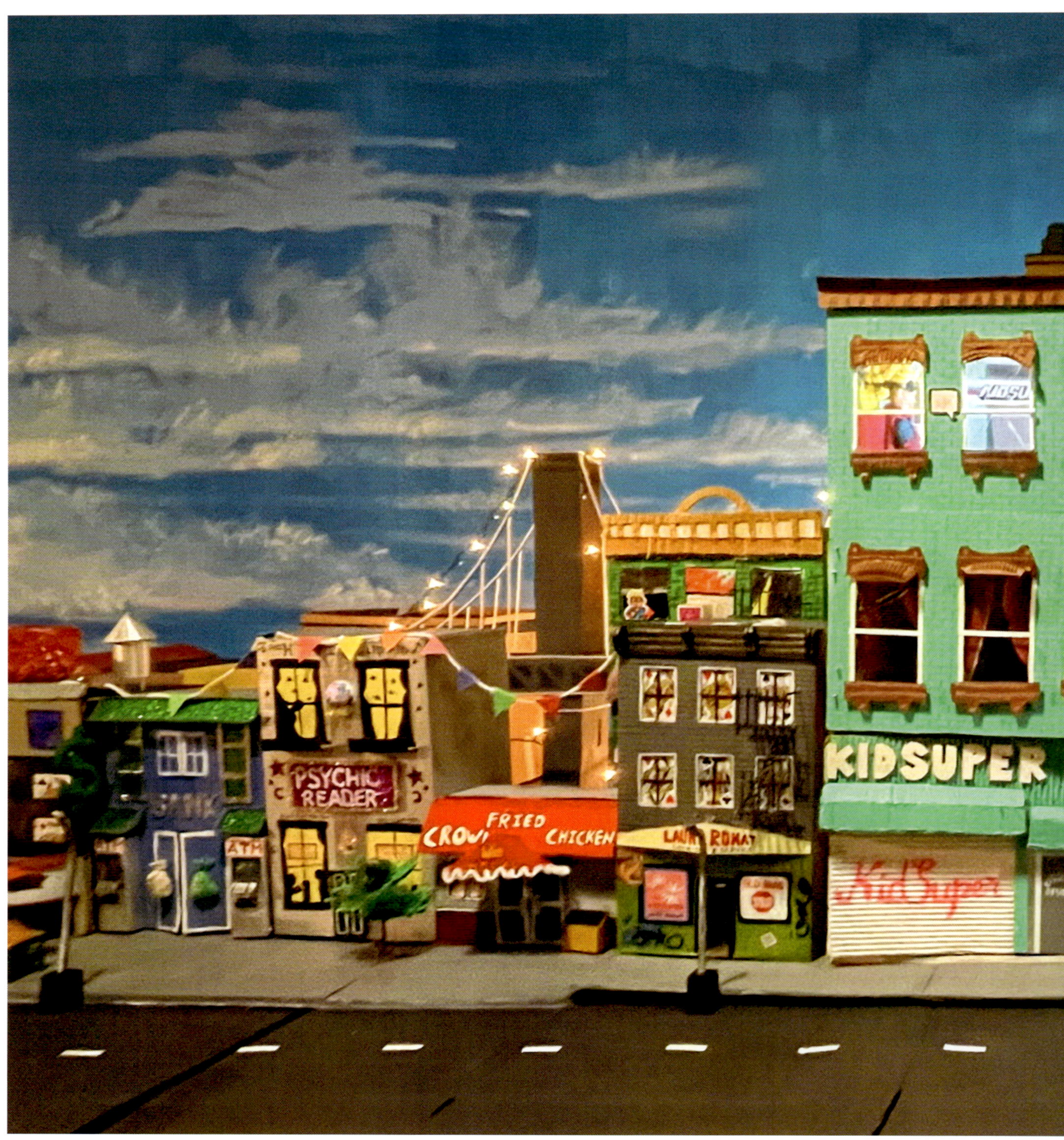
PSYCHIC
READER
ATM
FRIED
CHICKEN
KIDSUPER
KidSuper

Neighborhood and KidSuper Building reenactment for the Claymation scene within the pilot episode. I got a whole bunch of people to come build cardboard houses.

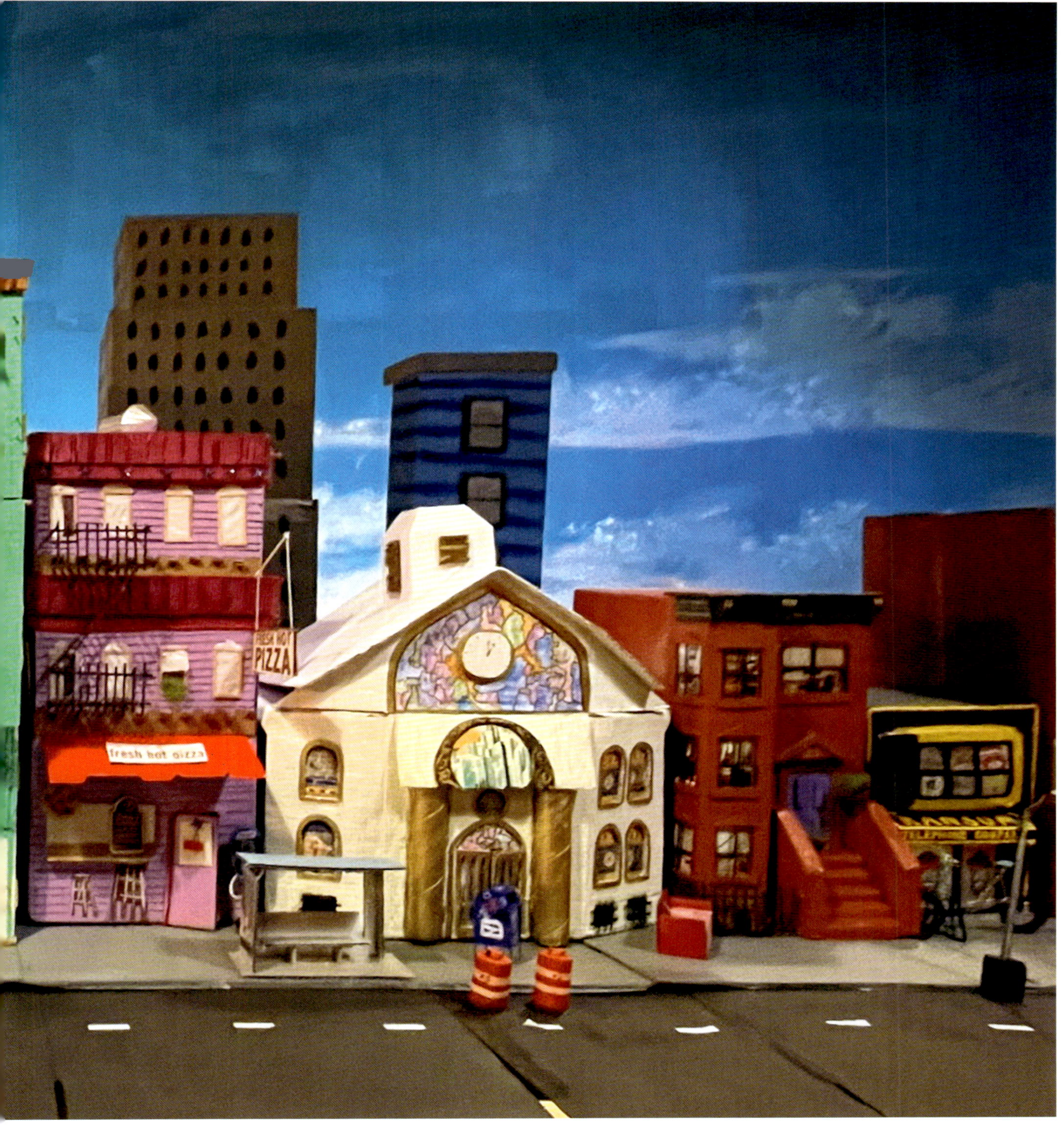

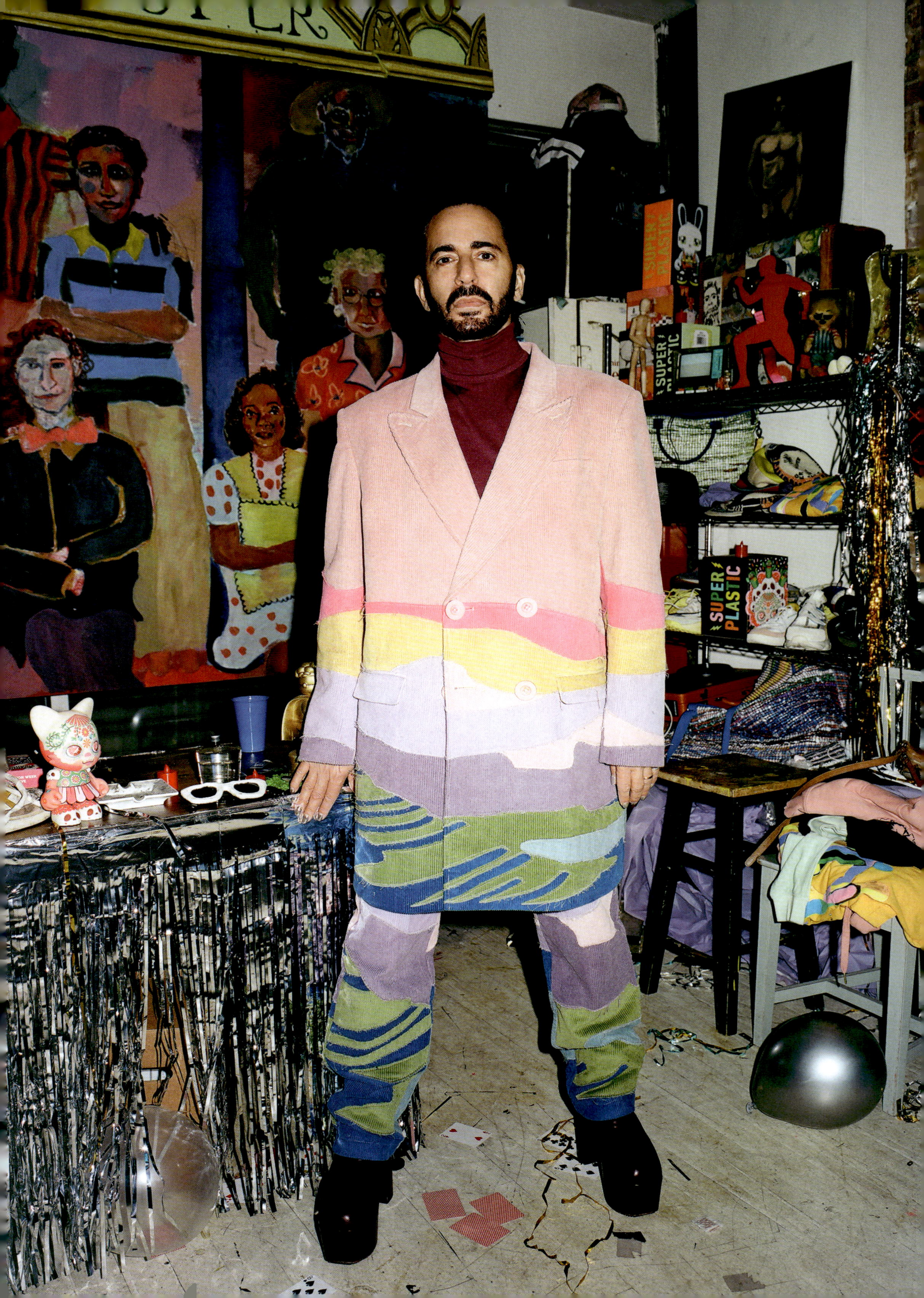
SUPER
PLASTIC

But Rob hits me with reality: "Well, first I'd have to show my producing partners. If they're in, we'd pitch a network. If the network likes it, they'll fund a pilot. If the pilot works, maybe they'll greenlight a season . . ."

So I asked, "Why can't we just shoot the pilot ourselves?" He laughed. It wasn't the nature of the business to shoot a full pilot as a pitch, and it especially wasn't for someone like Rob, who had already had hit TV shows. I told him I was already planning to spend a big budget on my last virtual fashion show—so why not roll the dice? One last show and a TV pilot.

Rob thought I was insane. But in a good way. And off I went.

At this point, KidSuper was doing better than ever. I'd just won the prestigious Karl Lagerfeld Prize awarded by LVMH. The virtual shows had finally earned me respect from the "real" fashion world. And for the first time, I was dropping clothing consistently and had a little money to play with.

I called up my friends who produced music videos and had made the first short film with me—guys itching to break into narrative work. They were all in. I had the script. Now I needed clothes, a cast, and well... everything else.

I called everyone I knew. Joey Bada$$. Big Body Bes. Princess Nokia. And they all agreed to be in it.

Part of the award for winning the Karl Lagerfeld Prize was mentorship with some of the biggest names in fashion, one of which was Marc Jacobs. I contacted him knowing he was somewhat inclined to help me: "Marc, would you be in my fashion show-slash-pilot episode? Just forty-five minutes of your time. That's it. You won't have any lines."

To my surprise, he agreed. I wrote him in as the celebrity cameo at one of our parties.

We planned everything down to the wire. The clothes arrived Wednesday. We shot Thursday, Friday, Saturday. Edited Monday, Tuesday. Submitted to our allotted Paris Fashion Week slot on Wednesday.

It was my first time ever shooting a full 16-minute narrative. I was in way over my head. Every hour we ran over schedule bled thousands of dollars. But I didn't care—I was all in. I knew this was going to be a piece of work that I referenced constantly and could build on top of it. I wanted it to feel KidSuper through and through: it was stylish, it had stop-motion scenes, and there was this optimism in it that was palpable.

When we finished shooting we went straight to the edit. There were three of us editing at the same time; as I fell asleep, one would wake up and take over. It was a 72-hour nonstop crunch. Miraculously, we pulled it off. Paris Fashion Week aired it, and the next week my phone exploded.

Talent agents—UTA, WME, CAA—all calling, all wanting to sign me. I picked whoever represented *Entourage*. Then Vimeo named us Staff Pick of the Year. And Rob? He called, genuinely shocked. "I can't believe you actually did it . . . and it's good."

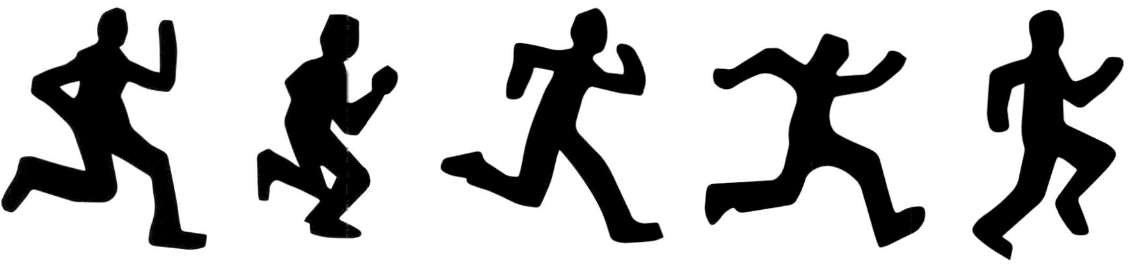

Marc Jacobs. Thank you so much for being a part of this and tripling the production value

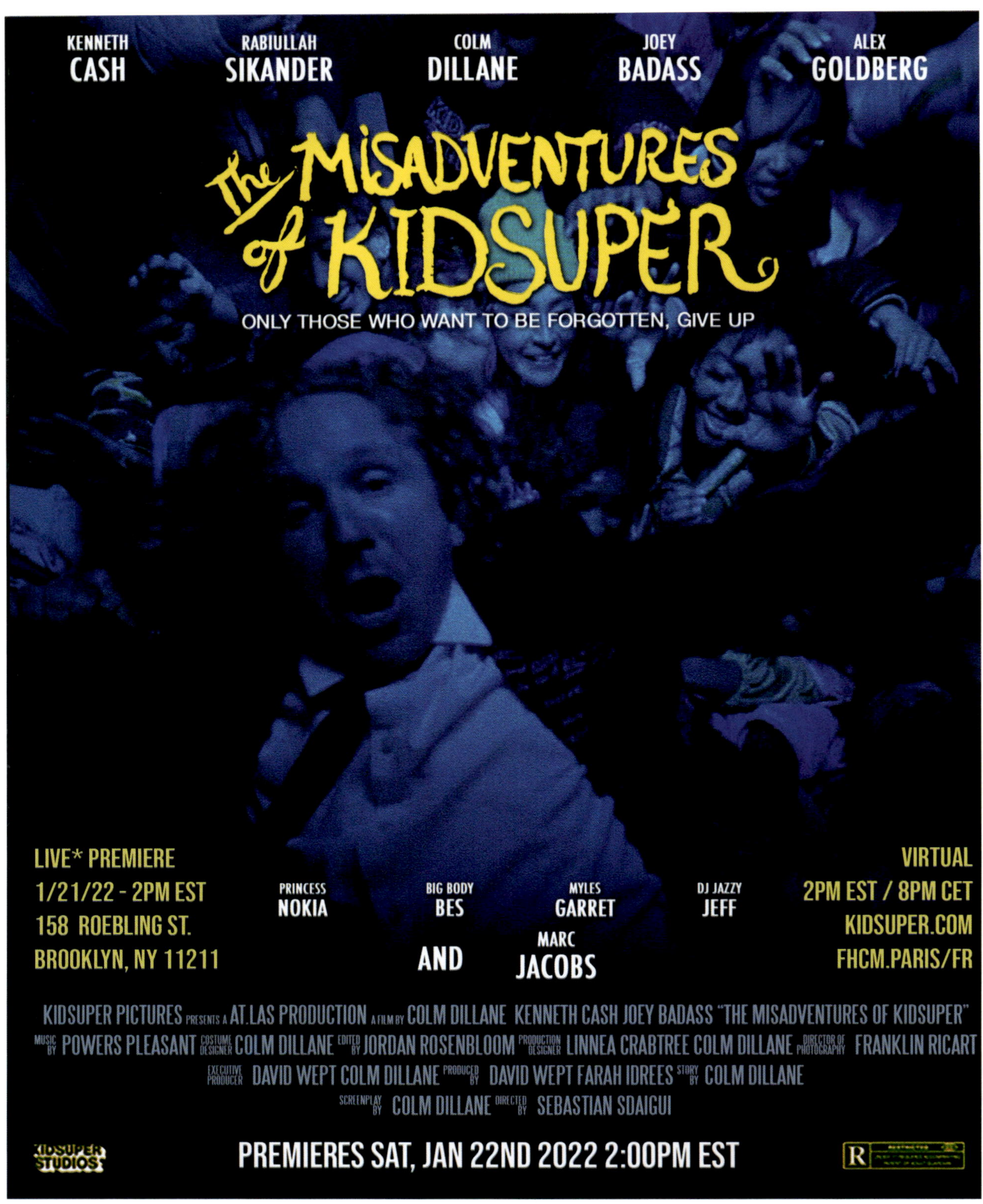

Fake movie posters for invites to the Paris show screening

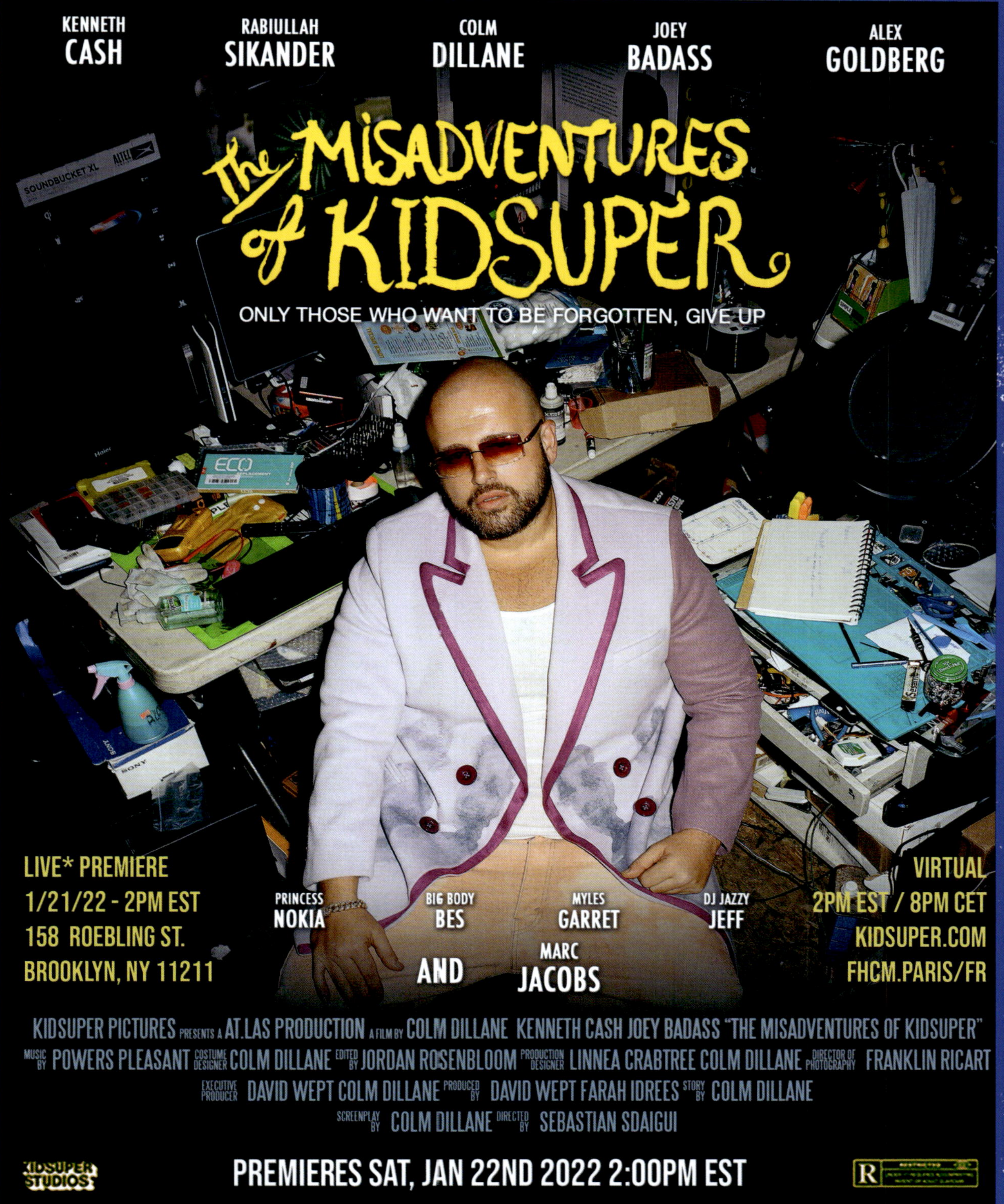
KENNETH CASH
RABIULLAH SIKANDER
COLM DILLANE
JOEY BADASS
ALEX GOLDBERG
The MISADVENTURES of KIDSUPER
ONLY THOSE WHO WANT TO BE FORGOTTEN, GIVE UP
LIVE* PREMIERE
1/21/22 - 2PM EST
158 ROEBLING ST.
BROOKLYN, NY 11211
PRINCESS NOKIA
BIG BODY BES
MYLES GARRET
DJ JAZZY JEFF
AND
MARC JACOBS
VIRTUAL
2PM EST / 8PM CET
KIDSUPER.COM
FHCM.PARIS/FR
KIDSUPER PICTURES PRESENTS A AT.LAS PRODUCTION A FILM BY COLM DILLANE KENNETH CASH JOEY BADASS "THE MISADVENTURES OF KIDSUPER"
MUSIC BY POWERS PLEASANT COSTUME DESIGNER COLM DILLANE EDITED BY JORDAN ROSENBLOOM PRODUCTION DESIGNER LINNEA CRABTREE COLM DILLANE DIRECTOR OF PHOTOGRAPHY FRANKLIN RICART
EXECUTIVE PRODUCER DAVID WEPT COLM DILLANE PRODUCED BY DAVID WEPT FARAH IDREES STORY BY COLM DILLANE
SCREENPLAY BY COLM DILLANE DIRECTED BY SEBASTIAN SDAIGUI
KIDSUPER STUDIOS
PREMIERES SAT, JAN 22ND 2022 2:00PM EST
R

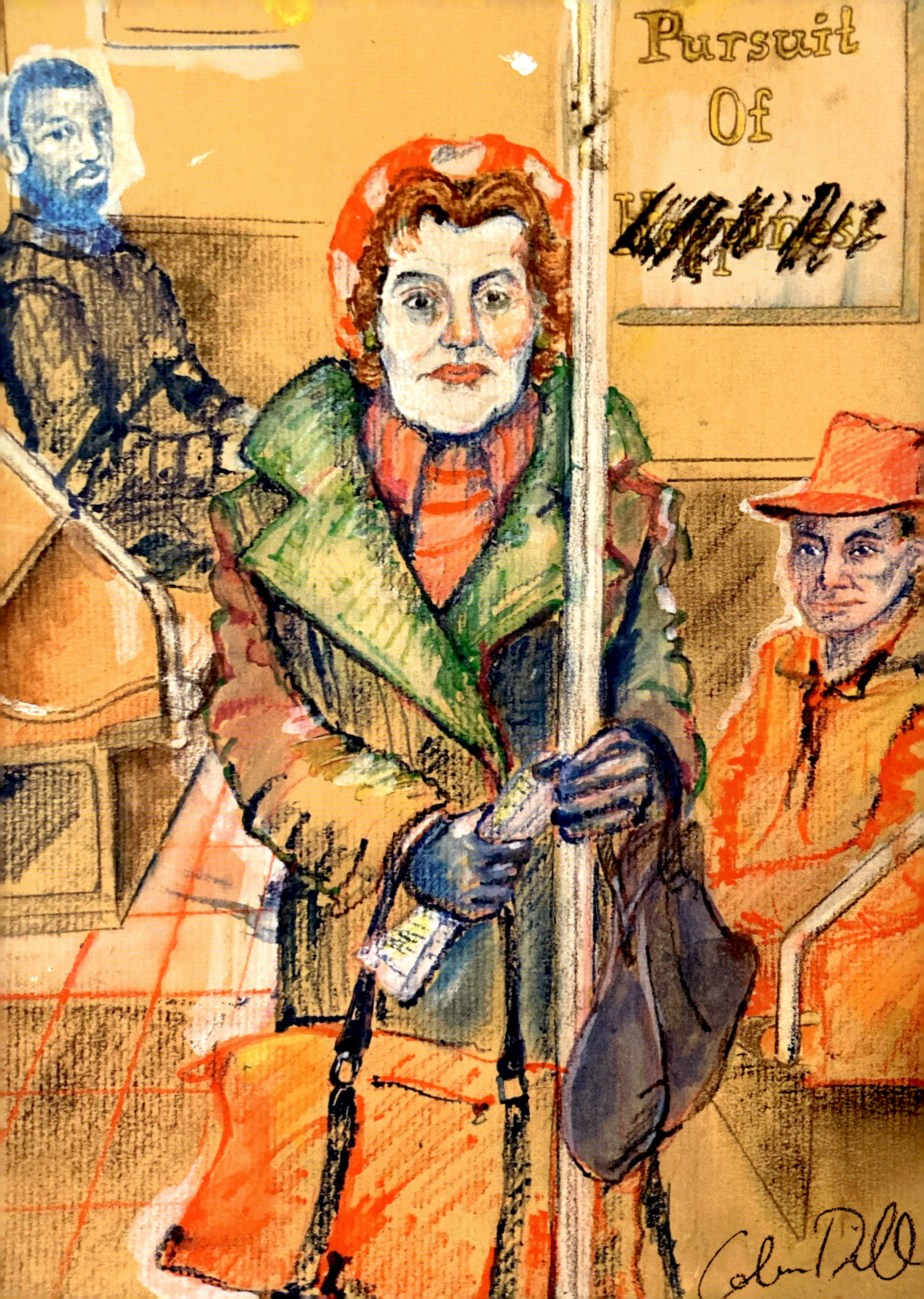
Pursuit
Of

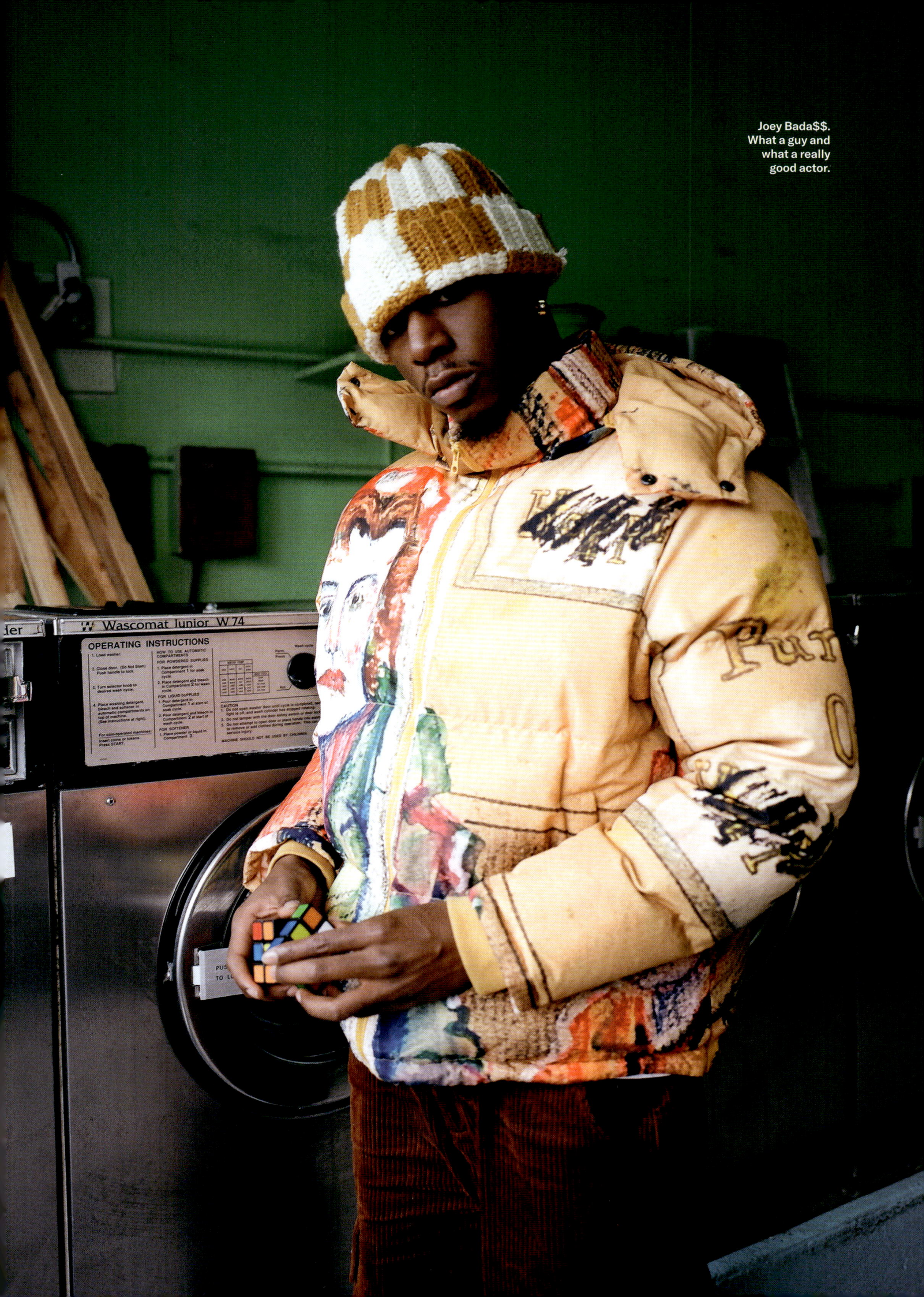

Joey Bada$$. What a guy and what a really good actor.

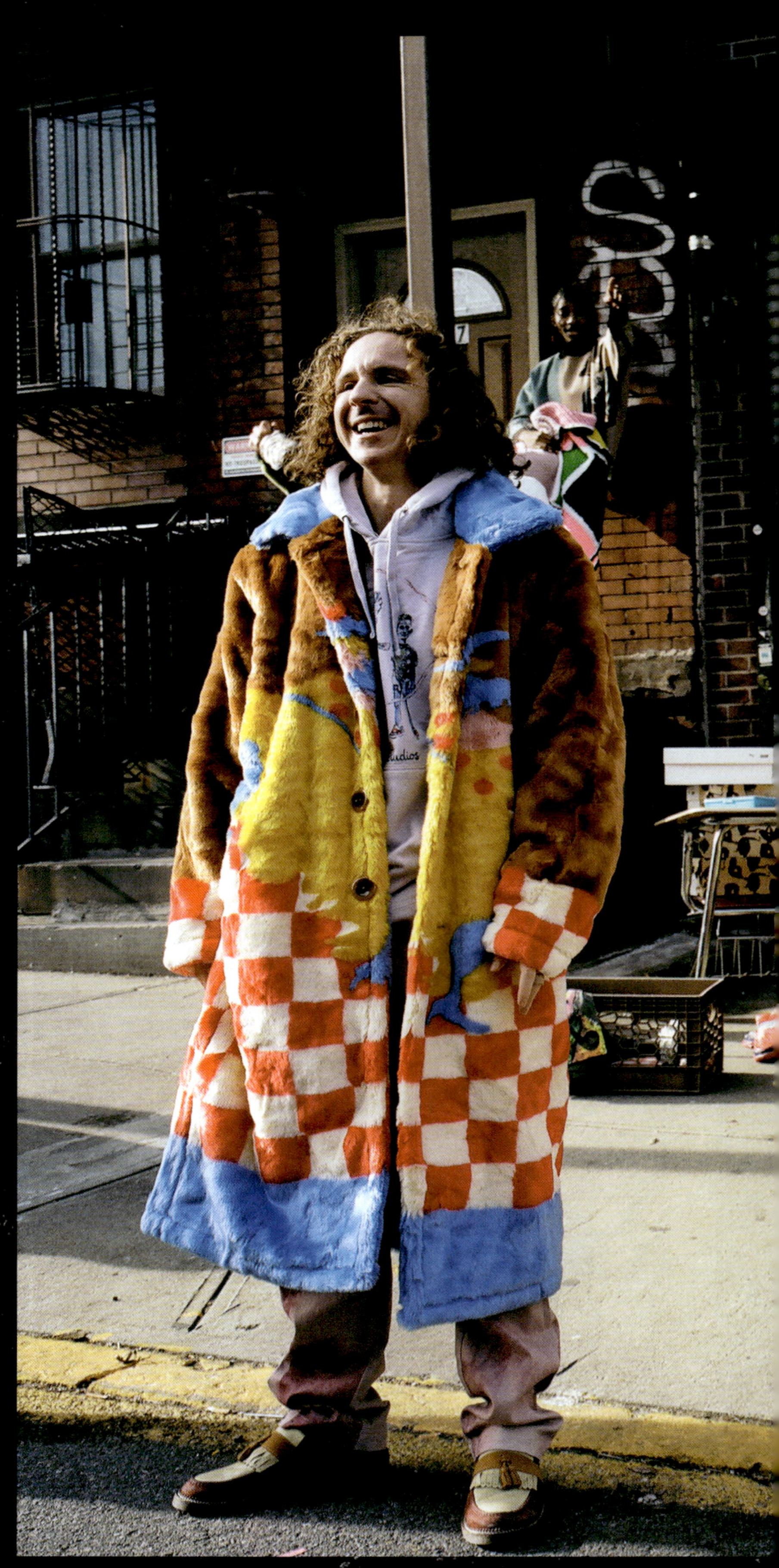

Go watch the pilot
on the internet!

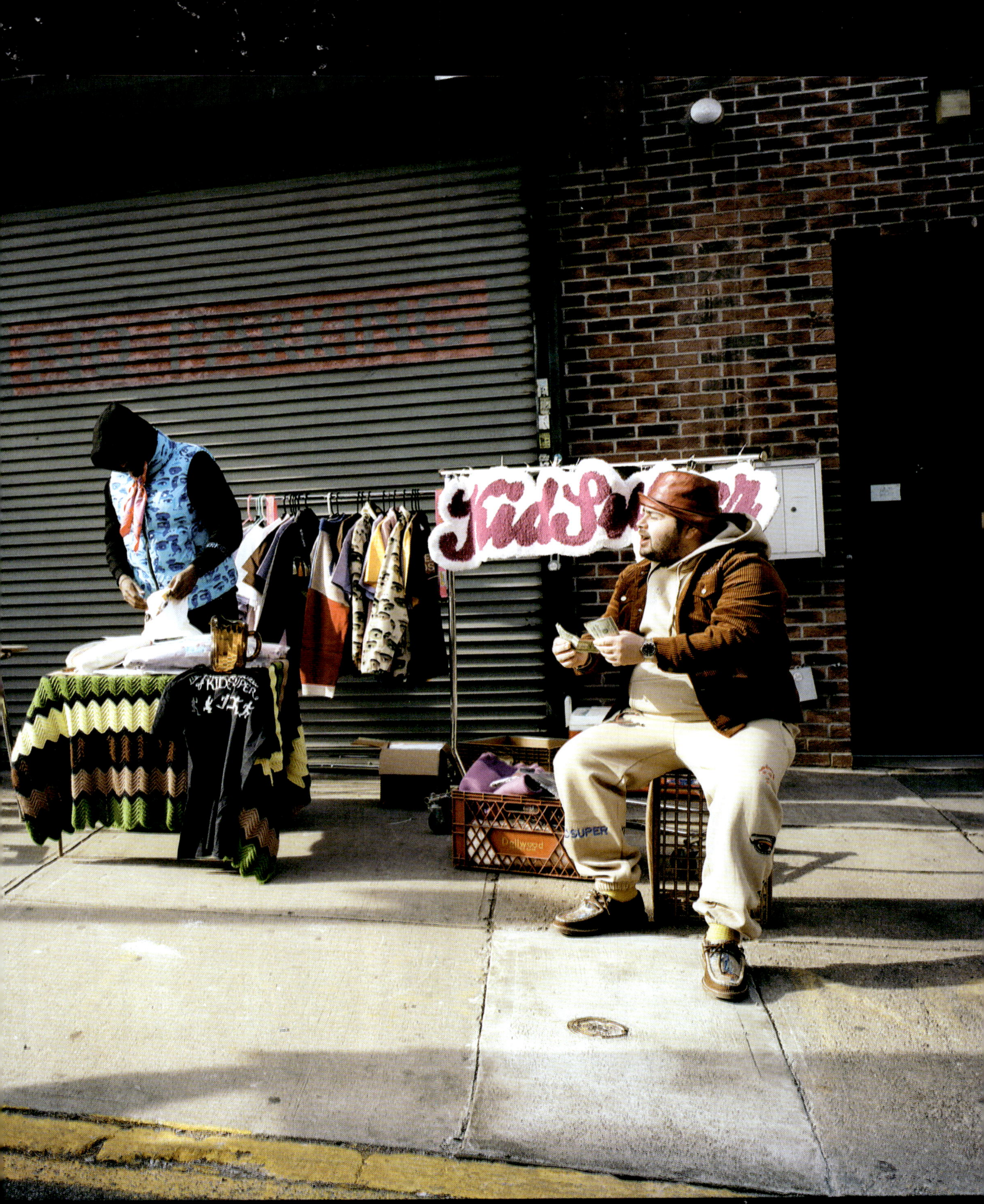
KIDSUPER
SUPER
Dellwood

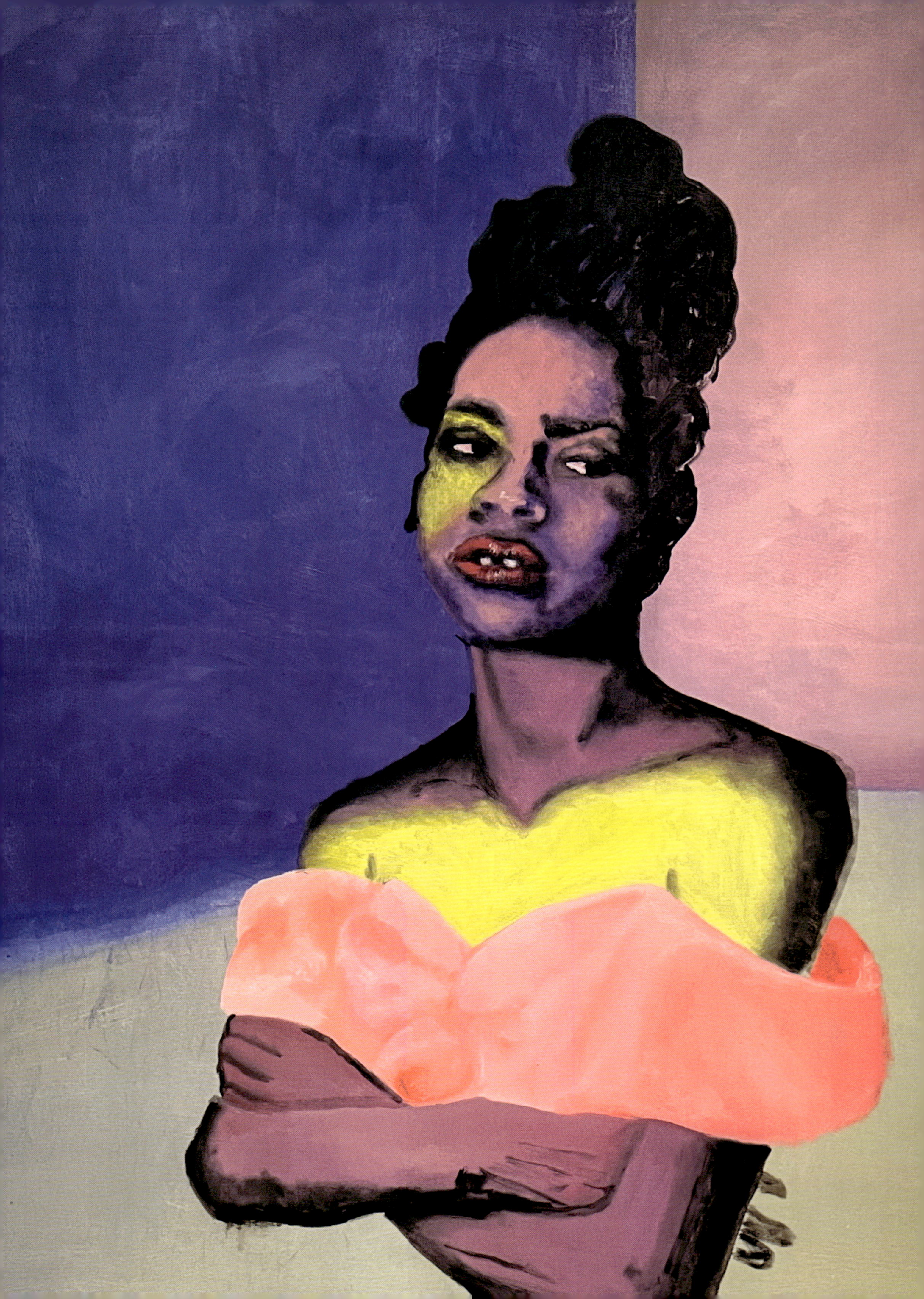

SUPERBY'S AUCTION HOUSE

Look at things
differently.

SS23

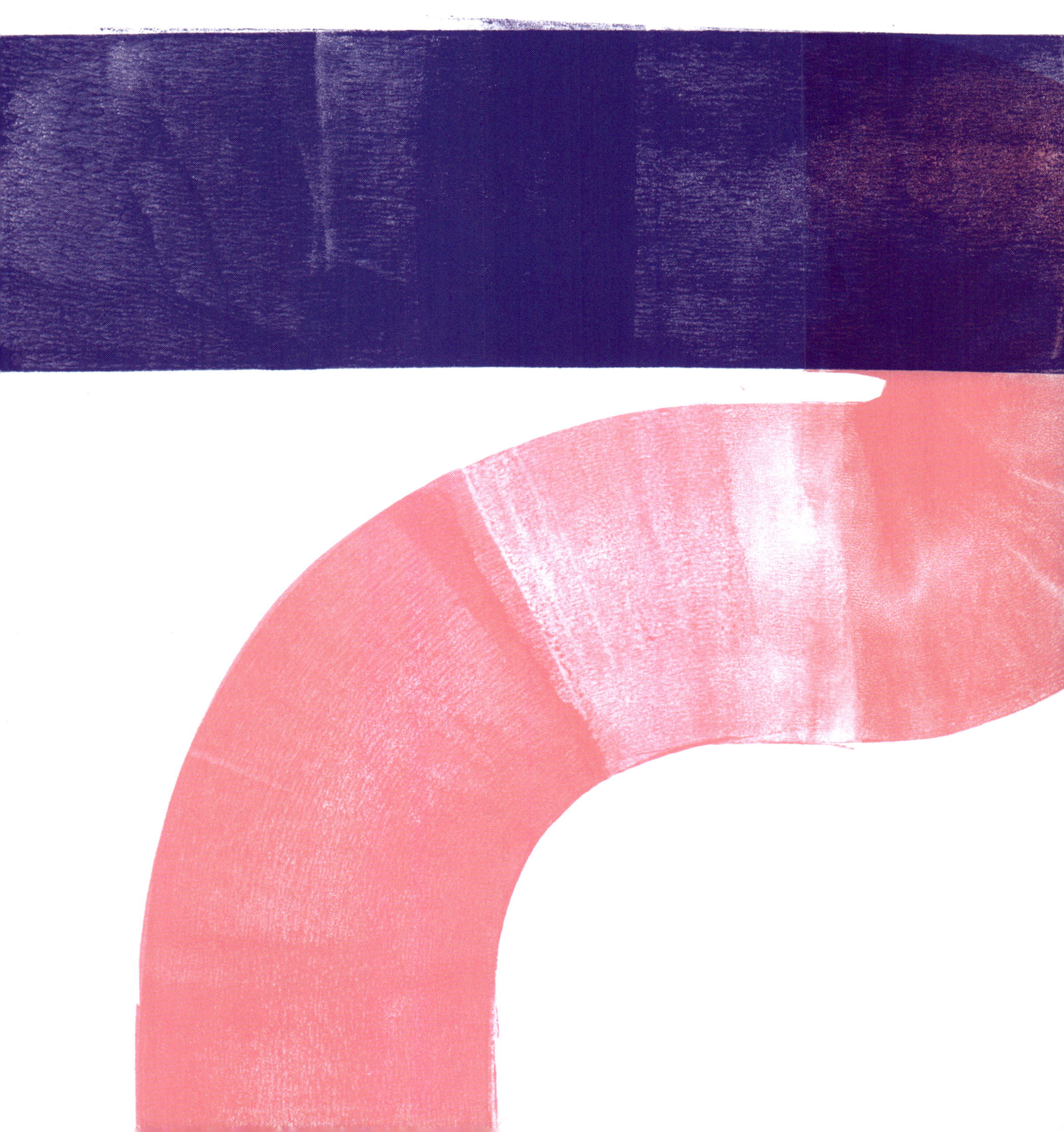

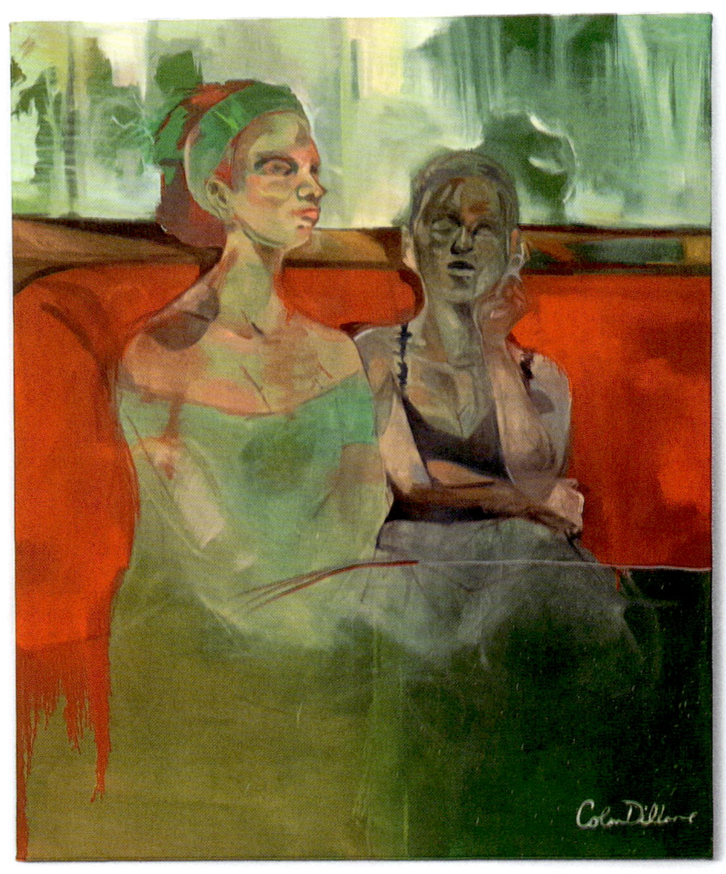

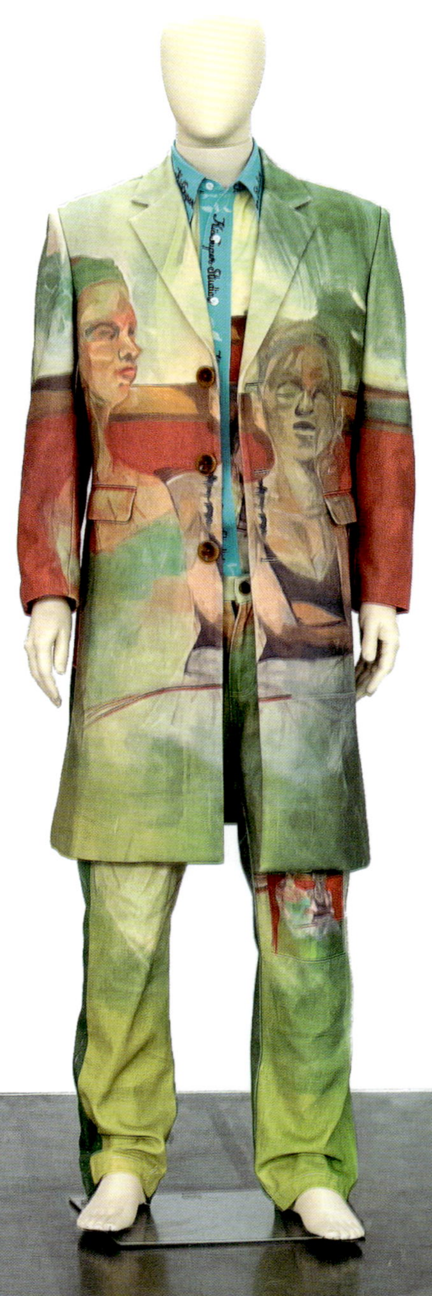

PARIS FASHION WEEK was back in person for the first time in two years. In that time, I'd gone from being rejected twice and completely off the calendar—an outsider—to on the official calendar and LVMH prize winner and someone everyone was watching, curious if I could live up to the hype I'd built during the virtual fashion weeks. Yet despite the newfound attention, I still felt like an outsider. I wasn't conventionally trained, had no insider connections, and was always fighting to prove I deserved my spot. I needed to show off my talents.

One of my talents was painting. From the start, KidSuper's identity—the embroideries, tags, graphics—had come straight from my hand. Fashion was full of imitation, and I stressed originality. I thought if I used my own art, something that came from my hand, good or bad, it would be original. So as I brainstormed how to merge my art with my fashion show, the idea hit me: twenty-four paintings and twenty-four looks, each painting inspiring a unique look. I still had never gone to a fashion show that wasn't mine—not because I didn't want to but because I had never been invited. As a kid I would go to galleries and museums, and I always would get yelled at for touching the art. I did not really understand the idea of not being able to interact with the work. When I saw something beautiful, my initial reaction would be to create, touch, participate. I think this has become a theme of KidSuper: getting the audience to participate in my work. Allowing anyone and everyone into my world. So I thought about how I could have the audience take part in this show.

That's when the auction concept was born. Each painting would come down the runway with its corresponding outfit, and the audience could bid in real time—without knowing it was an auction beforehand. All they knew was that the invitations were simple paddles with numbers on them. No explanation. Just intrigue.

I reached out to Lydia Fenet, then Christie's top auctioneer, and pitched the idea. She loved it. But executing it was another story. Not only did I have to design twenty-four looks and paint twenty-four canvases, but I also had to figure out how to get the massive paintings from New York to Paris without breaking the bank. The solution? We rolled them up, stuffed them into ski bags, and flew them over as oversized luggage. It actually worked.

A painting and the corresponding look

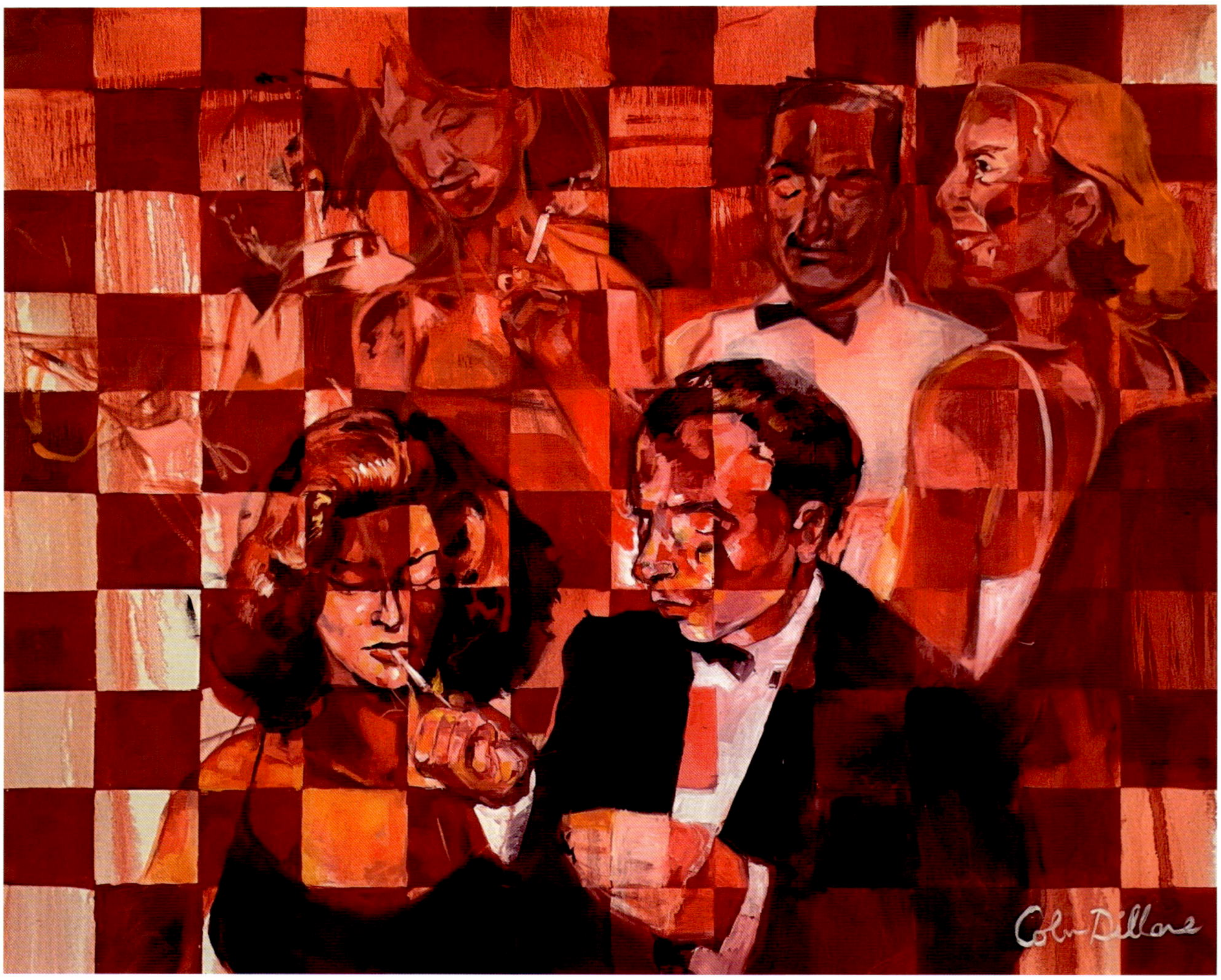

Showtime arrived. The venue was set up like a gallery, paintings surrounding the runway. Lydia stepped up and confidently announced, "Welcome to Superby's! Our first bid starts at $7,000."

Silence. Then laughter. No one moved. From backstage, my heart sank. I'd made a huge mistake not explaining the concept. The crowd thought it was all a gimmick.

But Lydia, ever the pro, didn't flinch. "Do I hear $1,000? Two?" she called out, pointing at nonexistent bids in the crowd. Slowly, the confusion lifted. People glanced at their paddles, realized they were part of the show, and started bidding—timidly at first, then with competitive energy.

By the end, the final painting bid for $210,000. I stood there, speechless. We sold every painting. After the show, I went up to the buyers; half the buyers laughed, thinking it had all been performance art. The other half casually asked for wiring instructions. It was as real as they wanted it to be. I ended up making around $400,000. Insane.

It was more than just a fashion show—it was a social experiment, a perfect collision of art, fashion, and psychology. And in the crowd, watching it all unfold, was an LVMH executive. Foreshadowing, as it turned out, what was to come.

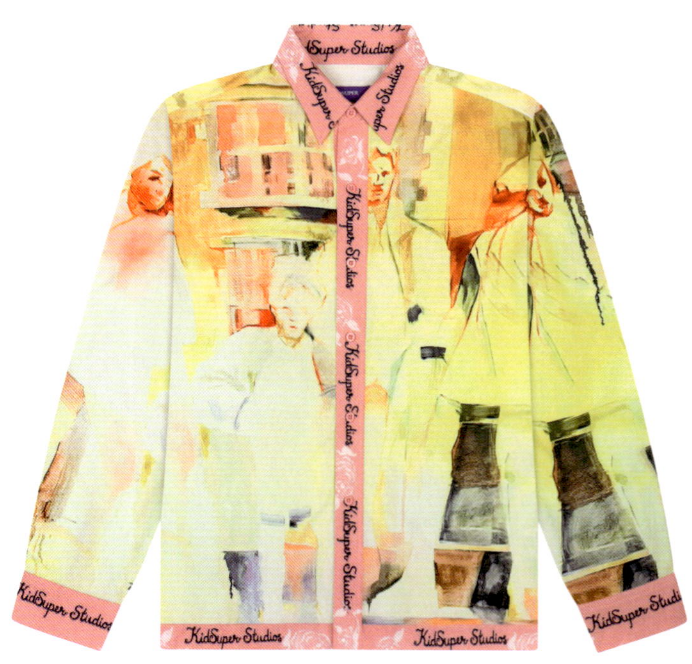

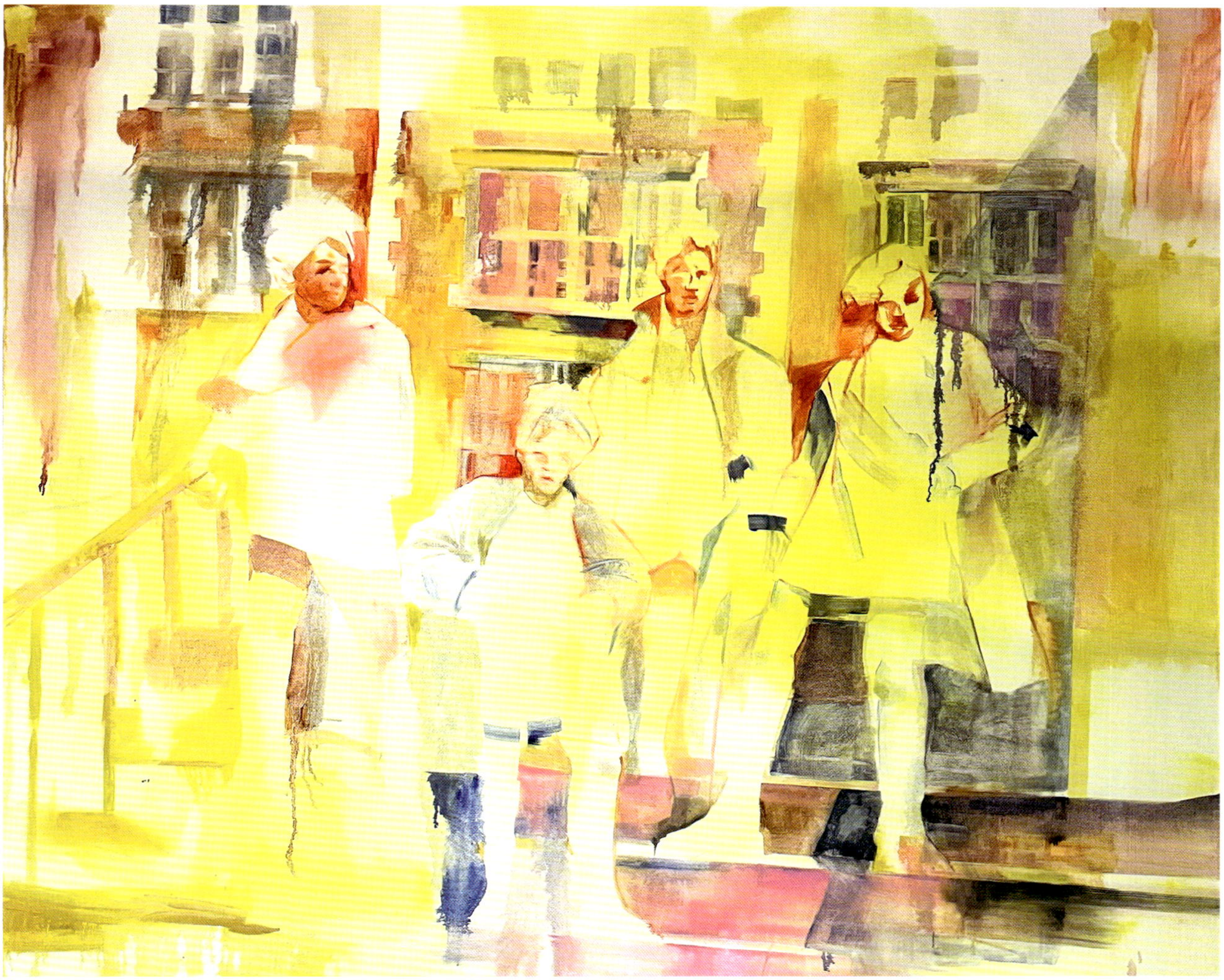

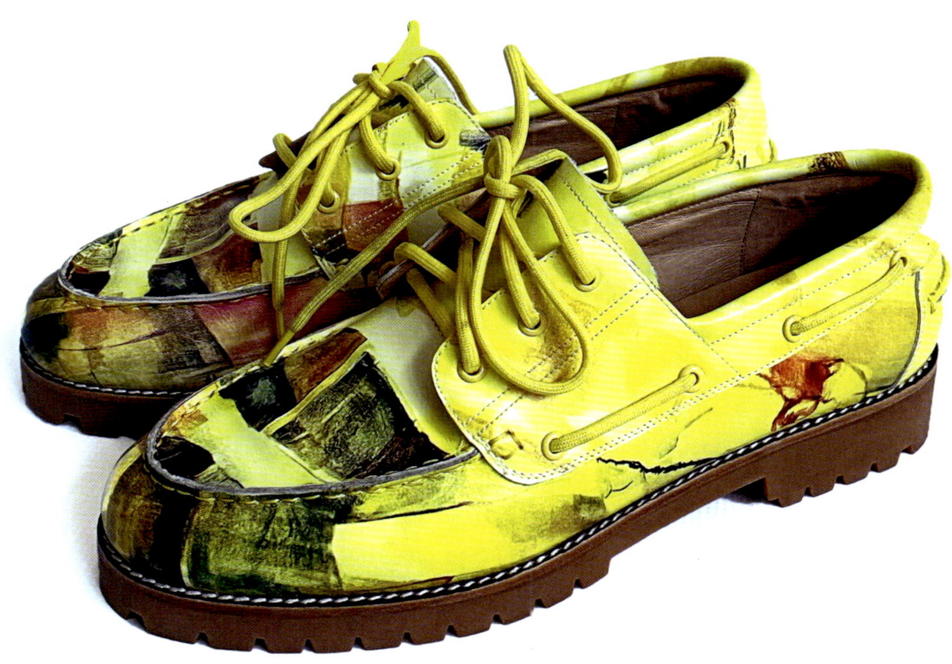

How the painting
is adapted to the
clothing items

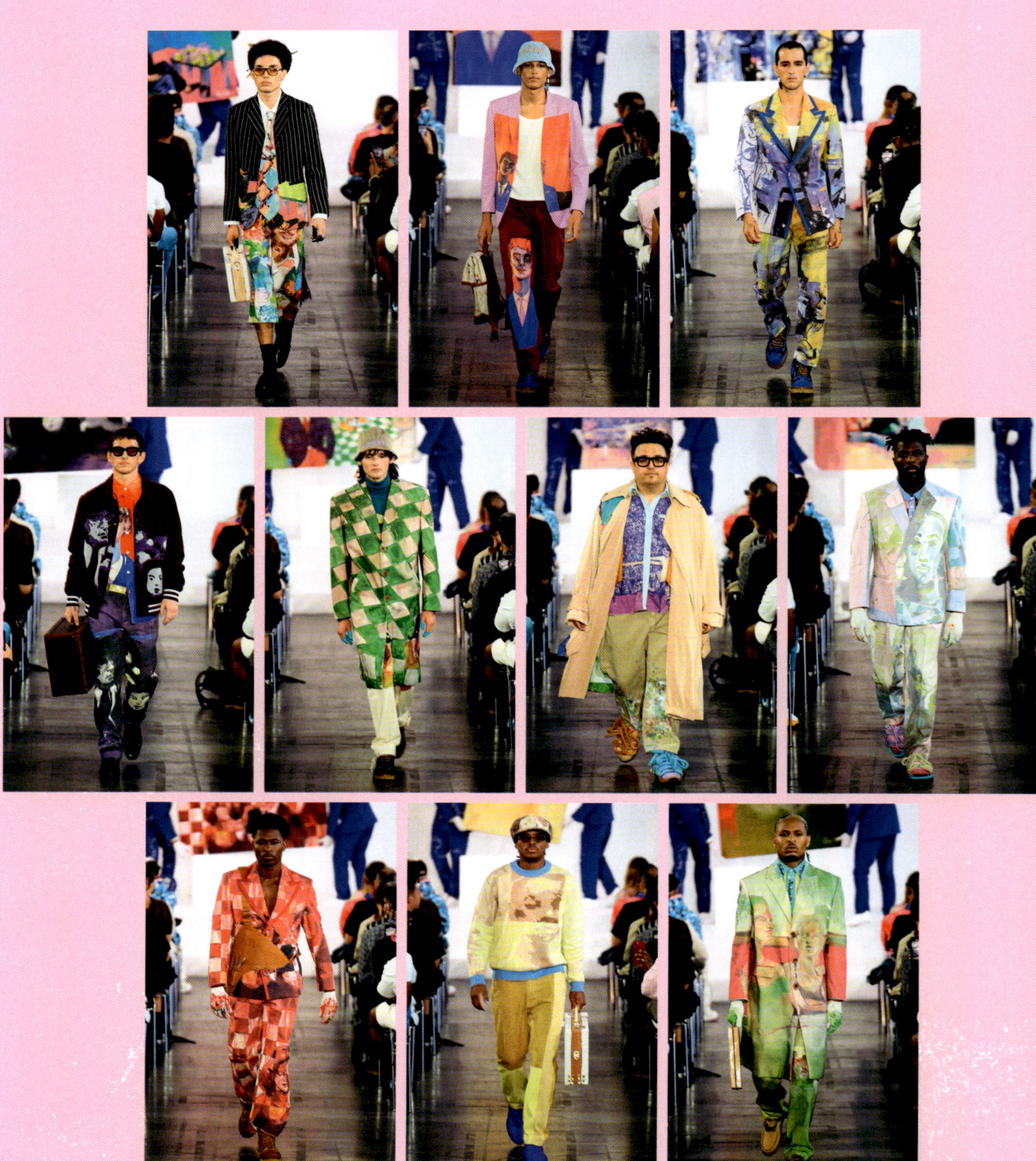

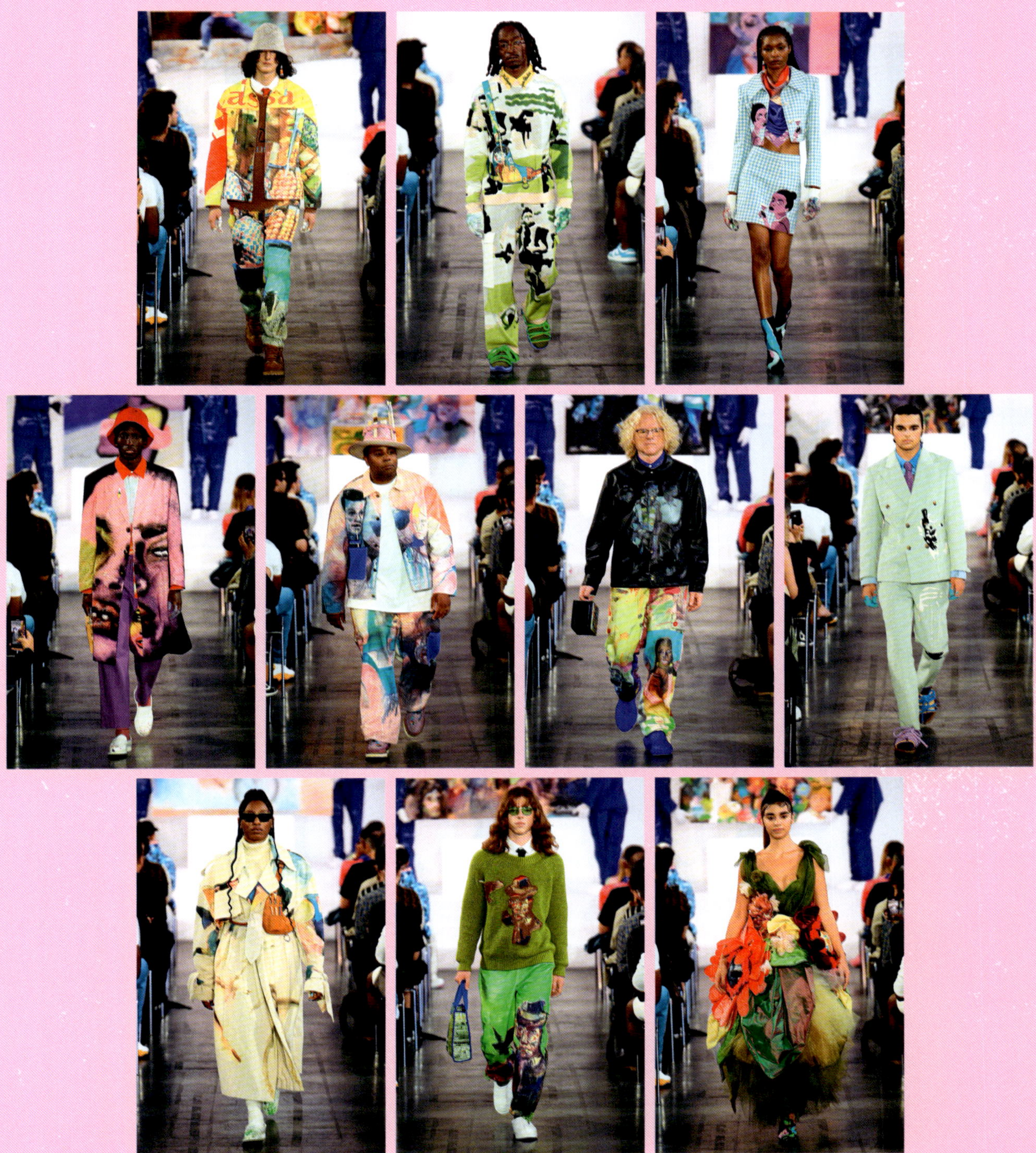

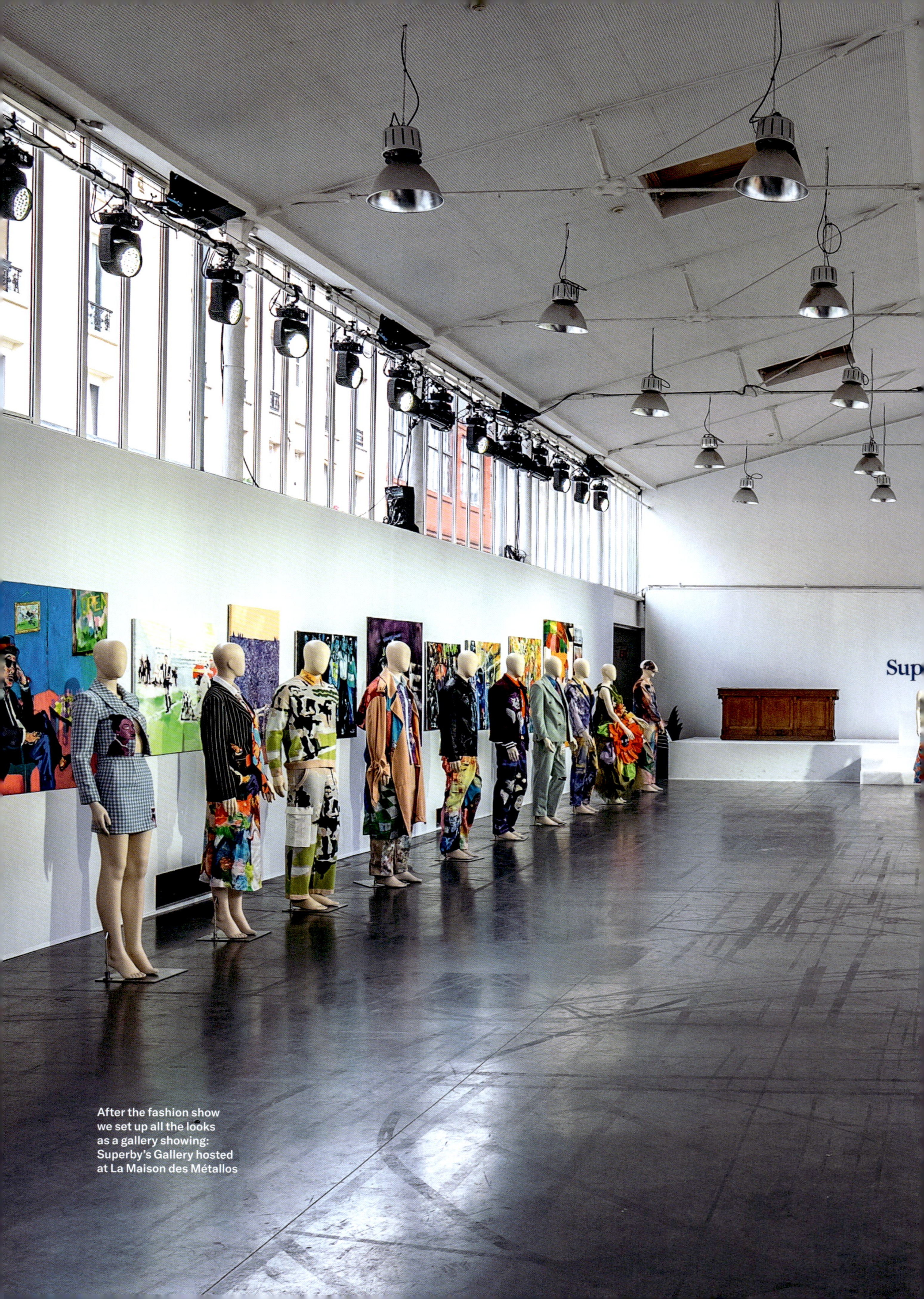

After the fashion show we set up all the looks as a gallery showing: Superby's Gallery hosted at La Maison des Métallos

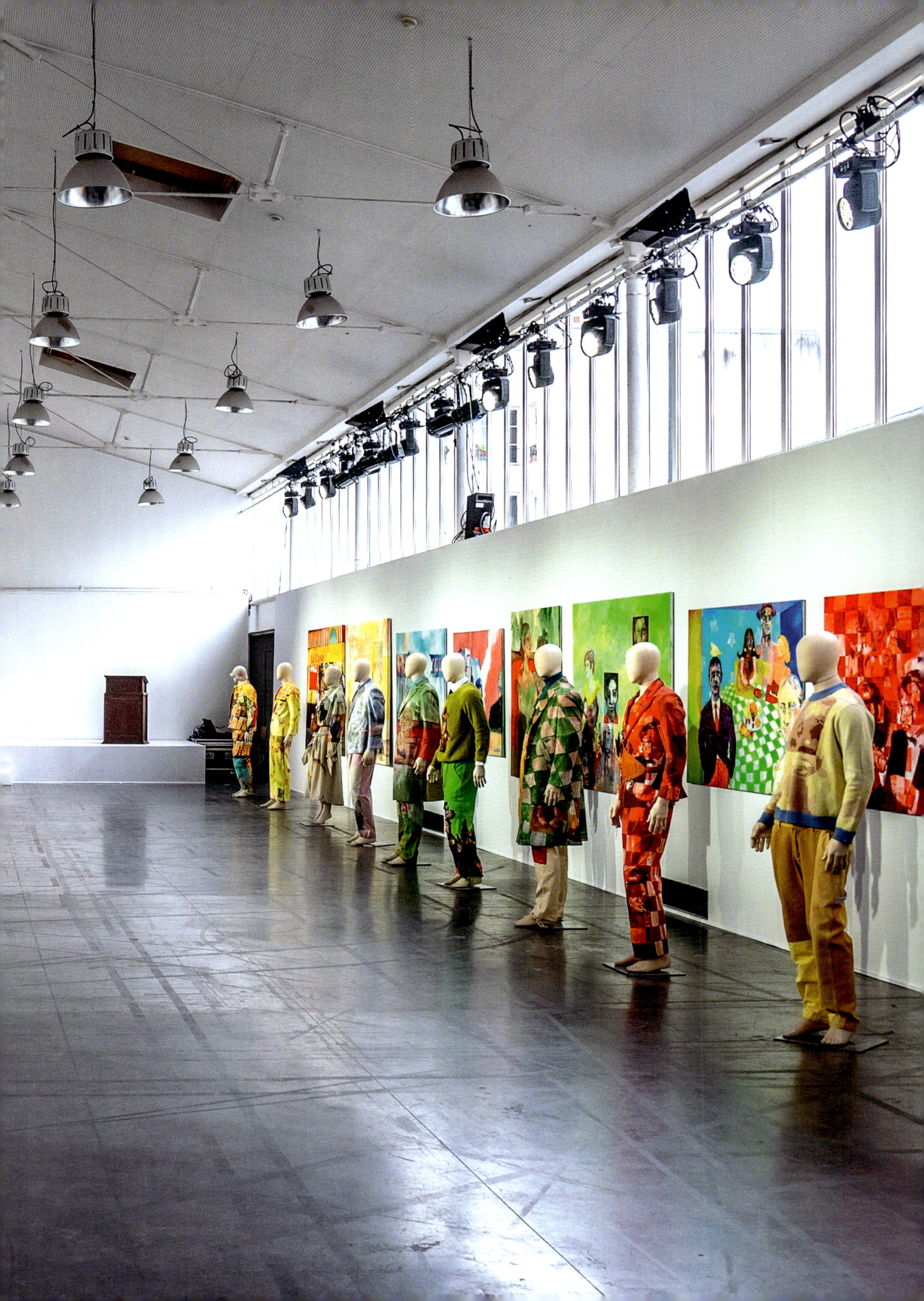

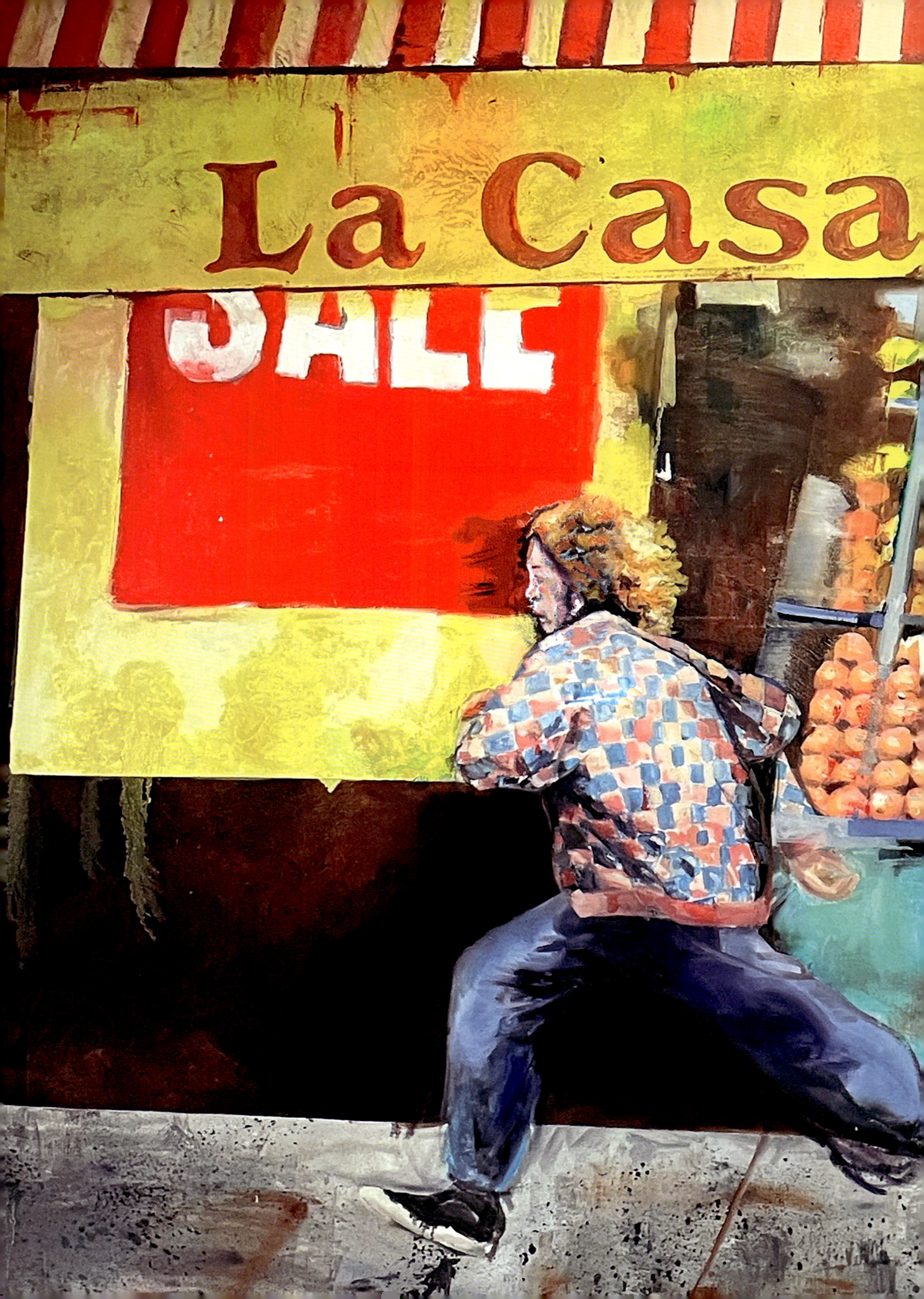
La Casa

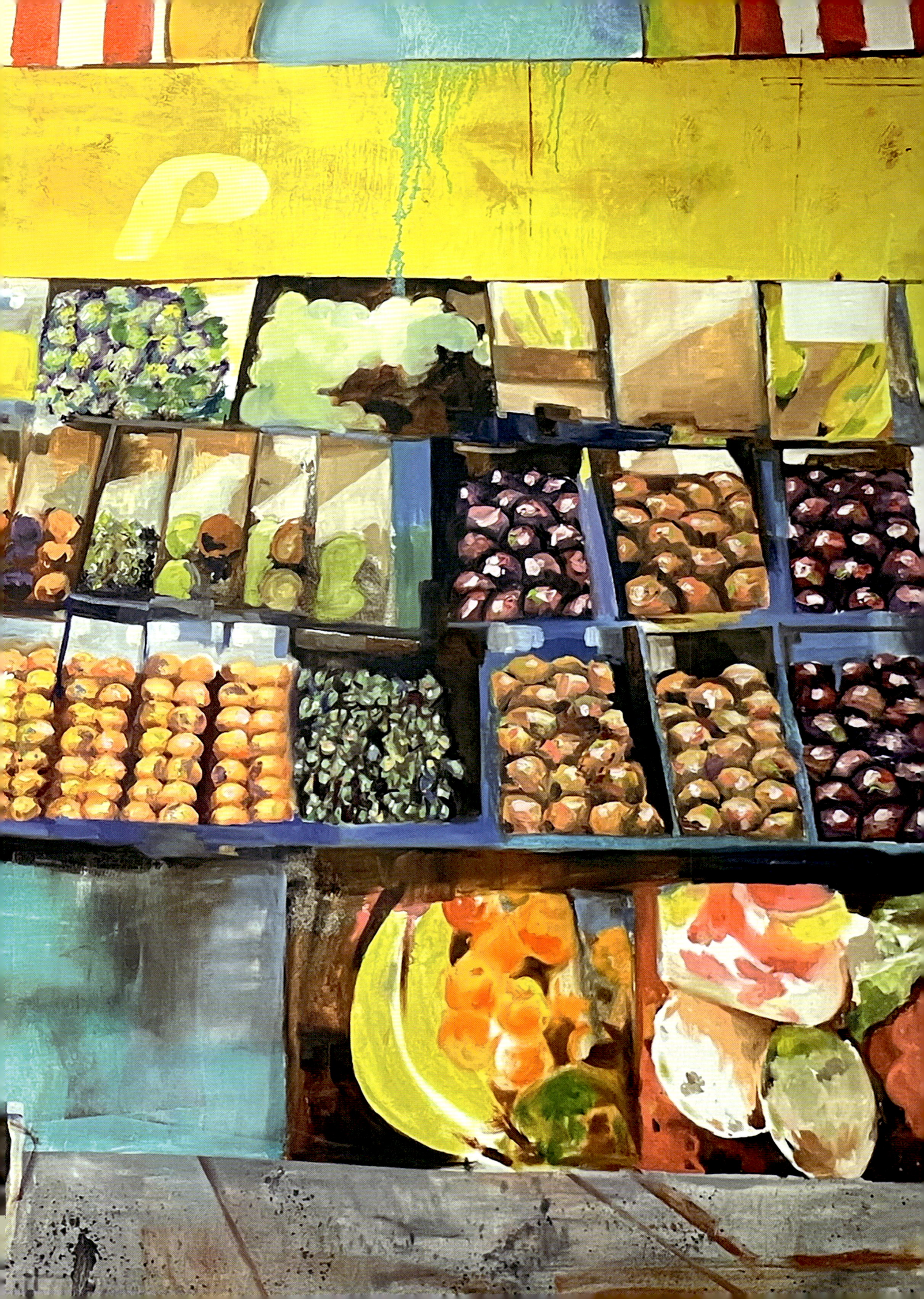

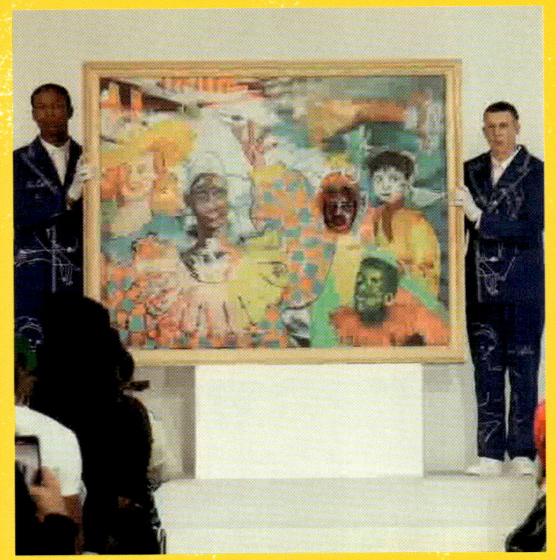

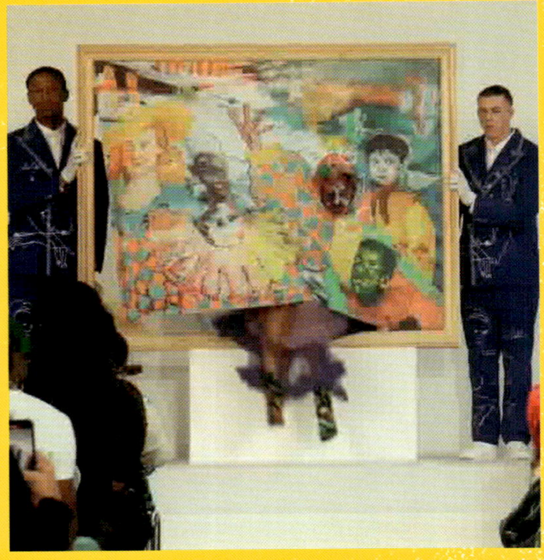

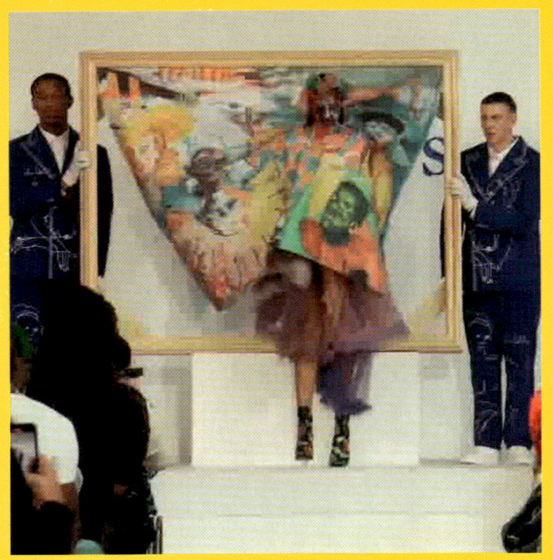

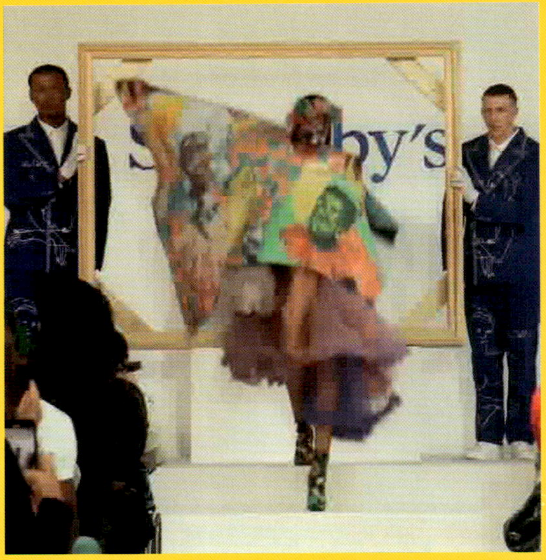

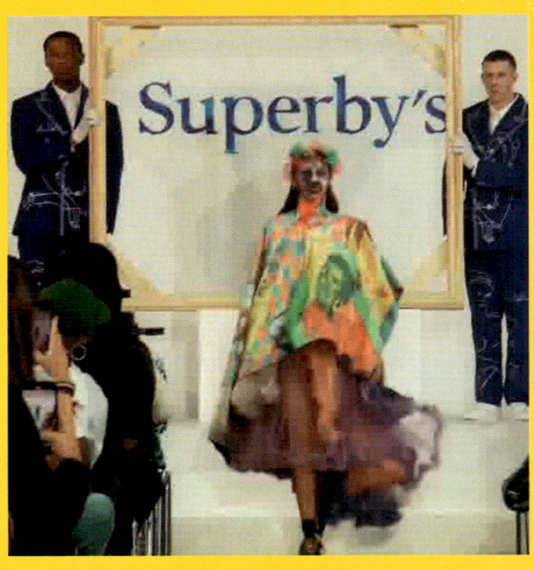

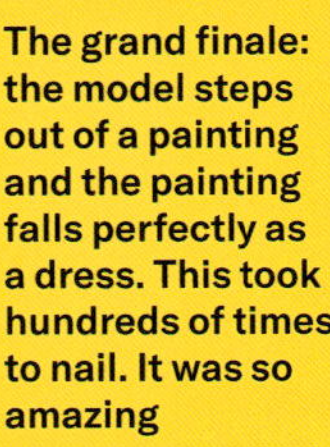

The grand finale: the model steps out of a painting and the painting falls perfectly as a dress. This took hundreds of times to nail. It was so amazing

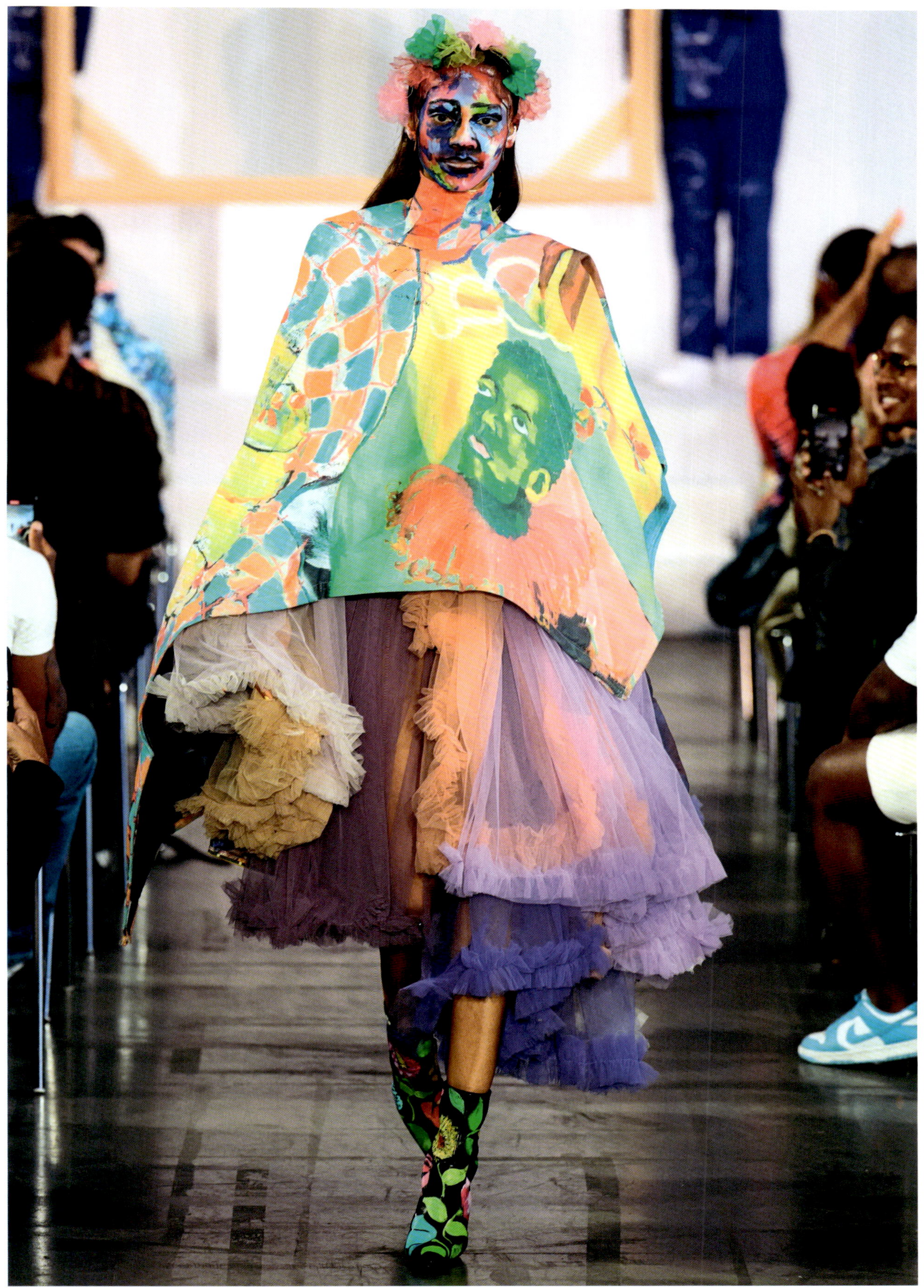

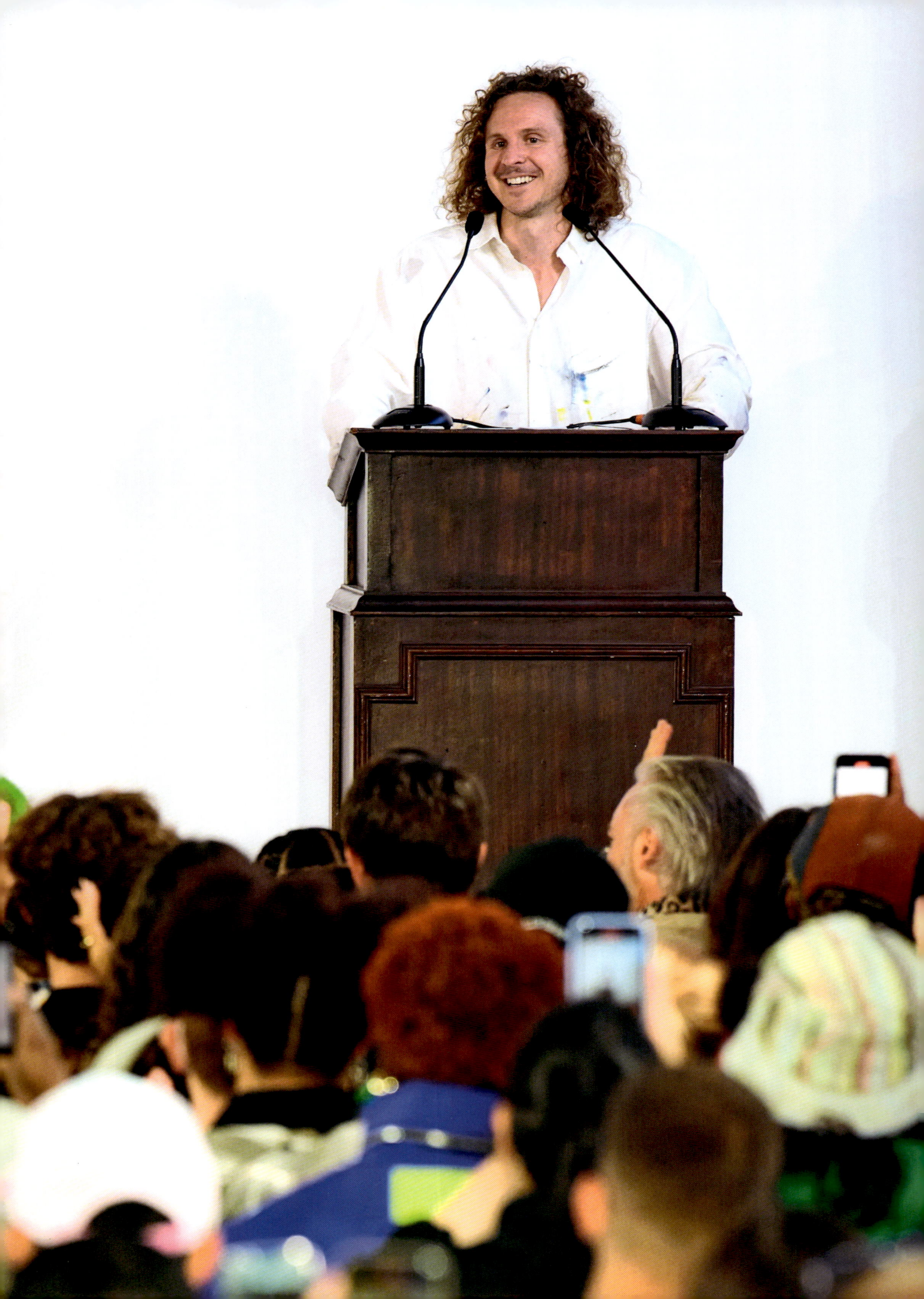

Back to delivering speeches

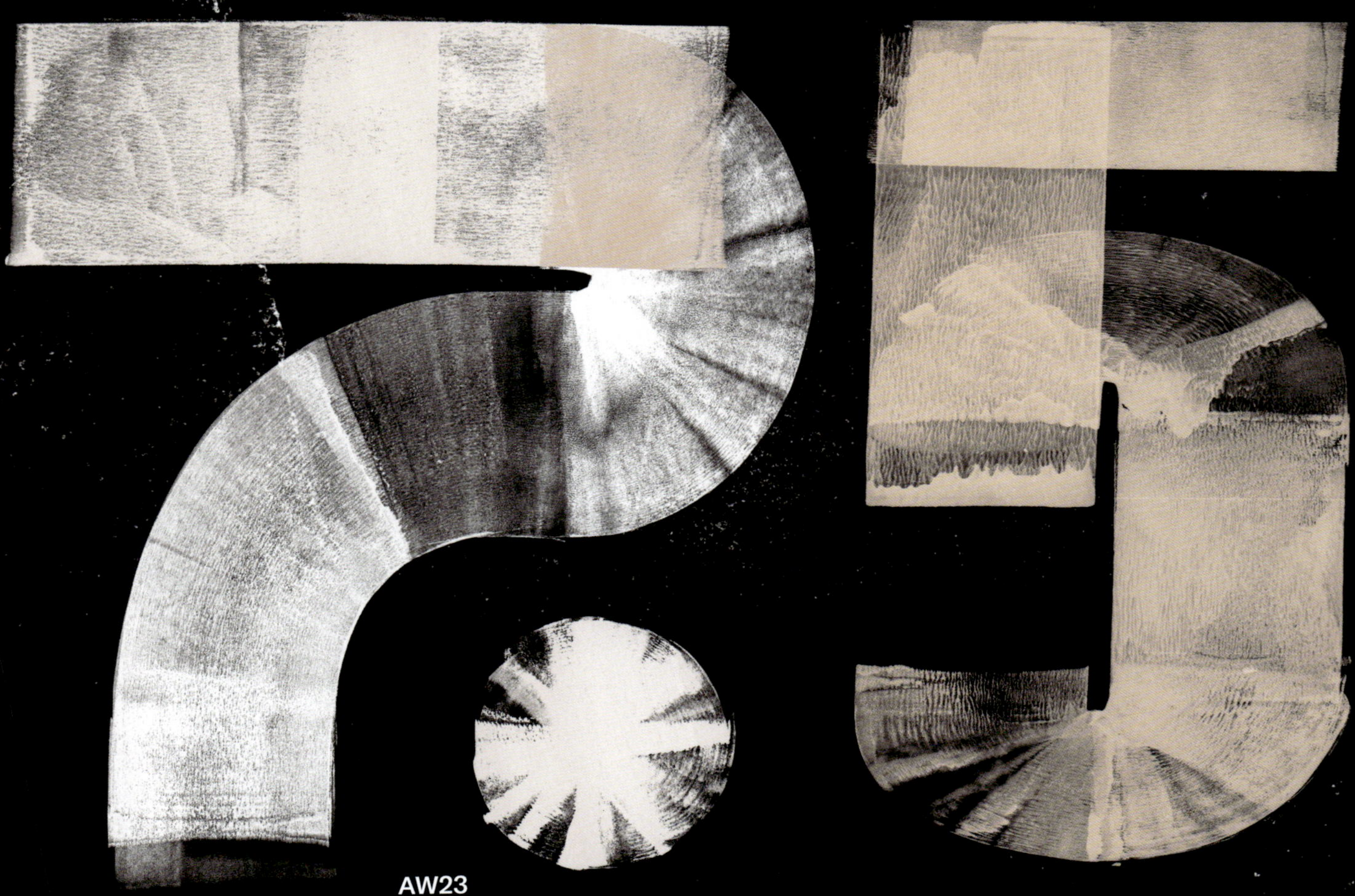

AW23

LOUIS VUITTON: GROWING UP

Be prepared.

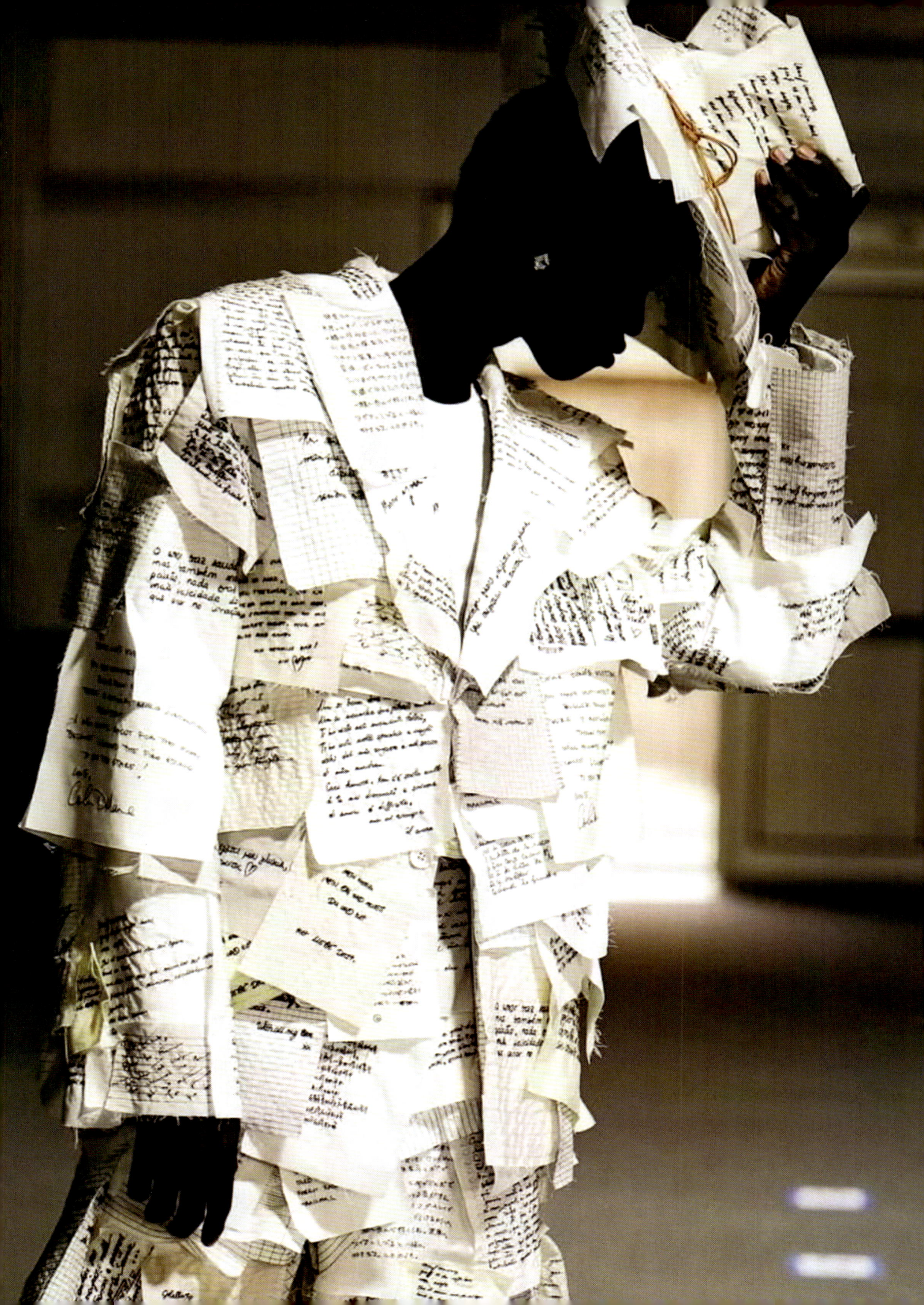

Dear Louis Vuitton,

You have motivated me to dream bigger than ever.

There is nothing more substantial than that.

I will always shoot for the moon because I climbed the fire escape to see the stars!

Love,

Colman Domingo

I GUESS THIS WAS the show heard around the world. It was my first big break—the kind that shifts everything. There was a lot of skepticism about how I even got the job, how it happened, and whether I was the right choice. And honestly, I don't know if I'm supposed to reveal the exact details, but to keep a long story short, I was interviewed and had to pitch—three different times—to different people within Louis Vuitton.

When I first got the call to pitch, I was completely shocked. I couldn't believe it. But I also remember telling the interviewers that Louis Vuitton was so smart to even consider me. Not to sound arrogant, but I didn't fit the typical mold. I wasn't classically trained. I wasn't incredibly famous. I wasn't driving insane sales numbers. But I had won the LVMH prize, and I had something arguably more valuable: original ideas and an unconventional approach to fashion. The fact that they were willing to take a risk on pure creativity over prestige or tradition made me respect them even more.

After the initial call they gave me two weeks to come up with the pitch. I called every friend or person I knew that could help and for two weeks I did not sleep. I set up a room with white boards on every wall and in true *Good Will Hunting* style scribbled every idea I had. I wanted to be beyond prepared. I didn't just show up with sketches—I went all in. I along with a rag tag group of friends created a 500-page book, shot three commercials, redesigned their website, 3D-printed shoes, made baseball cards of the C-suite executives, and made new bags from Chinatown fake bags. I didn't

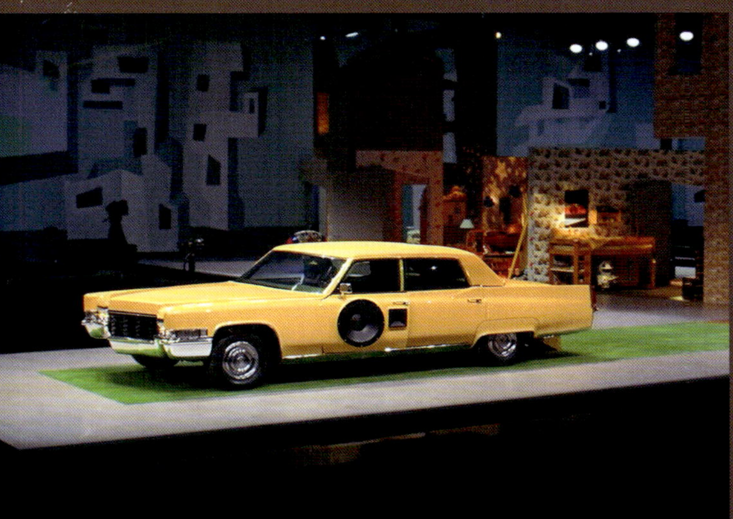

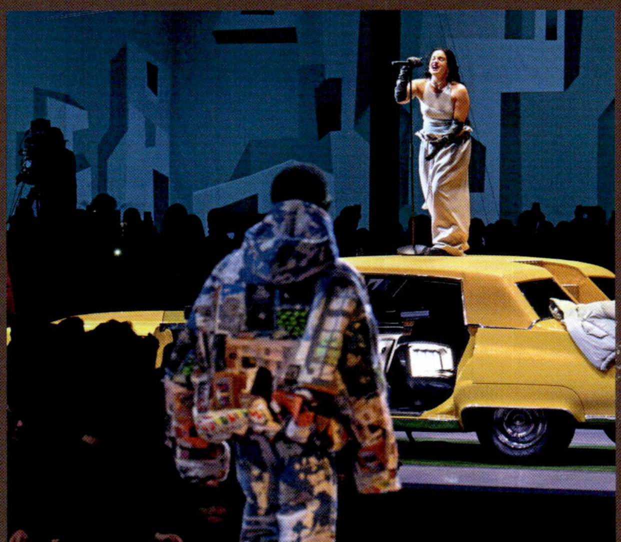

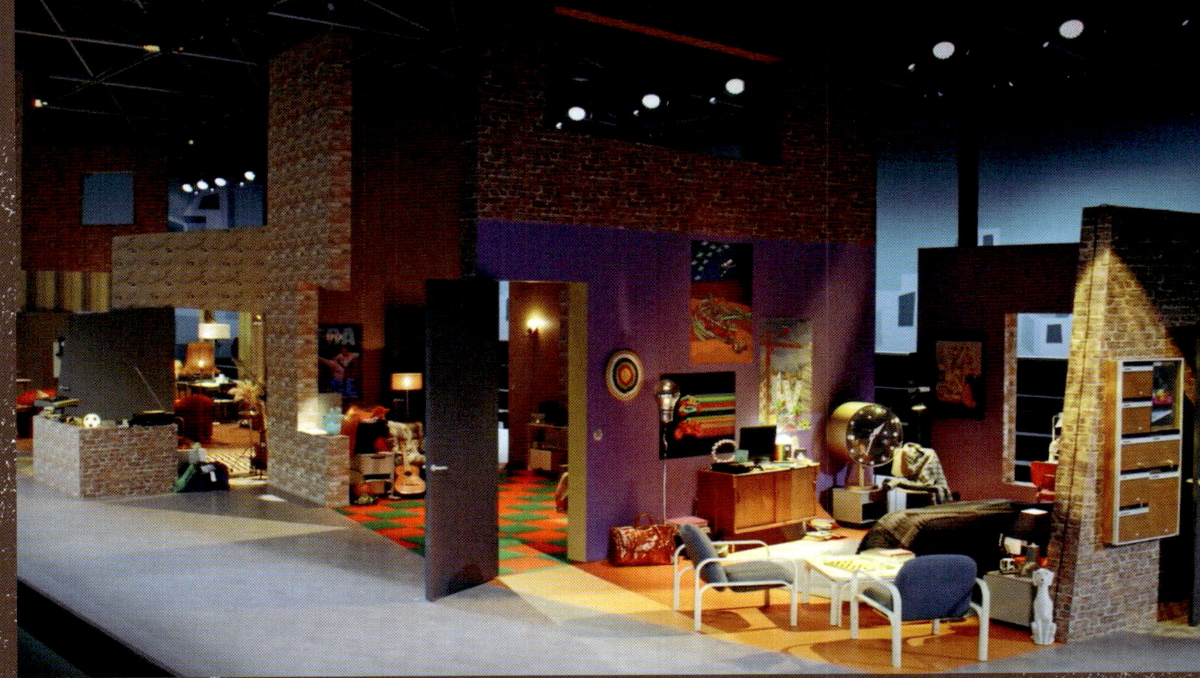

Rosalía and the runway set, reimagining a child bedroom through the eyes of Micheal Gondry

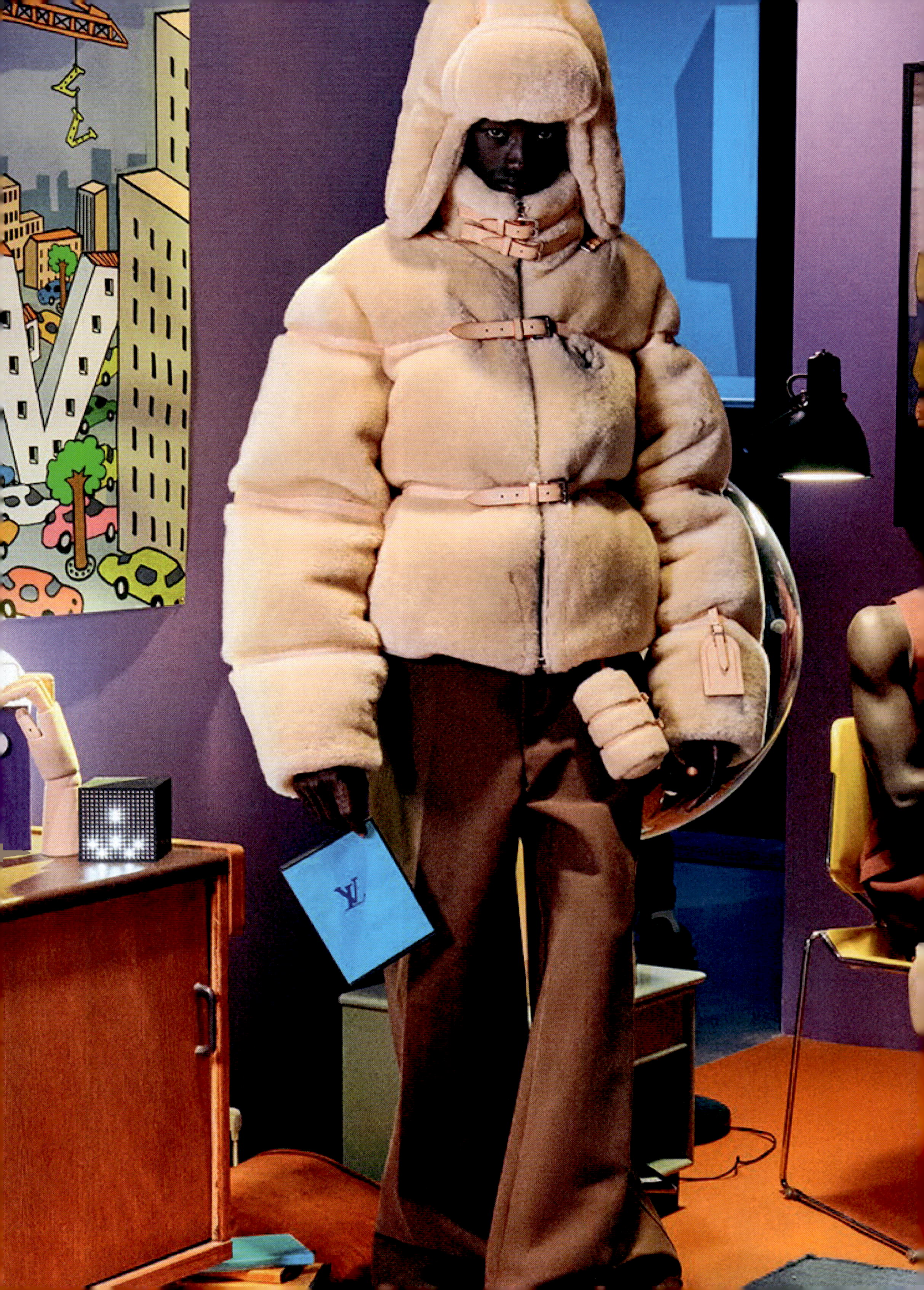
LV

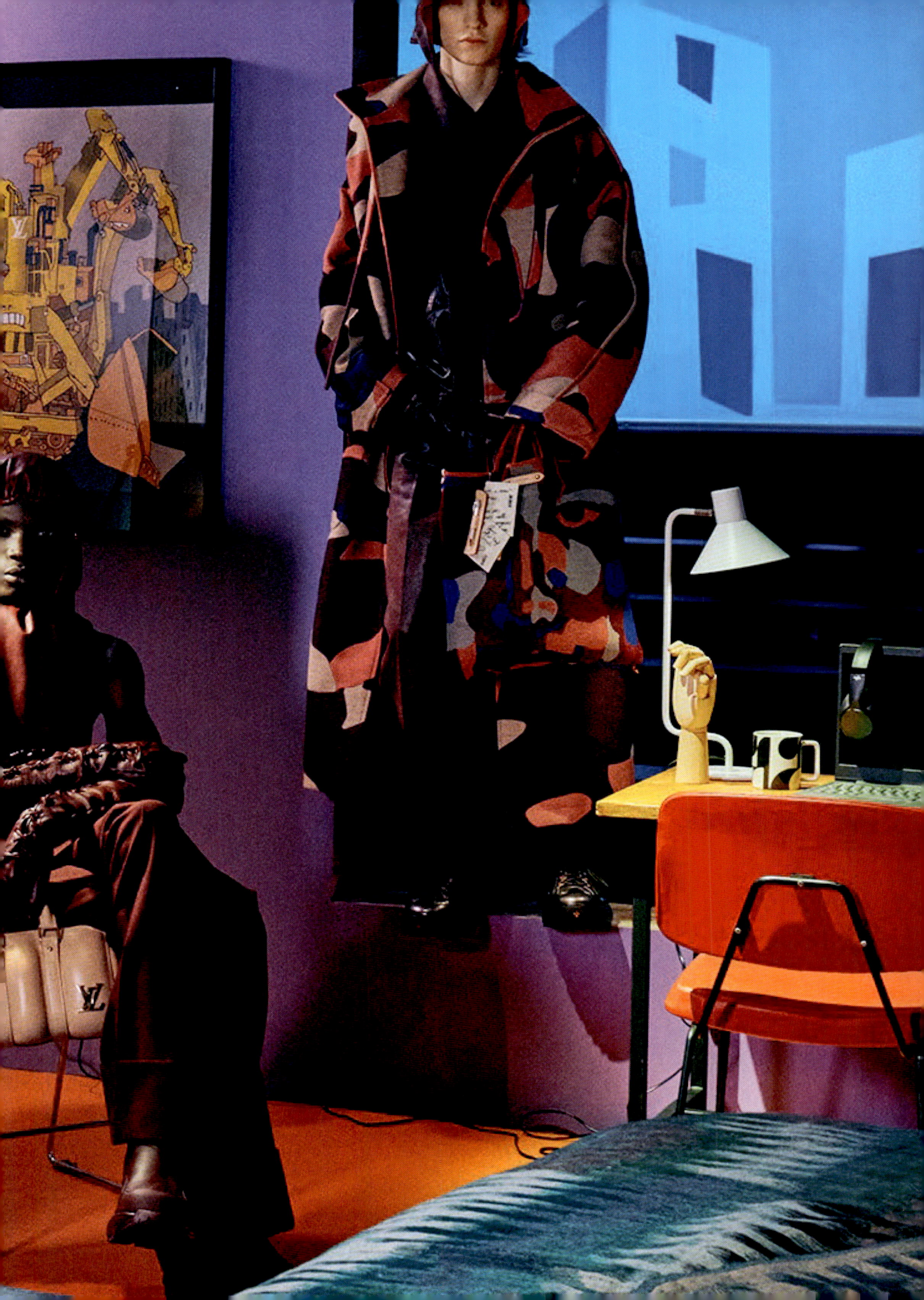

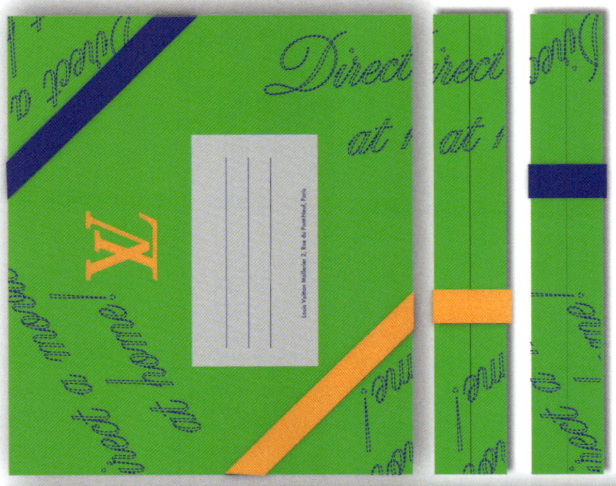

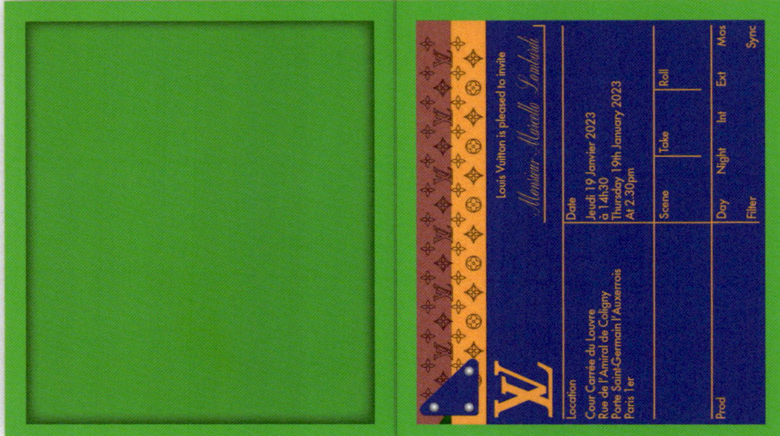

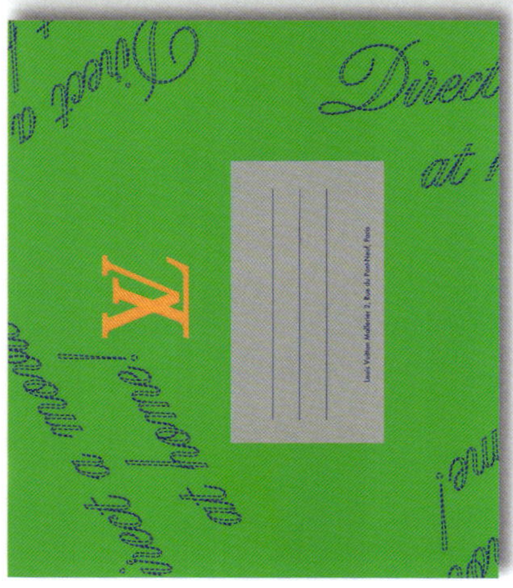

This was the invitation that was sent out the day of the show. It is in the shape of a film clapboard. Foreshadowing.

just want to present ideas; I wanted to prove I was the right choice. If you get an opportunity like this, you have to go big or go home, which should be the motto of this book.

So I went from a basement in Brooklyn to Louis Vuitton's headquarters in Paris (on a middle seat budget airline flight because I was too embarrassed to ask them to book my flight and I was afraid they would think I didn't have enough money to buy my own flight). I pitched my final pitch and after a couple more weeks/months of silence I got a call "we want you to creative direct the next collection, you start tomorrow."

My only two real fashion jobs: running KidSuper and designing for LV. Two worlds on completely opposite ends of the spectrum. And yet, somehow, they collided at this moment.

When I arrived at the studio, it was like walking into a new world; I had never experienced anything like it. But luckily any question, any design need, any last-minute decision that they asked about, I had an answer because I had done so much preparation for the pitch. Do you need some designs? Well I have 500 pages of designs. I would get to work as early as I could, and stay as late as possible, and absorb everything. I would then work all night designing the KidSuper collection. I was doing two jobs in two different time zones. I would leave the LV offices around 8 p.m. and then work from 9 p.m. to 3 a.m. on KidSuper, then wake up at 9 a.m. to go back to LV. I was a machine and I loved it. The LV team, members who had been part of the brand for years, were now coming to me with questions and ideas. It was surreal.

I wanted the collection to feel like me. I didn't know if this was a one-time thing, so I had to make sure that KidSuper's essence was there. I had to make sure that Colm had a touch. And I think I did that. This collection will be one of those moments people look back on in 10, 20 years as a turning point. If KidSuper's entire journey is about climbing to the top of the mountain, this was a flag at one of the highest base camps.

One of my favorite pieces from the collection was the "Letters" look. Louis Vuitton's history is rooted in travel—they were originally a luggage maker. So I thought: What do people do when they travel? They send letters home. That inspired a series of pieces centered on love letters.

To make it personal, I asked the LV staff—many of whom had come from different parts of the world—to write love letters to their families back home. I then embroidered those letters onto fabrics and turned them into boots, bags, and garments. There was something whimsical, almost magical, about it. The idea of carrying someone's heartfelt words, someone's story, as part of fashion—it made the designs feel alive.

And of course, I had to write my own letter. What I wrote couldn't be more true:

This collection wasn't just about fashion—it was about wonder. And that's what I try to create in everything I do.

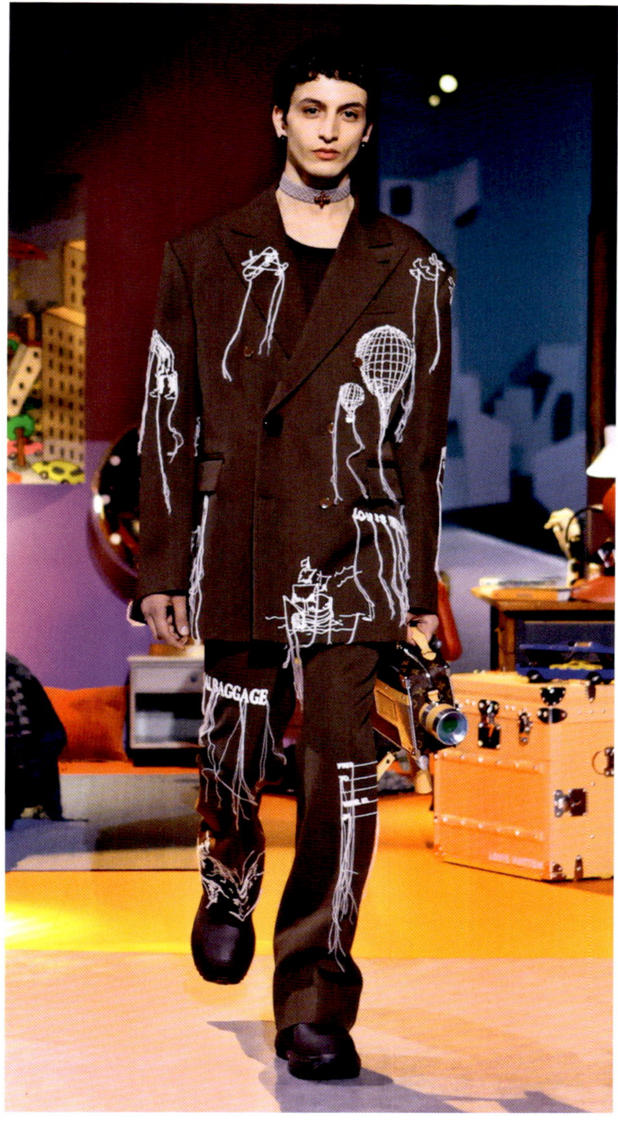

The Super 8 camera bag. We added a GoPro in the bag so it actually worked and filmed the runway set. I wanted to make an old camera as the invite to the show: you would open it up and it would have a video only available to those who received the camera. It wasn't possible in time... but one day!

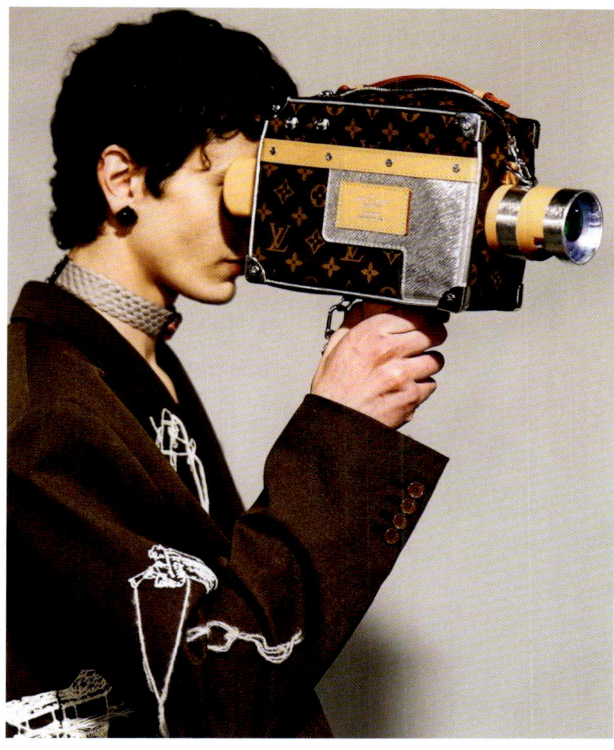

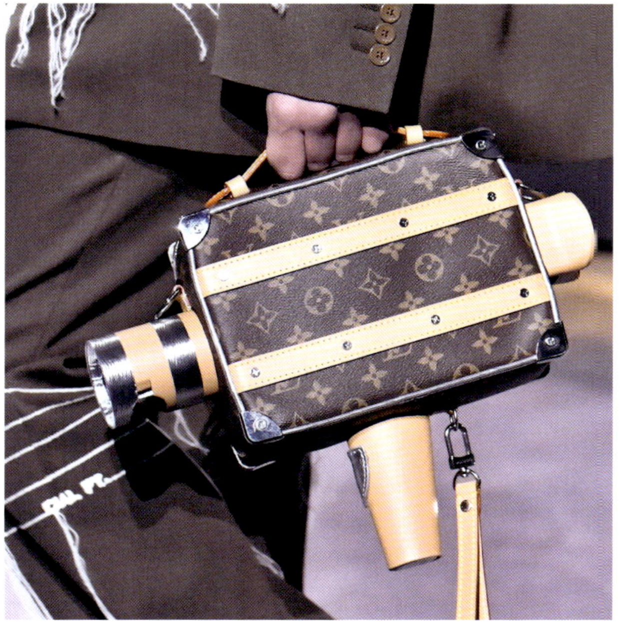

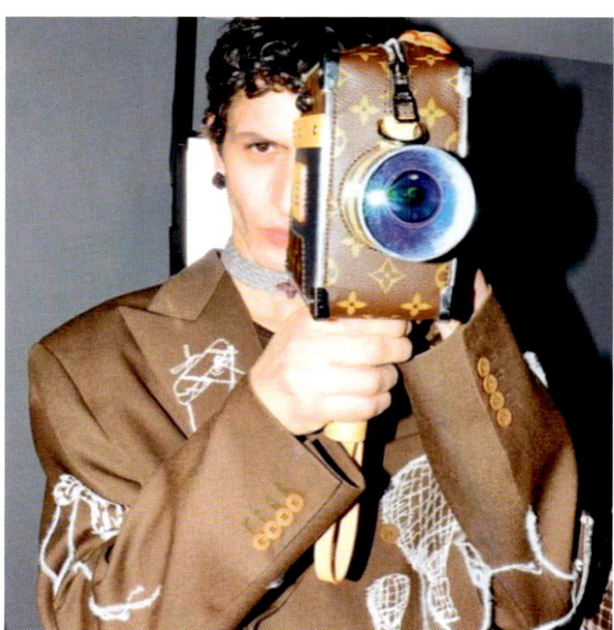

KidSuper Face Camo interpolated LV Monogram Print. I think some of the most iconic LV luggage of all time.

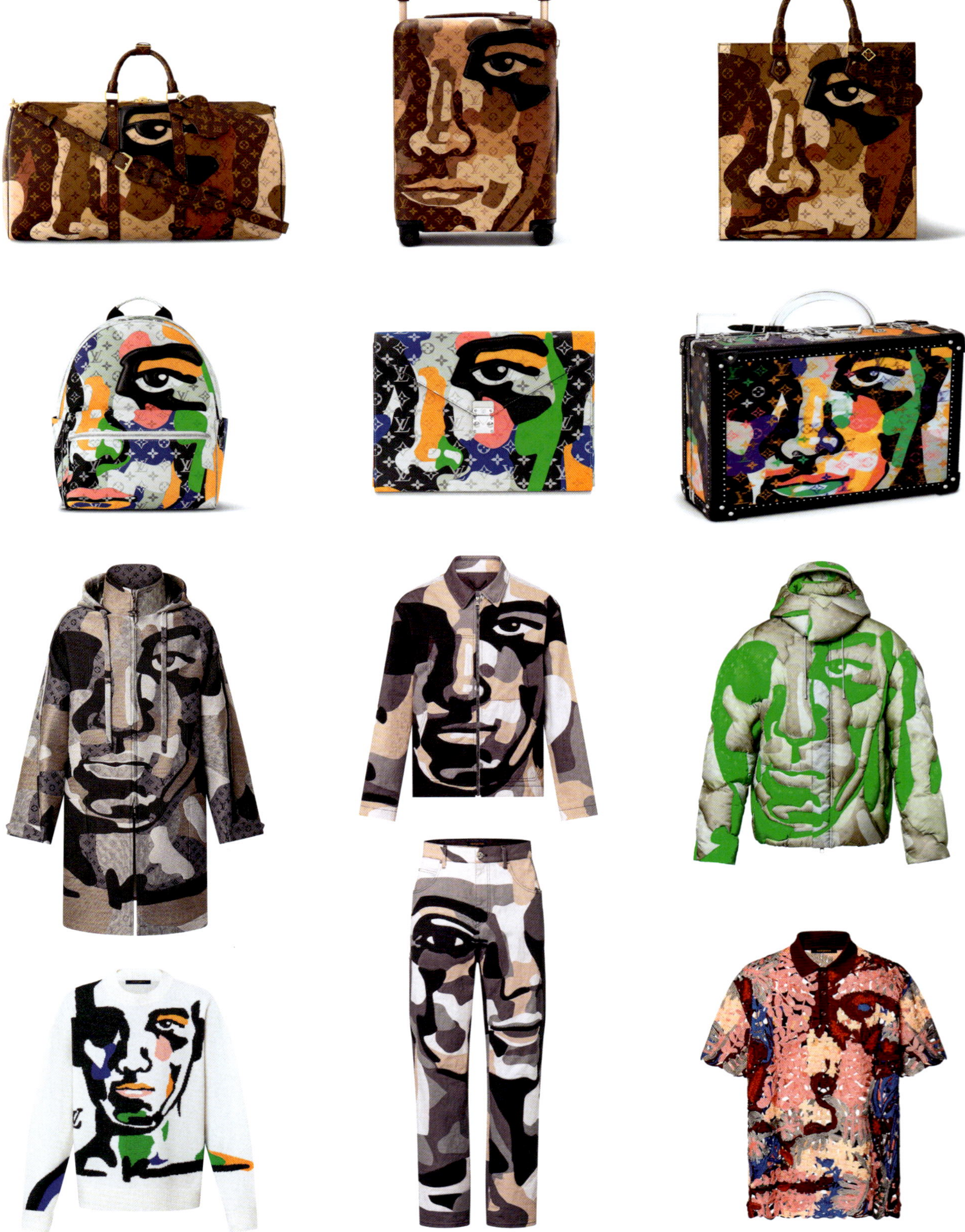

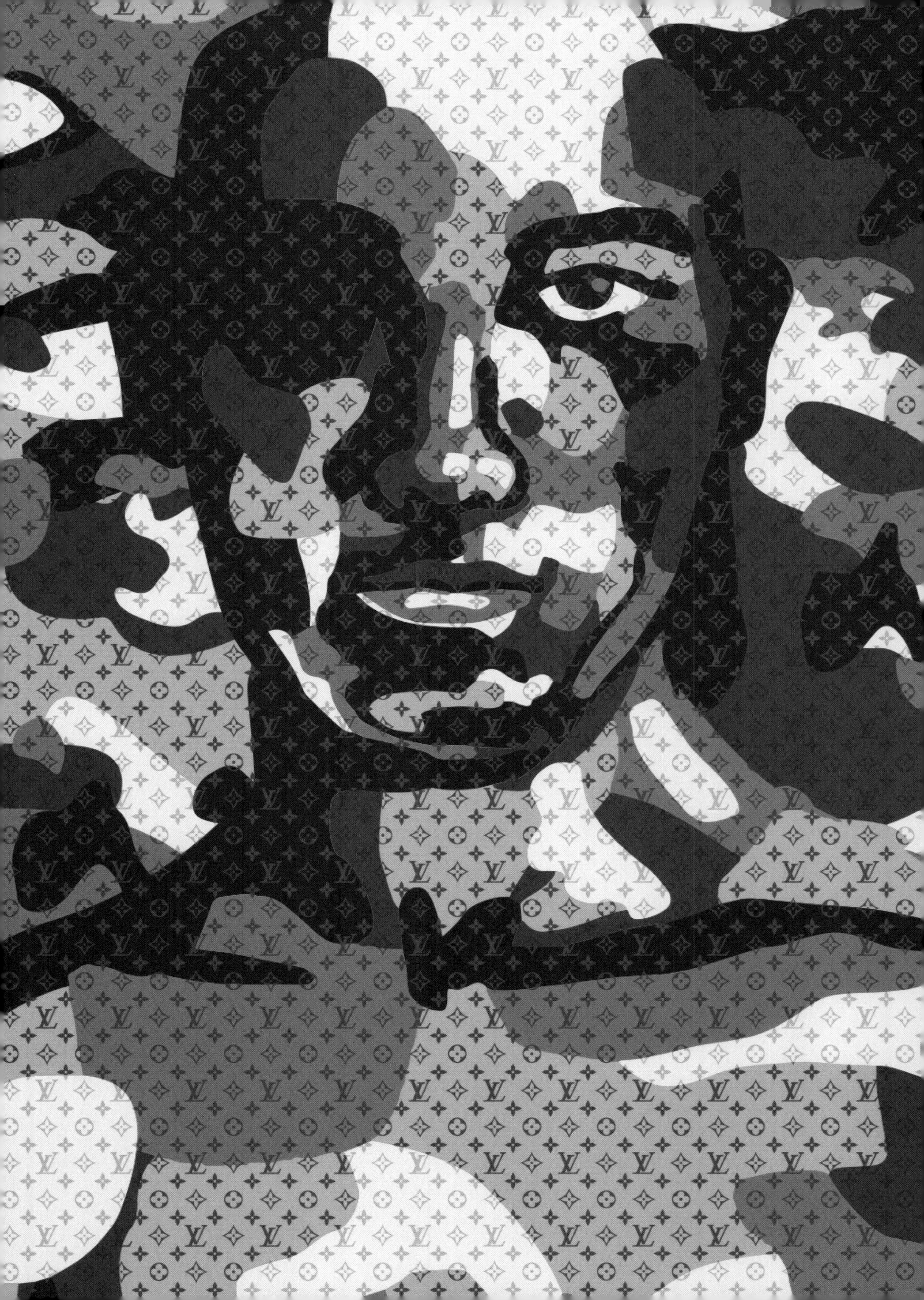

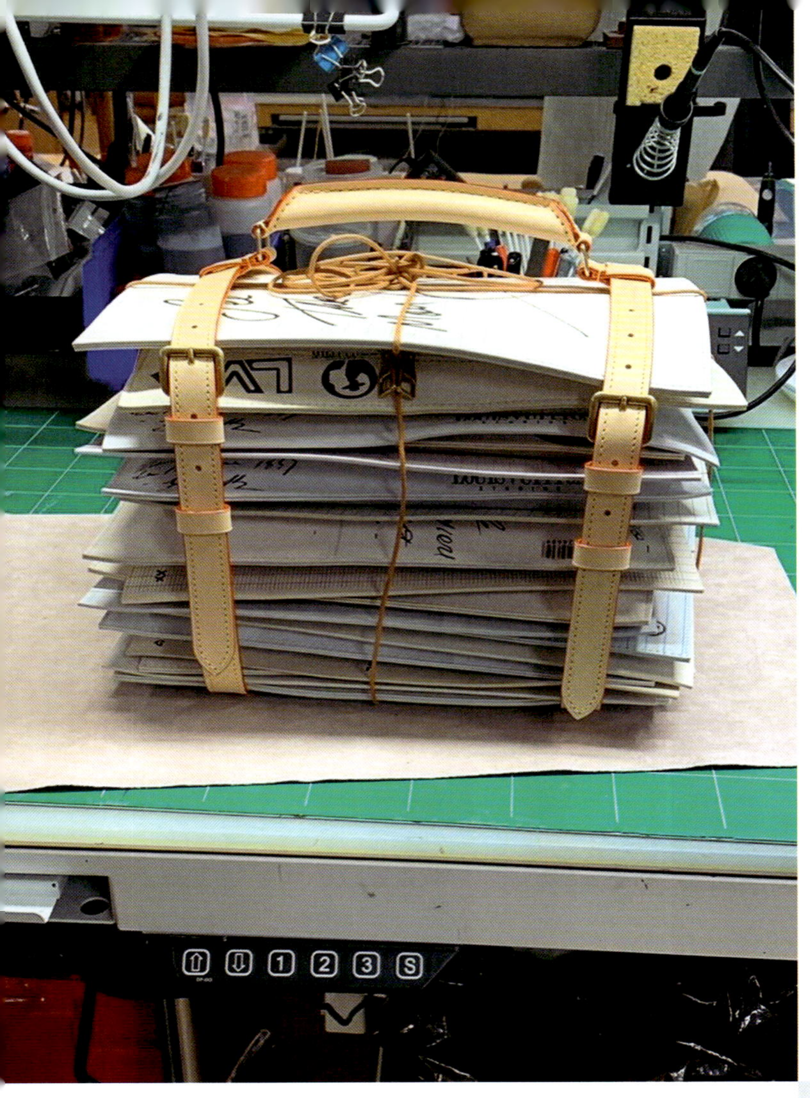

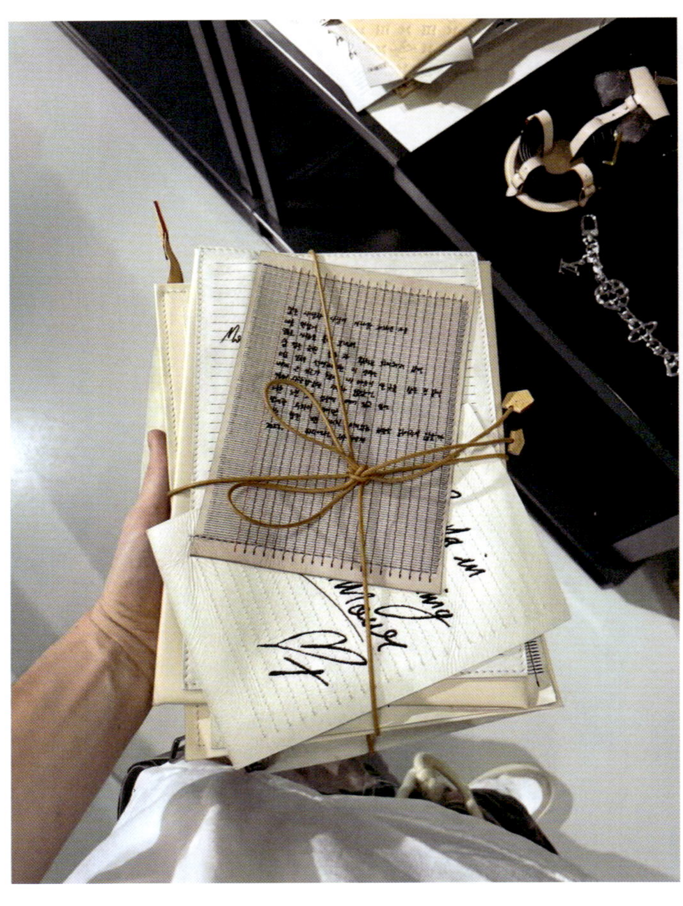

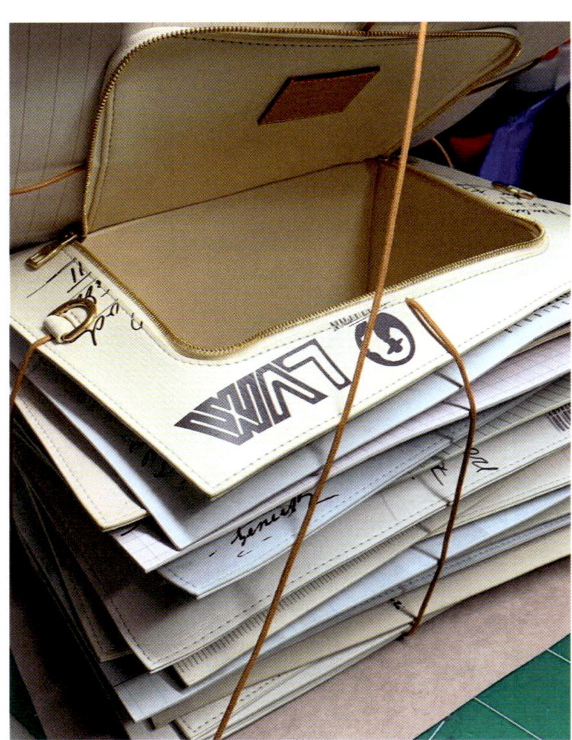

A stack of letters converted into a bag.
One of my favorite pieces made with LV.

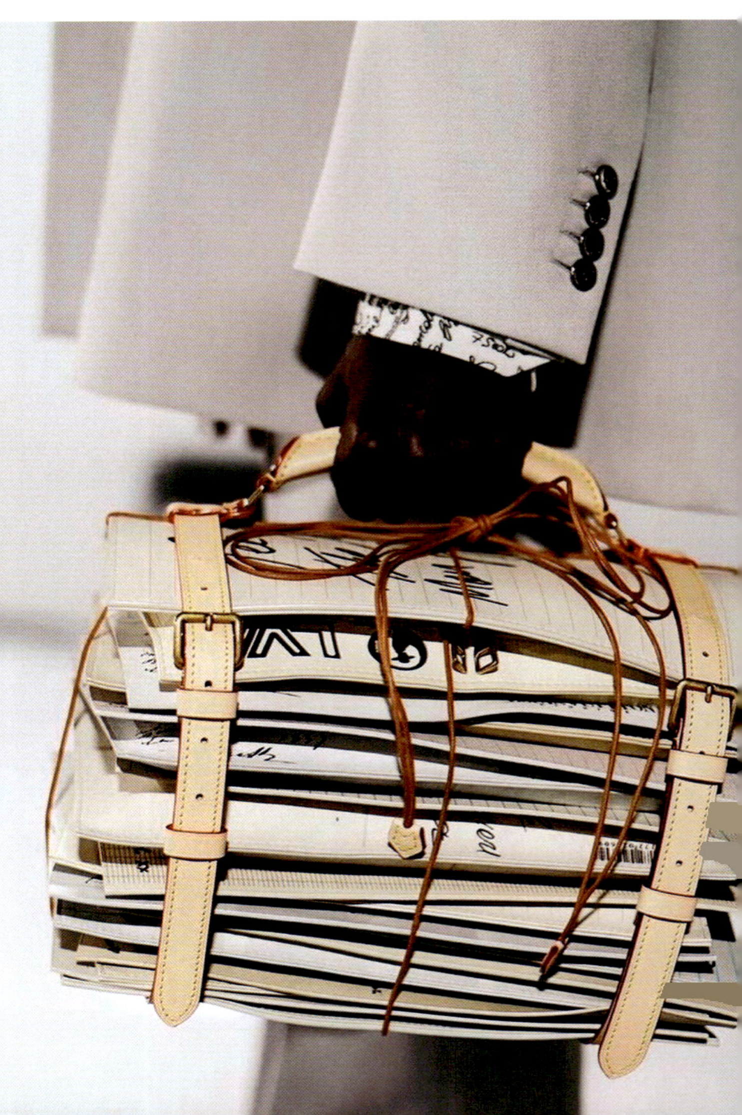

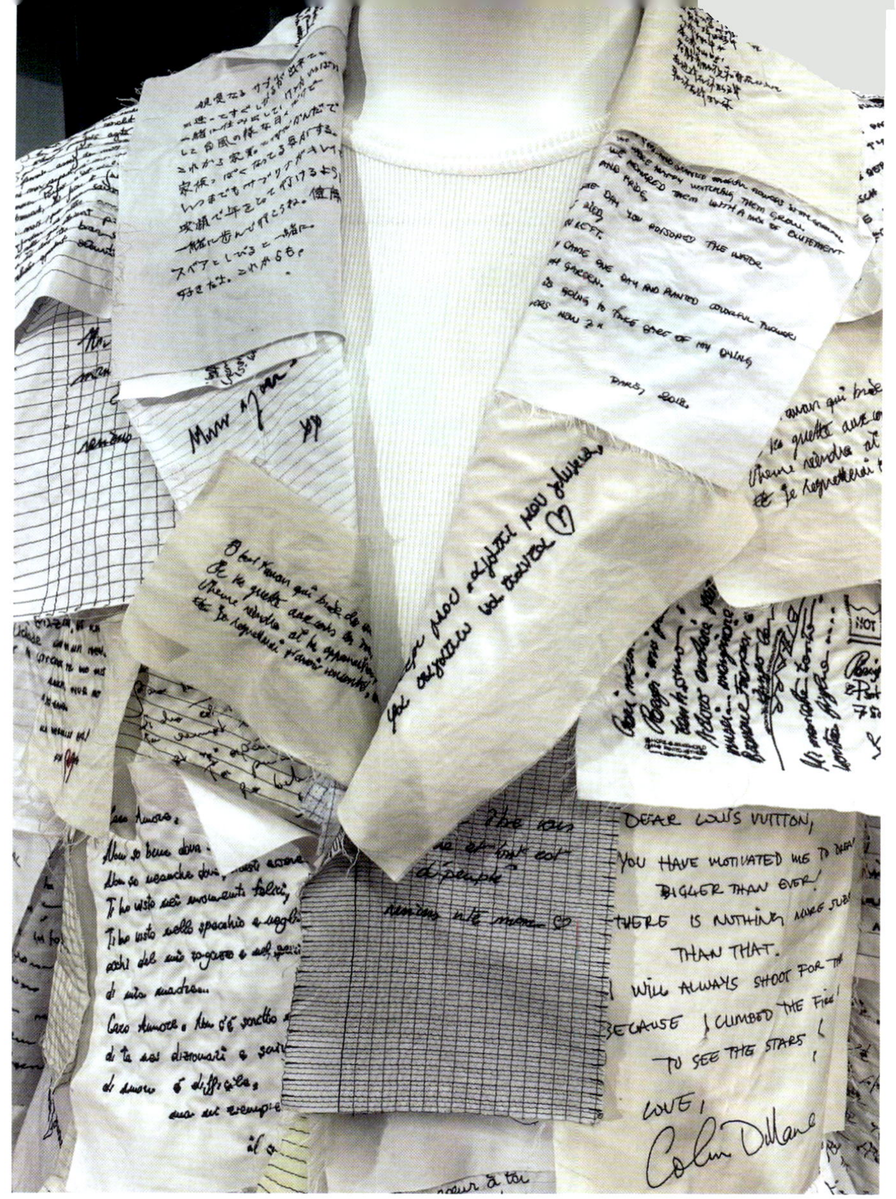

This is the Letter Suit, consisting of embroidery love letters from the LV studio members. We then sewed together all the letters to make a full suit.

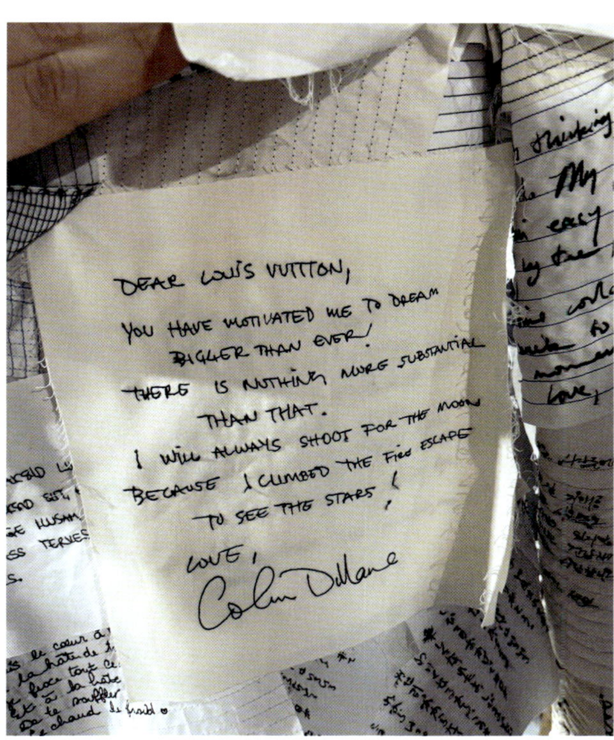

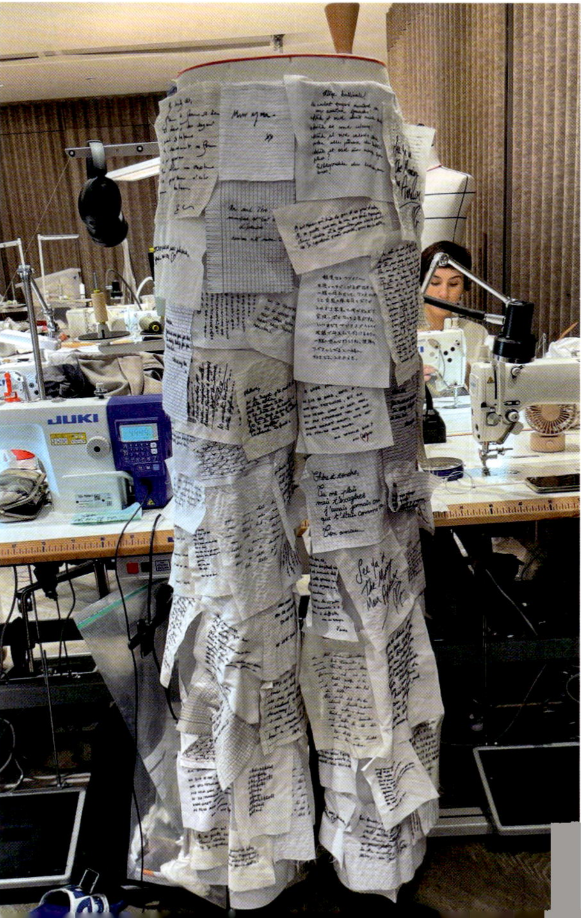

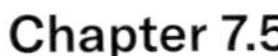

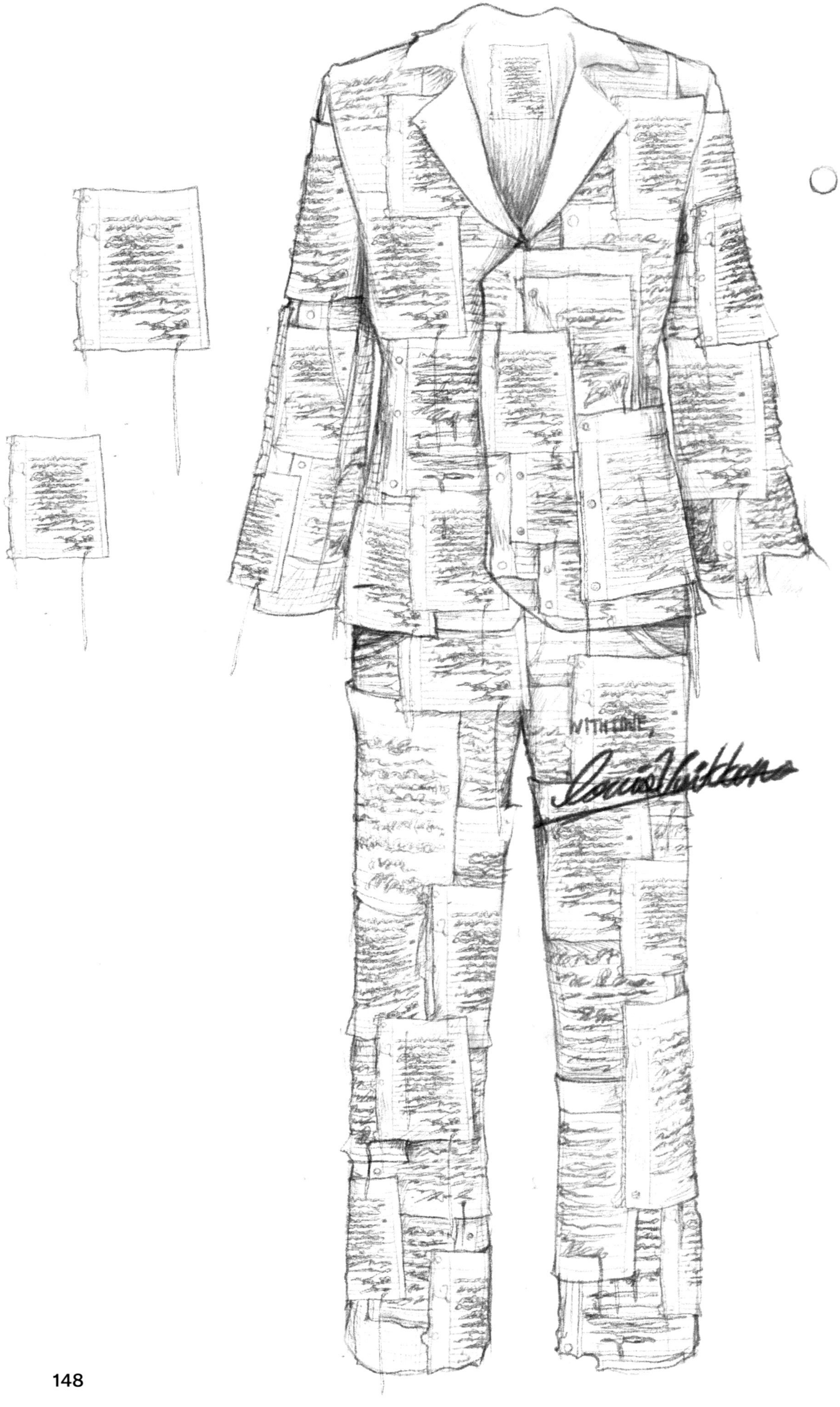

WITH LOVE,

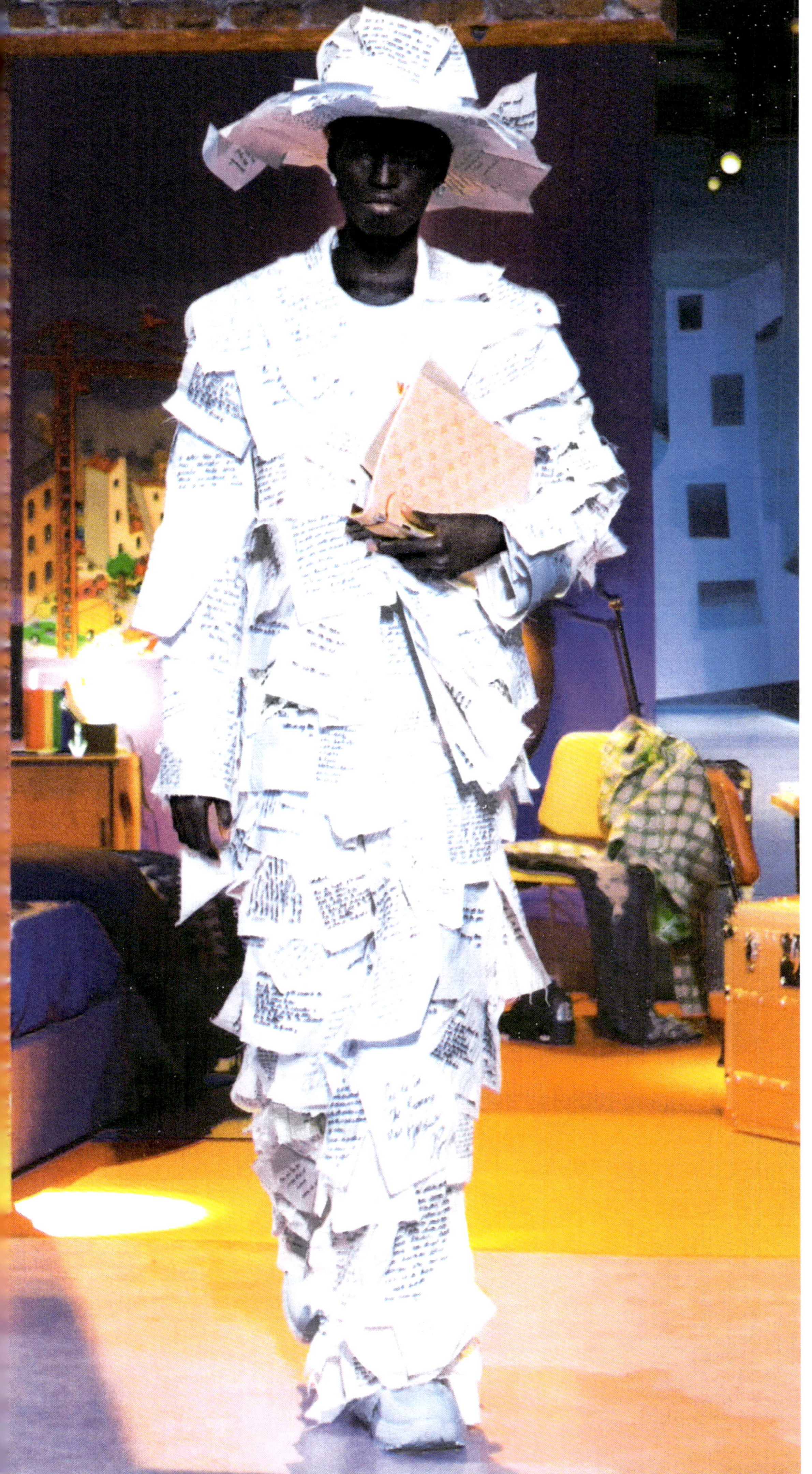

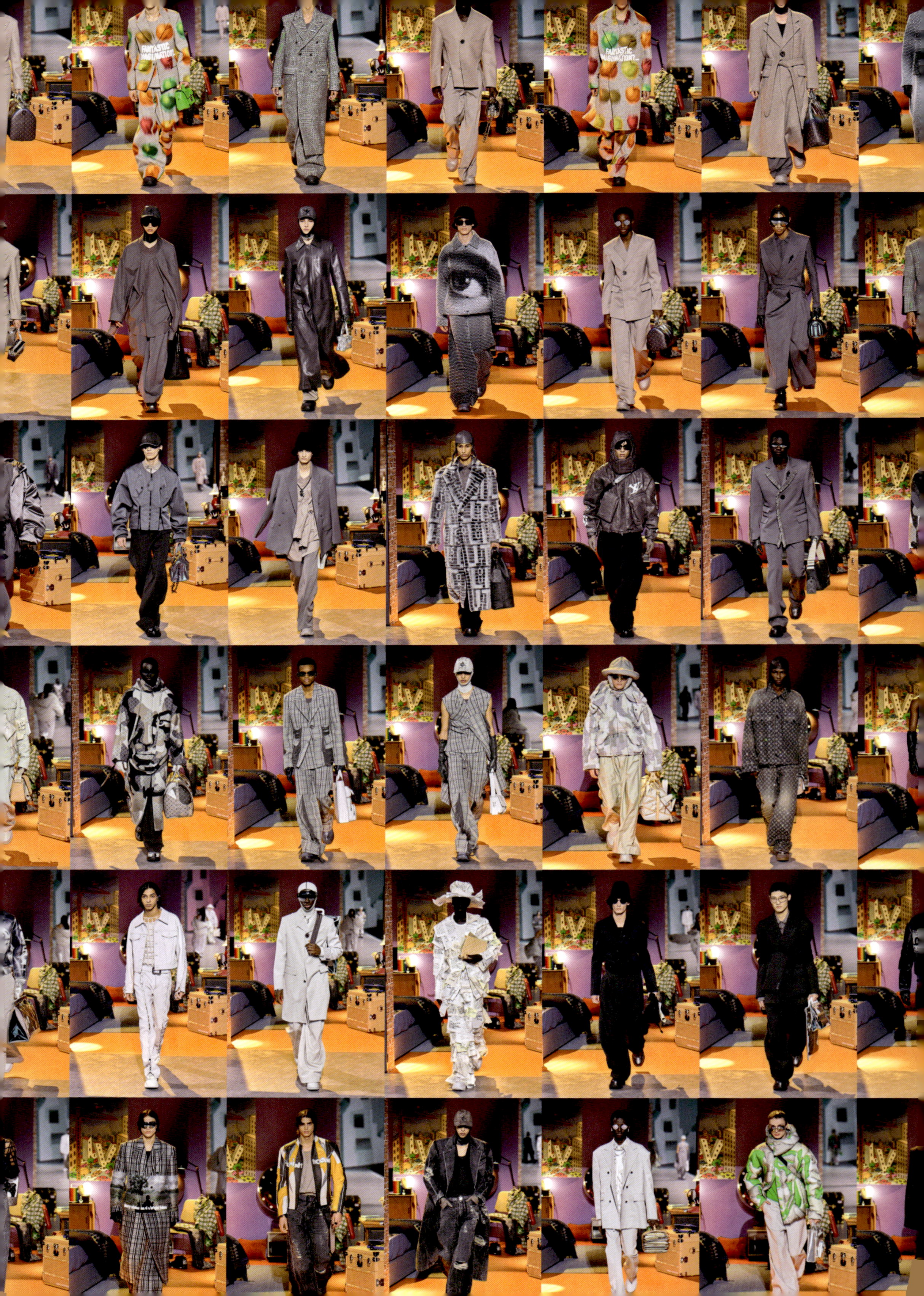
FANTASTIC

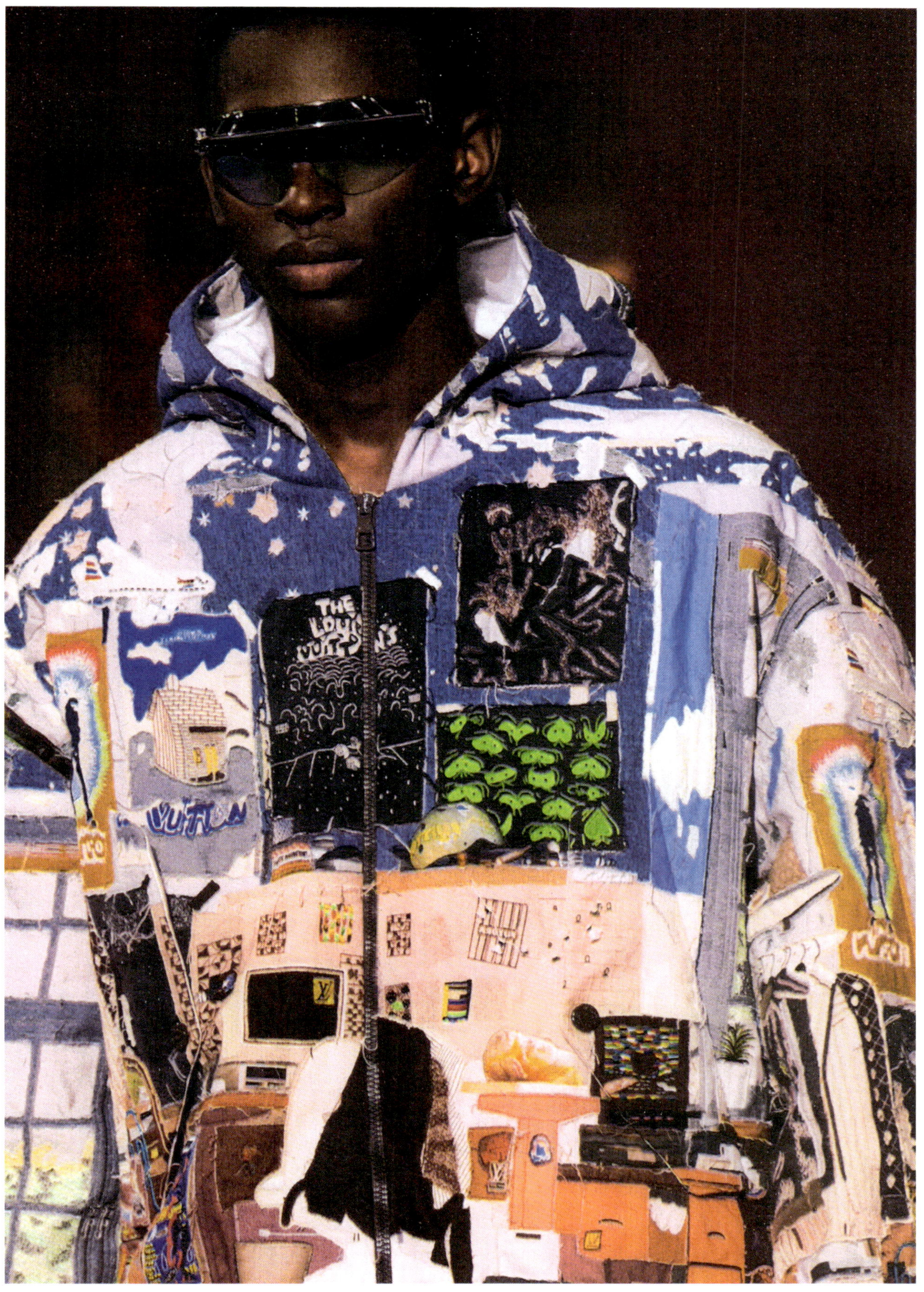

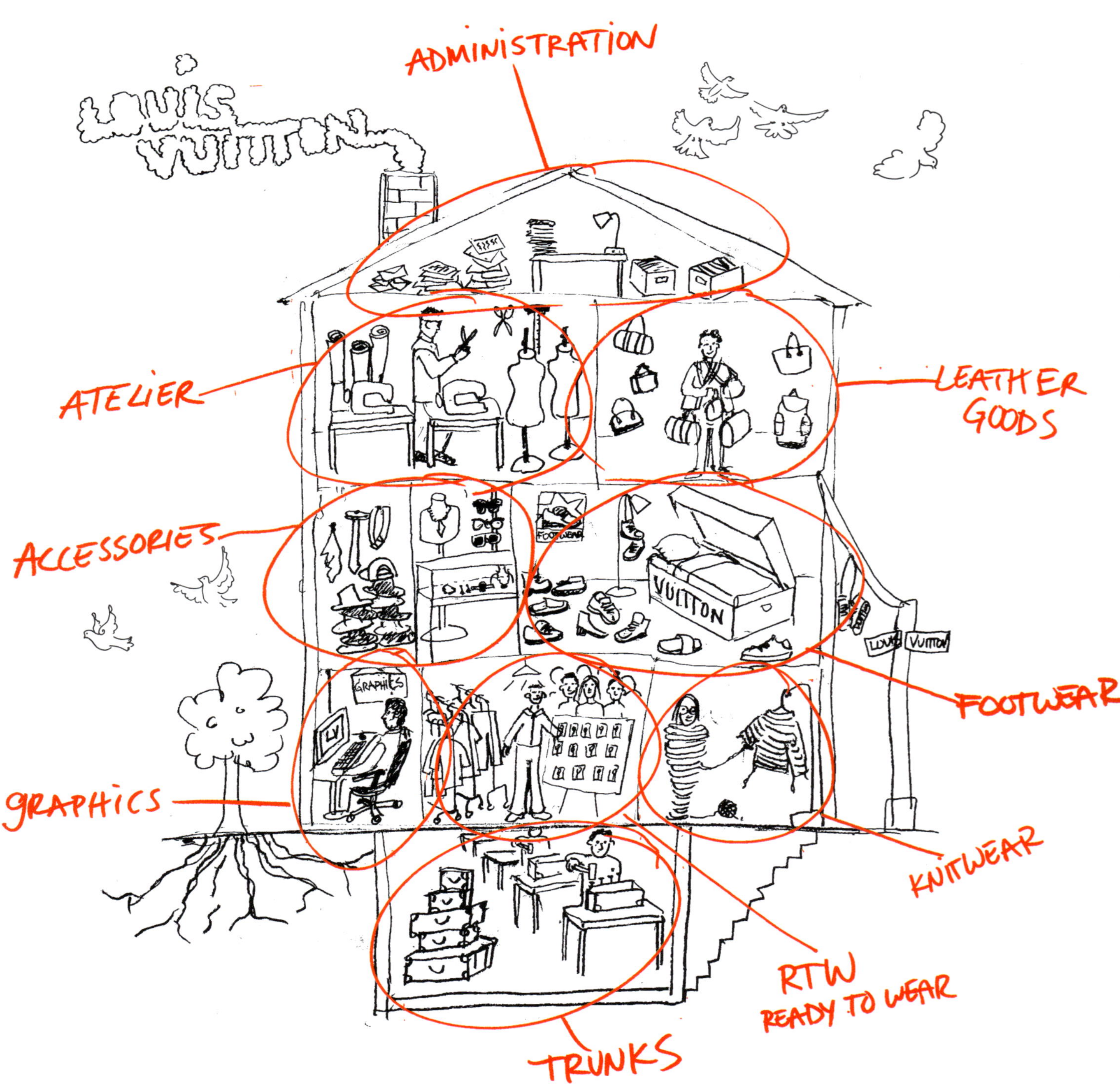
ADMINISTRATION
LOUIS VUITTON
ATELIER
LEATHER GOODS
ACCESSORIES
FOOTWEAR
VUITTON
GRAPHICS
LV
KNITWEAR
RTW
READY TO WEAR
TRUNKS

SPELLBOUND

COLM DILLANE IN CONVERSATION WITH MICHAEL BURKE

COLM DILLANE: The name of this book is *The Misadventures of KidSuper*, which I think is a title that goes true to the spirit of KidSuper, which is all of the different adventures and mistakes that have led me to where I am. Do you remember any crazy mistakes and what you've learned from them? Have you made mistakes in hiring?

MICHAEL BURKE: Wow, tough first question. Nobody bats a thousand when you're hiring people. And that's kind of a given when you're a leader, that means you're going to make a lot of mistakes, you're going to make a lot of hires you shouldn't have made.

CD: What are you looking for? I'm now in the position of hiring people. What are the qualities you're looking for in hiring, because I'm struggling with it as well.

MB: The number one thing I look for is agency. I mean, everybody says they want power, right? Everybody says they want to be empowered.

Truth is, most people don't. Most people want to hide behind somebody else. They want to hide behind a process or procedure. They want to hide behind rules and regulations, behind titles and whatnot. So it's actually much more difficult than you think. You want to say "yes" in an interview. The tough part of the interview is flushing out the people that say "yes," but don't really mean it, because what we need are people that love autonomy.

They love having authority too. They don't abuse it, but they do love it. I mean, they know very well that without authority, it's tough to get things done. Agency to me is being really convinced when you wake up in the morning that you're in the right place at the right time, doing the right job.

CD: I guess a follow up question to that is when you decided to hire me for a short time [at Louis Vuitton] I was fairly unknown. What were you thinking? Why?

MB: I mean you really were under the spell of what you were doing. You were spellbound, come hell or high water. I was looking for somebody that was spellbound and convinced that you'd reach the top. You want big dreamers.

CD: Some people clearly saw it as a risk. How important do you think it is to be taking risks? Because you've been one of the few people in fashion that to me has been a risk-taker throughout your career.

MB: Well, I like to say the only risk is not taking the risk.

Risk is a mandate. It's not something to be minimized or avoided. You look for it. I actively seek out risk. It doesn't find me. I go out and find it. It's the thing that comes out of left field. Risk is you. It's what we do. We're not here to guarantee anything. Nothing's guaranteed. It's creativity driven, it's beauty driven. It's quality driven.

And if you want to be creative, you have to, by definition, do something differently. Which means taking a risk. You're not replicating, you're not part of the ME generation. You're part of your own cohort. You're one person. You have to prove yourself by taking risks. Nobody gets hired for these top jobs to replicate what's existing. You are hired to take it to the next level.

Not necessarily disrupting, but at times, yes. You don't have to disrupt every season, but at the very least, you have to, you have to do things differently every season.

CD: And you've been a mentor. There's way too many people in the industry lately that don't protect us. And if you were going to give any advice, what are things to do and not to do? Because this book has a little bit of a self-help aspect to it.

MB: Don't be afraid.

CD: Yeah...

MB: Surround yourself with people that have positive energy.

I wouldn't even say with loyal [people], because your typical career path would be working in a studio, then branching out on your own. So it's not a straight line. Life is not going to be a straight line. You're going to have to stop working with people and find new people. And a couple years later, you work together again. But loyalty as a key element, when it comes to that.

CD: I think we met because of the LVMH prize, right? A lot of people reading this book would want to know how to stand out, to get on the radar of someone like you.

MB: Travel. Don't stick to your hometown. You got to go west. Wherever west is, and then you have an opportunity to be seen.

Go for it. Take all the risks. Don't be safe. Last thing we need is another safe designer.

CD: When I was pitching for Louis Vuitton, I think I was taking as many risks as possible. I did a book and a commercial and all of these things. What was that like for you, being on the opposite side? I'm curious what your thoughts were on that.

MB: I felt it was authentic. It was you. You weren't trying to be somebody you're not. I thought it was refreshing. It was a different approach. It was a little bit less deferential.

CD: Yeah, it was a pretty nervous experience for me, obviously not knowing what was going to come of it, or if I was doing the right job... but I definitely threw everything at the wall, in two weeks, which is in the KidSuper spirit of "go big or go home."

MB: If it leads to a full-time gig, that's serendipity. You can't guarantee that that's going to happen. All you can do is be yourself, be in somebody's face, make noise and be noticed. If there's some brand out there looking for somebody like you, then of course, magic happens.

CD: Yeah. It definitely felt like magic. And obviously it transformed my life.

MB: There's a lot of boredom right now. Everybody's complaining that there's not enough creativity going on, not enough news. I spoke to Vanessa Friedman last night. She was just going home and was complaining that there was nothing to write about.

CD: You didn't get to see my most recent show, but I had an indoor tornado.

There's a Brooklyn-based artist that had figured it out on a small scale, and so we worked together to make it a giant. Yeah, weirdly it worked, but it took a lot of IT engineering and figuring out the fans and the amount of smoke. It was exciting. The first model walked around it. But the finale was a girl walking through, or coming out of the storm, which was visually captivating.

MB: What was the diameter of the storm?

CD: Nine meters (27 feet) in height, so it's pretty tall, and it was probably around five meters (15 feet) wide. I'll send you videos of it. Fashion shows have always been a fun place for me to experiment.

On that note, what do you recommend for someone that's not in the beginning, but in the middle of their career, especially someone like me, for example, where I am?

MB: Let's say you are in the middle of your career, and you're very successful, you realize that some people are not able to keep up with you. That for your brand, at that moment, you need somebody else. When you have to cut somebody loose, if your business really needs it, those are some of the toughest decisions.

It shouldn't change who your friends are, but it might mean that some of your friends shouldn't be in the company. People mid-career, very often, what they'll do is they'll hang on to these people because of a sense of duty. It's tough. You don't want this. You don't want to sacrifice your friendships for your business, but you have to find a way to move forward, especially the people that were there from day one. Sometimes they're just not right anymore. They become frustrated. They're not with it. They're better off someplace else. But you don't cut your relationship.

CD: I can second that one, yeah... a lot actually. It is definitely, definitely difficult.

Another question. There are a lot of misconceptions about the fashion industry. What is something that people trying to get into the fashion industry should know that they don't.

MB: Know yourself.

CD: There are times where you need entire paragraphs, and sometimes there are the one-word or two-word answers, and those are good too.

This is also more of a personal question, as the book is kind of about me. I'm at a point in my life right now where I either go become a creative director or work on the KidSuper brand. Which brand should I take on to creative direct? If you're in my position, what would you do? Should I also take on investors or not?

MB: I was thinking creative direction. I think you're made for that.

It goes back to that very short answer before, you have to know yourself. Karl [Lagerfeld] could do anything, but he knew himself—that he was not going to be very good at being himself. He knew that he would be much more successful at Chanel and Fendi than at his own brand. He was very good at being somebody else. He was a master puppeteer. He navigated different interpretations of himself, and his strength was understanding what made a brand successful. How do you keep that going? Bring in somebody to continue the founder's work. He knew he was not strong as a founder. He was much stronger at taking something that existed and taking it to the moon.

Others like John [Galliano] are better at developing a big, individual aesthetic and bringing that to bear. And both approaches are needed. It depends on where that brand is. Does that brand require a reinvention because it's disappearing and losing its personality? Then bring in John. Is it a great brand and is just a little sleepy? Then bring in Karl.

Different people for different jobs, and one isn't more successful than the other. You need to know who you are. Are you better working for another brand and updating what that brand is, or are you better inventing a new brand?

CD: I think I know I have to figure out that question. I mean, for me, it's not obvious.

MB: It's still early and the answer is not obvious. Do a little bit of trial-and-error, but remember, those are two overriding approaches when you're trying to write a story, you're going to be, more or less, in for one and not the other.

Hard to do both. Are you good at understanding why somebody else was very good? And can you take that to the next level, which is commercially super, super important. That's actually where most of the money is. But most of the glory is inventing a new narrative.

So it's a little bit like being Coco Chanel, or are you successful because you understood Coco and you kept her alive, and even Coco herself could never have done that in another brand.

CD: And what kind of brand should it be? It's a tough one, yeah, but...

MB: —You gotta feel it.

CD: Do you think it's even possible to make a new brand at the level of these huge luxury brands from scratch?

And what are your thoughts on a streetwear brand versus a luxury brand? From my perspective, I find it kind of interesting that luxury brands get less criticism. I think people are less harsh on the collections and designs of an established luxury brand, whereas with smaller brands, you do something quite amazing and get burned for it because it's not deemed luxury.

It's an interesting thing, even for me in positioning KidSuper. Because kids say it's more of a streetwear brand. But since we've been doing all these fashion shows, do we want to raise our prices? And you know, it's kind of a tough positioning battle, because the customer is not ready to spend $5,000 on a bag. Our prices are quite affordable. It's an interesting position to be in as well because I don't know how you could get so expensive.

MB: It's quite obvious a lot of luxury brands went too far on their prices. There was a moment where everybody thought the more you raise your prices the more desirable it was. That's true for very few brands, and even for those few brands, you have to be very careful.

CD: Right now there's been a ton of changes in creative directors in the industry. And there was a moment where creative directors were stars, and brands were looking for star creative directors. And now it seems people are going for someone who isn't that far removed from working at a studio. Where do you see the creative directors going in a couple of years?

MB: It depends, it comes and goes. There's no permanence. People want a pendulum and want constant change.

CD: What do you do when you're stuck? How do you make up your mind? Are you flipping a coin? Is it in your gut?

MB: Go for it! What's the worst thing that can happen? You get fired? You're not going to die.

CD: I agree. That's the Colm motto, I think. And in over fifty years of being a professional, is there a common trait that you recognize as essential for success on a business, vocational and even a personal level?

MB: I think, fundamentally, you have to like your job. You have to like what you're doing.

CD: It's a good answer. I like that answer. Do you have any questions on your end? For me, I know you can learn so much from me [laughs].

MB: Maybe that's volume two. Make sure that you leave enough unsaid that you can follow it up with another book. Yeah, you're way too young to do something definitive, so I recommend that a lot of the stories you're giving them are the beginning and maybe the middle of the story. Leave some things for the next book.

Michael Burke is Fashion Group Chairman at LVMH and was CEO at Louis Vuitton from 2012 to 2024.

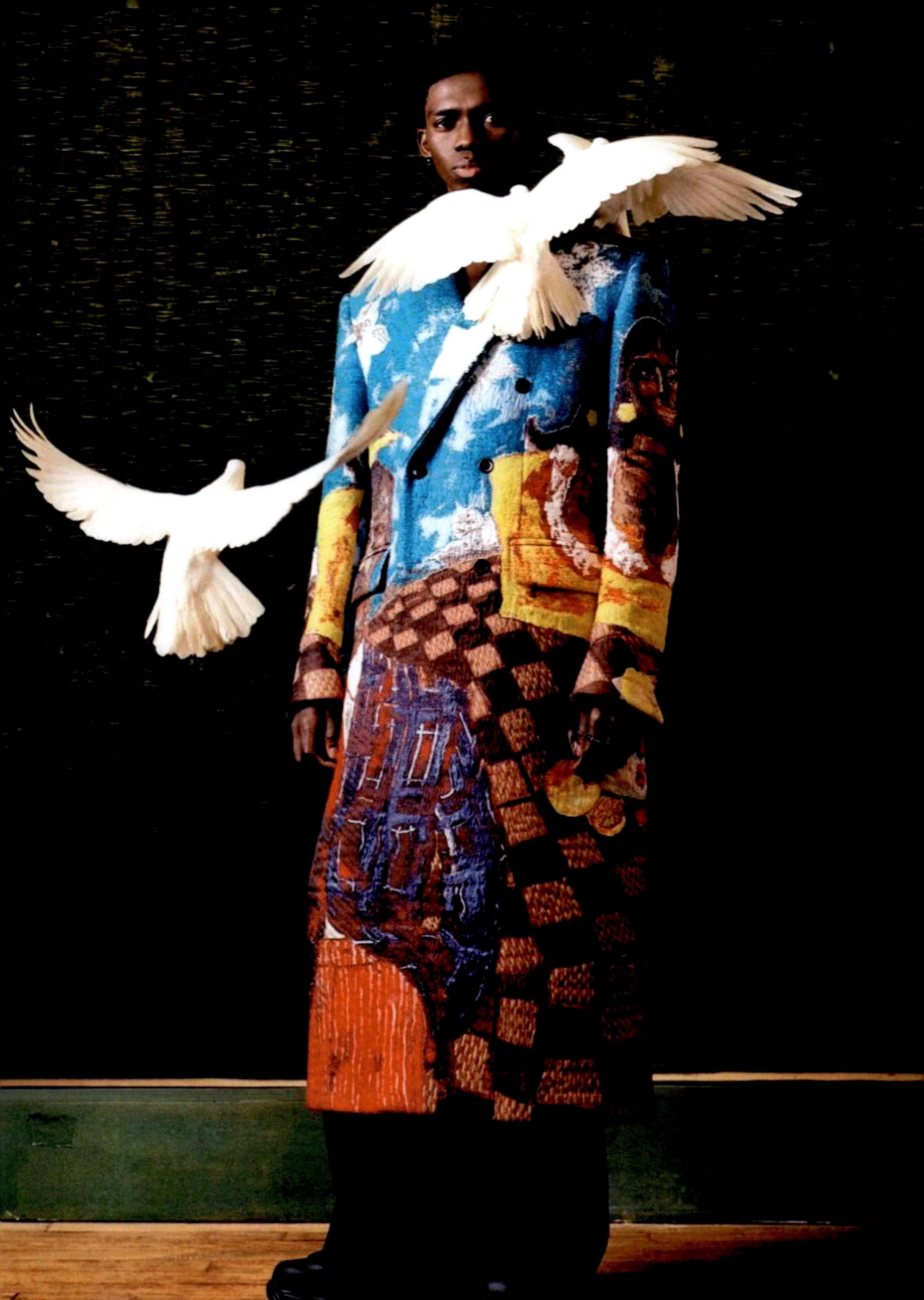

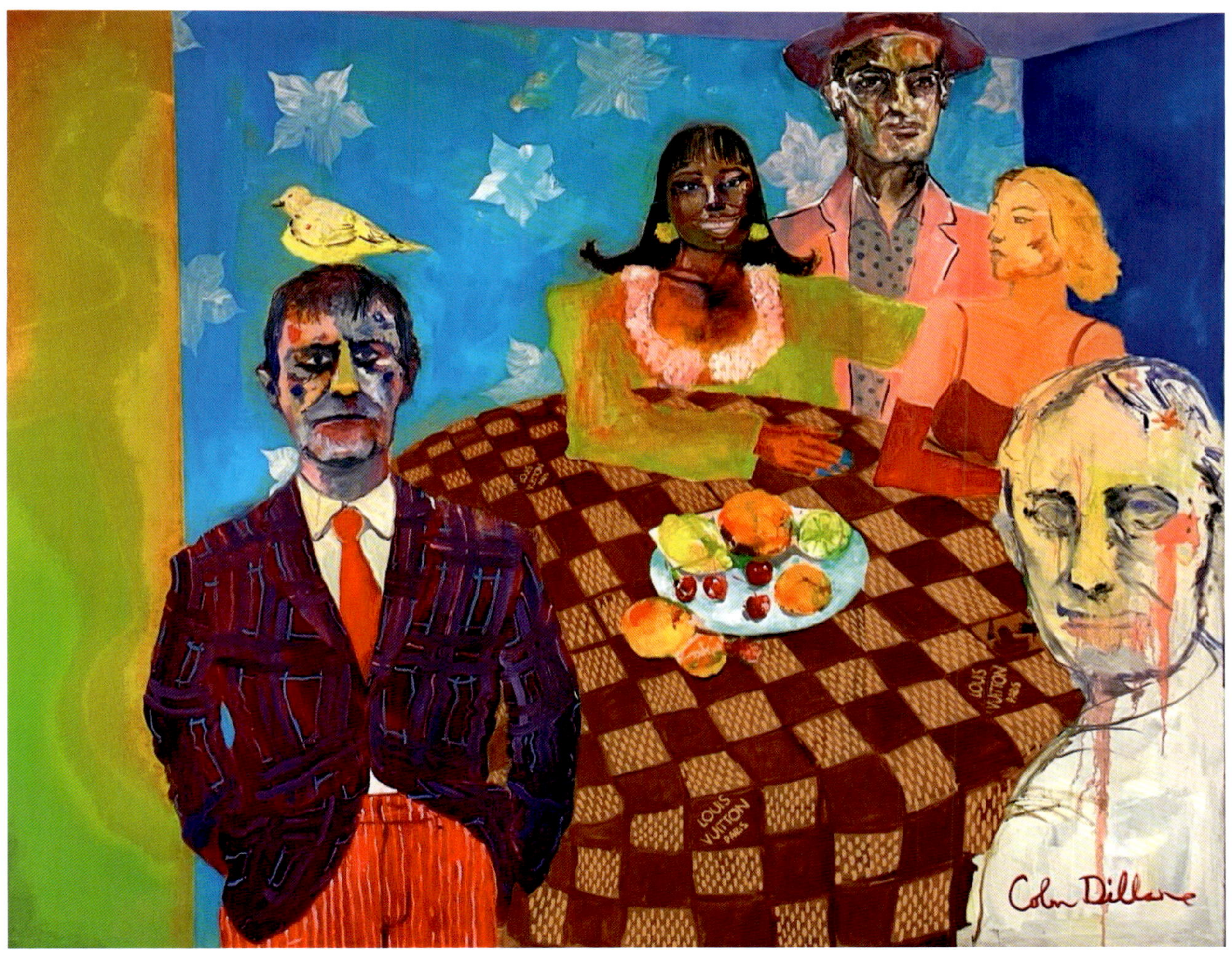
LOUIS
VUITTON
PARIS

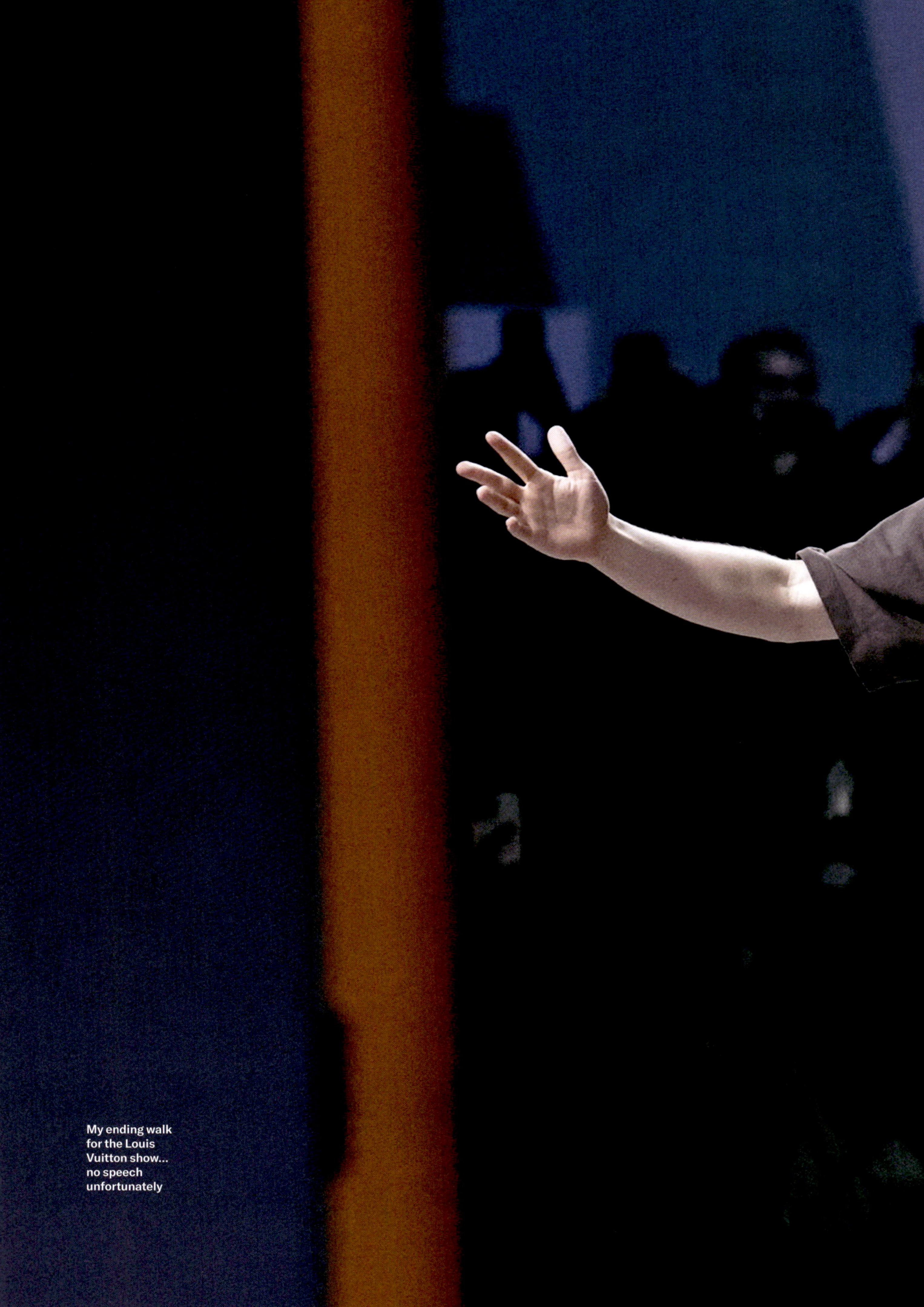

My ending walk for the Louis Vuitton show... no speech unfortunately

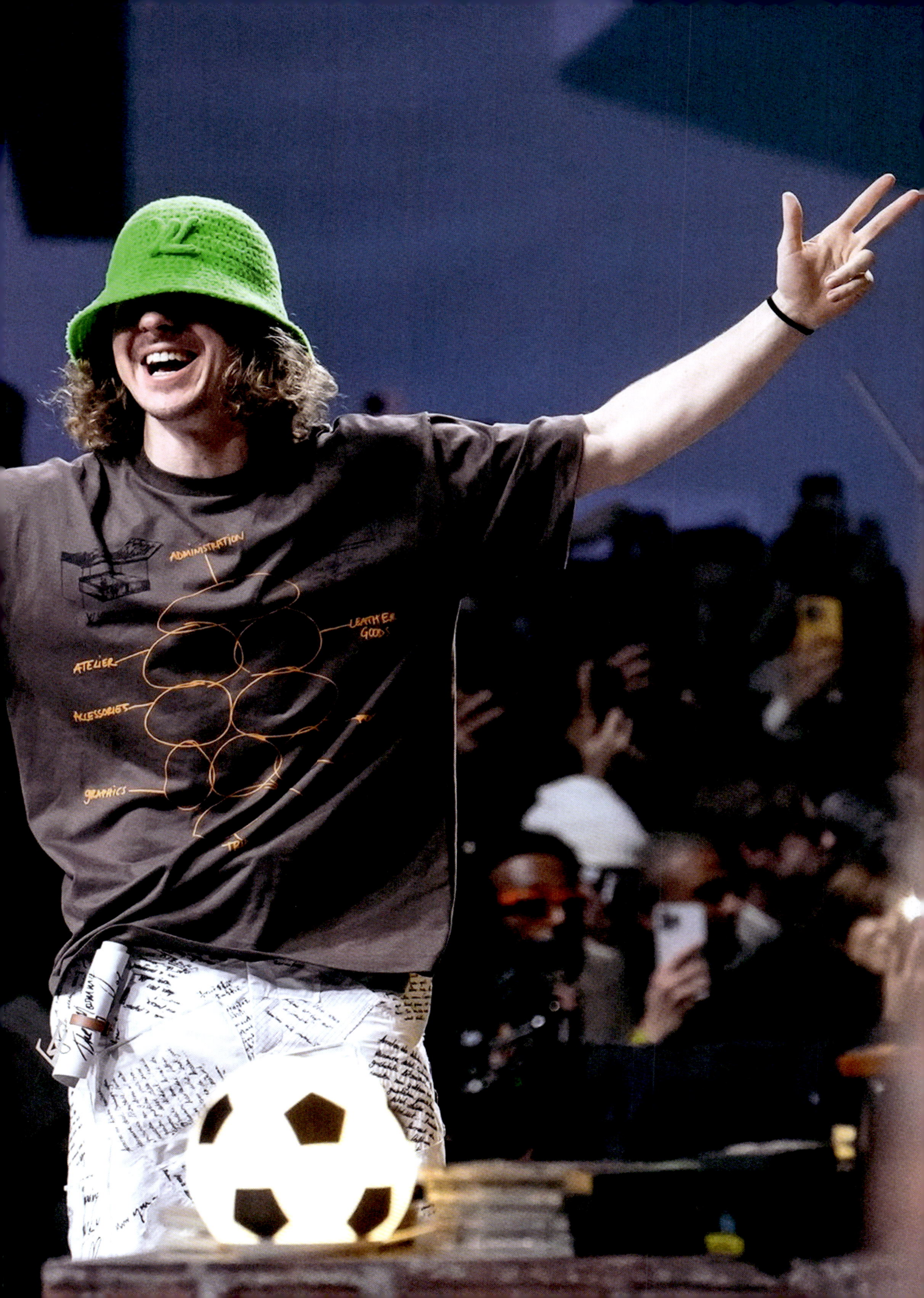
ADMINISTRATION
LEATHER GOODS
ATELIER
ACCESSORIES
GRAPHICS

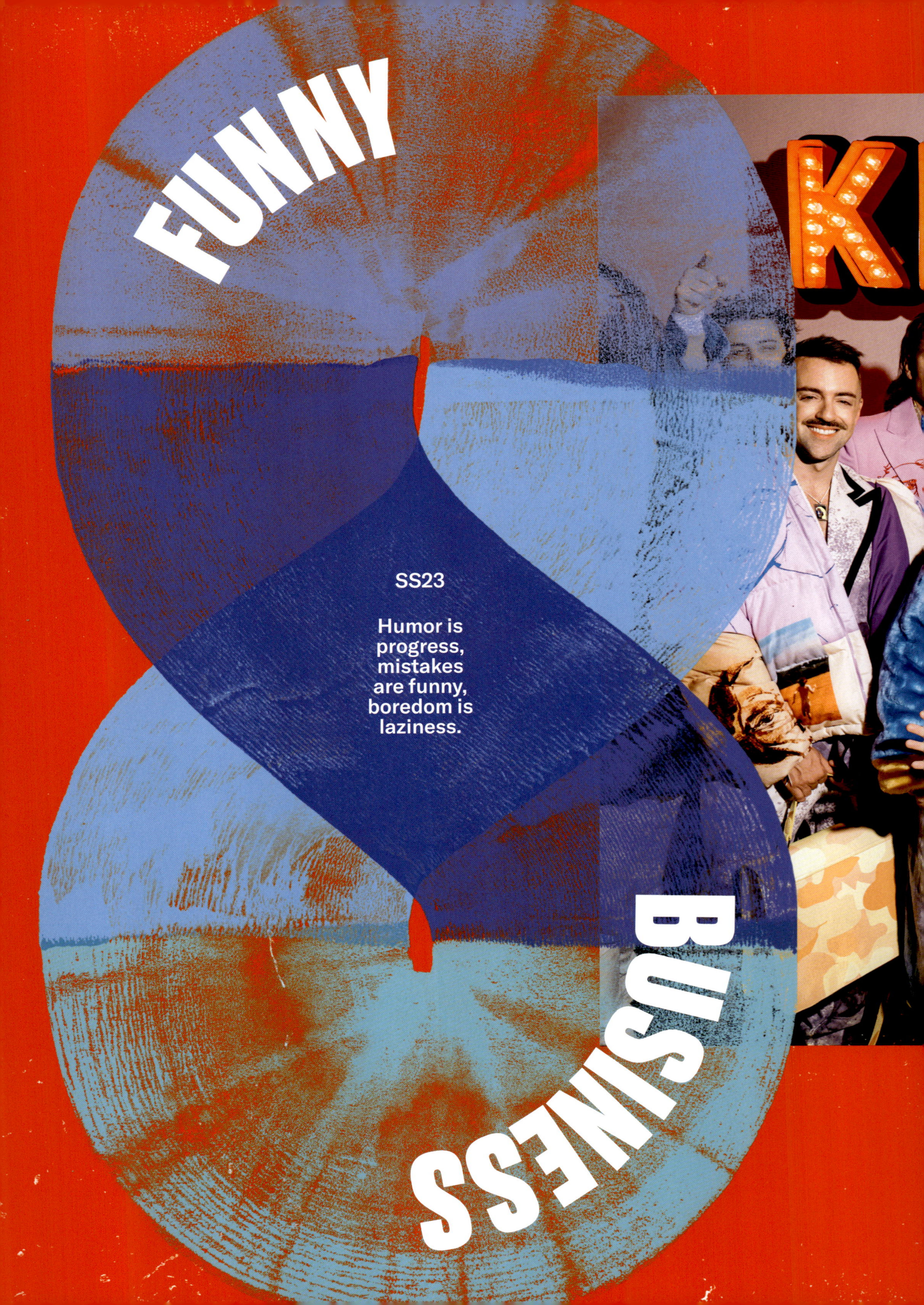
FUNNY
BUSINESS
SS23
Humor is progress, mistakes are funny, boredom is laziness.

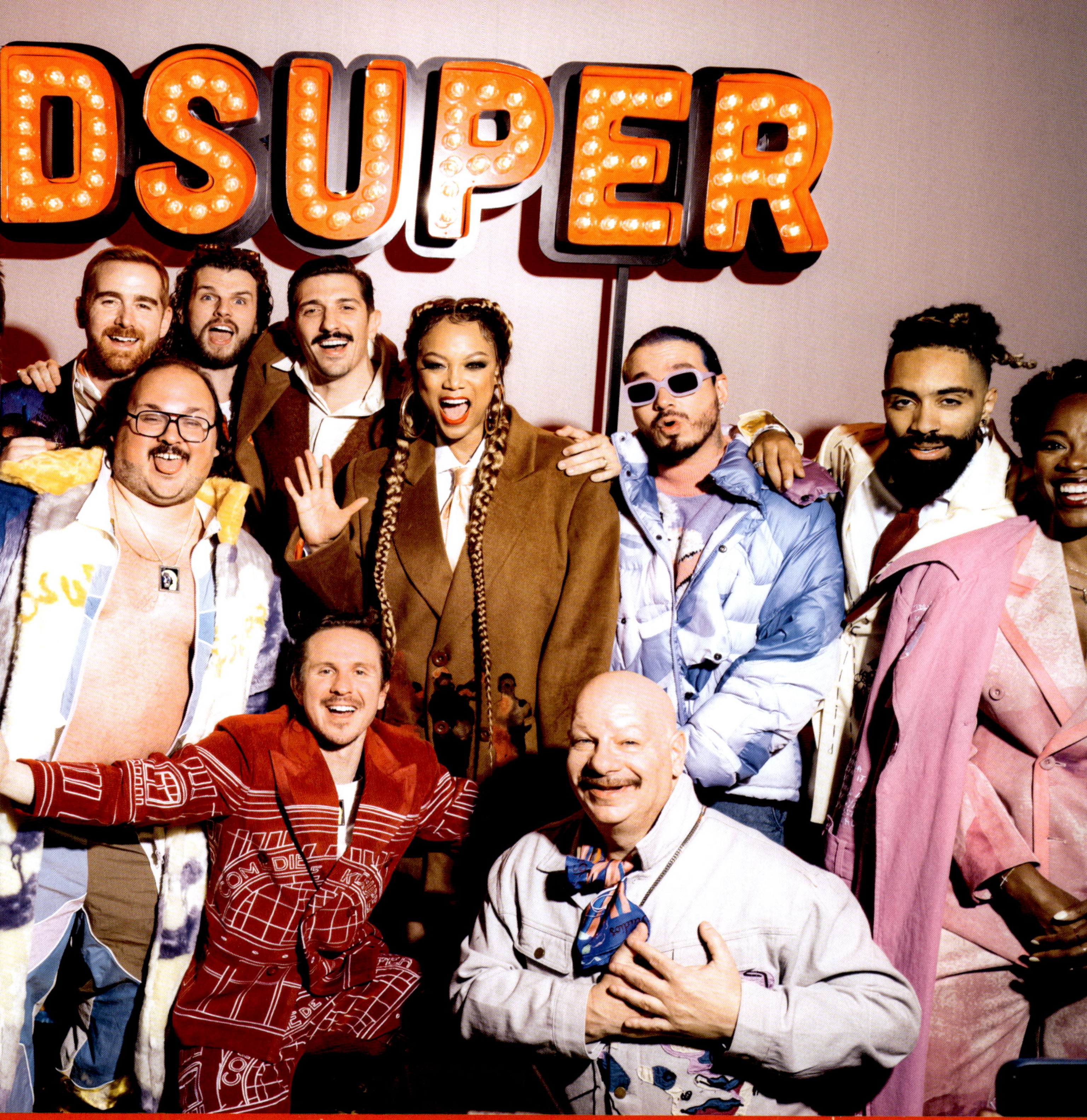
DSUPER

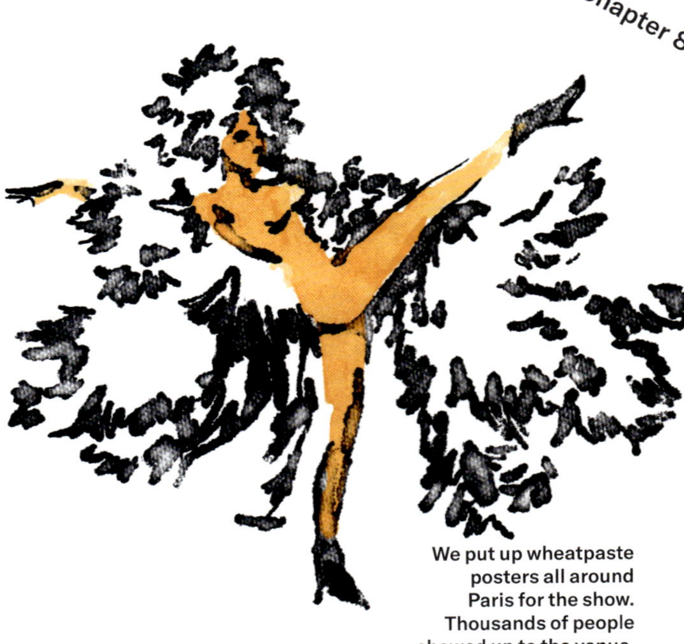

We put up wheatpaste posters all around Paris for the show. Thousands of people showed up to the venue.

ON THURSDAY, JANUARY 19, 2023, I creative-directed the Louis Vuitton show and two days later, on Saturday the 21st, I put on a KidSuper Comedy Fashion Show. Just for context, on Thursday I was at the pinnacle of high fashion, and by Saturday I was roasting fashion in a comedy show. Looking back, the contrast is hilarious—who else could go from Louis Vuitton to a stand-up comedy fashion show in the same week?

The comedy show idea had actually come about years earlier. Around five or six years before, I was doing all kinds of creative work in New York—art shows, music videos, posters, billboards, album art, record merch. I had been working with an artist organization called Wallplay, which partnered with landlords to use vacant storefronts as temporary art spaces. They gave me a space on Canal Street for three months, and I thought, Should I turn this into a KidSuper store and just make money? Or should I give back?

That's when I decided to build a theater and let artists, musicians, and comedians host and perform. I called it "The Apollo of the Streets." Ironically, years later, I actually ended up renting out the real Apollo to put on a KidSuper Comedy Show. The space became a hub for all kinds of creative events, and one night, after a party, I hopped on stage with a mic. It felt like a comedy show, so I posted on Instagram: "Anyone want to do stand-up at the KidSuper building tonight?" Real comedians showed up, and it was electric. From then on, it became a regular thing: The KidSuper Comedy nights at our makeshift theater.

I ALWAYS CONSIDERED myself one of the funniest guys (in fashion) and I had been planning this comedy fashion show concept for a while. But then Louis Vuitton called. I thought, Should I still do this? Will people think I don't take fashion seriously? I have a playful spirit— but it doesn't mean I don't work hard. So I pushed forward.

For the comedy fashion show, I reached out to Andrew Schulz, whom I'd met that year. He had been inspired by Russ's process of releasing one song a week, which led him to release one comedy clip a week—changing his career. He heard Russ mention staying at the KidSuper store and reached out to me. We became friends, and now his co-host, Mark Gagnon, even records his podcast at the KidSuper building. Once Schultz was in, I started reaching out to Theo Von, Andrew Santino, Stavros Halkias, and others. They didn't fully understand the concept at first, but once they started talking to each other, they got excited.

Then I thought, If we have too much comedy, we need a fashion host. Who better than Tyra Banks? She was the dream host. Whatever she wanted, we made it happen. I basically spent my entire Louis Vuitton paycheck on Tyra Banks—funny to say out loud, but totally worth it (to me).

I also didn't want the show to be just comedians. Enter J Balvin. He was the first major celebrity to reach out and support KidSuper in the early days. He actually messaged me "you are going to be big." It meant the world to me at the time and now.

After Louis Vuitton announced me as creative director for the season, J Balvin called me, emotional, saying, "I can't believe how far you have come, I need to walk for KidSuper. For the culture." But I told him, "Balvin, the next show is actually a stand-up comedy show." His response? "Oh, you don't think I'm funny? Bro, you don't think I'm funny?"

I couldn't tell if he was joking, I wanted him to walk more than anyone. I said, "Are you serious? I'll call all of the comedians to help write jokes." He wasn't joking. He was all in. An hour before the show, he came up to me and said, "I performed for 200,000 people last weekend and I haven't been this nervous to perform in 20 years." Twenty minutes before the show, we finally landed on a joke that worked. Every comedian—Jeff Ross, Theo Von, Schulz, Santino—kept pitching Colombia cocaine jokes, and Balvin was like, "No way, I can't do that to Colombia!" But we found something else, and it killed. The energy during fittings with J Balvin, Theo Von, and Tyra Banks was something no other brand could replicate. It still makes me smile thinking of those three preparing together for a Paris Fashion Week show.

Leading up to the event, I wasn't sure how many people would show up, so I put posters around Paris inviting fans. I expected maybe 200 people. Instead, thousands showed up. The police were called, and it was absolute chaos. But there was this electric, magical energy in the air.

The night before the show, the comedians arrived for their fittings and asked, "So, this is in front of, like, twenty of your friends, right?" I told them, "No, it's in front of 2,000 of the most elite people in fashion." They freaked out. "Why didn't you tell us?! We need to write fashion jokes!" They spent the night researching fashion scandals and fashion mishaps and ended up roasting fashion—and roasting me. Schulz closed the night with this beautiful tie-in about the whole experience. Then I dropped the mic with one final joke:

Knock, knock. Who's there? The new brand in town.

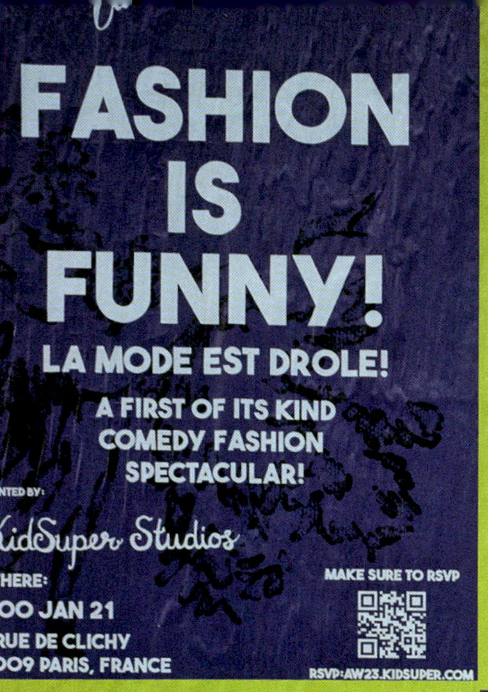
FASHION IS FUNNY!
LA MODE EST DROLE!
A FIRST OF ITS KIND COMEDY FASHION SPECTACULAR!
KidSuper Studios
MAKE SURE TO RSVP
RSVP:AW23.KIDSUPER.COM

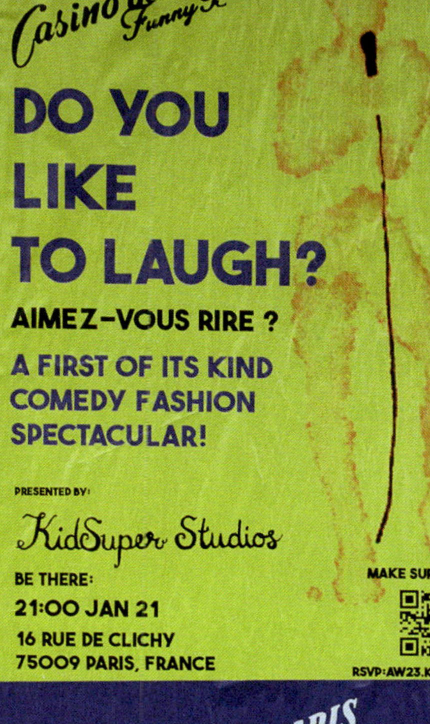
DO YOU LIKE TO LAUGH?
AIMEZ-VOUS RIRE ?
A FIRST OF ITS KIND COMEDY FASHION SPECTACULAR!
PRESENTED BY:
KidSuper Studios
BE THERE:
21:00 JAN 21
16 RUE DE CLICHY
75009 PARIS, FRANCE

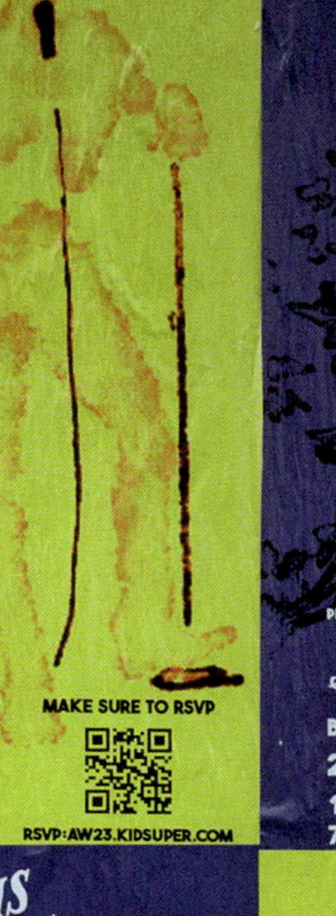
MAKE SURE TO RSVP
RSVP:AW23.KIDSUPER.COM

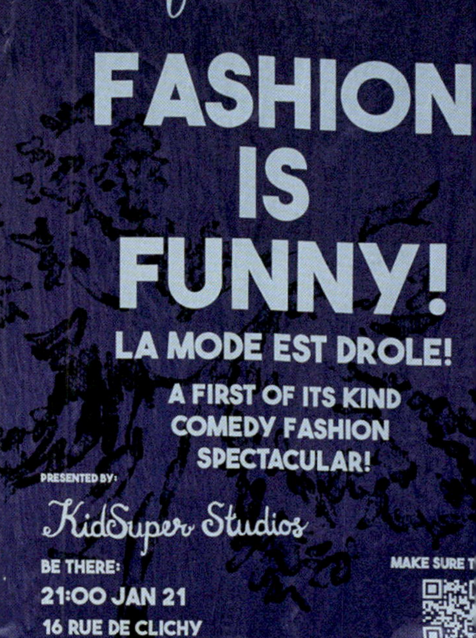
FASHION IS FUNNY!
LA MODE EST DROLE!
A FIRST OF ITS KIND COMEDY FASHION SPECTACULAR!
PRESENTED BY:
KidSuper Studios
BE THERE:
21:00 JAN 21
16 RUE DE CLICHY
75009 PARIS, FRANCE

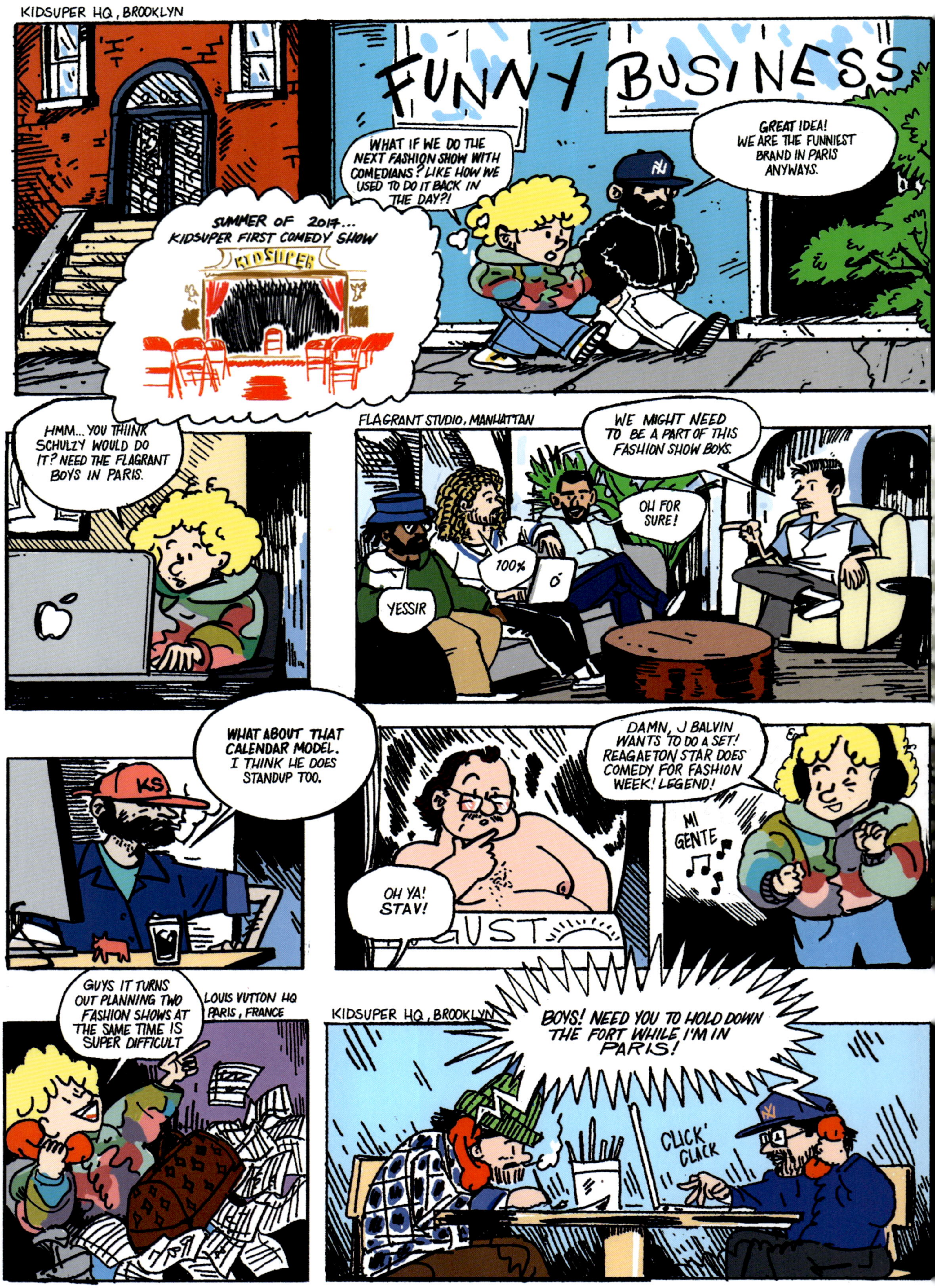

KIDSUPER HQ, BROOKLYN

FUNNY BUSINESS

WHAT IF WE DO THE NEXT FASHION SHOW WITH COMEDIANS? LIKE HOW WE USED TO DO IT BACK IN THE DAY?!

GREAT IDEA! WE ARE THE FUNNIEST BRAND IN PARIS ANYWAYS.

SUMMER OF 2017... KIDSUPER FIRST COMEDY SHOW

KIDSUPER

HMM... YOU THINK SCHULZY WOULD DO IT? NEED THE FLAGRANT BOYS IN PARIS.

FLAGRANT STUDIO, MANHATTAN

WE MIGHT NEED TO BE A PART OF THIS FASHION SHOW BOYS.

OH FOR SURE!

100%

YESSIR

WHAT ABOUT THAT CALENDAR MODEL. I THINK HE DOES STANDUP TOO.

KS

OH YA! STAV!

GUST

DAMN, J BALVIN WANTS TO DO A SET! REAGAETON STAR DOES COMEDY FOR FASHION WEEK! LEGEND!

MI GENTE

GUYS IT TURNS OUT PLANNING TWO FASHION SHOWS AT THE SAME TIME IS SUPER DIFFICULT

LOUIS VUTTON HQ PARIS, FRANCE

KIDSUPER HQ, BROOKLYN

BOYS! NEED YOU TO HOLD DOWN THE FORT WHILE I'M IN PARIS!

CLICK CLACK

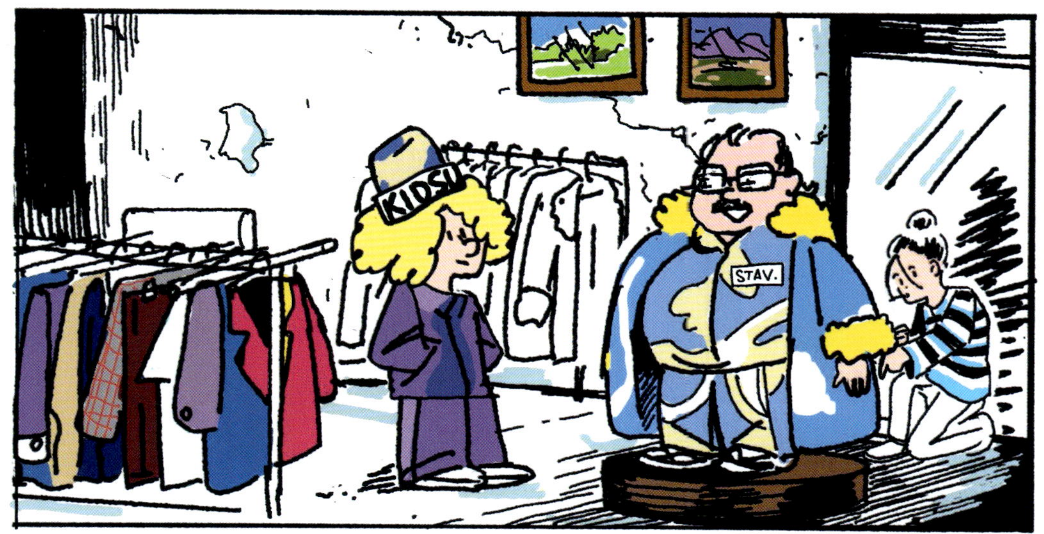

KIDSU
STAV.

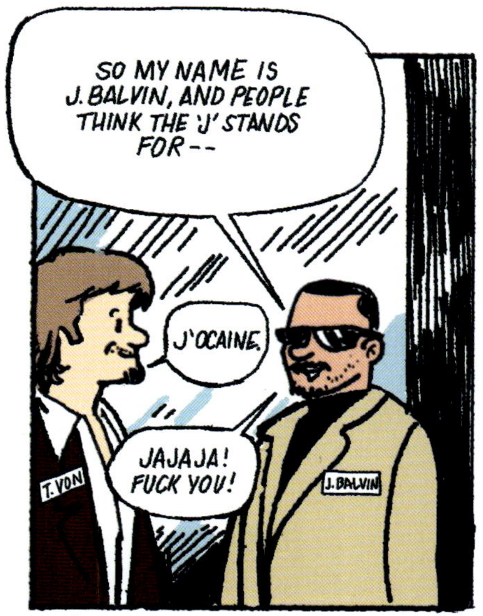

SO MY NAME IS J. BALVIN, AND PEOPLE THINK THE 'J' STANDS FOR--
J'OCAINE.
JAJAJA! FUCK YOU!
T. VON
J. BALVIN

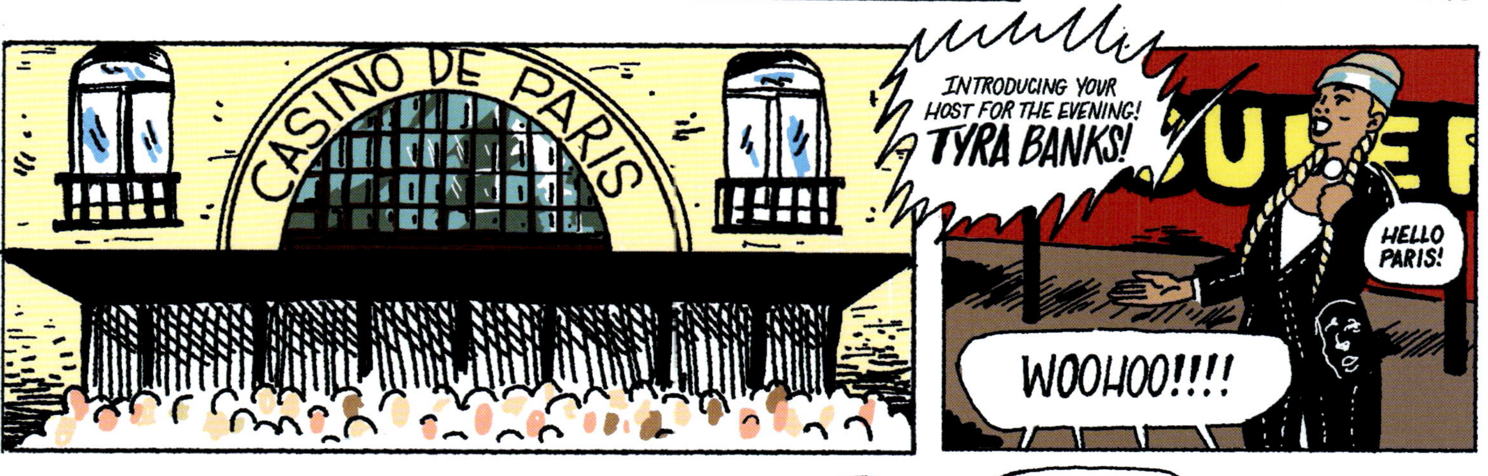

CASINO DE PARIS
INTRODUCING YOUR HOST FOR THE EVENING! TYRA BANKS!
SUPER
HELLO PARIS!
WOOHOO!!!!

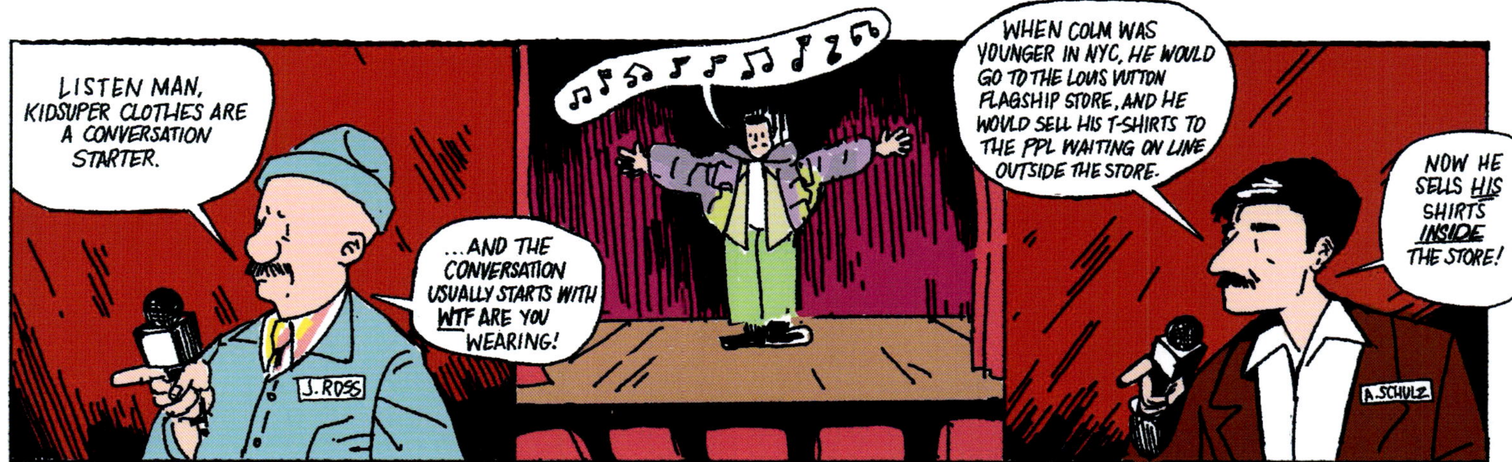

LISTEN MAN, KIDSUPER CLOTHES ARE A CONVERSATION STARTER.
...AND THE CONVERSATION USUALLY STARTS WITH WTF ARE YOU WEARING!
J. ROSS
WHEN COLM WAS YOUNGER IN NYC, HE WOULD GO TO THE LOUIS VUTTON FLAGSHIP STORE, AND HE WOULD SELL HIS T-SHIRTS TO THE PPL WAITING ON LINE OUTSIDE THE STORE.
NOW HE SELLS HIS SHIRTS INSIDE THE STORE!
A. SCHULZ

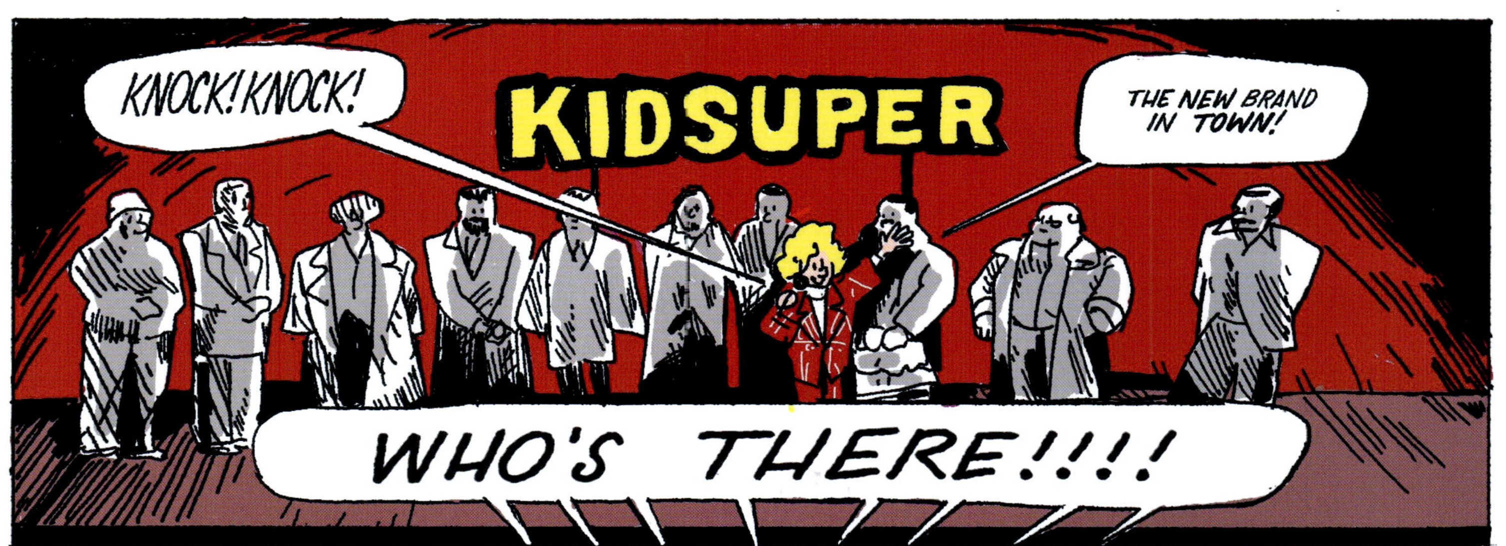

KNOCK! KNOCK!
KIDSUPER
THE NEW BRAND IN TOWN!
WHO'S THERE!!!!

"My agent said, There is someone named KidSuper who wants you to host his Fashion Week show, and my first response was, Who the hell is KidSuper? But I am a research-crazy geek, so I get on the computer and googled KidSuper and I'm like, Whoa, what the hell? He got, like, coats that're, like, tongue kissing and, oh my God, Louis Vuitton right? Louis Vuitton. This little Sour Patch Kid. He's actually kind of sweet."

Tyra Banks, the host of the show

"I'm not a comedian, you know. I'm not a comedian, but if you want, I can perform a song for you guys. I have the DJ right here. Are we ready? Are you ready, kid? Oh never mind, they didn't pay me enough."

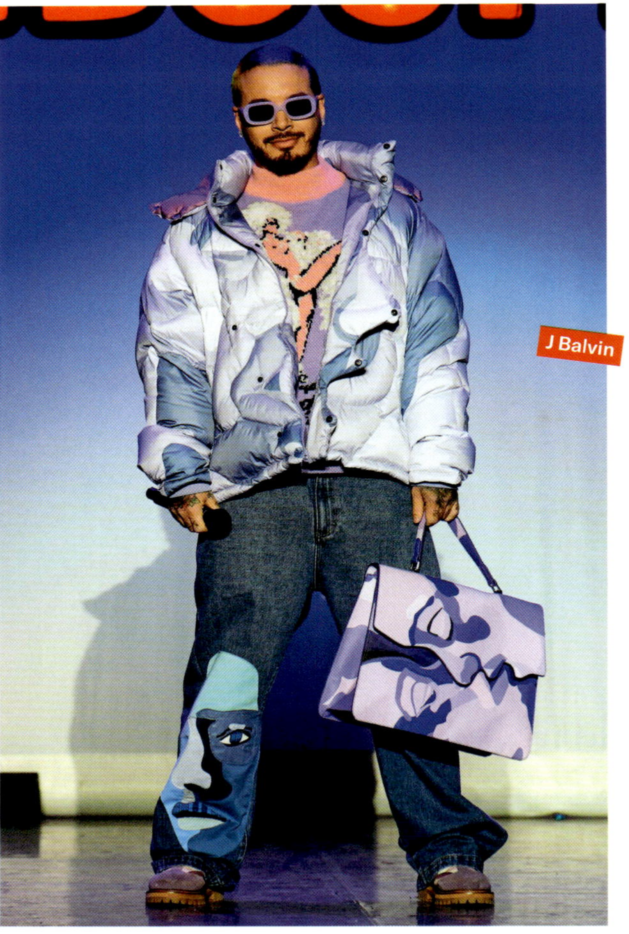

J Balvin

"I'm French so, first time in English—uh, yeah, yeah. I mean, not my first time performing in English—first time speaking English. I'm kidding. I'm not gonna do it in English, okay?"

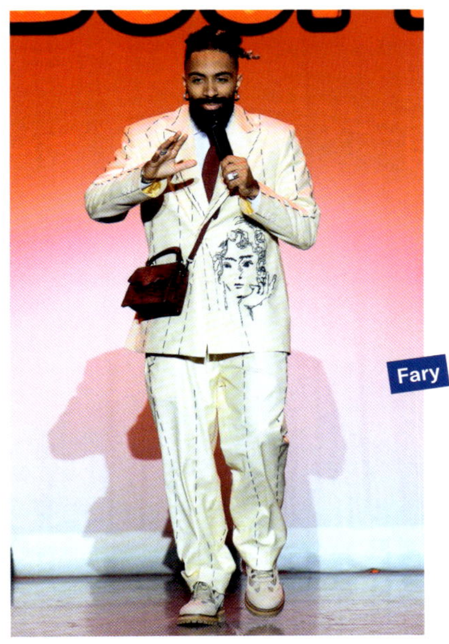

Fary

"The French, man. People are rude in France, man. I said hello to a guy . . . he said no, umm, my cousin got bit by a gay guy . . . so, we'll see. I'm Theo Von, baby. God bless y'all."

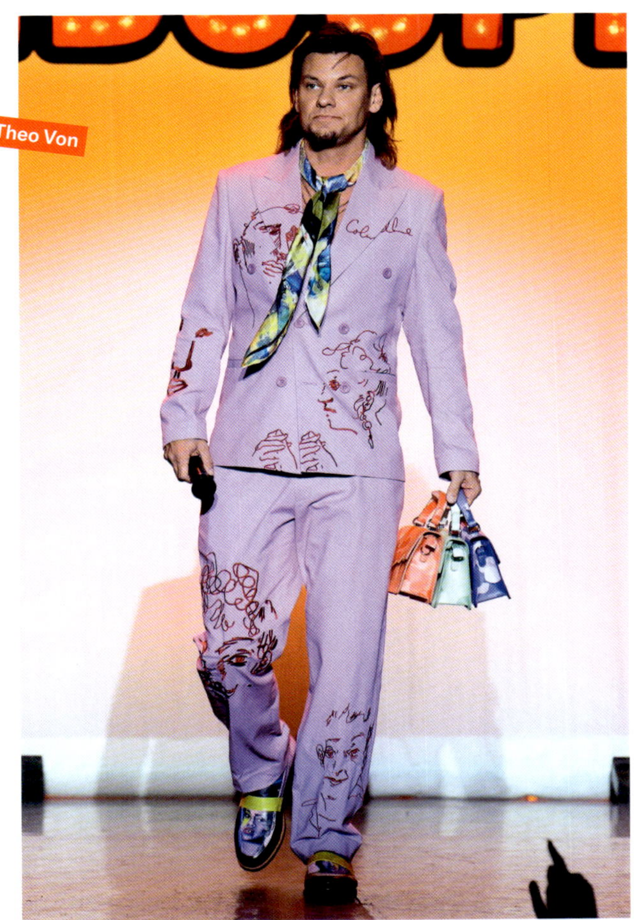

Theo Von

"Before I go—it's crazy, though. I didn't realize that the streetwear game is very reminiscent of the drug game. Like, it's easier to score cocaine, so I hear, than to score some sneakers."

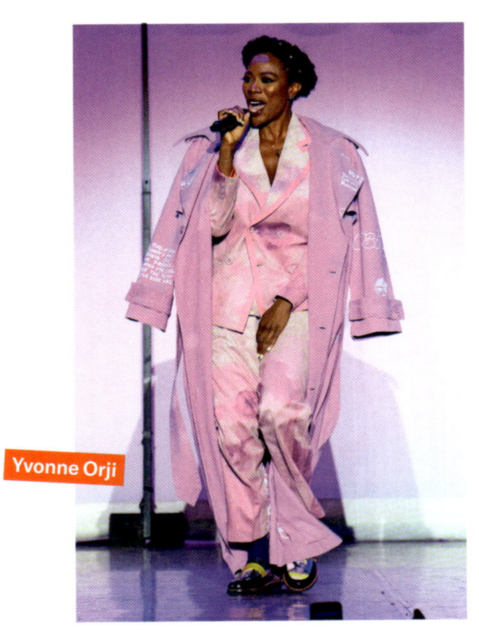

Yvonne Orji

"I don't understand the outfit because I'm not a smart man. I don't get the culture but I appreciate it. I don't know if this is impressionism or autism."

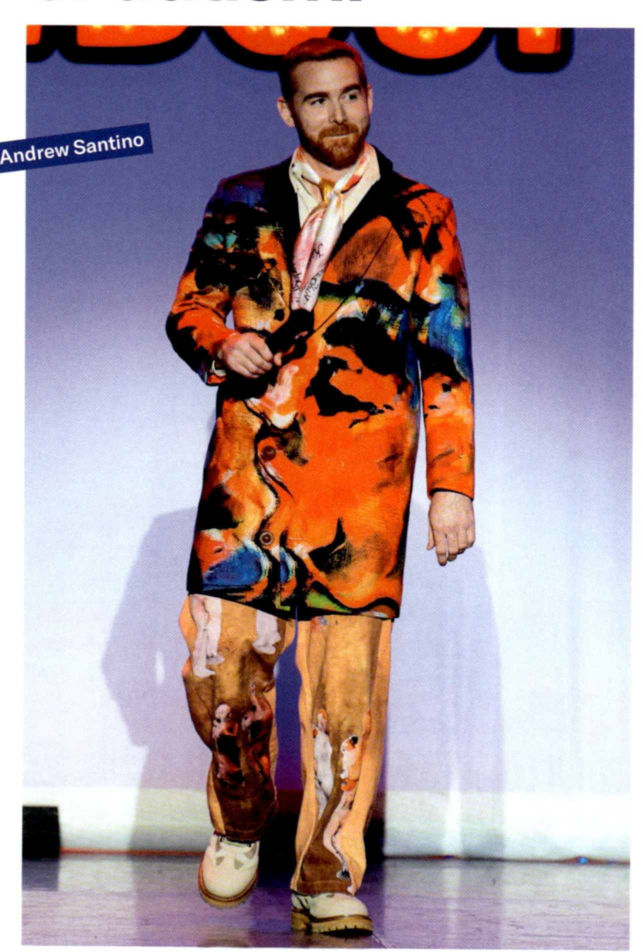

Andrew Santino

"Coming to Europe, like—I mean in New York, people dress well but, like, they dress really well here. Spain, Italy . . . every time I go to Italy, I cannot tell who's gay. I look like I'm crushing p***y."

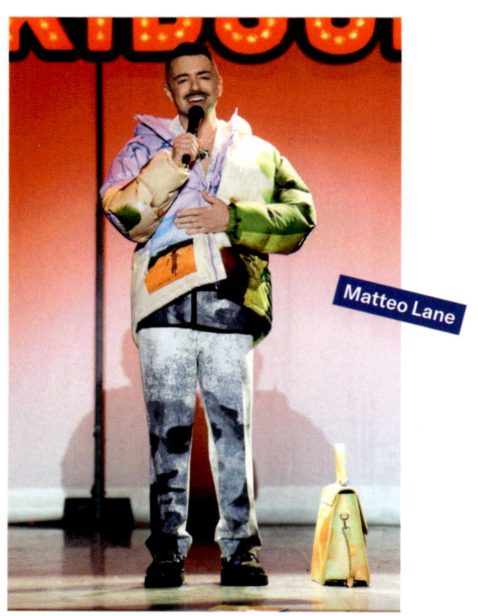

Matteo Lane

"How do I look? I'm looking cute, huh? I look like a bisexual mafia boss right now, dude. Oh man, hilarious that we're here. This makes no sense whatsoever. The f**k am I doing here?"

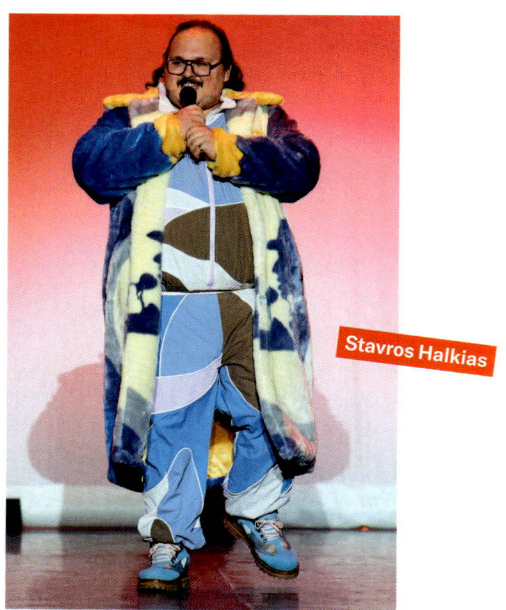

Stavros Halkias

"Before I go any further, I want to shout out all the ushers and all the bathroom attendants here at the theater. Just a few short weeks ago they were running PR for Balenciaga. F**k yeah, f**k yeah, crew. We're going for it tonight."

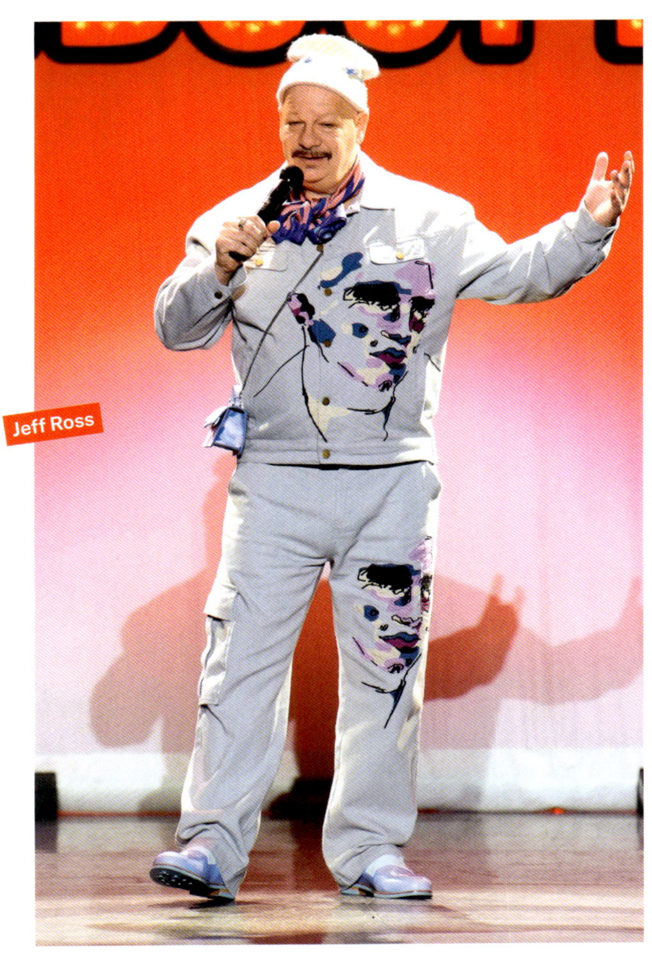

Jeff Ross

"When Colm was younger in New York he would go to the Louis Vuitton flagship store and he would sell his T-shirts to the people that were waiting on line outside the store. And now he sells his shirts inside the store. Anything is possible. Thank you guys so much. Have a great night."

Andrew Schultz

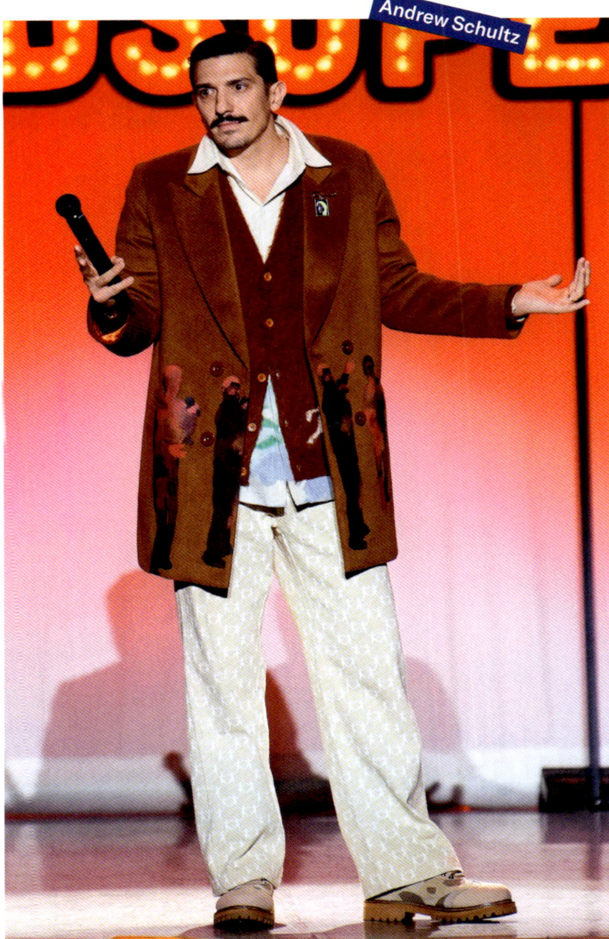

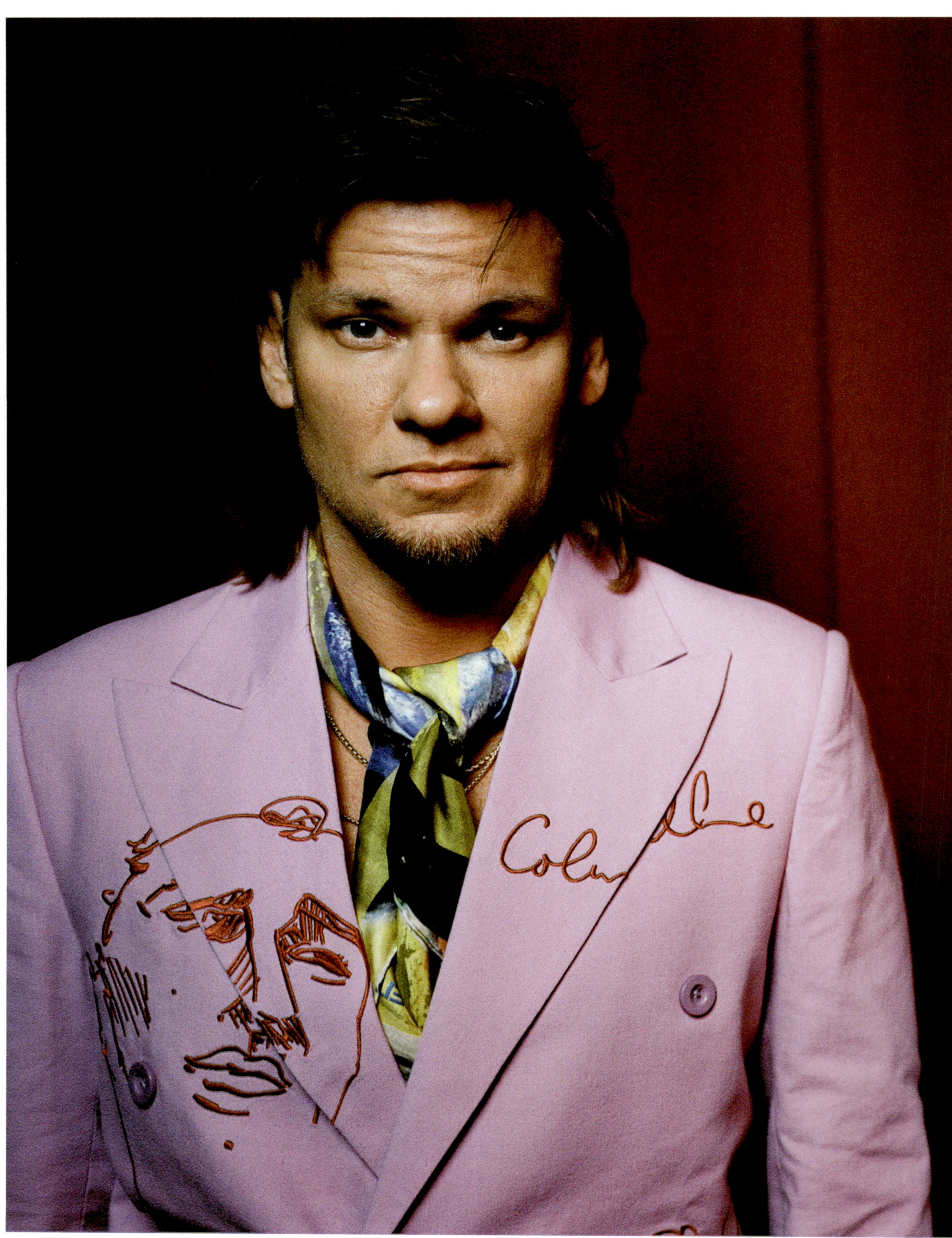

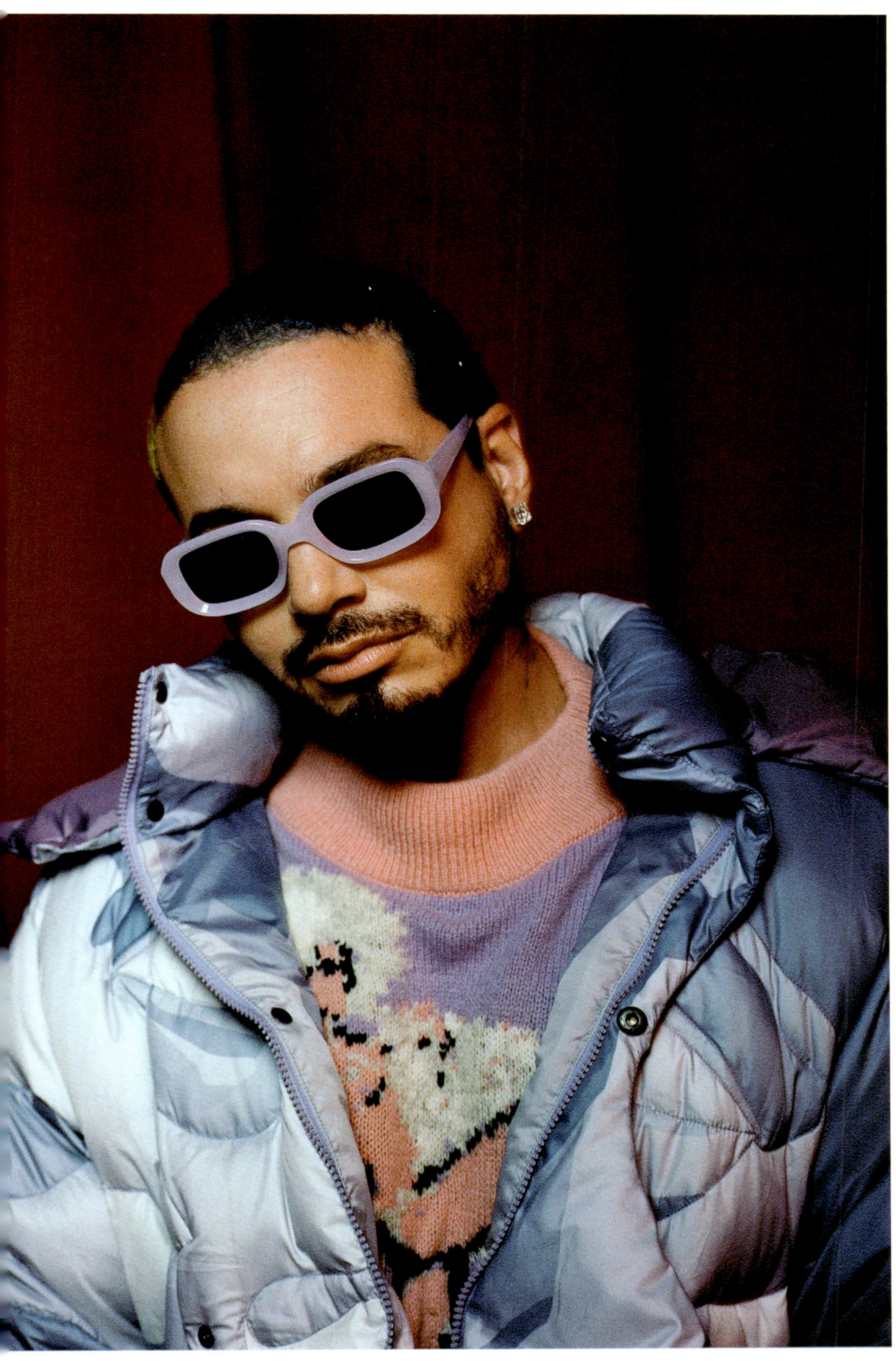

Theo Von and J Balvin, an unexpected duo who look like the start of an upcoming buddy cop movie

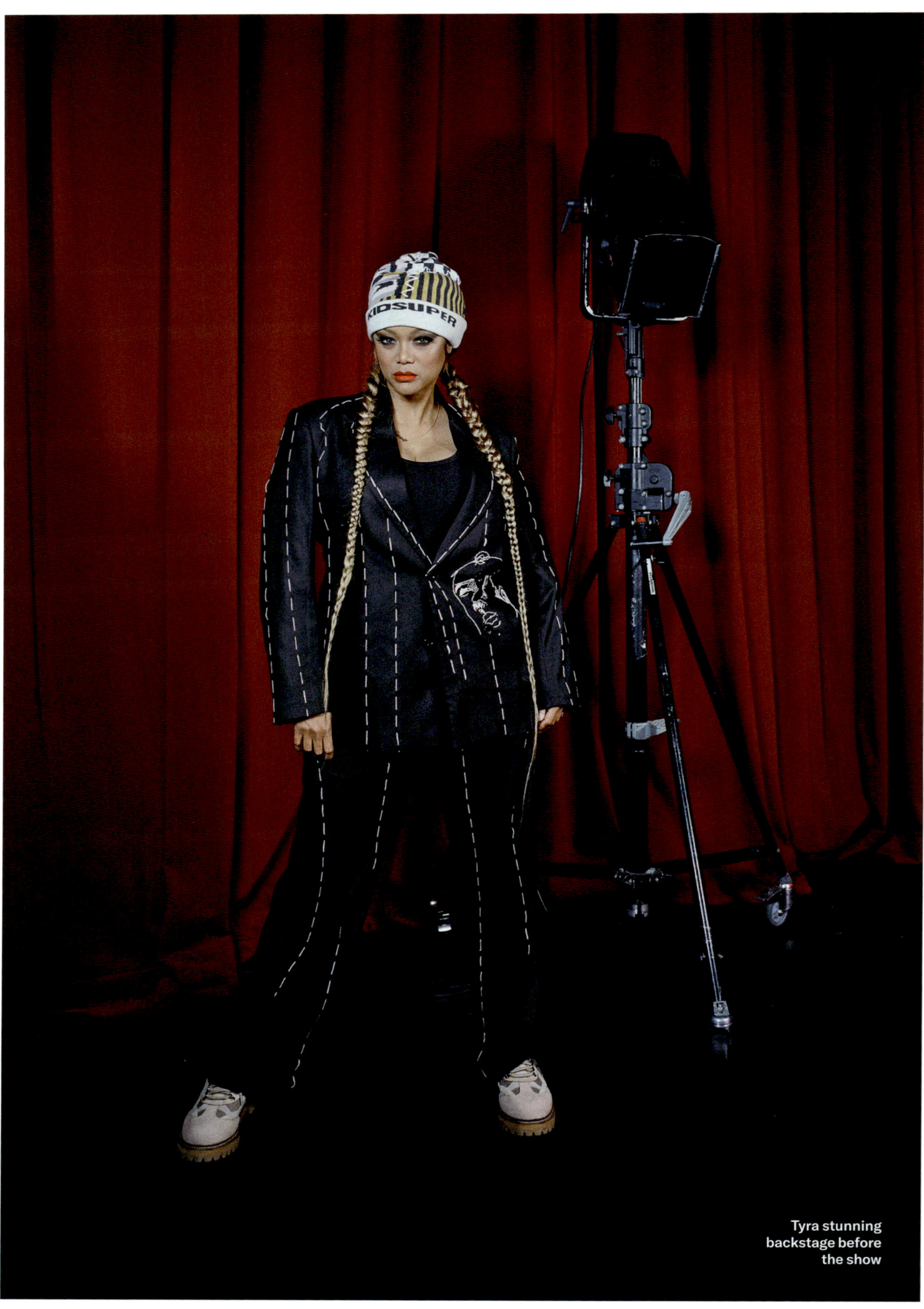

Tyra stunning backstage before the show

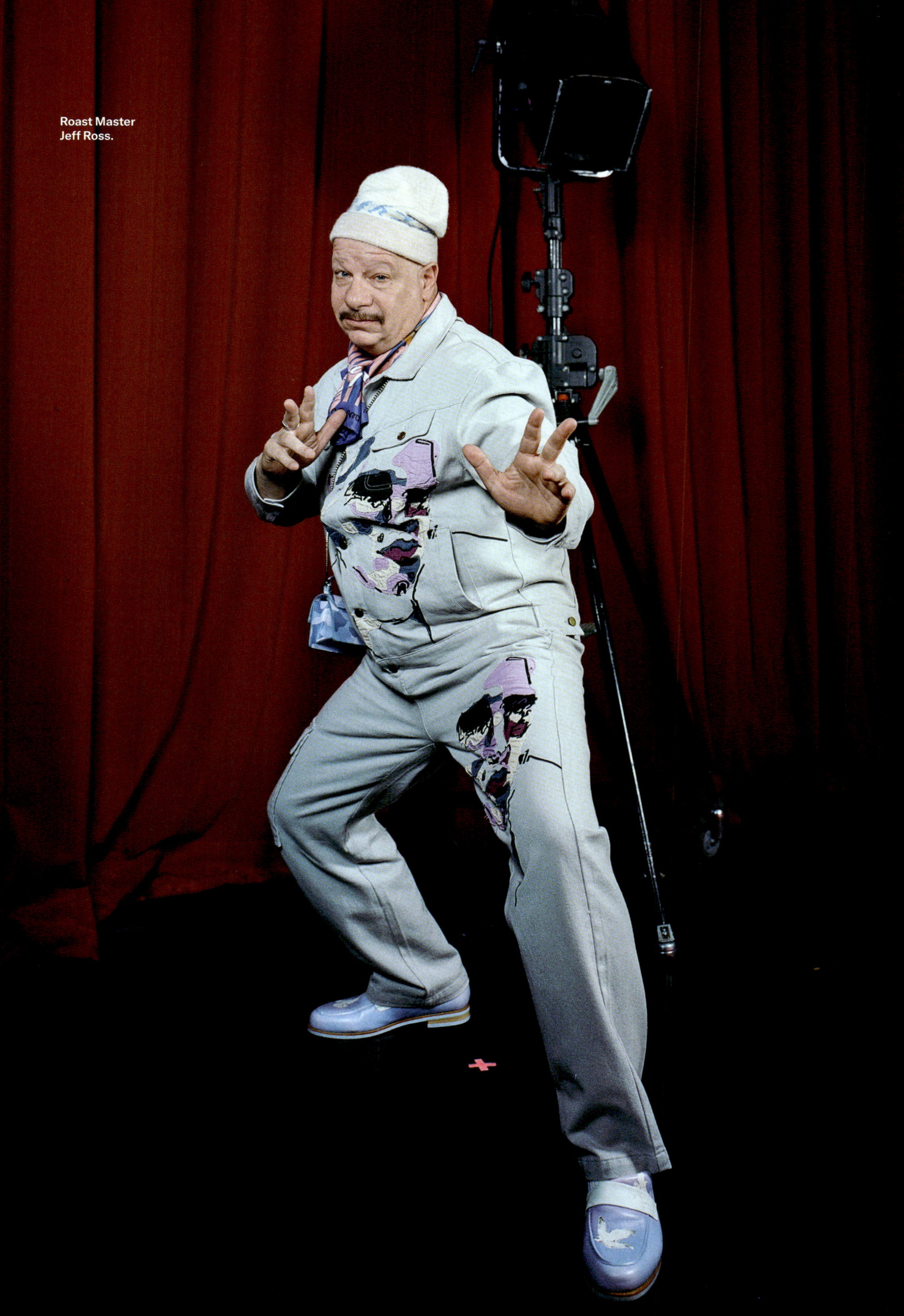

Roast Master
Jeff Ross.

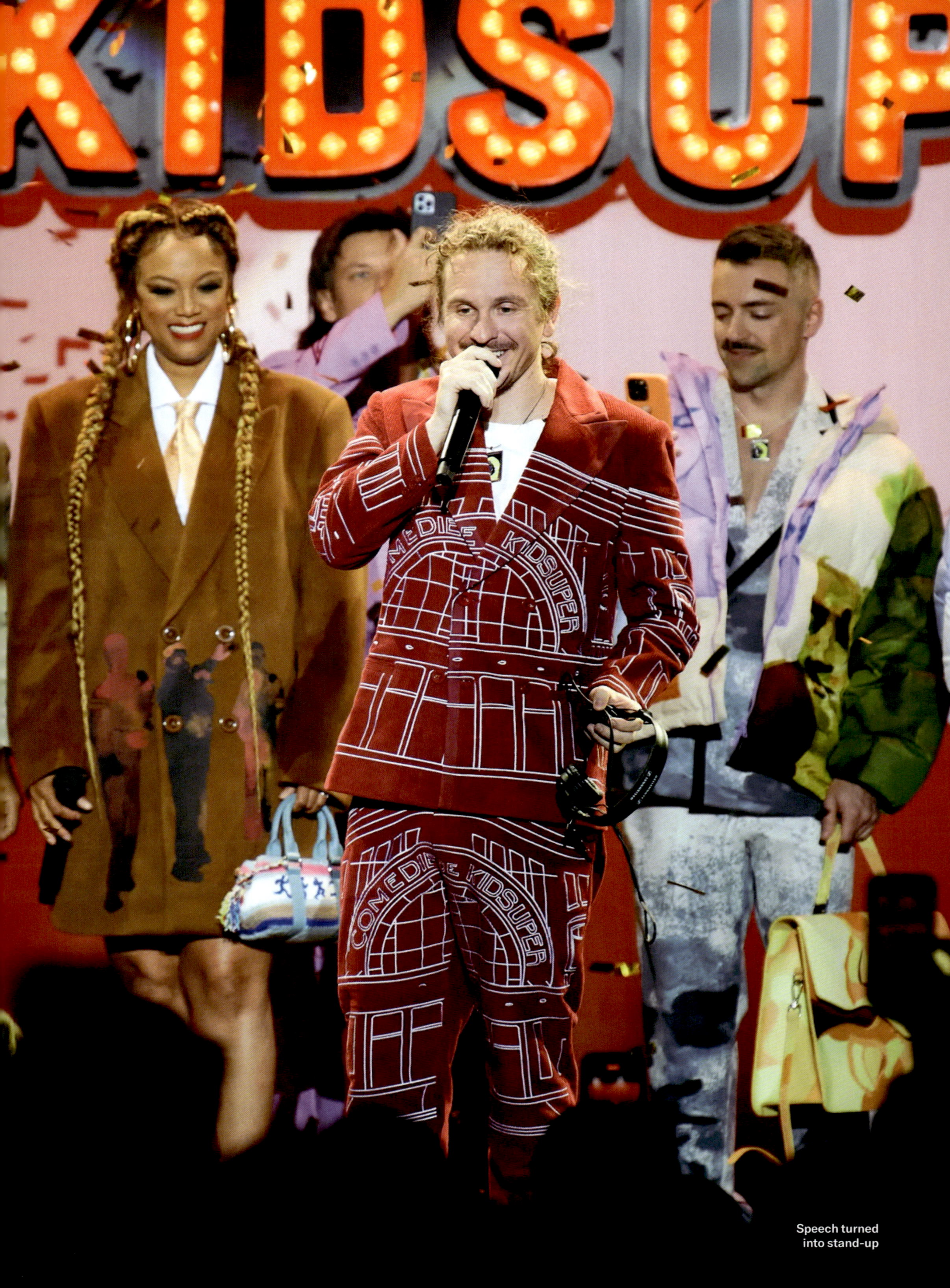

Speech turned into stand-up

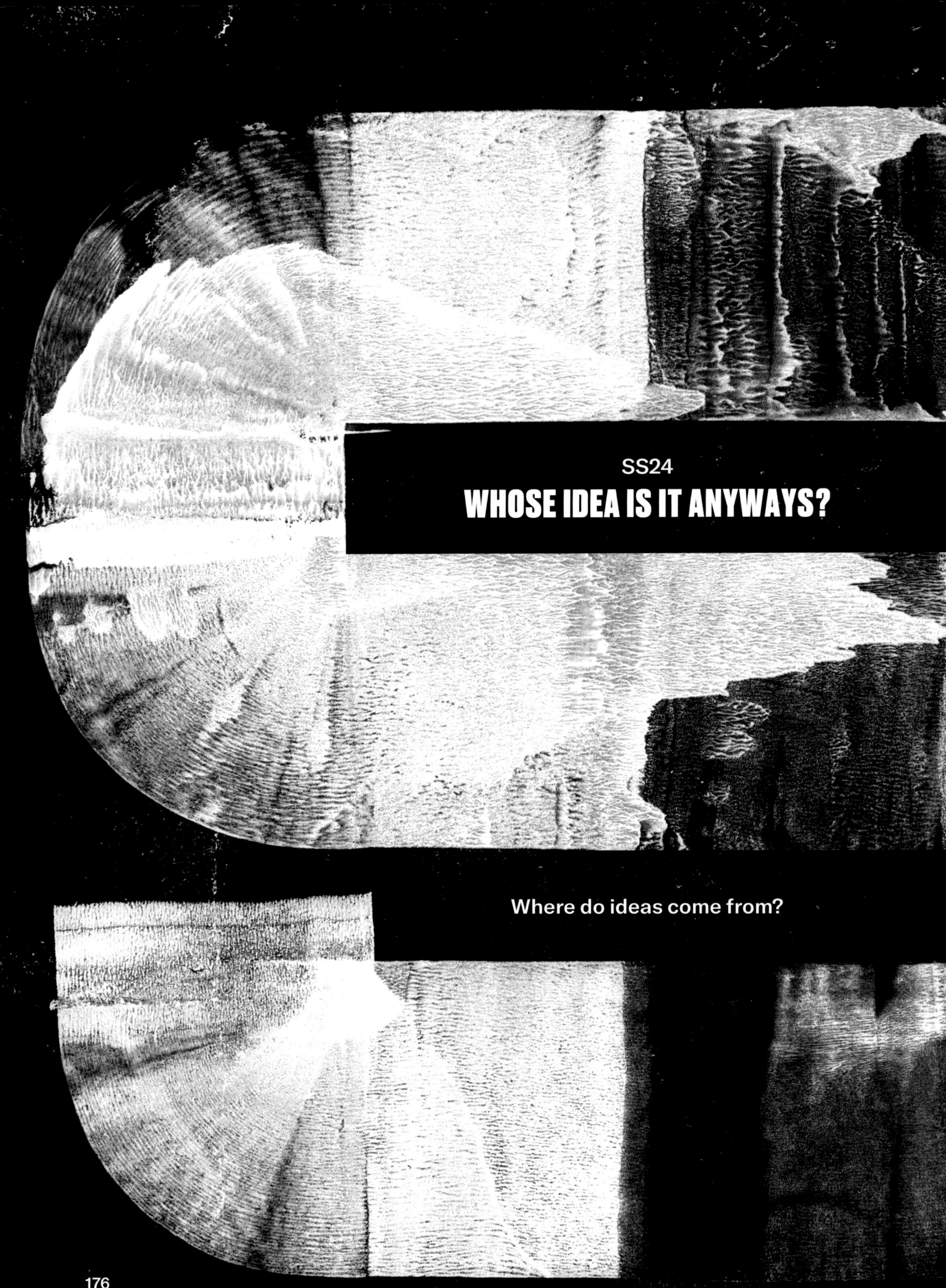

SS24

WHOSE IDEA IS IT ANYWAYS?

Where do ideas come from?

SUPERBILL

ODÉON-THÉATRE DE L'EUROPE

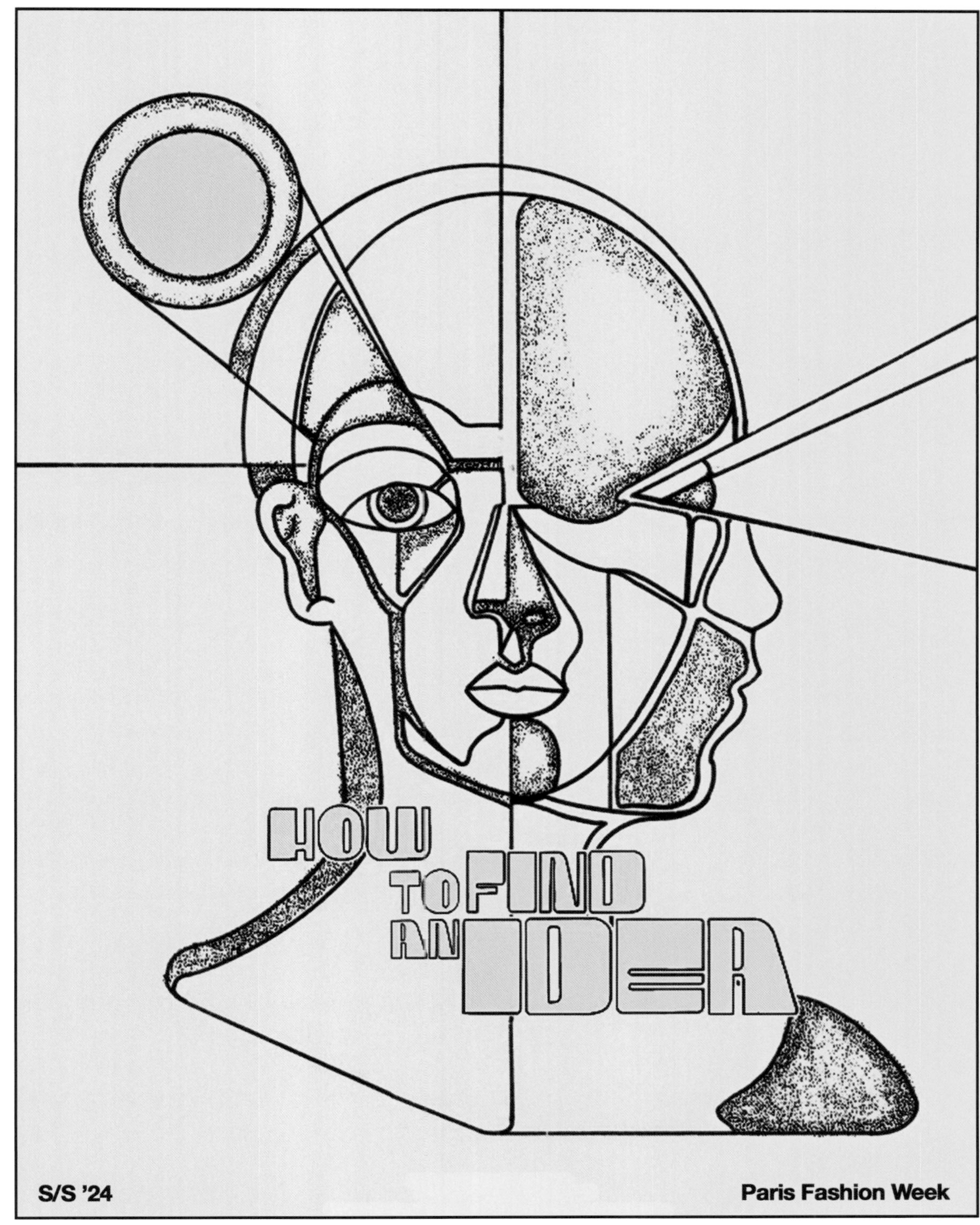

S/S '24

Paris Fashion Week

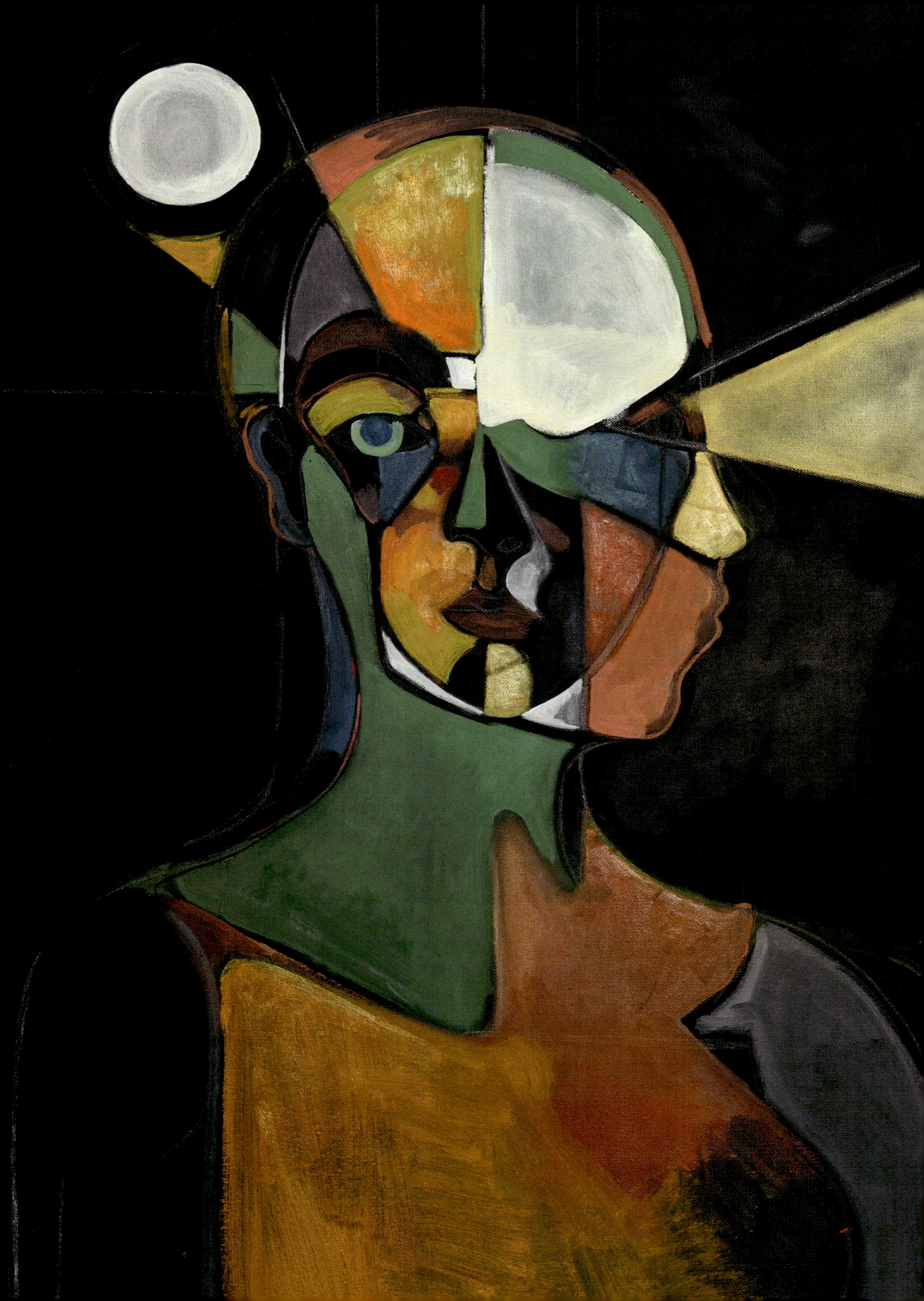

AFTER DOING EIGHT fashion shows where I constantly pushed the boundaries of what was possible, I kept asking myself, What's next? How do I keep one-upping myself? I was researching creative manifestos, where do ideas come from? Is there a specific process that I can outline to help me come up with new good ideas? That search became the driving force behind this show concept.

I HAD ALWAYS believed that theater and fashion would be the ultimate collaboration. If you've ever seen *Broadway*, the costume design is almost as impressive as the show itself. That thought led me to my next project—a play about ideas and where they come from.

I wrote a nine-part show, representing the different parts of my brain that I go through when coming up with ideas. The first scene was me searching, walking into my own ear, entering a space where ideas bounced around like in the string room. One of my biggest inspirations in creating is putting myself in a position where failure isn't an option—like being trapped in a burning house. That metaphor became a set piece: if you're in a burning house, you have to find a way out. Another scene portrayed the insecurity that comes with new ideas, represented by a game show where I stood in my underwear, exposed to judgment. There was also the absurdity room, inspired by Dadaism, where I explored the most outlandish and unconventional concepts.

The play had a laundry room scene where I played with the idea that everything—every idea—is ultimately made up. It tied into the concept of spontaneous, absurd if-then scenarios. I crafted an entire thirty-page script with nine sets, searching for the right cast. We jokingly considered actors like Timothée Chalamet, Vincent Cassel, but either they were unattainable or they declined. Eventually, I realized I had always imagined myself playing the lead, so I stepped into the role.

Check your messages.

Art arranges elements that appeal to the senses and emotions.

this is not working

Are Words enough.

It's a commodity. It's a bicycle. It takes you places,

tik tok tik tok tik tok

we are not working

When the voices and music hit the ultimate crescendo (please see audio attached) the HERO screams and falls back

HERO
STOPPPPPPPPP!!!!!!

The theater goes completely silent and black.

PAPER MACHE EAR

The paper-mache ear set gets pushed into scene from right to left. The ear stops at the table. Our hero steps on the chair, table and books to enter into the massive paper mache ear. At this point the ear begins to move toward stage right, slowly pushing the table, chair and dustbin. He crawls very hesitantly into the ear and the ear tube. As our HERO crawls through the ear, the music sounds as if it is crawling through a cave with echoing voices. When the ear box is in the center between the two curtains, the hero should be midway, he stops to breath like this is super difficult and waits for the ear to begin moving again. The voices seem like they are getting closer as he climbs through. The closer he gets too the end of the tube we hear some of the similar voices. As the HERO crawls through the ear tube, the next room enters into frame. For almost every time our HERO switches from one room to the next he is in the center stage so we see the transition.

THREAD ROOM

Our HERO falls out of the tube into a room filled with thread. Our HERO is confused and shocked.

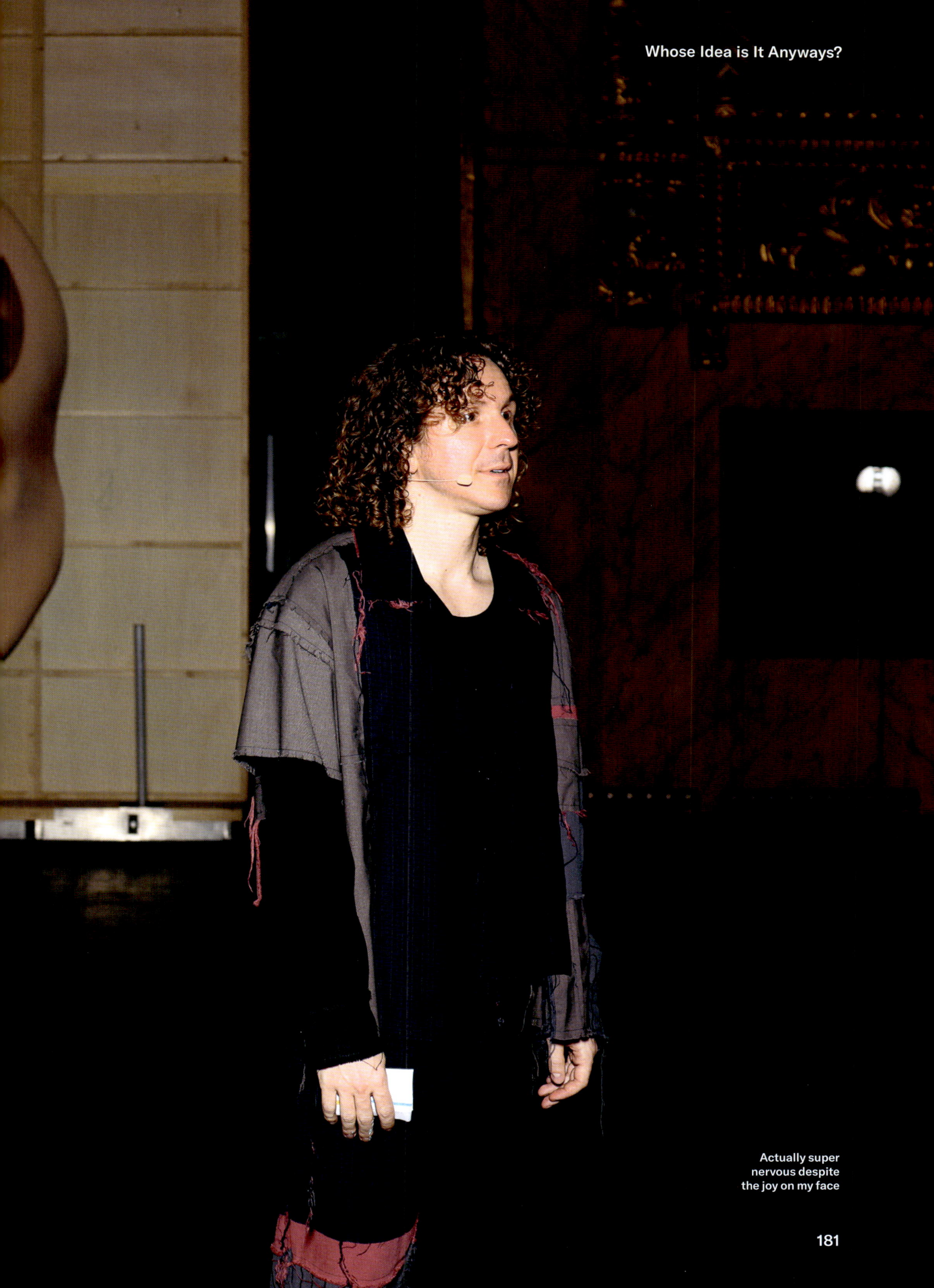

Actually super
nervous despite
the joy on my face

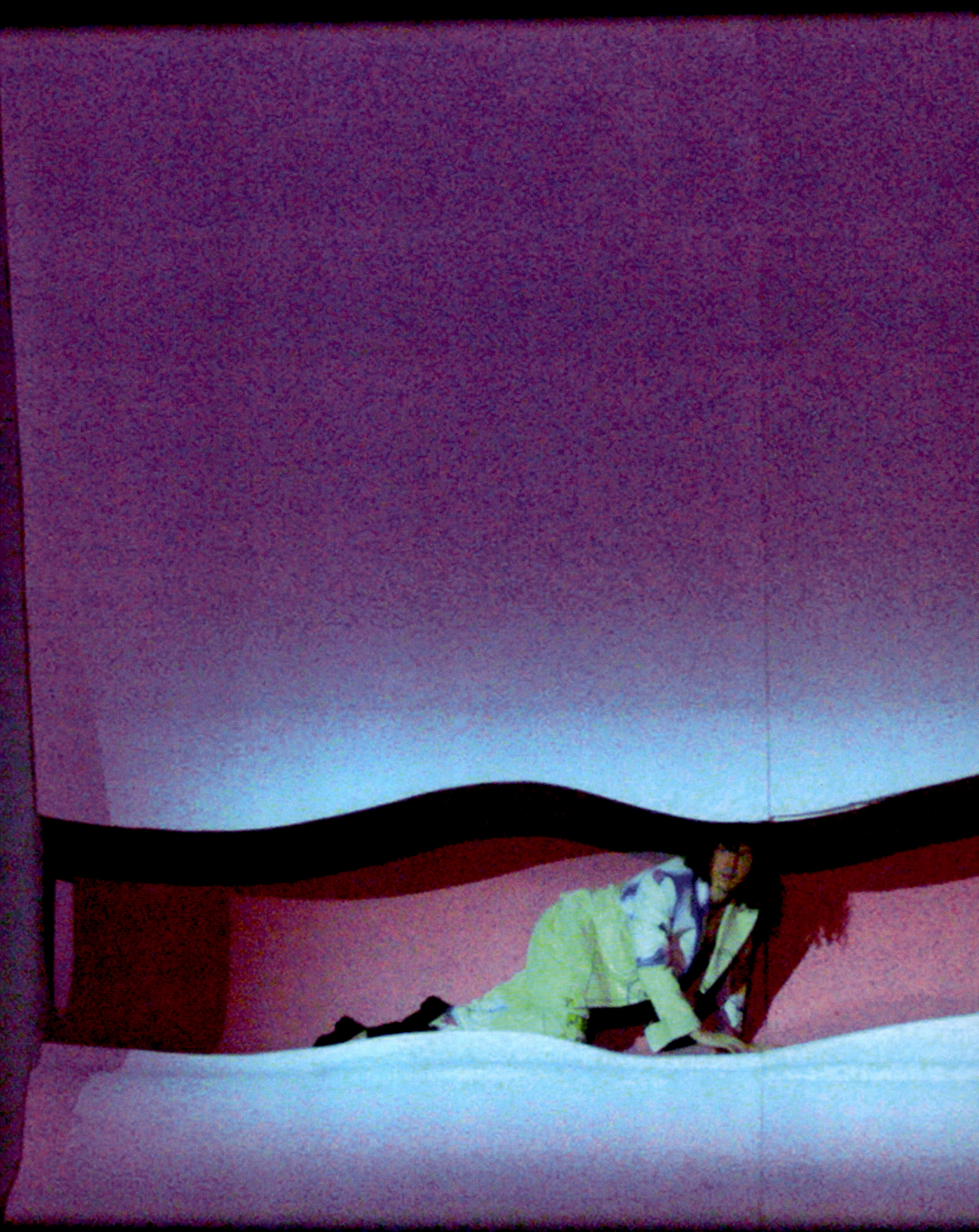

Full set design of the ear canal, entering the brain to conjure up ideas

When we arrived in Paris, I had to finalize the casting, oversee set designs, and manage rehearsals. But nothing was going according to plan. A fashion show alone is a logistical nightmare, but a theatrical play within a fashion show—with thirty actors, lines to memorize, and nine massive sets that needed to move in perfect unison—was nearly impossible. We were performing at the Odéon, the oldest operating theater in Europe (crazy to even think about in retrospect), which was an incredible honor, but it had a small stage. The complexity of our setup meant one set could only move if all nine sets moved in unison. We were supposed to have five rehearsals, but on the day of the show, after just one incomplete attempt where everything went wrong, I was talking to my friend, genuinely considering pulling the fire alarm to cancel the whole thing.

But then there was this KidSuper moment—this "fuck it" attitude that has always been part of the brand. Taking risks, putting yourself out there, attempting the impossible. I had written the script, designed the sets, cast the actors, choreographed the movements—every single aspect of the production was my responsibility. So I thought, If it fails, then at least I gave it my all.

The curtains rose. I was nervous, not just for my performance but for whether the show would even function. And then—it worked! It wasn't perfect, but it worked. At the end of the show, I had a monologue where I said, "There's nothing quite like a 3:00 a.m. idea." But in that moment, my mind went blank. I was standing in front of 2,000 people, the spotlight on me, and I completely forgot the next line. I just repeated, "There's nothing quite like a 3:00 a.m. idea." And somehow, as I said it again, "There's nothing quite like a 3:00 a.m. idea," and all my lines came rushing back. No one noticed the slip, but for me, it was symbolic—I had put everything into this show, exposed my soul, and faced the ultimate challenge.

The reviews came in. *Vogue* published a negative review, saying they couldn't see the clothes, that it didn't work. And while I don't normally care about reviews, this one stung—not because of their opinion, but because it shaped how others saw the show. What they failed to recognize was that this wasn't just another fashion show; it was an absolute feat, a personal and creative triumph. To the *Vogue* writer: go fuck yourself. I am joking but I think you need another watch!

But to everyone else—this show was one of the most meaningful, difficult, and rewarding things I've ever done. I hope that one day, everyone gets to see it.

MOM
you were always a fighter ever since a little kid

THEAD VOICE 2
You'll never seen a U-haul behind a hearse

When the voices speak, a spot light is pointed at them. They do not interact with our hero, it is as if he is not there.

THREAD VOICE 1
What if you do a fashion show thats a auction,

THREAD VOICE 2
A comedy show?

THREAD VOICE 3
A TV show?

THREAD VOICE 1
A claymation show?

THREAD VOICE 3
A movie show?

The voices start to overlap and accelerate.

THREAD VOICE 2
A circus show?

THREAD VOICE 3
A theater show?

THREAD VOICE 1
A robot show?

THREAD VOICE 2
A soccer show?

THREAD VOICE 1
A café show?

THREAD VOICE 3
An art show?

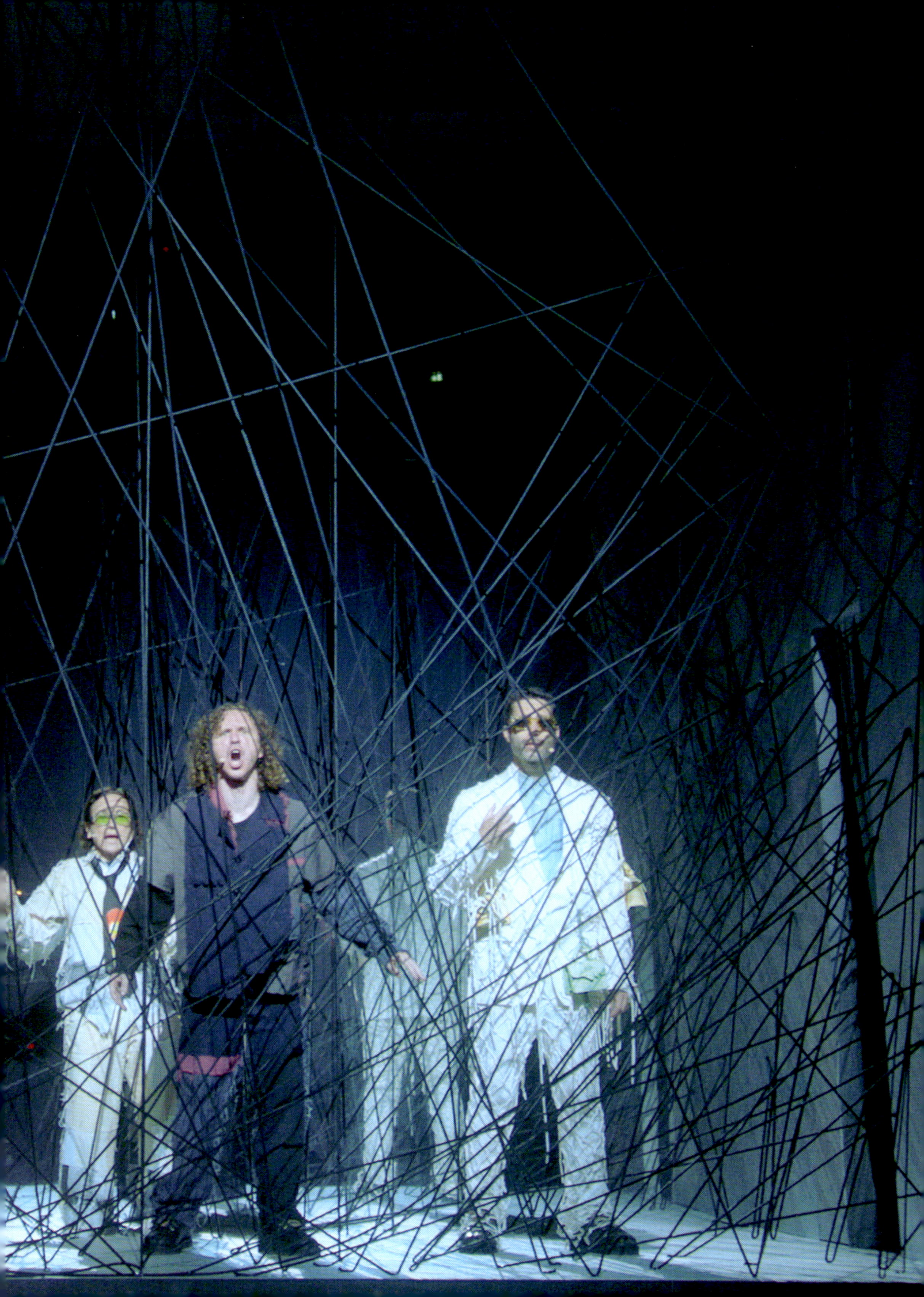

GODFATHER
to assume there is a fire is almost more powerful than there being a real fire. Though the same physical experience being in a room and being LOCKED in a room are very very different. The mind can be a powerful enemy or ally.

The sounds of the fire rise, we see smoke coming from the room.

HERO
I can feel the heat. I can see the smoke. I can hear the flames. this isn't a game! Why are you so calm?

The Godfather gets up and is walking to the opposite side of the room as our HERO.

GODFATHER
AHH but I have been here before, many times.

HERO
I haven't and I do not know why I am here but but I know I didn't come here to die!

GODFATHER
so you came here to what?

HERO still nervously looking around..

HERO
what

GODFATHER
why are you here, did you come here to die or...

HERO
what do you mean I obviously fucking came here to live!

GODFATHER gets excited

GODFATHER
(excited and professing)
Yes! That is it! You came here to live! You said it!

This is life! You can fucking feel it! The energy through the walls! This is what its all about! Isn't that funny, now that the house is burning you feel more alive?! You can feel life in these burning walls.

The GODFATHER gets up and walk out the room to Stage Right. As soon as The Godfather closes the door, the box begins to move. Our HERO, somewhat startled by their abruptness, gets up and follows. He realizes the door is locked. He is banging on the door, shaking the door knob. There is a door on the other side of the room, our HERO walks to the other side, as the stage moves, and tries the other door. The door opens and we enter into an office space.

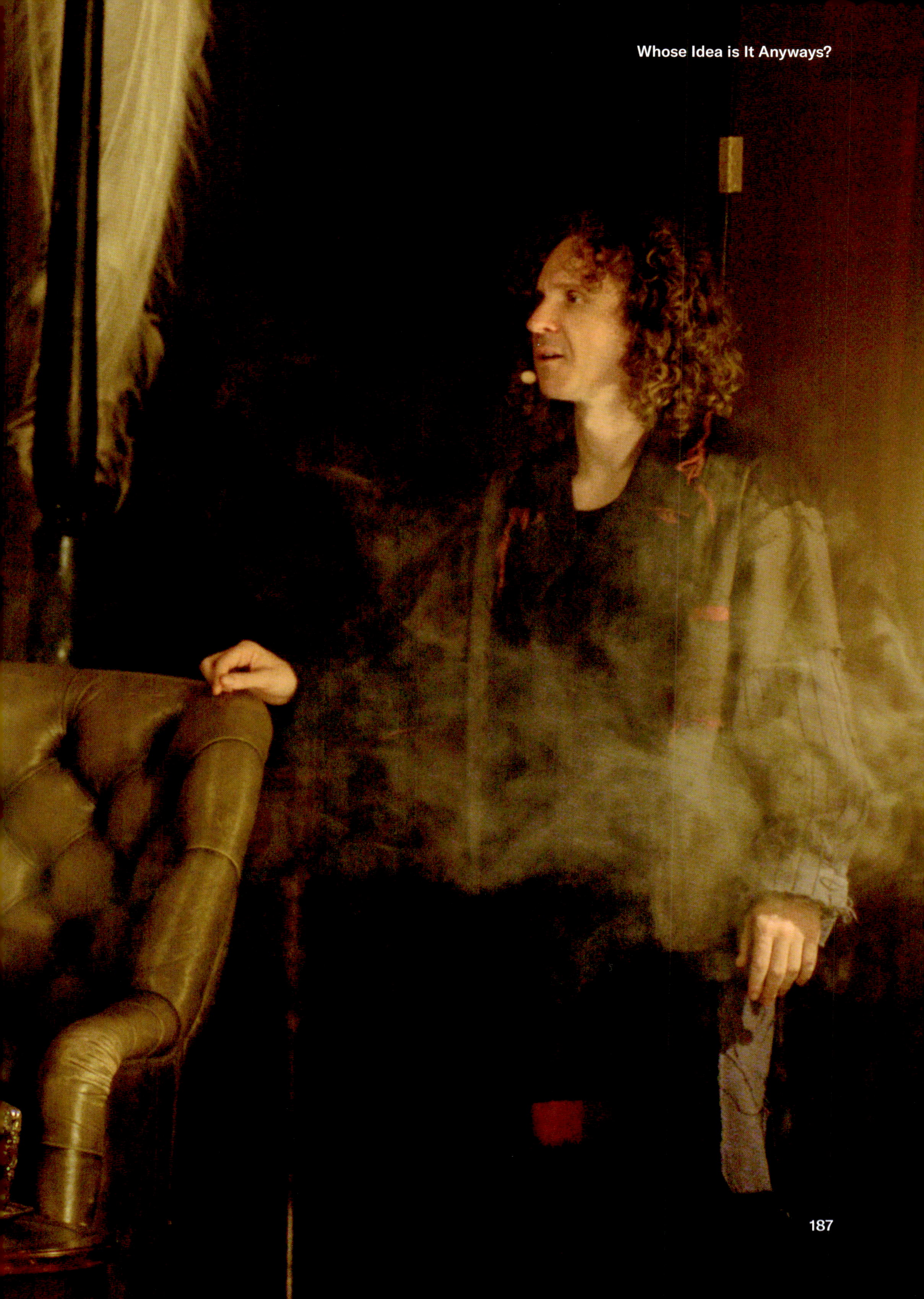

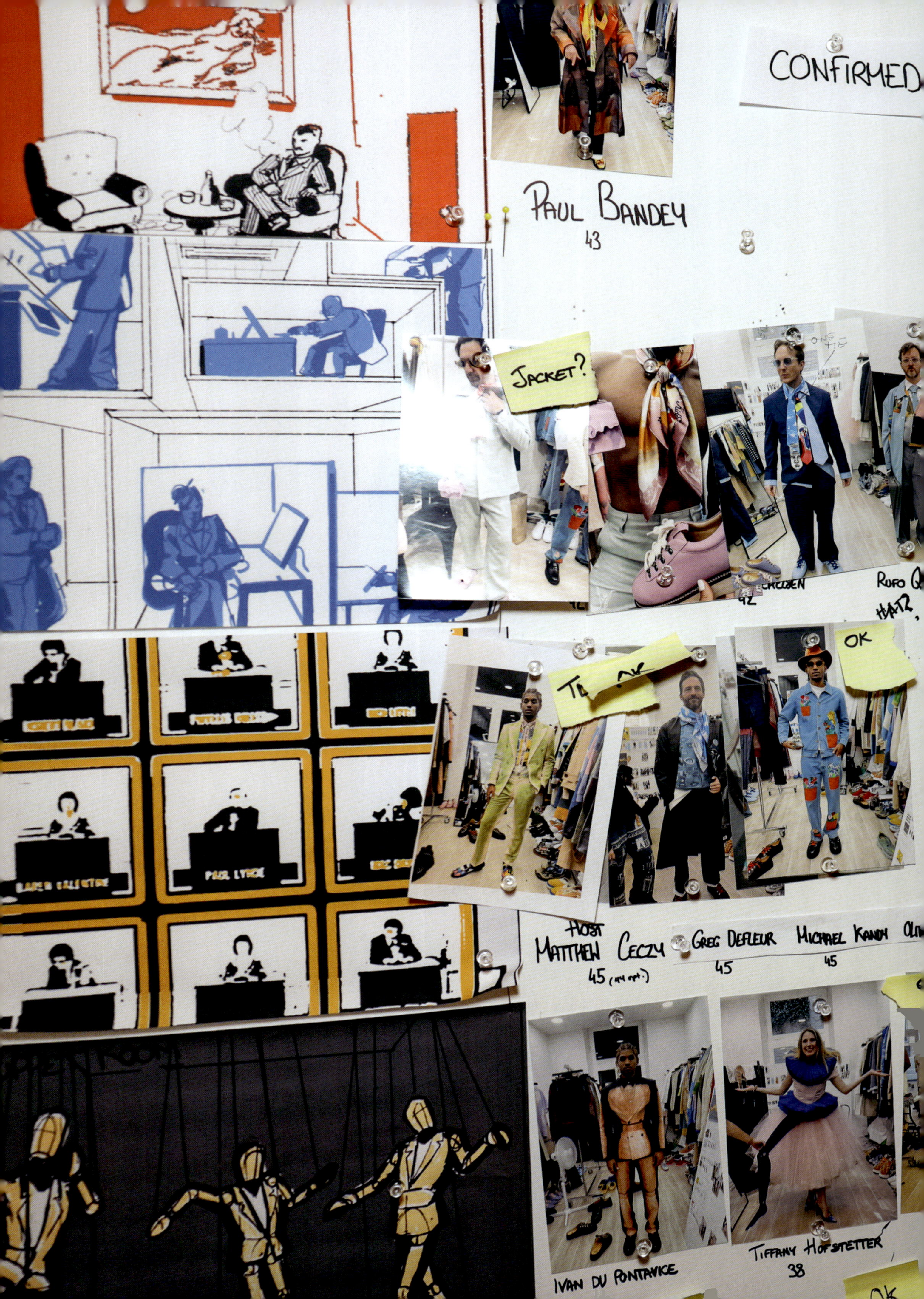
CONFIRMED
PAUL BANDEY
43
JACKET?
OK
HOST
MATTHEW CECZY
45
GREG DEFLEUR
45
MICHAEL KANDY
45
IVAN DU PONTAVICE
TIFFANY HOFSTETTER
38

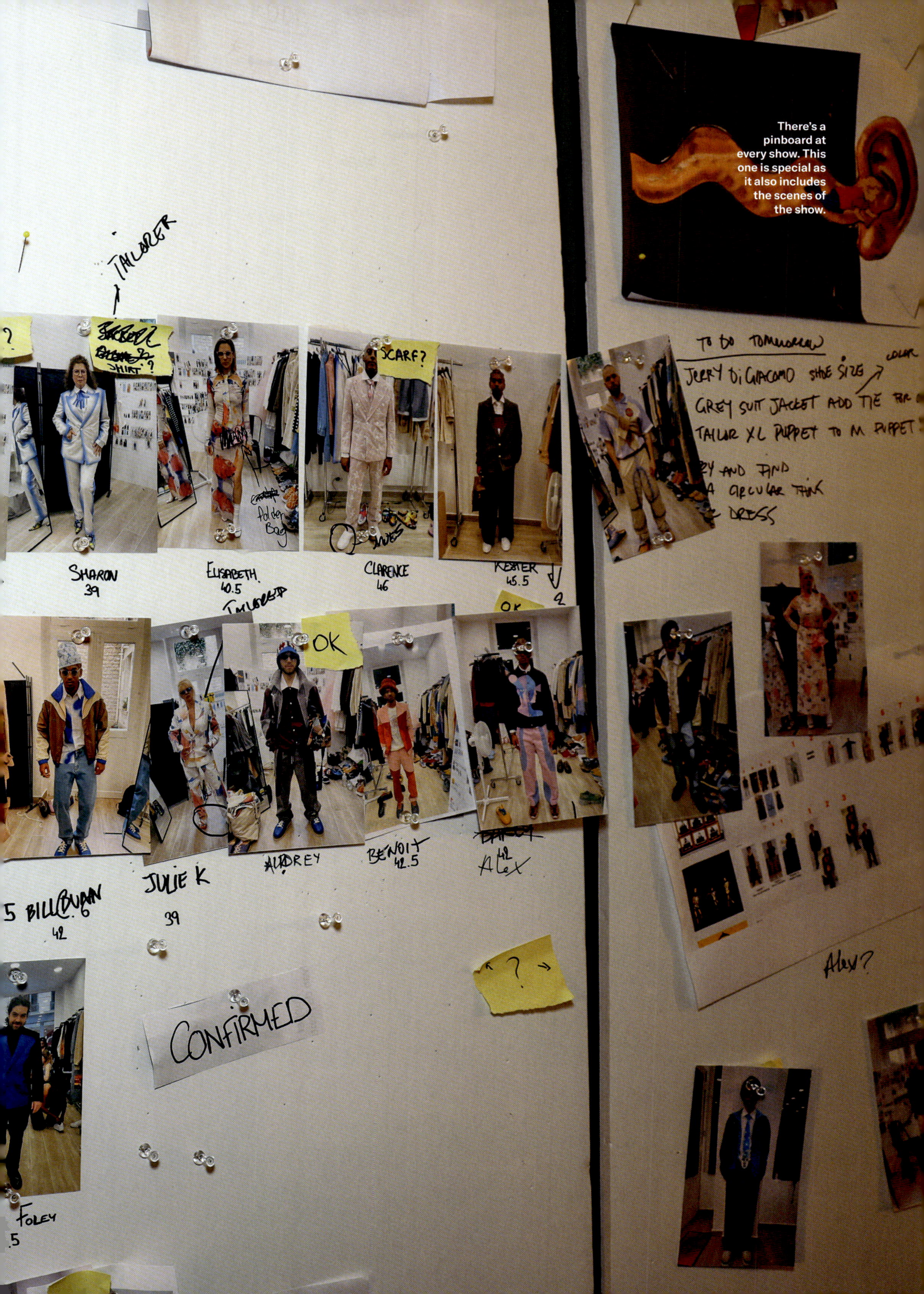

There's a pinboard at every show. This one is special as it also includes the scenes of the show.

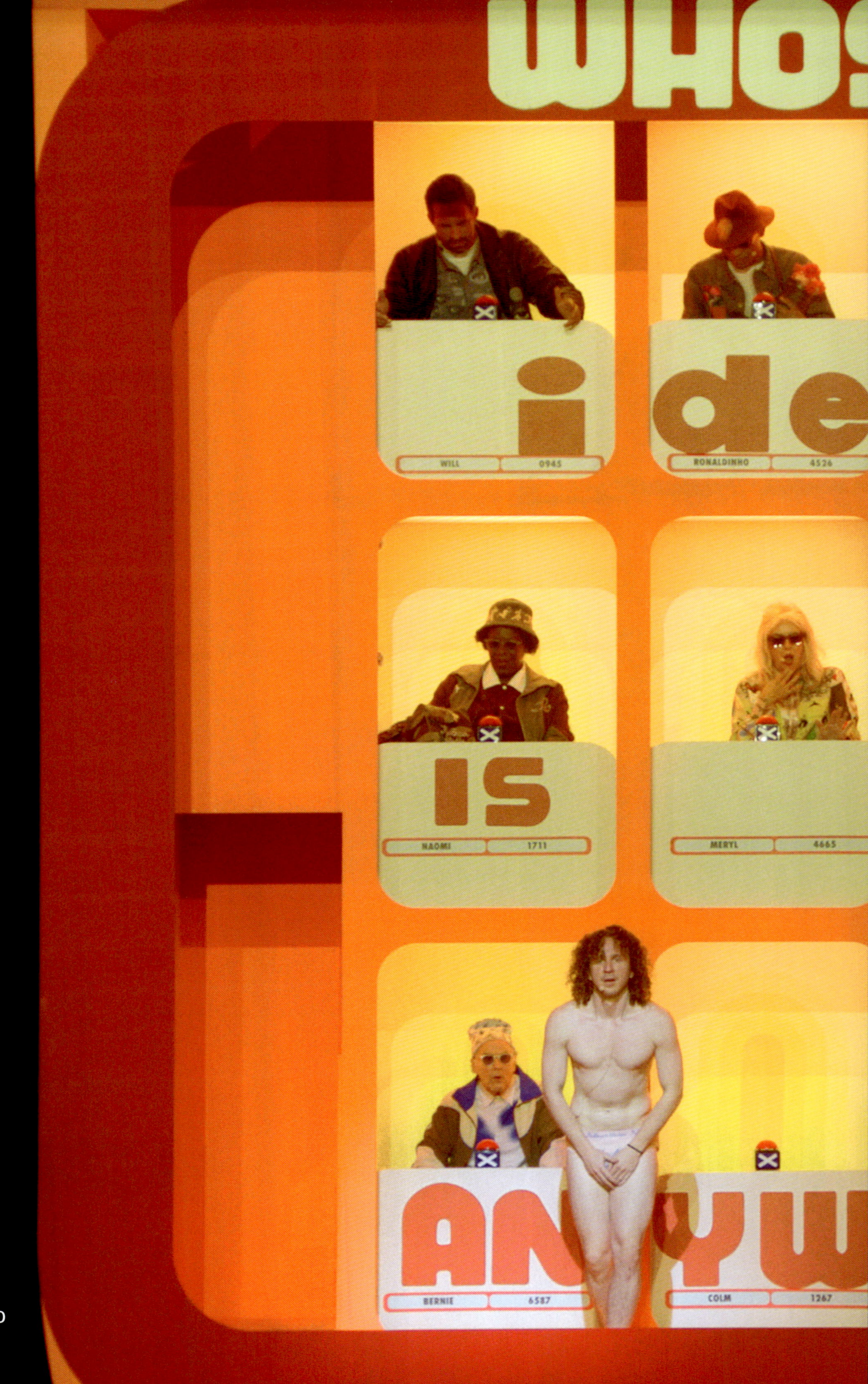
WHO
i
de
WILL 0945
RONALDINHO 4526
IS
NAOMI 1711
MERYL 4665
BERNIE 6587
COLM 1267

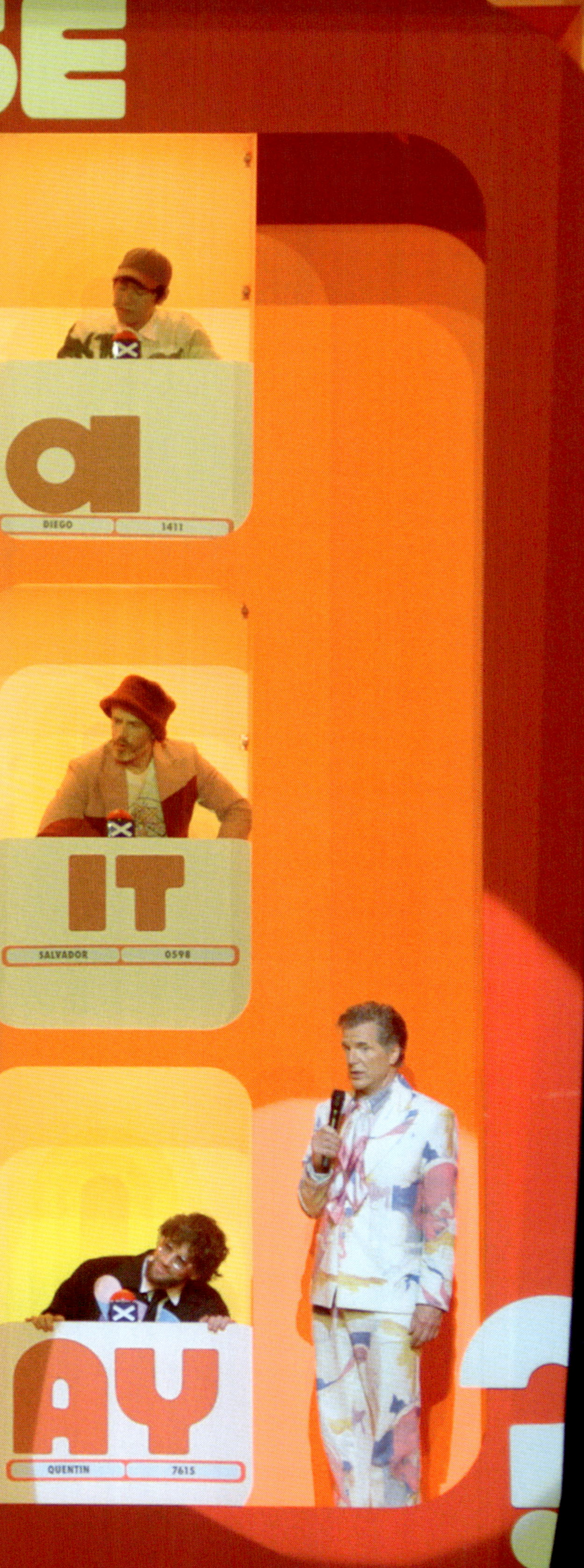

I was gonna go naked but they wouldn't let me so I wore some KidSuper underwear samples.

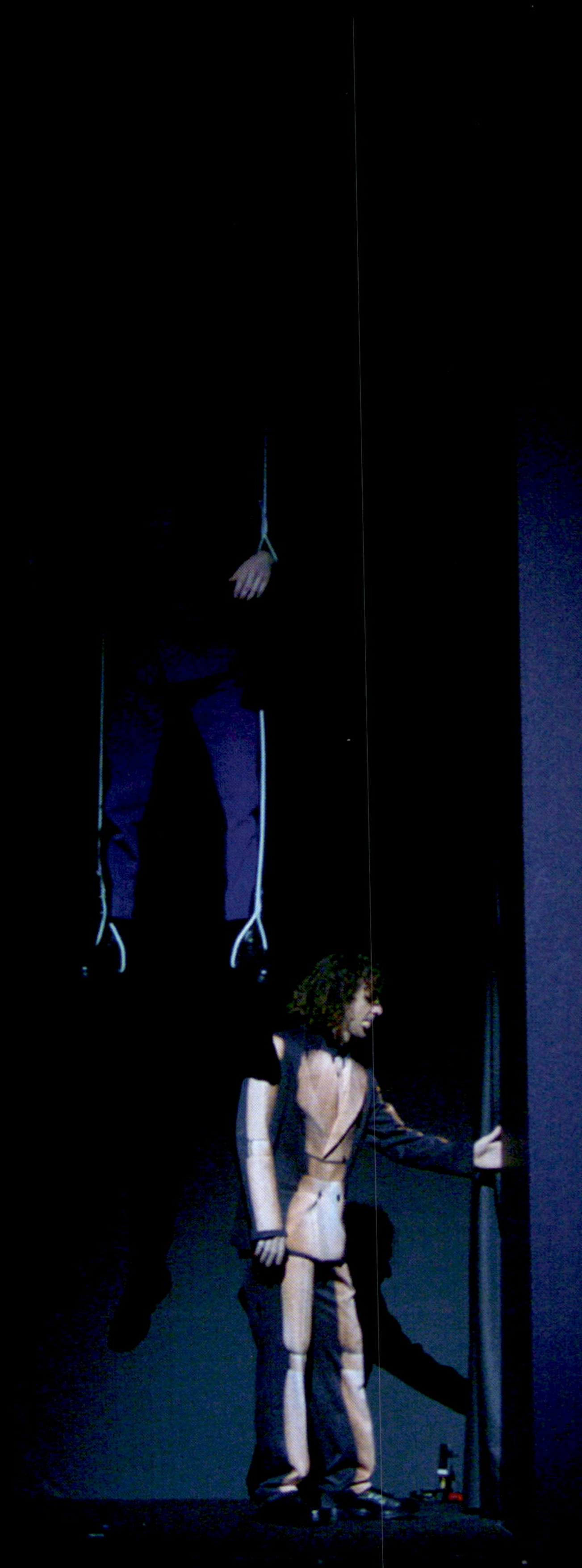

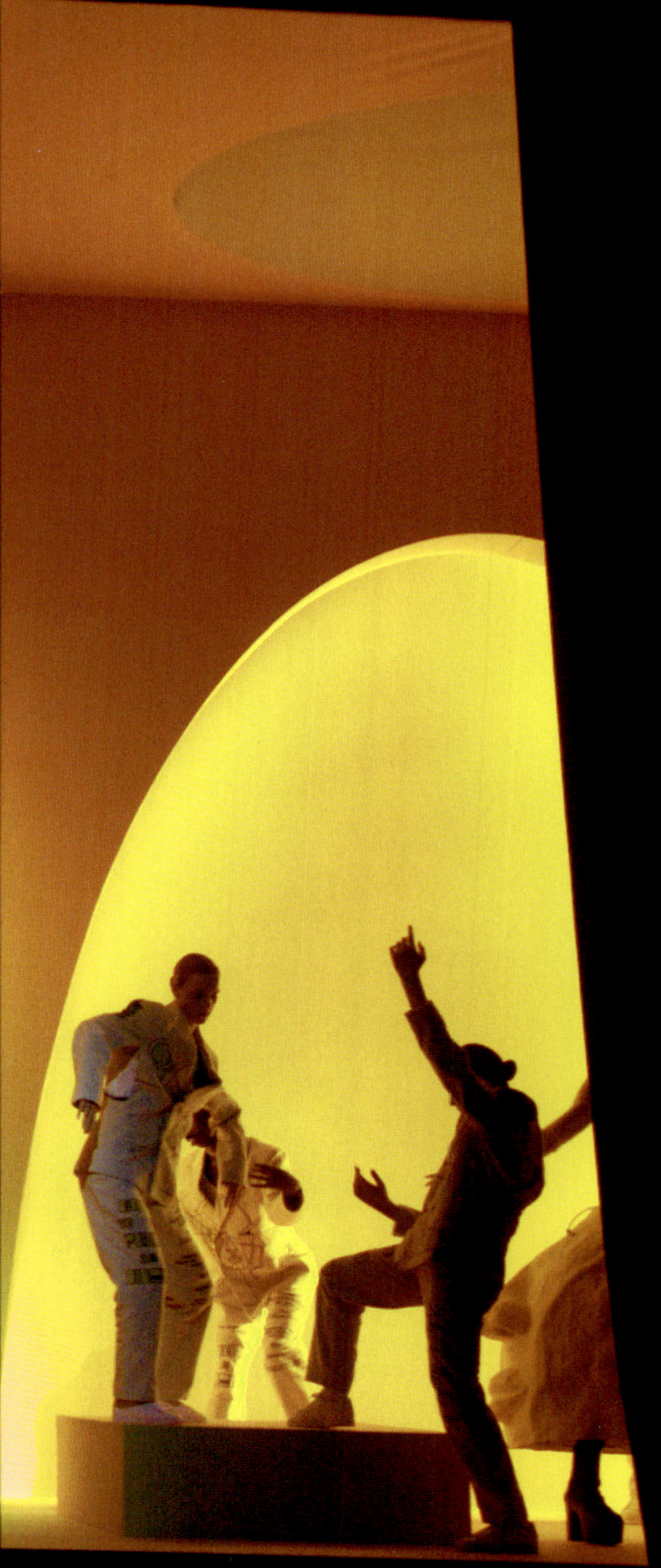

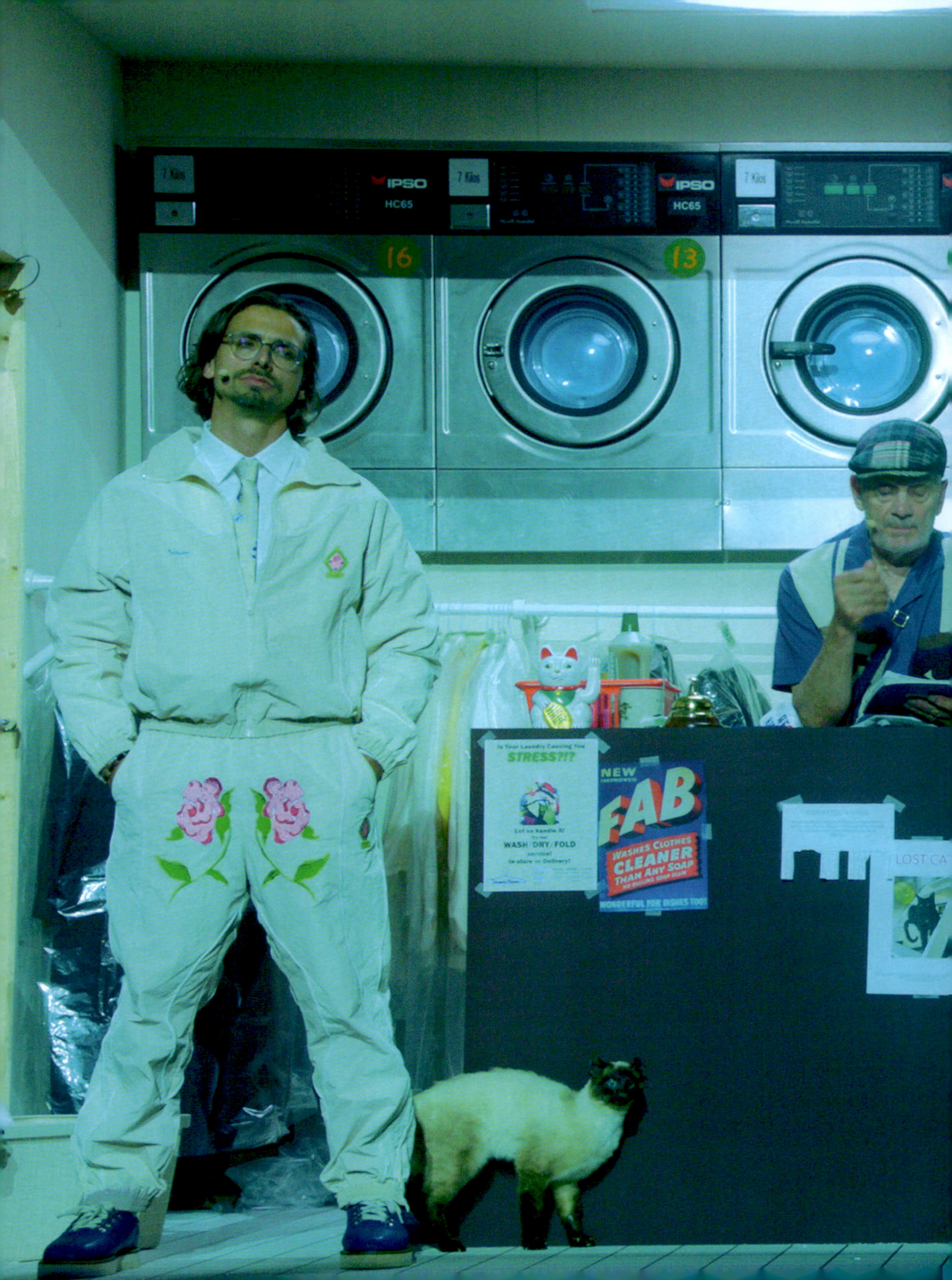
7 Kilos
IPSO
HC65
7 Kilos
IPSO
HC65
7 Kilos
16
13
Is Your Laundry Causing You
STRESS?!?
Let us handle it!
WASH/DRY/FOLD
NEW
FAB
WASHES CLOTHES
CLEANER
THAN ANY SOAP
WONDERFUL FOR DISHES TOO!
LOST CA

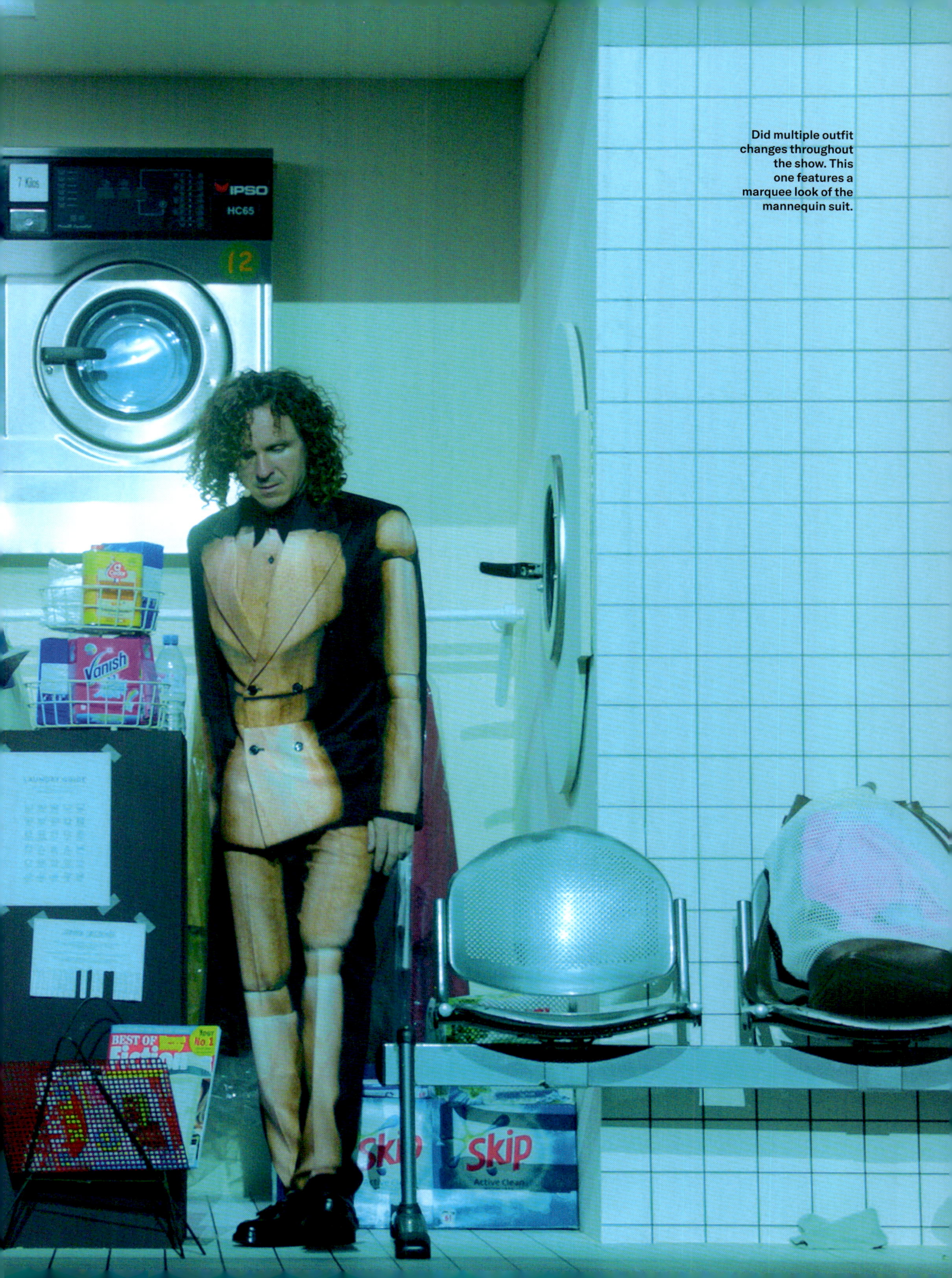

Did multiple outfit changes throughout the show. This one features a marquee look of the mannequin suit.

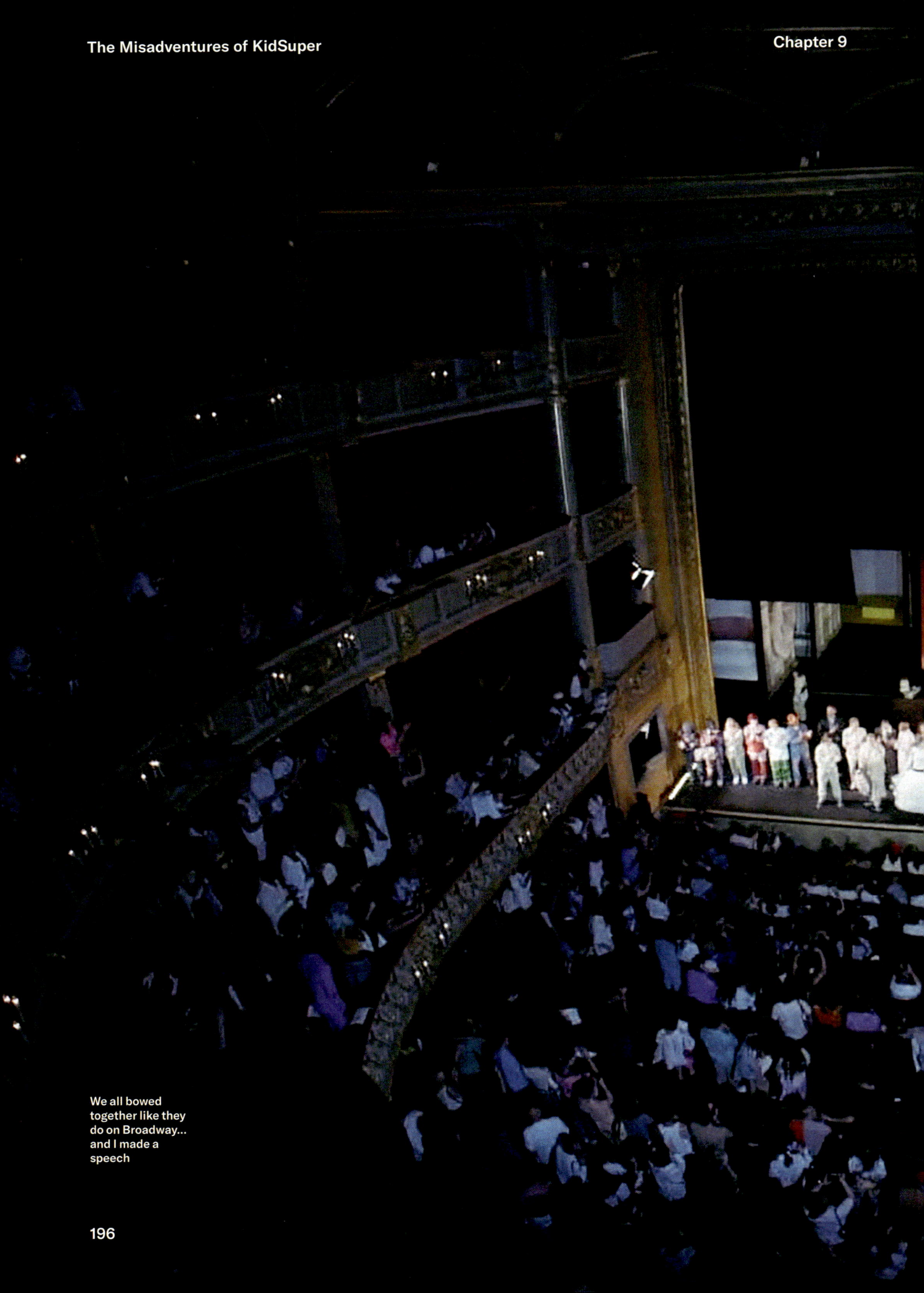

We all bowed together like they do on Broadway... and I made a speech

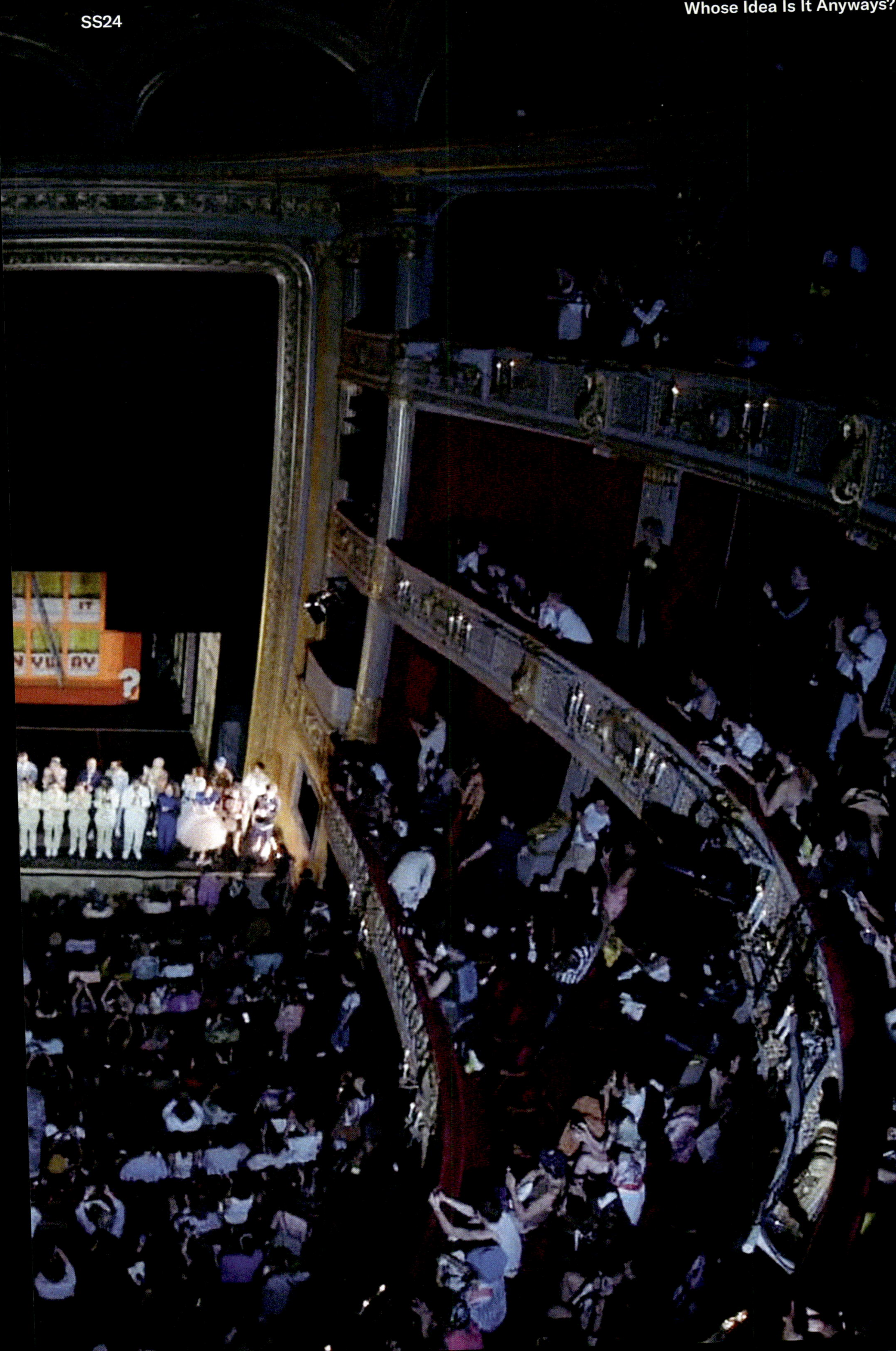

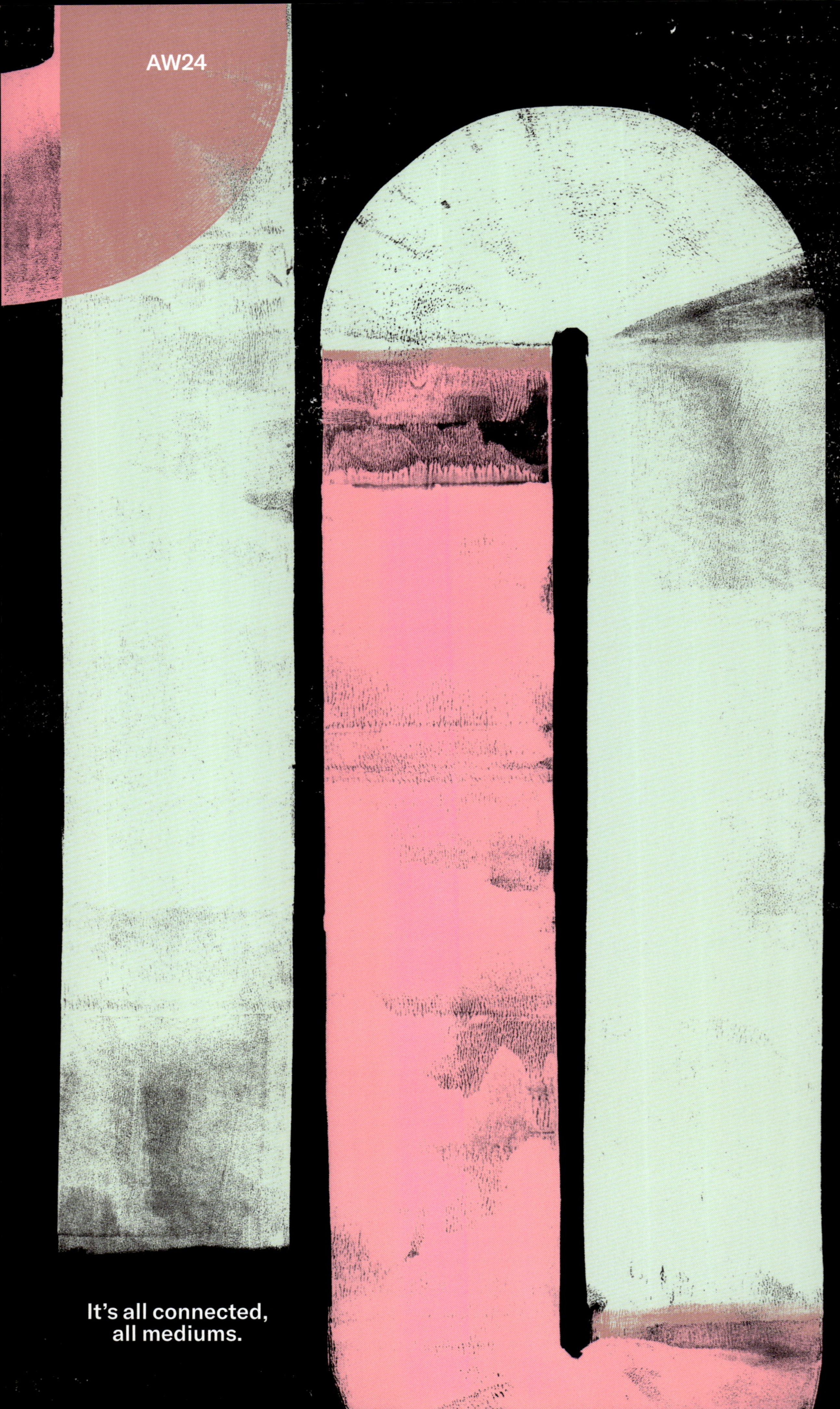
AW24
It’s all connected,
all mediums.

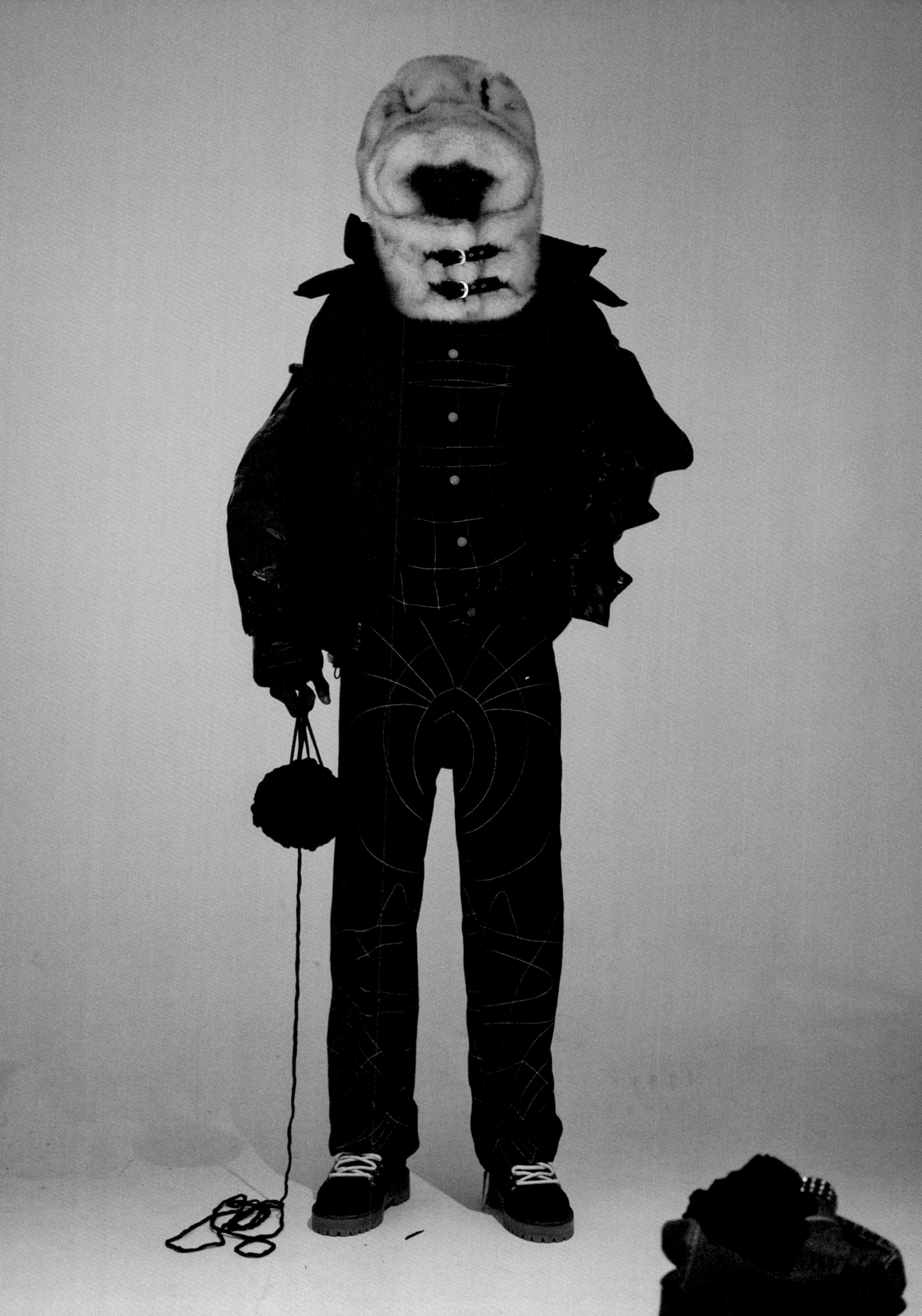

DURING MY TIME at Louis Vuitton, I had access to an incredible range of artisans and talent, which opened up so many possibilities for creative exploration. One of the themes I became obsessed with during my time there was the concept of letters—writing letters home and staying connected. This led me to experiment with embroidered letters, and I noticed that every time letters were embroidered onto material, a thread would always hang from the leather connected to the words. That visual—the connecting thread—became a metaphor for maintaining ties across distances.

From there, I started thinking about unraveling that thread, pulling it to see where it would lead. Since LV had an entire knitwear team, I pitched the idea of knitting a sweater that could unravel when you pulled the end of a string. We worked on it for weeks and finally got it to function, but it was still inconsistent. With so many moving parts in that LV show—from Rosalía and Michel Gondry to the various set designs—it ended up getting cut. That was disappointing because I thought it was such a compelling visual.

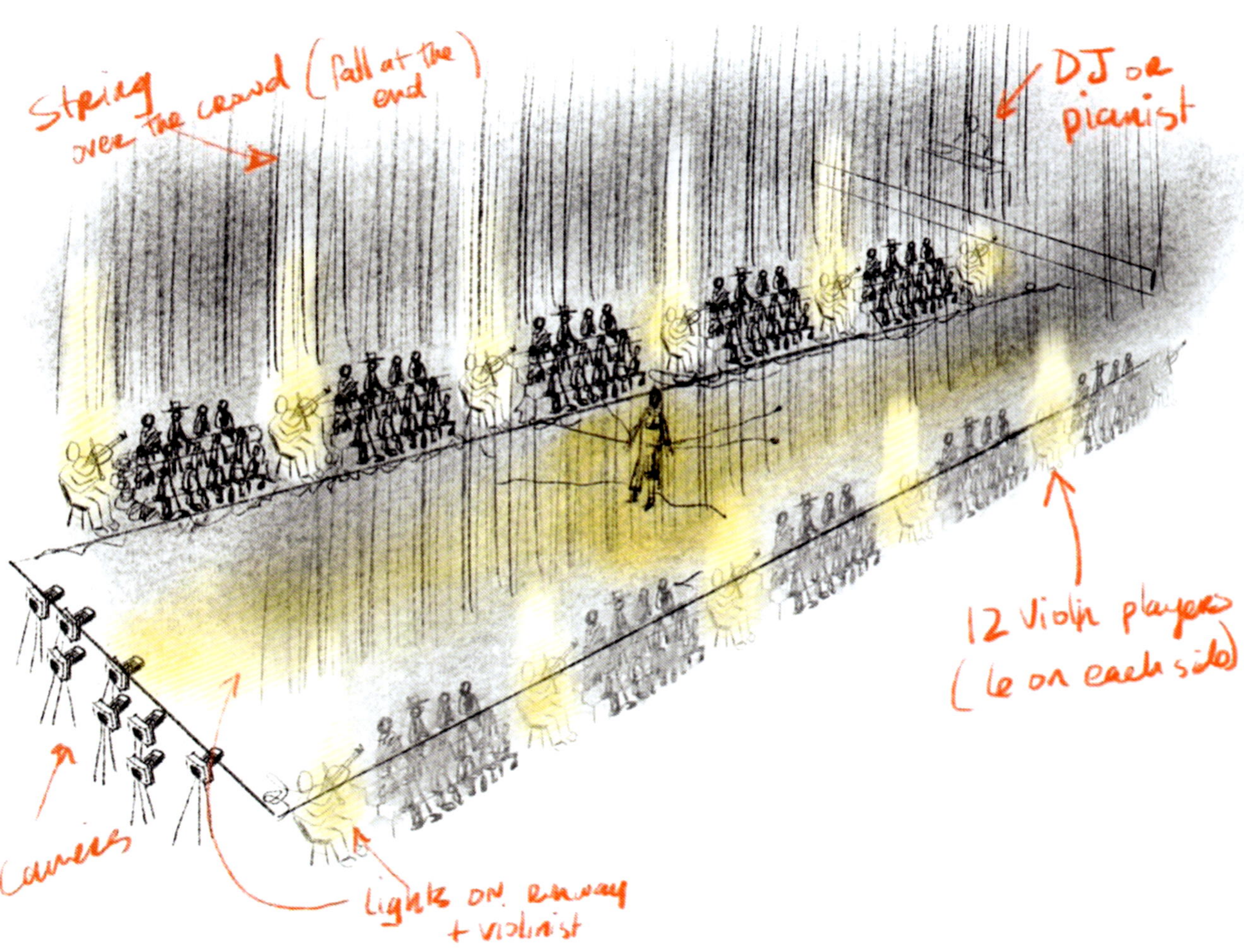

Men's Fall/ Winter Fashion Show

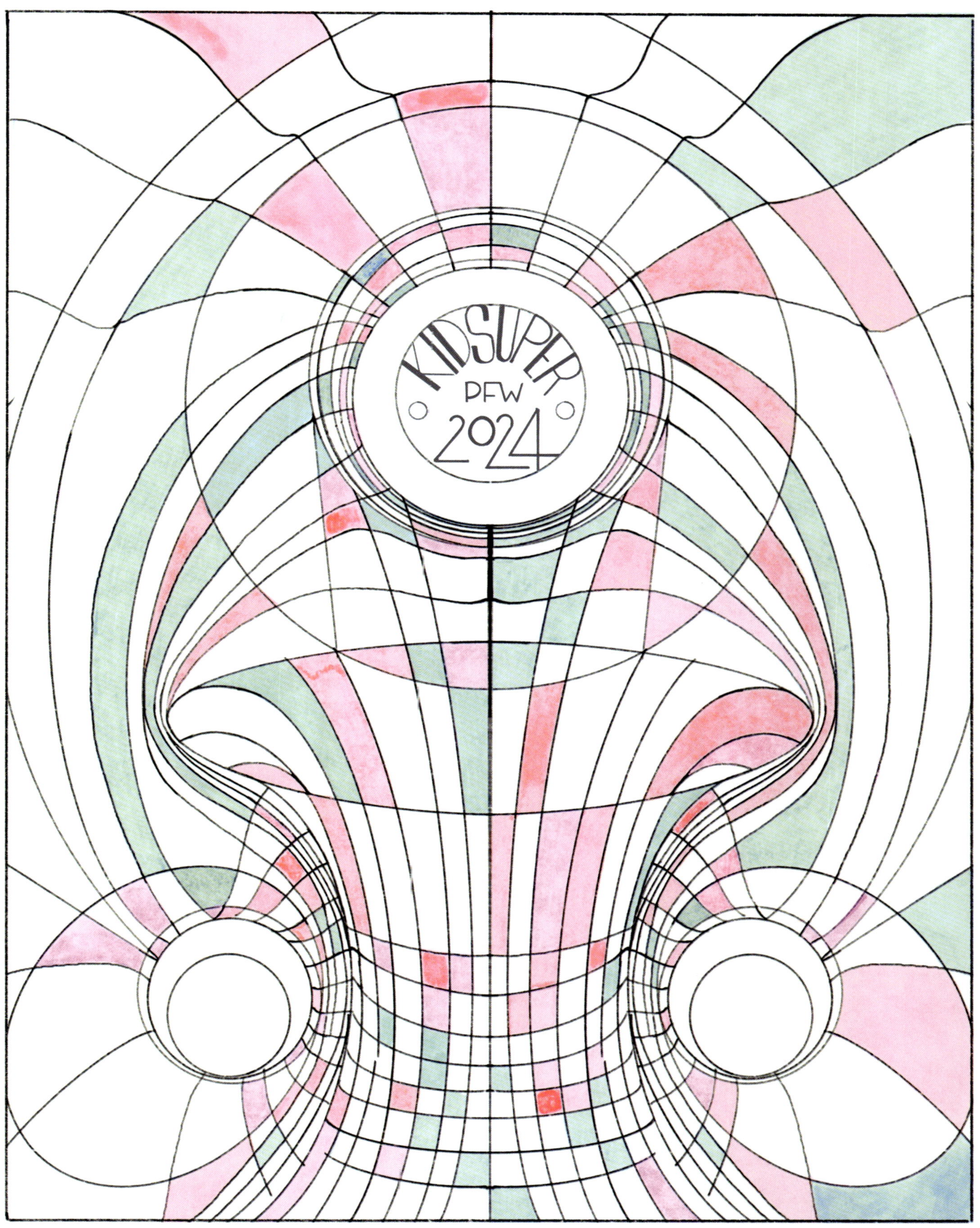

Saturday January 20th 2024 4: 30 CET
15 -17 Rue de Faubourg Poissonniere
75009 Paris

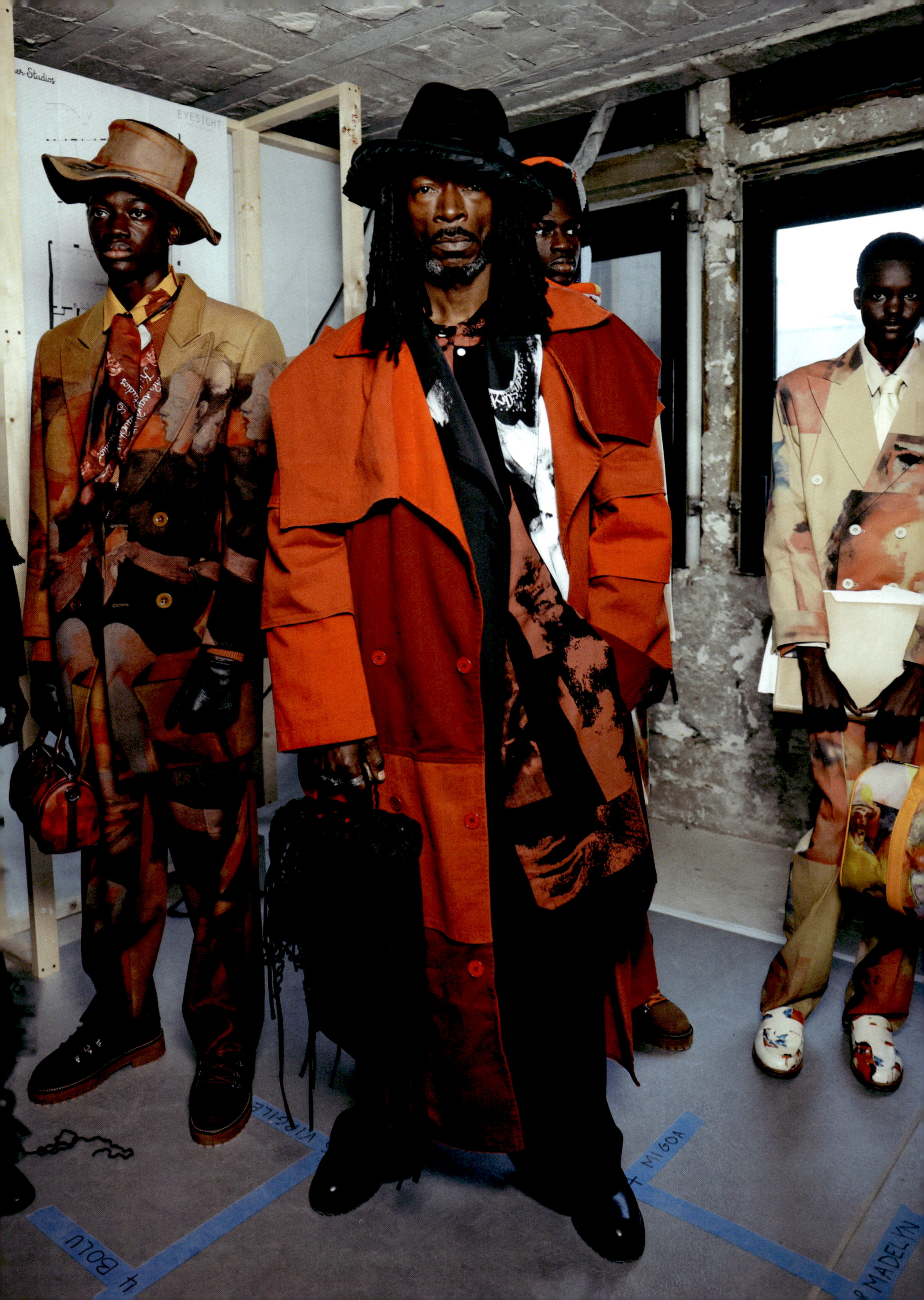
EYESIGHT
4 BOLU
VIRGILE
MIGOA
MADELYN

Backstage at the show. One of our favorite looks, and a model we cast every time. KidSuper is known for its range of model types.

When the next show came around, the theatrical play, the theme of connectivity and unraveling strings still resonated. The threads visually resembled the synapses of a brain, unraveling to reveal the finale—the idea. However, given the complexity of the play, adding the string concept felt unnecessary. Looking back at that theater play, Mike Amiri told me, "Every single one of those rooms could have been its own fashion show." That stuck with me, making me realize I could have expanded on each idea further.

For this fashion show, I was determined to finally bring the unraveling string concept to life. I made it the sole focus, which forced me to figure it out. In a way putting myself in a metaphorical burning house to get results. This led me to "String Theory," a theme inspired by the scientific theory that suggests everything at the most microscopic level consists of vibrating strings. The beauty of string theory is that it's just a theory—it has never been proven or disproven. In a way, KidSuper operates similarly: it's a theoretical concept that I'm always trying to prove is real.

I envisioned the entire ceiling being covered in string that would unravel and fall onto the audience at the end. Logistically, we couldn't figure out how to execute that affordably, so it was cut. However, I always want the audience to experience something unexpected, even if it's a playful prank.

Ten days before the show, ballerino Julian MacKay messaged me on Instagram about collaborating. Within two days, we planned for him to open the show with a ballet performance that unraveled in its own way.

But the true magic of this show—the most monumental moment of my life—was having Ronaldinho walk the runway. I've been drawing, posting about, and admiring Ronaldinho for as long as I can remember. He was always the person I wanted to meet, collaborate with, and have dinner with. And I actually got him to walk my fashion show.

The way it happened was surreal. A kid on Instagram said he knew Ronaldinho and his brother, who had met this kid's father at a soccer store in Chicago back in 2000. They stayed in touch over the years, and the kid created a group chat with me, Ronaldinho's brother (his manager), and himself. Every time I did something cool, he'd mention it in the chat. After about six months of this, Ronaldinho's brother finally responded, "Okay, we'll meet him if he's in Miami." Even though I lived in New York, I immediately said, "I'm a little tied up right now, but I can meet in four to five hours"—which really meant me rushing to the airport, hopping on a flight, and heading straight there.

At lunch, we were chatting in Portuguese (I picked up the language when I played soccer in Brazil after high school), and they eventually asked, "So what do you want?" The funny thing was, in a way, just having lunch with Ronaldinho was already more than I could have dreamed of. But if I was going to dream big, I said, "It would be amazing to collaborate with Ronaldinho and have him walk in my fashion show." And just like that, Ronaldinho, being the spontaneous legend he is, agreed.

During the fitting, I brought a soccer ball because I wanted Ronaldinho to see my touch. As he was trying on clothes, I passed him the ball, he passed it back, we started to juggle together and he said, "Oh wow, your touch is good." That was the greatest compliment I had ever received. Afterward, they invited me to play in celebrity soccer games with Ronaldinho, which meant not only did I get him to walk my show, but I also got to play soccer with my childhood idol multiple times—an absolute dream come true.

As for the show itself, everything hinged on the unraveling knitted suit at the finale. We had about five of these knitted looks made, and every rehearsal required a fresh suit because the unraveling was a one-time effect. Each practice was nerve-wracking—every time we unraveled, a new problem would arise. An hour before the show, our last rehearsal failed. The strings got tangled, and it didn't work. The only time it actually worked perfectly was during the actual runway show—a true KidSuper moment.

To ensure success, I even built a drill-powered machine from Leroy Merlin (the French Home Depot) to speed up the unraveling process. Backstage, one of the machines broke, so we had people pulling by hand. I had also given the violinists

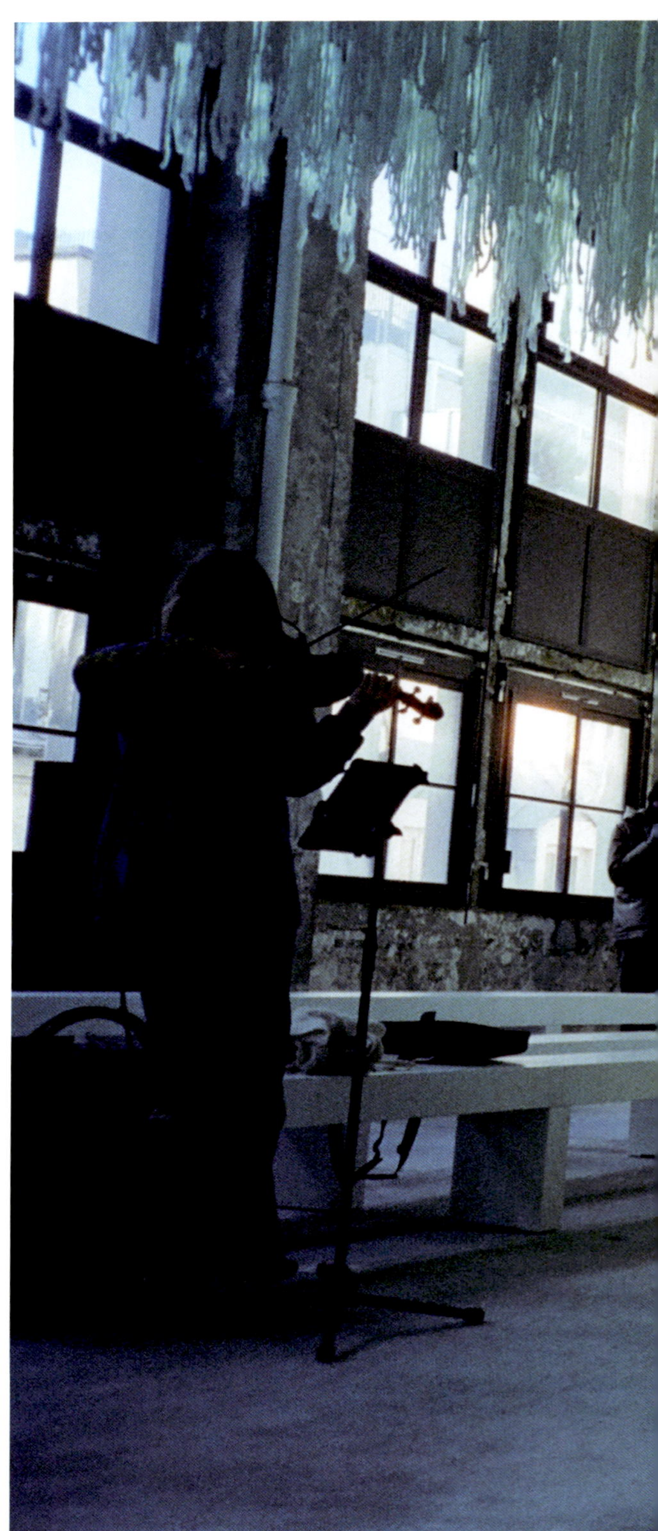

Principal Dancer Julian MacKay warming up with me in the background before the show. One of the best dancers in the world, like Nutcracker good.

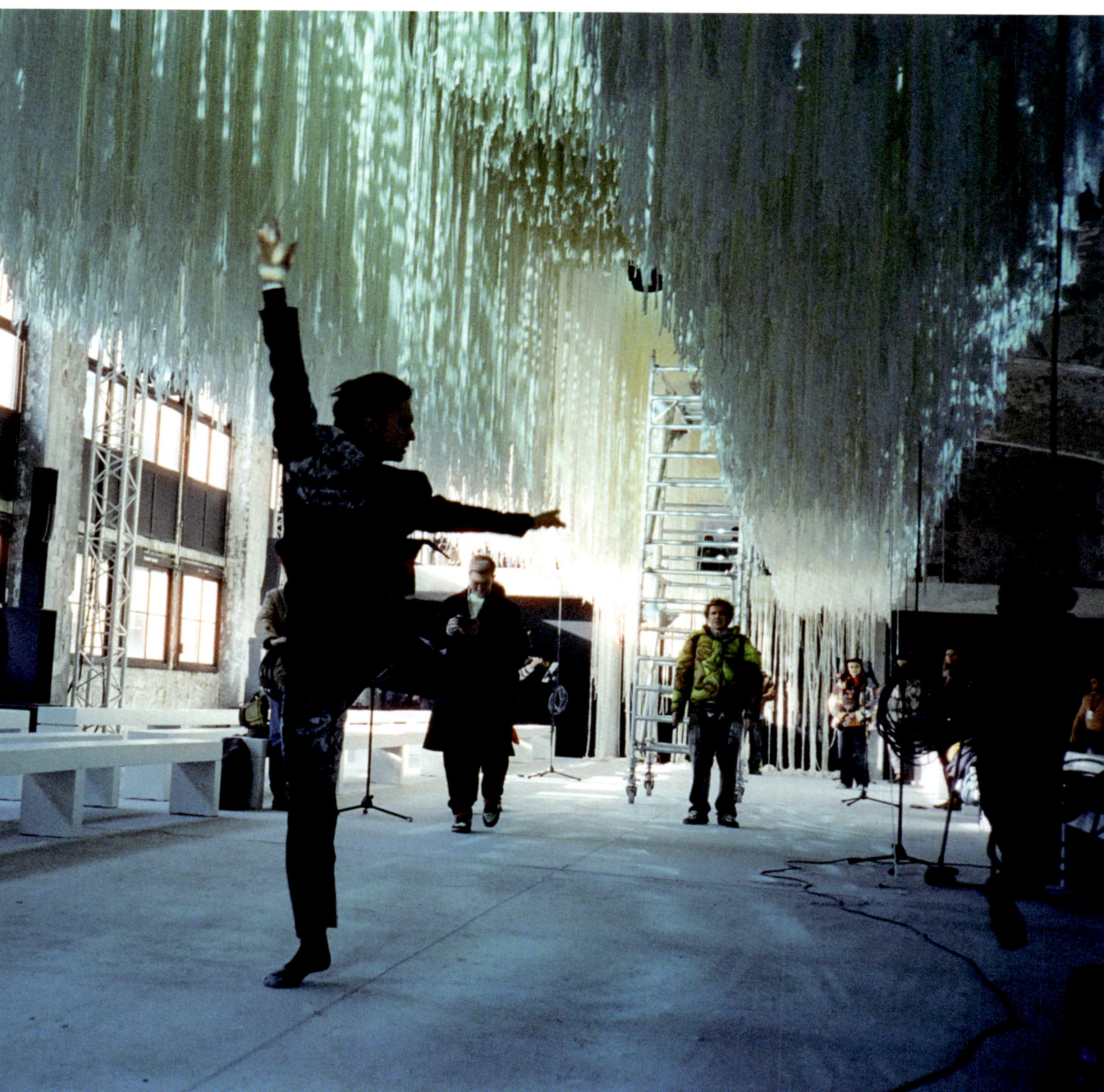

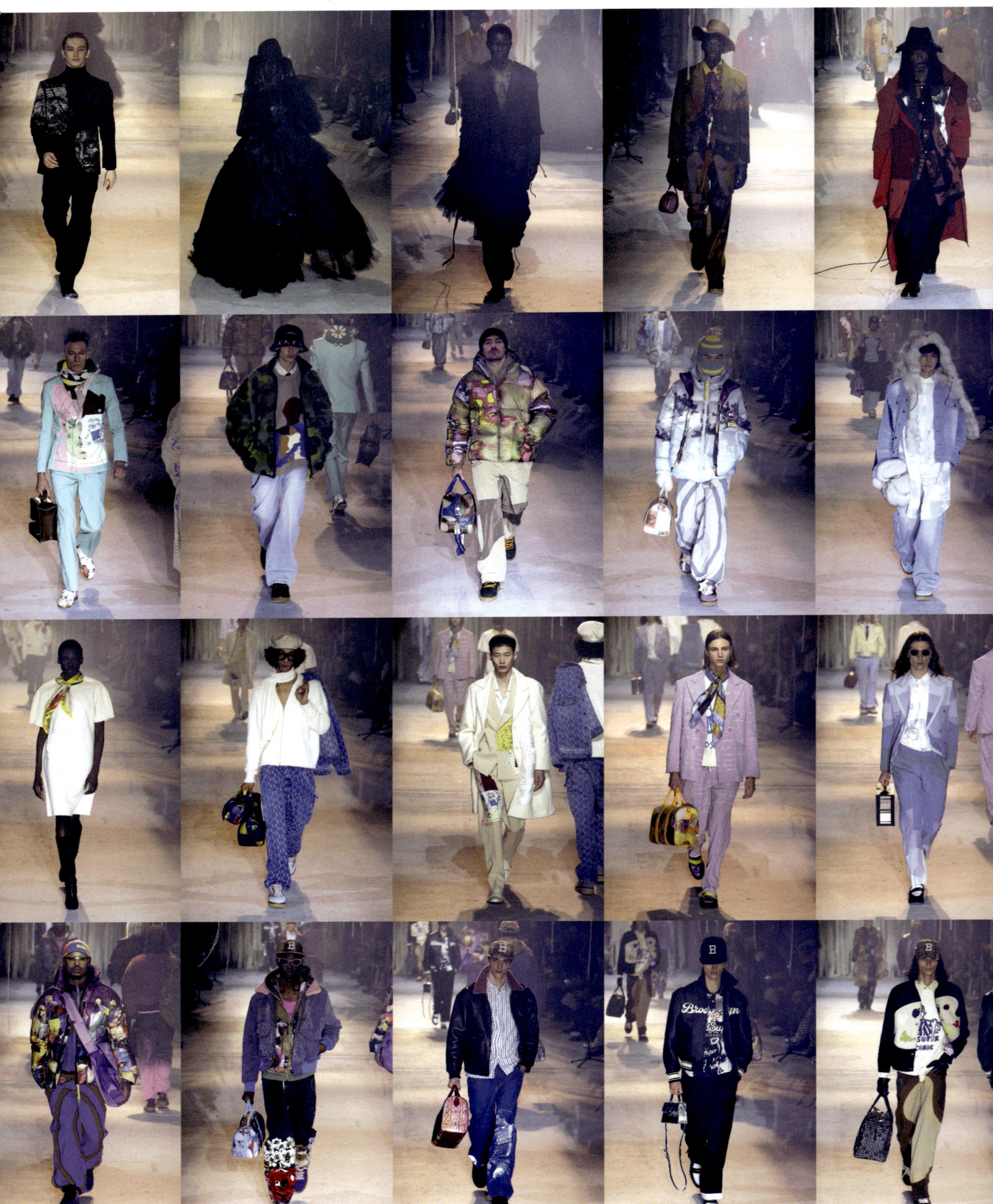

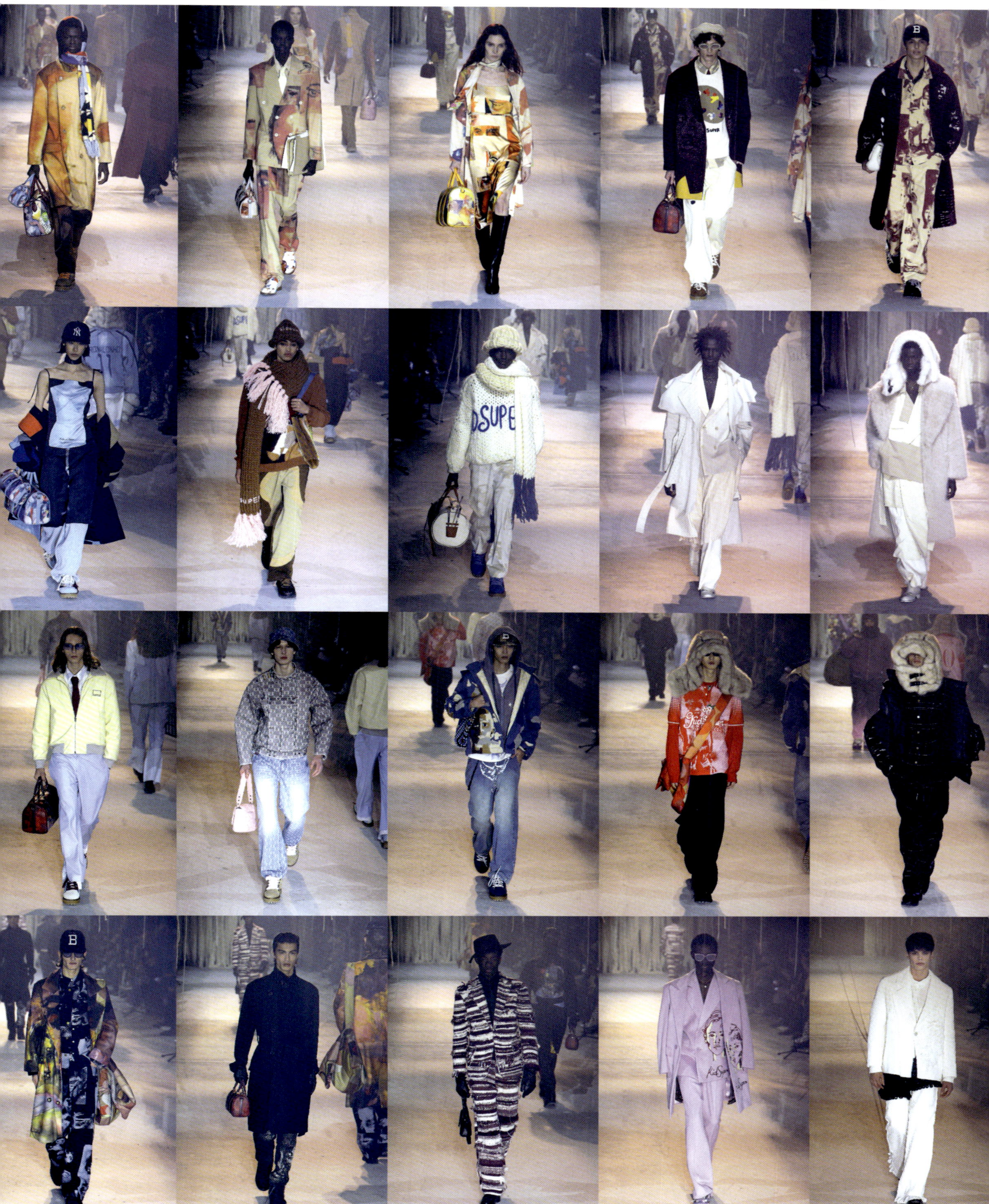

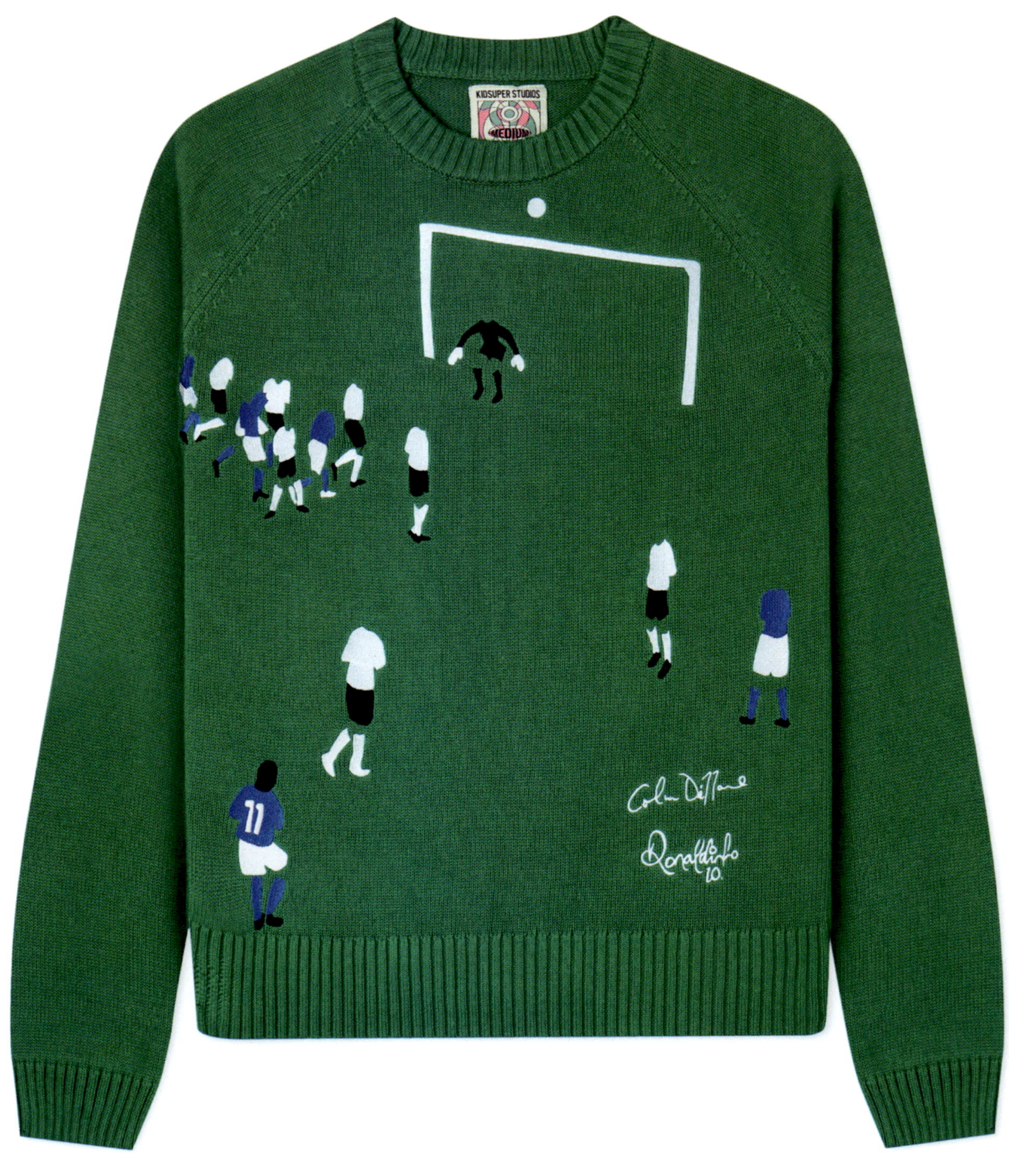

Sketch of Ronaldinho's Free Kick Goal v England | 2002 FIFA World Cup.

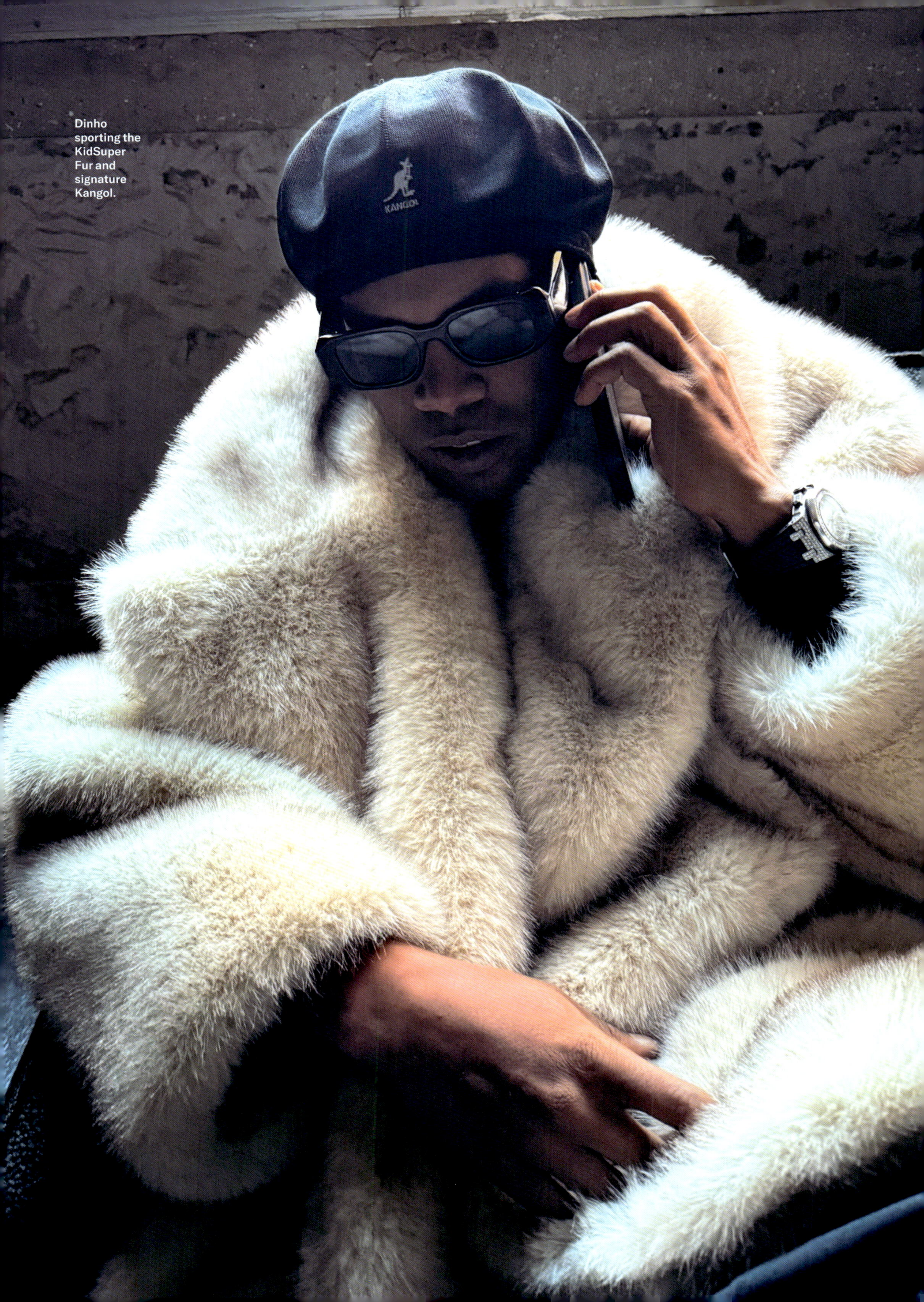

Dinho sporting the KidSuper Fur and signature Kangol.

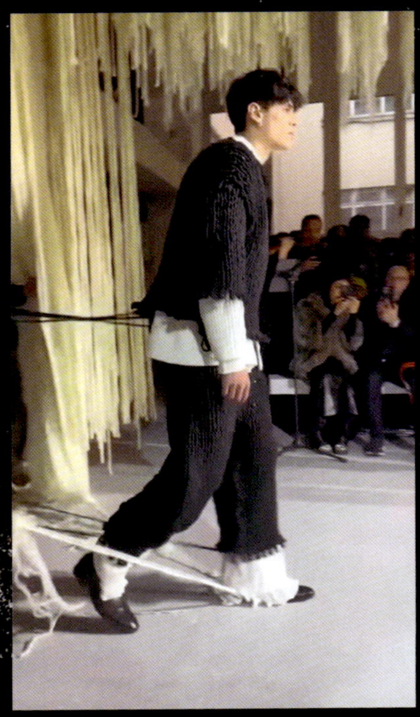
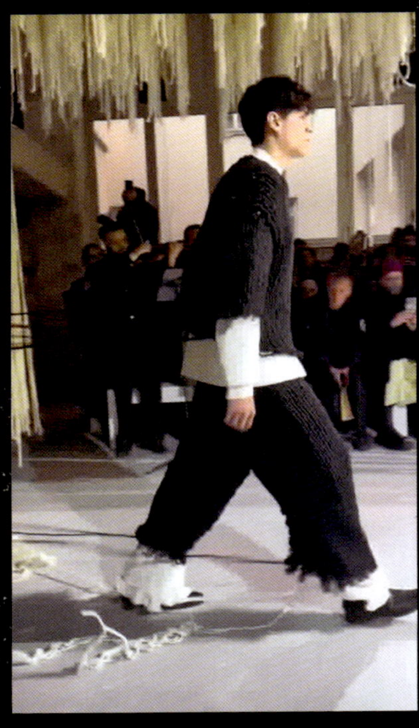
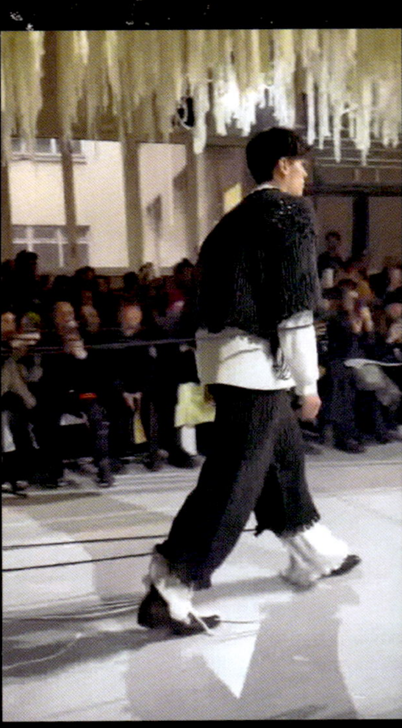

The unraveling look took so many tries to get right...
Actually the only time it ever fully worked was during the show.

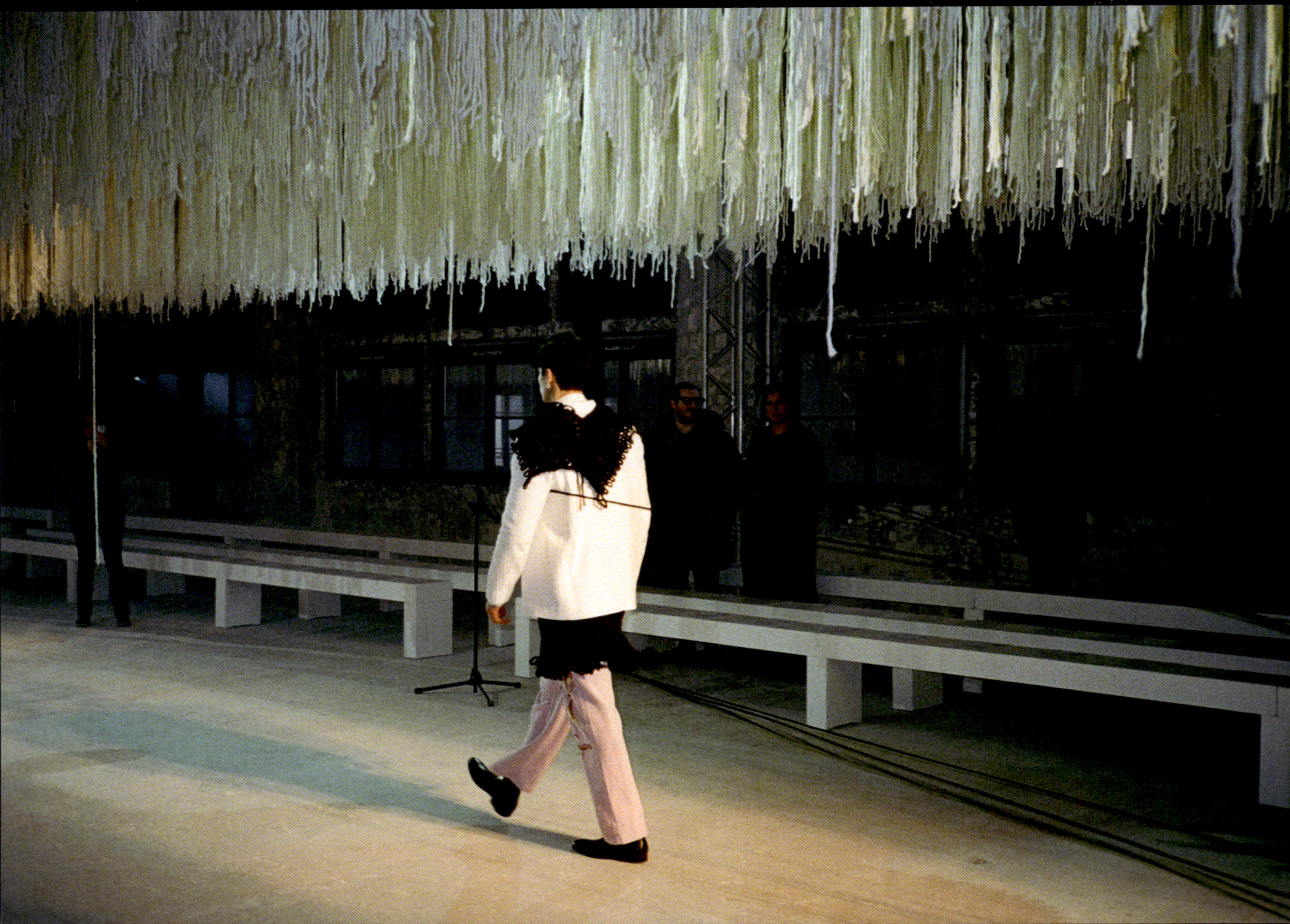

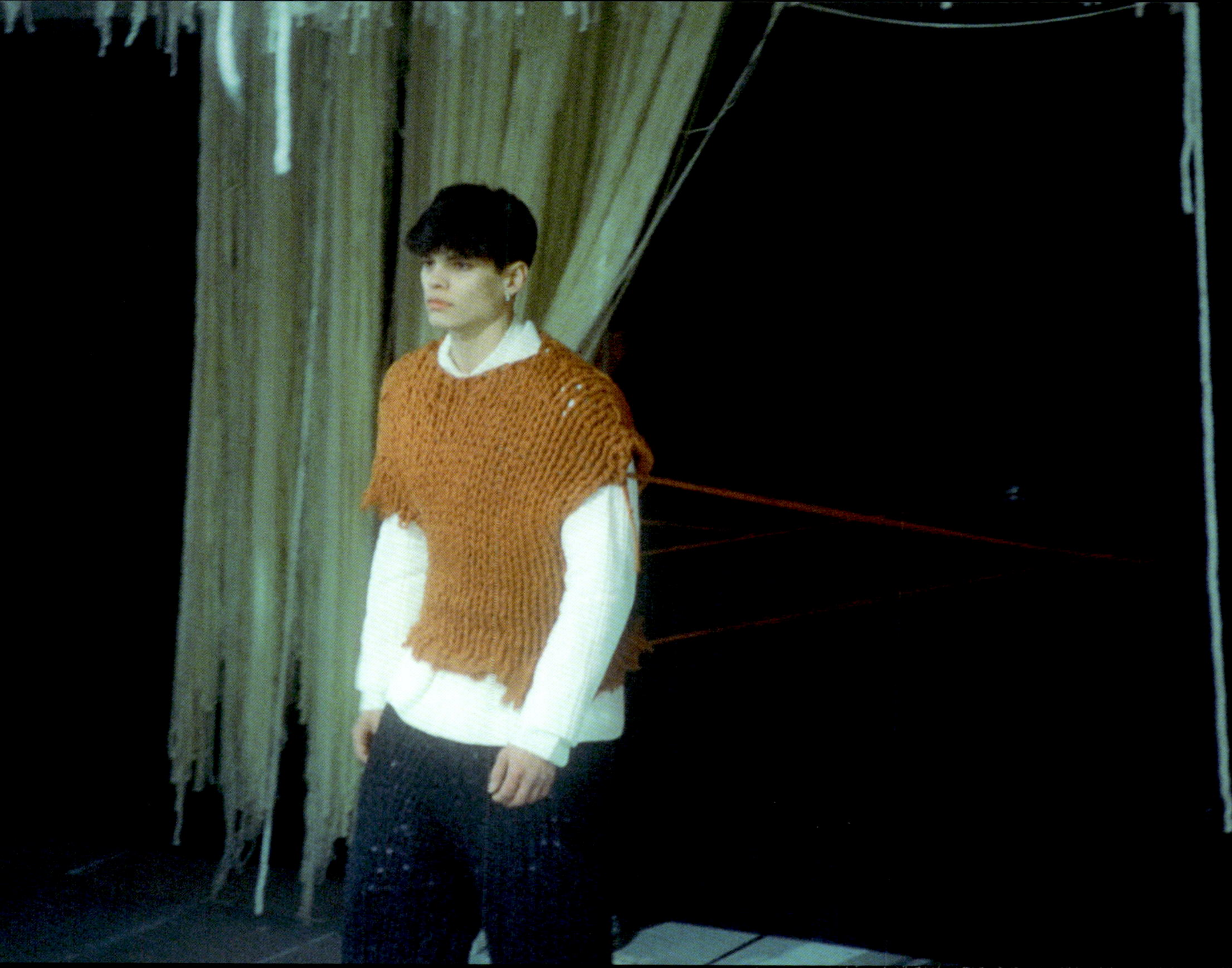

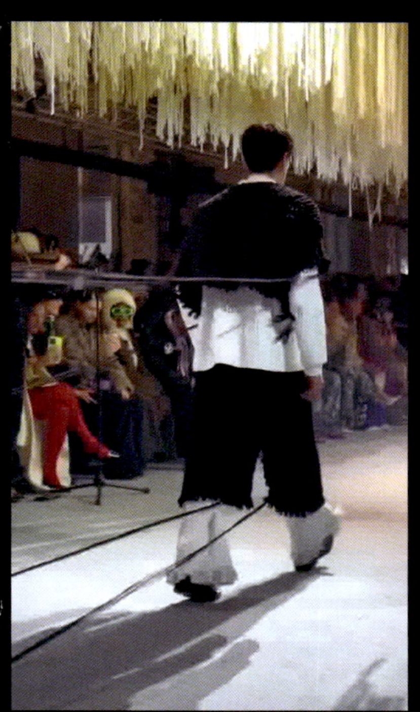

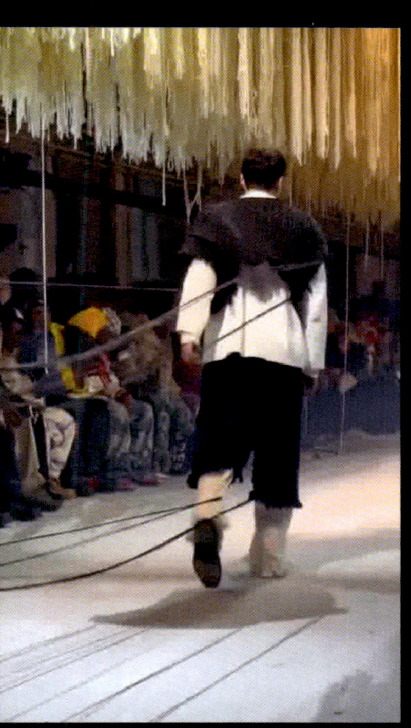

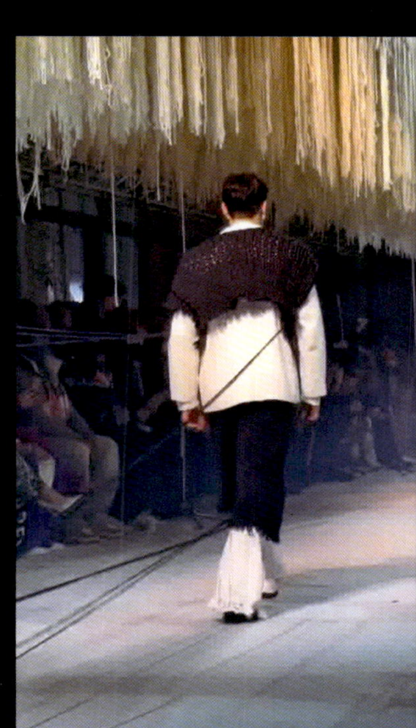

KIDSUPER PRESENTS

BIG IN DA GAME

QUAVO GIGGS

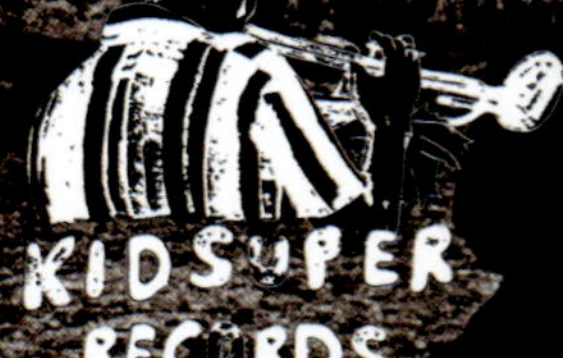

along the runway scissors, instructing them to cut the suit if the unraveling failed—so the audience would never know what was planned and what wasn't.

That moment of pure magic went viral, gaining around 100 million views on Instagram—not that virality is the goal, but it's gratifying when something you worked so hard on gets recognized.

For past fashion shows, we always created original soundtracks to reinforce the show's themes. This time marked the inception of KidSuper Records. A month before the show, Giggs visited the KidSuper building for a video shoot with Dave East. He loved the clothes, we clicked personally, and he mentioned he had never been to Paris Fashion Week but wanted to be part of it. I told him we always make custom music for our shows, and it would be amazing to have him on a track. I sent him some beats, and within days he sent back an incredible song. We played it on the runway while he sat front row, and during the afterparty he performed alongside Quavo and Jim Jones. Quavo loved the song so much he wanted to jump on it, and a month later we shot a music video—marking the first-ever KidSuper Records song: "BIG IN DA GAME."

This entire journey—from conceptualizing the unraveling thread to Ronaldinho walking the show to the music—was a testament to the KidSuper spirit: a mix of creativity, risk taking, and relentless pursuit of making the impossible real. Magic.

Poster for "Big In Da Game," the first song released by KidSuper Records. We shot a music video for it in *Peaky Blinders*-inspired looks. See us and looks from the collection

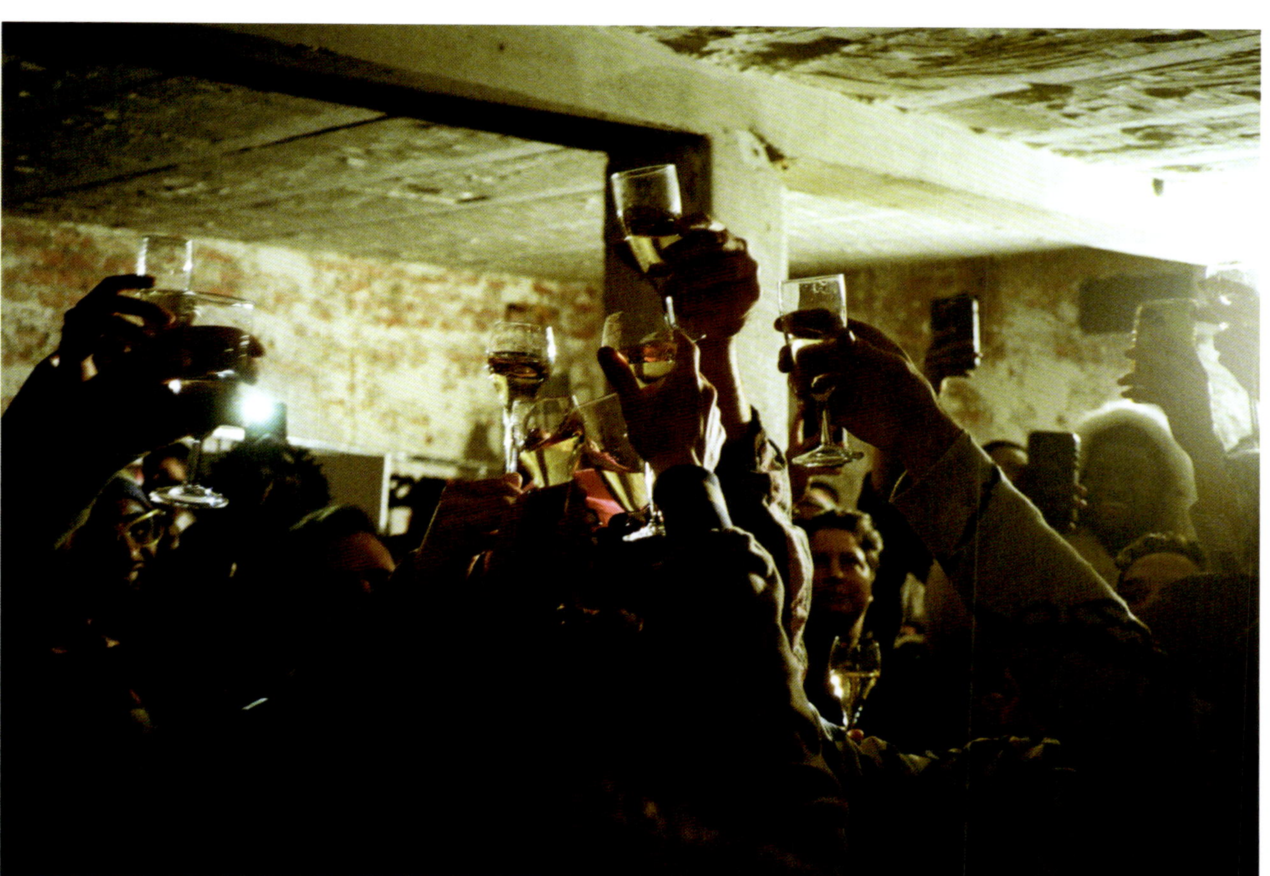

"Oh wow, your touch is good."

—RONALDINHO ON COLM'S SOCCER SKILLS

That was the greatest compliment I had ever received.

Afterward, they invited me to play in celebrity soccer games with Ronaldinho, which meant not only did I get him to walk my show, but I also got to play soccer with my childhood idol multiple times—an absolute dream come true.

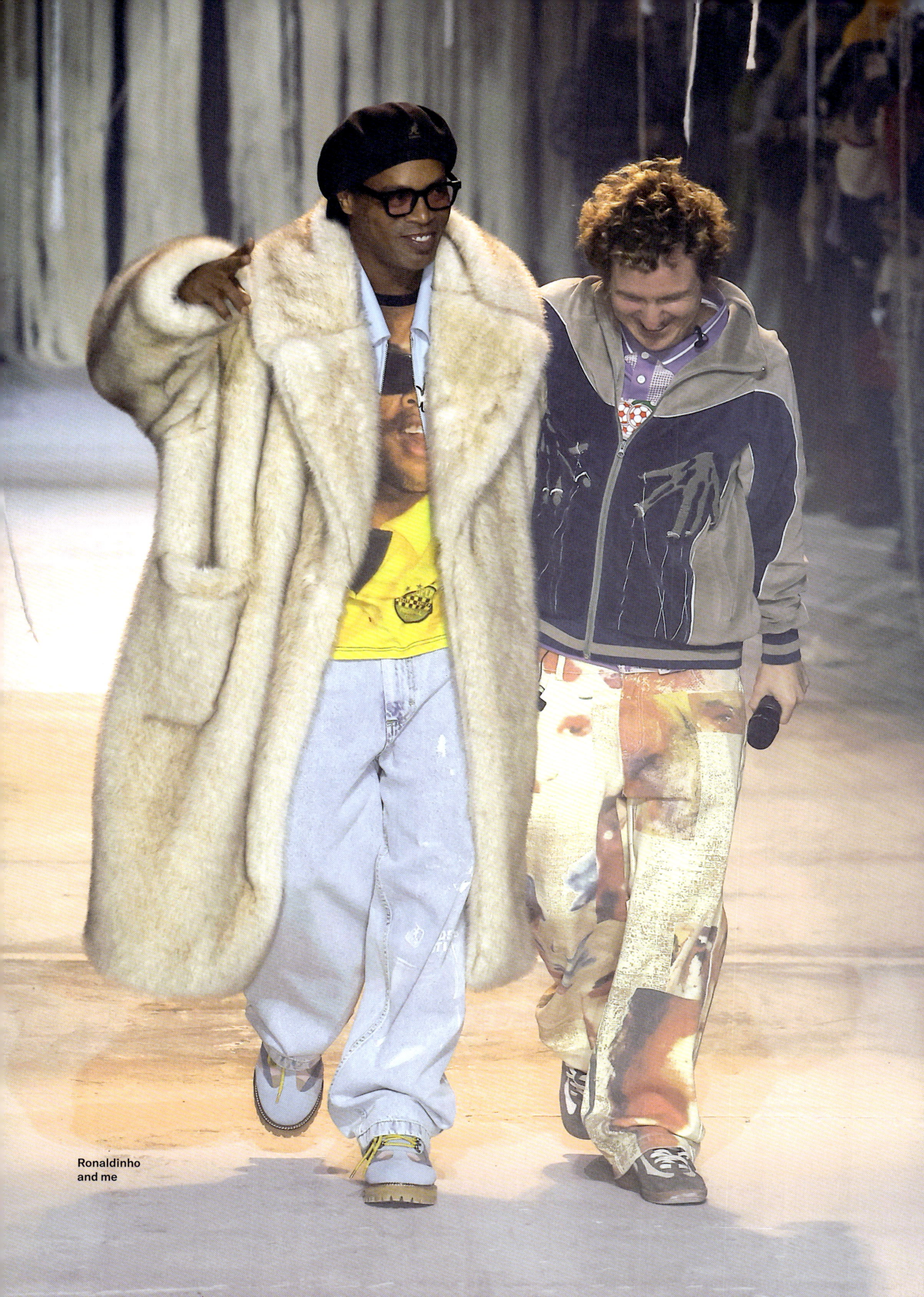

Ronaldinho
and me

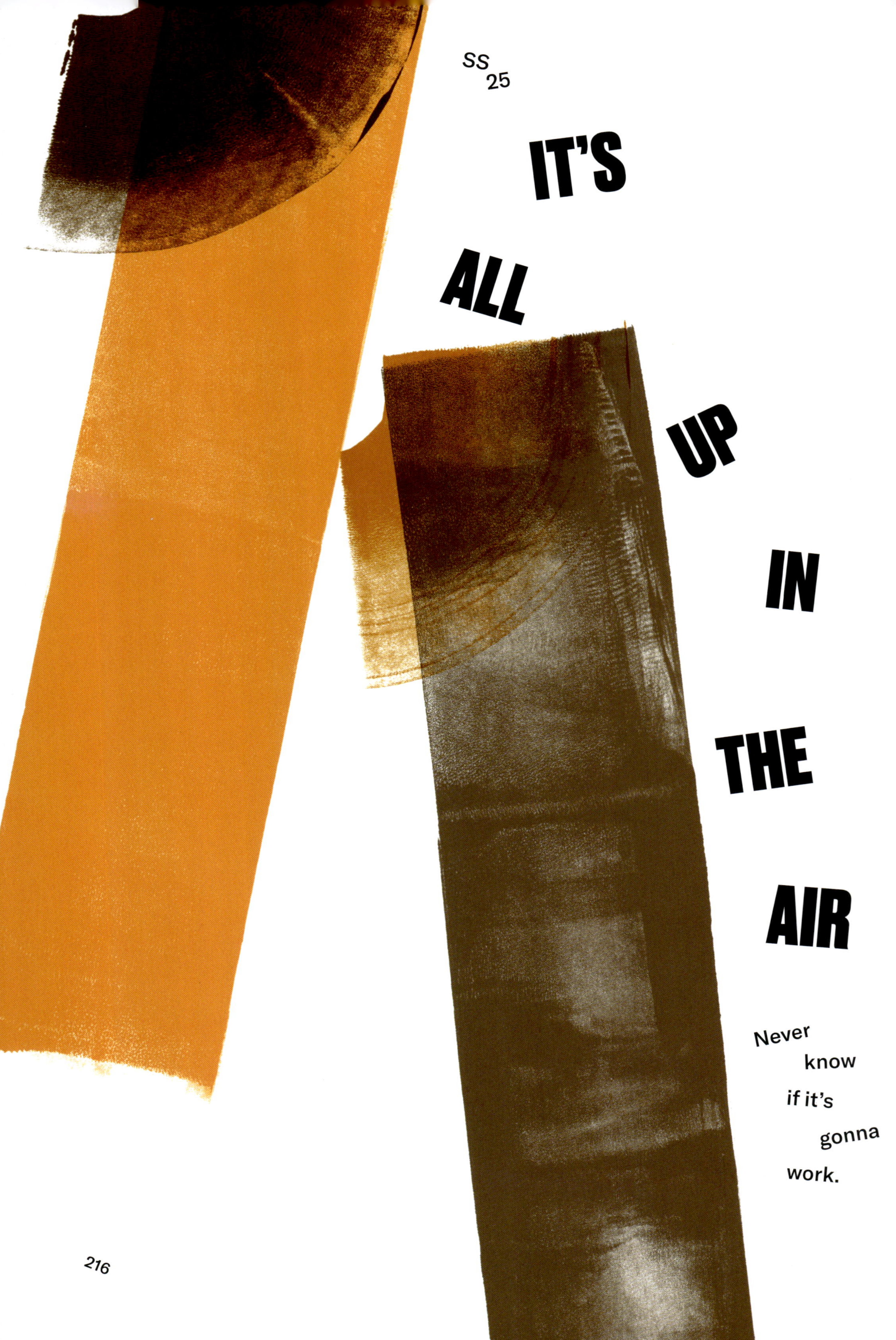

SS 25

IT'S ALL UP IN THE AIR

Never know if it's gonna work.

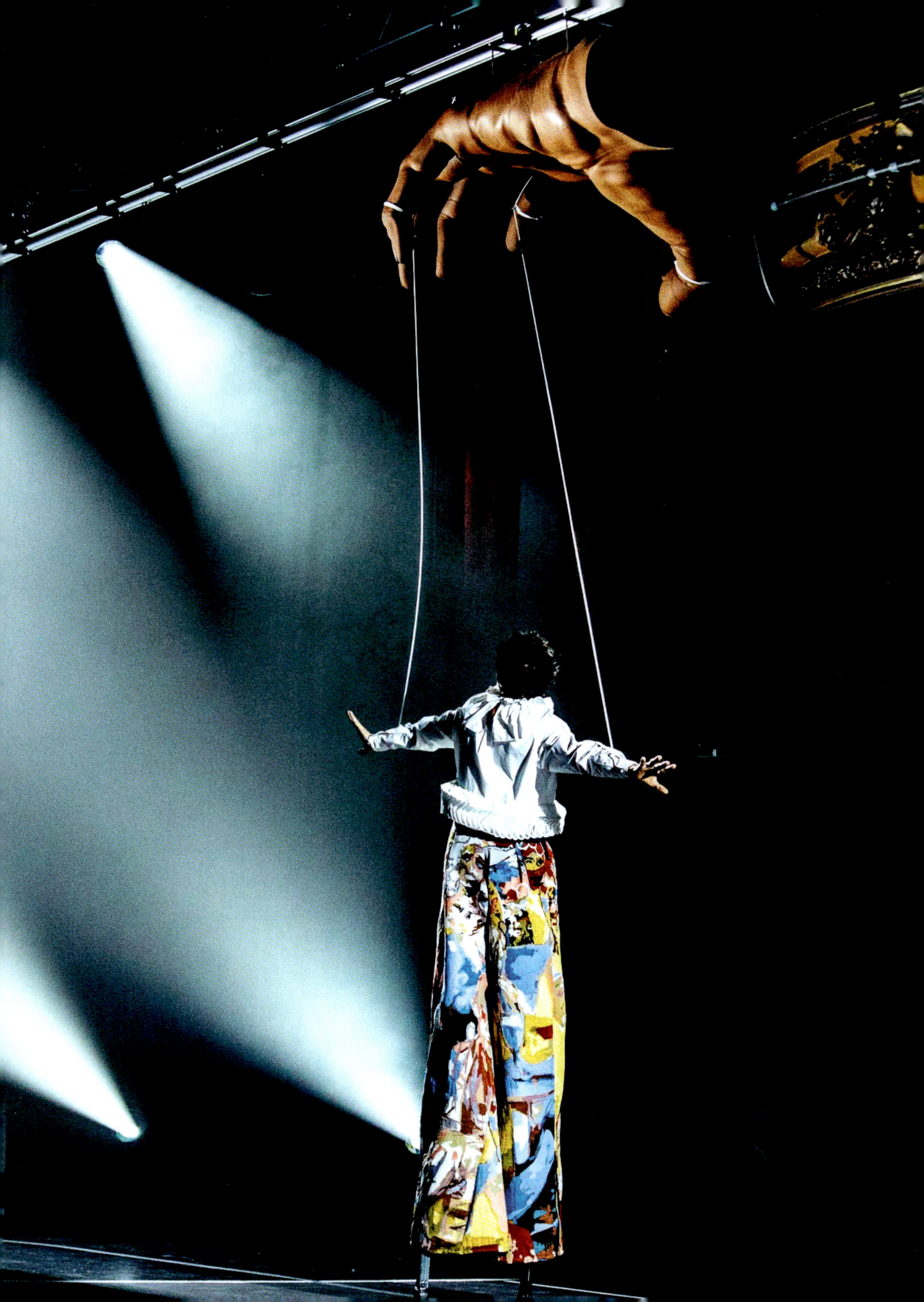

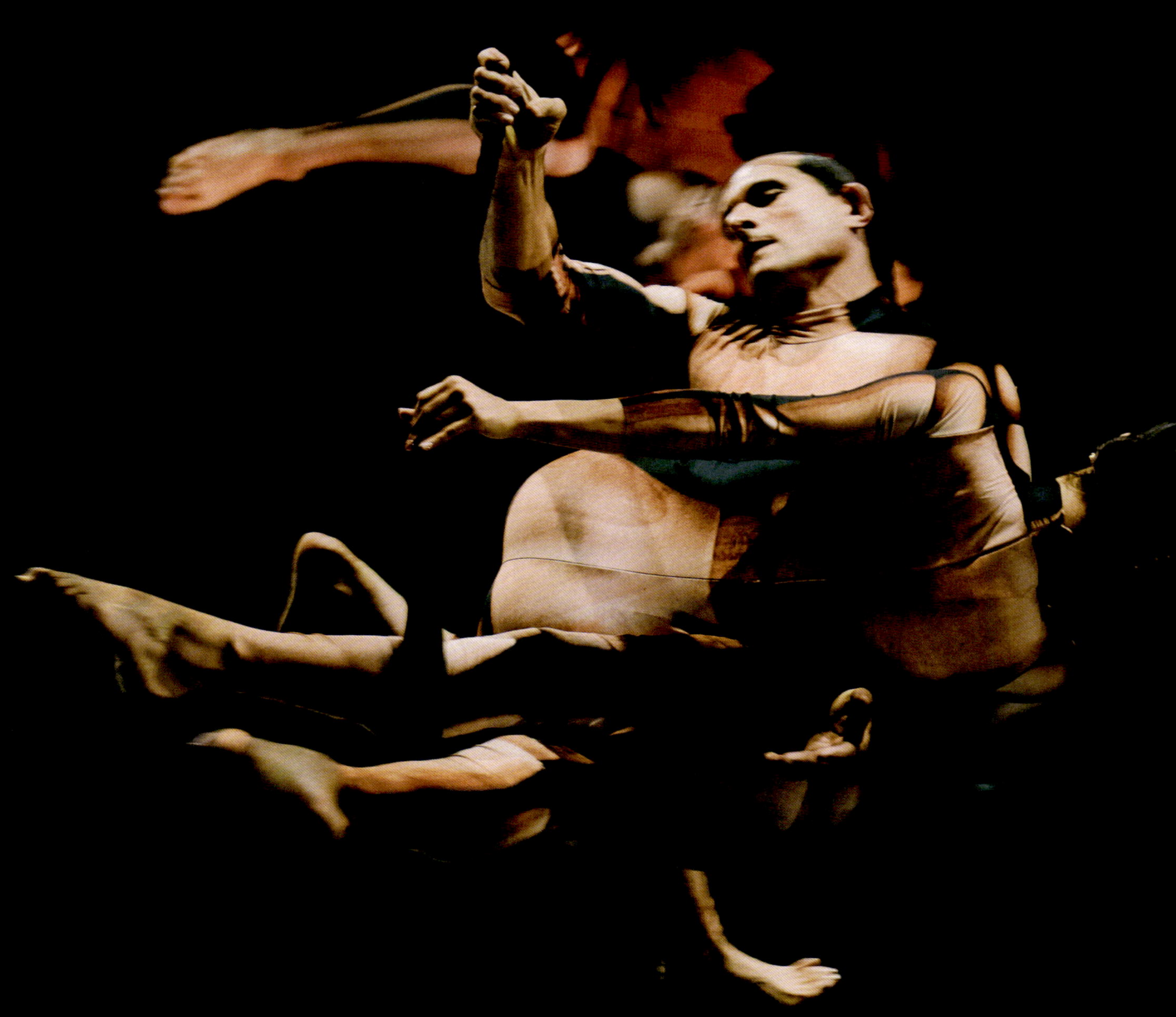

Cirque du Soleil trapeze performers opening the show. Just pulling off some moves we taught them earlier in the week.

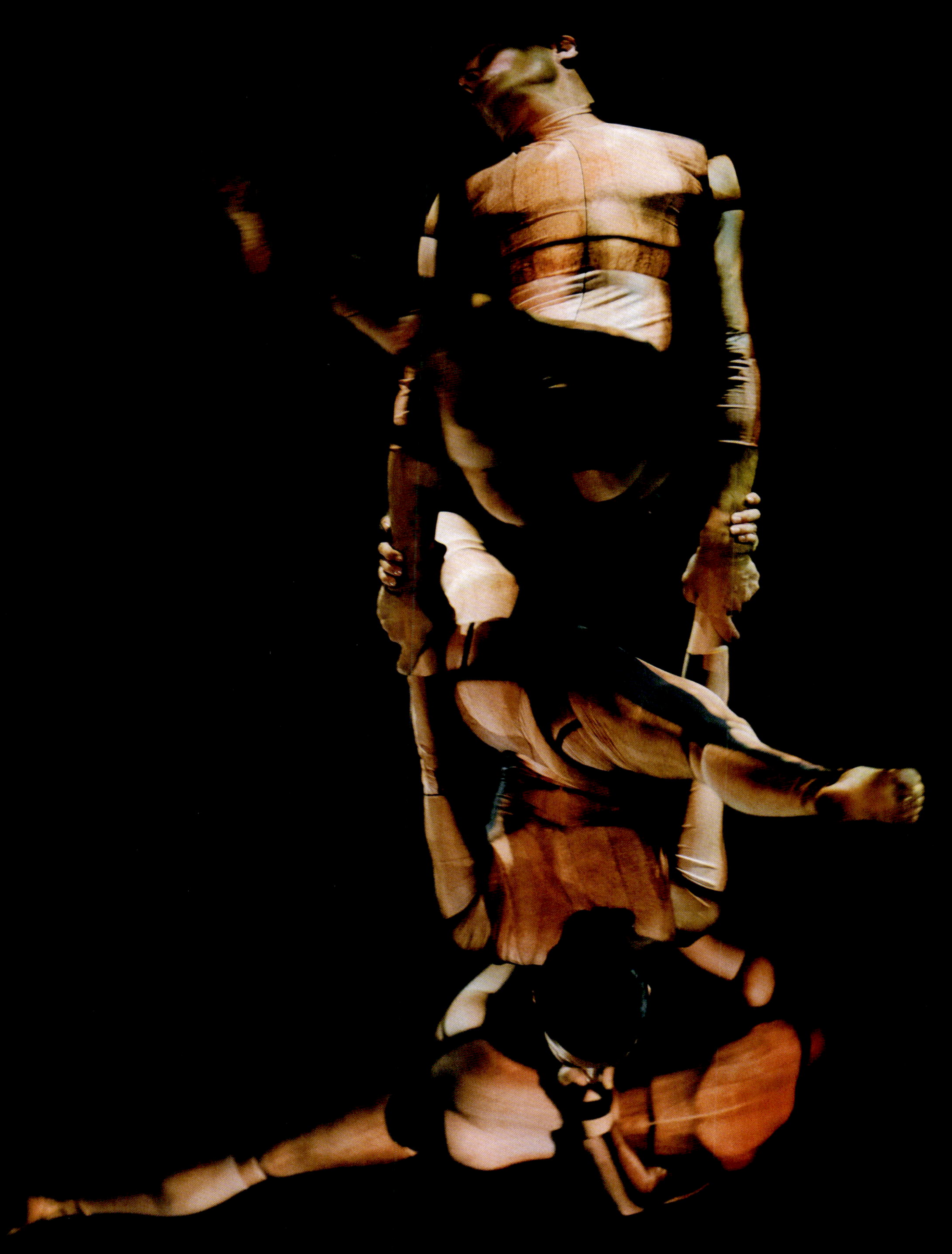

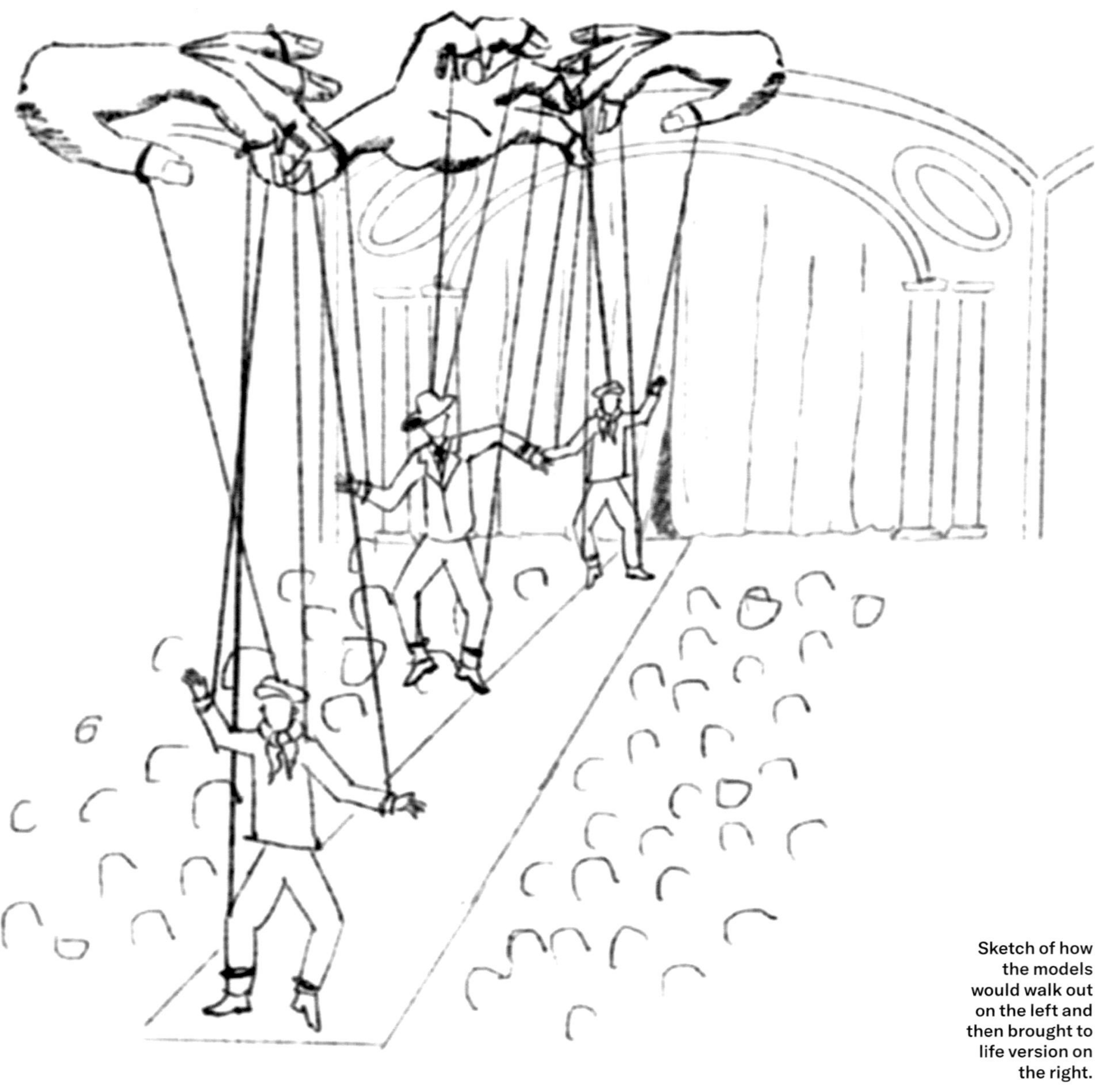

Sketch of how the models would walk out on the left and then brought to life version on the right.

ONE OF MY FAVORITE shows—and possibly my all-time favorite—was the stop-motion fashion show featuring dolls. I had always envisioned bringing these dolls to life as life-size figures and wondered: How could I translate the stop-motion aesthetic into a live performance? Could I make the models move like they were animated frame by frame?

As I explored this idea, I was drawn to the concept of puppeteering. The question of control fascinated me: Are we truly in control of ourselves, or is there an unseen force guiding us? Not necessarily in a spiritual sense, but in the sense of can we change—can we evolve? The visual of giant hands maneuvering human puppets felt both striking and conceptually rich—the perfect foundation for a KidSuper fashion show.

At the same time, Cirque du Soleil had been on my mind. It had come up in past discussions about collaborations, and the idea of incorporating their incredible performers in an unexpected way intrigued me. When we finally connected, we discovered that they didn't have a venue in Paris during the timeframe we needed. So I asked myself, If it's not at their venue, then what is it? That's when it clicked: Cirque performers could be the puppets coming to life, their incredible acrobatic skills reenacting the inhuman movements of puppets.

I traveled to Montreal to meet the Cirque du Soleil team,

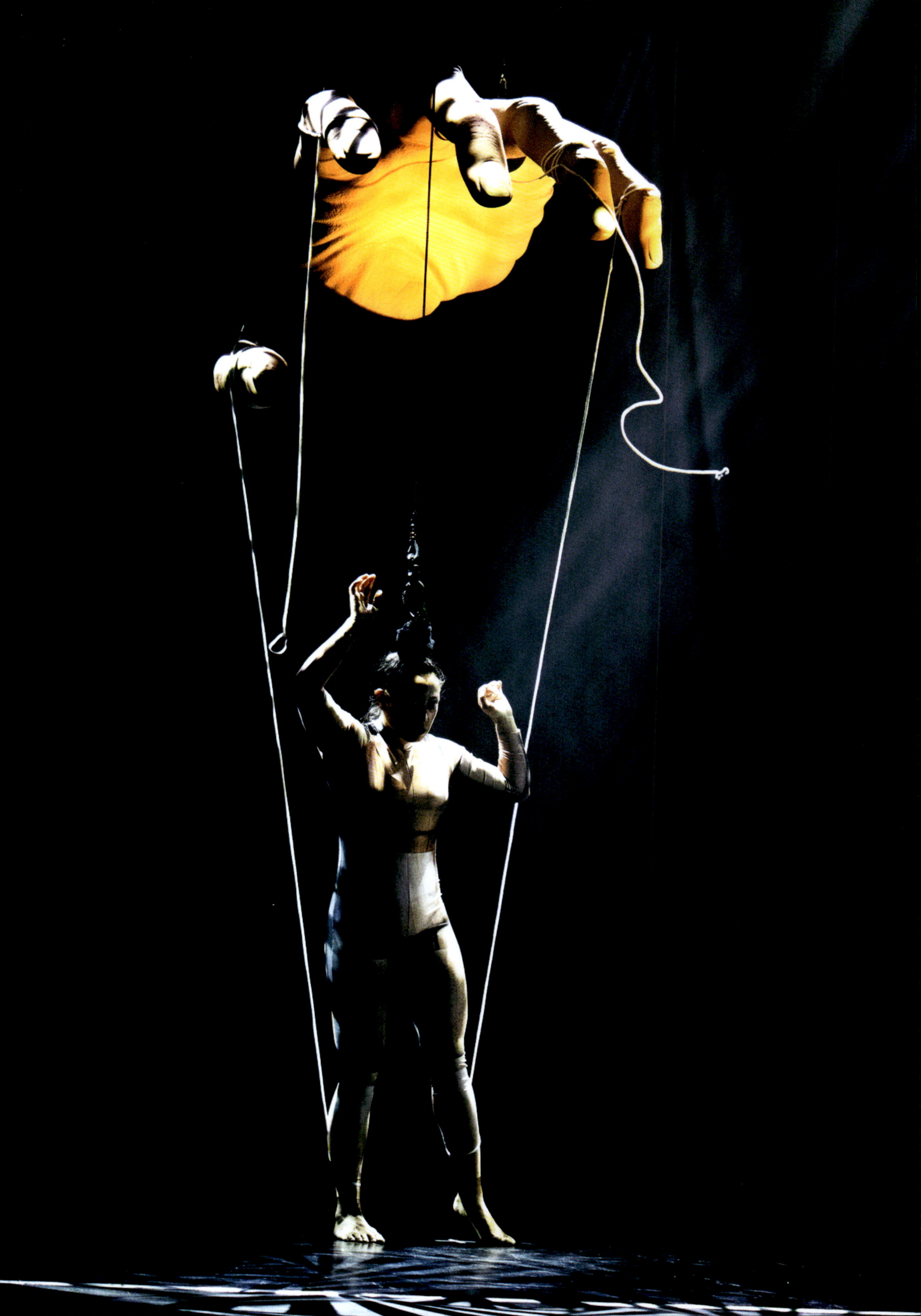

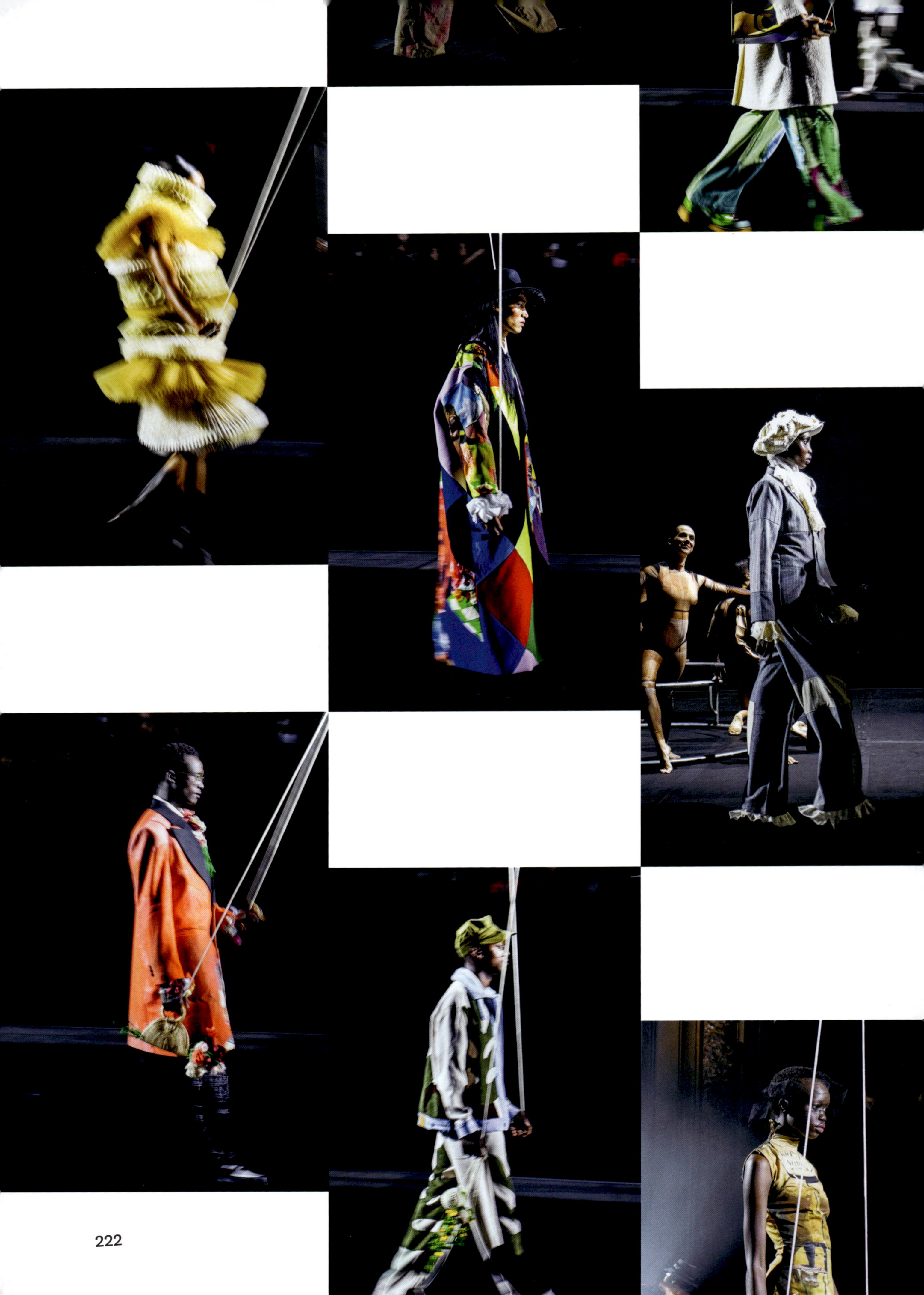

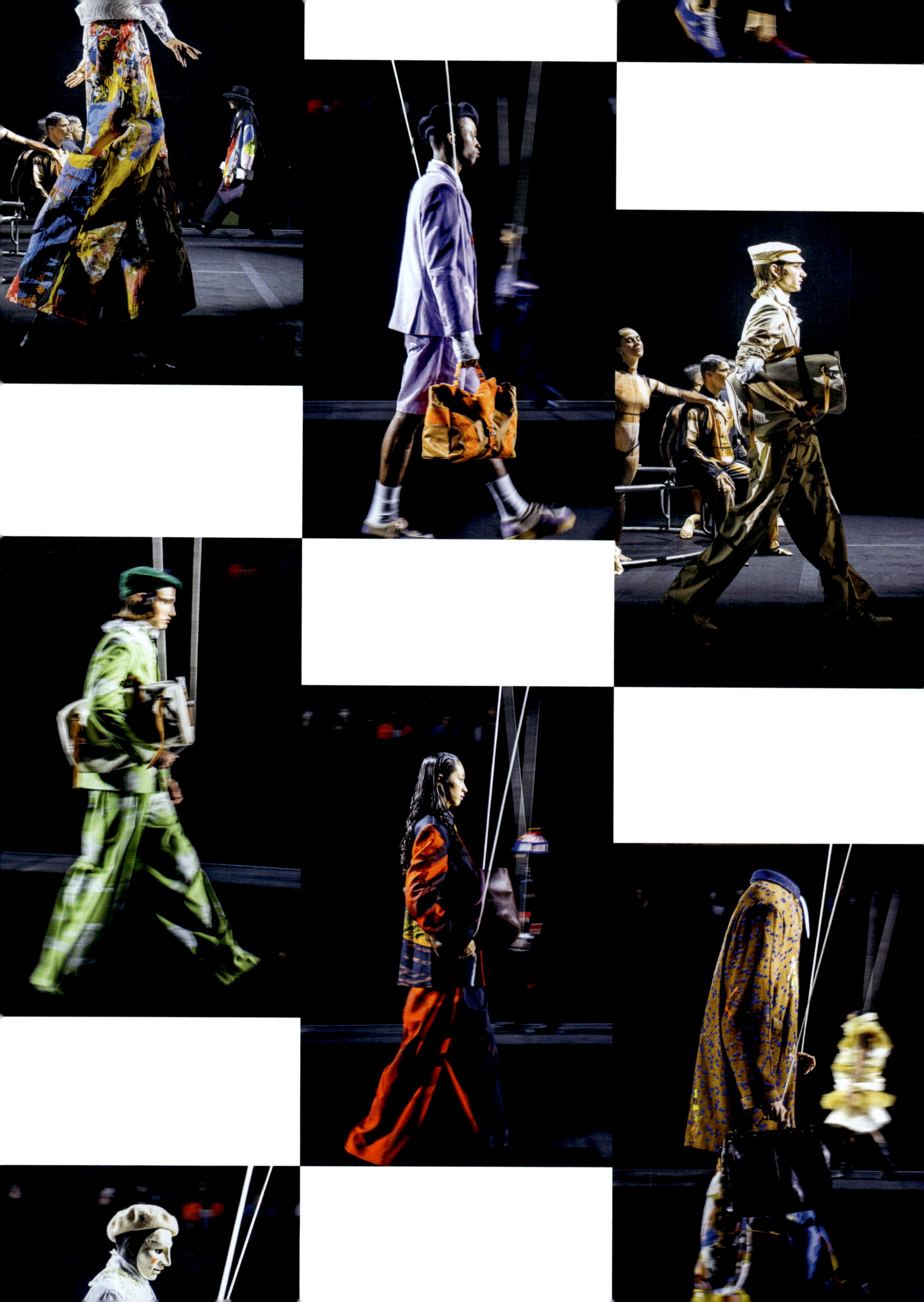

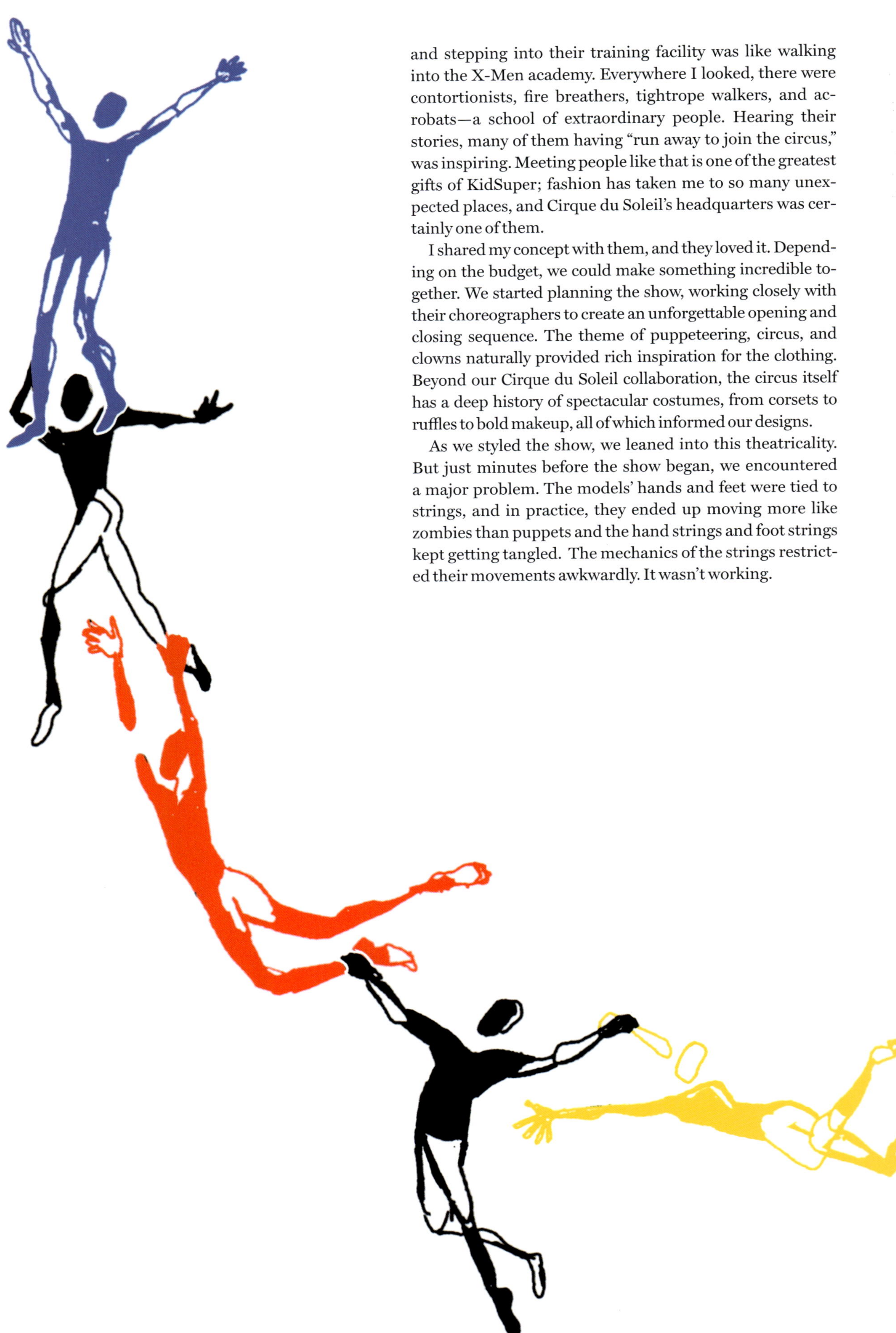

and stepping into their training facility was like walking into the X-Men academy. Everywhere I looked, there were contortionists, fire breathers, tightrope walkers, and acrobats—a school of extraordinary people. Hearing their stories, many of them having "run away to join the circus," was inspiring. Meeting people like that is one of the greatest gifts of KidSuper; fashion has taken me to so many unexpected places, and Cirque du Soleil's headquarters was certainly one of them.

I shared my concept with them, and they loved it. Depending on the budget, we could make something incredible together. We started planning the show, working closely with their choreographers to create an unforgettable opening and closing sequence. The theme of puppeteering, circus, and clowns naturally provided rich inspiration for the clothing. Beyond our Cirque du Soleil collaboration, the circus itself has a deep history of spectacular costumes, from corsets to ruffles to bold makeup, all of which informed our designs.

As we styled the show, we leaned into this theatricality. But just minutes before the show began, we encountered a major problem. The models' hands and feet were tied to strings, and in practice, they ended up moving more like zombies than puppets and the hand strings and foot strings kept getting tangled. The mechanics of the strings restricted their movements awkwardly. It wasn't working.

With only four minutes before showtime, I made a last-minute call: cut the feet loose and keep just the hands tethered to the giant overhead puppeteering arms. These projects are full of chaotic, down-to-the-wire decisions like that.

The models moved seamlessly—fluid and elegant—while still holding onto the puppeteer illusion. What most people don't see is the insane complexity behind the scenes. For this show alone, we built an entire mechanical rig just to guide the oversized hands across a track suspended above the stage.

THE FINAL LOOK of the show was the "Headless Man," which was adapted from one of Cirque du Soleil's own performances. We used their preexisting internal structure to achieve the effect, a true testament to the power of collaboration.

As for the show's title, that was another serendipitous moment. A friend asked me what I was going to name it, and I casually replied, "Ah, it's still all up in the air." Then I looked at that phrase again and thought, Actually, that's it.

Naming my shows is always important to me. I want them to be phrases that inspire, that capture the essence of the journey. "It's All Up in the Air" felt perfect—it spoke to uncertainty, to taking risks, to embracing the unknown. That's what KidSuper is about: diving headfirst into ideas, even when you don't know exactly how they'll land. And in this case, I think we stuck the landing beautifully.

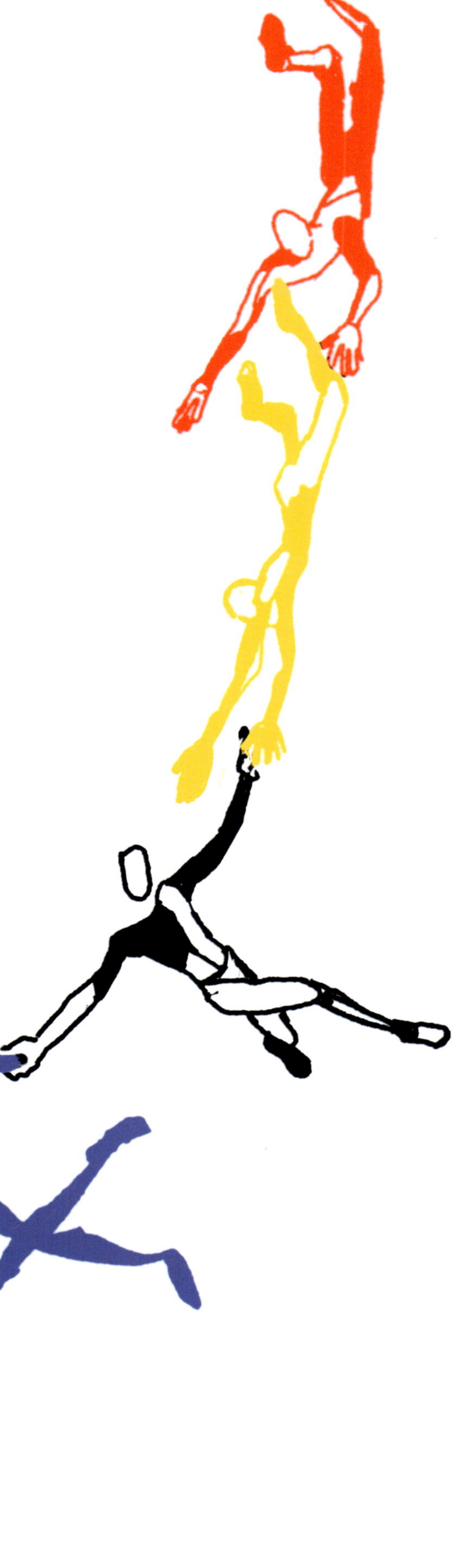

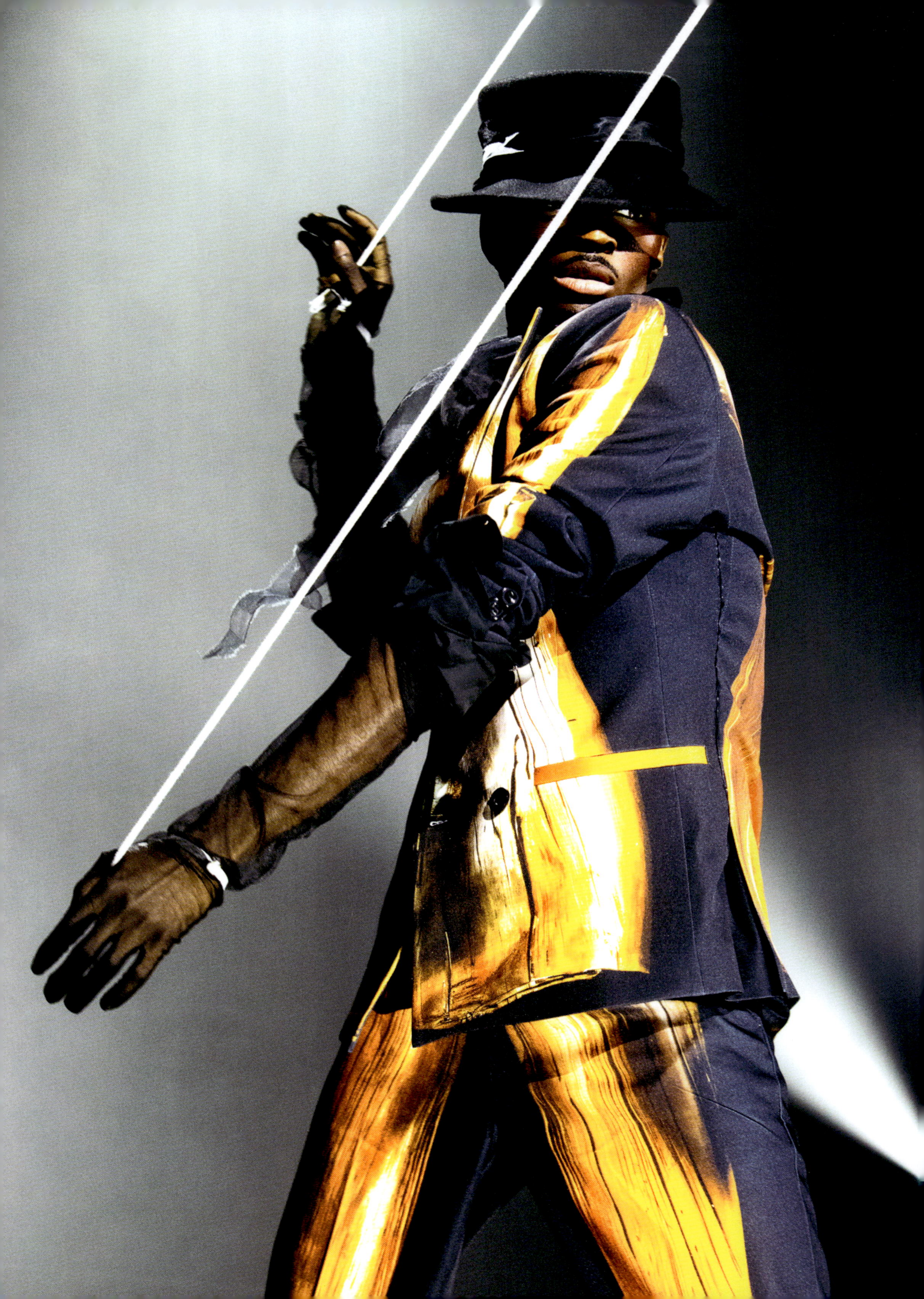

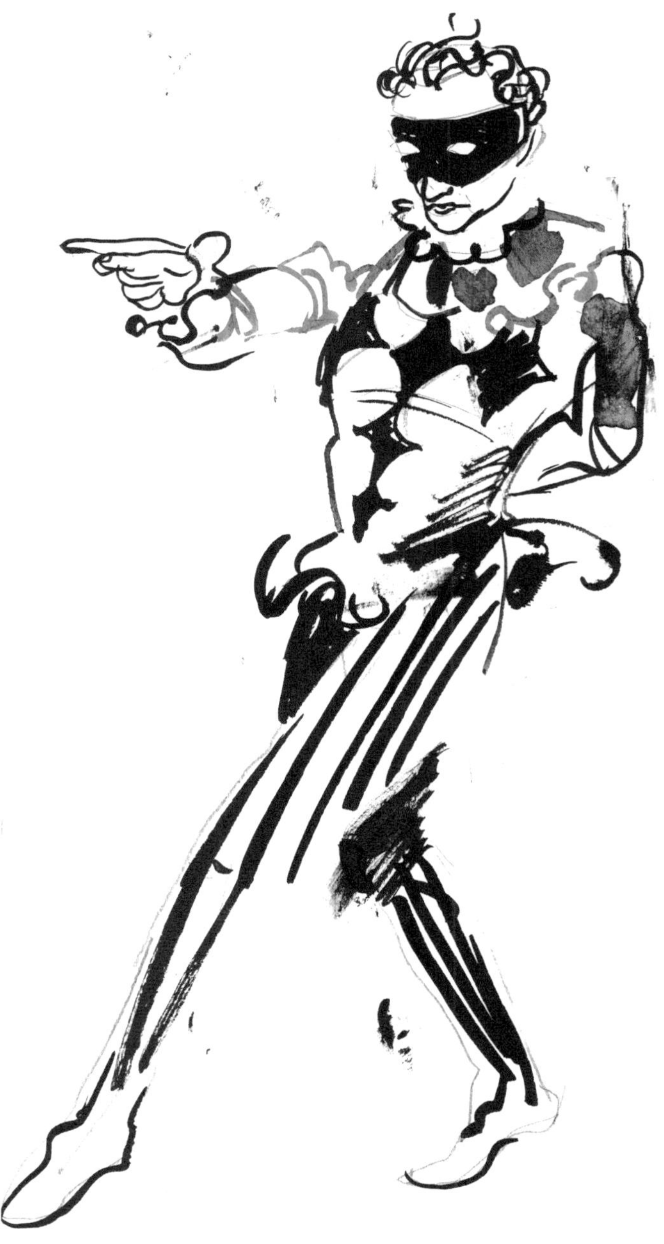

Alton Mason looking absolutely incredible. He opened the show with an incredible dance/walk.

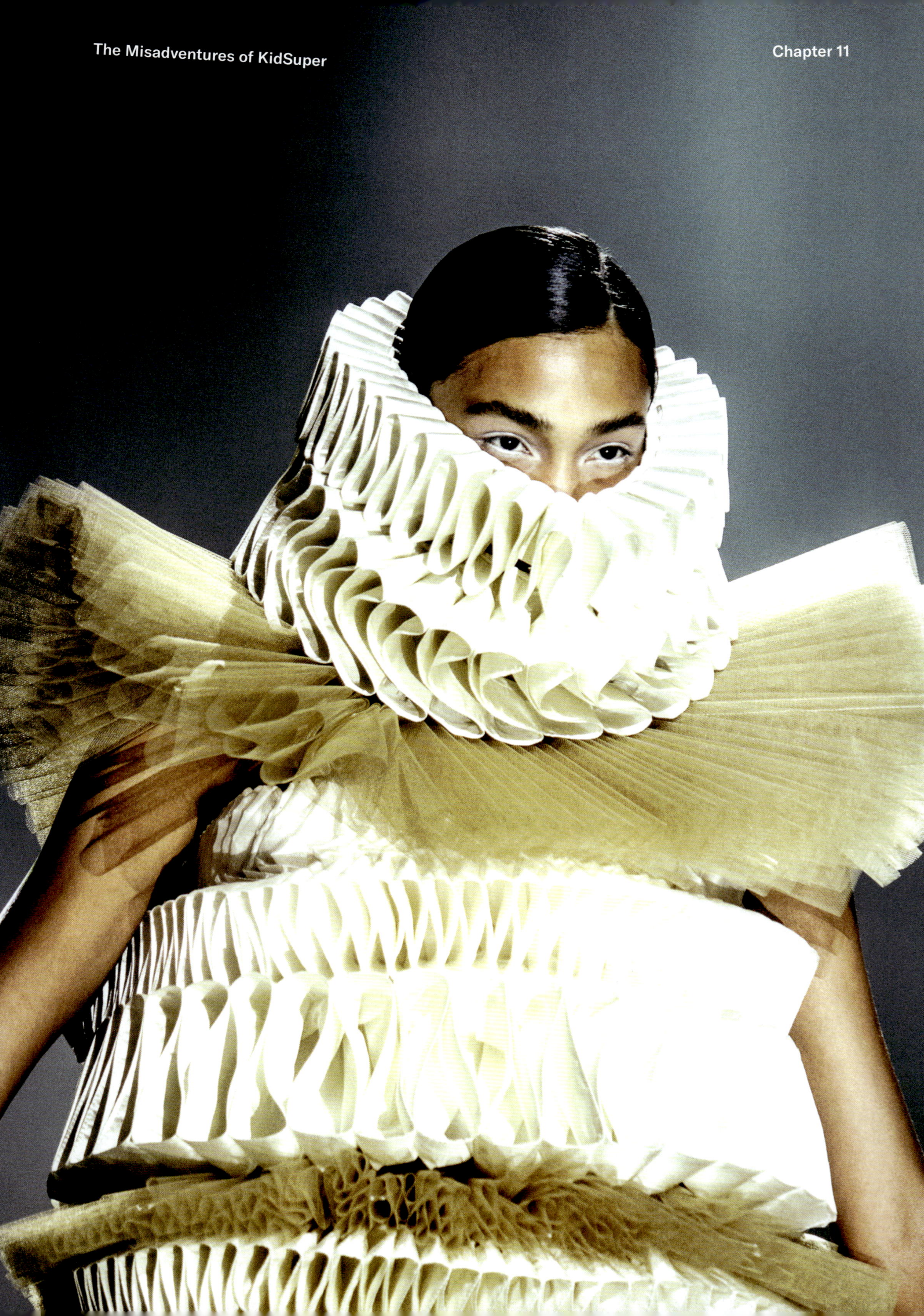

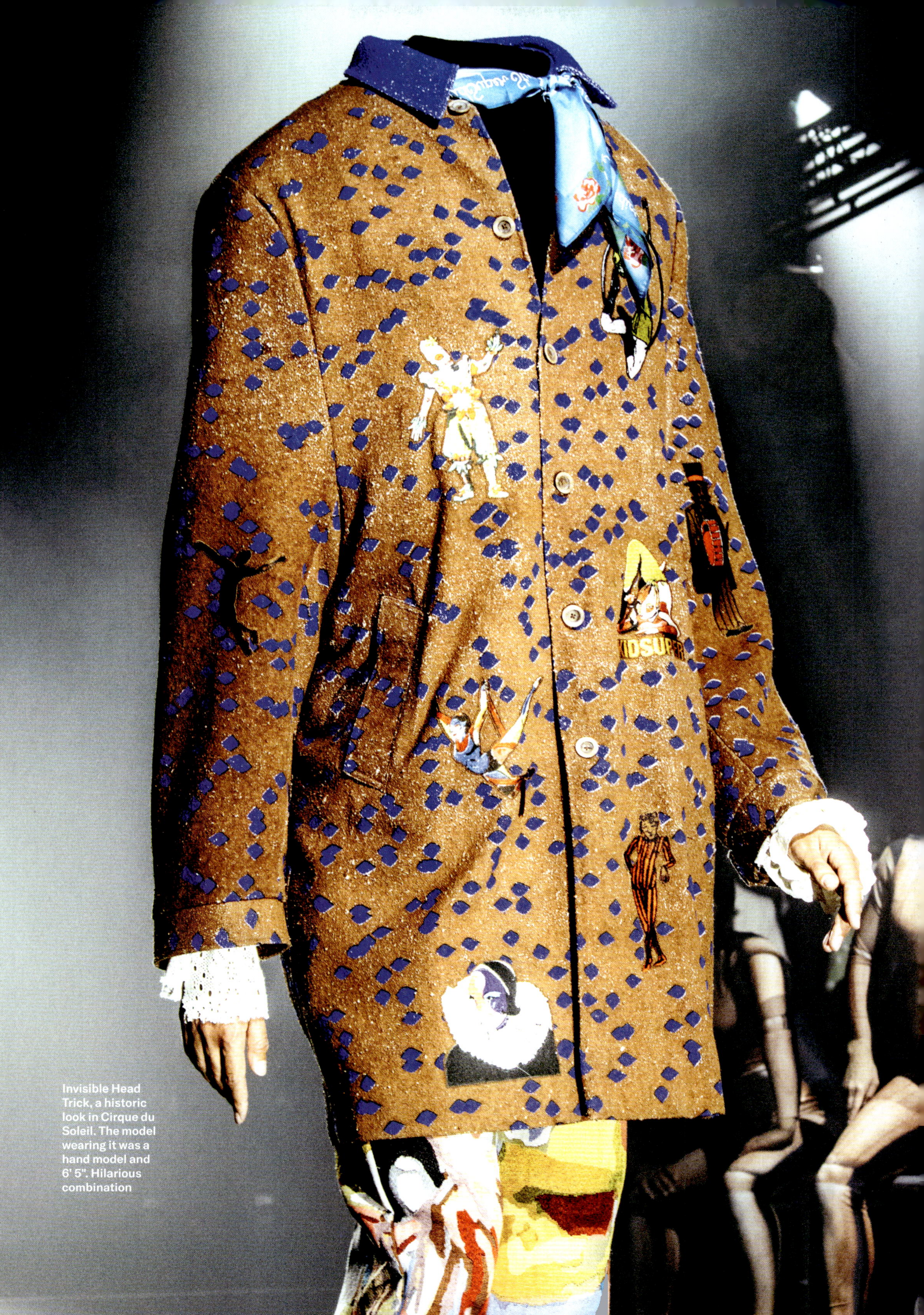

Invisible Head Trick, a historic look in Cirque du Soleil. The model wearing it was a hand model and 6' 5". Hilarious combination

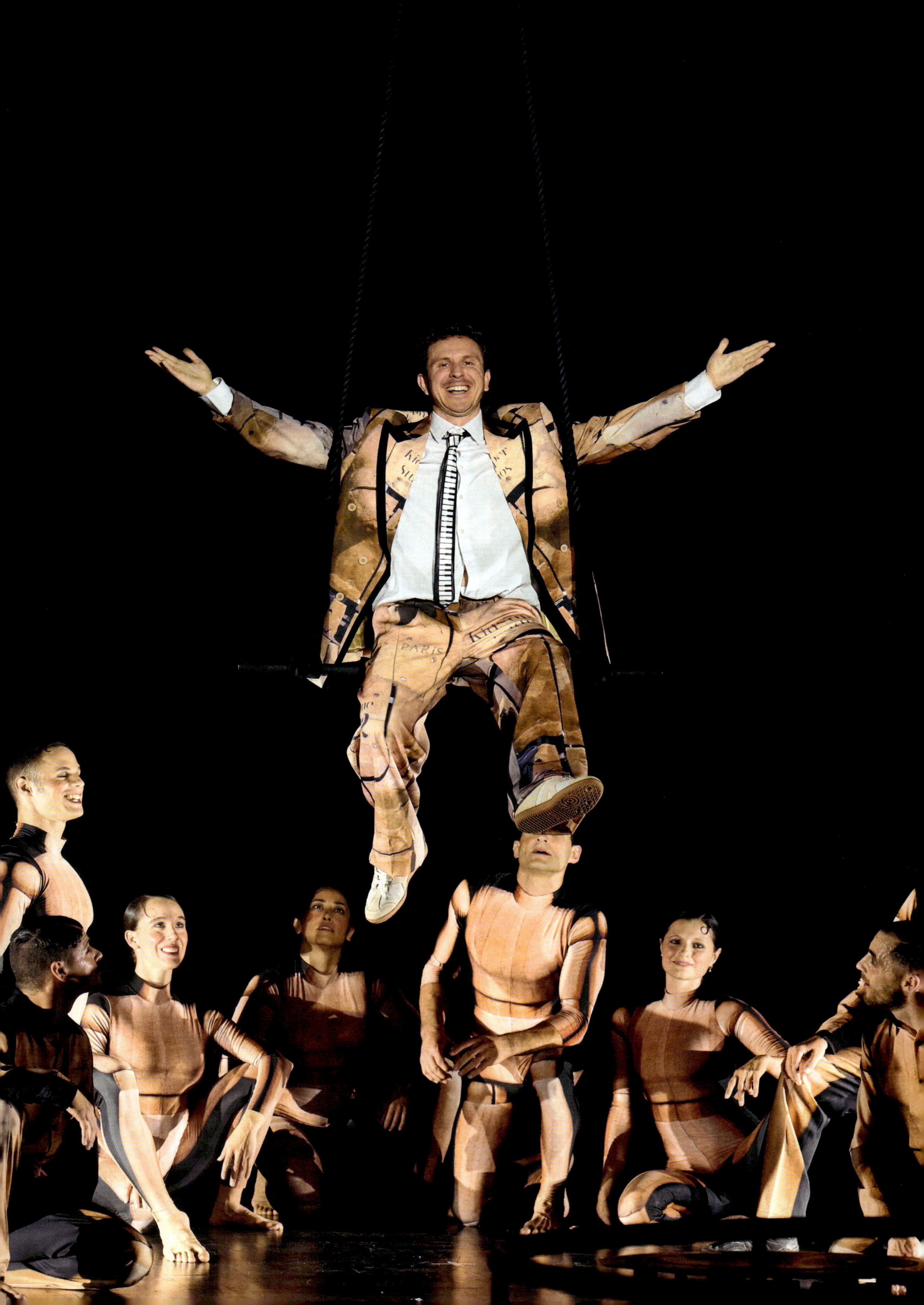
PARIS

A speech,
a cartwheel
and hoisted
up in the air

AW25

FROM A PLACE I HAVE NEVER BEEN

Step into the unknown.

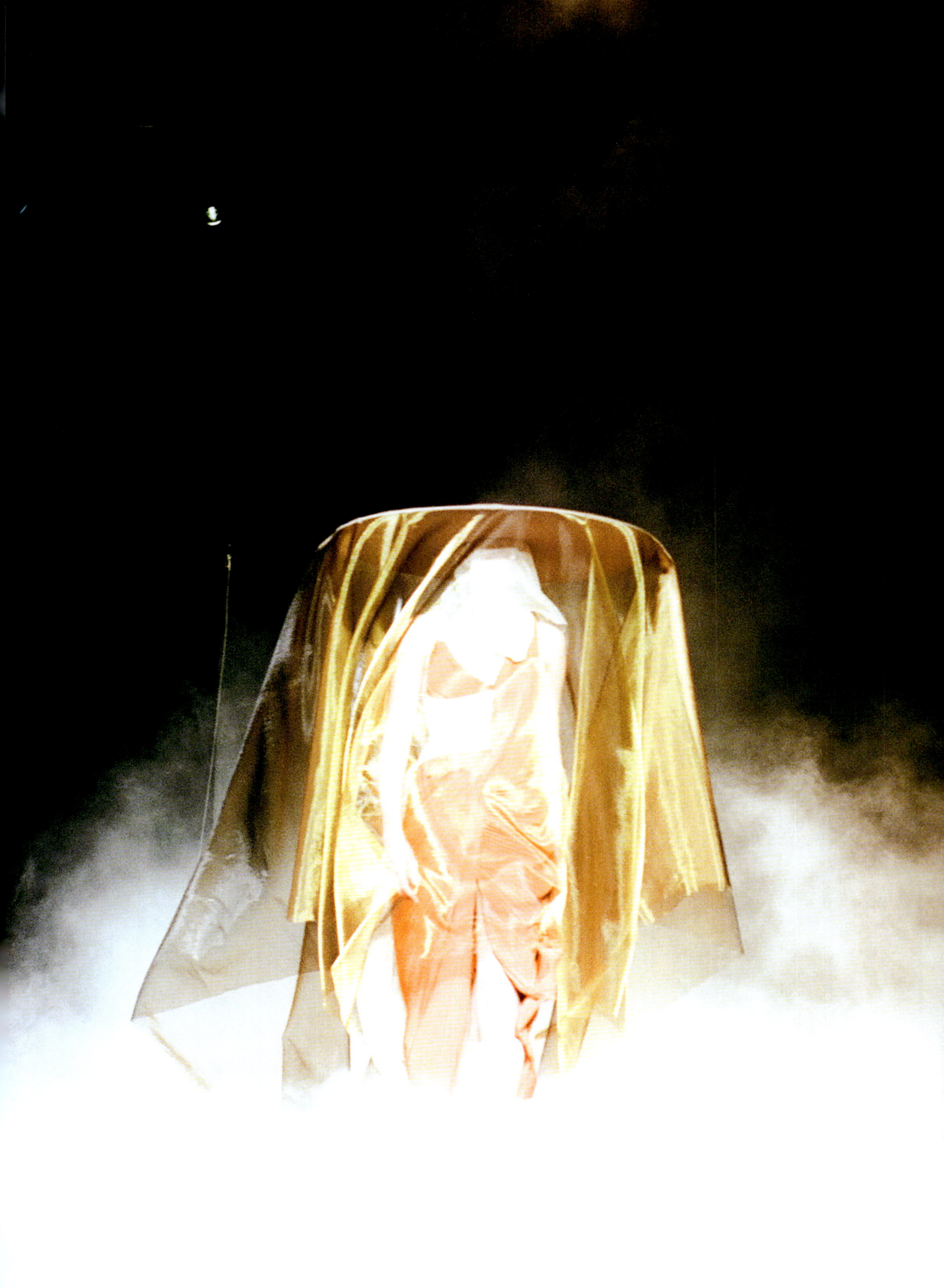

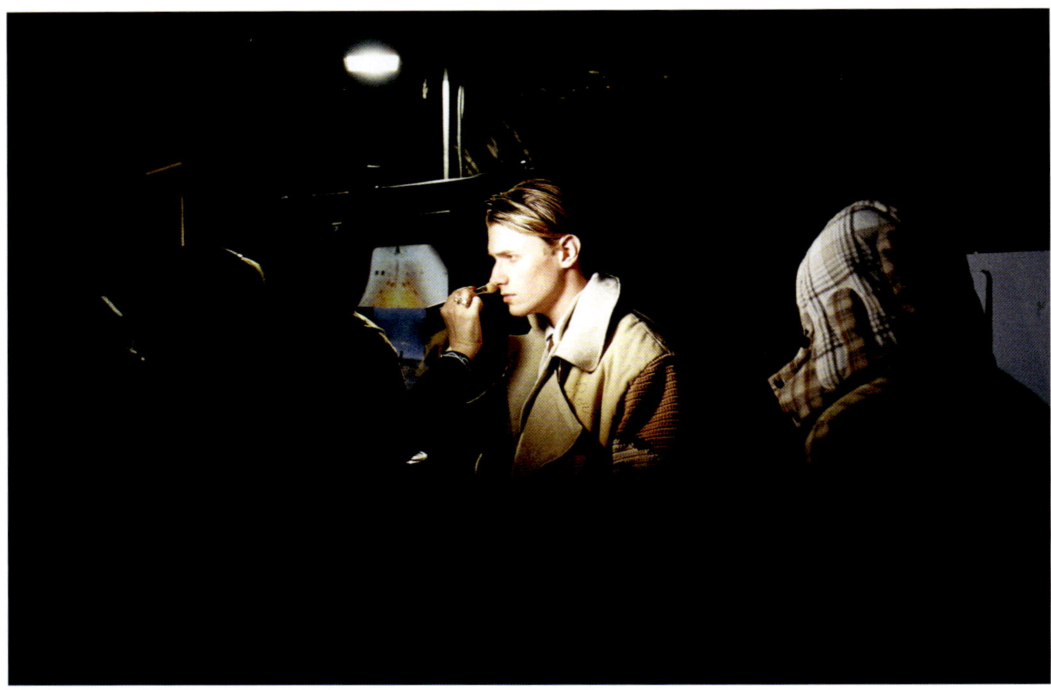

Debuting BAPE® X KidSuper collaboration

THIS IS STILL fresh in my mind because it happened just two weeks ago [January 25, 2025]. And I think I've been underselling how difficult these shows are—how much goes into them: physically, emotionally, mentally, all of it. Right now, because the show was so recent, it's still vivid in my head, but so is the massive sigh of relief that comes at the end of each one. The tension and intensity leading up to it is always overwhelming, so once it's over, there's this release.

WITH EACH SHOW, I've always felt the need to push boundaries, to do something unexpected. Every time, I try to reinvent the format—whether it's turning a fashion show into a circus, a comedy act, a theatrical play, or even an auction. But at some point, you start running out of ways to break the mold. So for this one, I shifted my approach. Instead of starting with a concept and building clothes around it, I started with the clothes. I wanted to design pieces that were different from my usual work—less about patterns and colors, more technical, more distressed, experimenting with washes and textures. And from that, I thought, what kind of world should these clothes exist in? What if, when people walked into the venue, they felt like they had stepped into another dimension?

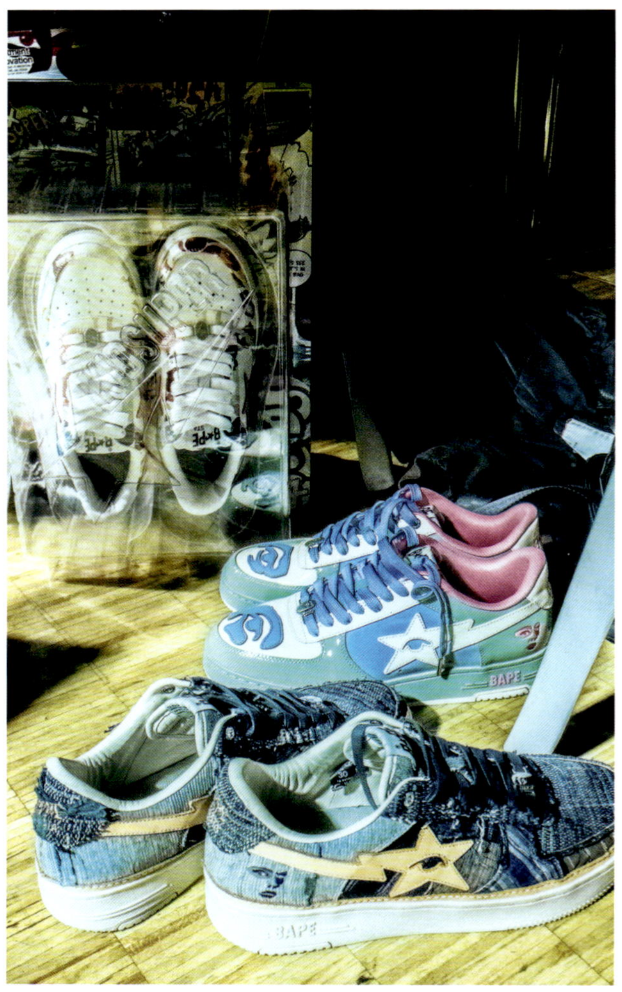

I STARTED EXPLORING ideas of the otherworldly. Was it smoke? A storm? A tornado? Could I create an indoor tornado? I went deep into YouTube, researching how to build one, but hardly anyone had attempted it. Eventually, I came across an artist who had created a small tornado—about eight feet tall—in his studio. I looked him up and, unbelievably, his studio was just ten blocks from where I lived in Brooklyn. So I cold-called him.

PFW
AW25

Paris Fashion
Week **AW25**

Saturday 1.25.2025
8PM CET

HALLE CHARLIE PARKER
211 Avenue Jean Jaurès
75019 Paris

I ENJOY WALKING INTO THE UNKNOWN
HAPPY HOLIDAYS FROM A PLACE
I HAVE NEVER BEEN

KIDSUPER 2025

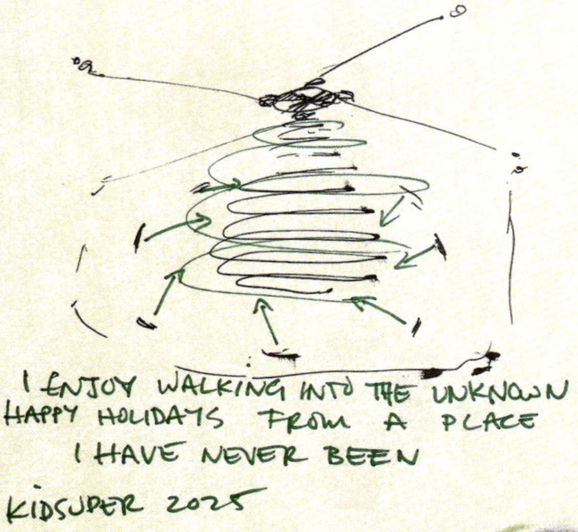

KidSuper Studios
presents:

From A Place I Have Never Been.

Saturday January 25th
8PM CET

HALLE CHARLIE PARKER
211 Avenue Jean Jaurès
75019 Paris

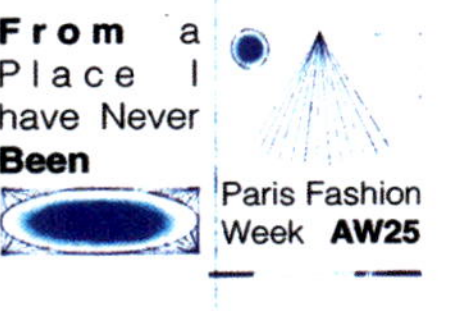

8PM CET

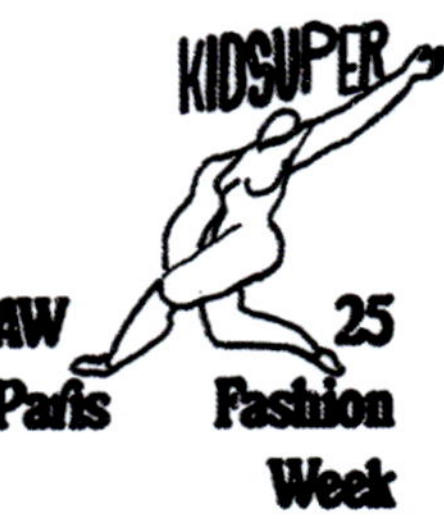

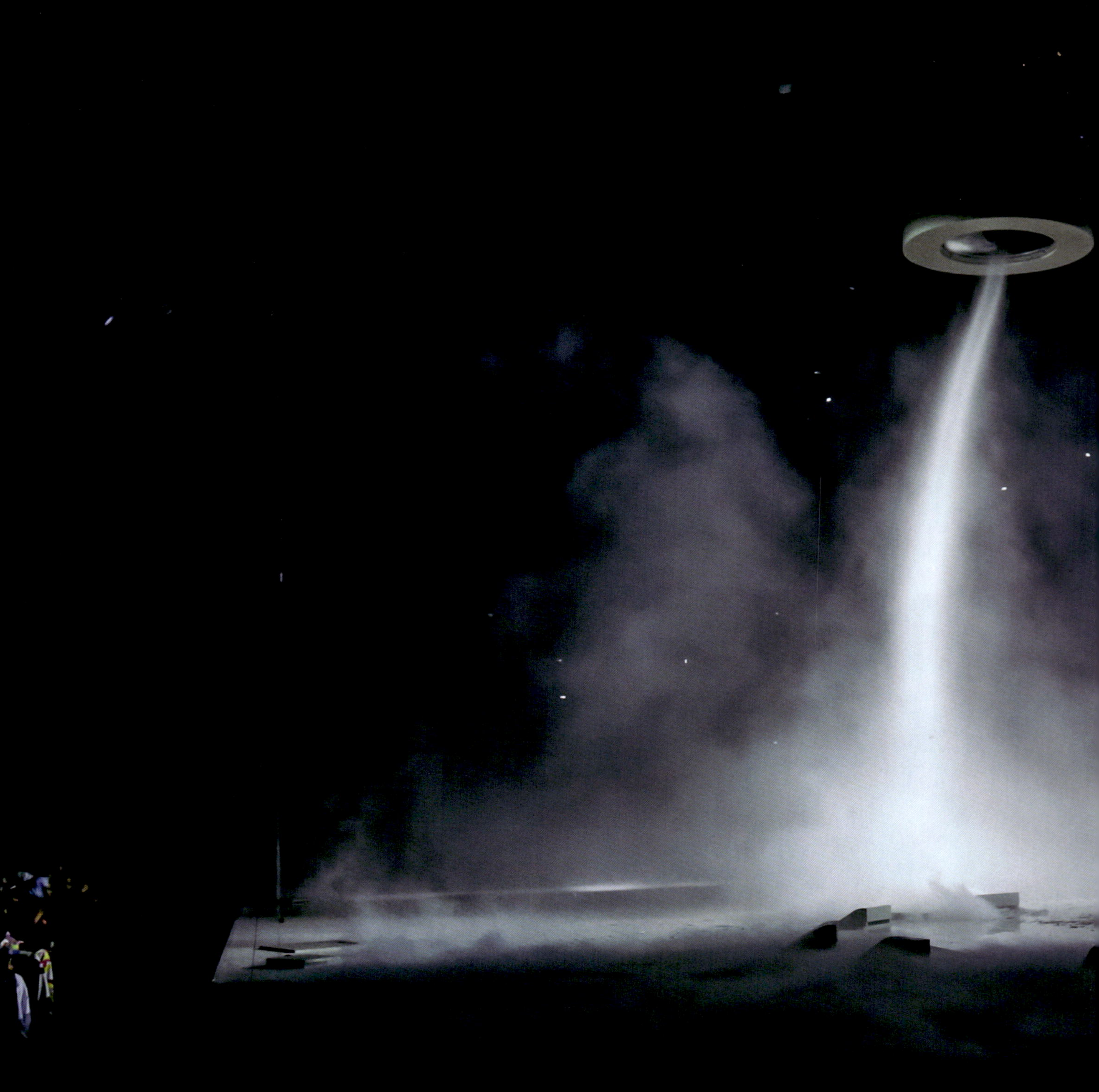

An indoor tornado for
the runway set design.
I repeat... I MADE
AN INDOOR TORNADO!
In collaboration
with Daniel Wurtzel.

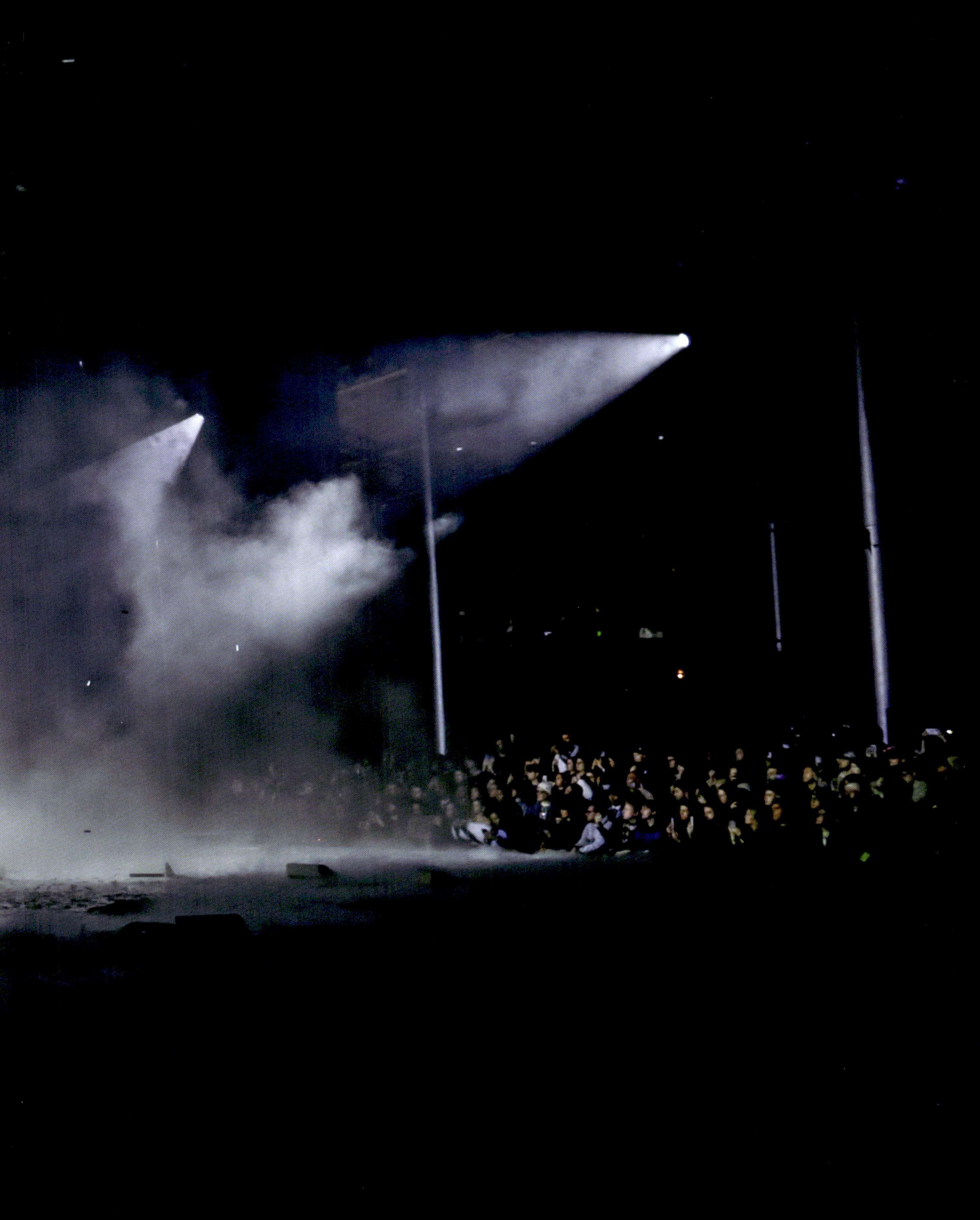

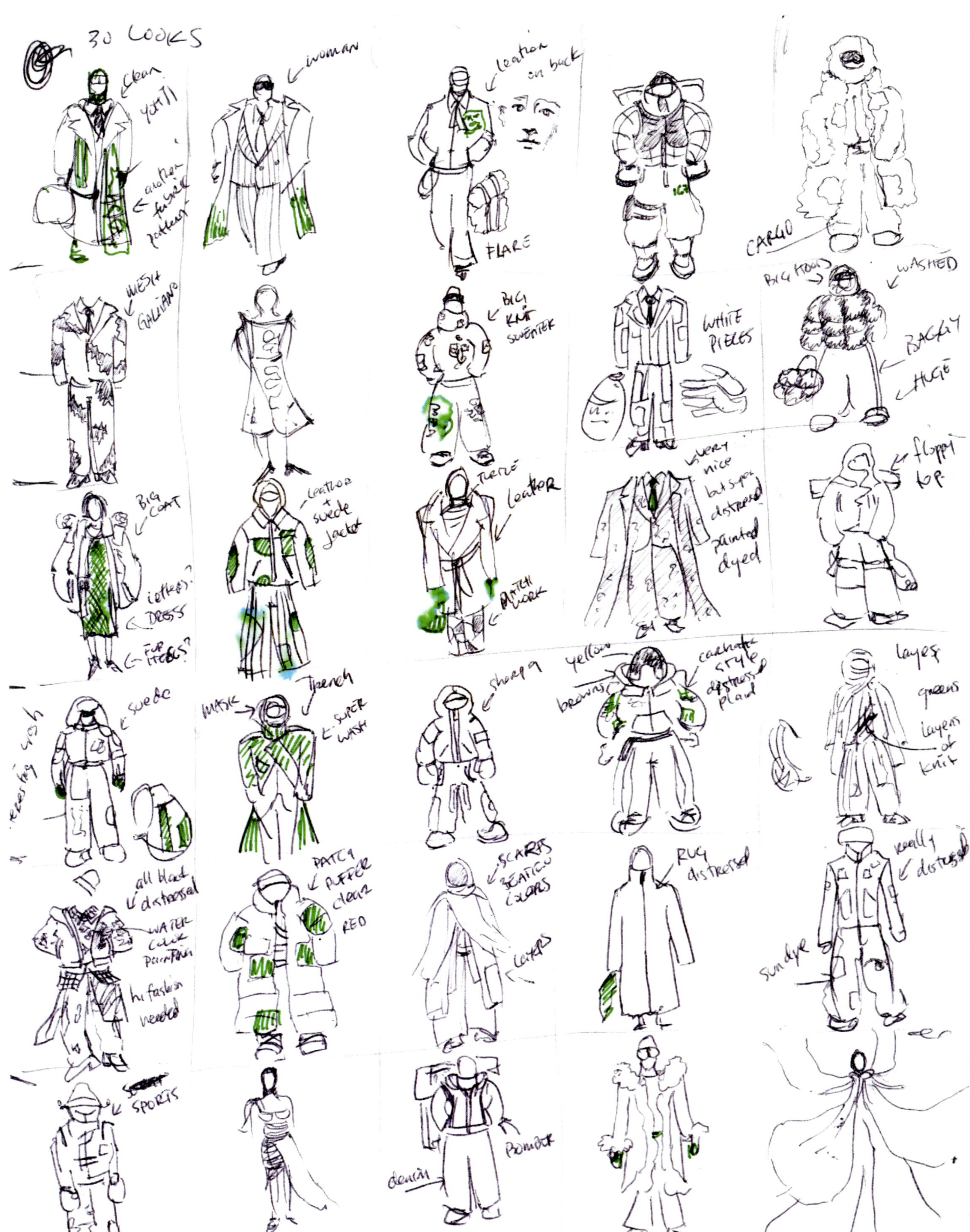
30 LOOKS
clean yeti
woman
leather on back
FLARE
CARGO
BIG HOOD
WASHED
BAGGY
HUGE
MESH GALLIANO
BIG KNIT SWEATER
WHITE PIECES
floppy top
BIG COAT
DRESS
leather + suede jacket
leather
PATCH WORK
very nice but super distressed
painted dyed
suede
MASK
trench
SUPER WASH
sherpa
yellow
browns
carhartt style distressed plaid
layers
greens
layers of knit
all black distressed
WATER COLOR PAINTING
hi fashion needed
PATCH PUFFER clear RED
SCARFS SEASONAL COLORS
layers
RUG distressed
really distressed
sundye
SPORTS
denim
BOMBER

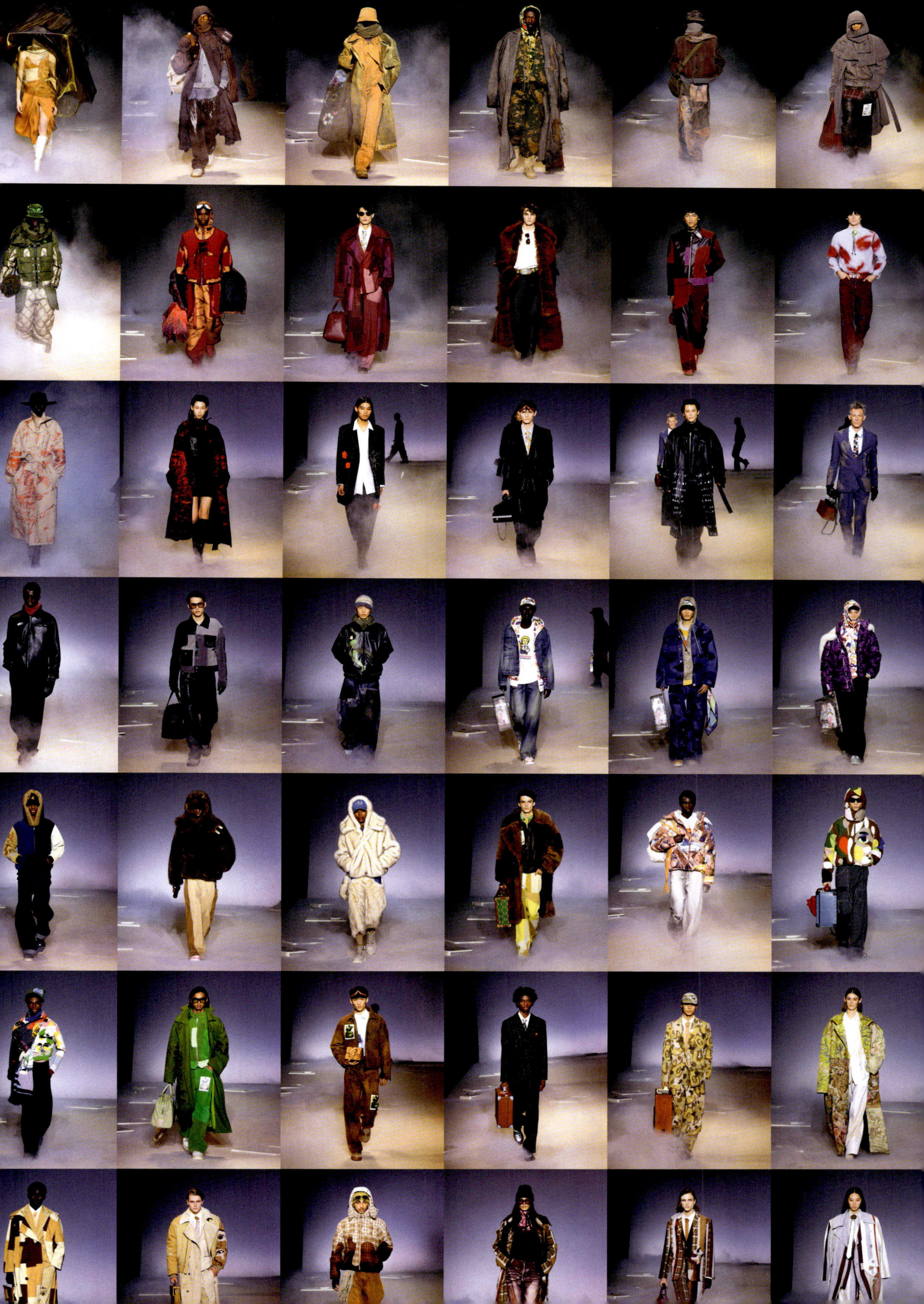

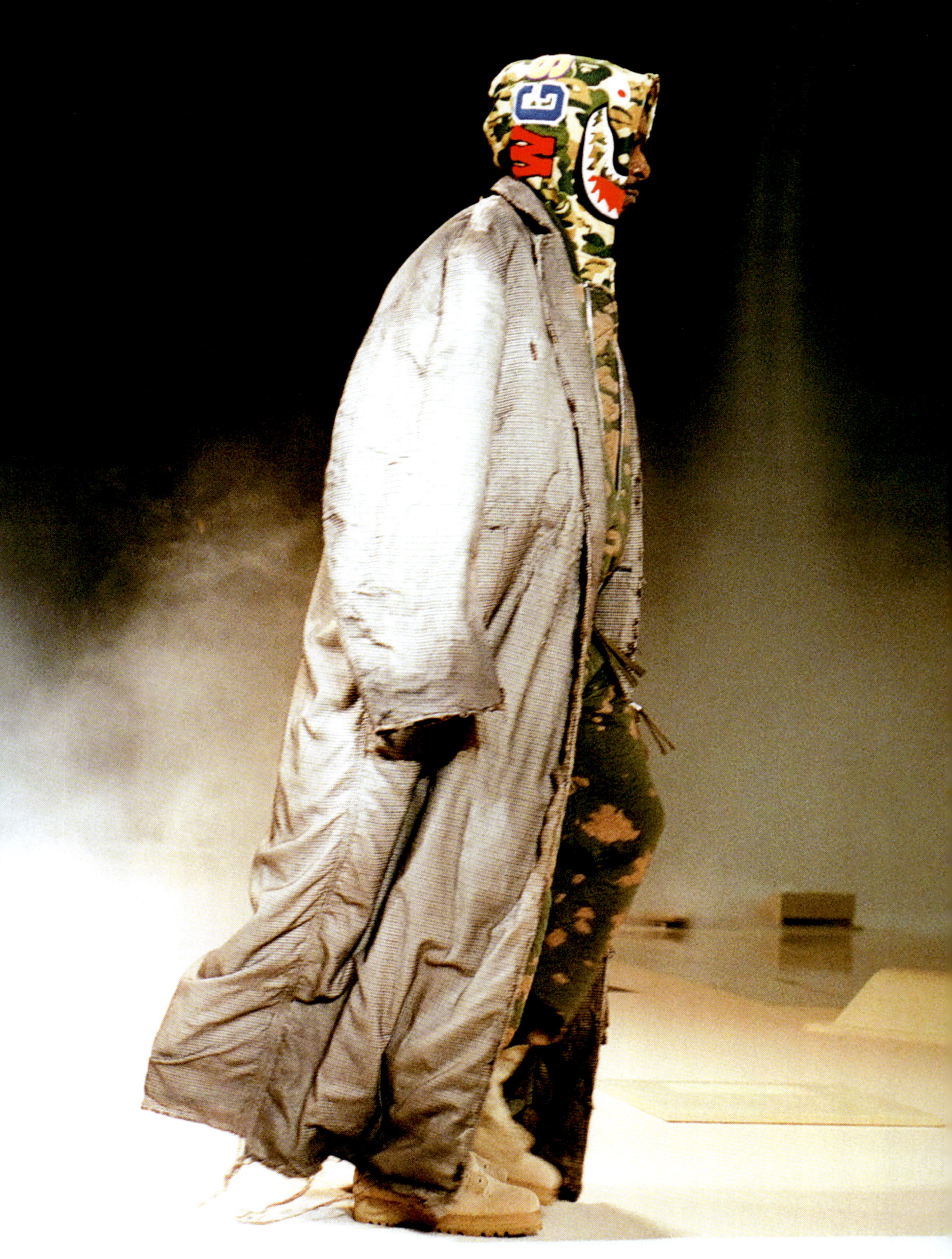

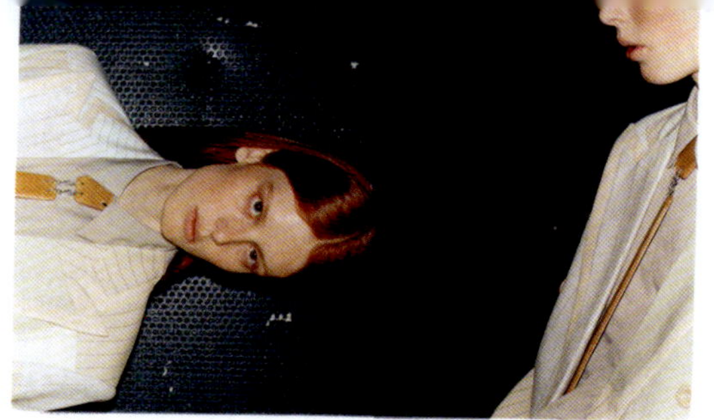

KIDSUPER FW25

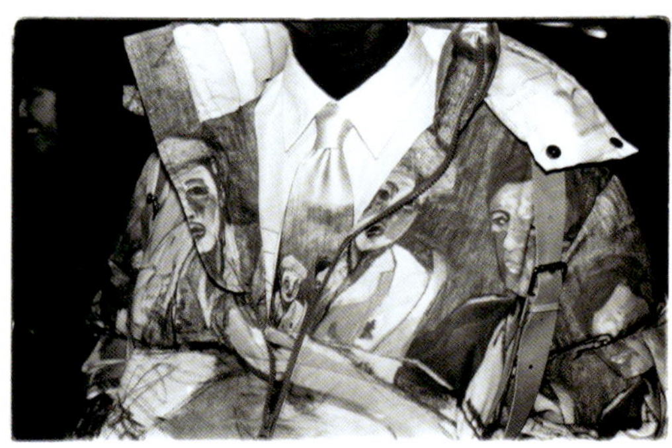

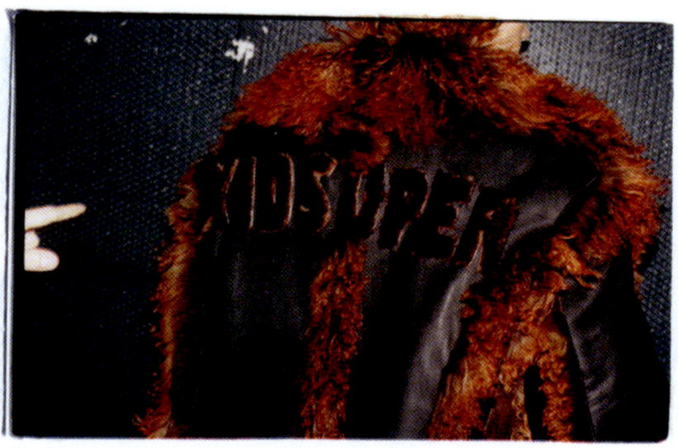

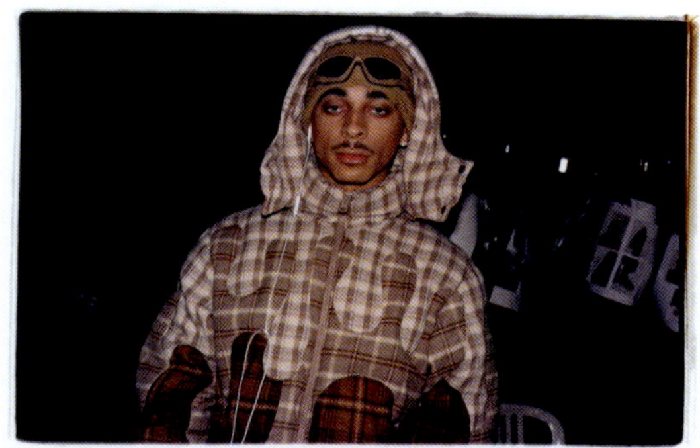

"Hey man, I'm a fashion designer. I have this idea for a show. I'd love to talk to you about it."

TURNS OUT, he had just moved upstate, about 45 minutes outside the city. I told him, "I'll come up."

That's one of the magical things about New York—the creative energy, the sheer number of potential collaborators. So I made the trip. And this felt different from my past collaborations. It wasn't like working with Cirque du Soleil, which was huge in scale. This was one artist to another. He was in his 50s or 60s, and as we talked, I realized this was someone who lived and breathed art. He wasn't just making tornadoes—he was creating moving sculptures, fabric that danced, material storms. I had studied his work before we met, and when I explained the arc of my show—the beginning, middle, and end, the emotional highs and lows—he understood immediately.

We hit it off. It felt good to talk to someone I considered a true artist. I've always struggled with calling myself an artist, but talking to him, I saw what it really meant. I mean, you have to be a true artist if you've been experimenting with fans for twenty years just to perfect the movement of air.

WE STARTED FIGURING out logistics. Could we make the tornado 20 feet high? 30? 40? He had attempted something big before, so we called an engineer he had worked with. Then came the challenge of executing it in Paris. I didn't want the mechanics to be visible—I wanted people to experience the magic without seeing how it worked. That meant building a stage that concealed the fans that formed the tornado. I think people who attended the show saw something seamless, but behind the scenes, this was one of the hardest shows I had ever done.

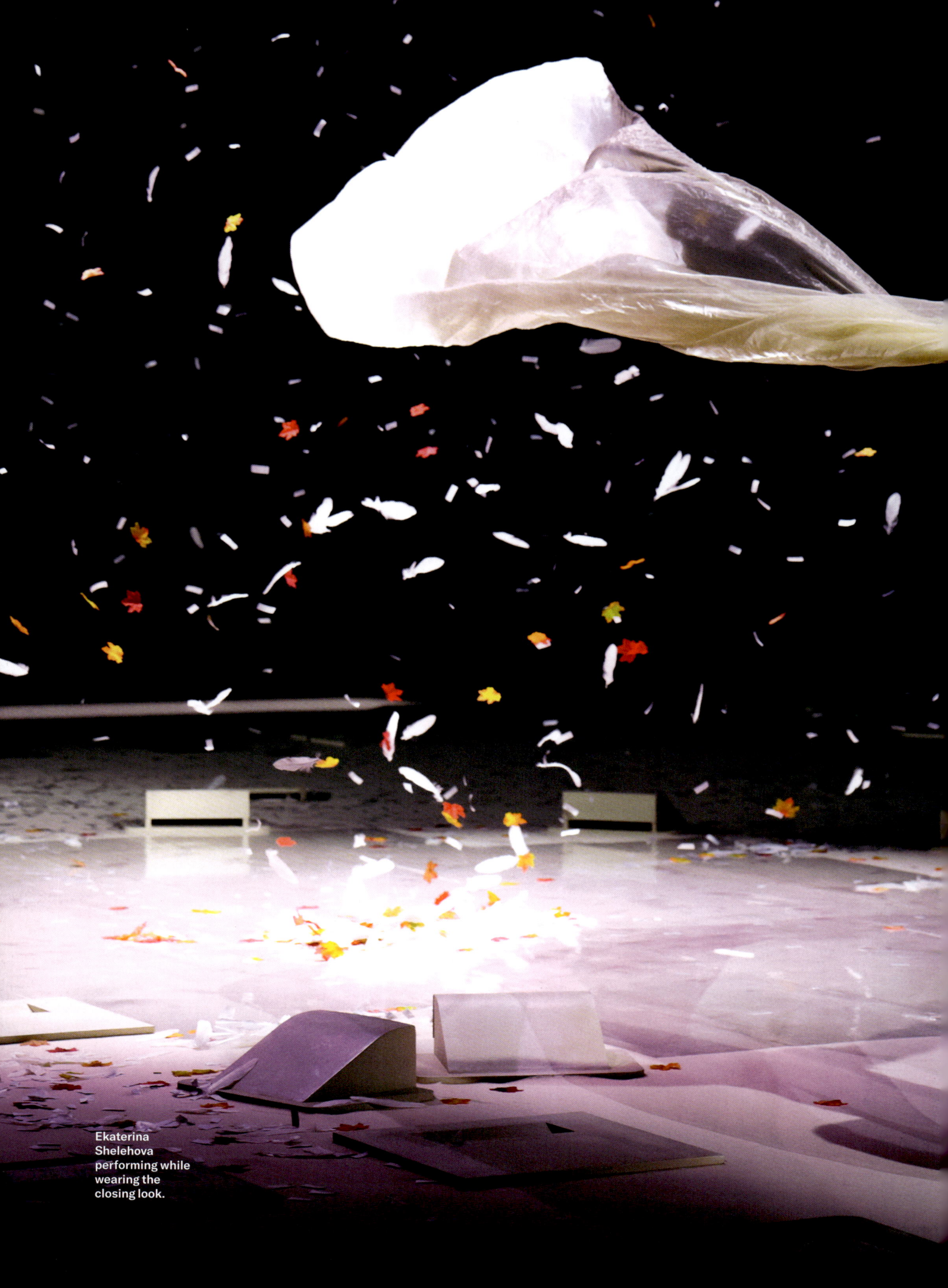

Ekaterina Shelehova performing while wearing the closing look.

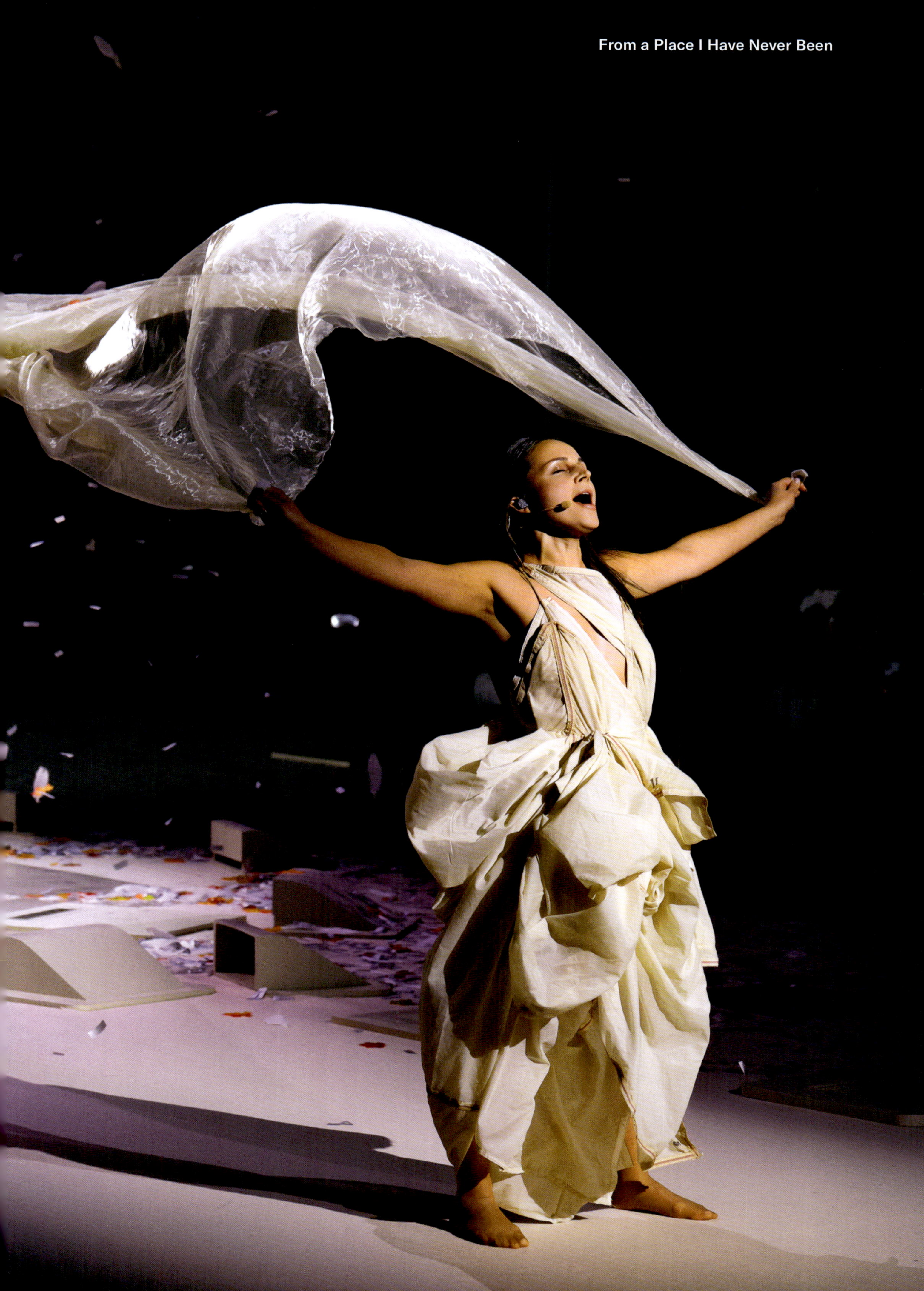

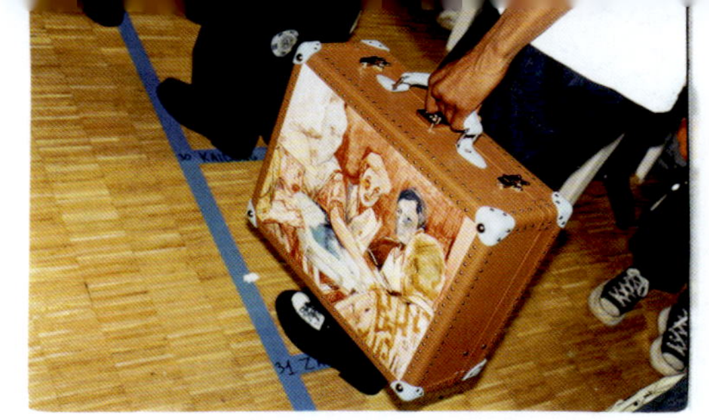

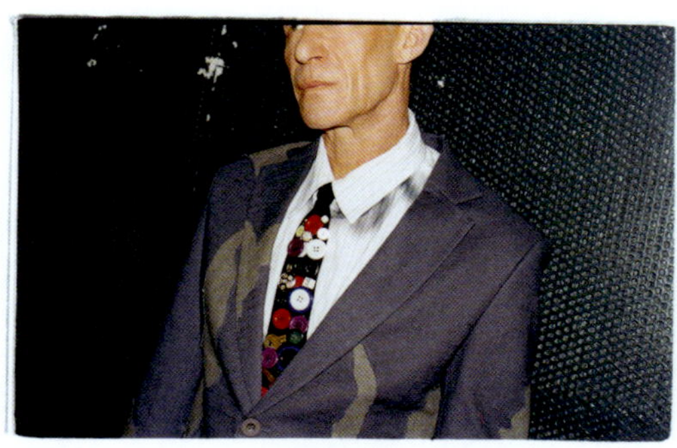

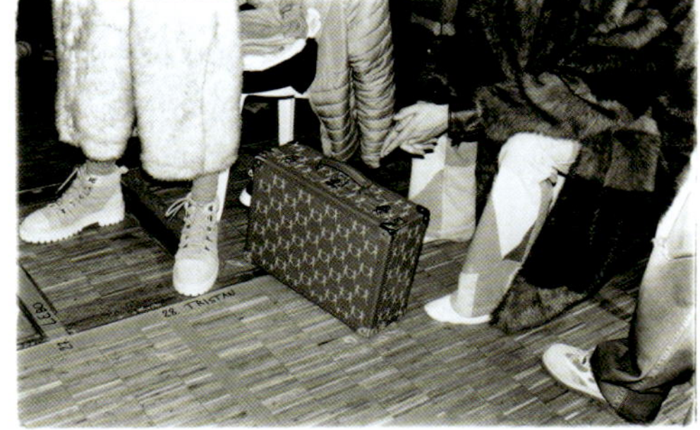

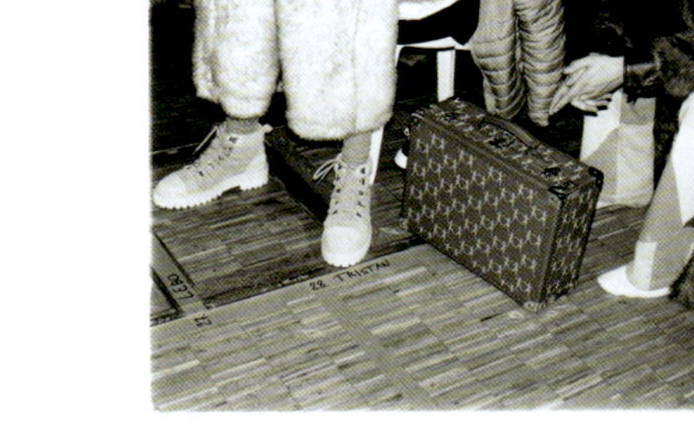

MAYBE IT FELT that way because I came up with the concept so last minute. I put so much pressure on myself to outdo each show, and sometimes the ideas just don't come. I kept waiting for inspiration. Then, suddenly—tornado. And because it came to me late, I started designing late. I went on a two-week bender, barely sleeping, just designing. I didn't even realize it, but I had created 60 looks—twice the usual number. For the first time ever, we showcased 50 full looks.

On top of that, our stylist got insanely sick. We didn't even know how bad it was at first. He was basically bedridden and couldn't show up, so my friends and I had to take over styling at the last minute. And then, another curveball—the backdrop was supposed to be this smoky red, inspired by Blade Runner, evoking another planet. But just before the show, the LA fires happened. I didn't want the imagery to feel insensitive, even if it was a stretch, so I scrapped the red last minute.

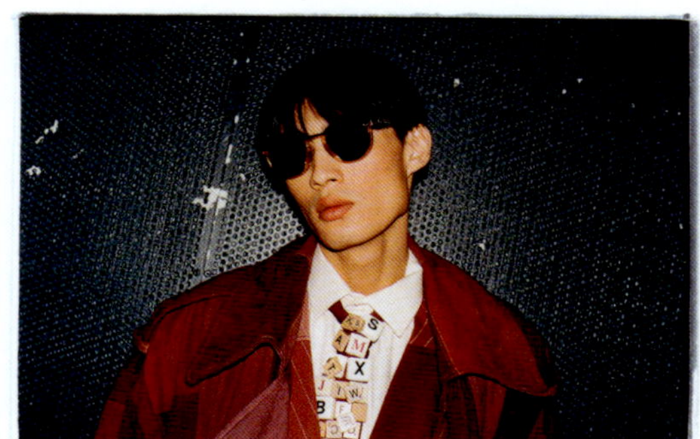

EVERY GREAT SHOW comes down to last-minute decisions, improvisations, and problem-solving. Somehow, we pulled it off. The music came together beautifully—we had Fuerza Regida perform. And in the end, it became one of my greatest shows.

We called it "From a Place I'd Never Been." The name came from a random Instagram caption. I had spent New Year's in Georgia (the country) with my parents, posted a photo, and wrote, "Coming from a place I'd never been." A friend commented, "That sounds like a cool fashion show name." And just like that, the show had its title.

Sometimes, things just fall into place.

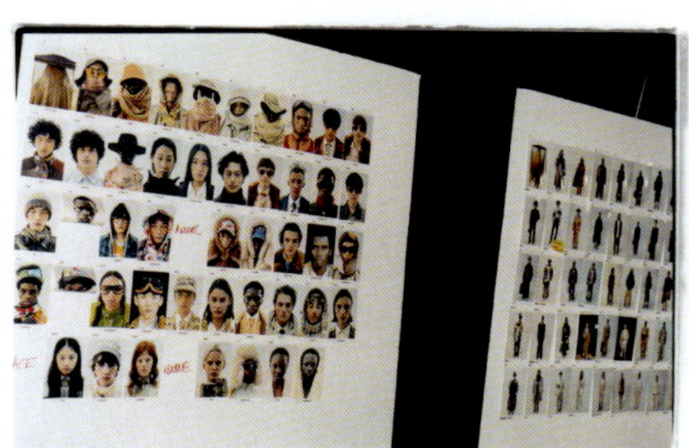

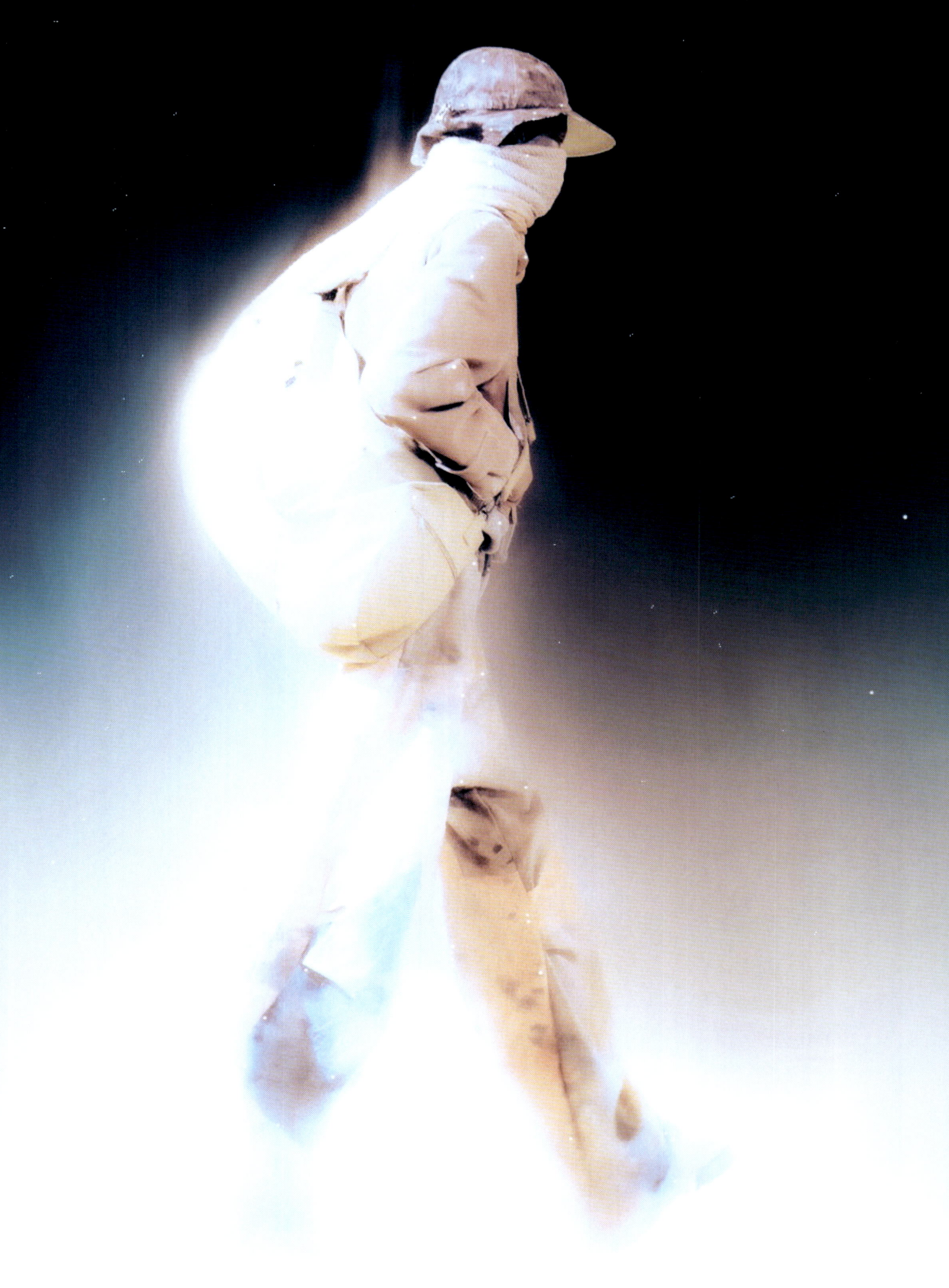

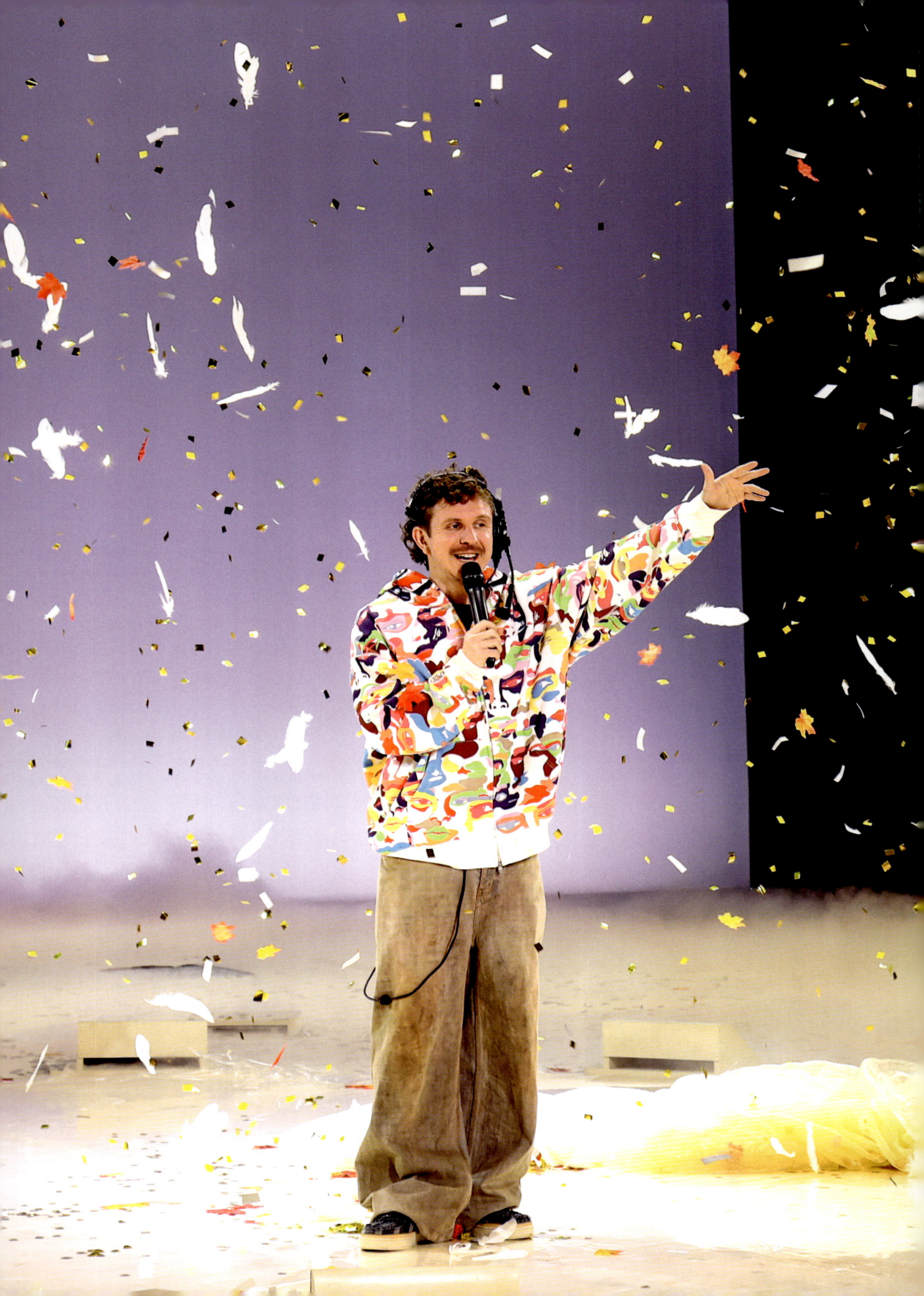

With each show, I’ve always felt the need to push boundaries, to do something unexpected.

Every time, I try to reinvent the format—whether it’s turning a fashion show into a circus, a comedy act, a theatrical play, or even an auction.

— Quoted from ending speech

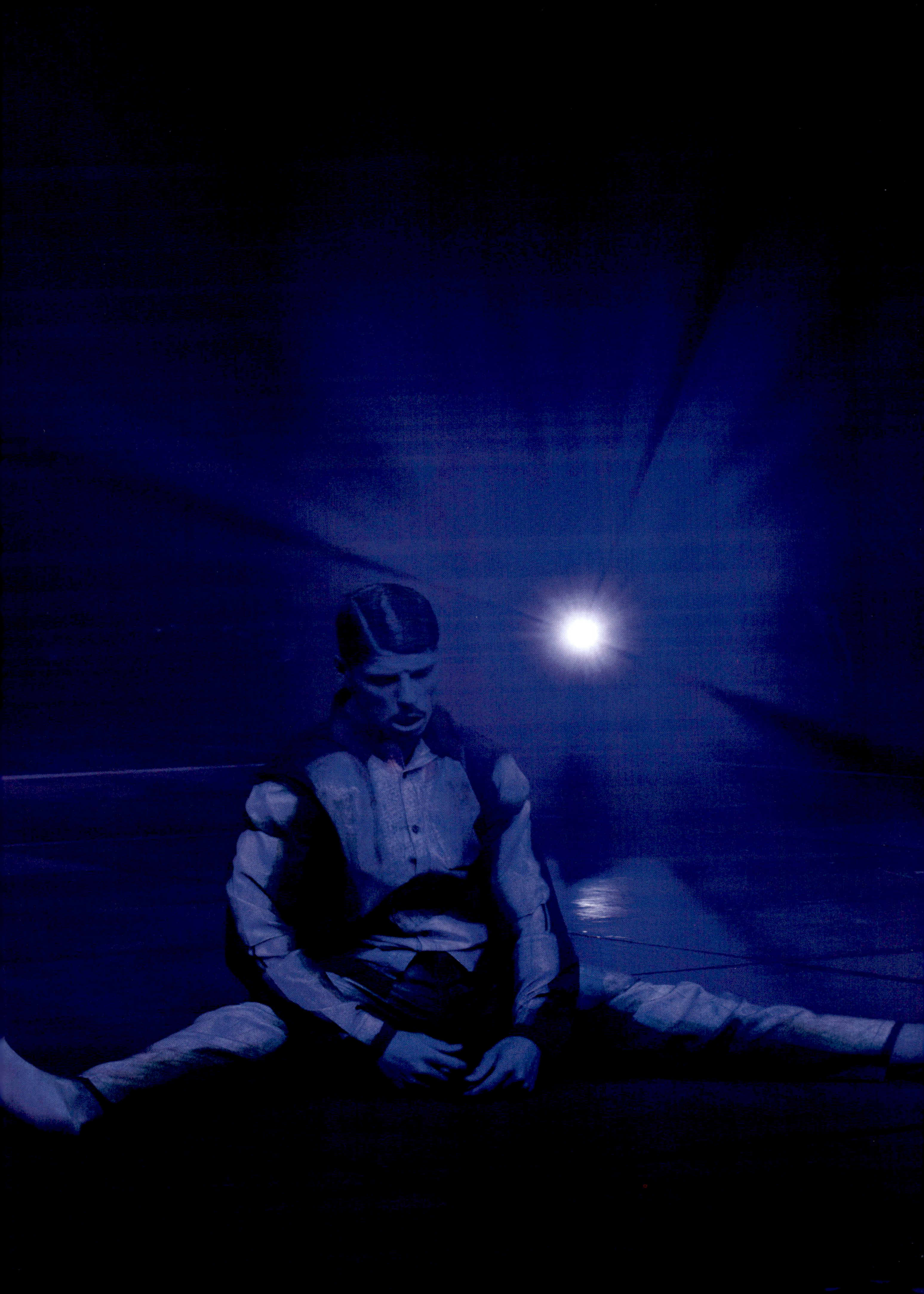

FINALE:

YOU DON'T KNOW what can't be done until you accidentally do it. That's been the theme of everything I've made. These weren't planned like a perfect arc—they just became one because I kept going. Every show left me with something: a new friend, a broken camera, a *Vogue* article, a missed payment, a standing ovation. And somehow, it all adds up to a life I couldn't have storyboarded better.

So if you take anything from this—take the risk. Say yes before you're ready. Build the raft before you know exactly where you are going. And when it all goes sideways (and it will), call it a prototype and keep moving.

The people who get anywhere aren't the ones with a perfect plan. They're the ones just crazy enough to believe in the idea—and run straight at it, spellbound.

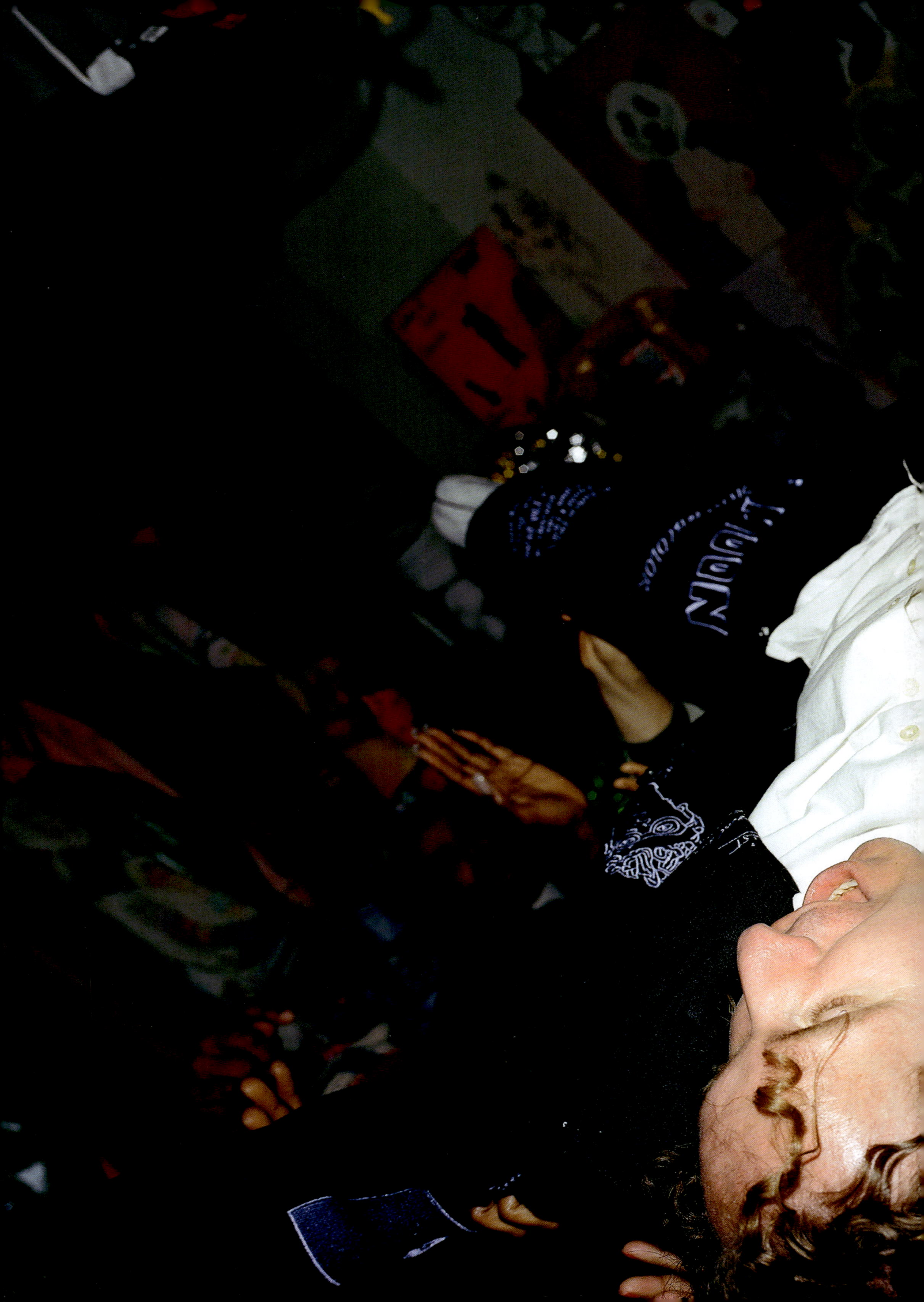

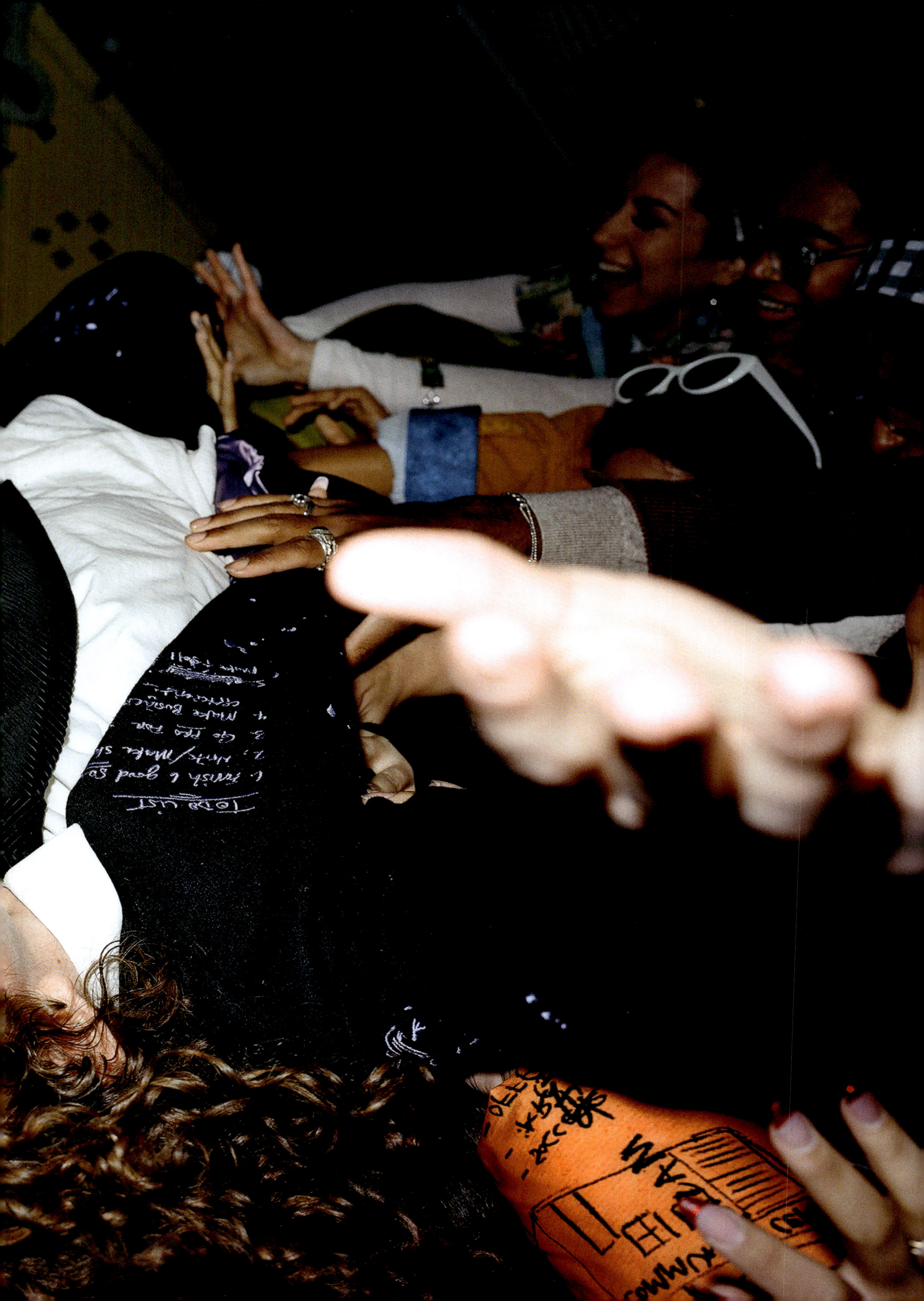

ILLUSTRATION CREDITS

Unless otherwise specified, all illustrations not credited below appear courtesy of KidSuper. Every effort has been made to contact all the rights-holders of all the images that appear in this book. Any errors will be corrected in subsequent editions provided notification is sent to the publisher.

Photography Credits

Principal photography courtesy of BFA: 31; 41; 42; 133; 180–181; 182–183; 184–185; 188–189; 192–195; 202; 206–207; 215; 233; 236–237; 239; 242–243; 245; 246; 248

Images courtesy of Mike Vitelli: 5; 18 (bottom left); 37; 46 (top left); 49; 52; 75; 76; 78–79; 82–83; 84; 86–87; 90–91; 93; 94; 95; 96–97; 99; 100–101; 102–103; 104–105; 107; 112; 115; 117; 124–125; 160–161; 170–171; 172–173; 250–251

Images courtesy of Bijan Sosnowski: 13; 17; 21

Images courtesy of Vikram Valluri/BFA: 20 (left)

Images courtesy of Matteo Prandoni: 31; 42

Images courtesy of KidSuper: 47; 51; 58; 60; 61; 63; 64; 65; 68; 69; 72; 73; 75; 80–81; 86–87; 89; 92; 98; 108–109; 110–111; 114; 116; 118–119; 122; 126–127; 132–134; 182–187; 190–191; 197; 199; 204–205; 209; 210–211; 213

Images courtesy of Seto Kiswoyo: 128–129

Images courtesy of Louis Vuitton: 137–159

Images courtesy of Courtnee Daly: 212

Images courtesy of Ik Aldama: 166–169; 174

Images courtesy of Astra Marina/BFA: 180–181

I would like to thank Ronaldinho.

— Colm Dillane

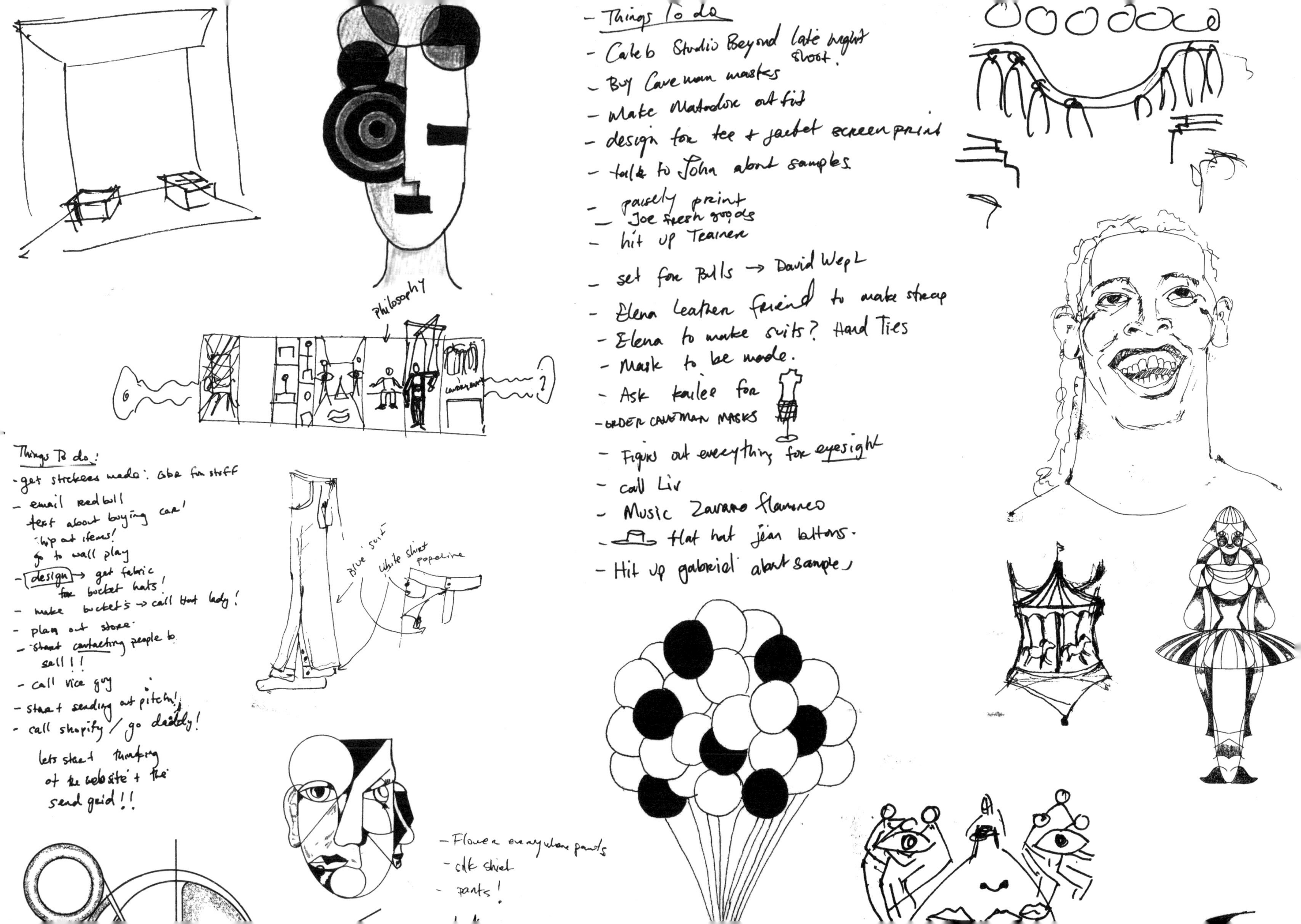

Things To do:
- get stickers made: Abe for stuff
- email redbull
text about buying car!
tip out items!
go to wall play
- design → get fabric for bucket hats!
- make buckets → call that lady!
- plan out store.
- start contacting people to sell!!
- call vice guy
- start sending out pitch!
- call shopify / go daddy!
lets start thinking of the website + the send grid!!
Philosophy
Blue suit
White shirt poplin
- Flower everywhere pants
- silk shirt
- pants!
- Things To do
- Caleb Studio Beyond late night shoot.
- Buy Caveman masks
- make Matador outfit
- design for tee + jacket screen print
- talk to John about samples
- paisely print
- Joe fresh goods
- hit up Trainer
- set for Bulls → David Wepl
- Elena leather friend to make strap
- Elena to make suits? Hand Ties
- Mask to be made.
- Ask Kailee for
- ORDER CAVEMAN MASKS
- Figure out everything for eyesight
- call Liv
- Music Zarano flamenco
- Flat hat jean buttons.
- Hit up gabriel about samples

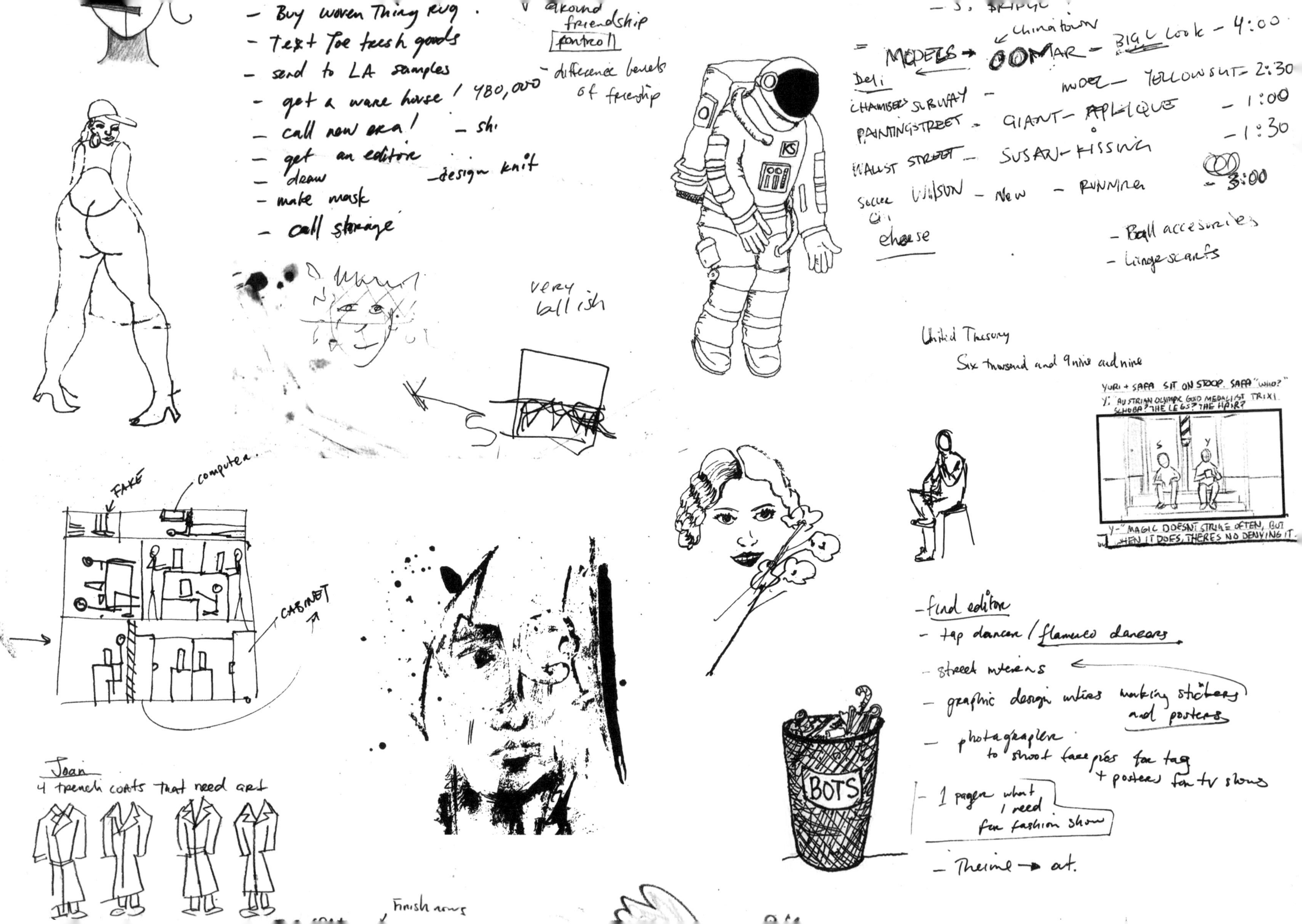
- Buy woven Thing rug
- Text Joe fresh goods
- send to LA samples
- get a ware house / 480,000
- call new era!
- get an editor
- draw
- design knit
- make mask
- call storage
around friendship
difference levels of friendship
very bullish
FAKE
computer
CABINET
Joan
4 trench coats that need art
Finish rows
MODELS
chinatown
BIG Look - 4:00
Deli
CHAMBERS SUBWAY
MODEL - YELLOW SUIT - 2:30
PAINTING STREET - GIANT - APPLIQUE - 1:00
WALL ST STREET - SUSAN - KISSING - 1:30
WILSON - New - RUNNER
3:00
cheese
- Ball accessories
- Lingerie scarfs
KS
United Treasury
Six thousand and 9 nine and nine
YURI + SAFA SIT ON STOOP. SAFA "WHO?"
Y: AUSTRIAN OLYMPIC GOLD MEDALIST TRIXI SCHOBA? THE LEGS? THE HAIR?
S
Y
Y- "MAGIC DOESN'T STRIKE OFTEN, BUT WHEN IT DOES, THERE'S NO DENYING IT."
- find editor
- tap dancer / flamenco dancers
- street wreckers
- graphic design writers making stickers and posters
- photographer to shoot face pics for tag + posters for tv shows
- 1 pager what I need for fashion show
- Theme → art.
BOTS